T0133104

An Architectural Approach to Level Design, Second Edition

An Architectural Approach to Level Design, Second Edition

By

Christopher W. Totten

CRC Press
Taylor & Francis Group
Boca Raton London New York

CRC Press is an imprint of the
Taylor & Francis Group, an **informa** business

AN A K PETERS BOOK

CRC Press
Taylor & Francis Group
6000 Broken Sound Parkway NW, Suite 300
Boca Raton, FL 33487-2742

© 2019 by Taylor & Francis Group, LLC
CRC Press is an imprint of Taylor & Francis Group, an Informa business

No claim to original U.S. Government works

Printed on acid-free paper

International Standard Book Number-13: 978-081-5361-374 (Hardback)
International Standard Book Number-13: 978-081-5361-367 (Paperback)

This book contains information obtained from authentic and highly regarded sources. Reasonable efforts have been made to publish reliable data and information, but the author and publisher cannot assume responsibility for the validity of all materials or the consequences of their use. The authors and publishers have attempted to trace the copyright holders of all material reproduced in this publication and apologize to copyright holders if permission to publish in this form has not been obtained. If any copyright material has not been acknowledged, please write and let us know so we may rectify in any future reprint.

Except as permitted under U.S. Copyright Law, no part of this book may be reprinted, reproduced, transmitted, or utilized in any form by any electronic, mechanical, or other means, now known or hereafter invented, including photocopying, microfilming, and recording, or in any information storage or retrieval system, without written permission from the publishers.

For permission to photocopy or use material electronically from this work, please access www.copyright. com (http://www.copyright.com/) or contact the Copyright Clearance Center, Inc. (CCC), 222 Rosewood Drive, Danvers, MA 01923, 978-750-8400. CCC is a not-for-profit organization that provides licenses and registration for a variety of users. For organizations that have been granted a photocopy license by the CCC, a separate system of payment has been arranged.

Trademark Notice: Product or corporate names may be trademarks or registered trademarks, and are used only for identification and explanation without intent to infringe.

Library of Congress Cataloging-in-Publication Data

Names: Totten, Christopher W., author.
Title: An Architectural approach to level design : processes and experiences / Christopher W. Totten.
Description: Second edition. | Boca Raton : Taylor & Francis, CRC Press, 2019. | Includes bibliographical references and index.
Identifiers: LCCN 2018059043| ISBN 9780815361367 (pbk. : alk. paper) | ISBN 9780815361374 (hardback : alk. paper) | ISBN 9781351116305 (ebook : alk. paper)
Subjects: LCSH: Level design (Computer science) | Software architecture.
Classification: LCC QA76.76.C672 T679 2019 | DDC 005.1/2--dc23
LC record available at https://lccn.loc.gov/2018059043

Visit the Taylor & Francis Web site at
http://www.taylorandfrancis.com

and the CRC Press Web site at
http://www.crcpress.com

For Adeline and Margaret, our little player 1 and 2

Contents

Foreword

B RIAN UPTON, FREELANCE GAME Designer, Owner—Upton Games
You never know what's going to turn out to be useful.

Part of what makes designing games so challenging is that the skill set required to do it well is essentially unbounded. It's hard to draw a clean line around a body of knowledge and say "this is all you need to know to design games" because, depending on the type of game you're making, all sorts of strange and unusual knowledge can turn out to be extremely useful.

Maybe it's an encyclopedic knowledge of the politics of the late Roman Empire. Or maybe it's a fascination with the economics of nineteenth-century railroads. Or maybe it's a lifelong obsession with romance novel tropes. Having a head packed with all sorts of obscure and seemingly irrelevant facts can be incredibly helpful if you're a professional game designer.

And that's true even if the game you're working on doesn't have a direct connection to your personal mental trivia collection. Knowing about the fall of Rome doesn't just help you make games about the fall of Rome, but about any game set in a world where central power is on the wane and local strongmen are stepping in to fill the vacuum. Knowing about railroad robber barons doesn't just help you make games about railroad robber barons, but also about any situation involving exponential economic grown and the struggle between capital and labor. Knowing about romance tropes doesn't just help you create period dating simulations, but also any game where players are expected to develop an emotional attachment to the NPCs they encounter.

You never know what's going to turn out to be useful.

Architecture is one of those things. At first glance, it might not seem as though real-world architecture would matter much to game design. After all, video game levels are constructed out of polygons and textures, not bricks and mortar. We don't have to worry if the structures we invent for our games are structurally sound or economically feasible. With a few mouse clicks we can create mile-high skyscrapers that would bankrupt any real-world developer who tried to build them, and that would collapse under their own weight if they actually were built. The physical constraints that determine so much of the geometry of real-world buildings simply don't apply to virtual structures.

Video game levels also serve different needs than real-world buildings. A real-world building could be designed to be a comforting place to sleep, or an efficient place to work, or a safe place to take refuge in, but it probably won't be designed to showcase a series of combat encounters or jumping challenges. Real-world spaces often have poor gameplay flow. They're too open and interconnected, with too many unlocked doors and uncluttered hallways and too many routes you can take to arrive at the same destination. And, at the same time, they're too closed off and fragmented, with multiple dead ends and bits of dead space where nothing interesting happens.

(I first discovered this back in the late 1990s when the original Rainbow Six team made a model of the Red Storm offices as an Easter Egg. We thought it would be fun to run around and shoot each other in the actual space where the game was developed. We quickly discovered, however, that a bunch of single-person offices connected by straight hallways to a few wide-open team rooms made for a really boring first-person shooter space. The level never made it past the gray box stage.)

So why is knowing about real-world architecture useful for making games?

The answer to this question is two-fold. First off, even though video game spaces shouldn't directly copy real-world spaces, they do need to evoke them. We spend most of our lives living in architected environments, and without even realizing it, we've internalized a great many rules for how buildings are supposed to be laid out. We know how big a standard door is, and how doors are typically placed in relation to each other. We know how long hallways typically are, and how steeply stairs usually rise. We know that a dining room feels different from a kitchen and how both of those feel different from a factory floor.

There's a subtle internal logic to real-world buildings that flows from the purposes for which they were designed and the uses to which they are put. And if a building in a game ignores this logic then we find it disturbing on a subconscious level. It's the Uncanny Valley for level design. Game levels may need to deviate from architectural realism to accommodate particular gameplay situations, but if they deviate too much then our suspension of disbelief collapses. We no longer feel like we're playing inside a real space, but rather a collection of arbitrary textured boxes.

(The uncanniness of improperly constructed spaces is sometimes deliberately used in horror games to put players on edge. Corridors that are unnaturally long, rooms that are unnaturally tall, spaces with too many doors or too few—all of these architectural sins have the accumulated effect of making the player wary and uneasy.)

So, one reason to study architecture if you're going to design games is to give yourself a better understanding of what real buildings look like and how they function. However, the second and more important reason to do it is that architecture gives us a language for talking about how humans perceive, talk about, and interact with space.

Real-world buildings are more than merely utilitarian shelters. How a building uses space and how it situates itself within the space of its surroundings is also a way of encoding meaning. Climbing up a broad flight of stairs to an imposing bronze door encodes a different meaning than descending along a dark, twisting passage to a rusty iron gate. Different architectural forms set up different expectations as we move through and within them. The constraints that they impose upon our actions and perceptions have a powerful material effect upon our understanding of what's happening around us.

This is the primary reason why studying architecture is so useful for game design—because the semiotics of space are the same whether you're talking about a real-world building or a virtual one. Game levels may need to be laid out in unrealistic ways to accommodate the flow of their accompanying gameplay, but they still possess the same capacity to influence the player's attitudes, emotions, and expectations as real-world buildings, and architecture as a discipline has a much longer history of grappling with these issues than game design does. Human beings have been thinking seriously about how to build meaningful structures for at least 5000 years and probably longer. Game design has only started to grapple with the same question for a few decades.

(Of course, games themselves have been around for at least as long as people have been building buildings, and probably longer. But until very recently no one gave much thought to the principles behind designing new ones. New games emerged out of the folk tradition, designed by trial and error and honed through innumerable play sessions. The notion that there are abstract game design principles you can draw on to design a new game from scratch didn't exist until very, very recently. In contrast, people have been writing books/papyrus scrolls/clay tablets about how to build buildings for millennia.)

So, if we're trying to understand how to build our game levels to be both meaningful and comprehensible, it makes a great deal of sense to borrow liberally from the vast body of knowledge that has already been assembled to explain the structure of real-world spaces.

This is where *An Architectural Approach to Level Design* really shines. Drawing on thousands of years of architectural knowledge and practice, Chris Totten neatly condenses this wealth of expertise into memorable and useful nuggets for the practicing level designer. He assumes that the reader has no prior knowledge of architectural design, explaining basic concepts like elevation, section and contour with clarity and precision. But he also delves quite deeply into the semiotics of space, devoting entire chapters to how level design can be used to evoke emotions, tell stories, and builds communities.

As he navigates this critical landscape, Totten continually grounds abstract theory in concrete practice. Design principles are clearly explained using examples from actual games, and accompanied by cleanly-drawn architectural illustrations. In fact, early in the book, he even provides a brief practicum in how to draw such illustrations yourself.

This illuminates another strength of this book. Totten doesn't just explain how spaces can be used to make meaning; he also lays out a comprehensive methodology for making it happen. He not only describes the basic steps of producing an architectural concept, but he beautifully spells out the workflow required to translate a raw concept into a playable level.

The result is a book that is both theoretically exciting and imminently practical. It not only teaches the reader a wealth of useful architectural knowledge, it also encourages them to think about level design in new and creative ways. Even after having read it through several times myself and teaching it in a classroom setting, I still find myself coming up with new ideas whenever I crack it open. It's also, I have to say, a book that resonates deeply with my own approach to both level design (in particular) and game design (in general). I've long thought that existing design theory tends to focus too much on what the player is doing and too little on what the player is thinking. The play space of a game consists of more than just its accumulated interactions and mechanics. There is simultaneously a broad country of play that exists entirely in the mind of the player, a landscape of expectation and anticipation and interpretation that is just as rich and ramified as the moment-to-moment challenges that the game itself poses. *An Architectural Approach to Level Design* directly addresses the challenges of designing for this internal mental play space. Totten hardly discusses dynamic game mechanics at all. Instead he focuses almost entirely on how the static geometry of a game level can nevertheless structure engaging and playful experiences. A game level (like a real-world building) doesn't have to do anything to be playful. Rather it evokes a feeling of playfulness within the mind of any player who actively engages with it. Although Totten doesn't spell this principle out directly, such an approach to thinking about playfulness represents a radical change in how we think about both play and the design of play.

Acknowledgments

I'M FRANKLY BLOWN AWAY to be doing a second edition of this book. When I was writing the first edition in 2013–2014 I could not have imagined the positive response it would earn from many in the industry that I would consider heroes. I am humbled to have the support of so many in this project, so I want to first acknowledge everyone who has expressed their support for me and my level design work. Thank you!

I have also had the privilege to work closely with a number of people who directly impacted my work and I want to acknowledge them here (sorry if I miss anyone).

I thank the staff at AK Peters/CRC Press for allowing me to develop this project for publication, especially Rick Adams and David Fausel (project manager of the first edition) and Jessica Vega, project manager for this new edition and my last book *Level Design: Processes and Experiences*. I thank my wonderful reviewers from back in the first edition, Jeff Howard (who also got me in touch with the publisher) and Helen Stuckey, whose direction was of great benefit to the quality of this book. Also thanks to the contributors for this edition, Dr. Umran Ali, Robin-Yann Storm, Melanie Stegman, Jerry Belich, Kelli Dunlap, and Camden Bayer, for offering their insight into their game and level design processes. A special thanks also goes out to Brian Upton for being a supporter of the book since the first edition and for writing the foreword to this edition.

Thanks to the organizers of the Game Developers Conference (GDC) for sponsoring an event that allows game developers, writers, teachers, and students to meet and make valuable networking connections, some of which made this book possible. Thanks to the GDC Conference Associate program for being such a wonderful part of my life and allowing me to get to GDC in the first place those many years ago.

I certainly would not have had the courage to pursue such a project were it not for the valuable opportunities to discuss the concepts in this book in several venues beforehand. For this I owe a great deal of gratitude to Christian Nutt at Gamasutra, who helped get me started in game criticism. I also thank the organizers of the East Coast Game Conference in Raleigh, North Carolina, and the Digital Games Research Association (DiGRA) for allowing me to speak and properly "playtest" the information contained here.

I had the courage to continue writing about level design thanks to the positivity of several important groups in the level design world. I want to acknowledge The World of Level Design staff for being a great cheerleader for my online design ramblings. Thanks also to the organizers and mentors of the Level Design Workshop at GDC, especially Joel Burgess, Lisa Brown, Mateusz Piaskiewicz, Jim Brown, Claire Hosking, Blake Rebouche, David Shaver, and Andrew Yoder for all the wonderful level design discussion over the past few years. I include Liz England in that list as well, but I wanted to spend an extra sentence also thanking her for her most excellent Twitter bots.

Many thanks to my supportive colleagues at Kent State University, especially Dr. Nicole Willey for running our on-campus writing group that helps ease the terror of impending deadlines. Thanks also to Mike Treanor, Josh McCoy, and Benjamin Stokes for your continued support in my research. Thank you to the staff of the Smithsonian American Art Museum, especially Kaylin Lapan, Lauren Kolodkin, and Gloria Kenyon for helping me explore the intersections between games and the arts as well as letting me put on a showcase of game worlds! Thanks to the D.C. chapter of the International Game Developers Association (IGDA), especially Trey Reyher and Taro Omiya, who have been wonderful collaborators on many gaming endeavors. Also thanks to my new game development community in Ohio, such as the Cleveland Game Developers and in particular Jarryd Huntley and Matt Perrin: your support has meant a lot while I work on projects like this! I certainly cannot forget the faculty of the Catholic University School of Architecture, who have supported my efforts since I began this journey.

Lastly, I thank my parents, without whose guidance I would not have become the person to conceive of a project like this, and my amazing wife, Clara, whose encouragement and support have allowed me to make this book something tangible.

About the Author

CHRISTOPHER **T**OTTEN IS AN Assistant Professor in the Modeling, Animation, and Game Creation program at Kent State University Tuscarawas. He is the founder of Pie for Breakfast Studios, an award-winning Northeast Ohio independent game company, and has done work as an artist, animator, level designer, and project manager in the game industry. He holds a Master's Degree in Architecture with a concentration in Digital Media from the Catholic University of America in Washington, D.C.

Chris is an executive organizer for the Smithsonian American Art Museum (SAAM) Arcade and lifetime member of the International Game Developers Association (IGDA). Chris has written articles featured on Gamasutra, Game Career Guide, and other publications and is a frequent speaker at game industry conferences such as GDC, GDC China, East Coast Game Conference, GDEX, and others. He is the author of *Game Character Creation in Blender and Unity*, released by Wiley Publishing in 2012. He is also the editor of the collected volume, *Level Design: Processes and Experiences.*

Introduction

GAME DESIGNER AND THEORIST Ian Bogost has been quoted as saying that game design is a bit of a "black art."[1] While many people outside the field underestimate the amount of work, expertise, and personnel required to make video games, many inside the industry are humbled by game design's staggering complexity. The International Game Developers Association (IGDA) 2008 curriculum framework for game design education is a testament to this complexity. Over twenty-seven pages of its forty-one-page length are devoted to a list of suggested topics to cover in an academic program on game design.[2] In *The Art of Game Design: A Book of Lenses*,[3] designer Jesse Schell highlights nineteen fields from which a successful game designer must draw knowledge. Both documents cite topics including business and economics, programming, art, psychology, and theater performance theory. Clearly, the entirety of modern game design is a daunting beast.

Perhaps this is why an important part of the game design process, level design, is only now becoming a topic of serious study. Andrew Rollings and Ernest Adams highlight level design's difficulty in their book *Andrew Rollings and Ernest Adams on Game Design* by arguing that there is no one standard way to design levels.[4] Jay Wilbur and John Romero have great respect for the level designer's work, saying "level Design is where the rubber hits the road"[5] and "the level designer is largely responsible for the implementation of the game play in a title."[6]

Level design is not only an important part of game development, it is also one of the most exhilarating. Many aspiring game designers get their start by creating their own custom levels, called mods, in toolsets for existing games. This act of creating the environment for a game and then playing inside your creation is one of the most empowering parts of video games, as both a hobby and a profession. Some games, such as *The Sims*,[7] *Mario Maker*,[8] and *Little Big Planet*,[9] even tout their level creation tools on their packaging to entice potential buyers.

The importance of level design in a game project is exactly why it deserves careful consideration as a subject of both academic and professional study. This book is such a study.

WHAT IS THIS BOOK ABOUT?

This is a book about level design. It is also about how to look at designed space, which game levels, environments, and worlds most certainly are. Real-world architecture, urban environments, and gardens are also designed spaces. At some point, a designer (it doesn't matter which kind; design is mostly universal) sat down to solve a problem that could only be solved by designing an interactive space. This problem could be how to best capture sunlight coming through a window, embody a religious idea, accentuate an important clue to solving a puzzle, or provide the best position for fragging competitors in an online game. Sometimes these spaces are loved by the people who use them, whether it is a home to raise a family, a plaza to enjoy a latte and some people-watching, or a city in which to shoot gangsters and jump cars off of piers.

Comparing level design and architecture can be very simple. It can also reveal things about both fields that we have not seen before. This book reflects on how both level design and architecture solve problems and create meaningful experiences for those using them. From these reflections, it provides an architectural approach to level design that emphasizes spatial design for maximum user engagement.

WHAT CAN WE LEARN FROM ARCHITECTURE?

The topic of game and level design blending with the field of architecture is popular in industry discussions, articles, and conference talks. When people think of integrating architectural thought with game design, they often turn to environmental art styles or references to famous buildings. While these things help create interesting level experiences, they are also the tip of the iceberg in terms of game design's current relationship with architectural design. Rather than simply turning to architecture as a reference for surface level visual elements, we can study how architects conduct space and occupant movement. We can also look to architecture and the many fields it references for inspiration, to understand spatial planning, organization, and how to manage relationships between a space and its occupants.

Many seminal books on game design and many seminal game designers do not base their methodologies for creating experiences in game design alone. To do so is very difficult and risks limiting the body of knowledge we can learn from. While games have arguably existed as long as modern humans, video games have only existed for about forty or fifty years. While the current video game design texts have done well in building a critical discourse in that amount of time, there is still much work to be done.

The books and designers that do, however, pull from other fields often do so to fill in blanks that game design itself cannot fill. How do you create a meaningful succession of rewards to entice players through your game and teach them how to play? Look no further than B.F. Skinner's theory of operant behavior.[10] Need a narrative structure for your hero's epic quest? Try Joseph Campbell's monomyth of the hero's journey.[11] What about a way to make little computer people happy in their little computer environment? Try Christopher Alexander's *A Pattern Language*.[12]

This book will do the same for level design, taking architectural principles and using them as inspiration for video game levels and environments. Like the above examples, level design does not need to stand on its own, but can pull from thousands of years of human knowledge that came before it was a professional field. As designed space, game levels have much to learn from their precursors in real-life architecture, including the development of sight lines, lighting conditions, shade and shadow, exploration, orientation, spatial rhythms, and even how to get epic spaces to be even more epic—among other things.

BUILDING A BRIDGE BETWEEN GAMES AND ARCHITECTURE

All of this discussion of level design and architecture is well and good, but it is ultimately meaningless unless the spaces that result fit into the context of a game. A game, as defined by Katie Salen and Eric Zimmerman, is "a system in which players engage in an artificial conflict, defined by rules, that results in a quantifiable outcome."[13]

To design a game, therefore, is to create the system, the rules by which it runs and by which a player interacts with it, the artificial conflict it is meant to embody, and the criteria by which an outcome is reached in the system. This closely reflects Salen and Zimmerman's definition of *design*: "the process by which a designer creates a context to be encountered by a participant, from which meaning emerges."[14]

This definition can mean the design of either games or architecture. In architecture, the architect is the designer, the building or urban space is the context, the participant is anyone who occupies the space, and the experiences that the occupant has while in the space are the meaning that emerges from it. However, establishing a parallel is not enough; a true link must be established between the design of games and the design of architecture.

Consider Rudolf Kremers's definition of level design: "This is a basic purpose of level design, to interpret the game rules, and to translate them into a construct (a level) that best facilitates play. Another way of expressing this is by stating that 'level design is applied game design.'"[15]

Kremers's definition is a good one that addresses a level's function as a facilitator of a game's rules, as expressed by Wilbur and Romero, and as a construct created by a designer. Where Kremers's definition falters, however, is in the expression of the level as a medium for creating gameplay *and* for using spatial design principles to facilitate meaningful user experiences. These experiences can be created through cognitive interactions with the player or through emotional means—all executed through spatial methods that will be discussed in later chapters. A better definition for the purposes of this book would be: "Level design is the thoughtful execution of game*play* into game*space* for players to dwell in."

The best level designers do not only take the contents of a game's ruleset and embody them in an interactive space. They also thoughtfully employ spatial articulations that enhance a player's journey through that space. These articulations give previews of what's to come, allow players to orient themselves in the environment, provide narrative clues without the need for overt storytelling methods such as cutscenes, and entice further exploration.

Such spaces are gamespaces—spaces that both embody gameplay and facilitate the player's journey through it, allowing him or her to better experience the game's mechanics. These spaces do so in such a way that players spend more time having fun and less time figuring out how to use the space. As a field that has perfected these kinds of spatial experiences over thousands of years, architecture is the perfect precedent to teach us how to create better gamespaces.

WHAT THIS BOOK WILL TEACH YOU

This book explores architectural techniques and theories for level designers to use in their own work. The utilized approach connects architecture and level design in different ways that address the practical elements of how designers construct space and the experiential elements of how and why humans interact with this space. Throughout the book, you will learn the skills listed below.

Spatial Layout

Learning how to create a spatial sequence is paramount to the study of architectural design. Over centuries of work, the field of architecture has developed methodologies for going from design idea to constructed building. These methods include sketching and modeling crude forms to generate a building idea. They also include more sophisticated renderings of buildings through plan, section, elevation, perspective, and even modern 3D visualization techniques. While this book avoids exploring the nuances of drafting, these techniques will be used to illustrate how to get both macro and micro views of your gamespaces for the sake of event layout and pacing.

Beyond the types of media used to plan buildings, the book also explores how architects deal with materials not just from a structural standpoint, but also from an aesthetic one. While level designers deal with materials primarily on a visual level, the practical concerns of material use can be very useful for level designers. For example, many newer level designers wonder how to make the box-shaped spaces inherent to many level editors seem less boxy. They also wonder how to make their realistically textured surfaces feel more like the real-world materials they are conveying in the eyes of players. Understanding how architects use these materials will help create better gamespaces.

Evoking Emotion through Gamespaces

If using spatial layout techniques is how we create contexts for users to inhabit, then the emotions these contexts create are what give these contexts life. Many buildings in the architectural canon are there because they evoke some greater idea or emotion from occupants. The same can be said of great game levels. Using the arrangements of space as a jumping off point, this book will explore how these arrangements respond to emotional factors of game players.

One way in which game designers and architects are inherently different is in the functions of their spaces. While architects typically design for pure function or for the embodiment of positive emotions, game designers are free to utilize negative emotions such as anger, aggression, or fear. Architects have developed a set of rules not only for what to do in design, but also what not to do. Game designers can look to both sets of rules for inspiration, arranging the "what to do" spaces among the "what not to do" spaces to create an emotionally exhilarating sequence of gameplay.

Creating Better Levels through Architectural Theory

Rollings and Adams are correct in saying that there is no one way to design levels. For example, a common level design technique such as *grayboxing*, which is discussed throughout the book, can mean different things to different designers. On the other hand, there are common truths to spatial arrangement that transcend concerns about software techniques. By studying spatial arrangement techniques utilized in great architecture and the kinds of experiences these create, level designers will be able to create similar experiences in their own work regardless of the tools they are using.

The effect that level design has on games is profound. As Kremers points out, "Bad level design can ruin a good game."[16] In current level design practice, playtesting—evaluating a level by having people play it many times to test for experiential and technical functionality—is the standard way of ensuring that levels are good. Utilizing architectural principles of spatial design in addition to playtesting can do two things to make this process easier. The first is allowing designers to utilize historically successful spatial sequences at the outset of design rather than having them only reach success through experimentation or by copying previous games. Second, having a knowledge of architectural design can give level designers a broader vocabulary with which to create gamespaces. As is common in many branches of design, level designers may be aware of many successful spatial layouts through their experiences in the field or through playing games. However, gaining a vocabulary for these layouts transforms them from vaguely understood secrets to concrete tools that can be used over and over again to great effect.

WHAT THIS BOOK WILL NOT TEACH YOU

While this book attempts to offer a broad exploration of design concepts that can enrich level design, there is also a lot of information that is outside of its scope. Some of these topics are addressed here to quell any confusion over the material in this book.

Environment Art

Many game designers confuse level design with the field of environment art. While both contribute to one final finished game level, we will treat these as two distinct disciplines for the purposes of this book. Level design is concerned with the sequence of spaces in a game level and how they create a better gameplay experience for users. Environment art, on the other hand, is the creation of art assets (3D models, 2D sprites, tiles, or textures) that create the look of a game environment. Neither is more or less important than the other, as good environment art will enliven the sequence of spaces that a level designer creates and often give it a context within the game's narrative. Likewise, a good level can utilize environment art assets as part of its system of visual communication—communicating to the player through the repetition of specific assets that come to mean things within the context of a game.

While this book explores how to best use environment art to communicate to players, it does not cover how to create 3D models or 2D textures, sprites, or tiles in art asset creation programs such as 3D Studio Max, Maya, Blender, or Photoshop. There are, however, many other great books on these topics, which you should explore if you are interested in creating environment art in these programs.

CAD Software

This book will also not teach you how to utilize computer-aided design (CAD) or building information modeling (BIM) software. As with art asset creation software, teaching these software packages is outside the scope of the book.

As for the use of this software to level designers, CAD is discussed in Chapter 2, "Drawing for Level Designers," as a potential tool for level design, though for different reasons than how architects use it. BIM, on the other hand, is of little use to level designers, as it is much more tightly connected to the construction management functions of real-world architecture. BIM programs such as Revit or ArchiCAD allow designers to create drawings of buildings using premade elements—doors, windows, structural elements, etc.—and store construction information in each specific element that can be used for ordering materials and directing contractors.

Game Engines

In most applications, level design occurs within programs, known as game engines, that are used to create video games. Modern game engines provide a framework for rendering assets on-screen, responding to player input, facilitating artificial intelligence (AI) interactions, and simulating real-world physics, among other things. In the industry, many different game engines exist, with some studios building their own for internal use. While there are popular ones, there is no universally agreed-upon industry standard as with other types of software.

This book describes a selection of engines that are popular at the time of its writing, but it avoids providing in-depth software tutorials for using these engines. This is done for two reasons: one is the aforementioned lack of an industry standard. If this book contained tutorials in the Unity engine, for example, it would be a "Unity book," rather than one approachable for users of Game Maker or the Unreal Engine. Engines come and go as technology advances, so it is hoped that readers can get more evergreen knowledge from this book even when today's engines are historic footnotes. As with environment art, a wide selection of books that teach the use of these game engines is available that interested readers can explore.

UPDATES FOR THE SECOND EDITION

Hello from the future! Or rather… several years after I wrote parts of this introduction. What you are holding in your hand is the second edition of *An Architectural Approach to Level Design*. In the years since the first edition's publication, the area of level design writing and criticism has progressed by leaps and bounds thanks to some really excellent people in the game industry. I have also grown as a designer and continue to find new things to talk about as I make more and more levels. For anyone looking at this second edition and wondering what is different from the first, I wanted to take some time to cover the updates I have made to the book.

New and expanded content: First and foremost, the book has expanded to include two entirely new chapters on designing tutorial levels and procedural generation systems. In these sections, you will find information for level designers on how to design for these challenging and nuanced areas of games. Along with these come deeper dives into areas of architectural theory relevant to these topics such as approaches, overviews, and pattern languages.

Another major addition are the contribution sections from industry professionals representing areas from big studio game development (or "triple-A") to indies and academics. In this book, I talk a lot about my own experiences as a level designer and games I have worked on, but level design is not something one designer can define alone. With this in mind, I have worked with level designers to bring their techniques into this book so readers can learn from a variety of sources.

Lastly, I have revisited several chapters from the first edition to clarify their language and update them with new techniques that I have been using in recent years. What was previously the second chapter ("Tools and Techniques for Level Design") is now two separate chapters, "Drawing for Level Designers" and "Level Design Workflows." This allowed me to expand the techniques found in each to provide even more useful information to readers. I have also reconfigured several other chapters to include new topics and principles.

Updated references: An inherent challenge of writing about the games industry is that what is "current" can change pretty rapidly. This is very different from architecture, where famous buildings are referenced well beyond their dates of occupancy. I have tried to take a blended approach with this: there are games that I have played in the time between the first and second editions that I know should be referenced to keep the work current. However, I am also a big believer in the staying power of great level design, so you will find many old favorites still mentioned in the text. I have tried to add references to more recent games in addition to old standards, rather than instead of them, so readers can experience the spatial concepts in a variety of games.

In the years since the first edition, there has also been a lot of activity in level design writing, both in professional contexts from more fan-accessible sources (YouTube videos, games journalism, blogs, etc.) I have found some of these ideas, like Mark Brown's diagramming method from his "Boss Keys" YouTube series, particularly earth-shattering. In this new edition, I have documented my findings from applying other designers' concepts in my own work. Readers looking for a place to find great level design criticism should keep an eye on the "works cited" section of each chapter as I've tried to update them with the newest resources.

Exercises: I have been very thankful and humbled to have level design instructors approach me to say that they have used the first edition of this book in their classrooms. Professional developers have also sent me games they made to practice concepts from the book, which is absolutely mind-blowing. With that in mind, I have added exercises to each chapter. These exercises suggest ways to integrate techniques listed in the book such as the diagramming methods, design principles, and others into actual classroom assignments or self-directed practice sessions.

As a teacher myself, I have written these as more general "design prompts" rather than prescriptive tutorials so as to not interfere with anyone's teaching methods. In this way, users can try these exercises in software or tools that work for them: 2D, 3D, sketchbooks, writing, and so forth. Keeping the exercises away from specific software also addresses the desire for the book to remain evergreen long after the current selection of software tools is gone.

WHO SHOULD READ THIS BOOK

This book looks at level design through the lens of architectural and spatial experience theory. While matters relevant to game art are discussed, it is not a book on environmental modeling or how to create 3D game assets. If you have not yet bought this book and are perhaps reading it in a bookstore, then you may want to see if you fit into one of the following groups:

The level designer who wants to understand architecture better and bring elements of it into his or her work. Many discussions of game levels and architecture focus on environment art creation, with statements of how "cool" certain architectural styles or layouts would look in the art for a game. This book brings level designers into the fray by discussing spatial concepts that have bearing on the layout and arrangement of gamespaces relevant to their gameplay goals. It also features advice from industry veterans who have spent time building game levels and worlds, or who have contributed to the field in other ways.

The environment artist seeking to better communicate with players through his or her work. The environment artist is not forgotten in this text. Visual communication with players involves the graphics, colors, forms, and textures that constitute a game's environmental art assets. Throughout the book, methodologies for utilizing a game's artistic presentation together with its spatial gameplay design are proposed for creating memorable player experiences.

Teachers and students studying level design. This book approaches level design from a point of view that synthesizes several bodies of knowledge into one source and employs them through case studies. With the advent of the game design degree, a danger facing the industry is the loss of the eclectic experiences of designers who come from other backgrounds to join the gaming industry. By viewing an important element of game creation, level design, through topics relevant to architecture, this book gives teachers and students in game design programs a broad landscape to pull from. Students especially can look to designer interviews to gain insight into the process from industry veterans. The book also includes exercises designed to spur deep analysis and discussion.

Architects. While this book mainly focuses on the practice of level design as educated by architectural principles, it is also written to enliven architectural design through the implementation of game design methodologies. This book recommends an iterative workflow focused around playtesting and audience interaction in interactive spatial simulations. Many architects today find themselves frustrated by the confines of 2D space and the guesswork that comes with trying to create meaningful spatial experiences with plan, elevation, and section drawings. This book discusses space and architecture as an interactive medium dependent on user input, much as it was throughout history.

Overall, if you have an interest in game design, level design, or architecture, this book will provide a focused and practical approach to level design that cannot be found elsewhere. Whether you are a professional level designer, artist, or teacher looking for another perspective on your craft; a game design student looking for input from other industries; or an architect trying to learn what all these interactive technologies can do for your own industry, this book has something for you. As games approach that murky and difficult-to-define status known as art, they should be studied in the light of other fields that create meaningful user experiences or even as brave new examples for the established canon.

HOW TO USE THIS BOOK

This book is separated into a variety of topics on experiential concepts in architectural and video game level design. These concepts are approached in a general manner rather than focusing on specific game types or genres. For example, there are no chapters with names such as "Sight Lines for First-Person Shooters," but rather ones on spatial design elements that can be applied to many game types. This was done purposefully so that the techniques are explored in a less prescriptive manner, and so that designers can implement them in any way they choose.

While the subject of each chapter can be understood without reading the chapters that came before, each portion of the book builds on the knowledge from previous sections. As such, it is recommended that readers read chapters in order to avoid confusion when a chapter refers to information given in one preceding it.

This book has exercises for designers who wish to practice the concepts in the book or teachers and students who wish to use the book in their classroom. These exercises are meant to be approached as design and analysis prompts rather than tutorials. The goal of these is for designers to integrate these prompts into their processes (or pedagogy in the case of teachers) as seamlessly as possible. In them you will find writing prompts (appropriate for design journals), drawing exercises (useful if you keep a sketchbook), paper prototyping exercises, game-testing exercises, and digital exercises (suitable for any game engine).

HARDWARE AND SOFTWARE REQUIREMENTS

This book practices some software agnosticism by not making tutorials in a certain application a requirement. However, readers may wish to practice the level design methods in one of several popular game engines. Many of the most widely used game engines for both independent and commercial game development offer free versions, often for non-commercial use. Check their websites to find out the exact terms of how they may be licensed. Here are a few links to websites where you can learn about acquiring free game engine software:

Unity 3D: www.Unity3D.com

Unreal Engine: www.unrealengine.com

Source SDK: https://developer.valvesoftware.com/wiki/SDK_Installation

Game Maker: http://www.yoyogames.com

Construct: https://www.scirra.com/construct2

The hardware specifications for each of these tools can be found on the following pages:

Unity hardware specs: https://unity3d.com/unity/system-requirements

Unreal hardware specs: https://wiki.unrealengine.com/Recommended_ Hardware

Source SDK hardware specs: Source SDK shares the same system requirements as any game that it comes with.

Game maker requirements: http://www.yoyogames.com/get

Construct system requirements: https://www.scirra.com/manual/6/ system-requirements

You may want to download some other tools for creating architectural map drawings, and 2D or 3D art assets:

Blender 3D (free 3D art and animation program): www.blender.org

GIMP (free 2D art program): www.gimp.org

Draftsight (free CAD software): http://www.3ds.com/products/-draft sight/overview/

WHAT'S INSIDE THIS BOOK

This book explores an architectural approach to level design through a variety of topics on spatial design. Each topic is accompanied by studies of both game level and real worldbuilding cases. Through these studies, the book proposes spatial design principles for game levels in 2D, 3D, and multiplayer applications. Each chapter is also accompanied by a level design exercise so users can practice what they've learned. The chapters and the topics they cover are as follows.

Chapter 1, "A Brief History of Architecture and Level Design"

This chapter gives a brief overview of the architectural history that is relevant throughout the rest of the book. This includes a listing of styles and techniques from prehistory through Postmodernism. This chapter also discusses several milestones in how the spaces of games evolved from single-screen games with limited movement into the sprawling 3D worlds of current games.

Industry Perspective: Dr. Umran Ali

This contribution features Dr. Umran Ali, Senior Lecturer at the University of Salford, describing his research project called *Virtual Landscapes*. In this groundbreaking project, he observed the development and trends of game environments that simulate natural landscapes from their infancy in the early days of game consoles to today.

Chapter 2, "Drawing for Level Designers"

This chapter further explores our definition of level design and provides an overview of some useful drawing and diagramming techniques for level designers. It also covers digital tools that designers can use to plan their game environments including industry standard ones and ones from architecture.

Industry Perspective: Robin-Yann Storm

In this contribution, Guerrilla Games Tool Designer Robin-Yann Storm describes the qualities of a good toolset that will help level designers do their work efficiently. He describes how different features affect a level designer's workflow and what designers should expect when using these features.

Chapter 3, "Level Design Workflows"

This chapter approaches level design from a project management standpoint, describing how designers can formalize their processes in stages to go from concept to creation. It describes how level designers develop mechanics over the course of several levels to create satisfying difficulty curves. It also describes how designers create game worlds that are easily read by players, which will be a theme throughout the rest of the book.

Chapter 4, "Basic Gamespaces"

This chapter teaches lessons on architectural spatial arrangement, starting from basic principles and then applying these principles to several famous types of gamespaces, such as linear and sandbox spaces. It then analyzes spaces in famous games to discover spatial types that can be used among a variety of games. Lastly, it discusses how game cameras accentuate level spaces in games based on their positioning in relation to the player character.

Industry Perspective: Jerry Belich

In this contribution, experimental game and experience designer Jerry Belich showcases his games that blend digital and electronic technologies and real-world spaces and objects. Not only does his process include planning games based on mechanics, but also within the metrics of things that players can directly interact with.

Chapter 5, "Communicating through Environment Art"

Chapter 5 moves beyond overviews of how spaces are used in games and investigates how creating repeatable architectural forms allows designers to communicate with players. Such techniques are demonstrated as methods for changing player behaviors and teaching players game mechanics through subtle in-level tutorials. They are also discussed as methods for helping players retain and develop their knowledge of how to play through a game through level design.

Industry Perspective: Interview with Greg Grimsby

In this interview, George Mason University Assistant Professor and four-teen-year game industry veteran Greg Grimsby describes his influences, his processes for environmental design, and how fine art inspires him. He offers his insight from his time as an art director on games like *Dark Age of Camelot, Ultima Forever,* and *Warhammer Online: Age of Reckoning.*

Chapter 6, "Building Exciting Levels with Dangerous Architecture"

This chapter introduces spatial arrangements and techniques that allow designers to evoke emotions connected with human survival instincts and contrasting elements. It shows how arrangements of specifically sized spaces entice players to move along paths. It also shows techniques for using lighting to engage curiosity or fear responses.

Industry Perspective: Camden Bayer

In this contribution, Arkane Studios Level Architect Camden Bayer describes the day-to-day work of a level designer and the benefits of having a shared language in the industry. He describes how playtesting, paying careful attention to the needs of players, and doing usability research has helped him refine his maps.

Chapter 7, "Enticing Players with Rewarding Spaces"

Chapter 7 utilizes psychological theories popular with game designers to discover how game levels can reward players. It explores the architectural principle of denial to show how spaces and sight lines can be used to make levels that entice players to move through them.

Chapter 8, "Level 1–1: The Tutorial Level"

This chapter encourages designers to take a step back and focus special design attention on the first levels of games. Utilizing concepts from the preceding chapters, this chapter explores how game levels teach players how to play a game. It also describes the building blocks of building excit-ing and non-intrusive tutorial content with architectural approaches, effective spatial communication, and effectively utilizing game assets. It also describes how several educational games teach in their levels so level designers can learn how to turn lesson plans into gameplay.

Industry Perspective: Melanie Stegman

In this contribution, Molecular Jig founder Melanie Stegman provides a detailed project report from the development of her game *Immune Defense*. This report shows her process of determining how, over the course of several levels, her game should model processes from molecular biology to best teach players about how cells defend the body.

Chapter 9, "Storytelling in Gamespaces"

This chapter addresses narrative elements of games and explores the different ways that built spaces can tell or facilitate stories. It discusses how changes in materials and environment art can assist the storytelling process. It also explores how storytelling opportunities can be rewards for passing through difficult gameplay sequences.

Industry Perspective: Kelli Dunlap

In this contribution, psychologist and game designer Kelli Dunlap, PsyD analyzes the ways that levels can develop psychologically complex game characters. She describes the choices the player can make about characters in levels from the *Halo* series. This contribution goes beyond environment art storytelling and into the realm of interactive and moral character-building through interactivity.

Chapter 10, "Possibility Spaces and Worldbuilding"

This chapter discusses how game levels can be built to accommodate different player styles and create robust worlds with many play choices. It discusses how some gamespaces expand based on the abilities players have and that they acquire during gameplay. It also shows how some architects and game designers provide visual overviews of the spaces they create, and how ancient practices of Japanese garden design can inform the designs of game worlds.

Chapter 11, "Working with Procedurally Generated Levels"

This chapter outlines approaches for level designers to work with systems that generate levels while still maintaining the human-centric element of handmade levels. It describes the types of procedural generation systems used for level design. It then describes architectural theory for designing chunks of space that can be mixed and matched. The chapter then shows case studies from several games that blend procedural systems with hand-made design.

Industry Perspective: Interview with Chris Pruett
In this interview, Oculus VR Head of 3rd Party Publishing and Head Task Master of Robot Invader Chris Pruett describes the levels that inspire him and works outside of games that he finds impactful. He also describes his process for designing and testing levels for several different styles of games from platformers to adventure games.

Chapter 12, "Influencing Social Interaction with Level Design"
Chapter 12 explores how urban designers arrange buildings of different use types to facilitate social interaction and unforeseen in-game events. These studies can influence quest structure in single-player games, or even how players interact in massively multiplayer online (MMO) games.

Chapter 13, "Sound, Music, and Rhythm in Level Design"
Chapter 13 addresses an often overlooked part of spatial design in games: sound design. It explores how architects have used acoustic design to create different spatial experiences and how rhythms in space and sound can drive gameplay. It also explores how sound can enhance many of the spatial types found elsewhere in the book.

ENDNOTES

1. Fullerton, Tracy, Christopher Swain, and Steven Hoffman. *Game Design Workshop: A Playcentric Approach to Creating Innovative Games.* 2nd ed. Amsterdam: Elsevier Morgan Kaufmann, 2008.
2. Gold, Susan. *IGDA Curriculum Framework: The Study of Games and Game Development.* PDF file, version 3.2 Beta. February 2008. http://www.igda.org/wiki/images/e/ee/Igda2008cf.pdf.
3. Schell, Jesse. *The Art of Game Design: A Book of Lenses.* Amsterdam: Elsevier/Morgan Kaufmann, 2008.
4. Rollings, Andrew, and Ernest Adams. *Andrew Rollings and Ernest Adams on Game Design.* Indianapolis, IN: New Riders, 2003.
5. Saltzman, Marc. *Game Design: Secrets of the Sages.* Indianapolis, IN: Macmillan Digital, 1999.
6. Shahrani, Sam. *Educational Feature: A History and Analysis of Level Design in 3D Computer Games—Pt. 1.* Gamasutra. http://www.gamasutra.com/view/feature/131083/educational_feature_a_history_and_.php (accessed October 20, 2012).

7. The Sims. Maxis (developer), Electronic Arts (publisher), February 4, 2000. PC game.

8. Mario Maker. Nintendo (developer and publisher), September 10, 2015. Nintendo Wii U game.

9. Little Big Planet. Media Molecule (developer), Sony Computer Entertainment (publisher), October 2008. Playstation 3 video game.

10. Salen, Katie, and Eric Zimmerman. *Rules of Play: Game Design Fundamentals.* Cambridge, MA: MIT Press, 2003, p. 345.

11. Campbell, Joseph. *The Hero with a Thousand Faces.* 2nd ed. Princeton, NJ: Princeton University Press, 1968.

12. Donovan, Tristan. *Replay: The History of Video Games.* East Sussex, England: Yellow Ant, 2010. Will Wright was famously inspired to create *The Sims* after reading *A Pattern Language* by Christopher Alexander. The game was originally about building architectural spaces according to Alexander's language of architectural patterns. *The Sims* characters' original purpose was to score the player's use of the patterns.

13. Salen, Katie, and Eric Zimmerman. *Rules of Play: Game Design Fundamentals.* Cambridge, MA: MIT Press, 2003, p. 80.

14. Salen, Katie, and Eric Zimmerman. *Rules of Play: Game Design Fundamentals.* Cambridge, MA: MIT Press, 2003, p. 41.

15. Kremers, Rudolf. *Level Design: Concept, Theory, and Practice.* Wellesley, MA: A.K. Peters, 2009, p. 18.

16. Kremers, Rudolf. *Level Design: Concept, Theory, and Practice.* Wellesley, MA: A.K. Peters, 2009, p. 3.

CHAPTER 1

A Brief History of Architecture and Level Design

A LOT OF GAME DESIGNERS think of architecture as a thing to study when they need historic precedents to enhance their environment art or create an epic backdrop for their game. Using architectural forms that the player recognizes but may associate with exotic places is one way to enhance the experience of your game. These experiences enhance a game's ability to bring players into its make-believe world and provide the feeling that the player's actions have some sort of effect on important events. These can be good uses for architectural history, but by truly understanding humanity's built past, we can learn more exactly how space affects interactivity.

Looking to historic precedents can have other important effects for designers, too. Beyond being inspirations for backdrops, historical spaces have many lessons to teach about how space is composed. While form has always been a consideration of architects, historic buildings were also built with a great focus on the experience they created for visitors. As such, level designers looking to architecture for insight into their own work can learn a great deal about composing sight lines, telling stories with levels, inviting social play, and many other spatial design principles by carefully studying historic structures.

This chapter provides a brief overview of architectural history with a focus on the buildings that are important for our explorations in the rest of the book. We look at the evolution of gamespaces to discover how game rules and technological limitations have created interesting design opportunities. Finally, we explore some guidelines for visual analysis that will influence how we play gamespaces.

What you will learn in this chapter:

Breaking the rules of level design

An experiential history of architecture

The history of gamespaces

Ways of seeing for level design

BREAKING THE RULES OF LEVEL DESIGN

Let us get something out of the way early on: is level design a field that one enters by learning software or by learning theory? As a follow-up question: is level design a field that should be advanced through new software or new theory? These are not really easy questions to answer and for most developers, what is most important might change over time.

On one hand, the limitations of the platform upon which a given game is developed or the workflow that a game engine supports have a great impact on how a designer works. For many designers, understanding how technology impacts design brings a wealth of intrigue. Digital game development has traditionally been seen as a discipline related to science, technology, engineering, and math (STEM), so the idea that technology is core to understanding game worlds is not far off from many designers' feelings. You hear lots of industry veterans speak poorly of "game studies" as a discipline because it often fails to include the practical use of game-making software. For designers in a tools-first camp, level design is something one studies by opening an engine like Unreal and mastering the building process.

Theory-focused designers, on the other hand, see technology as a means to an end, a tool for creating experiences that are otherwise described by intangible ideas like spatial psychology and game feel. For these designers, studying other games is important: learning from the successes and failures of previous designs is a way to build new and better ones. This allows them to decode the more mysterious elements of game experiences through theoretical guidelines rather than technology "best practices."

Among the many facets of game design, level design is one of the most difficult to isolate as having one correct methodology. The tools and techniques that build a great level for one game do not always translate into other games or genres. Saying that all designers should focus on technology or theory fails in a lot of ways: there are lots of games designed around theoretical goals that ignore basic playability or bug-fixing. There are also wonderful showcases for technology, such as recreating a real-world building or city in a game engine, that fail because these places don't make very interesting game levels.

Level design cannot be learned in the same way something like 3D game art can. With few exceptions, there is an accepted way of creating 3D art, just as there are accepted ways of creating game sound or specific classes one would use for defining inputs when scripting in a game engine. Software-based tutorials for level design typically utilize engines geared toward specific game types (often first-person shooters). While these demonstrate software-specific methods that get developers started with a tool, they often do little to teach developers what makes spaces memorable.

Confused yet? That's okay: at the time of this writing, level design is undergoing an identity crisis that game design has been undergoing for several decades. Prior to 2003, books on the general design of games and game design theory were rare, and many books on "game design" were actually software or coding manuals. One of the earliest examples of a book devoted to game design theory is *The Art of Computer Game Design*[1] by Chris Crawford. Written in 1984, it was one of the few game design theory books for many years. In the 2000s, publications such as *Andrew Rollings and Ernest Adams on Game Design*,[2] *Rules of Play: Game Design Fundamentals*,[3] *The Art of Game Design*,[4] and *Game Design Workshop*[5] advanced the field from purely computational to an aesthetic practice. These books take a much more generalist approach to game design, showing readers how to conceive of games through their mechanical, narrative, or experiential elements. Ian Schreiber and Brenda Brathwaite's *Challenges for Game Designers*[6] has readers actively deconstruct games to learn new things about them. In this way, games become modular systems that can be shaped by designers rather than the result of specific how-to manuals. Many of these books draw from fields outside of game design to influence their material. Salen and Zimmerman discuss not only the design of famous games, but also the work of psychologists, designers, architects, and others to synthesize how one might create games.

We need to similarly break the rules of how we understand level design if we are to advance it. While it can be beneficial to explore the design of levels for games of specific genres, there is also a lot of room for generalization. For example, if we were to say, "In first-person shooters, it is tactically advantageous to have a high position to shoot from," this could be a good criterion for designing deathmatch maps: having lots of sniping positions and crisscrossing catwalks. If we remove the specificity to first-person shooters, however, we can say, "It is advantageous to have a high position when in a game level." This can then be applied to stealth games, fighting games, platformers, first-person shooters, and many others (Figure 1.1). Understanding this, a developer working in a specific engine can apply this spatial knowledge in whatever way works best for it: creating a tall BSP Brush geometry in Unreal, importing a tall level object into Unity, building a tall structure with tiles in Game Maker, etc. This is how I approach level design in this book: as information that designers can utilize in the context of their software of choice.

In this way, architectural history has a lot to show us about how gamespaces can be constructed. Some of the most famous pieces of architecture are the result of a designer taking an intangible idea and embodying it in a structure that has to support occupants, withstand the elements, and not fall down. Architecture is a field built on *practical theory* that can provide level designers with insight in both how humans perceive space, and cool ways to construct space. If we understand level design as the application of a broad set of general spatial theories applied to playable games, we can use experientially rich architecture—that means to elicit

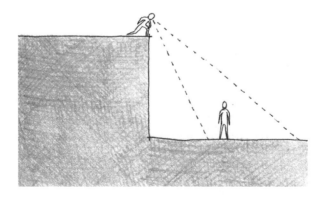

FIGURE 1.1 Height generally offers strategic advantages to players in game levels. This is a guideline that can apply to many game genres and types.

an emotional response from occupants or affect their behavior in some way—as a precedent for our own level designs.

AN EXPERIENTIAL HISTORY OF ARCHITECTURE

There are many ways to understand the history of architecture. Some writers focus on a history of structural components: post-and-lintel construction, column types, arches, domes, vaults, etc. (Figure 1.2). Others focus on the evolutions of styles over time. Some styles have philosophies that impact how one explores works in that style, but often they focus on the formal or sculptural aspects of buildings. Lastly, there is the evolution of architectural experiences. These can be closely related to cultural factors of the times and places in which they were built. They often most closely reflect the ideas of the designers and builders of space. Experientially focused buildings utilize space to create specific experiences or evoke some idea broader than the architecture itself.

Understanding these varied outlooks on architectural history can be useful to game and level designers. Having proper structural elements in a level adds to the *structural believability* of a gamespace. If a column does

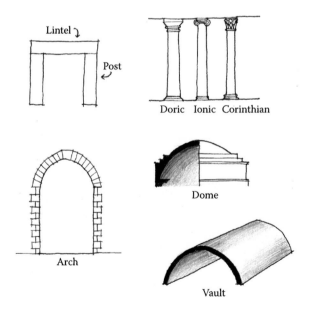

FIGURE 1.2 Standard structural elements found in architecture. These can be useful to game designers and environment artists seeking to have believable architectural components in their game levels.

not look like it would reasonably support a building in real-life players will notice—breaking player engagement. Knowledge of architectural style and form also helps art directors create the look of games. Some games utilize fictional architectures inspired by real styles. The *Halo* series, for example, often utilizes Gothic-inspired motifs for game levels,[7] such as in *Halo 4*'s[8] Requiem mission (Figure 1.3). Architectural allusions can be a good way to theme your gamespace or give it a sense of epic otherworldliness. In the case of *Halo*, the vertical elements of Forerunner buildings lend to the Forerunner race's perceived power and mythical presence in the series. Style and form will be an important part of the discussions in this book, as they contain the language through which we communicate with players.

It is, however, the experiential elements of architecture that most of this book focuses on. In many ways, level design is about how players utilize space. Level spaces in games are about creating cohesive, engaging experiences for players. This is why we focus not on the entirety of architectural history—that is a topic for an entire book, several of which already exist—but instead on a selection of architectural pieces that have some important experience to talk about. Some of these pieces will also have structural or formal elements worthy of note, which is discussed later in the book. However, a building's inclusion in this historic overview is ultimately to serve our own spatial design goals: creating a meaningful and emotionally evocative user experience.

FIGURE 1.3 The Gateway structure at the end of *Halo 4*'s Requiem mission features Gothic architecture-inspired elements such as tall pointed arches and a reliance on vertical linear elements.

Elements of Architecture and Level Design

The Roman architect Vitruvius, who lived around 40 BCE, considered *firmitas* (firmness), *utilitias* (utility), and *venustas* (delight) to be the vital elements of architecture.[9] This book, based on spatial design theory while addressing practical elements of level construction, utilizes elements similar to those outlined by Vitruvius.

Functional Requirements

First and foremost, your game must work. This is the *firmitas* of level design. It is for this reason that this book will keep theory discussions grounded in level construction methods. Chapter 3, for example, discusses practical elements of level design, including overviews of level construction methods for several engines. Later chapters discuss theory with an eye toward how game assets may be used to fulfill experiential goals for level design.

Usability

Next, gamespaces must be usable. In this way, we should concentrate on how players see gamespace through points of view, game cameras, and how they navigate levels. This element of level design concentrates on navigation and teaching. As we will see, levels are an opportunity for game designers to have an indirect conversation with players. As such, our game levels should teach players how to use themselves and speak in easily understood language.

Delight

Lastly, our gamespaces should be rewarding to go through. For this, we must engage the psychological elements of level design and understand how levels guide players through emotional experiences. Note that I am avoiding the word "fun" here. Many games strive for playful, visceral, and thrilling experiences, but games can also be enormously scary, personal, heartbreaking, funny, and even tragic. For this reason, we will discuss successful levels as being emotionally resonant: that great art can bum you out, make you think, or produce empathy is what makes it great. By challenging and rewarding players, we offer them opportunities to have agency over the climactic elements of games in ways no other media form can offer. For this, we should strive to create the most engaging experience possible.

It is important to note that these experiences are not mutually exclusive, nor is any one hierarchically more important than another in level design (Figure 1.4). It is also important to understand these elements, as they are the lens through which we will explore our experiential history of architecture.

The Beginnings of Architectural Sight Lines

In its earliest form, architecture was simply a means of shelter—the ultimate in fulfilling functional requirement. Fitting early humankind's migratory lifestyle, early dwellings were in caves or were constructed from temporary, portable materials such as animal skins and poles. As humans became increasingly agricultural, they settled in a single place and their shelters became more hut-like. This occurred about 12,000 years ago, during the Holocene period.[10] Over time, settlements became large cities, one of the earliest being the biblical Jericho, originally settled in around 8000 BCE in what is now Palestine.

With the rise of urban living came the rise of non-hunter/gatherer roles for occupants. Among these were priests and other hierarchically important persons who oversaw the settlement's links to deities and the afterlife. Concentration on the spiritual elements of one's life also necessitated the construction of buildings for spiritual purposes, especially worship and burial. The architecture of these buildings reacted to sacred elements in the lives of their builders. Western European sites such as the Newgrange passage grave in County Meath, Ireland, and Stonehenge in

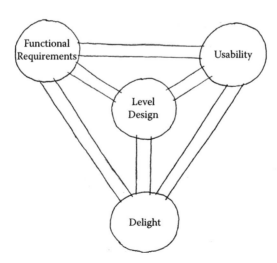

FIGURE 1.4   A diagram of the three elements of level design and how they correspond to one another.

Salisbury, England, are examples of this type of architecture. A transom-like opening in the Newgrange grave allows the light of sunrise during the winter solstice to enter and illuminate the grave's inner chamber (Figure 1.5). Stonehenge is oriented such that the sunrise during the summer solstice occurs directly over a heel stone at its eastern end. This has led some to conclude that the site was a giant observatory for prehistoric peoples (Figure 1.6). The examples of Newgrange and Stonehenge illustrate the early acknowledgment of designed sight lines in architecture. In both cases, architectural elements were carefully planned such that they

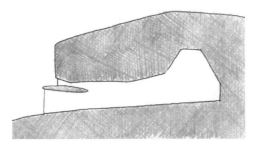

FIGURE 1.5 A sectional diagram of the Newgrange passage grave in County Meath, Ireland (constructed ca. 3100 BCE), showing the transom-like passage that allows light to enter the inner chamber at specific times of the year.

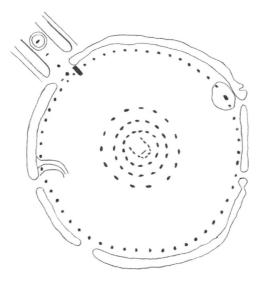

FIGURE 1.6 Stonehenge, located on the Salisbury Plain in England (constructed ca. 2900–1400 BCE), utilizes architectural elements to establish sight lines to important astrological phenomena.

were positioned for best observing specific astrological phenomena. Even in these early stages, we can see how designers utilized architectural forms to direct the attentions of occupants. This will be vital to us as we study user interaction in level design.

Architecture as Representation in Ancient Mesopotamia

The invention of written language by the Sumerians in 3500 BCE is largely considered the border between prehistoric and historic periods in human history. The Sumerians were one of several civilizations that began in Mesopotamia, a territory in modern-day Iraq, Iran, Syria, and Turkey considered the cradle of Western civilization. Mesopotamia was home to several peoples, including the Sumerians, Akkadians, Assyrians, and Babylonians.

The Sumerians worshipped many deities, and thus greatly influenced the development of temple forms. During the Neo-Sumerian period (ca. 2150–2000 BCE), they developed the *ziggurat*, a temple raised on an artificial mound, often built of kiln-fired brick. The development of the ziggurat is important in the development of architecture as a system of representation. The ziggurat form (Figure 1.7) is said to have fulfilled two functions: elevating temples closer to the gods, and recalling the mountains from which the Sumerians migrated. In this way, the Sumerians were using shapes or ornamentation of buildings to convey a larger idea.

Later Mesopotamian civilizations, such as the Babylonians and Assyrians, would also use architecture as representational forms. The constantly warring Assyrians especially utilized their architecture as a means to convey their power and ferocity. They made great use of the ziggurat form to elevate their palaces above surrounding villages. In Sargon II's royal city of Korsabad, built in 720 BCE, realistic sculptures

FIGURE 1.7   The Ziggurat at Ur (built in the city–state of Ur, modern-day Iraq, ca. 2100 BCE) typifies the ziggurat form. These buildings brought temples closer to the gods and are said to have been constructed to resemble the mountainous regions from which the Sumerians came. The city of Ur is also notable for having one of the first known board games: the Royal Game of Ur.

of animals—bulls, eagles, etc.—and of conquering armies warned visitors of the dangers of defying Assyrian power. The spatial layout of the palace utilized circuitous sequences of rooms for reaching important chambers such as the throne room. This was to confuse and further accentuate the absolute power of the Assyrians (Figure 1.8). The representational systems utilized by Mesopotamian cultures will be useful as we study how to build game worlds and use art and sound assets to set environmental tone.

Architecture as Statement in Ancient Egypt

Ancient Egyptian civilization began in ca. 3000 BCE with the uniting of Upper and Lower Egypt by Pharaoh King Menes. Egyptian monumental architecture focused heavily on establishing links between the pharaohs and the gods. It was believed that during life, the pharaohs were manifestations of the falcon-headed god Horus. Upon death, they were linked with Osiris, lord of the underworld. Both gods were linked with Ra, the sun god. It was for this reason that many Egyptian architectural works utilize the *pyramid* form, either as an entire building or as the tops of obelisks (Figure 1.9), as it was believed to establish links between the pharaohs and the sun god.

Imhotep, court architect to the pharaoh Djoser, designed one of the first pyramids in 2630 BCE. The building was begun as another traditional Egyptian form, a *mastaba*—short stone tomb—but was elaborated on by

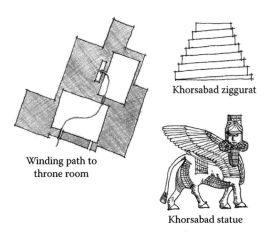

Khorsabad ziggurat

Winding path to
throne room

Khorsabad statue

FIGURE 1.8 Sargon II's palace at Korsabad (built ca. 720 BCE) utilized architectural form, sculptural ornament, and disorienting spatial sequences to assert the dominance of the Assyrians to visitors.

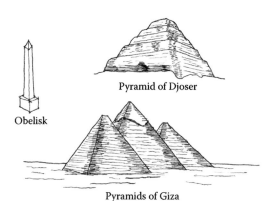

FIGURE 1.9 The pyramid form was used in ancient Egypt to establish links between pharaohs and the sun god Ra. This image of a typical Egyptian obelisk, the step pyramid of Djoser (built in 2630 BCE), and the Great Pyramids of Giza (built between 2550 and 2460 BCE) demonstrates uses of the form.

stacking several mastabas on top of one another. Other notable pyramids include the famous Great Pyramids at Giza, built between 2550 and 2460 BCE for the pharaohs Khufu, Khafre, and Menkaure. The chambers in these pyramids have symbolic associations based on their materials. The physical positioning of chambers has symbolic significance, such as those bored into the bedrock below the pyramids, representing the underworld. Similarly, special materials such as red granite are used to emphasize important spaces such as the king's chamber in Khufu's pyramid. The constructions of early Egyptian monuments and tombs, from form to materials, were carefully planned to communicate the importance of their patrons.

Later Egyptian works would move away from the pyramid form and toward temple forms with sequential spaces. The mortuary temple of Queen Hatshepsut, built between 1473 and 1458 BCE, utilized a sequence of terraces and colonnades to emphasize depictions of the queen's life embedded in the walls of the temple. These temples also utilized *hypostyle* halls, spaces with a dense grid of columns holding up a stone roof. Experientially, these halls created the feeling of a vast expanse with dim lighting to make the room feel ethereal (Figure 1.10). Evidence suggests that the Egyptians' use of such columns, especially those with faceted sides, would later influence Greek column styles.

The architectural styles of the Egyptians can likewise influence our own understanding of space. On one hand, they standardized forms such

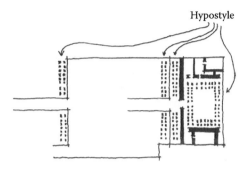

FIGURE 1.10 Hypostyle halls like those found in the mortuary temple of Queen Hatshepsut create the feeling of vast space through rhythmic, closely spaced columns and dim lighting.

as the pyramid and the column to create the beginnings of modular architectural language. On the other, they associated ideas with these modular pieces such that they were universally recognizable within the culture.

Spatial and Symbolic Relationships in Greek Architecture

In the West, Classical Greek civilization is credited with many advancements in art, architecture, philosophy, politics, science, and other fields. It is no wonder then that Greek architecture helps us understand how relationships between objects and environments drive our experience of space. The Greek philosopher Plato, for example, sought inner beauty through the expression of *form*, the perfect embodiment of proportional geometries that humans attempt to recreate through art and architecture.[11]

Greek architecture emphasized ratios and dimensions to establish forms. The relationships between buildings often occurred on carefully planned axes or sight lines. During Greece's Archaic period, ca. 800–480 BCE, temple architecture was established following the form of *megarons*, rectangular spaces with entrances on the shorter sides so the space was perceived as very long. In Greek temple architecture (Figure 1.11), this established a processional sequence of spaces from the temple's *pronaos* (entryway) to a *cella* or *naos* (long interior space) where the statue of the deity would reside, and an *opisthodomos* (additional rear room). This period also saw the establishment of what the Roman architect Vitruvius would later call the *orders* of architectural columns: *Doric*, *Ionic*, and *Corinthian*. These three orders represented the proportions of men (Doric), women (Ionic), and young maidens

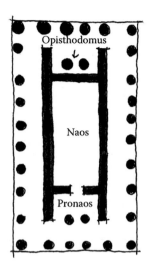

FIGURE 1.11   Greek temples use a procession of spaces and long rectangular rooms to guide viewers to statues of their gods and goddesses.

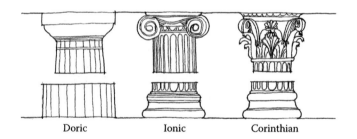

FIGURE 1.12   The three orders of Greek columns. They allowed for the creation of different proportional effects in building construction and form the basic language of Greek architecture.

(Corinthian) in their forms and ornamentations (Figure 1.12). The use of these columns allows the creation of subtle proportional effects in temple design. Doric columns, for example, lend a weighty and assertive nature to buildings, while Ionic columned buildings "feel" light, as though they were being lifted from the ground. More important than their formal qualities is the fact that these columns are among several elements that founded the Greek *architectural vocabulary*. Architectural vocabularies, often referred to as *vernacular*, are consistent elements utilized throughout the structures of a specific culture or aesthetic. Architectural vocabularies throughout history allow specific formal arrangements to become associated with specific building ideas or uses. Buildings with recognizable forms and vernacular elements are known as *types*. As with the Egyptians, the Greeks' use of these linguistic architectural elements exemplifies how we will develop languages of level forms and art assets to create game worlds.

Later Greek public architecture during the Classical period (between 479 and 323 BCE) brings concepts of spatial hierarchies and arrangements even more to the forefront. The Athenian Acropolis, built in 479 BCE, utilizes a carefully planned spatial sequence to guide visitors around and into its primary buildings, the Temple of Athena Nike, the Propylaea, the Erechtheion, and the Parthenon (Figure 1.13). The approach to the Parthenon seems random, but was a carefully planned sequence of perspectival experiences. First, visitors would see the Acropolis from far away as they approached the hill on which it sat. Next, they would enter the entrance portico of the Acropolis, the Propylaea. This building offered a choice: continue onward to the Acropolis proper or divert slightly to the Temple of Athena Nike. Those who continued to the Acropolis proper would view it from behind a screen of columns, framing the statue of Athena. The Parthenon itself was viewed at a slight

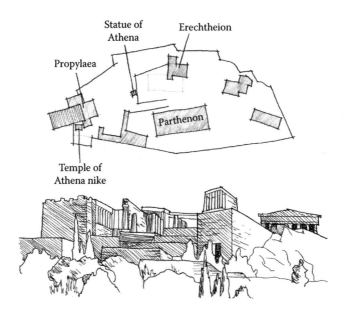

FIGURE 1.13 The plan of the Athenian Acropolis and a simulated sketch view of the approach to it. The designers previewed the visitor's arrival at the Parthenon several times in this spatial sequence.

angle. This was intentional, as designers intended for it to be viewed three-dimensionally by walking around it and seeing it in perspective rather than seeing it straight on. This also made the *composition* of views more dynamic, as viewing the building straight on would give it a static feel. Visitors of the Erechtheion are likewise reminded of the Parthenon's dominance of the site, as it utilizes architectural language similar to the larger building and features a porch that offers yet another composed view of the famous building.

Later Greek urban architecture, such as the Athenian Agora—built in 150 BCE—offered not only similarly planned approaches, but also articulations of public and private space through the use of stoa, columned structures used for meetings and commerce (Figure 1.14). People could mingle as they circulated through the large open spaces of the agora, which was on the road to the Acropolis, or stay and linger in the stoa. These dichotomies of public/private, motion/pause, and large/intimately sized space will be of great use as we explore how gamespaces influence player actions.

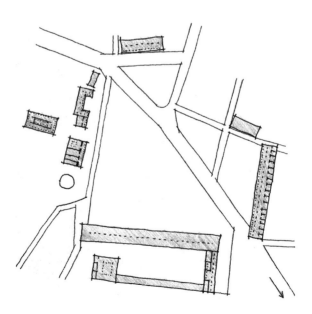

FIGURE 1.14 The Athenian Agora offers a mix of public and private spaces. The large, open public spaces are generally used for circulation and travel, while the covered private spaces lend themselves to meetings and other stationary activities.

Indian, Southeast Asian, and Asian Representational Architecture

While Western civilization was growing in Mesopotamia, pockets of civilization were also growing in the Indus Valley of what is now Pakistan and Afghanistan. For much of the early history of these civilizations, cities were laid out in regular grids of houses with raised citadels.

The architecture of these regions would be influenced by the rise of several important religions around the sixth century BCE, especially Hinduism and Buddhism. These religions all believed in the transmigration of souls and the ability to transcend the sorrows of physical existence. Key to Buddhist architecture was a symbolic verticality based on ideas of a vertical world axis. There was a belief in the cyclical nature of existence; thus building forms were hemispherical, symbolizing the earth under the dome of the heavens (Figure 1.15).

The architecture of Hinduism also links gods and worshippers through sacred forms. Hindu temples serve as homes for these gods, who were believed to enjoy mountains and caves. As such, ancient Hindu temples utilize mountain-like verticality to enclose cave-like interior chambers. Hindu temples were often places where worshippers could visit representations of the sacred mountain and holy cave important to Hindu theology (Figure 1.16).

Religion also had a great impact in the experiential architectural histories of East Asian cultures. In China, the scholars Laotzu and Confucius

FIGURE 1.15 Buddhist architecture, such as the Great Stupa in Sanchi, India (built between 250 BCE and 250 CE) utilizes form for embodying important religious beliefs.

FIGURE 1.16   Angkor Wat (built in 1120 CE in Cambodia) utilized representational forms to evoke sacred locations in Hindu theology.

developed their own philosophies, Daoism and Confucianism, which would greatly influence lifestyles in the region. Daoism focuses on finding harmony with the outside world by studying nature. This would have great influence on later Chinese and Japanese garden design, where gardens became simulations of natural landscapes. Confucianism, on the other hand, focused on a respect for authority, the state, and people of superior wisdom.

Daoist ideas can be found in the concept of *feng shui*, which has designers adjust a building's features to the conditions of a specific site. Similar ideas have risen in Western architectural theory as *genius loci*, the spirit of place, which is discussed in later chapters. Principles of city planning, on the other hand, often coincide with Confucian ideas on hierarchical authority. Beijing's Imperial and Forbidden Cities are exemplary of this idea, as access to the central Imperial Court was denied to visitors by several layers of outer walls and gates (Figure 1.17).

Chinese and Japanese domestic architecture focused largely on a modular and consistent language of architectural forms: columns, mats, screens, and other elements. The garden designs of both countries allude to natural landscapes through the orientation of rocks, trees, herbs, and other features. Despite representing natural, organically arranged forms, these spaces demonstrate how even exterior scenes can be directed experiences for occupants. The architecture of Asian temples and cities demonstrates how symbolic

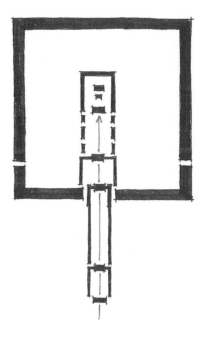

FIGURE 1.17 This diagram of the layered gates in Beijing's Imperial and Forbidden Cities (built in the fifteenth century CE) typifies Confucianist urban planning ideas with layers that deny visitors access to the emperor's Hall of Supreme Harmony in the center of the city.

forms and layered experiences can be used to preview experiences to come, but deny them to viewers until they explore the space further.

Linear Experiences in Roman Architecture

If the cultures already mentioned were developers of experiences that offered choice and expansive simulated landscapes, the Romans were designers of linear experiences. Following the architectural forms and language of the Greeks, the Romans—whose empire lasted from the first century BCE to around 337 CE with the end of Constantine's reign— would deliver primarily engineering and structural innovations to the field of architecture. The Imperial Forums in Rome, constructed in the first century CE, utilized spatial language consistent with Greek stoa and agora constructions (Figure 1.18). Forums such as the ones in Rome utilized public and private articulations, as well as axially arranged landmarks that moved visitors through the public spaces.

Roman temples such as the Pantheon focused mainly on a single, hierarchically important view rather than a variety of three-dimensional

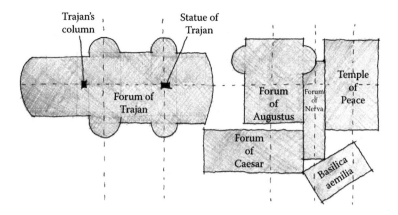

FIGURE 1.18 The Imperial Forums of Rome. This project was a collection of several forums, including the Forum of Trajan, and landmarks that are arranged axially from one another.

views, as seen in the Greek Parthenon. Instead, these temples offered visitors who entered rewarding interior vistas (Figure 1.19) that predict how game designers can surprise players with rewarding level views. Large interior spaces were an important element of Roman architecture, owing to their refinement of the arch, vault, and dome that allowed expansive spaces. Emperor Hadrian's Villa in Tivoli, built between 117 and 38 CE,

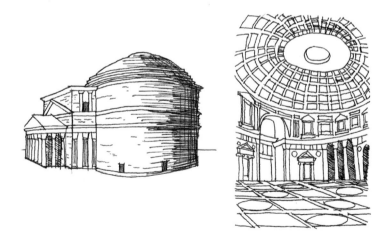

FIGURE 1.19 Interior and exterior sketches of the Pantheon (built in Rome ca. 125 CE), which utilizes a singular embellished façade to guide visitors into a climactic interior space. This focus on one impressive façade leading into a rewarding interior was typical of Roman architecture.

featured climactic interior spaces built around water features. The architectures made possible by the Romans' engineering power would greatly influence later cultures, who utilized the Greek and Roman architectural languages to embody spiritual ideas.

Medieval Christian and Islamic Symbolic Architecture

During the Roman Empire, a new religion rose to prominence based on the teachings of Jesus of Nazareth—Christianity. Early Christians were persecuted by Roman authorities and had to keep their beliefs a secret. This changed with the conversion of Emperor Constantine in 313 CE to Christianity and his making it the state religion. From 610 to 633 CE, Islam took root in the Arab world following what is said to have been an appearance by the angel Gabriel to the prophet Mohammed in Mecca. These religions, their development, and their interactions with one another would have great impact on Medieval architectures.

Like the Romans, Christians utilized modular architectural elements and axial arrangements in their buildings. Christians used these to evoke symbolic ideas of the kingdom of heaven and the hierarchical relationship between priest and congregation (Figure 1.20). The use of *clerestory* windows, windows raised above the heads of viewers to let light in from above, created the feeling of an ethereal space on the interiors of the churches through the manipulation of lighting conditions.

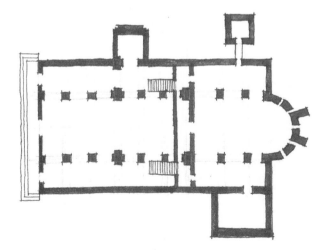

FIGURE 1.20 The plan for San Miniato al Monte in Florence, Italy (built between 1062 and 1090) typifies Christian basilica planning with a hierarchically planned procession space toward the altar at the back of the church.

Throughout Western Europe, church architecture continued to evolve even as the Roman Empire fell, taking on other meanings beyond worship spaces. From about 476 to the 1500s CE, Europe was in what is now considered the Middle Ages or Medieval period. While this was not a prosperous time for Europe, there were nonetheless many developments in literature, philosophy, art, and architecture during the period. Regardless, the societal shift caused by the fall of the Roman Empire to barbarian tribes left much of Western Europe illiterate. Builders of Medieval churches, in this context, focused their efforts on embedding biblical narratives into their designs with relief sculpture and mosaics (Figure 1.21). Builders also became more adept at creating structurally efficient churches. The zenith of Medieval architecture, the Gothic style, was marked by the use of minimal structural stone on the interior of churches so there could be an increase in stained glass clerestory and *rose windows*. These filtered light into the church to create an atmosphere that made patrons feel as though they were closer to God.

Islamic architecture was focused on the embodiment of religious ideas and narratives. Unlike in Western civilizations, the Medieval period was

FIGURE 1.21 Relief sculptures and mosaics were used in medieval churches to pass biblical narratives on to a largely illiterate populace.

a prosperous time for Islamic culture that saw advances in art, architecture, math, and science. Mosque design would reflect the five duties that each Muslim was to perform, especially praying in the direction of Mecca five times daily. This influenced the directional orientation of mosques and necessitated the construction of minarets, tall towers from which the faithful could be called to prayer. Like Christian architecture, Islamic architects utilized ornamentation containing passages from their holy book. The embodiment of narrative ideas would become an important one in Islamic architecture with works such as the Taj Mahal in Agra, India.

Both Christian and Islamic architectures fused the practical elements of their respective religions with the need for narrative expression. Both strove to create ethereal experiences through lighting and a separation of the outside world from the sacred space within. It is no wonder, then, that many of these structures would change hands between the two cultures over the course of many centuries, adding narrative elements unintended by the original builders. In these ways, Medieval Christian and Islamic architecture became important narrative and simulation spaces.

The Renaissance Return to Human-Centered Architecture

In the late fifteenth and early sixteenth centuries, an increased interest in classical influences, beginning in Italy, brought about a cultural, artistic, and scientific Renaissance. While Renaissance architecture returned to the architectural language of the classical period—arches, domes, and classical column orders, with elements learned from Medieval construction—there was also an emphasis on symmetry and a centralized floor plan in many Renaissance buildings.

More important for our exploration, however, is the Renaissance's emphasis on mathematical ratios inspired by the works of Plato. These studies led to an increase in *humanist* architectural forms, which stemmed from the belief that the human body was derived from divine ratios (Figure 1.22). Many Florentine palaces utilized different proportions for demarcating public and private spaces. Beginning with the architecture of Michelozzo Bartolomeo and Leon Battista Alberti in the mid-1400s, it was common for first stories of wealthy families' palaces to have a taller ground floor with rusticated materials from which the family could conduct business. The second floor was where the family could entertain guests. This floor, known as the *piano noble*, had a shorter height than the ground floor, but was often emphasized via more elaborate windows (Figure 1.23). The Renaissance emphasis on

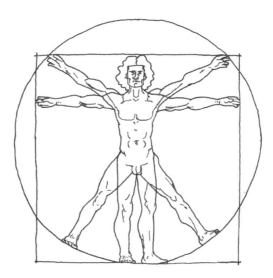

FIGURE 1.22 Leonardo da Vinci's *Vitruvian Man,* drawn around 1485, exemplifies the belief that man is proportioned according to divine ratios. Such beliefs led Renaissance architects to pursue geometries that responded to the proportions of the human body.

FIGURE 1.23 Alberti's Palazzo Rucellai (built in Florence between 1446 and 1451) emphasizes the height of the ground floor, while using more ornate classical language on upper floors to emphasize their importance to the owners.

human proportion shines through the architecture of Andrea Palladio. In many of his works, particularly in his villas, Palladio emphasized rhythmic classical elements and consistent room size ratios. He utilized Greek temple forms to emphasize porticos from which inhabitants could look out onto impressive vistas (Figure 1.24). In many ways, the Renaissance emphasis on space based on human proportions is vital to our own level design work. Understanding the metrics of human interaction forms the basis of our own level measurements throughout the book.

Ornamental Reformations and Material Revolutions

The centuries following the Renaissance saw many societal changes that were reflected in the architecture of the period. Beginning with Martin Luther's nailing of his ninety-five theses to a church in Wittenberg, Germany, a period of Reformation occurred within the Christian Church, resulting in the establishment of Protestantism. The Catholic Church responded with a Counter-Reformation movement focused on internal reforms and bringing people back to Catholicism. One of its primary

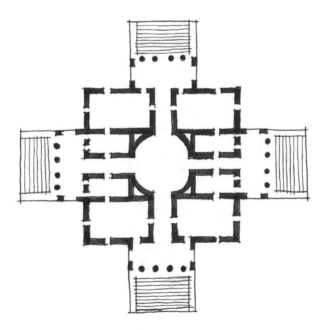

FIGURE 1.24 Palladio's Villa Rotunda in Vicenza (built between 1566 and 1570) utilized both carefully proportioned spaces and rewarding porticos that allowed viewers to look out onto their surroundings.

weapons was a new emphasis on ornamental art, which gave rise to the Baroque style.

Baroque architecture has two main facets that will become important to us as we study level design. The first is the previously mentioned use of ornamental elements in the architecture. Works such as the Jesuit home church of Il Gesu or Borromini's S. Carlo alle Quattro Fontane in Rome utilized layered exterior ornamentation and new façade compositions that reflected interior conditions of the church to recreate the grandeur of old Rome. In many ways, the church was utilizing ornamentation not only as a system of narrative communication, as it had in the Middle Ages, but also as a system of advertisement.

Another facet of Baroque architecture useful to level designers is Baroque city planning. The first major work of this kind was the replanning of Rome done by Pope Sixtus V in the late 1580s and implemented over the next century. Axial streets linked many of the major pilgrimage churches in the city (Figure 1.25). This was to aid the navigation of pilgrims from landmark to landmark. Large urban plazas, such as the Piazza del Popolo, were constructed to accommodate visitors. This type of planning would be evident in other projects such as the gardens of Versailles, which later influenced the axial street and node-based plan of Washington, D.C.

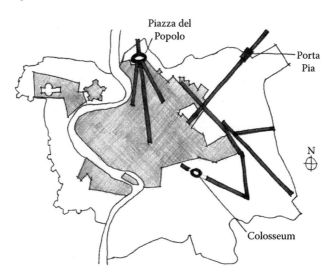

FIGURE 1.25 Baroque city planning utilized sight lines and planned axes to link important nodes, gathering spaces, and landmarks.

The eighteenth-century period of Enlightenment, during which intellectuals in Europe challenged ideas based on faith in favor of those based on reason and scientific enterprise, would return architectural styles to a focus on classical forms. It was during this time that Neo-Palladianism, Neo-Classicism, and a rationalization of Gothic architectural ideas flourished. The Industrial Revolution beginning in the late-1700s to mid-1800s influenced building styles, allowing architects to build higher and wider expanses thanks to the innovations of iron and steel. The materiality and construction of buildings became something of a controversial topic during this time. In response to the engineered rationalism of industrial architecture, the arts and crafts movement also rose. These artists and designers advocated for a refocusing on artistic quality rather than on manufactured goods. In *The Seven Lamps of Architecture* (1849), John Ruskin laid out seven lamps, or principles, of architecture for the design of great buildings.[12] Among these were the Lamp of Truth, which argued for the acknowledgment of handcrafted structural materials, and the Lamp of Life, which demands expression of the human mind and hands. Ruskin's work was a great influence on architects such as Philip Webb, whose Red House in Bexleyheath, Kent, England, built between 1859 and 1860, utilized warm, natural materials such as brick and wood. The plan of this building was a reaction to the needs of occupants for light and proximity of household functions (Figure 1.26). Such explorations of naturalistic building materials and forms would be evident in later arts and crafts architects, as well as those from the art nouveau movement such as Antonio Gaudi, who merged Gothic revival language with natural ornamental forms (Figure 1.27), and Louis Sullivan, who integrated natural ornament into the structures of his buildings.[13]

The clashing of ideas that occurred in the centuries following the Reformation—ornamentation as a system of rhetoric, the refocusing of cities around user experience, and the industrial innovations that ultimately led to the reassertion of natural materials—would come to a head during the twentieth century in various interpretations of Modernist architecture. The architects of this movement, including many who are discussed later in the book, would utilize architecture as an intervention into human society. Their works would influence the actions of occupants in ways that should not be ignored by level designers, who should seek to create gamespaces catering to the relationship between game players and mechanics.

FIGURE 1.26 Philip Webb's Red House utilizes more natural materials than its industrial contemporaries and focuses its design on the needs of occupants.

FIGURE 1.27 Antonio Gaudi's Church of the Sagrada Familia in Barcelona, Spain, begun in 1882 and still ongoing, utilizes naturalistic forms expressed in a Gothic style.

This overview of architectural history through the lens of user experience is the basis for how we will understand gamespace in this book. Unconcerned with formal expressions, prehistoric builders emphasized sight lines and responses to human experiences of celestial phenomena. Early civilizations and religious cultures, on the other hand, focused on form as a system of remembrance and communication, building structures that represented important landscapes or that asserted their own cultural ideas. Classical cultures utilized these elements in directed spatial experiences, using axial and experiential relationships between buildings to create sequences that influenced user movement. These rules were later combined with embedded ornamentation to create spaces that emphasized both the mechanics of their use and spiritual narrative ideas. Lastly, new industrial building technologies created a backlash from designers interested in preserving natural and treasured building methods and materials. These elements—user views and experience, representation, communication, lighting conditions, materials, and others—all have a great impact on how we conduct our own players' spatial experiences.

In the next section, we briefly look at the history of gamespaces to build comparisons between user-based architectural experiences and those found in games.

THE HISTORY OF GAMESPACES

Like much of architectural history, the history of gamespaces has been influenced by the purpose of the space (i.e., the game being played) and the limitations of materials for constructing these spaces. In many ways, games are as old as the architectures that we have just explored, with early examples of both occurring in the same locations around the same periods. Even then, it was important that gamespaces corresponded to the rules of play.

While the history of games has been well documented (several times), the history of level design is less clear. There are databases such as Level-Design.org's screenshot and article archives,[14] but historians have not used these resources to form a full narrative for the field. Since such an effort could easily fill its own book, I will not attempt one here, but like our architectural history, I will review some areas that will give context to the discussions in the rest of the book.

Board Design for Early Games

Ask most digital game designers, and they will tell you that they have done some form of non-digital game design: either for prototyping, hobby projects, or even as a side job supplementing their other income. Likewise, many game design classes start with some form of tabletop game design as a way to understand the way games work without the need for computers. Understanding non-digital design is not only a great way to test games quickly, though: it's also a way to understand the history of how game spaces are linked to game experiences. Many early games wove game mechanics and board design together for uses beyond entertainment: religion, military, and cultural.

Two of the earliest known games are the Royal Game of Ur and Senet, created in Sumeria and Egypt respectively, between 3500 and 2500 BCE. These were race games whose boards reflected the pattern that players had to traverse to win the game, precursors of what we know now as backgammon. Senet, in particular, evolved into a tool for religious ceremonies: the pathway created by the board represented the pathway through the netherworld.[15]

Later games would marry board design and game mechanics to demonstrate military strategy. Chess and Go are about territorial control and the capturing of opponents' pieces based on the movement rules of one's own pieces. Chess, created in India during the Gupta Empire (240–590 CE), features pieces that may only move in very specific ways across a checkered battlefield. These pieces were originally based on the four divisions of the Gupta military and eventually evolved into the pawn, knight, bishop, and rook that we know today.[16] The pieces each have individual ways of moving, and the board is built to allow these movements to mix into infinite possible strategies. Go, referred to in writings as early as the fourth century BCE, alternatively features a few simple rules that apply to all pieces equally. This vastly increases the possible board combinations that can occur. As such, the spaces embody not only the rules of play, but also the potential for unique player reactions to these rules. Like chess, playing Go contains elements of scholarly pursuit: mastering it requires years of time and practice. In ancient China, it was one of the Four Arts required for acceptance in the scholar–gentleman social caste.[17] This mastery is embodied in how players progressively use more of the board to play as they learn: beginners use a 9×9 or 13×13 grid, while skilled players use the full 19×19 grid.

Physical Gamespaces and Architecture

Physical gamespaces such as playing fields and arenas are another case where the needs of a game are embodied in the space where it is played. Ancient analogs to modern sports such as football (soccer), basketball, lacrosse, and others utilize spatial elements in their design: goals, defensive lines, etc. When these games were eventually codified into their modern forms, they gained even more direct spatial elements: boundaries, zones for which there are rules of how or whether the ball can be possessed, and others (Figure 1.28). Once they were organized, these games often also gained spectator areas, which added out-of-game elements to the overall experience, making these games simultaneously game and performance. Modern sports facilities have even incorporated ancillary parts of games into their architecture. No modern baseball stadium, for example, would be without a bullpen, the space where relief pitchers warm up before entering the game to replace a tired starting pitcher.

In *Man, Play, Games*, anthropologist Richard Caillois[18] identifies fundamental categories of play, one of which is *mimicry*, which includes theater and other staged productions.[19] Like spectator sports, these events are performed in spaces whose performance area (the field for a game or the stage for a play) caters to the performance needs of the event. Boundaries and field markers in sports embody the rules of play. Likewise, the stage

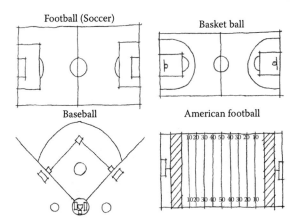

FIGURE 1.28 Fields for various sports: football (soccer), basketball, baseball, and American football. Each of these fields has spatial elements for which there are rules governing how players may utilize them. Scoring is often related to guiding a ball to, or hitting it such that the player can reach, scoring territories.

for a theater production anticipates the choreography of the production: how will the lighting be arranged to best show the performance? Is there an orchestra pit or choir area? Is there room for dancing if the production calls for it? How do scenery and lighting describe the setting? In addition to architecture, modern theatrical set design could also be an area of interest for level designers.

Ancient Greek amphitheaters utilized many of the elements common in theater design today, a circular area for the orchestra, a *skene* building that acted as the backdrop and backstage, and the *proskenion*, from which the performance occurred. These theaters were reactions to the needs of the theater productions and allowed for the development of performance innovations not originally intended. This included utilization of the skene as a place from which an actor could deliver lines as an unseen supernatural character or change costumes between scenes.

This modularity of uses was also reflected in stadiums such as the Flavian Amphitheater, popularly known as the Roman Colosseum. Famous as a venue for gladiatorial combat, it was also the site for animal hunts and scenic recreations that utilized real tree and animal life.[20] Tunnels for the preparation of gladiators and the transportation of scenic elements were located under the spectator areas, and even in some cases under the floor of the stadium itself. The tunnels beneath the performance space featured elevators and trap doors for the introduction of animals into events. Like Greek theaters, the Flavian Amphitheater was a space for basic contests, but also allowed for elaboration based on the imaginations of organizers. Several possibilities are imagined in the 2000 film *Gladiator*: gladiator fights, chariot battles, historic recreations, fights with dangerous animals in a ring around combatants, and others.[21]

Digital Gamespaces

In the twentieth century, the invention of electronic computers and subsequent development of games for them began the concept of designing digital spaces for games. A common theme through the history of level design in digital games is how the technology used to build the space influences how the space works. Today, this might mean that the nuances of a particular game engine influences the construction method or how lights and textures are rendered. The early history of game spaces, however, is also the history of technical advancement in games: specifically how much territory could be displayed in a game at one time.

One of the first visually displayed electronic games, 1952's *Noughts and Crosses*—a translation of tic-tac-toe—has the same spatial rules as the non-digital version: line up three of your own shapes while preventing your opponent from doing the same. The game was created to show how information could be displayed on the small screens of the Electronic Delay Storage Automatic Calculator (EDSAC). Another early electronic game from 1958, *Tennis for Two*,[22] borrowed its simulated gamespace from the sport tennis. It displayed the game from the side rather than the top down, necessitating a simplification of tennis's rules to focus on getting the ball over the net, leaving out some specific rules based on court lines (Figure 1.29). The display of the ball's arc fit well onto the oscilloscope used by William Higinbotham to create the game. Later tennis-like games such as Ralph Baer's *Tennis*[23] or Atari's *Pong*[24] would depict the game abstractly from the top down, excluding shooting over the net as a challenge and concentrating on keeping the ball in play by moving a paddle on the screen (Figure 1.30).

In 1962, *Spacewar!*[25]—created by a group of MIT students led by Steve Russel—simulated a battle between two ships in space around a gravity well. Like *Tennis for Two* and the later games *Tennis* and *Pong*, this game occurred on one screen, but introduced a wraparound feature where a ship leaving one side of the screen would appear on the other (Figure 1.31).

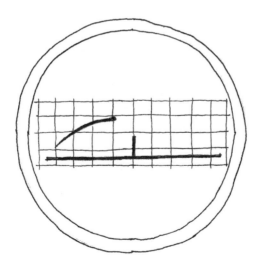

FIGURE 1.29   *Tennis for Two* had to edit the rules for tennis to accommodate the 2D point of view of the game. Player positions or court boundaries are not an issue for players, who must instead focus on hitting the ball over the net.

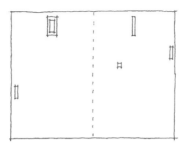

FIGURE 1.30   *Pong* edited the rules of ping-pong, similarly to how *Tennis for Two* edited the rules of tennis, to take advantage of its top-down point of view. Players do not have to worry about the net in this game, but must move their paddle to avoid missing the ball.

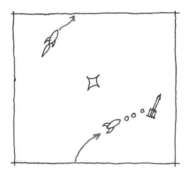

FIGURE 1.31   Apart from being one of the first computer games and multiplayer digital games, *Spacewar!* was also the first game to feature a gamespace that wrapped from one side of the screen to another.

This feature, which simulates the infinity of space, would become popular with later games, notably *Asteroids*[26] in 1979, *Pac-Man*[27] in 1981, and more recently the indie fighting game *Towerfall.*[28] It allows players to formulate complex strategies within the confines of a single-screen space.

For much of the early history of digital gamespaces, action occurred largely on one screen. This was due to technical limitations of hardware, as well as the engagement time of many arcade games. One of the first popular games to have a scrolling environment was Williams's *Defender.*[29] Its use of an environment several screens long is considered a breakthrough, though that environment is not very detailed. Konami's *Scramble,*[30] released in 1981, was one of the first games to feature multiple scrolling environments that were distinct from one another. Other arcade games would not join the scrolling bandwagon, but did begin differentiating their single-screen areas from one another. 1981's *Donkey Kong*[31] and 1982's *Ms.*

Pac-Man[32] are two notable examples where each screen in the game is distinct from the one that preceded it, giving the impression of progression.

In the arcades, having more screens meant that your game was more advanced than the competition, but in the home market, expanding gamespaces served a different purpose. While single-screen games worked for short play sessions in arcades, home games needed to be expansive enough to provide value for the consumer's investment. Warren Robinett's *Adventure*,[33] published on the Atari 2600 in 1979, addressed the problem of single-screen gameplay by displaying rooms of the gamespace one at a time (Figure 1.32). *Adventure*'s solution would be standard for many years in graphical adventure games such as *King's Quest*,[34] where players could travel from screen to screen within a larger world. Another method of creating large game worlds on limited hardware was to move away from graphics entirely and express environmental information through text. This type of gameplay had its roots in computers whose output was teletype printers rather than screens. Games such as *Colossal Cave Adventure*[35] and *Zork I*[36] would utilize this type of space to create engaging imaginary worlds.

The spatial languages established in these earlier games were used to create bigger worlds as computers and game consoles became more powerful. *Pac-Land*[37] and *Super Mario Bros.*[38] utilize the screen-scrolling of

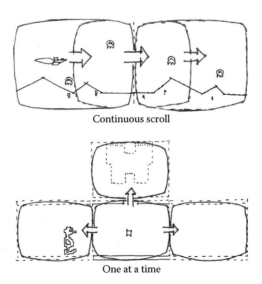

Continuous scroll

One at a time

FIGURE 1.32 Games like *Defender* and *Adventure* addressed the problem of creating multiscreen worlds in unique ways.

Defender to create lengthy and colorful obstacle course worlds, but adds *Adventure*-style rooms to create secret bonus levels both above and below the main gamespace to delight curious players (Figure 1.33). These models continued to grow and expand into bigger, more complex, and more visually interesting 2D game worlds.

Three-dimensional game worlds were also evolving at this time. One of the first was *Battlezone*,[39] a tank game where players could move around a 3D vector world. This game was so successful that the U.S. Army even contracted Atari to build tank simulators similar to the game. Other 3D games mainly utilized perspectival or axonometric projections (both of which are discussed in more detail in Chapter 2), mainly for aesthetic novelty. A true 3D successor to *Battlezone* emerged in 1992 when developers at id Software created *Wolfenstein 3D*,[40] one of the earliest first-person shooter games (Figure 1.34). id and other companies would continue developing 3D software, enabling bigger and more interactive game worlds to become possible.

The history of gamespaces is a combination of building spaces to accommodate specific game rules and play styles and allowing for unique implementations of the spaces later. This history involves overcoming the

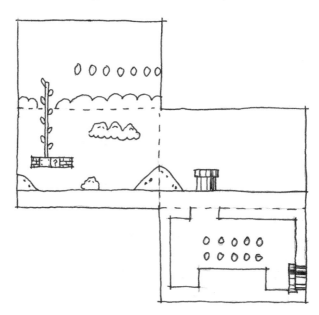

FIGURE 1.33 *Super Mario Bros.* utilizes different 2D spatial types—side-scrolling and connected rooms—to create bonus levels for surprising and delighting players.

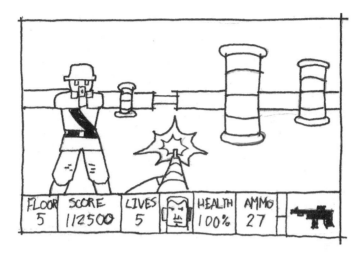

FIGURE 1.34 *Wolfenstein 3D* was one of the first games to usher in the transition to 3D games that eventually resulted in the vast gamespaces of today.

limitations of the platforms these games were built upon, especially for digital games. These earlier spaces, however, can still show us how meaningful and rewarding game experiences were created even from limited hardware.

In the next section, we examine how level designers can look at both architectural space and gamespace in ways that allow us to learn from their examples.

WAYS OF SEEING FOR LEVEL DESIGN

To fully understand spatial design principles for level design, precedents from both real-world architecture and video games must be analyzed. The next chapter discusses drawing techniques for doing this type of analysis, but first we must understand how to best view designed space. Hal Box, FAIA, professor emeritus and former dean of the School of Architecture at the University of Texas at Austin, argues for an educated form of *seeing* architecture based on study and analysis. In this case, seeing is used not only to describe using the visual senses, but also to process the spatial, formal, contextual, and historical elements that make a building unique.

For level designers, this type of seeing can be transformative for how we learn from the levels of previous games—and not just the good ones: learning what makes bad levels bad can be hugely educational. To *see* in this way may involve breaking some habits common to game players. For example, gamers don't usually look up when playing games. As designers, the verticality of gamespaces can be an important element in establishing the grandiosity of a setting or for communicating direction with players. For players, it is common to run directly to the next action scene rather than pause to explore game environments. Designers should look for ways to direct the pacing of a game environment in subtle ways—placing narrative elements in the way of player pathways or incentivizing exploration with rewards.

In his book *Think Like an Architect*, Box proposes ten ways for exploring and understanding a building:

1. Learn why a building was built, what it was for, and what it is now.

2. Look up as you walk around—noticing visual elements, layering of forms, and materials.

3. Sense the space by its size, shape, and how it interacts with light, sound, and other spaces.

4. Train your eye to understand the structure of the building and how it holds the building up.

5. Determine how materials are working—in compression or tension—or if they feel heavy or light.

6. Determine how the building was constructed and from what materials.

7. Examine the historical precedents of the building.

8. Analyze the composition, proportions, and rhythms of building elements.

9. Observe the appropriateness of the building to its setting.

10. Analyze what makes the building special from others.[41]

Obviously, not all of these apply to game levels. While the environment art of a level can represent structures that are in compression or tension, the game art itself will not. Many elements of game levels stand up because they are not defined as rigid-body objects in the game engine, and thus do not fall according to the engine's physics system. Still, many of these proposed ways of seeing are applicable to game levels in their current form, or may be modified slightly to fit our purposes. Level designers can modify their ways of seeing with the following methods:

1. Identify what gameplay occurs in the space. What are the game mechanics supported?

2. Look up as you walk around, noticing visual elements, especially art that contrasts the rest of the environment or somehow calls attention to itself. Also look down—is the space's verticality used in reverse to make you feel in danger?

3. Sense the space by its size, shape, and how it interacts with light, sound, and other spaces. How do the lighting or sound conditions make you feel?

4. Analyze the pacing of the level. Does the level usher you through itself quickly, or are there opportunities to explore? Are these required or are they bonuses for extra curiosity?

5. Is there one gameplay style reflected in this level, or are multiple supported? (For example, does a deathmatch map have places for snipers, offensive players, defensive players, etc.? Does a game level play well for barbarians but poorly for mages?)

6. How does the space express the narrative of the game? Is it a backdrop, or does exploring the level tell you about the game world in some way? Are narrative events scripted to occur around the player, or are there cutscenes?

7. Examine any historical or gameplay precedents. What kinds of spatial experiences were in those games?

8. Analyze the compositions, proportions, and rhythms of environment art elements.

9. How does level geometry compare with the movement abilities of your avatar? Is everything well within its capabilities, or does the level space challenge these measurements? Is there anything that is outside of these capabilities? If so, does the game offer any way to expand these abilities?

10. What environment art elements are repeated? Are they interactive? If so, do they correspond to a specific gameplay mechanic?

These ways of seeing for level design, as well as the architectural and gamespace precedents found earlier in this chapter, will guide our explorations of spatial design principles for level design.

SUMMARY

This chapter has been an introduction to the mindset of studying architectural space, with insight into how game levels are designed. We discussed how theory could be utilized to enhance our practical level design activities. We also discussed how exploring the principles of fields outside of game design can give us a framework from which to better understand existing gamespaces.

To form the foundations of our studies throughout the book, we examined Vitruvian elements of architecture and discovered how they can help us frame our own elements of level design: functional requirements, usability, and delight. These also framed our explorations of historic architecture through a number of civilizations. Our explorations followed an emphasis on the experiential elements of architectural design—use of architectural language, spatial sequences, communicative art, materials, and others—that will be useful as we move forward through the book. We also looked at the development of spaces within games, from board and physical games and play spaces to electronic games that evolved with expanding technology. We looked at how the design of these spaces was influenced by game elements: rules, settings, and the drive to create expansive worlds. In later chapters, we will see how experiential elements of architecture can help us enhance our own game levels.

Finally, we explored how we see spaces in both architecture and games. Following the suggestions of experienced architects, we formed ways of seeing for level analysis that will allow us to better identify the elements that create memorable level experiences. In Chapter 2, we explore methods not only for recording these analyses of architectural and level spaces, but also for constructing our own, both on paper and on the computer.

EXERCISES

1. **Writing prompt**: Name a game with fictional architecture that is based on a real-world architectural style covered in this chapter (an example from this chapter being the Forerunner architecture from *Halo* being based on Gothic Cathedrals). What does the use of that style convey about the in-game builders of that architecture? What mood does it create?

2. **Writing prompt**: Analyze the board or field for a non-digital game such as a tabletop game or a physical game (sport, playground game,

etc.) How does the design of the board and/or the boundaries of the field help define gameplay?

3. **Writing prompt**: Play a territory control board game such as Chess, Go, or other strategy games. How does the game utilize the board to define the movement of pieces and the game's win conditions? How do players use space to create strategies?

4. **Writing prompt**: Choose a popular commercial digital game. How would the experience of the game change if you changed the point of view? (Example: *Pong* is a game that views tennis in a top-down view while *Tennis for Two* imagines tennis from the side).

5. **Writing prompt**: Choose a level from a popular commercial game or one you are designing and try to answer the "ways of seeing for level design" questions for it.

ENDNOTES

1. Crawford, Chris. *The Art of Computer Game Design*. Berkeley, CA: Osborne/McGraw-Hill, 1984.
2. Rollings, Andrew, and Ernest Adams. *Andrew Rollings and Ernest Adams on Game Design*. Indianapolis, IN: New Riders, 2003.
3. Salen, Katie, and Eric Zimmerman. *Rules of Play: Game Design Fundamentals*. Cambridge, MA: MIT Press, 2003.
4. Schell, Jesse. *The Art of Game Design: A Book of Lenses*. Amsterdam: Elsevier/Morgan Kaufmann, 2008.
5. Fullerton, Tracy, Christopher Swain, and Steven Hoffman. *Game Design Workshop: A Playcentric Approach to Creating Innovative Games*. 2nd ed. Amsterdam: Elsevier Morgan Kaufmann, 2008.
6. Brathwaite, Brenda, and Ian Schreiber. *Challenges for Game Designers*. Boston: Charles River Media, a part of Course Technology, 2009.
7. *The Art of Halo 3*. Roseville, CA: Prima Games, 2008.
8. *Halo 4*. 343 Industries (developer) and Microsoft Game Studios (publisher), November 26, 2012. Xbox 360 game.
9. Fazio, Michael W., Marian Moffett, and Lawrence Wodehouse. *A World History of Architecture*. 2nd ed. Boston: McGraw-Hill, 2008, p. 1.
10. Barker, Graeme. *The Agricultural Revolution in Prehistory: Why Did Foragers Become Farmers?* Oxford: Oxford University Press, 2006.
11. Bloom, Allan David, and Plato. *The Republic of Plato*. 2nd ed. New York, NY: Basic Books, 1991.
12. Ruskin, John. *The Seven Lamps of Architecture* (Dover Architecture edition). New York, NY: Dover Publications, 1989.
13. Fazio, Michael W., Marian Moffett, and Lawrence Wodehouse. *A World History of Architecture*. 2nd ed. Boston, MA: McGraw-Hill, 2008.

14. Piaskiewicz, Mateusz. http://level-design.org/. October 25, 2009. Accessed May 12, 2018.
15. Piccione, Peter A. "In Search of the Meaning of Senet". *Elliot Avedon Museum & Archive of Games*. July 6, 2007. Accessed through the Internet Archive Wayback Machine May 17, 2018. https://web.archive.org/web/20080918080211/http://www.gamesmuseum.uwaterloo.ca/Archives/Piccione/index.html
16. Murray, H. J. R. *A History of Chess*. Oxford: Clarendon Press, 1913. Accessed on the Internet Archive May 17, 2018. https://archive.org/details/AHistoryOfChess
17. American Go Association. "A Brief History of Go". Accessed May 17, 2018. http://www.usgo.org/brief-history-go
18. Callois, Roger. *Man, Play, and Games*. New York, NY: Free Press of Glencoe, 1961.
19. Salen, Katie, and Eric Zimmerman. *Rules of Play: Game Design Fundamentals*. Cambridge, MA: MIT Press, 2003, p. 307.
20. Claridge, Amanda, Judith Toms, and Tony Cubberley. *Rome: An Oxford Archaeological Guide to Rome*. Oxford: Oxford University Press, 1998.
21. *Gladiator*. DVD. Directed by Ridley Scott. Universal City, CA: DreamWorks Home Entertainment, 2000.
22. *Tennis for Two*. William Higenbotham, October 18, 1958. Oscilloscope game.
23. *Tennis*. Ralph Baer, August 1972. Magnavox Odyssey game.
24. *Pong*. Atari (developer and publisher), 1972. Arcade game.
25. *Spacewar!* Steve Russel et al., 1962. PDP-1 computer game.
26. *Asteroids*. Atari (developer and publisher), November 1979. Arcade game.
27. *Pac-Man*. Namco (developer and publisher), 1981. Arcade game.
28. *Towerfall*. Matt Thorson (developer and publisher), June 25, 2013. Ouya game.
29. *Defender*. Williams Electronics (developer and publisher), 1980. Arcade game.
30. *Scramble*. Konami (developer) and Stern (publisher), 1981. Arcade game.
31. *Donkey Kong*. Nintendo (developer and publisher) July 9, 1981. Arcade game.
32. *Ms. Pac-Man*. Midway Manufacturing (developer and publisher), January 1982. Arcade game.
33. *Adventure*. Atari (developer and publisher), 1979. Atari 2600 game.
34. *King's Quest*. Sierra Online (developer) and IBM (publisher), 1983. Computer game.
35. *Colossal Cave Adventure*. William Crowther (developer and publisher), 1976. PDP-10 game.
36. *Zork I*. Infocom (developer and publisher), 1980. Computer text adventure.
37. *Pac-Land*. Namco (developer and publisher), August 1984. Arcade game.
38. *Super Mario Bros*. Nintendo (developer and publisher), September 13, 1985. Nintendo Entertainment System game.
39. *Battlezone*. Atari (developer and publisher), 1980. Arcade game.

40. *Wolfenstein 3D*. id Software (developer) and Apogee Software (publisher), May 5, 1992. Microsoft DOS game.
41. Box, Hal. *Think Like an Architect*. Austin: University of Texas Press, 2007, pp. 13–17.

INDUSTRY PERSPECTIVES: REFLECTIONS ON GAME LANDSCAPES

Dr. Umran Ali

Senior Lecturer in Creative Media, University of Salford

INTRODUCTION

I am an active higher education academic who has developed, written and taught on a range of programmes in the areas of creative and digital media, with a specific interest in computer and video game theory and practice. For over a decade I have taught on a games degree, and taught game design and game production. The natural world, in particularly scenic landscapes, has captivated and held my attention for many years; as a result I have been an active and keen walker, and have developed an interest in nature landscape photography.

I am also a keen and passionate video game player. My practice as a designer and artist over the last two decades has involved undertaking a range of technical and creative problems at the forefront of artistic and commercial practice. Many of these challenges are only ever partially solved or left fully unexplored due to project limitations such as resource constraints. For a practitioner, these "unsolved" challenges can be frustrating, and after a number of projects many residual tasks, both creative and technical, remained.

This led to the first major part of the research: virtual natural environments (VNE)—in particular game landscapes—were examined through a contextual review, a combination of previous professional practice in addition to a selection of digital games across a variety of platforms and genres over the last thirty years. The contextual review involved a detailed textual and visual-based historical survey of virtual landscapes, resulting in a practice-based exploration of virtual natural environment design.

One problem was identifying an appropriate entry point into these digital games from which to collect visual data and use as a basis for later analysis. This is where British Landscape Photographer Jay Appleton's book, *The Experience of Landscape*, which discusses the relationship between landscape and environment, helped focus the research. Simply put, "Landscape is not synonymous with environment, it is the environment perceived, especially visually perceived." So, focusing on virtual landscapes within the larger virtual environments would perhaps be manageable (given the scope of the study), and more effective at illustrating the dominant or emerging environment design paradigms than simply trying to analyse entire virtual environments in digital games.

The next problem was framing: how would I "frame" the digital natural landscapes? Well, I was partly inspired by Charlie Waite's *Landscape Photographer of The Year* books, and Professor Joan I Nassauer, who in *Framing the Landscape in Photographic Simulation* argued that the choice of framing could elicit different viewer responses: "Different photographic framing choices can elicit different viewer responses to a landscape. Framing formats that create large images with broad horizontal ranges may be superior for simulating field experience." I chose to then adopt panoramic framing as a manner in which to present the virtual landscapes. So, using Appleton's and Nassauer's assertion, what emerged was the above thinking: panoramic framing was the closest to how we naturally perceive landscapes, which in turn are strongly representational of how we perceive the wider environment.

MAIN RESEARCH QUESTION

Question 1: How have VNEs evolved in computer and video games over the last thirty years in both technological and design innovation and what (if anything) has been the dominant design paradigm?

Question 2: Given the rapid evolution of computer and video games in design and technology, how does one propose any improvements to the design process or technique or a new future framework for VNE design?

Observations

From the review of landscapes in computer and video games over three decades (1980–2010) what emerged were three relatively distinct eras or periods, each one exemplifying particular traits in how landscapes were portrayed and designed.

VIRTUAL LANDSCAPES: THE EMBRYONIC ERA (1980–1990)

The representation of natural environments in the Embryonic Era begins with nothing more than simple shapes and forms. The non-existence of colour, at first, meant natural environments and landscapes were limited to black and white, with later developments allowed the use of several colours (albeit in a very limited range). Early in the era, natural environment design was largely limited to simulating entire environments rather than depicting a series of smaller landscapes. In later games such as Sierra's *King's Quest* (1990) the limited screen space illustrated the use of traditional composition techniques. Larger game environments were broken down into smaller screen spaces, i.e. mirroring traditional representations of landscapes. These processes used the tools and techniques developed in other disciplines, such as matte landscape painting, within fragmented 2D space (i.e. hotspots) to simulate 3D environmental depth.

Landscapes in the Embryonic Era can be defined in these ways:

1. The representation of natural environments began with nothing more than simple shapes and forms, no colour, no lighting and in simple 2D space. Block forms were used to present key natural environment landscape features. Cosmi Corporation's *Forbidden Forest* (1983) illustrates this: a green solid colour background represents the forest backdrop with vertical rectangles of brown used to represent trees.

2. The representation of 3D space was minimal, and was abstracted due to technological limitations to an "ant farm" view. This abstraction would have a profound impact on the recreation/representation of existing and fictional 3D space in all games including those attempting to recreate natural environments. There was very limited portrayal of "landscape" in the classic sense but rather crude attempts at simulating larger natural environments.

3. Natural environments during this era were static; dynamic movement was severely limited (e.g. trees did not sway, grass did not move) and players were unable to interact with any part of the environment. However, early attempts at simulating a dynamic environment such as the day/night cycle (Cosmi Corporation's *Forbidden Forest*) and rockfalls or flowing water (Atari's *CaveLord*) illustrate the potential of the medium.

4. Despite relying on the "ant farm" view, Namco's *Dig Dug* (1982) design illustrates an early attempt to use the environment with gameplay through a uniquely designed mechanic. The natural environment becomes an integral part of the game by becoming embedded as a gameplay feature. The avatar moves through the ground by digging through it. Tunnelling through the terrain was reduced to the onscreen

removal of pixels (a high level of abstraction is present since the digging results in the "dug space" becoming an empty black void).

5. Early indicators of the use of the environment beyond a merely aesthetic consideration started to emerge. Bullfrog's *Populous* (1989) serves as a prime example of the successful coupling of agency and natural environmental design, laying the foundations of how meaningful interaction (agency) could enrich immersion.

6. The limited screen space forced the use of traditional composition techniques; larger game environments were broken down into smaller screen spaces, e.g. traditional representations of landscapes, using the same tools and techniques in the creation of these virtual spaces.

VIRTUAL LANDSCAPES: THE TRANSITION ERA (1990–2000)

The use of idyllic and specific "landscapes" was lost from the Embryonic Era (they were used mainly due to hardware and software technology constraints). Nevertheless, during the transition era these constraints were removed and hence the design process changed, using more expansive environments as gamespace. The modern era has seen an evolution of this back toward recognising landscapes as a vital feature within the environment.

Landscapes in the Transition Era (1990–2000) can be defined in these ways:

1. Technological advancements such as digital scanners and increased memory capacity allowed game environments to make the leap from the simple two-dimensional, block-pixel-based forms to environments that utilized detailed digitised landscape paintings. Sierra On-Line's *King's Quest 5* (1990) and Westwood Studio's *The Legend of Kyrandia* (1992) demonstrate the transformation of the visual quality of these virtual environments from crude simulations to rich detailed spaces.

2. The introduction of pseudo 3D technologies (e.g. isometric, pre-rendered 3D) led to an inevitable decline in the portrayal of game landscapes as designers struggled to fully utilise the new software and hardware.

3. Developments of new software technologies such as Mode 7 allowed the creation of pseudo 3D environments. Platforms such as the Sega Megadrive and Nintendo Super NES heralded an evolution of the "ant farm" perspective with graphic technologies allowing the simulation of three-dimensional depth, creating richer and more detailed environments.

4. Simulations around environmental changes further evolved and started to become increasingly integrated with the visual elements in natural environments. In addition games such as Bethesda's *Daggerfall* (1996) illustrate technological advancements in lighting (such as day and night cycles), and crude weather cycles started to be incorporated into these virtual environments.

5. Game landscapes evolved further as designers started to realise that natural environment design is more than just the geometrical representation of an environment but one that includes a variety of other features. Weather, climate, etc. started to be increasingly combined with visual elements to produce more convincing and dynamic environments.

6. The "ant farm" view was reinterpreted into three dimensions. Natural environments on platforms such as the Nintendo 64 exemplify this with extruded block form geometry used to simulate hills and mountains on terrain. This approach was used as a system by designers to restrict access to the specific parts of the environment in order to align progression with the gameplay/narrative.

7. With the emergence of 3D there was a loss of design and traditional art disciplines (like landscape painters) into pure spatial design.

8. The transition era also marks a deviation away from simply replicating the natural environment to one where the natural environment begins to cross over into fictional works.

9. Despite the emergence of 3D technologies, natural environments were essentially still limited to a flat, horizontal x,y plane. However, early indicators point to depth (the Z axis) to be the next era's key differentiator in virtual environment design.

10. Throughout the Transition Era, water simulation was also problematic: game environments for the most part lacked water. Rivers, waterfalls, lakes and other water bodies were essentially non-existent due to technological constraints of simulating them. Water bodies that were simulated were restricted to block "volumes," carefully placed discrete sections of water that were often crudely detached from the terrain, with players unable to interact with it.

VIRTUAL LANDSCAPES: THE MODERN ERA: 2000–2010

The Modern Day Era (2000–2010) can be defined in these ways:

1. The Modern Era heralded a leapfrogging in both the design and technologies surrounding virtual environments, resulting in revolution in complexity and richness of VNEs.

2. The early indicators during the Transition Era of height becoming the differentiator in modern 3D natural environments was realised:

game environments were now fully simulated as detailed three-dimensional spaces with players being able to move on all three axes. The size and scale of these natural spaces also increased exponentially.

3. The compartmentalization of the space within game environments that was apparent in the Transition Era reduced significantly as players were now able to traverse a greater variety of natural environments (spanning several virtual square miles in some cases). Players were now able to traverse high mountains and dense forests or go to underwater caves/tunnels without the need to formally progress through structured "levels."

4. Early indicators of trans-disciplinary approaches towards natural environment design started to emerge. Bethesda's *Oblivion* (1996) illustrates this as the developers approached the University of Maryland's Geology department to help inform the design of the environment (in this case natural erosion of rocks for *Oblivion*'s natural landscapes).

5. Complex environment systems further evolved, developing alongside the form (geometry) and aesthetic (graphics) elements of the natural environment. Weather systems now simulated a variety of complex weather and seasonal patterns. Crytek's *Crysis* (2007) and CD Projekt Red's *The Witcher* (2007) illustrated weather systems that included fog, dust, complex cloud simulations and unique weather phenomena (whirlwinds, tornados, etc.)

6. The concept of weather and seasons developed further and deeper into virtual natural environment design. The use of seasonal changes went beyond changes in the environment aesthetics into design considerations; for example, a seasonal change provided a chance for a designer to link an environmental change to gameplay and for players to explore an alternative environment. Eidos Interactive's *Soul Reaver 2* (2001) illustrated this as players were able to experience gameplay differently in the same natural landscape but within different seasons like spring or winter.

7. Additional systems around environmental simulations such as dynamic flora (i.e. physics systems linked to flora in order to simulate movement linked to wind speed) were now integral parts of the natural environment simulations. Early indicators (such as the Dunia Engine) pointed to dynamic flora growth cycles being a future implementation within natural environments.

8. The Modern Era also marked a major milestone with water simulation no longer presenting a major technological constraint, the result of which is now a wider, greater and richer use of water bodies in natural environments. Rivers, lakes and other water bodies have become

more prevalent with the transition between water bodies and the terrain done much more subtly. Games such as Nintendo's *Zelda: Wind Waker* (2002) highlighted both the technological developments and a design progression away from VNEs being solely based around a large central landmass as players navigated a natural environment that was based around a large ocean occupied by smaller archipelago type islands.

9. The cultural domination of Western-influenced representations of the natural environment also appeared to be shifting. Games such as Sega's *Phantasy Star Universe* (2006) demonstrated the growing popularity of home-grown development coupled with a growing preference of players for culturally aligned content.

CHAPTER 2

Drawing for Level Designers

I N THE INTRODUCTION, I gave the working definition of level design as "the thoughtful execution of game*play* into game*space* for players to dwell in." As we move from discussing historic precedents from both architecture and game design, we will explore the methods we will use to design game levels according to this definition. In this chapter, we discuss what game levels do to create user experiences. We will then discuss different tools used for level design both on and off the computer. With the tools in this chapter, you can analyze historical precedents the way architects do to inform their own designs and implement your ideas in your own gamespaces.

What you will learn in this chapter:

Level design goals

Non-digital level design techniques

Digital level design tools

LEVEL DESIGN GOALS

There is something exciting about the act of creating. This is what many people who aspire to be architects and game designers are ultimately looking for—fulfillment in the act of creation. A sure way to excite a group of novice game designers is to let them create things in a level editor. Much less technological but still very powerful is sketching your ideas—putting the creations of one's mind on paper. Improvising a new gamespace from a blank sheet of paper or an empty void in a game engine can be exhilarating.

However, levels made without a concrete plan or based only on "wouldn't it be cool" design ideas often turn out to not be very fun when actually prototyped. In the same way an architect should never begin pouring a foundation without doing a site, budget, or load analysis, game designers should never begin work without taking a very important component of games into account—players. Great or even simply good levels should be planned—not only to get an image of what the level will look like, but also to understand the kind of experience the designer hopes to create for players. Therefore, before exploring the different digital tools for level design, it is important to know that game levels are the primary tool of communication between game makers and game players.

If game levels are executions of *gameplay*—the system of rules that create a user experience—then levels are also the medium that game designers use to express this gameplay to players. It is important to know this, because so often novices in level design open a game's level editor and simply begin placing objects in a scene like a child with a new box of LEGOs. While LEGOs *are* incredibly fun, planning your work in them or in your game levels with a goal in mind is the difference between building a masterpiece and having a disorganized mess.

As the primary tool for communication between game designers and game players, game levels should be built with three goals in mind. By reaching these goals, designers can better direct players through games and create meaningful user experiences:

Adjusting player behavior

Transmitting meaning

Augmenting space

Concepts that help you reach these goals form the content for much of the rest of this book. Gamespaces that reach these goals can deeply affect players while also allowing players to create their own interactions with the game system. Before moving forward, let us briefly explore these goals of level design.

Adjusting Player Behavior

Many designers argue that a level's primary function is to teach players how to play a game. Referencing his game *Super Meat Boy*, indie game designer and artist Edmund McMillen has said in interviews that the placement of early obstacles builds both skills and knowledge.[1] McMillen places obstacles in the player's path that require the player to use each of Meat Boy's abilities, one at a time, to pass. In these areas, players not only learn Meat Boy's different properties, but also gain a sense of accomplishment for figuring out how to play. Repetition of these situations, he argues, both reinforces gameplay lessons so they are retained and teaches players how to combine abilities, such as running and jumping, into new moves (Figures 2.1 through 2.4).

Rudolf Kremers argues a similar point in his book *Level Design: Concept, Theory, and Practice*, with the concept of *skill gates*.[2] Skill gates are required challenges that block a player's progress unless he or she performs a specific action to pass. Such obstacles can be very simple, such as an enemy or object that players must jump over (Figure 2.5), or more complex, such as games that require you to use new abilities to escape from the room where you acquire them (Figure 2.6).

While behavior adjustment can be accomplished in these very planned ways, another way to adjust behavior is to build your levels to support or encourage unplanned play. One celebrated (and sometimes demonized) aspect of games is how they let players have a choice of how to play. If a game allows players the choice of many things to do, especially in massively multiplayer online games, players will find inventive ways to make levels fit their play style. This is especially important for games where players can

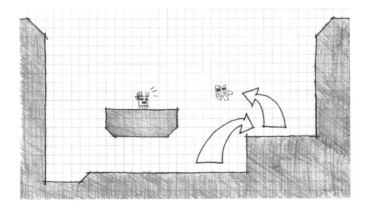

FIGURE 2.1 The first level of *Super Meat Boy* requires players to jump to save Bandage Girl.

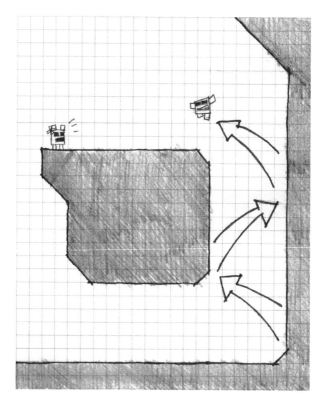

FIGURE 2.2   The second level requires the player to use Meat Boy's wall-jumping ability.

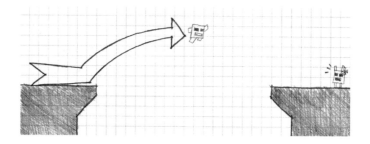

FIGURE 2.3   The third level requires players to combine running and jumping into a long jump.

choose from multiple character types, such as Blizzard's team-based game *Overwatch*. Again, gamespaces can help facilitate interesting interactions between players by providing environments that provide spaces designed for different play styles.

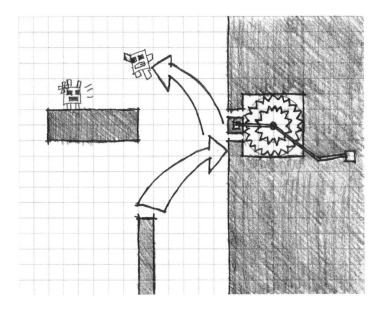

FIGURE 2.4 The final level demonstrates saws to the player in a non-interactive fashion before they become obstacles in future levels.

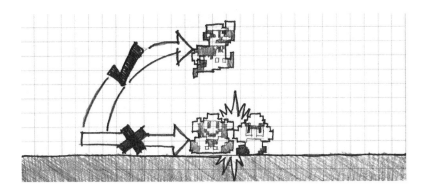

FIGURE 2.5 An early skill gate in *Super Mario Bros.* requires you to jump over or onto an enemy Goomba to pass. This teaches the player to jump.

Architecture provides great precedents of how to make spaces for multiple types of users. In different cultures and throughout history, architects and builders have used spatial configurations to channel occupant activity. Throughout this book, we discuss the psychological methods that both games and buildings use to adjust user behavior.

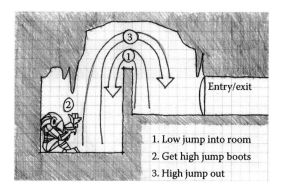

FIGURE 2.6 After getting new powers in *Metroid* games, players must often solve a puzzle related to the new power to escape the item room.

Transmitting Meaning

Once upon a time, a hot debate in game studies was whether games should be understood according to gameplay mechanics (ludology) or by their storytelling capabilities (narratology). Over time, these two factions have settled their differences and games are now often understood for how they utilize both rule-based systems and meaningful structures together. Through explorations of this combination, new genres of games have emerged, such as persuasive games. These games communicate a message or teach players something through gameplay.

Embedding meaning in structural systems is a hallmark of architectural design. Much of architectural history is focused around sacred structures. Built for occupants who were often illiterate, pictorial representations of biblical scenes or figures of deities helped communicate the idea of what the structure was supposed to represent. Some structures, such as Gothic churches, were built in ways meant to simulate the architect's idea of spiritual places such as the kingdom of heaven.

In games, narrative descriptors contained within a game's dialog, art, and symbolism interact with formal and structural elements of game levels—rules of movement and level geometry. Understanding how these work together helps create meaningful game levels. Rather than simply turning to cutscenes for storytelling, designers can make their game levels do a lot of narrative legwork for them. This turns game levels into systems of *rhetoric*, the art of communicating ideas through discourse. Game theorist Ian Bogost argues that while writing and debate are classical forms of rhetoric, and while art and graphics make arguments through *visual rhetoric*, games and interactive media can make statements through *procedural rhetoric.*[3] In Bogost's model, games make their arguments through the cause-and-effect relationships between player actions and game rules. This is explored throughout this book to show how gamespaces can help encapsulate narrative or meaningful ideas.

Augmentation of Space

Tied in with the idea of transmitting meaning is the concept of augmenting space with information. In video games, user interfaces and on-screen icons connect players to databases of in-game information (amount of ammo, enemy information, etc.) In some games, levels can give information to players in ways that allow them to make informed decisions about what is coming next. Lighted signs in Valve's *Portal* tell players what mechanics a given puzzle will involve at the entrance to every chamber. Patterns in level design can inform players when bosses or other significant enemies are coming (Figure 2.7).

Patterned spaces can be powerful ways to communicate with players. In architecture, formal *symbols* are often used to communicate the function of a building (Figure 2.8). Establishing a set of formal or spatial symbols allows players to understand what's next in a level, or even what objects are interactive (Figure 2.9). Through this type of formal interaction, gamespaces build their own "languages" that can assist in directing player behavior or communicating meaning and narrative.

It is impossible to talk about how to design game worlds with layers of information without mentioning *augmented reality* (AR), technology that

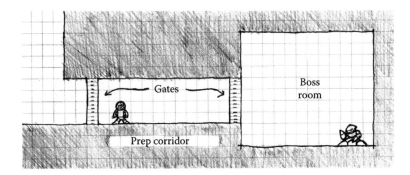

FIGURE 2.7 Games in the *Mega Man* series typically use a double set of gates and a hallway to mark the entrance to a boss room. This pattern trains players to know they are about to fight a boss and builds anticipation for the encounter by slightly delaying it. Knowing that a boss fight is about to happen also allows players time to arrange their resources for the battle.

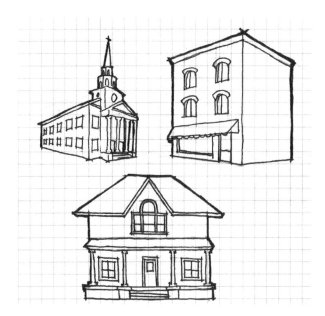

FIGURE 2.8 Look at these building sketches. What types of buildings do you suppose they are? Symbolic forms like these help demonstrate to observers what the purpose of a structure is without the need for signage or verbal indicators.

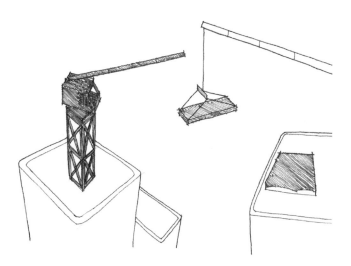

FIGURE 2.9 In many games, interactive objects such as buttons, grappling hooks, switches, and others follow similar visual language throughout so players know when to use their abilities. The game *Mirror's Edge* uses an interesting approach of color-coding interactive objects in the otherwise whitewashed world.

overlays digital information on the real world. With AR-capable devices, game worlds can expand to include real-world environments. Like creating symbols in digital environments, AR apps are often programmed to recognize certain images in real space and then pair digital information with them. Similarly, to how players learn to "read" the geometry of digital game levels, AR apps can be designed so players learn to recognize important structures around them. As games like *Pokémon GO!* have shown, properly placed waypoints direct players to places where positive social experiences can happen.

So, what kinds of spaces should be augmented with AR to create meaningful game situations? Is it enough to put a digital layer on any real-world environment, or are there ways to plan interesting interactions through spatial awareness? Theories of urbanism may hold the key to understanding how functions of AR, alternate reality games (ARGs), and big games (large-scale physical games played in real environments) can meaningfully communicate serious ideas to players.

NON-DIGITAL LEVEL DESIGN TECHNIQUES

Now that we have established some goals for level design, we can discuss tools. Like many things in the game industry, there is no one perfect tool for level design: many large studios have their own proprietary tools and independent developers often use third-party software. Since there are so many options, game-making is a very open medium: games can be made with many tools, even non-digital media. However, it can also make breaking in confusing for anyone looking for one set path to game development.

Due to the non-standard state of game production, developers should take time to find a tool that fits their own workflow and process. The most popular tool is not always necessarily the right tool: using a 3D-capable engine that gives you fine control over lots of options may be overkill for a quick 2D retro side project. This book is about architectural approaches, so we're going to start our two-chapter look at the practical side of level design with some foundational architecture tools. This means that we're going to start in a place that surprises many new game designers: with pen and paper drawing.

When designing levels, especially 3D ones, designers should prototype their levels in interactive form as soon as possible. In this way, there is tremendous value in using non-digital tools for level design. While they do not get designers onto the computer and generating work right away, non-digital sketches and maps answer a lot of questions without taking up a lot of production time.

To be clear, this section is not focused on the perspective drawings that are typically used for concept art, though those certainly play a part in planning. Instead, drawing in this context refers to diagrams used to communicate ideas and construction drawings used to show how buildings will go together in very plain visual language. Many experienced designers will understand non-digital level sketching as drawing what their level will look like before making it on the computer, which is a good way to plan your work. However, architectural sketching is also a powerful tool for analyzing the levels in games you are playing, a practice that can make you a better designer.

Basic Drawing Techniques

University of Washington Professor Emeritus Francis Ching said that drawing both "invigorates seeing"[4] and "stimulates the imagination."[5] Drawing is a core component of not only how architects make construction documents, but also how they learn from other designers' works. It is therefore vital to understand the basics of architectural design drawing if you want to incorporate it into your level design workflow. Know, though, that while drawing for artwork is similar to that for architectural analysis, there are quite a few differences.

In architectural drawing, you are trying to capture the *shapes*, the two-dimensional boundaries of objects; *forms*, three-dimensional masses of objects; and *relationships*, how each object interfaces with others in space. Perhaps the biggest difference is that architectural drawing is meant to be more communicative than regular sketching. These drawings describe the forms, shapes, and relationships of spaces, and therefore must be neater and more precise—free of chicken scratch, hurried shapes, and timid lines (Figure 2.10).

FIGURE 2.10 These are examples of how not to draw lines or shapes in architectural sketches. Chicken scratch lines and hurried shapes can distract from the meaning of a drawing.

How to Draw a Line

Even if you are an excellent artist, we are going to start from square one: making clean lines and marks so we can make readable sketches. Two techniques can help in drawing clean, straight lines. One is beginning and ending each line with a dot or dash. These dots and dashes should over-shoot where the line actually ends, so lines coming to a corner should intersect slightly. Another technique is to squiggle your lines as you draw them. This will provide straighter lines. While this seems counterintuitive, wiggling your pen slightly while you draw a straight line will cause you to concentrate more on the squiggle and less on making your line perfectly straight; the result is a line that is more directionally straight (Figure 2.11).

When creating shapes that are not linear, such as circles, it is useful to create straight *reference* lines and measure out the shape rather than simply attempting to draw it correctly. To draw a circle, first draw a square. Then, draw lines through the square horizontally and vertically. Now, draw arcs between each midline so that you end up with a circular shape (Figure 2.12). When drawing in perspective, circles become ellipses, so draw these by either using the sides of an object as endpoints for the ellipse or measuring the ellipse out with a square drawn in perspective.

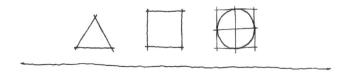

FIGURE 2.11 These line sketches show several different techniques, including adding a start and end to each of your lines, how these are used to neatly intersect lines, and how squiggled lines create directionally straight sketch lines.

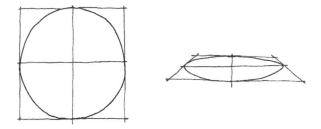

FIGURE 2.12 To sketch a circle correctly, create a reference square and reference lines, and use them as a base to draw a properly proportioned circle. Circles in perspective flatten and become more elliptical.

Contours and Line Weights

The types of drawings discussed so far in this chapter are *contour* drawings. Contour drawings follow the edges of shapes and forms, describing where objects are in space (Figure 2.13). Contour drawing is what people often start with when learning how to draw. Contours also offer a quick way to document spatial conditions when in the field.

When sketching in contour and when drafting, *line weights* communicate object distance. Line weight refers to the thickness or darkness of a line used in a drawing (Figure 2.14). When drawing with line weights, the thickest weights are assigned to edges that do not immediately connect with others, such as the outer contours of an object or group of objects. Contours of objects that directly meet other objects are given very light line weights.

FIGURE 2.13 This contour drawing shows the placement of buildings, trees, and other natural features in relation to one another.

FIGURE 2.14 This sketch utilizes line weight to communicate the distance edges and contours are from one another. The outer contours of objects are therefore the thickest lines in the drawing.

Drawing with References

When sketching designed spaces, reference lines can be used in much the same way as when you are sketching shapes. If the point of sketching is to understand the spatial conditions of the scene you are observing, then it is helpful to use light reference lines to line up elements of scenery or architectural forms that line up with one another in space. Ching also recommends using your pencil as a *viewfinder* to observe spatial relationships. Holding your pencil with your thumb halfway up the shaft allows you to measure the image you are seeing. Holding the pencil further down toward the eraser allows you to use the shaft of the pencil as a *straightedge* to determine angles and relationships between objects so you can draw your reference lines[6] (Figure 2.15).

Shading

Despite the usefulness of contour drawing, you will occasionally want to describe the *surface conditions* of forms you are observing or the *lighting conditions* of a space. To do this, use *shading* to describe these conditions. Shading is using your drawing tools in such a way that describes light as well as *tonal* information related to color.

There are several different methods for shading. One of the most commonly used is *hatching*, where the artist uses a series of parallel lines to describe tonal value. When hatching, darker values are created by spacing lines closely together, while lighter values are created by spacing lines farther apart. *Crosshatching* is a similar technique to hatching where two sets

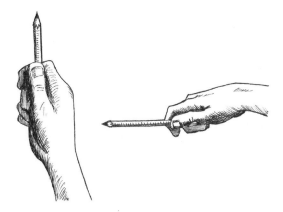

FIGURE 2.15   Techniques for using your pencil as a measuring tool and viewfinder. From these exercises, you can create reference lines that help you understand the relationships between objects you are drawing.

of lines are crossed over one another to create values. Crosshatching and hatching can be used interchangeably in the same drawing to create many different tonal and textural values.

In his book, Ching describes another useful method, called *scribbling*, that has artists putting down more random lines to denote tonal value than one would while hatching and crosshatching. Scribbling is useful for on-site drawing situations where not a lot of time can be devoted to creating neat hatch lines. By keeping scribbling methods consistent, artists can still create neat and communicative drawings[7] (Figure 2.16).

Hierarchical Drawing

With all these methods, it is important to remember the purpose of your drawings—communication of the spatial conditions of places you are observing. In this way, you must remember to create your drawings in a *hierarchical* fashion, that is, in such a way that best communicates the information you are trying to convey without getting caught up in extraneous details. For example, when trying to sketch details on the façade of a Gothic church, it is better to focus on the church itself rather than sketching people and landscape elements around the church. Such elements can be abstracted with scribbles or rough contours.

When trying to establish your visual hierarchy, it is also important to draw in such a way that accentuates the most important part of the drawing. For example, shading or outright blacking out the unimportant elements of a drawing can have the adverse effect of seeming hierarchically more important. Intricate details or dark values capture the eye of a viewer much better than lightly drawn lines, so you should focus details and dark tones on the part of a drawing you wish to accentuate (Figure 2.17).

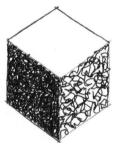

FIGURE 2.16 The two described types of shading—hatching/crosshatching and scribbling. Three-dimensional forms can be described in sketches by capturing tonal values through these methods.

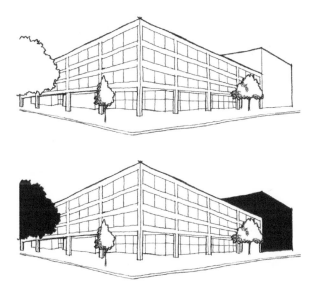

FIGURE 2.17 Two versions of the same sketch. One shows the proper way to establish visual hierarchy by focusing more attention onto the subject of the sketch. The other shows how silhouettes of unimportant details can take attention away from the drawing's subject. The subject of these sketches is the Martin Luther King Memorial Library in Washington, D.C. It was designed by Ludwig Mies van der Rohe and completed in 1972.

Types of Architectural Drawings

Now that we have covered techniques for design drawing, we can look at the types of drawings that architects use to describe space. Each type is used to show specific information about a building design from a specific point of view. The types of architectural drawings that we will utilize are:

Plan

Section

Elevation

Axonometric

Perspective

Plan

Plans are top-down drawings of a space that show spatial relationships between the elements of a design (rooms, hallways, stairs, gardens, lawns, landscaping features, etc.) from above (Figure 2.18). Like the other construction drawing types we will discuss, they are drawn without perspective. They are drawn assuming that the viewer is observing the design from 4½ feet above the ground level. Masses such as walls or other objects that pass through this viewing plane (it is best to imagine a giant saw blade cut through the space at 4½ feet above the ground) are darkened either through hatching or *poché*, the complete blacking in of the contours of the cut form. Sometimes, architects use different types of hatching to color in cut forms instead of poché to indicate the type of material a wall or object is made from.

Franco–Swiss architect Le Corbusier is famously quoted as saying that "the plan is the generator" in his book *Toward an Architecture* (popularly known as *Towards a New Architecture*).[8] Indeed, plans are typically the first drawing that an architect creates when designing a building. Plans show the arrangement and flow of spaces in a design. They provide a useful top-down view of spaces that make them suitable for diagramming (Figure 2.19). When designing levels, many designers will draw at least one plan diagram or sketch to visualize how their gamespaces will be arranged. Often viewed simply as maps, carefully drawn plans can provide meaningful spatial layouts for viewing things like level challenges and pacing, which are covered later in the chapter.

Despite these strengths, plans have major downsides: the primary one is a lack of any three-dimensionality. To describe spatial conditions above

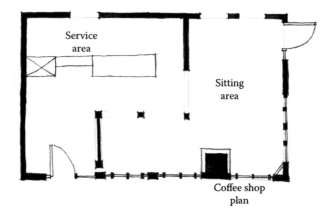

FIGURE 2.18   Plans show the flow and relationships between spaces in a design. Blacked-in masses show built elements. This plan shows a simple coffee shop layout.

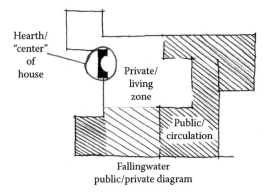

FIGURE 2.19 This drawing shows how plans can be used to diagram spatial articulations in a design.

and below the level shown in a drawing, dotted lines are typically used, but to properly capture multilevel spaces, a different type of drawing is used.

Section

In terms of technique, building sections are very similar to plans, as they depict a design cut along a plane. However, rather than the design being cut horizontally to show a top-down view, sections show views into the building as though they had been cut through vertically (Figure 2.20). Like plans, cut-through masses are colored in with poché or hatching.

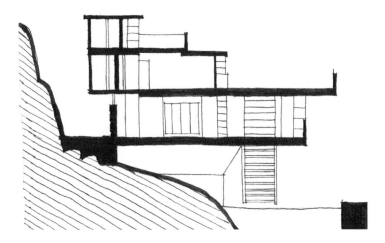

FIGURE 2.20 A building section of Fallingwater by Frank Lloyd Wright. It was built between 1936 and 1939 in Mill Run, Pennsylvania.

Most sections show the *elevation*, perspective-less drawings of the side of an object, of forms and objects past the cut line, though sectional perspectives and other combinations are quite common.

Sections are often used in tandem with plan drawings to describe three-dimensional space. According to architectural writer Matthew Frederick, "Good designers work back and forth between plans and sections, allowing each to inform the other."[9] Sections can help a level designer map out vertical spatial arrangements for things like multilevel puzzles or battle positions in multiplayer maps. As many 2D games are viewed from the side, sections can offer the same overview of side-scrolling game levels for better planning of level pacing.

Plans are especially important for 3D titles. If you design in a two-dimensional plan, your game level will be two-dimensional, even in a 3D game (i.e., have very few areas where the player looks or travels up or down). Having several sections of the major play spaces in your levels will allow you to visualize alternate ways of transitioning from play space to play space. Sections allow you to better utilize height-based spatial transitions such as ramps, overhead bridges, cliffs to jump down, and similar structures that are difficult to encompass in a plan drawing.

Elevation

Elevations are the third type of architectural drawing. Elevations are similar to sections, but instead of cutting through a design, the viewpoint is from the outside of the building. Elevations are used to show exterior views of a building's sides (Figure 2.21).

Architects use elevations primarily to visualize the exteriors of buildings. For real buildings, this is vital. However, game levels often lack the

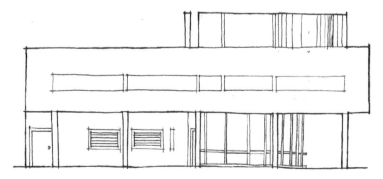

FIGURE 2.21   A building elevation of Villa Savoye by Le Corbusier. It was completed in 1931 in Poissy, Yvelines, France.

need for real building conditions like having both an exterior and an interior. Instead, the designer will only create those surfaces that the player will look at. Even so, elevations are still important for designing good building exteriors for scenery. Elevations in level design fall more under the category of concept art rather than spatial planning.

Axonometric

When planning 3D video games, plans and sections must work together to correctly show 3D space. However, *axonometric* drawings can be used to represent a design's three-dimensionality. To create an axonometric (axon) drawing, artists take an already-made plan drawing and turn it either 30 or 45 degrees, and then project the plan upward to create 3D forms of the design (Figure 2.22).

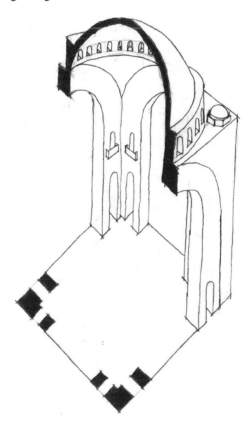

FIGURE 2.22 An axonometric drawing. This one is a *sectional axonometric*, showing the extruded interior geometry of the design and the plan that forms the base of the drawing.

Axonometrics are powerful spatial planning tools. They often combine plan and elevation drawings, and can even combine plan and section to create *sectional axonometric* drawings like the one seen in Figure 2.22. As drawings that are derived from others, axonometrics are often a question of time for level designers. On one hand, they can help visualize 3D space. On the other, the time taken to produce an axon drawing could be used for creating level prototypes in your game engine.

Level designers that use axonometric drawings tend to create semi-planned axonometrics. These show the three-dimensionality of a gamespace but may or may not fully follow a plan of the level. They can be done for several different purposes. One is to create spatially planned concept art for a game level space, combining plan and elevation to communicate what the final level geometry may look like. Another is to use axonometric-like drawings, or *axons*, of levels to demonstrate three-dimensional gameplay concepts; a technique that Valve used to plan several of its games.[10] These axons create the level space only as a visual guide. Rather than a plan of the actual level, they instead use this visual guide as a backdrop for sketches of gameplay events that will happen in the level in a three-dimensional way—allowing for the mapping of vantage points, sniping spots, or spatial puzzles. In this way, axons become both concept art and a game design tool (Figure 2.23).

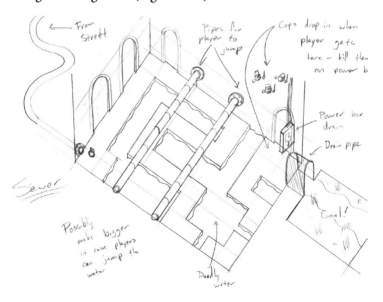

FIGURE 2.23 These axonometric drawings diagram a level with added notes for gameplay situations.

Perspective

Finally, there are *perspective* drawings. Like axons, perspective drawings show 3D space. However, unlike axons, which are drawn without distortion, perspective drawings show how an object distorts based on the viewer's positioning relative to a *vanishing point* (Figure 2.24).

Perspective drawings can be drawn with multiple vanishing points. Drawings based on one vanishing point, where one side of an object is drawn without distortion in an elevation style, is called a *one-point perspective*. Drawings that utilize two vanishing points to distort more than one side of an object are called *two-point perspectives*. Two-point perspectives are the views most commonly seen from a human's eye level. Drawings using three vanishing points, most often done for views of tall buildings from above or below, are *three-point perspectives*.

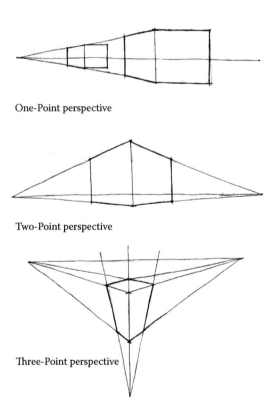

One-Point perspective

Two-Point perspective

Three-Point perspective

FIGURE 2.24 Diagrams of perspective drawing, showing how objects are drawn to distort toward one or more vanishing points. These diagrams show one-, two-, and three-point perspectives.

Perspectives are most often used for concept art, as they are the least useful for actual spatial planning but most useful to develop the visual art of a level. They can either be drawn manually or generated through *3D underlays*. Three-dimensional underlaying is when an artist creates a simple version of his or her concept art scene in a 3D art program, then paints on top of it using a digital art program like Photoshop. Such underlays are helpful for creating many versions of the same scene to develop a game's final art style (Figure 2.25).

Now that you know a few different drawing techniques and the types of drawings used to understand spatial design, we will show how these techniques can be applied in order to better understand and plan game levels.

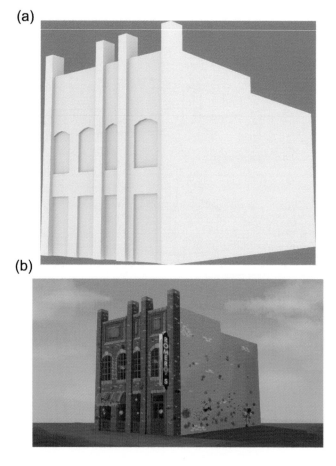

FIGURE 2.25 This perspective sketch of a building was painted over a simple 3D rendering. Such underlays can be used to create multiple looks for the same model.

Sketching and Journal Writing

What use are drawing techniques without a place to actually use them? One of my most important tools for level design is my sketchbook: a graph paper booklet small enough to be carried easily or slipped into a backpack. It's where I do all of my non-digital level design and idea collection. For the architect, sketching is an important way to both capture design ideas and record elements he or she has seen while studying a piece of architecture (Figure 2.26). The drawing techniques covered in the two previous sections are a big part of creating your own design sketchbook. By sketching your ideas as you have them, you can more easily remember or communicate them to others later.

In Chapter 1, we discussed a way of seeing for game levels and buildings. The guidelines for seeing include things like understanding why the level is

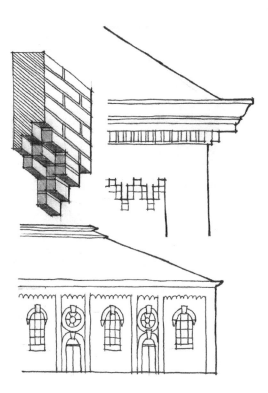

FIGURE 2.26 Sketches such as these are important tools for both aspiring and professional architects for understanding buildings. Sketching allows the architect to both highlight elements he or she finds important in the design and gain a greater understanding of the building by recreating its forms through manual drawing.

created the way it is, what gameplay experiences it creates, what its historical precedents are, and what its spatial composition is. Early in an architect's education, he or she is taught to record these kinds of observations in sketchbooks. Using the level design ways of seeing that were isolated in the previous chapter as a guideline, we can also do similar studies for game levels. Having such a sketchbook can be vital for understanding design precedents that will be inspirations for your own levels (Figure 2.27).

Granted, for many games, it's really hard to sketch and analyze while being attacked by waves of enemies. In these cases, keeping a gameplay journal and sketchbook concurrently can help players retain their memories of gameplay. When I play a game whose level design I want to learn from, I write my thoughts down on paper or in a word processor immediately after a play session or after each level. On computers, taking screenshots or videos during gameplay and adding them to your journal is also an excellent way for marking what to analyze later on. From your screenshots and notations, analysis sketches can be derived.

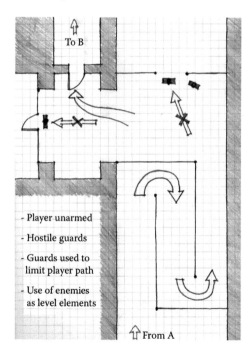

FIGURE 2.27 Here are some sketches of *Half-Life 2* environments derived from gameplay journals recorded during gameplay sessions. Writing down how you feel during gameplay sessions and taking screenshots can help designers mark what they will analyze with sketches like these later on.

Designing on Paper

Beyond recording precedent analyses, sketching is useful in level design for working on your own ideas. In architectural design, initial ideas are often sketched out in sketchbooks or on trace paper. A standard way of forming design ideas on paper is to do *parti* sketches. An architectural parti is a simple formal study that seeks to isolate the shape a building will eventually take. These studies can be done on paper or as architectural models, in both two and three dimensions. For buildings, these are important for understanding the formal principles that will govern a design and how a building will interact with its *site*, the place where it is built (Figure 2.28). Perhaps as importantly, parti studies are noncommittal, meaning that a designer can quickly create a large number of them without having to commit a lot of effort and detail into any one design, only to realize it was the wrong choice later. They also lack measurement in most cases, so designers can focus more on spatial and formal ideas rather than sizing. Parti is explored later in the chapter as an element of level design workflows.

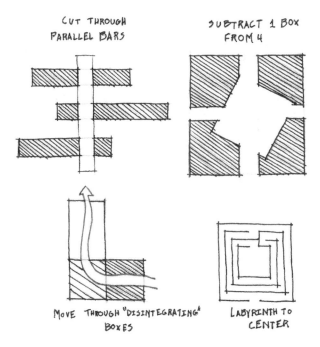

FIGURE 2.28 Architectural parti sketches allow designers to quickly understand how their design will interact with site conditions. They also help designers try different spatial and formal compositions quickly without having to commit to any one design.

For more measured level design drawing, a useful tool for generating paper level ideas is *graph paper*. Graph paper is commonly used to plot various mathematical functions—thus the name. It comes in many types, but the type most commonly used by building engineers is *Cartesian graph paper*, which features a regular grid. While not always used by architects, engineers use graph paper as an aid when drafting tools like rulers and triangles are not handy. It is especially useful for figuring out the proportions of objects in a sketch. To do this, builders stipulate that one square on the paper represents a specific unit of measurement (1 square = 1 yard, for example), and use that as a base for generating quick but accurately measured sketches.

Spatial design for games also has a close relationship with grids and graph paper. It is the primary tool of many who have created their own maps for the role-playing game *Dungeons & Dragons*. In video game design, many engines inherently use grid-based units of measurement to measure space. Creating architect-like graph paper drawings is therefore not only great representationally, but also helps the designer figure out proper proportions for game worlds. A common mistake that new designers make is to generate game levels on the computer that do not appropriately fit around a player character. In some extreme cases, this can mean that the player character cannot even go through doors.

To properly design levels, a level designer must understand a player character's *metrics*. Metrics are gameplay-based measurements expressed in in-engine units that describe size and movement properties of characters in games. Measurements that could be considered metrics include the size of the character, the space traversed by jumps, the space taken up by attacks, the distance traveled over time when the character runs or walks, and many other movement-based things. Many game engines employ their own basic units of measurement; 1 unit in the Unity game engine, for example, equals 1 meter, which can allow designers to understand the distance that player characters need to do things.

Graph paper can help designers figure out proportion before the design is created on the computer. By stipulating that a square or group of squares on graph paper is equal to a specific unit of measurement, level designers can plan their levels according to player metrics similarly to how architects design according to specific units of measurement (Figure 2.29).

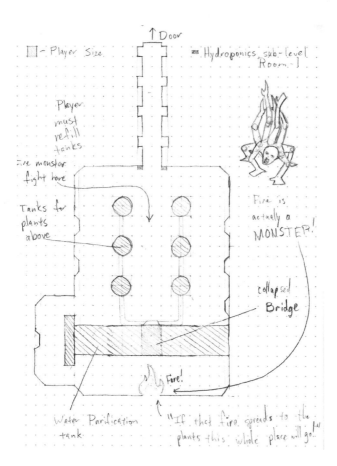

FIGURE 2.29 This design sketch, showing the plan of a level, utilizes graph paper to help the designer match gamespace measurements against the size of the player character in a 3D game.

Notation Methods for Level Design

Not all drawing methods are used to describe the "physical" (as physical as spaces in a digital game can be) aspects of game levels. Architects and game developers have also developed shorthand diagramming methods for describing non-physical aspects of space. These methods describe how users flow from one place to another, the "pace" at which users travel from one place to another, or other types of relationships.

Proximity Diagrams

When a property owner wants to build a building, he or she outlines a *building program* to give to potential architects. The program is a list of necessary functions the building must perform and spaces the building must have. This form-follows-function approach allows us to relate our level designs to the mechanics of the games we are designing them for.

Once they receive the building program, architects translate the program requirements into building spaces with *proximity diagrams.* Proximity diagrams are made up of bubbles and connected with lines. The bubbles represent rooms or spaces that are to be part of the building and are sized according to square footage requirements for these spaces. Likewise, lines connecting the bubbles are sized according to how important it is for them to be adjacent[11] (Figure 2.30). It is important to note that proximity diagrams are not actual spatial plans. They are a tool for analyzing the functional idea for a building but should not be understood as its final spatial plan.[12]

Proximity diagrams can be used for level design as they would be used for real-world architecture. Rather than each bubble having the name or square footage for a functional building space, it has the name of a gameplay space, such as boss room, sniping spot, or finish line. The sizes of these bubbles can stand for their size type. The size and type of line used to connect the bubbles can describe proximity priority and the type of connection spaces have. For example, it may be important for sniping positions to have a view of a large prospect space in a map, even if the player must actually travel a long set of corridors to get there (Figure 2.31).

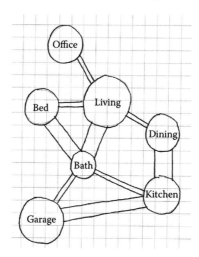

FIGURE 2.30   A building proximity diagram. Each bubble is sized according to the required square footage of a space. The sizes of lines show the necessity of spaces being adjacent in the final building.

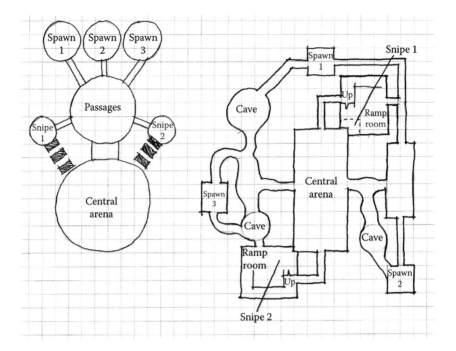

FIGURE 2.31 A proximity diagram for a multiplayer first-person shooter (FPS) level. In this example, it is important for each sniper position to have a view of the main competition area for each spawn point to have access to gear. Despite the layout of the diagram, the final design can (and should) look drastically different.

Concept Diagrams

Proximity diagrams are a very specific type of architectural diagram, but with the right visual language it is possible to express many different types of information in diagrams. Creating an exhaustive list of diagramming symbols and language could be a book in and of itself. Instead, we will adopt the term *concept diagram*, used in architecture studios for diagrams that show a design's core idea, to describe diagrams that show a variety of spatial conditions similar to the parti sketches shown in Figure 2.28.

A hallmark of concept diagrams is not any particular symbol or spatial description, but rather the use of one or more symbols to illustrate conceptual aspects of a space's design. A popular concept to diagram might be the amount of *public space*, where occupants dwell among large crowds, versus *private space*, where occupants can be alone or in small groups. A *public–private* diagram is usually a simplified floor plan with rooms hatched in with varying levels of density.

Hatching is useful for showing spatial concepts that occur in different levels throughout a design, as shown in Figure 2.19, a public/private diagram of Fallingwater. Hatching is a useful symbol for describing varying levels of a spatial condition like public–private, lighting, or the functions of spaces. Since hatching can be drawn with lines of different orientations or patterns, there are many possibilities for communication. For example, the diagram of a house designed with some rooms for parents (den, office) and some for children (play room) might be diagrammed with vertical hatch lines in the parents' rooms and horizontal hatch lines in the kids' rooms. In general-use rooms like the kitchen or dining room, the hatches would intersect to form a cross-hatch.

Other visual elements useful for diagramming include arrows: these are useful to show the direction of foot traffic, major sight lines, or a design's *axes*, imaginary lines that inform a building's shape (Figure 2.32). Color is another useful tool to describe the function of spaces or as an alternative to hatching (Figure 2.33). Finally, shapes and forms are used in lots

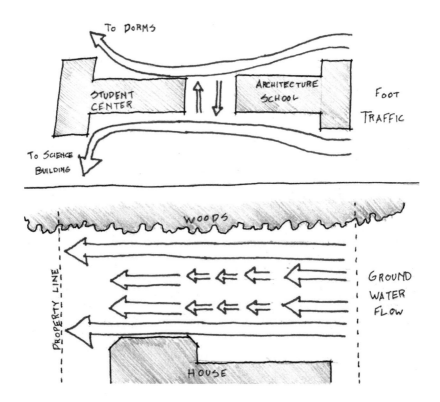

FIGURE 2.32   Some diagrams that make different use of arrows.

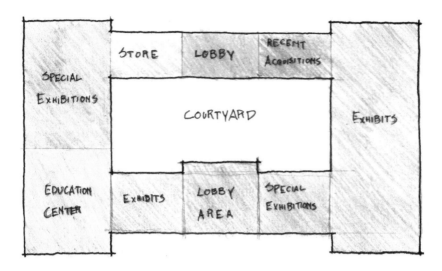

FIGURE 2.33   A museum diagram that uses color-coding instead of hatching to describe what happens in each part of the building.

of architectural diagrams, either as an abstraction of the spaces within a building or as a *parti* illustration of what a shape might eventually be (Figure 2.34). Depending on how the shapes in such diagrams are filled in, the emphasis can also be on the diagram's *negative space*, or the space between drawn elements.

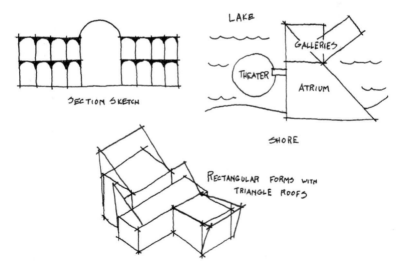

FIGURE 2.34   Some diagrams with shapes and forms blocking out building spaces in different ways. Some of these have the shapes filled in with black poché to emphasize the white space in the image.

It is tempting to think that there are predetermined "recipes" for paring symbols and concepts to make diagrams. In reality, diagrams are made by architects to record their ideas and observations in whatever way feels right at the time. As such, you should experiment with different techniques when you make diagrams of levels from your or others' games to find a "grammar" that works for you.

Game-Mapping

Somewhere between diagramming game levels and more exact types of drawing, like drafting or graph-paper planning, lies *game-mapping*. Before many games came with *auto-maps*, portions of a game's user interface that show the player a map of the game's world, game players had to record the areas they visited on paper. While not explicitly an architect's technique, the style of mapping that most game players use has a lot in common with graph paper maps from games like *Dungeons & Dragons* and the architect's plans and sections.

Game critic and historian Jeremy Parish has taken a particular interest in mapping as a "forgotten art."[13] In a series of YouTube videos which he calls *Cart-ography*, a portmanteau of cartography (map making) and cartridge (the physical media of retro games), he plays games with particularly large worlds and draws room-by-room maps of them. The shared nostalgia for these maps is what keeps audiences coming back to retro-game mapping blogs like *Mapstalgia*,[14] where readers can submit their own maps for curation on the site. In 2014, *Polygon*'s Ben Kuchera similarly called for the site's readership to share their own game maps—either drawn during the "mapping" era of the 1980s and early 1990s or in response to the article.[15] These maps, he argued, represent not only the actual layout of game levels, but also the player's memories of these spaces. I had a similar experience once when buying a used copy of *The Legend of Zelda* for the NES: the "maps and strategies" insert that came with copies of the game had the blank areas of the map filled in by the previous owner (Figure 2.35). It was like holding someone else's childhood in my hands.

Beyond their personal value, maps are important because they represent yet another method of recording our own experiences and precedents for planning our own game spaces. Parish's *Cart-ography* maps, for example, are drawn with a lot of care and feature color-coded keys to signify doors, item pick-ups, and other significant objects in the environment. Each square of the paper represents a predetermined unit of measurement, so the maps he makes are accurate, to-scale representations of

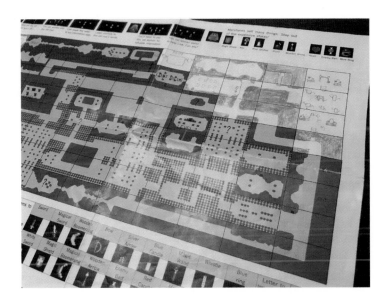

FIGURE 2.35 The "Maps and Strategies" insert of a used copy of *The Legend of Zelda* that I bought several years ago with the previous owner's hand-drawn maps filling in the blank sections—an artifact of a bygone era in game-playing.

levels. Measuring in this way helps designers analyze how levels take character metrics into account and plan the same in their own work.

Maps can be combined with diagrammed information: the graph paper drawings in this book combine mapped representations of game levels with arrows, shading, and other diagramming symbols. My own childhood maps were drawn in this way: I vividly remember sketching individual rooms where I had found secrets with notes of how to find them again. The graph paper maps in this book are a combination of that bygone practice with the techniques I learned from architecture.

Flow Charts

Now we head back into the abstract with *flow charts*. Used by many game and software designers, flow charts map the progression of decisions that a user can make when operating a system (Figure 2.36). Where previous diagram styles represent the "physical" reality of levels in some way, flow charts try to approximate what a user thinks while playing.

Flow charts are great tools for planning games with branching stories or where players have to manage complex systems. However, they can also work well mapping important nodes or gameplay points in a level. For example, if a player needs to find a specific item that will help overcome

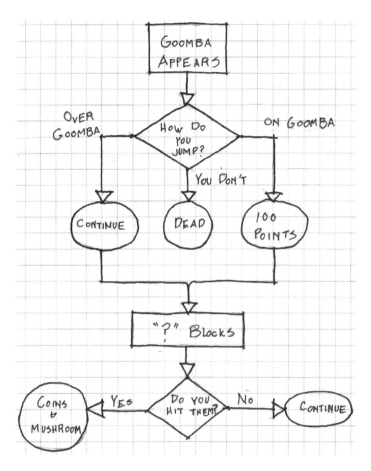

FIGURE 2.36 A flow chart of the decisions a player might make in the first screen of *Super Mario Bros.*

a later challenge, the designer can use a flow chart to "map" out how to inform the player to go back and search (Figure 2.37).

To properly draw a flow chart, a designer starts at the beginning of the level (a "start" node) and draws a line to the next node where a player will make a decision or where the game will require something of the player (like having a key or performing an action). Again, these are not the "physical" locations where things will happen in level geometry, but abstract representations of events. From the start node, the designer will draw lines to several other nodes representing each possible decision a player can make or condition that could exist (example: "has key" or "doesn't have key"). From each of these, the designer draws the next event in the sequence or next node where multiple outcomes can occur.

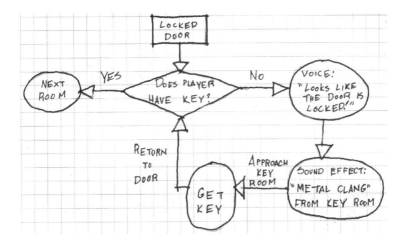

FIGURE 2.37 Using a flow chart to map out the progression of a level when the player has a required item and when they do not.

When drawing a flow chart, it's best to use differently shaped bubbles to represent different types of nodes. Like any diagram, establishing and maintaining a consistent visual language is important to ensure usability. The content of flow charts is usually short text, but as we will see with the final type of diagram we'll cover, creating them with symbol-based languages makes a powerful analysis tool.

Mark Brown's Boss Keys diagrams

One of the most impressive developments in the game industry's understanding of spatial design is game design critic Mark Brown's video series *Boss Keys*.[16] As a spinoff of his *Game Maker's Toolkit* series on YouTube, Brown devotes *Boss Keys* to analyzing the dungeons from *The Legend of Zelda* series. Each episode covers a single game in the *Zelda* series, and analyzes the dungeons based on their *linearity*, *lock-and-key progression*, and *player progression*.

In his video on the 2001 Game Boy Color *Zelda: Oracle* games,[17] Brown develops what he calls an "objective and universal" way to diagram these spaces. Each *dungeon graph* resembles a flow chart, drawing a straight *critical path* between the entrance and exit of the dungeon. Next, the number of *locks* existing on the critical path is drawn on the path itself. Branching from this critical path are sub-paths with *keys*. Laid further on top are places in the sequence where *puzzles* or significant *obstacles* exist blocking player progression (switches requiring special items, etc.) (Figure 2.38). In

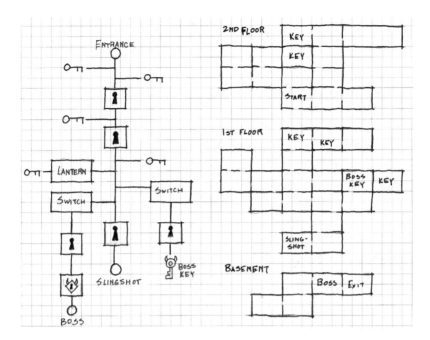

FIGURE 2.38 A recreation of Mark Brown's dungeon graph of the Dancing Dragon Dungeon from *The Legend of Zelda: Oracle of Seasons* shown next to the actual dungeon map.

special cases where dungeon-specific obstacles block player progress, they are treated as *unique locks*: drawn with the same notation as locks but with a label of what the obstacle is instead of a keyhole symbol.

Like a flow chart, Brown's dungeon graphs do not resemble the map of these levels, but describe structural relationships between gameplay elements. These diagrams reveal a lot about these levels that might not be immediately apparent when drawing a map, such as when players have multiple ways to unlock a door or reach an item. One of Brown's major analysis criteria, linearity, is tracked by showing how many locks or keys are in front of a player at one time: multiple keys on the graph preceding one lock or one key before multiple locks implies open-ended exploration. In Brown's own words, these graphs are also handy for showing how much "explorable space" is in a dungeon at one time as well. Viewers of these graphs need only observe how many paths and keys are available before the player encounters a lock or item-requiring puzzle (Figure 2.39). It is also worth mentioning that Brown applies this method to both two-dimensional and three-dimensional *Zelda* games, showing the versatility of the method.

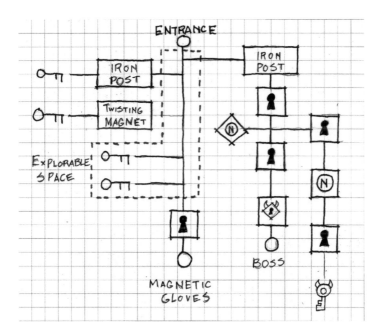

FIGURE 2.39 Brown's graph for the Unicorn's Cave dungeon, showing a significant "explorable space" at the beginning of the dungeon where the player has access to many rooms and multiple keys.

If you are not a fan of *Zelda* or are merely wondering what a diagramming method for such a specific game series has to do with general tools for level design, keep reading nevertheless. Despite the video series' focus on *Zelda* games, Brown's method is easily applicable to any game with "lock-and-key" progression mechanisms such as roleplaying games or point-and-click adventures. At the time of this writing, Brown has begun adapting his method for "Metroidvania"-style games—2D side-scrolling games with persistent maze-like worlds like those from the *Metroid* and *Castlevania* series. Going a step further, levels in other types of games can be analyzed if the types of obstacles or "locks" graphed are changed. Figure 2.40 imagines what a level from id's 2016 reboot of *DOOM* would look like drawn as a *Boss Keys* graph. Major objectives and "kill arenas" take the place of locks and puzzles in this diagram, which shows how elements are organized to avoid the "hallway"-like design found in other first-person shooters. If you are trying to create non-linear levels, these diagrams help objectively evaluate the number of choices players have within your designs.

With Brown's *Boss Keys* graphs, other diagramming methods, and the drawing techniques described in this section, level designers can

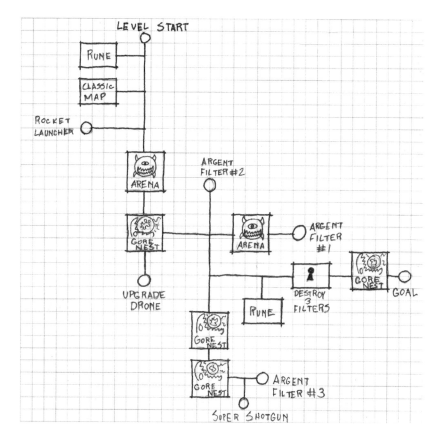

FIGURE 2.40 A *Boss Keys*-style graph of *DOOM*'s Argent Facility level. The diagram shows how this level has a significant "explorable space" and presents players with several objectives that they can accomplish in any order.

accomplish quite a lot before ever turning on a computer. Drawing maps or diagrams is a great way to learn as you play. Likewise, design drawing is a great way to set goals and plan the work you will do once you move to digital production. The next section will cover just that: the tools and techniques that level designers use when they implement their levels in the digital world.

DIGITAL LEVEL DESIGN TOOLS

Eventually, non-digital sketches and diagrams of levels need to become interactive. Off-computer design is vital to establish project goals, but digital prototyping is what helps you *playtest* the level design. Playtesting is when a designer plays a game to evaluate whether it fulfills its original design goals.

There are many great digital tools available to level designers that can be used for everything from planning to implementation. One might wonder why additional planning may be needed after spending time doing architectural sketches of levels on paper. As we will see, digital tools can help plan spatial conditions beyond the geometry of a level, including the materials of different surfaces and lighting conditions. Some of these tools also offer ways to plan out the measurements of environmental objects during the drawing phase.

Like the last section, this is not a prescriptive list, but rather a list of tools, what they are used for in terms of architectural drawing, and how they can help the process of level design. Again, your choice of tools should be based on your own process or the process that is most appropriate for your own games.

CAD Programs

Although this book does not give level designers tutorials on computer-aided design (CAD) software, CAD programs can be a useful next step for level designers that want their drawings to demonstrate more information than a single sketch can. The traditional software used by architects is Autodesk's AutoCAD. However, free alternatives like Dissault Systemes' DraftSight are also excellent, especially if CAD is used only occasionally by a designer (Figure 2.41).

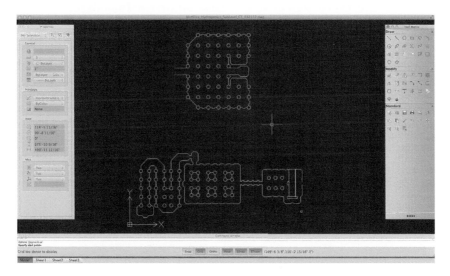

FIGURE 2.41   DraftSight provides everything a level designer would need from a CAD program.

There are several potentially useful applications of CAD software for level designers. The most obvious is that digital drawings have great advantages in clarity over hand drawings, as shown in Figure 2.42. Clear drawings can convey information much better than rough ones. When drafting, CAD programs produce clearer results than most of us do when hand-drafting and in a shorter amount of time. Additionally, CAD programs have features that force designers to work in logical ways that translate well into game engines.

One such feature of many CAD programs is *snapping*, where the drawing cursor locks, or snaps, to a point in space when within a certain radius. Like graph paper, CAD drawings can be set up on a grid of dots that can be set as snapping points for the drawing cursor. Another useful part of this system is that the grid spacing can be set to real-world units. Designers working with game engines that have specific unit measurements, such as Unity or Game Maker, can greatly benefit from grids and snaps. With these features activated, designers can draw in regimented ways that are similar to the logic of game engines—working out measurement problems in the drawing phase. Beyond the workspace advantages, CAD programs also allow drawn lines and shapes to be copied, stored, and modified in various ways so that designers can edit quickly without redrawing things by hand (Figure 2.43).

Another useful feature of CAD software that is applicable throughout the entire level design process is *modular design*. In both professional architecture and level design, many designs are created out of prefabricated pieces that are ordered from a manufacturer and installed. In architecture, many components of buildings come prefabricated: plumbing fixtures, windows, doors, structural elements, curtain wall systems, etc.

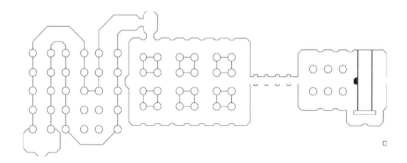

FIGURE 2.42 This simple CAD plan of a level shows the clarity at which level maps can be created.

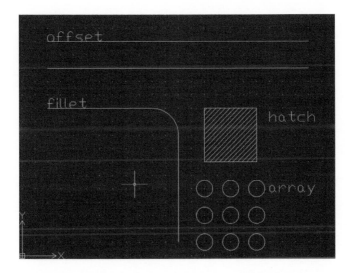

FIGURE 2.43 This image shows just a few drawing modifications that are standard to many CAD programs. Pictured are lines and shapes that have been offset, filleted, hatched, and arrayed.

Many CAD programs allow designers to store components that will be used many times, such as doors or plumbing fixtures, as *blocks*. Blocks are drawings that are stored as a separate document so they can be inserted in future drawings at whatever size the designer needs (Figure 2.44).

Where this applies to level design is in the discovery of what pieces of a level will be utilized multiple times. Level designers might use CAD software or graph paper to sketch out their levels and find themselves using a certain wall shape or environmental object multiple times. When this happens, they might decide that the object should be prefabricated for repeated use. When levels go into production and 2D and 3D art is being made, the designer can then have a list of the most important assets that the environment artists will need to produce. Preproduction planning of levels allows for a LEGO-like construction rather than having to custom build each environment.

A final useful application of CAD software in level design is as line drawings for use in digital art programs. As great as line drawings are for planning levels from plan, section, and elevation, they often miss the mark in planning atmosphere. This is where rendering your drawings can be handy. If a designer is using CAD software, he or she can base a digital painting on a clean drawing that can become a very communicative rendering.

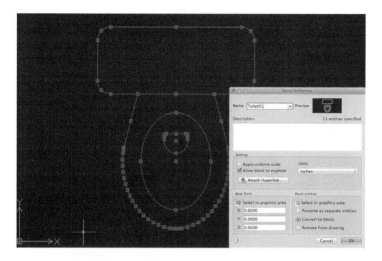

FIGURE 2.44   This toilet image has been stored as a block and can be inserted into drawings as the designer likes.

Digital Art Programs

Rendering is the process by which a designer enhances a drawing with color and lighting information through artistic media—often watercolor paint or colored pencils. Digital art programs like Adobe Photoshop, the GNU Image Manipulation Program (GIMP), or Krita are popular digital alternatives to traditional art media. In the game industry, they are used to create concept art of game environments: often perspective drawings of what a level will look like. Some architects also use these tools to also render their 2D design drawings. Doing the same with level design diagrams, plans, sections, and elevations adds new information only found in concept art.

Like more traditional concept art, rendered plans can be used to convey the atmosphere of game levels in ways that concept perspectives cannot. While concept perspectives are excellent at conveying the general atmosphere of a level, they cannot properly convey changes in atmosphere unless additional design perspectives are done. With an architectural drawing of a level, designers can show the progression of a level's atmospheric effects or materials with a single drawing (Figure 2.45). Macro views like those provided in plan drawings allow designers to visualize the *atmospheric progression* of their levels over time.

When using these types of programs, it is wise to understand their most powerful feature: *layers*. Starting with Photoshop, digital art programs

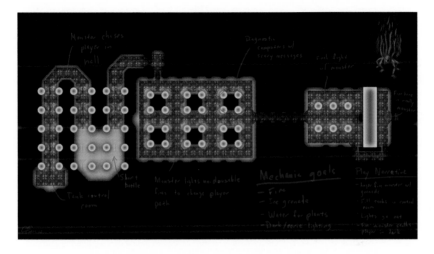

FIGURE 2.45 This rendered version of the CAD map from Figure 2.31 demonstrates how additional information such as textures and lighting can be used with digital art programs.

have allowed users to divide their images into separate layers that can each have their own special effects or adjustments (Figure 2.46). Like in most other pieces of concept art, layers are useful both for adding effects to an image and controlling what information is visible. For example, having notes on their own separate layer allows written information like that in Figure 2.45 to show for design discussions or be hidden for clean displays of the art.

If your game is two-dimensional and a digital art program is where you will be creating your final art assets, you can utilize a pixel-based measurement system for sizing game objects. For example, let's say you are creating a character that on paper or in CAD is 1 grid square wide by 2 grid squares high and jumps at a distance of 8 grid squares horizontally. You can easily say that each grid unit represents a power-of-2 (16, 32, 64, 128, 256, 512, 2048, and 4096) pixel measurement used as the basis of grids in many game engines. Using these proportions, you could make a character that is 16 pixels wide, 32 pixels tall, and can jump 128 pixels horizontally. You will thus know to proportion any level assets and their spacing to these measurements so that the game functions correctly.

Engine Primitives and Placeholder Art

Now to game engines. A common mistake many new designers make is to assume that gameplay cannot be tested until there is art to put into the

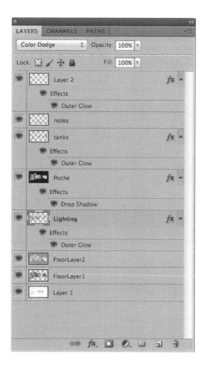

FIGURE 2.46   The layers window from Adobe Photoshop. Layer effects like those applied to the layers in this image can greatly enhance level map concepts.

engine. It is much more efficient, however, to design the spaces of a level and create any required *scripts*, pieces of code that make game elements work, while art is being developed. In this way, a level designer can test whether his or her paper designs effectively create the game experience he or she wants.

To do this, game prototypes can be created out of *engine primitives*, the simple geometric forms that come with some game engines. In a typical engine, this consists of cubes/rectangular solids, spheres, cylinders, and planes. Some engines may also include stairs, cones, and other shapes (Figure 2.47). Engine primitives can create a surprising variety of level geometry, and in fact, many engines' level editors are robust enough that most of the larger spatial geometry of a level can be created entirely out of primitives. For engines without primitives, like many 2D game engines, designers can use *placeholder art* (often also called *programmer art*) in the same way. Placeholder art typically consists of simple shapes—squares, circles, triangles, etc.—that are used to test gameplay until final art is imported.

Primitives are a great tool for designers using graph paper or CAD programs for sketching: they usually adhere to an engine's grid-based

FIGURE 2.47 The primitive shapes in the Unreal Engine.

measurements and are easy to translate from paper to computer. Some older level editors, like Valve's Hammer level editor (part of the Source engine) actually require users to design on a grid with snapping always activated. These editors did this to avoid holes or "leaks" in a level, which will prevent the level from compiling. Some even snapped automatically to power-of-2 measurements: computers process those measurements more easily and textures are still made in those units. Objects in Hammer, therefore, had unit lengths of 16, 32, 64, 128, and so on (Figure 2.48). Modern engines offer more flexibility in how levels are created, but disciplined use of grid-based units still makes it easier to create levels that respond well to movement metrics.

Another benefit of getting right into primitives is that designers will have full access to an engine's systems, such as particles, lighting, and others that can influence the look of a game. In this way, they can begin to test gameplay scenarios against their atmosphere as early as possible. Combined with scripting, designers can create rather robust prototypes of their games without the need for developed artwork (Figure 2.49).

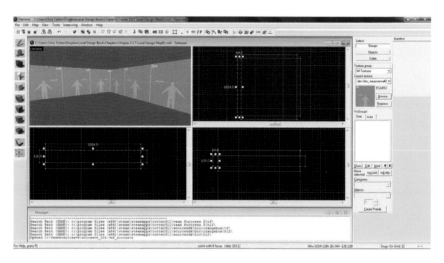

FIGURE 2.48 Building with primitives in the Source engine forces users to use grid snaps similar to those found in CAD programs.

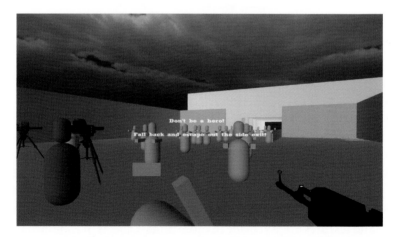

FIGURE 2.49 This prototype of a zombie FPS was created entirely out of Unity engine primitives. Enemies and allies were scripted to create a defense scenario where players had to hold off a horde as long as they could before being overwhelmed.

3D Modeling Programs

In 3D game engines, environmental objects are designed in 3D modeling programs and imported into the engine itself. Like working with 2D level assets or level primitives, these 3D assets can be created according to measurement systems defined during planning stages. The degree to which you will have to use 3D programs to generate level geometry will vary by engine. For engines with rich level editing power, you will mainly be importing decorations or specialty items: furniture, mechanical parts, alien architecture, etc. In these cases, scale is less of a factor. However, if you are using an engine where most of your level geometry, including the actual rooms of a level, must be imported from a 3D modeling program, managing scale between the 3D program and the engine is very important.

Like engines, 3D content creation programs have their own scales and measurement systems that designers can build their models to, typically defined as a generic unit. If the environment artist translates level geometry measurements from paper into the 3D program's unit system (for example, 1 grid square = 1 unit), then objects can be built to proper scale with one another.

One simple methodology for maintaining the scale between imported 3D objects when you go between content creator and engine is to model your whole level in your 3D program (Figure 2.50). This can

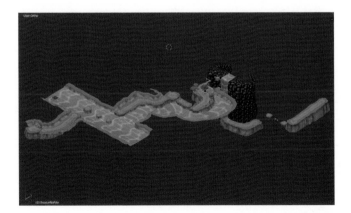

FIGURE 2.50 This jungle level was modeled in its entirety in a 3D program and then imported into the game engine as individual landmasses. Aesthetic elements like the river that flows through the level were modeled to fit around the pieces. This created a system that was prescriptive, but that allowed for adjustments to be made in-engine without having to go back into the 3D program.

be convenient as you build environmental decorations, as they can be built and arranged in context with the rest of a level (Figure 2.51). This method offers memory advantages: importing as a single model is easier to render for weaker consoles, tablets, and phones. The problem, however, is that you are modeling your level in a non-interactive program, so testing can be very slow. Proper planning of your unit metrics (the character can jump 4 units far, for example, so gaps should accommodate that) can help alleviate this problem, but testing your level layout requires awkward exporting and importing. An alternative that I've used in several games is to build a system of "tiles" in the 3D program that can be assembled in your engines in different ways (Figure 2.52). This way you get the best of both worlds: consistent scale between objects when importing and exporting, and the modularity of a level editor. If memory is an issue, we've used scripts to "pack" the tiles so that the engine thinks of them as one model.

If you are modeling all of your level objects at a standard scale in your 3D program, such as the previously mentioned 1 grid square = 1 unit, then all of your level geometry should import at the same scale. If, for example, you find that your objects are importing at 1/20 of the size they are supposed to be, you can import each of your similarly proportioned objects at twenty times their size. If you modeled at the same scale, then each

FIGURE 2.51   In this close-up shot of the model from Figure 2.39, environment décor can be seen. Each was modeled on the landmass to check for proper proportion, and then exported individually into the game engine where it could be copied and arranged as needed.

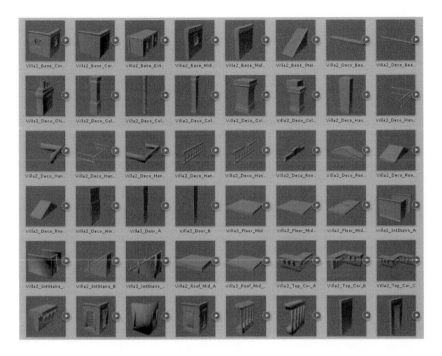

FIGURE 2.52 A tile-based building system for *Dead Man's Trail* levels. These were created in a 3D art program and imported into the engine so a few parts could be used to create many level designs. Models are from the Flooded Grounds mesh pack by Sandrot.

object should import at the same scale, requiring you to remember one scale factor.

An alternative to scaling objects when you import them is figuring out the proportions between units in your 3D program and units in your engine. For example, 1 unit in both Maya and Blender = 1 unit in Unity. This is not always necessarily true for 3D Studio Max. Max can use real-world units, so designers can model in proper scale if they utilize the metric system, such as 1 Unity unit = 1 meter. Other engines have similar proportions. Once they are figured out, you can even build a *scaling model* for your 3D program, which is often just a box built at the standard scale of a character or unit that is used as a "measuring tape" for building level geometry (Figure 2.53).

Now that you understand the digital tools of a level designer and how they are implemented in level-building, you can use them to generate your own game levels.

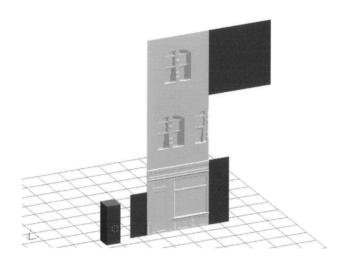

FIGURE 2.53 This screenshot shows some level geometry tiles for the side of a building alongside some reference models, shown in a darker color. The rectangular solid model is scaled to the size of a character, while the planar level geometry reference models are scaled to be 1 unit by 3 units and 3 units by 3 units in the game engine. Also pictured is a reference model for a door.

SUMMARY

There is a wide variety of tools for the study, planning, and execution of game levels. These tools allow designers to plan out the experience they'd like players to have and make modifications quickly as they go from paper to polygons. By understanding the different methods for drawing and diagramming space, we can become better observers of gamespaces. By planning levels in such a way that we focus on measurements, we can prepare for the realities of gameplay. Implementing these findings in game engines and prototyping them in an iterative process can ensure that our game levels meet our original experiential goals.

In the next chapter, we will see how these tools are integrated into various level design workflows.

EXERCISES

1. **Drawing exercise**: Set up a still life, a scene made up of everyday objects arranged together, of things around you. Draw the still life in pencil or ink, and try the following techniques: measuring and referencing to make sure your drawing is properly proportioned, lining weights to depict how far or near objects are from one another, shading or

hatching to describe lighting conditions, and completing a hierarchical drawing to focus attention on specific objects in the scene.

2. **Drawing exercise**: Visit an architectural space either in a game or in the real world, no bigger than a lobby or courtyard. The space can be interior or exterior. Draw at least three of these types of drawings to record the space: plan, section, elevation, axonometric, or perspective. Feel free to write notes or draw diagrams to highlight any important details.

3. **Drawing exercise**: Using graph paper, map a small portion of a game's world (about enough space that takes thirty seconds to a minute to travel). Use concept diagrams and notes to highlight at least three places where the level emphasizes a specific mechanic.

4. **Drawing exercise**: For either a popular commercial game or a game you are working on, create a flow chart that shows the player's choices in a level or portion of a level.

5. **Drawing exercise**: For either a popular commercial game or a game you are working on, create a *Boss Keys*-style diagram analyzing the level's structure.

6. **Drawing exercise**: Play a popular commercial game. Sketch modular objects or tiles that you see repeat in the environment to understand how the level is assembled.

7. **Digital exercise**: Create a set of modular pieces—either 2D or 3D level tiles or environmental objects—that can be used to create a level for a game you are working on.

ENDNOTES

1. *Indie Game: The Movie*. Directed by Lisanne Pajot, performed by Jonathan Blow, Phil Fish, Edmund McMillen, and Tommy Refenes. Flutter Media, 2012. Film.
2. Kremers, Rudolf. *Level Design: Concept, Theory, and Practice*. Wellesley, MA: A.K. Peters, 2009, p. 33.
3. Bogost, Ian. *Persuasive Games: The Expressive Power of Videogames*. Cambridge, MA: MIT Press, 2007.
4. Ching, Francis D.K., and Steven P. Juroszek. *Design Drawing*. New York, NY: John Wiley & Sons, 1998, p. 6.
5. Ching, Francis D.K., and Steven P. Juroszek. *Design Drawing*. New York, NY: John Wiley & Sons, 1998, p. 8.

6. Ching, Francis D.K., and Steven P. Juroszek. *Design Drawing*. New York, NY: John Wiley & Sons, 1998, pp. 29–31.

7. Ching, Francis D.K., and Steven P. Juroszek. *Design Drawing*. New York, NY: John Wiley & Sons, 1998, pp. 43–45.

8. Le Corbusier. *Towards a New Architecture*. New York, NY: Dover Publications, 1986, p. 47.

9. Frederick, Matthew. *101 Things I Learned in Architecture School*. Cambridge, MA: MIT Press, 2007, p. 68.

10. *Half-Life 2: Raising the Bar*. Roseville, CA: Prima Games, 2004.

11. White, Edward T. *Space Adjacency Analysis: Diagramming Information for Architectural Design*. Tucson, AZ: Architectural Media, 1986.

12. Yatt, Barry D. Assessing Program. In Draft. *Parti Planning: A Guide to Pre-Design Analysis*. Washington, DC: Catholic University of America, 2006, Chapter 7, pp. 7-35–7-54.

13. Parish, Jeremy. "Rediscovering the (mostly) lost art of mapping". *Retronauts*. July 27, 2017. https://retronauts.com/article/437/rediscovering-the-mostly-lost-art-of-mapping. Accessed February 6, 2018.

14. Millard, Josh. *Mapstalgia*. http://mapstalgia.tumblr.com/. Accessed February 6, 2018.

15. Kuchera, Ben. "Hand-drawn video game maps are physical memories, so let's see yours". *Polygon*. May 23, 2014. https://www.polygon.com/2014/5/23/5745002/zelda-maps-gaming. Accessed February 6, 2018.

16. Brown, Mark. *Boss Keys*. YouTube video series. https://www.youtube.com/user/McBacon1337/playlists.

17. Brown, Mark. *Boss Keys: The Legend of Zelda Oracle of Ages and Seasons' Dungeon Designs*. YouTube video. September 25, 2016. https://youtu.be/fqKGl6exyyY. Accessed February 9, 2018.

INDUSTRY PERSPECTIVES: TOOLS AND DESIGN

Robin-Yann Storm

Tools Designer, Guerrilla Games

Tools will affect your level design, whether you realize it or not.

This means the differences between your perfect idea for a level and the level you actually create will largely be determined by the tools you use. There are many examples of this happening, and it is not true only for level designers, but also for other disciplines. Below I've included some examples that you can look out for so you can spot when tools are subconsciously affecting your work. And if you recognize them: speak up. Let the developers of the tool know your use case, your problems, and your lost time—whether these tool developers are in your studio or in a company many miles away. The developers of the tools might just be able to fix the issues and prevent so many headaches down the road.

Here are seven examples on how tools affect level designers:

1. **Geometry & Grids**

    If you work with a square grid, you will make more square-ish buildings. Not because you want to, but because the simpler and easier things to build are on right angles. Especially if it's hard to iterate off-grid geometry you will be less inclined to make the awesome geometry shapes your level needs to look and feel interesting.

2. **Snapping**

    If snapping is difficult, like snapping two pieces of geometry together, or fitting two modular assets to each other, then sooner or later you may be forced to cover gaps up with filler. You may also end up with texture or geometry overlap without realizing it; or even worse, if two walls have only a slight gap in-between them, the player may be able to walk through them and into the void outside your level. This could completely break the game and there is no easy way to check if this is possible apart from hiring a team of QAs or playtesters to walk into every wall of your game. Instead, having a snapping system that makes it easy and clear to snap two objects perfectly together helps you prevent bugs, while also making sure the art is represented as beautifully as possible.

3. **Texturing**

   If it is difficult or annoying to texture geometry in your tools, you will miss out on vital data when playtesting (Figure 1). A player needs to be able to quickly see what mockup geometry is representing, such as rocks, grass, water, or lava. Even just varied solid colors on geometry faces can accomplish this goal (Figure 2).

   Also, if you cannot quickly change your textures or scale them correctly, you are again limited by what is possible: this will limit what you create, which in turn will affect how testers play through your level, and ultimately the final quality of your level.

4. **Lighting**

   If it takes a while to see the results of your lighting, like having to compile/render first to see any kind of indication of lighting, your lighting will suffer for it. Nobody wants to spend time compiling for hours on end, going back and forth with lighting options to see if that new spotlight is better than the last one. You may have even forgotten what the old version looked like because you went on YouTube or Twitter while the new one was compiling!

FIGURE 1   Level geometry with simple textures.

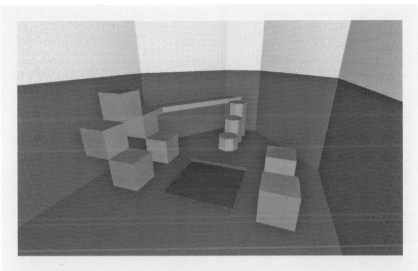

FIGURE 2   Using simple colors to mock up the materials that will eventually be applied to level geometry.

5. **Editor Visibility Settings**

   If it isn't simple to turn the visibility of helper objects—3D triggers, physics colliders, and other objects that perform a function but won't be visible in the final game—on and off in the editor you're using, you're going to miss critical errors until it's too late (Figure 3).

FIGURE 3   A level with colliders and volumes set to be invisible.

For example: volumes, both big and small, can trigger incredibly important events, but volumes are also often used for placing clipping/physics colliders that make sure players cannot reach areas they are not supposed to reach or get stuck on cool looking geometry. If you can't quickly see those volumes without a gigantic amount of clutter on your screen, you will run into trouble later in development if any of them are not perfectly placed (Figure 4).

Imagine being an animator and not being able to easily see what bones are located where in a rig. It would be disastrous. The same goes for a level designer's volumes.

FIGURE 4   A level with colliders and volumes set to be visible.

6. Asset-Browsing

If the asset browser does not easily allow you to see what assets are in your project, what their scale is, what they look like in 3D, and what you could/should use in your current level, then you are having a problem that decreases the work quality of even the best level designers (Figure 5). Without a good asset browser, you have to remember esoteric asset file names to find what you want to use and nobody can realistically remember hundreds or thousands of asset names! Limiting your palette of assets to only what you can remember results in you using only a few assets way too many times, which the players will notice. While that makes work easier

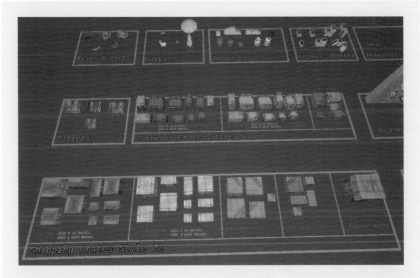

FIGURE 5   An asset browser.

and faster, it does not make your work of a better quality. This issue can also result in some good (and expensive!) assets never being used, because you happen to not know the name of them, or that they even exist.

7. **Camera Movement**

If moving the 3D viewport camera in your editor around is a pain, or it moves too fast most of the time and is hard to slow down, you will miss critical problems in your level. For example, if you are using orbit camera controls to navigate a confined dungeon-ish level that the player will play through in first person, you will not perceive the level the way the user is going to perceive it. Sure, playtesting makes you see it that way, but by that point the time has already been spent building the level. Why not build the level correctly the first time, and spot if a room is too large or not easy to navigate because you go through a doorway and see that nothing helps the player decide where to go next? You can iterate much more rapidly if you see the level as the player would see it while already in the editor. Having a camera control scheme in your level editor that is solid helps prevent these kinds of problems.

Now you may be wondering: shouldn't level designers just be good enough to work around these tool issues? Sure, that's a great end goal, but a bad tool will hold back the work of even the best designer.

Tool issues may be preventable through skill or hard work, but a bad tool raises the risk of issues popping up. So, keep these issues in mind, but also keep in mind that the tool itself, if not designed well, can cause problems in your level's design without you even realizing it. Again, if you recognize any of these issues in your tools: speak up! They are important issues and can be fixed.

CHAPTER 3

Level Design Workflows

N ow THAT WE HAVE researched some history and tools for level design, it's time to get to work! In this chapter, we will talk about the methods that professional level designers use in their work and how methods from architecture can inform them. This chapter also talks about how level design fits into the production of overall games and how to choose which content to develop first.

What you will learn in this chapter:

Form follows function

Level design workflows

Level design scheduling

FORM FOLLOWS FUNCTION

The American architect Louis Sullivan, credited as the creator of the skyscraper, once famously said, "Form ever follows function." This was shortened to the famous design idiom, "form follows function." With this phrase, Sullivan stated one of the driving principles of architectural *Modernism*. Modernism was an architectural movement of the early twentieth century defined by an emphasis on creating buildings whose form was derived from their purpose. In Modernist architecture, ornament was generally a product of the building itself or applied for a purpose, rather than simply for the sake of aesthetics. Similar to Sullivan, Le Corbusier stated, "The house is a machine for living in." Much of his architecture, as with the architecture of Frank Lloyd Wright, Walter Gropius, Louis

Sullivan, and others, was focused on purposefully creating an experience for the occupants.

The same can be said of level design. The best level designers work with a specific experiential goal in mind. In a 2008 interview, Valve level designer Dario Casali argued that "experience is key" when creating level design ideas.[1] We previously discussed some goals of level design that relate to how users use gamespaces and how we designers communicate to the user through those spaces. If experience is key to making game worlds, then we should construct for the purpose of creating great gameplay experiences: form follows function.

This section is all about planning: taking experiential ideas and translating them into gameplay. We will discuss how setting experiential goals works hand-in-hand with gameplay metrics, which in turn change how levels are eventually constructed. Lastly, we will discuss how levels may be designed to introduce and evolve gameplay ideas.

Form Follows Core Mechanics

The tenets of "form follows function" thrive in game design through a concept known as the *core mechanic*. A core mechanic is defined as the basic action that a player makes throughout the course of a game. In his doctoral dissertation, game designer Aki Jarvinen created a core mechanic-centered design method where designers begin from verbs.[2] If core mechanics are the basic verbs of what a player does in a game, we can say that they are the foundational elements of what builds each game's unique experience. For example, *Super Mario Bros.*[3] is about jumping, *The Legend of Zelda*[4] is about exploring, *Katamari Damacy*[5] is about rolling a ball, *Angry Birds*[6] is about flinging, and so on. Beginning from this core, other actions are added that define the rules of the final game product.

When designing levels, having a core mechanic idea in mind is necessary. While many new designers assume that individual levels should simply follow the core mechanic of the game, it is possible to define level core mechanics to make each unique. An example is the Badwater Basin level (Figure 3.1) of Valve's *Team Fortress 2* (*TF2*).[7] In this level, the "BLU" team must push a bomb into their opposing "RED" team's base via a mine cart on a track. The mine cart mechanic of "Payload mode," for which Badwater Basin is a map, takes *TF2*'s standard team-based first-person shooter mechanics and adds a twist. This changes not only the mechanics of gameplay, but also the conditions of the level's spatial geometry.

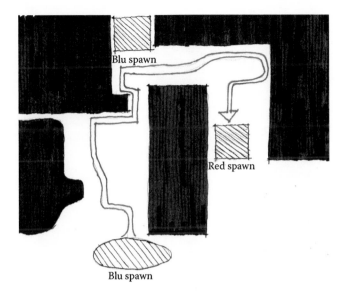

FIGURE 3.1   A plan diagram of Badwater Basin from *Team Fortress 2*. RED and BLU team bases are marked on the map, as are major circulation areas and BLU checkpoints between the two bases.

One example cited by Casali, who helped design Badwater Basin, was the level's tunnel. In the first prototypes of the level, designers made the mine tunnels a standard width that they had used for other basic maps. However, upon playtesting the level with the mine cart-pushing mechanic in place, they realized that tunnels had to be widened to accommodate both players and the cart. This seems like a small change, but it prevented a lot of aggravation from players that had been getting blocked out of tunnels by the cart (Figure 3.2).

This ties back to the idea of utilizing measurement systems for levels based on gameplay metrics. As level designers, it is our job to design to the realities of how player avatars and other gameplay elements move through levels. Traversing levels is comfortable when level spaces comfortably accommodate metrics. As we explore in later chapters, gameplay drama can be achieved when we create spaces that push metrics to the limit. Such spaces include gaps that require the farthest possible jump a character can make, such as the one found in world 8–1 of *Super Mario Bros.* (Figure 3.3) or tight corridors that restrict movement in horror games, such as *Resident Evil*[8] (Figure 3.4).

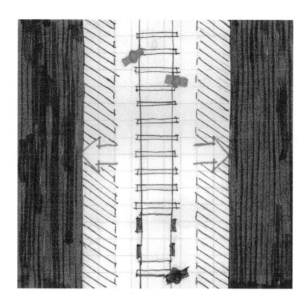

FIGURE 3.2   Modifying the width of the tunnel in Badwater Basin allowed for better circulation of both player and mine cart through the level and made gameplay less aggravating for the offensive team.

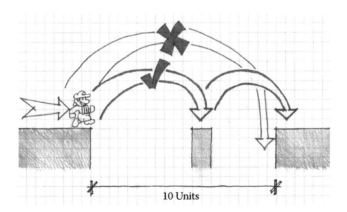

FIGURE 3.3   This section of *Super Mario Bros.*'s level 8–1 pushes Mario's jumping metrics to their limit. The gap is ten blocks wide, one block longer than Mario's running jump distance of nine blocks, so using the one-block-wide middle island is necessary. Most strategies for crossing this gap call for a running jump to the middle island, and then another quick one off the one-block-wide island so Mario's landing inertia doesn't launch the player into the pit.

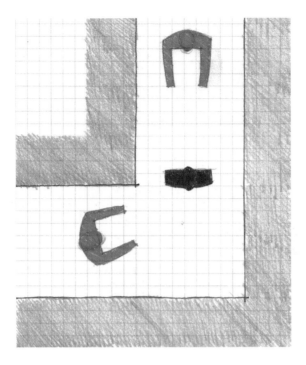

FIGURE 3.4 Many hallways in *Resident Evil* are barely wide enough for two characters standing shoulder to shoulder. In this way, a single zombie in these hallways can become a significant threat for players trying to get past. This spatial condition also gives the game a claustrophobic atmosphere.

Designing to gameplay does not solely have to involve measurements either. It can also mean designing to specific character *abilities* such as special attacks or movement modes. Stealth games like *Metal Gear Solid*[9] provide a great example of how to construct levels based on different types of character movement. In *Metal Gear Solid*, the player character, Solid Snake, has the ability to hide behind walls and look around corners. This vastly changes the meaning of 90-degree corners when compared with other action games—they are strategic hiding places rather than just level geometry. As such, the nuclear weapons facility that makes up *Metal Gear Solid*'s environments has lots of these corners so players can sneak from place to place, looking around corners to find their next refuge. While not measurement or metric based, these kinds of layouts are based on the character's own *mechanics*, the gameplay actions that form the range of possibilities for how a character may act or interact with his or her environment.

Level Progression with Scaffolding Mechanisms

Lastly, focusing level designs on gameplay mechanics does not have to mean that everything is based on the player character's design. In an episode of Mark Brown's *Game Maker's Toolkit*,[10] he looks at how the levels from *Donkey Kong Country: Tropical Freeze*[11] follow a "form follows function" principle based on external mechanisms. Donkey Kong and his friends never change or power-up in the game, but the variety of platforms, switches, hazards, and other mechanisms in the game's levels help it feel constantly fresh. Brown starts by analyzing another game's level design, *New Super Mario Bros. U*,[12] showing how each level is built on a single level design mechanism: a special moving platform, an enemy that chases you, a glowing creature you must bring through a dark cave, and so on. In each level, the central mechanism is introduced early and in a safe way—away from pits or enemies—so players can learn how to use it. Educators call this *scaffolding*: introducing a concept and applying it in increasingly complex ways over the course of several exercises.

As *Mario U* levels progress, their core mechanism is used in increasingly novel and dangerous ways (above a small platform, then above lava, then above lava with enemies). *Tropical Freeze*, Brown argues, takes this idea and expands it by introducing two or three mechanisms in a level. It then mixes and matches them in novel ways in a similar scaffolding pattern to that used in the *Mario* series. In one level, the player must progress by jumping on large flowers whose stems tilt with the player's weight: when a flower is tilted enough, the player can jump to the next platform. This level also introduces rolling spiky fruits that damage the player. A twist comes at the end of the level when a giant spiky fruit appears and chases the player while he or she jumps across a series of tilting flower platforms. Many of the levels in *Tropical Freeze* follow the same pattern of introducing several mechanics, scaffolding them, then introducing and scaffolding combinations of them. This idea of taking game mechanisms and finding multiple interactions or functions for them is known as *juicing* in independent game developer circles. Trying to get every possible interaction out of a mechanic—juicing it—is an important part of creating rich gameplay experiences with concise sets of assets.

The games discussed here are 2D platformers, but scaffolding can also be applied across many different gameplay genres. In the 2016 version of *DOOM*, a first-person shooter game, enemy monsters fill the role that level mechanisms do in *Tropical Freeze*. When a new monster is introduced, you see it in a cutscene then face it alone or alongside much weaker monsters. Afterward, you face the monster alongside strong monsters or in new (often disadvantageous for the player) spatial conditions: narrower pathways or alongside hazards. Once you receive a weapon that makes the monster easier, a new monster is introduced that challenges these new powers.

The adage that level design is "where the rubber meets the road" in games is in full effect when studying how levels work with a game's core mechanics. It is the job of the level designer to create levels that give players a space to best utilize their characters' movement capabilities or to showcase mechanisms external to the player character. Making a core mechanic or mechanism the key to each level you create will help you make interesting levels with a natural sense of progression. In the next section, we will take these level progression ideas and see how they are implemented in actual level-building.

LEVEL DESIGN WORKFLOWS

Now, finally, we can talk level construction. The last section showed how a game's core mechanics influence the way we build levels and create experiences for players. It also showed how designers can take gameplay ideas and change them over the course of a level so that the level always feels fresh. This section is about what to do with those goals and ideas once you sit down at a computer. By discussing several methods that take a level from "sketched idea" to implementation, we will see how functional game mechanics can be turned into engaging gamespaces.

Level Design Parti

Earlier we discussed the architect's parti, basic formal explorations that architects utilize to determine what shape or orientation they want their building to take. For level designers coming off of determining the core mechanics of their level, a parti is another valuable tool for developing the spatial layout of their level.

Designing with parti is quite different than designing on graph paper or a computer. Partis are meant to be sketches, and therefore will lack measurement. While this may seem contradictory to the rest of everything we've discussed about player metrics, sketching without measurement allows designers to form ideas quickly before spending time planning measured versions of their designs. The key to a level designer's parti is to sketch *gameplay ideas as spatial diagrams*. For example, a level design parti of the Badwater Basin level would be two large masses (representing the teams' base areas) with thinner zones of circulation in-between the two to represent the mine cart track, and some smaller bases for BLU players to capture, similar to the diagram in Figure 3.1.

In his discussions of level design from *Indie Game: The Movie*, Edmund McMillen argues that once a designer has created *environmental mechanisms*, that is, interactive parts of a level that factor into gameplay, they should be usable in many different ways in order to be valuable. For a game I worked on called *SWARM!*,[13] a ball-roller/platformer game where players have to lure enemies into traps, programmer and fellow designer Taro Omiya created many such sketches. Figure 3.5 shows a series of drawings he did of the game's electric fence traps to visualize the different uses they could have. Likewise, Omiya and I made formal partis on the computer and on paper to visualize spatial orientations of levels, such as downhill slides, floating islands, and platforming areas (Figure 3.6). These images were not our final designs, but helped us visualize ideas that we thought might be fun before figuring out exactly how they would work in our game. From these formal visualizations of game scenes, we could then plan how these areas would specifically work.

"Scenes" and Readability

Parti is great for getting general ideas down, but if you want to think on an even more micro-level with how players will use your levels, then

FIGURE 3.5 Once designers for *SWARM!* created the electric fence traps, they sketched many gameplay partis of them to visualize how they could be utilized through different levels.

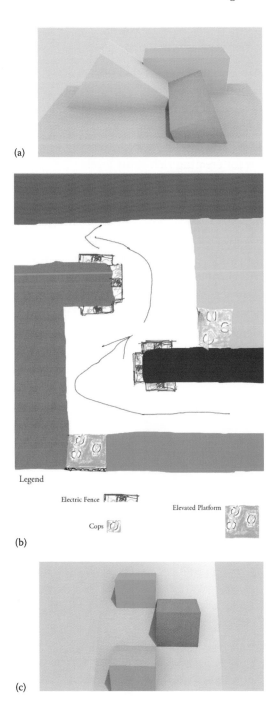

(a)

(b)

Legend

Electric Fence

Cops

Elevated Platform

(c)

FIGURE 3.6   Formal partis for *SWARM!* show the visualization of different spatial orientations such as hills, tilted ledges, and others.

thinking in *scenes* is the way to go. While several game engines call the files that represent levels or other parts of the game "scenes," the usage of the term I mean is a more conceptual one. A scene, as coined by Anna Anthropy in the book she co-wrote with Naomi Clark, *A Game Design Vocabulary,*[14] is a single screen's worth of designed level space that is currently confronting a player. Anthropy calls these scenes "the most basic unit of pacing in a game"[15] and indeed, they are one of the most useful concepts to follow for creating rich game levels.

Scenes combine several of the concepts we've already discussed into an easily usable design method. First of all, by designing in one-screen increments, designers can look closely at how a level's core mechanics are expressed in each moment of gameplay. I have used this method in my games *Lissitzky's Revenge*[16] and *Dead Man's Trail.*[17] The former is a reinterpretation of the Atari 2600 game *Yar's Revenge*[18] with an art style based on a 1920 Bolshevik propaganda poster by graphic designer El Lissitzky. In the game, each level is meant to be a single-screen "poster" of interactive graphic design elements, so each puzzle had to be designed in the space of one scene (Figure 3.7). On the other hand, *Dead Man's Trail* is a zombie game with 3D isometric environments that players can explore and loot

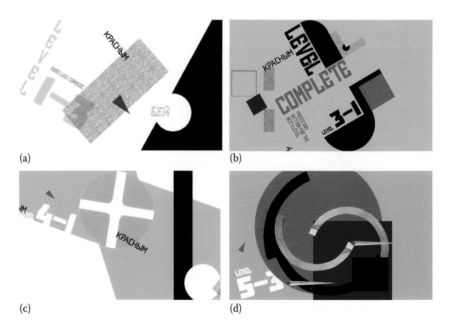

(a)   (b)

(c)   (d)

FIGURE 3.7   Screenshots of *Lissitzky's Revenge* showing several levels. Each level occupies one screen's worth of space, so was designed using the "scene" concept.

for supplies. When looting, the game generates levels by loading a group of randomly selected "tiles" to create a maze. Each tile measures three screen spaces horizontally by three screens vertically—nine scenes in all (Figure 3.8).

In both cases, scenes were a valuable concept for designers to make their levels readable by players. In *Lissitzky's Revenge*, having everything in the level contained within a one-screen space helped both designers and players cope with the game's abstract visuals. For designers this set an easily achievable goal of a one-screen puzzle and for players this meant that puzzles were understandable because everything was in front of them. The need to maximize the impact of each screen also led level designers to prioritize designing around game objects that had interesting interactions with one another. Especially for new level designers, a wide space makes a tempting place to throw every interesting switch, hazard, movable wall, etc. at the player. However, as emphasized by Anthropy herself, placing a few objects that have interesting relationships with one another in a small space can be equally impactful (Figure 3.9).

In *Dead Man's Trail*, a core mechanic of the looting levels was having players get supplies and leave quickly: the longer the player stayed in one place, the bigger the zombie horde in the level was. Playtesting showed

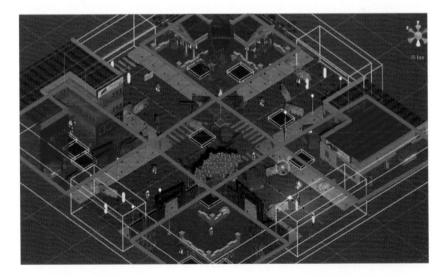

FIGURE 3.8 A level tile from *Dead Man's Trail* with a graphic overlay showing how one level "tile" is constructed of nine "scenes." The scenes are color-coded to show "scenes" where designers concentrated their work in red and other areas reserved for "circulation"—player and zombie movement through the tile.

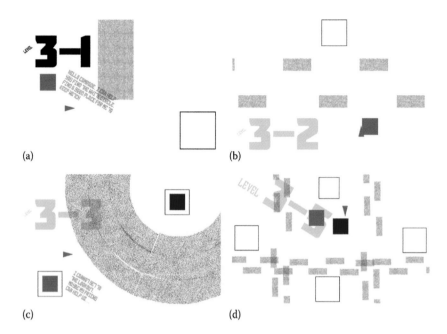

(a)

(b)

(c)

(d)

FIGURE 3.9 The third world of *Lissitzky's Revenge* is built around a few simple objects: a red square that activates switches, moving gray shapes that destroy the red square but do not harm the player, and a burgundy square that destroys the gray shapes. As these screenshots show, this combination alone can be "juiced."

that as zombies accumulated in a level, players needed clear pathways to escape moment-to-moment encounters. As such, each one-screen space in these levels had to be planned to be individually interesting and readable. Again, the concept of "scenes" was vital: designers could work with a limited scope of making one screen as mechanic-rich as it could be. If a designer wanted to stretch gameplay across multiple scenes for any reason, like making a long cornfield where zombies could surprise players, the designers placed environment art so that pathways between screen spaces were clear.

These two examples show how designing with scenes works in small-scale 2D and isometric environments, but what about full 3D worlds? 3D environments often do not have the same restricted cameras that 2D and isometric games do. Anthropy discusses scenes in terms of longer, continuous levels, so theoretically taking the approach to 3D could include making each architectural space interesting: a hallway, room, or other section of level. Alternatively, the scenes concept can be useful when designing *approaches* from one space to another. Approaches are a topic we will revisit several times throughout the book, but they are essentially transitions between spaces. In his talk, "Balancing Action and RPG in *Horizon Zero Dawn* Quests,"[16] from the 2018 Game Developers Conference (GDC), Blake Rebouche discussed how room designs in *Horizon Zero Dawn* were optimized for maximum *readability*. Because of its focus on observing a space from a specific angle, often an entrance or approach, *readability* features many of the elements that make for good scenes.

Horizon Zero Dawn[20] is an action–adventure game where players roam a large world and hunt mechanical beasts using survival tactics and sneaking. Rebouche discussed one enemy encounter in his talk in particular, where the player has to pass through a room with patrolling enemies. Successful design for this room meant two things: the first was that navigating and battling enemies in the room would be interesting. The second was that the player could see their goal, see the possible paths they could take to it, and plan how they would deal with enemies from a vantage point as they entered. An early prototype of Rebouche's design (Figure 3.10) came back with notes that suggested poor visibility: the exit from the room was difficult to see, large obstacles obscured enemies, and paths were not interesting enough. Rebouche's subsequent design was

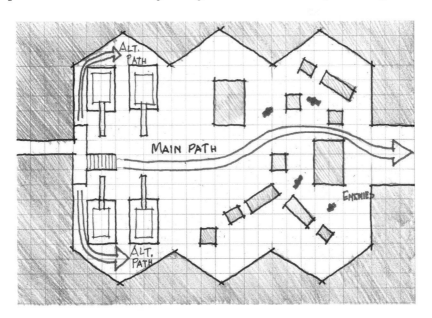

FIGURE 3.10 A sketch of Rebouche's "bad" prototype shown during his GDC 2018 talk. Notice the barriers that could obscure enemies and the narrow exit that limited readability and made the player's goal hard to see.

received much better: multiple places to encounter enemies, a more visible goal, multiple paths with opportunities to flank enemies, and variations in height. In addition to these elements, all enemies and pathways could be evaluated from the room's entrance, which now had a railed staircase on which players could pause without being seen (Figure 3.11).

It should be noted that readability is not a "one size fits all" approach to level and scene design in 3D. Another GDC 2018 talk by Hi-Rez Studios' Andrew Yoder, "The Holy Grail of Multiplayer Level Design,"[21] presented readability as a way to plan for players of different skill levels in competitive multiplayer levels. Yoder described the different levels of readability appropriate for different skill levels in terms of *scanning*, or how many times a player has to look at a space before they understand it. In a level suited for

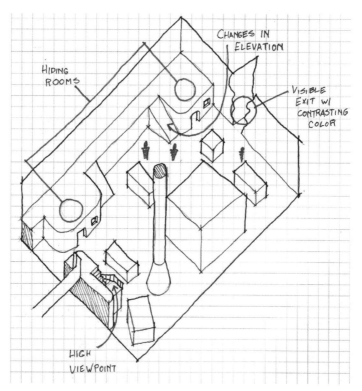

FIGURE 3.11 A sketch of Rebouche's final design from *Horizon Zero Dawn*. Enemy placement and pathways through the stage are more easily readable from the entryway, which now has a staircase that the player can hide on. Notice that I had to switch perspective from a 2D plan to a 3D axonometric drawing for the different versions of the level: good 3D levels make the most of 3D space (and need to be understood in 3D).

casual players, they should be able to stand in one spot and pan the camera around a space once to get a sense of who and what is in the room (Figure 3.12). This is a *single-scan* space. Alternatively, competitive players might want a space where there are places to hide and surprise players. Suddenly, elements that were less optimal in Rebouche's *Horizon Zero Dawn* (a single-player game) prototypes are now useful for high-level play. To get a sense of these spaces, players have to scan once, move around an obstacle, and scan again. Yoder calls these spaces *multi-scan* spaces (Figure 3.13). In Yoder's model for multiplayer levels, readability is an element of levels that can be adjusted to fit the needs of different types of players, showing that based on genre, there is nuance to readability and scene design.

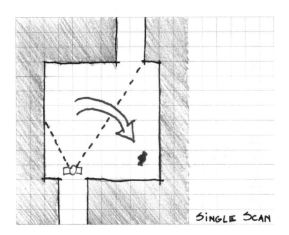

FIGURE 3.12   A "single-scan" space.

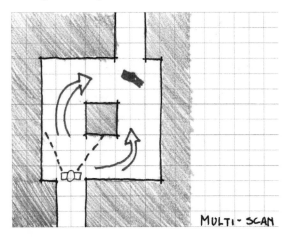

FIGURE 3.13   A "multi-scan" space.

A lot of what makes scenes work is that they address very core questions about how a level will feel to a player and what type of experience it creates. To test how effectively a level creates gameplay experiences, and to allow us to change things around if the level is ineffective, level designers do extensive prototypes. The next several sections will cover the types of prototypes level designers use in their work and how these prototypes become final designs.

Non-Digital Prototypes

For years, game developers did not playtest a game until it was in *beta* stage, that is, the stage prior to release where asset production is already complete. Most of the industry now thinks that this is a dangerous way to playtest a game: beta is far too late to fix fundamental design issues. Now, game designers use a myriad of testing methods that help them evaluate ideas at all stages of design, including when the game is a brand-new idea. In this section, we will talk about how early-stage level design ideas might be tested with non-digital prototypes.

Most publications on game-prototyping discuss non-digital prototypes as a tool for testing entire games. However, level designers can utilize non-digital prototypes as well. In her book *Game Design Workshop*,[17] Tracy Fullerton describes how EA utilizes a real-life sandbox to test levels for the *Medal of Honor* series. Designers use plastic trees, toy army men, and battlefield models to draft exterior levels. The authors also describe a board game prototype of a first-person shooter game, where the designers have defined movement rules for players moving army men around a hexagonal grid (Figure 3.14).

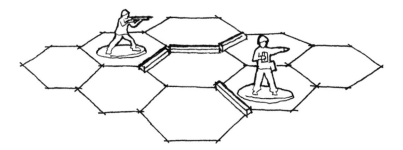

FIGURE 3.14 A non-digital prototype of a first-person shooter utilizing a hexagonal grid and army men. Designers place matchsticks on the board to define walls. The matchsticks are ideal for a simple prototype, as they can be easily picked up and moved to try different spatial articulations.

Non-digital prototypes can define gamespaces on both the macro (large, zoomed out) and the micro (small, close-up) scale. An exercise I often use in courses for new game designers is having them make a table-top game based on a favorite video game. This gets them thinking about how concepts they think are inherent to digital games might be conveyed with physical pieces. When done well, the resulting projects also reveal the spatial realities of different types of games.[18] In an iteration of this class from several years ago, one prototype required players to progress their knight character through different stages of a Candy Land-like board until they reached the princess at the end. The designers, seeking a story-heavy roleplaying adventure game, opted for a board with a linear path with minimal forks. In many ways, this board is an interactive parti for the entire game, showing the designer's intent of creating a linear experience based on specific story beats rather than player choice. As a demonstration of the game environment on a macro level, it allows players to play with the linear progression of general gameplay situations but not dig deeply into each one.

A different student project prototyped a stealth game where players must elude guards, rescue their fellow prisoners, and escape a prison yard. This game focuses on micro-level gameplay-prototyping by allowing designers to explore issues such as enemy movement and character interaction in a single room of the prison. The version demonstrated in the class utilized a completely open room devoid of any walls, as the designers were focused on defining how characters would move. However, further iterations of the board could potentially explore how the movement rules could work in more complex hallway and cell block-like environments.

While non-digital prototypes can offer an abstracted trial of macro and micro spatial gameplay, digital prototypes allow designers to test the gameplay of specific environments through a process called *grayboxing*.

Digital Prototypes with Grayboxing

When developers move from prototyping off the computer to prototyping in digital form, they create test levels through a process known as grayboxing. Grayboxing is when a level designer creates a level out of simple geometry, most often gray or quickly textured blocks (thus the name), to test whether levels accomplish the gameplay goals he or she wants. Early on in the design process, when designers are trying to define gameplay metrics of player characters and other things, grayboxing can help determine what gameplay measurements should be. Designers can draft the spatial characteristics of their levels in a parti-like way, testing the sizes and shapes of certain environments for different gameplay experiences, before specific environmental art is added to a level (Figure 3.15).

The geometry used to graybox level spaces is usually the simplest needed to simulate the *colliders* that will be used in the eventual final level design. Colliders are a component of objects in game engines that simulate the interaction between physical objects. A box-shaped collider, or *box collider*, attached to a piece of level geometry will cause that object to interact with other objects as though it is the shape of a six-sided box, regardless of the shape of the actual environmental art (Figure 3.16). Colliders can be simple geometric shapes or can be made to tightly fit organic shapes.

When building games like *Portal* or *Half-Life 2* Valve used grayboxing extensively in its level design process. The construction rules for engine primitives in their level editor, Hammer, allow rapid 3D level prototyping through simple and precise building. Hammer's primitives, called brushes, are used to roughly define level spaces, which are then playtested to see if the intended experience has been created. Level designers see what worked properly and what did not, and then change the spaces by editing the brushes. When the designers find themselves editing little of major spaces and instead focusing on smaller details, the level is ready for environment art.

As an iterative process, grayboxing has designers begin with almost parti-like interactive forms before transitioning toward more art and ornament-centric design once gameplay for the level has been refined. As level geometries become better defined, you will also discover how often you use certain objects. This helps define the list of environmental objects you should prioritize when creating environment art, as you will know which are more or less useful for your work.

Before we dive too far into micro-sized level design considerations like assets and environment art, however, we should take a look at how designers manage designing in micro- and macro-scales.

Pacing Your Levels with the *Nintendo Power* Method

A downside to planning out individual bits of gameplay is not understanding how they relate to one another within a level. This is where drawing techniques for graph paper and other measurement-based tools come in. Arranging gameplay properly is known by level designers as *pacing*.

Pacing is based on the concept that in order for gameplay action to seem exciting, it must be contrasted with moments of "quieter"

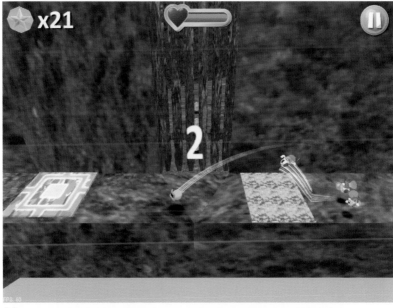

(a)

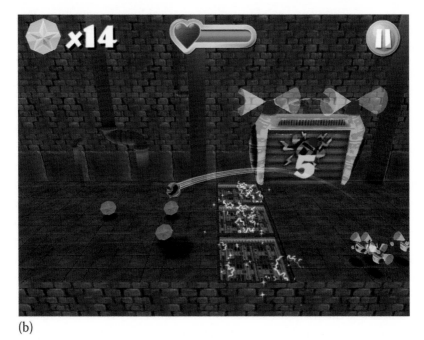

(b)

FIGURE 3.15 Grayboxing done for *SWARM!* shows how an important section of a level meant to teach players how to kill enemies was thoroughly tested in simple geometry before environment art was added.

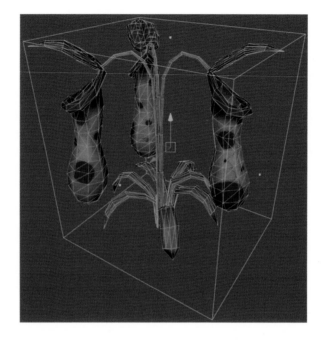

FIGURE 3.16 This plant has a box collider attached to it. Though its 3D model has an organic shape, player objects in a game will interact with it as though it were a rectangular solid.

gameplay, such as puzzle-solving, exploring, or even playing with a character's movement possibilities. As we show in later chapters, spatial contrast is very important for building meaningful experiences in both games and architecture. As such, we must learn how to control how we pace our levels in games.

In reality, the kind of top-down level design done on paper should occur from two different points of view: *macro-scale level design* and *micro-scale level design*. The parti for *TF2*'s Badwater Basin shown several sections ago is a macro-scaled design, as it shows the entire level and diagrams how it creates the intended gameplay. On the other hand, the partis of traps and level pieces from *SWARM!* are micro-scaled designs, as they show individual gameplay instances divorced from an entire level. Many new designers make the mistake of putting intense micro-scaled gameplay instances together in quick succession in their levels. Proper pacing would have gameplay points like this separated from one another by periods of quieter gameplay.

To circumvent this, I use something I call the *Nintendo Power* method of level design. *Nintendo Power* was a game strategy and news magazine published by Nintendo beginning in the late 1980s. For some time, it was a valuable source of secret codes, hints, and tips on how to beat games on Nintendo consoles. For many games, *Nintendo Power* would publish detailed maps of levels with caption balloons that would highlight particularly noteworthy or difficult points of gameplay (Figure 3.17). For level designers, these maps can be a valuable lesson on pacing.

Nintendo Power maps show a level from a macro-scaled point of view, so a reader can see a game level in its entirety. At the same time, it highlights important gameplay moments on the micro-scale so readers know what to look out for to reach secret rooms or beat difficult obstacles. It should also be noted that the highlight balloons on these maps were not butted against one another in quick succession, but rather spread evenly across a map. This is less a result of the magazine's publishing and more a result of proper pacing by the game designers. When designing levels, we can utilize the same mindset by treating our level drawings as ones from *Nintendo Power,* creating the overall scope of a level on a macro-scale and evenly spreading out micro-scaled areas of more intense gameplay across the entire map. In-between the "loud" gameplay moments should be circulation space—spaces for movement-based gameplay, movement-based obstacles, exploration, or even rest and recharging of the player character.

Without quiet moments to contrast moments of high action in a level, the game can turn into a never-ending slog rather than an exciting experience. Even with the most careful planning, however, a designer is bound to miss something. That is why it is important to play a game as much as possible and have others play it, which will take us to our next level design workflow.

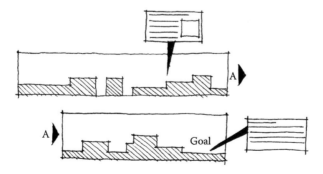

FIGURE 3.17   Maps in *Nintendo Power* magazine show the entirety of a level and highlight important points of gameplay on each map.

Iterative Design with Playtesting

Iterative design is a term borrowed from human–computer interface design. It describes a cyclical design process where the designer produces a prototype of his or her work, tests whether a user can properly interact with it, evaluates the results, makes changes to the design, and tests it with a user again. It is not unlike the scientific method, where a scientist tests a hypothesis with repeated experimentation.

Game designers test their ideas by holding playtests of their games. Salen and Zimmerman call game design a *second-order design* problem. They say in *Rules of Play*, "You are never directly designing the behavior of your players. Instead you are only designing the rules of the system."[19] Salen and Zimmerman are pointing out that designing a game is very different than designing a directly relatable object such as a cup or a chair— you are creating a context for players to inhabit. This directly ties to the idea that a game level is a medium of communication between players and designers.

Much like how an architect will bring clients in to see and evaluate work, game designers bring eventual clients—their players—in to playtest their game. To understand whether the experience you intend happens in your game levels, it is important to watch others play your game in both non-digital and digital forms, depending on your stage of development. As you watch people play your levels, keep these things in mind:

Do they understand how to play the level? When discussing adjustment of behavior, we saw that teaching is an important mission of level design. If a player does not understand a puzzle that you intend to repeat, he or she may need a better or more transparent introduction to the mechanic before reaching the iteration of it that he or she is stuck on.

Is the level too hard for the player? This mainly applies to early levels of a game, though you should always avoid sudden increases in difficulty without proper balancing or player preparation. If a player is getting stuck on a challenge or puzzle ten minutes into your game, you should perhaps place that challenge later in the game or build easier levels and put them before the challenge the player is stuck on. Playtesting is important because as you play your own game, you become very good at it and can no longer see when things are too hard.

Do not interfere with their play. When people buy your game, they will not have you there to explain how it is supposed to be played. Thus, you should not stop a playtester to explain what he or she is supposed to do. If he or she cannot figure it out, you should add more teaching moments to your levels.

Embrace happy accidents. Sometimes playtesters reveal a strategy, solve a puzzle in a unique way, or "game" the system to create new abilities. When you see players performing an action or using a level in a way you did not intend, evaluate whether it is game-breaking. If it is not, but could instead be an interesting secret to find, leave it in.

Playtest for the current stage of development. Lead playtesters to give you feedback on issues that match your stage in development. Major gameplay feedback should occur early, before assets are created, while late feedback should focus on finding *bugs*, errors that can inhibit the experience of, halt any progress in, or even crash the game. Feedback on gameplay mechanics or art, for example, has no place a month before launch when testing should focus on finding bugs. Ask playtesters prepared questions relating to the information you want from them or create a paper survey for them to fill out.

Ask for additional comments, but stick to your guns. While you want focused feedback, it is good to get additional comments in case playtesters have any happy accident statements that could help you out. Be prepared, though, for a slew of ridiculous suggestions. Playtesters are often very enthusiastic to help with the development of a game and will give design input of "things you should totally put in the game." Learn to properly vet these statements for things that can help in that stage of development versus the ones that will break your game's core vision. Also learn to dismiss bad ideas in a friendly and non-condescending way.

If the player does not understand something, it is not clear enough. I have had times playtesting where a player will ask how to do something or how they know when the game is in a certain state and all I can think is, "I clearly indicated that with x..." Over time, I have learned that no matter whether you have put in a bright neon sign, a particle effect, a sound effect, or any other gizmo that is supposed to draw player attention to an in-game event, you usually need to add at least two more before players actually perceive the event. For example, older versions of *Lissitzky's Revenge* indicated when the player could attack the white circle enemy with a particle effect, and a tester told me, "How do I know when I can do this? I wish there was a particle…" I wanted to scream that it was right there in front of them, but I realized this was completely wrongheaded and I should listen to the player. I added more particles AND sound effects AND made the character flash and finally the indicator was crystal clear. Seeing your game from the player's point of view is hard, especially for new designers, but having that bit of empathy instead of arguing makes your game better.

Playtest to learn what players will need to learn about your game. A lot of game designers assume that they should start their game by building level 1–1 right away. We will talk about this more later in the chapter, but for now understand that in early playtests, you should pay extra attention to the mechanics that players do and do not need help understanding. If you plan on using early levels to have a tutorial or otherwise teach players your game's mechanics, then you will want to know what tutorial content to put in those levels. Sometimes a mechanic you think will need teaching to players is intuitive, while others will remain hidden unless you teach players they exist. Playtesting helps you form a "lesson plan" for your game's tutorials so that you can best respond to player needs.

As playtesters try your levels throughout your process, document what went well with each prototype and what could be changed or improved. Change your design and have someone playtest your next prototype. As you iterate, your needs will change: where you once needed playtests to explore large-scale design questions, you eventually need them to polish individual moments of gameplay. At this latter stage, you will need to understand a player's relationship to individual pieces of level geometry and swap out what doesn't work.

Modular Level Design

An advantage of building levels with engine primitives is that these primitives are standardized within the engine and easily repeatable. They are *modular*, that is, premade parts that can be copied, assembled, disassembled, and moved easily. Since the Industrial Revolution, buildings have been made of modular elements. Many of these are *prefabricated*, created at a factory and assembled on the building site. Modernist architects were great proponents of modularity in their buildings. Phillip Johnson and Ludwig Mies Van Der Rohe, for example, are famous for designing buildings with prefabricated steel and glass components. Le Corbusier designed Unite D'Habitacion, an apartment building where the apartments were created as modular units and stacked together (Figure 3.18).

I have used LEGO building blocks as a metaphor for level design; modularity is the reason for this. Game development is a work-intensive process, and an intelligent designer will utilize easily repeatable game objects and textures to lessen the need for constant recreation of art assets. If designers create a set of modular pieces, levels can be assembled like sets of LEGOs rather than difficult-to-change custom artworks.

Creating modular assets can also aid the metric-based measurement methods discussed in the last chapter. For *SWARM!*, we utilized modular tiles for some of the game's non-organic level designs. Building in predefined tiles allowed for the easy measurement of game environments such as skate parks and mazes. As an example, we realized that 2-unit-wide tiles were the smallest unit that could be balanced on by players using the game's tilt controls without the game feeling unfairly difficult. For labyrinth-like puzzles where the player had to navigate a narrow maze without falling into electrified floors or pools of acid, the 2-unit tiles were used to build the ledges.

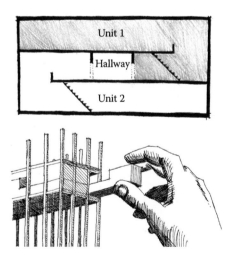

FIGURE 3.18 An apartment cross-section and model sketch of Unite D'Habitacion by Le Corbusier.

Even for less measurement-based pieces, such as organic landmasses and plants, having modular pieces made the construction of *SWARM!* levels simple. Less measurement-based objects like landmasses and trees could be scaled to any size without the art looking awkward compared to other objects. They could also be rotated in any way we wished should uphill or downhill areas be required for a level.

Architects track modular elements of their buildings through documents called *building schedules*. A schedule is a chart that specifies prefabricated products, such as doors, windows, or plumbing fixtures, the sizes of such products, and where they should go in the building (Table 3.1). The modular pieces used by level designers can be documented very similarly, especially if the pieces follow measurement-based construction systems.

In game art direction, it is common to utilize *style guides*—documents that establish color, graphics, measurement, and other artistic standards—for maintaining graphic consistency within a team. Level design schedules can offer similar utility for level construction. A schedule for the half-pipe shown in Figure 3.19 might look like that found in Table 3.2.

Even for scale-less pieces such as trees and plants, schedules can help establish the style guide for a level by listing the pieces that will make it up. In this way, schedules are useful for both listing the pieces that will make up certain environments and assisting with art direction.

Those are just a few workflows that I and other designers use in our levels. One of the reasons that level design is such a complex topic is that it can vary from person to person, game to game. While there's often no one-size-fits-all answer to level design problems, general workflows can be adapted to any situation. And when in doubt: playtest playtest playtest.

Speaking of playtesting, we've already discussed how playtesting can be used to determine what players will need to learn as they play your game. This is an idea we'll discuss in further detail in our next section, on determining the order in which you will design your levels.

TABLE 3.1   Door schedule

Quantity	Door Type	Door Material	Frame Type	Frame Material	Door Opening Size	HDW Set
1	1	Wood	A	HM	3'0" × 7'0"	05
2	10	WD and TG	A	HM	3'0" × 7'0"	14
3	1	Wood	A	HM	3'0" × 7'0"	03

FIGURE 3.19   A half-pipe level from a 3D game.

TABLE 3.2   Level 1-3 asset schedule

Quantity	Model Type	Model Name	Location
15	Half-pipe side	Skatepark01_2x2.blend	Skate park 2
8	Half-pipe ground	CityFloor_Concrete_2x2.blend	Skate park 2
4	Electric fences	CityTrap_ElectricFence02_2tile.blend	Skate park 2

LEVEL DESIGN SCHEDULING

Beyond wondering how level designers do their work, many new designers also ask where they should start. In *Level Up! The Guide to Great Game Design*,[20] Scott Rogers describes a level designer's opinion of "which level to make first," one that changes over time: new designers start with the first level while more experienced designers start in the middle and work back to the first level. In an appearance on the *Retronauts*[21] game podcast, *Iconoclasts*[22] designer Joakim Sandberg alternatively described his process as designing from beginning to end: starting from the first world and making levels in order.

While this may seem like a philosophical question, on a practical level the choice of what to make first affects your development schedule: which order to prioritize individual levels and how much time you'll leave for figuring out the contents of tutorials. In this way, the choices you make on level construction order might depend greatly on your own individual production process. Like anything in this book, I will stay away from prescribing things that you MUST do but will instead offer insights into processes that I have seen designers use. This way, you can figure out which approach works best for your game or your team.

The Toy Box

A common place to start level-designing is not a level at all, but a place to build and try level mechanisms. I call this the *toy box*. To build a toy box, take a scene, room, or whichever term is used in your engine of choice for a level file and set it aside to build and test the things that will go into your level (Figure 3.20). Toy boxes are for developers only, so they are typically not accessible from the rest of the game (i.e., selectable or reachable by players). Since they serve a mainly utilitarian purpose, you don't have to dress them up with polished environment art like you do a playable level.

Toy boxes are a good place to experiment with how your character interacts with level geometry and mechanisms, as well as how mechanisms

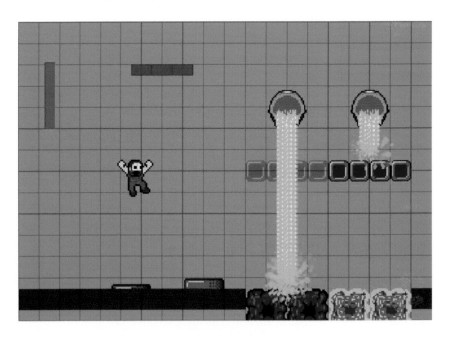

FIGURE 3.20 **A toy box level from my game *Ice Bucket Challenge*. I used this** space, inaccessible from any other part of the game except by selecting it as a file in the game engine, to build and test level mechanisms.

interact with one another. Figure 3.20 shows a toy box level I created for a game jam game: the character cannot cross lava blocks but can cool them off by letting water fall on them. The red and blue ledges block the water from falling on the lava, so the player has to use red and blue switches to turn the ledges on and off. Having a space like this in my game let me focus on building and testing how parts of my game interacted with one another before I started to implement them in the game's actual levels.

Other things you might test in a toy box level include how camera systems might work in your game, especially if the camera is an important feature of the game. In his GDC 2012 talk on the development of *Super Mario 3D Land*, Koichi Hayashida showed a series of test levels that his team used to experiment with the Nintendo 3DS's stereoscopic 3D screen.[23] Things they tested included what optical illusions could be achieved with the 3DS and finding the limits of what they could put in a scene's foreground before players lost track of Mario.

This is fine for testing mechanisms, but what about when you actually have to start making levels that a player will interact with?

Building from the Middle

It may not seem intuitive at first, but many studios start designing levels somewhere in the middle of the game and save their first levels—where players will learn how to play the game—for last. The reasons for this can vary: a studio might need footage from several levels for a trailer, a mid-game level might make the most exciting demo, budget or personnel concerns could play a factor, and so on.

In my own work, whether I build levels in order varies by project, but the reasons I build mid-game levels first usually have something to do with helping players best understand the mechanics in my games. Earlier in my career, it was not uncommon for me to make all of my level mechanisms and dump them into the first level I designed out of sheer excitement. This was anything but good level design: playtesters could not beat the level because concepts were hastily introduced and challenges were too punishing. In her article on *Super Mario Maker*, a Nintendo game that lets players make and share *Super Mario* levels, Boing Boing's Laura Hudson had this to say about the "everything at the wall" level design she saw from the game's online community:

> But wish fulfillment alone does not make for a particularly good video game experience, and if you're actually trying to make an entertaining level as opposed to merely demonstrating your

god-like power to make the goombas do your bidding, a better question is whether you should.[24]

The "kitchen sink" levels made by the *Super Mario Maker* community are an extreme example, but they still remind me of the lessons I learned when I started designing levels for games I wanted to sell. The levels I created that playtesters could not beat had some good ideas but were too complex to be a player's first encounter with the game. In this way, I designed from the middle of the game because I created a too-difficult first level out of inexperience then pushed it to the third or fourth level after testing. What I learned from these experiences was to create an ideal level that I wanted to achieve with my mechanics first then work backward so that I could introduce ideas to the player so he or she would be ready when that ideal level finally appeared.

Now when I work on mid-game levels first, it's in a much more deliberate way. For my company's game *Dead Man's Trail*, we iterated on the game's looting *mode* first, a part of the game where players navigate isometric 3D environments to find resources. Daniel Cook's article "*Steambirds: Survive*: Goodbye Handcrafted Levels"[25] talks at length about the concept of mode-first design: rather than designing a bunch of levels with unique mechanisms, design a strong central gameplay concept and create variation by changing the condition of the board every time you enter that mode. For Cook's game, a dogfighting strategy game, this meant varying the types of enemy formations players would see when missions started.

In the case of *Dead Man's Trail*, we created a mode where players have to loot supplies from a city quickly before a zombie horde comes. The main ideas or mechanics of this mode were limited item-carrying capacity, limited combat effectiveness, quick running speed, and a timer that counted down until the map filled with zombies. We then created levels that would challenge players' management of those mechanics with varied amounts of space to move, varying map complexity, and the number of exits from maps, among other things. We tested with a random assortment of level themes and conditions to see which players found intuitive and which they found overwhelming. We likewise kept track of which mechanics we had to teach to players and which they could figure out on their own. After months of this sort of testing, we finally arrived on a "curriculum" that we could use as a basis for designing the tutorial in the game's first level. We likewise understood what made an "easy" *Dead Man's Trail* level and what should be left for later in the game.

Building in Order

Not every project needs the designer to spend time searching for a perfect level order. In action games where gameplay mechanics have to be introduced along a difficulty curve, or games with a lot of complexity, building from the middle makes a lot of sense. However, if a game is simpler or has other methods for planning level order, designing from the first level and working in order has a lot of advantages.

At the beginning of this section, I mentioned the game *Iconoclasts* and how its developer talked about designing that game from the beginning. *Iconoclasts* belongs to the style of game known as a *Metroidvania*, named after the games *Metroid* and *Castlevania: Symphony of the Knight*. The term Metroidvania is commonly used to describe a game that is a side-scrolling platform game that takes place in a large contiguous maze that a player must escape from. Players progress in Metroidvania games by expanding their avatar's movement capabilities so they can access more of the maze. One way a designer might approach a Metroidvania game involves more than just the map itself, but also a plan for what upgrades players will get and when. In this way, designing from the beginning of the game makes sense: the game's map is an extension of a mostly linear chain of upgrades. In terms of player experience, building in order works well for Metroidvanias or other games where a strong linear element (such as a story) is central to the game's enjoyment. Part of what makes these games pleasurable is exploring a space to find the next item, completing the chain faster, or finding out what happens next.

Another reason to build your levels in order is that your game may be simple enough that you do not need to plan extensive teaching levels. Building your game levels starting with mid-game levels is great when the player is in control of complex mechanics and you need to learn what players will and will not understand quickly. However, some game designs are straightforward enough that this approach isn't necessary. In my experience, this applies when designing arcade-style games, ones with short levels and a small number of gameplay mechanics. Another element of these games is that their complexity is (usually, but not always) external to the player. This means that the player's avatar moves or otherwise operates in a very simple way, but complexity is added with level mechanisms that make the avatar move in different ways or via enemies and items that change the player's strategy.

Lissitzky's Revenge was a game that I designed in order: the core mechanic is that you are a red triangle that must kill the white circle in each scene by finding it, charging up, and delivering the death blow. In the first level, the player goes through this sequence with no opposition, and complexity is added by first having the white circle fire back at you, then use an escalating series of moving barriers and puzzles. Cook's "modes not levels" idea is very much in play here: at its core, *Lissitzky* has very simple mechanics, so it's easier to conceptualize what an "easy" configuration is vs. a difficult one.

Another game that embodies this idea is Interstellar Tortoise's *Interstellar Invaders*,[26] a mash-up of *Breakout* and *Space Invaders* where players bounce a missile off of a paddle at aliens. The game's initial waves of enemies are simple, but complexity is added in later levels with new power-ups, more enemies, and different enemy types. For both of these games, designing mid-game levels simply did not make sense: an initial tutorial level that taught players the core of the game was easy enough to build and iterate on. With a strong understanding of the game's core mechanics, a player can then respond to new enemies or mechanisms easily, since they only tweak the core idea.

While not exhaustive, the workflows explored so far provide a comprehensive list of ways to approach level design. The only remaining piece is software, and designers should explore different ones such as Unreal, Unity, Game Maker, Construct, Tiled, and others to discover what works best for them and their workflows. Together, the planning workflows described in this chapter and the affordances of different software packages will help you determine which pipeline works for you.

SUMMARY

There is a wide variety of tools for the study, planning, and execution of game levels that can work together to create better game experiences. By planning levels in such a way that we focus on measurements, we can prepare for the realities of gameplay. Implementing these findings in game engines and prototyping them in an iterative process can ensure that our game levels meet our original experiential goals. Indeed, player-centric design is key to these workflows, and seeing our levels as a series of scenes which help us clearly communicate with players is a trend that we will see throughout the book.

In the next chapter, we take these lessons and explore the different types of spaces found in both real and game worlds. Through this exploration we will discover how to utilize these spatial types, and the points of view from which we see them, to create meaningful gameplay experiences.

EXERCISES

1. **Drawing exercise**: Design a gameplay mechanism that a player character must react to in a level (like the tilting flowers or rolling spiky fruits in *Donkey Kong Country: Tropical Freeze*). Sketch individual areas of a level for each of these: (1) introducing the mechanism to the player under "safe" conditions; (2) having the player react to the mechanism with his or her character in a little danger; (3) having the player react to the mechanism while his or her character is in a lot of danger.

2. **Drawing exercise**: Play a commercial game and draw diagrams of three scenes that you find in the game. Detail what makes them effective scenes and what type of gameplay the scene creates.

3. **Drawing exercise**: Choose a commercial game. Choose three rooms or spaces from that game and diagram their readability. Determine what types of players or what challenge level those rooms are built for.

4. **Paper prototyping exercise**: Create a paper prototype of a level you want to create in a digital game. Invent movement rules for the non-digital pieces that will let you at least somewhat mimic the movement style of your digital game, and create rules for utilizing other core mechanics from your game. Try to balance the amount of time players spend traveling and with amount of time they spend interacting with players or practicing the non-travel core mechanics.

5. **Digital exercise**: In a game engine, graybox a level and focus the experience on a specific mechanic. If you created a non-digital prototype of a level for Exercise 2, you may graybox that level for use in the digital environment.

6. **Drawing exercise**: Create a *Nintendo Power Method*-style map of a level you are working on (including the graybox from Exercise 3) or of a level in a commercial game. Create call-out boxes for significant gameplay areas and observe how they are spaced out from one another. Use this to determine whether gameplay scenes are paced well.

7. **Game-testing exercise**: Run a playtest of a game you are creating (such as the one you grayboxed in the last exercise) or have a partner

play a commercial game they have never played before. Avoid interrupting them as they play but take thorough notes of where they get stuck, where the level is unclear, and other pitfalls that take away from the user experience.

8. **Digital exercise**: Choose a game engine that you are able to script in comfortably (non-coding or coding). Create a "toy box" level of at least three simple game mechanisms. Find at least two ways that these objects can work in tandem to create new interactions (i.e., having water put out fires, having fires ignite oil pools that slow down players, etc.)

ENDNOTES

1. Casali, Dario. Interview by author, personal. Valve Corporation, Bellevue, WA, October 27, 2008.
2. Jarvinen, Aki. GameGame. *GameGame*. http://gamegame.blogs.com/ (accessed January 3, 2013).
3. *Super Mario Bros.* Nintendo (developer and publisher), September 13, 1985. Nintendo Entertainment System game.
4. *The Legend of Zelda*. Nintendo (developer and publisher), February 21, 1986. Nintendo Entertainment System game.
5. *Katamari Damacy*. Namco, Now Productions (developer), Namco (publisher), September 22, 2004. Sony Playstation 2 game.
6. *Angry Birds*. Rovio Entertainment (developer), Chillingo (publisher), December 11, 2009. Mobile device game.
7. *Team Fortress 2*. Valve Corporation (developer and publisher), October 9, 2007. PC game.
8. *Resident Evil*. Capcom (developer and publisher), March 22, 1996. Sony Playstation game.
9. *Metal Gear Solid*. Konami Computer Entertainment Japan (developer), Konami (publisher), September 3, 1998. Sony Playstation game.
10. Brown, Mark. "Donkey Kong Country: Tropical Freeze – Mario's Level Design Evolved" *Game Maker's Toolkit*. https://www.youtube.com/watch?v=JqHcE6B4OP4. June 16, 2017. Accessed February 27, 2018.
11. *Donkey Kong Country: Tropical Freeze*. Retro Studios and Monster Games (developers), Nintendo (publisher). February 14, 2014. Nintendo Wii U game.
12. *New Super Mario Bros. U*. Nintendo EAD. November 18, 2012. Nintendo Wii U game.
13. *SWARM!*. e4 Software (developer and publisher), January 2, 2013. Mobile device game.
14. Anthropy, Anna and Naomi Clark. *A Game Design Vocabulary: Exploring the Foundational Principles Behind Good Game Design*. Boston, MA: Addison Wesley Professional, 2014.

15. Anthropy, Anna and Naomi Clark. *A Game Design Vocabulary: Exploring the Foundational Principles Behind Good Game Design*. Boston, MA: Addison Wesley Professional, 2014. p. 40.
16. Rebouche, Blake. "Level Design Workshop: Balancing Action and RPG in 'Horizon Zero Dawn' Quests". Game Developers Conference. San Francisco, CA. March 2018.
17. Fullerton, Tracy, Christopher Swain, and Steven Hoffman. *Game Design Workshop: A Playcentric Approach to Creating Innovative Games*. 2nd ed. Amsterdam: Elsevier Morgan Kaufmann, 2008.
18. From the Introduction to Game Design course at George Mason University's Computer Game Design Program. Taught by Prof. Christopher Totten.
19. Salen, Katie, and Eric Zimmerman. *Rules of Play: Game Design Fundamentals*. Cambridge, MA: MIT Press, 2003, p. 168.
20. Rogers, Scott. *Level Up! The Guide to Great Game Design*. San Francisco, CA: Wiley, 2014.
21. Parish, Jeremy. "The Metroid sisterhood – Scurge Hive and Iconoclasts". *Retronauts*. Podcast audio, April 9, 2018.
22. *Iconoclasts*. Joakim Sandberg. January 23, 2018. Multi-platform downloadable game.
23. Hayashida, Koichi. "Thinking in 3D: The Development of *Super Mario 3D Land*". Game Developers Conference. San Francisco, CA. March 2012.
24. Hudson, Laura. "Your Super Mario Maker level has no chill". *Boing Boing*. September 14, 2015. https://boingboing.net/2015/09/14/super-mario-maker-levels.html. Accessed April 24, 2018.
25. Cook, Daniel. *Steambirds: Survive:* Goodbye Handcrafted Levels. *Lost Garden*. December 3, 2010. http://www.lostgarden.com/2010/12/steambirds-survival-goodbye-handcrafted.html. Accessed April 24, 2018.
26. *Interstellar Invaders*. Interstellar Tortoise. May 1, 2018. Multi-platform downloadable game.

CHAPTER 4

Basic Gamespaces

Architecture is the thoughtful making of space.

—LOUIS KAHN

This quote from famous architect Louis Kahn, similar to our own for level design, brings us to our next discussion on gamespaces. In Chapters 2 and 3, we explored some of the practical tools and methods used to design game levels, from planning on paper to constructing level geometry in game engines. Now we will discuss basic spatial arrangements that will enable us to create better experiences within our game levels.

First, we will look at some simple spatial principles from architectural design: figure–ground, form–void, and so on. Next, we will explore historic gamespaces such as the maze and labyrinth, learning how these ancient space types influence modern game structures. From these core concepts, we will explore other popular spatial types found in modern games and discover how they are used to enforce different gameplay mechanics. Lastly, we will consider player point of view and discover what advantages and disadvantages are found in first, third, and other camera views.

What you will learn in this chapter:

Architectural spatial arrangements

Historic gamespace structures

Spatial size types

Molecule level spaces

Hub spaces

Sandbox gamespaces

Working with camera views

Enemies as alternative architecture

ARCHITECTURAL SPATIAL ARRANGEMENTS

So far, we've started each chapter by looking at relevant works and concepts from architecture that inform how we approach gamespaces, and this chapter is no different. Whereas we previously focused on tools and techniques that were useful in game engine environments, this time we will discuss commonly used spatial arrangements that can be useful in games.

Games and architecture differ in the fact that real-world architecture must conform to real-world rules. For example, real-world buildings must have both an interior and an exterior—with the shape of one influencing the other. Real-world architecture must also take into consideration weather, geology, zoning regulations, and structural realities. These are not things that gamespaces must deal with. To one extreme, this can mean experimental structures such as Atelier Ten Architects and GMO Tea Cup Communication, Inc.'s Museum of the Globe,[1] a large elliptical structure formed from cubes floating in space (Figure 4.1) or Hidenori Watanave's explorable database sculpture on the life of Brazilian architect Oscar Niemeyer[2]—both former structures within the virtual world *Second Life*.[3] For more day-to-day level design, however, this means gamespaces that are free from interior/exterior requirements. This results in more freeform spatial layouts based on player movement patterns, narrative events, or game mechanics (Figure 4.2). Indeed, *interior* and *exterior* are little more than descriptions based on the art used to decorate the gamespace.

With these differences in mind, spatial designers for games can take advantage of architectural lessons within the freedom of game design environments. Some of these lessons even have conceptual links to how levels are constructed in many modern game engines.

Figure–Ground

The first architectural spatial arrangement we will explore is *figure–ground*. Figure–ground is derived from artistic notions of the *positive* and *negative* space of a composition, where positive space describes the area

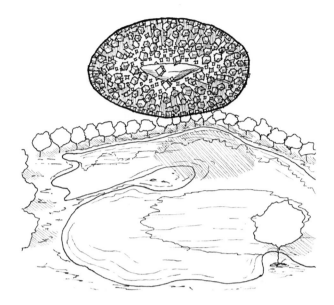

FIGURE 4.1 A sketch of Atelier Ten Architects and GMO Tea Cup Communication, Inc.'s Museum of the Globe. Since the building is built within a virtual world, it does not require any structure to hold up the hundreds of cubes making up its main body. The designers designed the building's form in Microsoft Excel and then generated the geometry in an automatic modeling program.

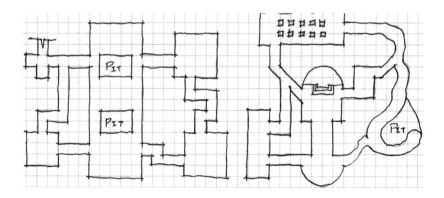

FIGURE 4.2 Parti diagram sketches of level plans. Game levels can take on unusual formal characteristics because they do not have to conform to a corresponding interior or exterior as real buildings do.

inhabited by the subject of a piece and negative space describes space outside of or in-between subjects (Figure 4.3).

Figure–ground theory in architecture comes from the arrangement of positive space figures, often pochéd building masses, within a negative space ground. When viewed in plan, the designer can see how the placement of building figures begins to form spaces out of the ground. Indeed, the formation of such spaces in figure–ground drawings is as important as the placement of the figures themselves (Figure 4.4). According to architectural designer Matthew Frederick, spaces formed by arranged figures become positive space in their own right, since they now have a form just as the figures do.[4] From an urban design standpoint, these framed spaces are often squares, courtyards, parks, nodes, and other meeting areas where people can "dwell," while remaining negative spaces are for people to move through.[5]

Frederick also points out that when utilizing figure–ground, both figural elements and spaces can be *implied*,[6] either by demarcating a space with structural elements or by creating negative spaces that resemble the

FIGURE 4.3 This illustration, known as Rubin's vase, shows the concept of positive and negative space and how they can be reversed. Based on whether the viewer is interpreting the black or white portions of the image as the negative space, this is either an illustration of two faces looking at one another or of a vase.

FIGURE 4.4   When mapping out spaces with figure–ground drawing, it is important to observe how the positive space figures create spaces out of the negative space
ground. These spaces, having forms of their own, are considered positive space.

form of nearby figures (Figure 4.5). This echoes theoretical neuroscientist
Gerd Sommerhoff, who, as quoted by architect Grant Hildebrand, said:

> The brain expects future event-and-image sets to be event-and-
> image sets previously experienced. When repetition of previous
> experience seems likely, the brain readies itself to re-experience
> the set. If expectances are confirmed, the model is reinforced,
> with a resultant sensation of pleasure.[7]

In this way, we can see how figure–ground becomes a powerful tool
for level designers to create additive and subtractive spaces within many
game engines. Many engines allow for the creation of additive figure elements to be arranged within negative 2D or 3D space. Gamespaces are
often based on mechanics of movement through negative space, using
positive elements such as ledges or supports for a player's journey. Under
other mechanics, forming spaces in-between solid forms allows for the
creation of rooms, corridors, and other spaces that players can run, chase,
and hide in. Additionally, designers can communicate with players via
implied boundaries or highlighted spaces that use figure–ground articulations like those described by Sommerhoff (Figure 4.6).

FIGURE 4.5 This illustration show how figure–ground arrangements can be used to imply spaces or elements.

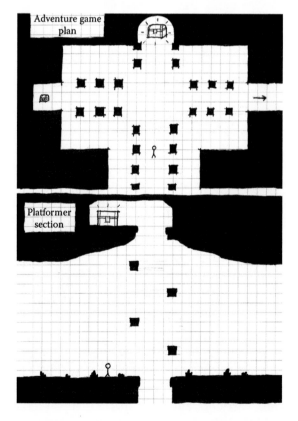

FIGURE 4.6 These illustrations show ways that figure–ground relationships can be utilized in many gamespaces, implying spatial relationships can be an effective way of relaying spatial messages to players.

Form–Void

Form–void (also called *solid–void*) is in many ways a three-dimensional evolution of figure–ground. It is the natural application of figure–ground in games where the gamespace will be viewed from a non-top-down perspective (Figure 4.7). In form–void theory, spaces that are carved out of solid forms are implied to have a form of their own.

Just as figure–ground is spatial arrangement by marking off spaces with massive elements, form–void is spatial arrangement by adding masses or subtracting spaces from them. The game engines described in Chapter 3 have features that reflect form–void, allowing designers to place geometric forms or carve them out of an endless mass. Similarly, 3D art programs allow designers to add or subtract forms from one another with *Boolean operations*, where mathematical equations are used to combine 3D models in additive or subtractive ways. Buildings such as Peter Zumthor's Therme Vals or Mario Botta's Casa Bianchi, both in Switzerland, use form–void relationships to carve out spaces for balconies, doorways, windows, private rooms, and other functions (Figure 4.8). In games, such additions and subtractions can be used for hidden alcoves, secret passages, sniping spots, or even highlighted level goals.

Arrivals

Based on what we have seen in figure–ground and form–void, level design is an art of contrasts. It is also an art of sight lines, pathways, dramatic lead-ups, and ambiguity about the nature of where you are going. All of

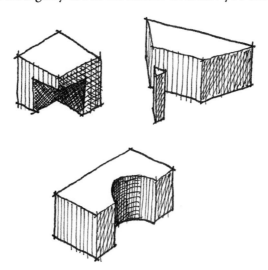

FIGURE 4.7   Some examples of form–void relationships between forms.

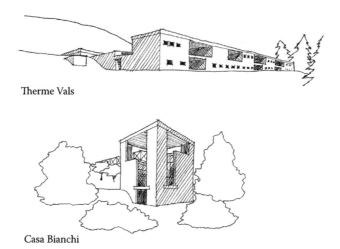

Therme Vals

Casa Bianchi

FIGURE 4.8 Sketches from Therme Vals by Peter Zumthor and Casa Bianchi by Mario Botta show how forms and voids can be used to define space.

these elements contribute to the experience of an *arrival*, the way in which you come into a space for the first time.

Much of how we will communicate with the player is through arrivals in space. It is also through arrivals that a space ushers players toward their next destination or allows them to choose their own path. Much of how you experience a space when you arrive in it comes from the spatial conditions of the spaces that preceded it: if you are arriving in a big space, the spaces leading up to it should be enclosed so the new space seems even bigger. Light spaces should be preceded by dark, safe by dangerous, sparsely populated by busy, etc. In their book *Chambers for a Memory Palace*, architects Donlyn Lyndon and Charles W. Moore highlight John Portman & Associates' Hyatt Regency Atlanta hotel as featuring such arrival in its atrium space. Dubbed the "Jesus Christ spot" by critics, it was not uncommon soon after the hotel was built for businesspeople to arrive in the twenty-two-story atrium from the much lower-ceilinged spaces preceding it and mutter "Jee-sus Christ!" as they looked upward.[8] Similar spatial experiences are common in exploration-based games such as those in *The Legend of Zelda* series or ThatGameCompany's *Journey* for leading up to important enemy encounters, item acquisitions, or story events (Figure 4.9).

Another important element of how players arrive at spaces is their point of view from the arrival point. As we will see later in the chapter, camera angles in games have a great deal of influence over how a player

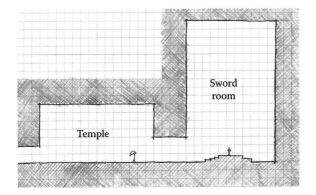

FIGURE 4.9 Many games use contrasting spatial conditions to highlight the approaches to gameplay-important spaces such as boss rooms or goals. This diagram of the Temple of Time from *The Legend of Zelda: Ocarina of Time*, where the player receives a narrative-important sword, shows how contrasted spaces and a Byzantine-esque basilica plan emphasize the importance of the sword chamber.

understands space. When a player looks through a doorway their ability to plan their next steps has a lot to do with how well they can "read" the space they've just arrived in. Controlling the information shown in a view is very important and if done well, can make a more satisfying experience. In classical architecture, the procession-like approach to the Parthenon in Athens, Greece, shows how an occupant's point of view is steered toward dramatic reveals. Visitors climbing up the steps of the Acropolis would first see the Parthenon from below. Then, passing through the Propylaea, the portico-like entrance building of the Acropolis, they would be greeted by a three-quarter view of the Parthenon from its northwestern corner rather than a more two-dimensional view from straight on. The path then forces visitors to walk around the building before they would wind back to the entrance of the Parthenon itself. From this forced path, visitors got a more theatrical approach to the Parthenon than if they had walked straight up to its entrance (Figure 4.10).

Genius Loci

Our last architectural spatial concept is less of an arrangement and more of another goal for designing your own spaces: *genius loci*, also known as *spirit of place*. This term comes from a Roman belief that spirits would protect towns or other populated areas, acting as the town's *genius*. Late-twentieth-century architects adopted the phrase to describe the identifying qualities or emotional experience of a place. Some call designing to the

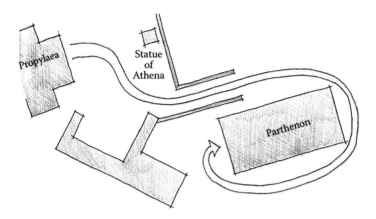

FIGURE 4.10 Diagram of the entry procession to the Parthenon. Visitors did not approach from the entryway side, but from a corner. They then had to walk around the building. Since all elevations of the building were equally intricate, it could be enjoyed from all sides as visitors walked around to the entrance.

concept of genius loci *placemaking*, that is, creating memorable or unique experiences in a designed space.

In Chapter 3, we discussed the *Nintendo Power* method of level design, where the designer creates a macro-scaled parti or plan of his or her level, and then distributes highlighted moments of gameplay as though developing a map for a game magazine. Each of these highlighted moments of gameplay—be they enemy encounters, movement puzzles, or helpful stopping points—has potential for its own genius loci. Are these places for rest or for battle? Should the player feel relaxed, tense, or meditative in these gamespaces? The answers to these questions depend highly on the game you are building, but can help you determine the kind of feel you want for your levels.

Beyond individual gameplay encounters, level designers can implant genius loci within the entirety of their gamespaces and use it as a tool for moving players from one point to another. Genius loci can be built through manipulations in lighting, shadows, spatial organization, and the size of spaces, which will all be discussed in detail later in the book. If you are building a level for a horror game, the genius loci you build should be one of dread, created through careful selection of environmental art, lighting, sound effects, and other assets. Spaces in a game with little or no genius loci can be *circulation* spaces, that is, spaces for the player to move through to get to the next destination. Depending on the gameplay you are creating, circulation spaces may be a chance to rest between intensive encounters or tools for building suspense before a player gets to the next memorable gameplay moment.

Now that we have discussed a few more general spatial concepts, we can move on to exploring some historical gamespace archetypes. These will allow us to take the tools and techniques we have learned thus far and employ them in classical gameplay structures.

HISTORIC GAMESPACE STRUCTURES

Many games and puzzles have been inspired by spaces described in classical literature or built in the real world. Beyond defining a specific spatial condition of a game environment, these classic spaces serve as important models for how game worlds can be structured: in linear, branching, or interconnected ways.

Labyrinth

The first of these spaces is the classical *labyrinth*. According to Greek legends, the Labyrinth was built by the architect Daedelus to hold the half-man half-bull Minotaur for King Minos of Crete. Representations of labyrinths in art dating as far back as the Roman Empire depict labyrinths as winding passages that loop around themselves, eventually reaching an endpoint (Figure 4.11). While labyrinths are often confused with branching mazes, artists and writers such as Hermann Kern have made

FIGURE 4.11 An illustration of a classical labyrinth.

the distinction that classic labyrinths are *unicursal*—consisting of a single winding path.[9] Labyrinths are also notable for their use as a floor pattern in many medieval churches, such as Chartres Cathedral, where walking the path of the labyrinth was a meditative experience.

Labyrinths are an important model for understanding gamespaces that are navigated in a linear fashion. As Salen and Zimmerman point out, games are often the least productive way to accomplish a task.[10] Labyrinths also demonstrate that even in linear gamespaces, both literal and gameplay twists, turns, and challenges can add interest to an otherwise straightforward pathway. Beyond singular levels, many games are themselves labyrinthian, requiring players to follow one set path of events. Such a structure is useful for games where an embedded narrative, theme, or argument is being communicated to the player.

Maze

Mazes are branching spatial puzzles where occupants and players must find their way through an elaborate set of pathways with multiple dead ends to find an exit point (Figure 4.12). Due to their branching nature, mazes are said to be *multicursal*, having more than one defined path, unlike unicursal labyrinths. The distinction between *maze* and *labyrinth* is important to level designers, because both are unique and useful spatial types that create different types of gameplay. Despite the name, the legend of the Minotaur and the Cretan Labyrinth actually describes a maze— thus the current popular interchangeability between the terms *maze* and *labyrinth*. Upon finishing the structure, Daedelus is said to have nearly gotten lost among its many branching paths. Thus the hero Theseus utilized a ball of thread to remind himself of the way out during his mission to kill the Minotaur.

From the Renaissance through the nineteenth century, architects also developed *hedge mazes*, multicursal pathways through tall bushes in the

FIGURE 4.12　An illustration of a maze.

gardens of large estates. Originally unicursal labyrinths, these structures evolved into branching paths that often contained several points of interest. Of note is the Labyrinth of Versailles, within which explorers could find thirty-nine sculptures depicting Aesop's Fables (Figure 4.13). The PC indie title *Slender: The Eight Pages*[11] uses a similar layout, where players must navigate a maze of pitch-black forest pathways to find notebook pages before they are captured by a malicious entity (Figure 4.14). *Slender* is noteworthy because the "maze" experience is created not by walls (though certain small areas are maze-like), but with ambiguous scenery and pitch-black darkness.

Mazes, and even recreations of European-style hedge mazes and their American derivative, corn mazes, are a very common spatial type in games. Their branching nature with potential dead ends implies a rich *risk–reward* structure, where the game asks you to weigh different uncertain options with the hope of choosing an advantageous answer. In terms of game mechanics, maze levels of games are often paired with features such as powerful enemies or time limits to create dramatic gameplay situations (Figure 4.15).

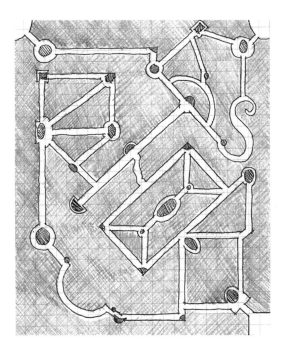

FIGURE 4.13   A plan of the Labyrinth of Versailles showing the many branching paths.

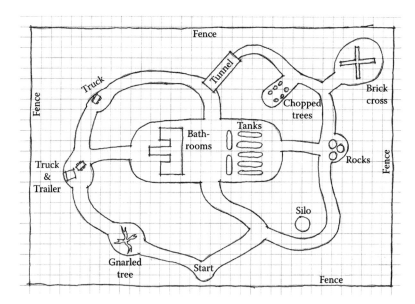

FIGURE 4.14 A map of the forest in *Slender: The Eight Pages*. Notice that it has a similar layout and node-based structure for places where players may find the titular pages.

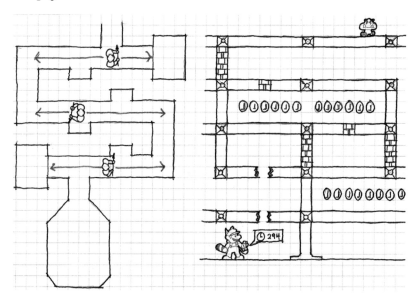

FIGURE 4.15 Two examples of in-game maze levels from *The Legend of Zelda: Ocarina of Time* and *Super Mario Bros. 3* show how designers use mazes to complement dramatic elements such as powerful enemies (*Zelda*) or a time limit (*Mario*).

The dead ends in mazes do not always have to be negative. Many games with explorable dungeons, such as *Final Fantasy* or *Zelda* titles, use branching paths and dead ends as incentives for exploration. Often these explorable branches yield treasure or other rewards. Games with even simpler worlds can also utilize small branching paths, such as in a mobile ball-rolling platform game I worked on, *SWARM!*. Within levels of this game, small diversionary paths off of a level's typical route can lead to caches of coins and other rewards (Figure 4.16).

Rhizome

While *maze* and *labyrinth* are architectural terms, *rhizome* is a term from botany. Rhizomes are networks of roots formed by underground stems of plants. This term was borrowed by philosophers Gilles Deleuze and Félix Guattari for their two-volume work *Capitalism and Schizophrenia*. As a philosophical concept, rhizomes describe a lateral representative structure

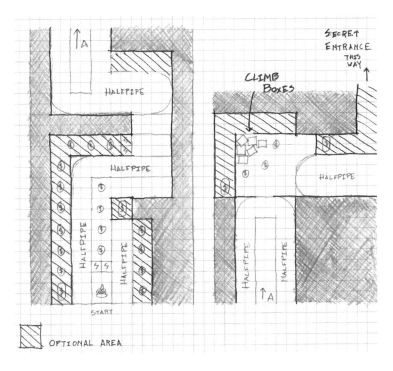

FIGURE 4.16   A plan sketch of level 1–3 of *SWARM!* showing small passageways off of the main level path. While not traditionally maze-like, these branching paths demonstrate in a small game the same methods for creating player curiosity found in much more complex titles.

of information and data without distinctive entry and exit points. At the beginning of *A Thousand Plateaus*, Deleuze and Guattari outline the guidelines of a rhizome, the most important of which, for our purposes, is that every point in them is connected to every other point at the same time[12] (Figure 4.17). In this regard, the term *rhizome* has been used to describe the Internet,[13] as users can access information on any website from any other website by typing in its Uniform Resource Locator (URL).

Spatially, the term *rhizome* can apply to any place that can be instantly traveled to from any other place. In the real world, air travel allows this to an extent. In games, a popular mechanic in large adventure games is to give players access to an instant transportation function that allows distances to be traveled quickly. In *Pokémon*, for example, players eventually gain an ability that allows bird Pokémon to transport them to places they have already visited. This ability also exists in many games in the *The Legend of Zelda*, *Final Fantasy*, and *Elder Scrolls* series to help players manage travel over large in-game landscapes. Making these features available to players early in a game is seen as a hallmark of "modern" open world design.

ActiveWorlds,[14] *Second Life*, and other large virtual worlds have similar functions, but make them part of the user's standard moveset by allowing him or her to type in coordinates of where he or she would like to go. In *ActiveWorlds*, this has turned locations along the x and y axes of the world map, such as points (45, 0) or (0, 45), as well as points along the center diagonal between the two, such as (45, 45), into major commerce and development thoroughfares[15] since they can be traveled to and remembered easily. Likewise, in *Second Life*, the interior of the Museum of the Globe can only

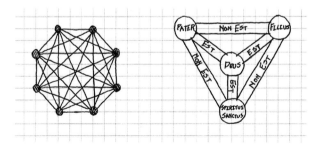

FIGURE 4.17 A diagram of a rhizomatic structure. Mathematically, these are referred to as *complete graphs*, where all vertices on a geometric object connect to all other vertices. These kinds of structures are often used in religious iconography, such as the Christian shield of the trinity[52] (also pictured).

be accessed through *Second Life*'s coordinate system—further making it a piece of architecture that can only exist within a virtual world. The ability of game developers to script such options into games makes rhizomes a unique option for creating world logic and geometry within digital games.

On a macro-scale, labyrinths, mazes, and rhizomes are very useful for describing the structures of both single levels and entire game worlds. Now we can discuss how even more micro-scaled portions of levels can emotionally engage users. In the next section, we look particularly at the sizes of gamespaces and discover how they affect a player's relationship with an environment.

SPATIAL SIZE TYPES

While size distinctions for gamespaces seem like rather banal information, they actually create some very interesting emotional scenes in game levels. Here we discuss three size types that level designers can use in their work. These types can be used in a variety of gameplay scenarios, such as contextual tutorials or creating drama through survival scenarios.

Narrow Space

The first size type we will discuss is *narrow space*, a spatial condition where the occupant feels confined and unable to move.[16] When considering the measurement techniques highlighted in Chapter 3, narrow gamespace is that which is not much larger than a player character's own size metrics—often with space for only two of such a character to stand in a passageway (Figure 4.18). Narrow space is a significant spatial type in video games that can be used for a variety of dramatic or skill-based gameplay scenarios.

Narrow spaces create tension by giving space *scarcity*, limited amounts such that space itself becomes a valuable resource. Under this model,

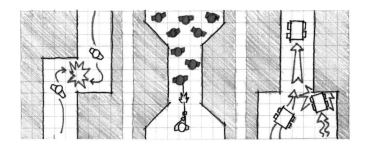

FIGURE 4.18 Plan diagrams of narrow space. These examples show how narrow spaces can be used to create conflict scenarios among players and NPCs.

conflict can rise from players' drive to keep space for themselves from other players or non-player characters (NPCs). In player vs. player conflicts, narrow space can be used to create bottlenecks for ambushes and traps or to provide tense "threading the needle" moments in racing games.

The narrowing of space close to the limits of player metrics creates a sense that the player cannot perform many of the actions he or she could under other conditions. This is significant for the other function of narrow spaces—evoking vulnerability by limiting player movement options. This is a common design feature of many horror games such as *Resident Evil*, where the hallways of the Spencer Mansion combined with the game's non-intuitive "tank controls" create a heightened sense of claustrophobia (Figure 4.19). The more modern *Resident Evil 7* loses the tank controls, but still creates tension by featuring a similar house of narrow spaces. The game even hints that the two mansions were designed by the same architecture firm: a unique instance where gameplay similarities are treated like an architectural style.

Stealth games use narrow space in interesting ways. Games in the *Metal Gear Solid* series offer a plethora of spaces to hide in. While some comfortably allow hero Solid Snake to scout out his next hiding spot, others, such as lockers, vents, or crawl spaces, limit both Snake's mobility and the player's ability to see the environment (Figure 4.20). This feature of many stealth games reinforces the idea that in stealth games, as in horror games, player characters are often weaker than their opponents.

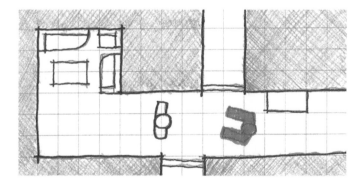

FIGURE 4.19 Diagram of a typical hallway space in *Resident Evil*'s Spencer Mansion. The narrow hallways create a claustrophobic environment. This causes enemy encounters to be a significant threat, as the player is less able to move around them.

FIGURE 4.20   Narrow spaces in *Metal Gear Solid* games offer concealment from enemies, but at the cost of both mobility and visibility.

Intimate Space

The next size type is known as *intimate space*. Intimate spaces are neither confining nor overly large[16] and are, in fact, what one might call *metric appropriate*, at a size that comfortably supports the size and movement metrics of player characters (Figure 4.21). Within intimate spaces, interactive surfaces or features are within reach of a player character's inherent abilities. In some games, the amount of space described in this way may

FIGURE 4.21   Intimate spaces are ones where everything within the space is accessible by the player character with its inherent abilities.

change if the abilities of player characters can expand through additions such as high-jump capabilities or others.

A great deal of gamespaces could be described as intimate space. In corridor shooters and in multiplayer arenas where players are on even ground with no significant vantage points above or below, the gamespace can be considered *multilateral intimate space* (Figure 4.22). In multiplayer situations, intimate spaces create a spatially even playing field shared by multiple actors. Player skill notwithstanding, no player has an advantage over any other. Racing game tracks with wide enough road space for multiple cars allow players to compete against one another for race position rather than track space. In these situations, contrasting narrow and intimate spaces creates interesting gameplay situations and allows players to build strategies of how to proceed.

Intimate spaces in single-player games can have several beneficial effects. Due to their comfortable accessibility, they are often "friendly" locations within the plot of a game. Princess Peach's Castle from *Super Mario 64* is an intimate space because the player can access many of the platforms inside without putting Mario at any significant risk. There are no pits or enemies to endanger the character and end the game. This space and others like it also act as a *tutorial space* for the game, allowing players

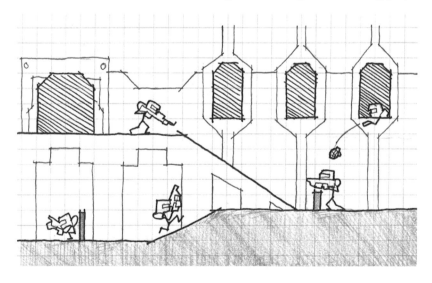

FIGURE 4.22 This sectional diagram shows multiplayer shooter characters battling within an intimate space arena. Architectural features like ramps, slight elevation changes, and occasional barriers do not interrupt the spatially even playing field of the level.

to experiment with Mario's abilities at their own pace. New Donk City in *Super Mario Odyssey* is another such space: the close distance between buildings lets players make free use of Mario's wall jump ability such that he can reach even the tops of skyscrapers with ease.

One game series that utilizes intimate space in interesting ways is the *Batman: Arkham* series. For the first game in the series, *Batman: Arkham Asylum*, developer Rocksteady coined the term *predator gameplay* to describe the game's stealth hunting. As a contrast to typical stealth games where the protagonist is somehow weaker than the enemies, the developer argued, Batman would be stronger and have better command of his surroundings, similar to his capabilities in the *Batman* comic books and films.[17] To complement Batman's abilities of gliding, grappling, and silently taking down foes, the level designers created level spaces that enabled these actions, with high vantage points and sight lines that allowed the player to capitalize on Batman's unique abilities (Figure 4.23). Unlike multiplayer games, where the focus of intimate space is to create comfortable spaces for many players, single-player games can utilize intimate spaces to give players an advantage over foes.

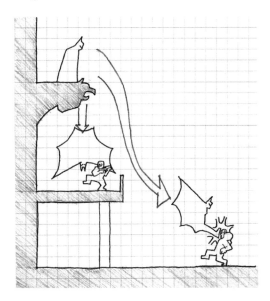

FIGURE 4.23   Intimate spaces in *Batman: Arkham Asylum* involve the use of vantage points and sight lines that are accessible through the abilities of the player character, Batman. These abilities allow for greater use of the level space by players than enemies, so intimate space in this case provides spatial advantages for this single-player experience.

Prospect Space

At times, games put players in the positions that Batman's foes in *Arkham Asylum* find themselves in: wandering through a large open space and open to attack. This third spatial size type is known as *prospect space* (Figure 4.24).[18] Hildebrand describes prospect space as that to which ancient humans had to make risky journeys for food, water, and other necessities—outside of the safety of caves and open to predators and the elements.

Prospects in gamespaces take many forms. Once again looking to the multiplayer map, prospects are found in any area where one player may take a spatial advantage over another, such as by having a vantage point from above. In single-player games, prospects are used as *boss rooms*: large open spaces where the player cannot use his or her abilities to take a spatial advantage but must instead fight a single powerful foe. Such spaces are used regularly in the *Mega Man* game series, where players must finish each level by battling a powerful Robot Master (Figure 4.25).

Prospect spaces are similar to narrow spaces in their potential for creating fear in the player. They do so through opposite means, however. If narrow spaces create a sense of claustrophobia, prospects create a sense of *agoraphobia*, an anxiety disorder that includes a fear of wide-open spaces. While there may be a general sense of vulnerability in prospect spaces of a multiplayer deathmatch map, this feeling can be heightened through the use of fog, music, shadows, and other atmospheric effects related to the forming of your gamespace's genius loci. The entire environment of *Slender: The Eight Pages* is a prospect draped in pitch-black darkness,

FIGURE 4.24 This illustration shows a basic idea of how prospect space operates in terms of a player's openness to enemy attack.

FIGURE 4.25 Boss rooms in the *Mega Man* series are often large and open so players must directly deal with the attacks of foes.

heightening the sense that the malevolent Slender Man has mastery of the gamespace and is waiting just beyond the player's field of vision. His artificial intelligence (AI) is scripted in such a way that he will randomly appear to the player at varying distances and move closer when the player is looking away (Figure 4.26). As such, Slender Man's movements across

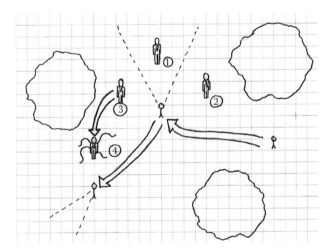

FIGURE 4.26 In *Slender: The Eight Pages*, the antagonist spawns randomly around the player, demonstrated in this plan diagram, giving the impression that he has complete control over the pitch-black prospect space (locations 1, 2, and 3 on the diagram). If the player turns away, the antagonist quickly pursues and further gives the impression of great speed (location 4).

the prospect space give the impression that he is supernatural and can move great distances quickly. To put this in terms of movement metrics: the space is built to enhance Slender Man's metrics while it makes the player's own movement metrics seem agonizingly slow.

Prospect spaces and the other spatial size types are much more complex than the qualities listed here. In later chapters, we discuss how they are mixed and matched with other types of spaces to create dramatic spatial articulations. Next, however, we explore a spatial type that connects the singular spatial atoms that we have thus far discussed.

MOLECULE LEVEL SPACES

Now that we have discussed several isolated gamespace types, we need to understand how to link these spaces together in interesting and meaningful ways. Designers Luke McMillan and Nassib Azar, who is himself a former architect, in their Gamasutra article "The Metrics of Space: Molecule Design,"[19] highlight a methodology for spatial organization based on the arrangement of gamespaces, how players reach one from another, and how designers can allow or disallow access between them for interesting play scenarios. Based on interpretations of mathematical graphing theory, which we delved into briefly during our discussion of rhizomes, they call this methodology *molecule design*. In this section, we discuss the basics of molecule design and enhance it by combining its functionality with proximity diagrams, which we saw in a previous chapter.

The Basics of Molecule Design

McMillan and Azar's concept of molecule design is primarily focused on the relationship between play spaces, treated in their graphs as *nodes* and *edges*. Nodes are the play spaces themselves—areas with significant enemy encounters, item pickups, spawn points, or opportunities for action. Edges describe the relationship between these spaces, be they visual or spatial (as in you can travel from one to another). These molecule graphs are similar to proximity diagrams, a tool used by architects to determine which rooms in a building should be near one another, which we discussed in Chapter 2. In proximity diagrams, the size and importance of spaces are described by the size of bubbles used to represent those spaces. The bubbles are connected with lines of varying thickness to show how important it is for spaces to be connected, much like how McMillan and Azar connect gameplay nodes with edges. For our versions of molecule graphs, we will borrow some ideas from proximity diagrams as well as concepts implied by McMillan and Azar's article to form a distinct *visual language*. In this way, we can use molecule diagrams to dictate what the proximities between nodes and the size or nature of edges mean. In Figure 4.27, dotted lines show that spaces are viewable from one another, and solid lines show that you can move from one to another. Arrows on the solid lines show if spaces are one way, and thick lines show that spaces between the nodes are direct paths. Level plan and section drawings are included to show a level space that may be designed from such a molecule.

It is important to note that the shapes of these molecules are not necessarily the layout of the level, but a description of how spaces interact with one another. To demonstrate this, Figure 4.28 shows another set of level drawings that can be derived from the molecule diagram in Figure 4.27.

Understanding the abstract nature of molecule diagrams is important for utilizing McMillan and Azar's last important concept: *Steiner points*. In graph theory, a *Steiner tree* is a spatial puzzle where the player must find the shortest point between two lines, constructed from points labeled A, B, and C, where A connects to B, B connects to C, but C does not connect to A. In McMillan and Azar's example, the answer to the puzzle is a slight cheat, where players can draw a node directly in the middle of the three that is connected to each. This is a Steiner point (Figure 4.29). Steiner points in level design can occur in any spatial scenario where a player may access play spaces vertically, that is, by climbing or jumping from a nodal gamespace to a Steiner point space, then into another nodal gamespace in the molecule diagram (Figure 4.30). Steiner points are essentially shortcuts in level paths. These can be utilized purely by jumping from high ledges onto lower ones to save time, or may even be incentivized with power-ups or other rare items.

Now that we have discussed the basics of McMillan and Azar's molecule design principles, we will see how we can further integrate them with our own architectural approach.

Spatial Types as Molecule Nodes and Edges

Molecule diagrams are very abstract. As such, they leave a lot of guesswork about what could be used as a significant gameplay node. We have already discussed many spatial principles that can be useful for defining these spaces. We have already established that in level design, form often follows core mechanics. Likewise, nodal gamespaces in your own molecule diagrams can represent areas where the player employs unique or intense applications of your core mechanics: big gun fights, sharp turns,

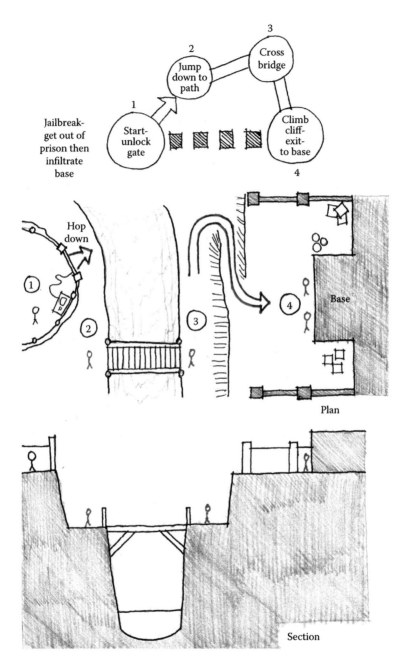

FIGURE 4.27 This molecule diagram establishes links between nodal gamespaces with the use of edges. A visual language has been established for edges to help describe elements of three-dimensionality as shown in the accompanying plan and section drawings of the level.

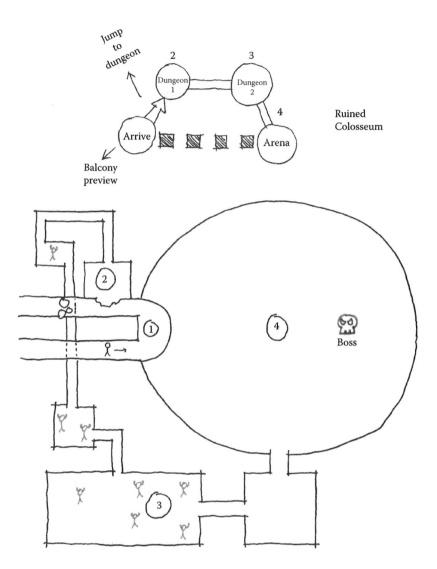

FIGURE 4.28 This level drawing is also derived from the molecule diagram found in Figure 4.27. Molecules describe relationships rather than actual level space.

boss battles, difficult platforming, etc. These nodes are also opportunities to emphasize the genius loci of your level. To once again use *Slender: The Eight Pages* as an example, each landmark in the wooded maze carries its own experience unique from the rest of the course. In the infamous bathhouse, for example, the normally prospect-structured space of the game world suddenly becomes a maze of narrow hallways where Slender Man

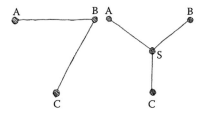

FIGURE 4.29   This diagram shows the Steiner tree puzzle and the answer utilizing a Steiner point.

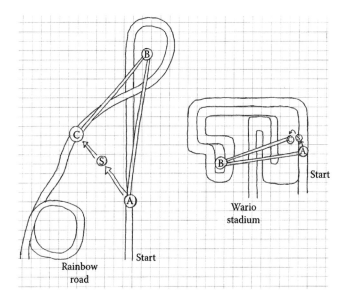

FIGURE 4.30   Steiner points in level design may be used to conceptualize secrets, or shortcuts. These diagrams of tracks from *Mario Kart 64* show how Steiner points (and some considerable skill) may be employed to skip large portions of the game's two longest tracks.

could be around any corner. While the transitional edges between such landmark nodes allow for encounters with Slender Man, they ultimately shuffle players between more notable gameplay nodes.

Slender also demonstrates an important distinction of using spatial types as nodes. While the game itself is structured as a Versailles-esque maze, several of the nodes contain their own smaller maze spaces. The circulation spaces that bring players from one node to another may be very linear, as may the nodes themselves. Figure 4.31 shows a level I created based on Washington, D.C.'s Sackler Gallery of Art, an underground

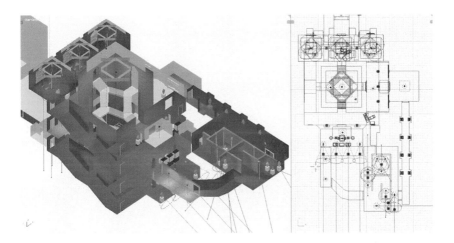

FIGURE 4.31 This image of a prototyped level shows how transitional spaces (the downward spiraling ramps) may be linear, while the nodal gamespaces may follow their own linear or branching pathways on a smaller scale.

museum with a downward-spiraling ramp system. The structure of this museum makes the node/edge contrast very apparent: the transitional spaces (the edges) utilize the downward ramps to take players from one intense gamespace to another. In the more intense sections (the nodes) are either unicursal corridors that use atmospheric effects or tight mazes for enemies to inhabit.

Molecule diagrams may also describe spaces where spatial size changes significantly. As described previously, size changes create their own special gameplay scenarios. McMillan and Azar pay special attention to *spawn points* in their article: the spaces where players begin a level or come back to life during multiplayer matches. These spaces may be large but intimate, allowing players to gather resources before rejoining battles. Likewise, transitional spaces may be equally intimate, keeping players on an even playing field when inside, but leading to large prospect spaces where players may gain spatial advantage over one another (Figure 4.32). In single-player games, where players can pay more attention to level details, transitions from intimately or narrowly scaled circulation to prospect spaces may describe changes in gameplay intensity and create "Jesus Christ spot" experiences.

If one reverses this dynamic, prospect-scaled transitional spaces allow for the generous usage of Steiner points. In the previous Sackler Gallery level prototype, the entire circulation space is a Steiner point that players may utilize within the limits of the player character's ability to fall from

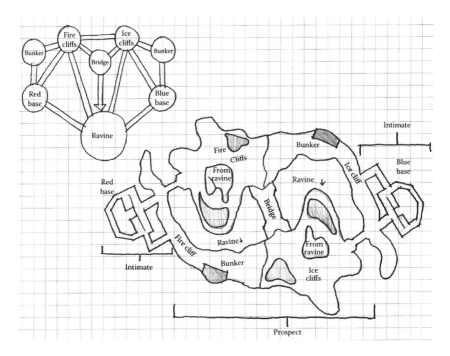

FIGURE 4.32 This drawing and molecule diagram of a multiplayer map from *Halo 4* shows how players move from intimate hallway spaces into prospect nodes where they may gain strategic advantages over one another.

heights without taking damage. Alternatively, *Metroid Prime 2: Echoes* utilizes prospect/circulation spaces as challenges. The Steiner point ability to jump from higher levels to lower ones is used as an obstacle in sections where players must scale a set of platforms to progress in the game (Figure 4.33). Later, if the player is returning from the higher gamespaces, the Steiner point becomes a shortcut again.

Now that we have looked at some methods for organizing spaces in levels, we will explore some common world configurations found in games to discover how they are organized for ease of use and enjoyment.

HUB SPACES

We have looked at some basic spatial concepts that will help us organize our levels, so now we can move on to common level structures. The first of these are *hub spaces*. Level designers also call these hub-and-spoke spaces, but we're mainly focused on the hub portion of this system. Hubs are a type of intimate space that behaves like a lobby where the player may access a game's different levels (the spokes). Many hubs are non-threatening and

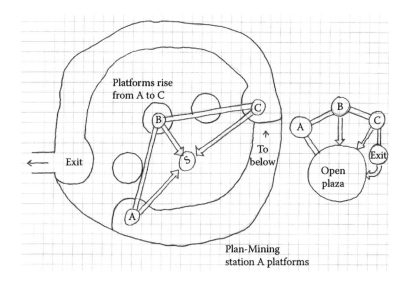

FIGURE 4.33 This drawing of the Agon Wastes environment from *Metroid Prime 2: Echoes* and the accompanying molecule diagram show how Steiner points are used as obstacles: failure to jump to platforms where one may progress results in a return to earlier areas.

offer players the ability to explore within the metrics of their character's abilities. Hubs distinguish themselves from other game world structures, such as sandboxes, which we will discuss later, by separating levels from more intense gamespaces through the use of portals, doors, or some other device (Figure 4.34).

Hubs became popular in early 3D games like *Super Mario 64* and *Banjo Kazooie* as a way to facilitate player travel between different environments. In this way, they are semi-rhizomatic: they offer a central point from which to jump from gamespace to gamespace. From a performance standpoint, these hubs allow levels to be loaded one at a time rather than all at once. Loading levels in this way is very efficient, but you lose the sense of seamlessness that one might expect in a large sandbox environment. Also, they offer a narrative "out" for games that wish to have characters travel to themed worlds such as ice, volcano, jungle, etc. when it would otherwise be illogical.

From a gameplay standpoint, hubs are notable for how they manage player goals. Hub-based games are typically structured around collecting resources, gold stars, puzzle pieces, etc. that facilitate travel through the game world and unlock portals. As players complete more intense

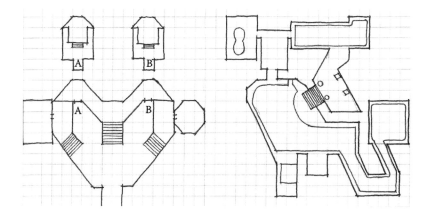

FIGURE 4.34   Hub levels include spaces such as Princess Peach's Castle from *Super Mario 64* and Station Square in *Sonic Adventure*. They both lead players from environment to environment while allowing them to backtrack and freely explore.

gameplay challenges, they collect more of the unlocking resources and can access new levels. While hub-based games offer an overall labyrinthine model through the general order in which one engages levels, they also offer great freedom to players in determining what missions to take, when and if to backtrack, or for how long they wish to explore each level (Figure 4.35).

In many ways, hubs offer the best of both linear and open styles of gameplay. In the next section, we will explore another type of space that offers players almost complete freedom over their gameplay experience.

SANDBOX GAMESPACES

Developers create the feeling of a large open world by utilizing *sandbox*, or *open world*, gamespaces. Sandbox worlds are named for their ability to have defined boundaries while also allowing players to play however they want in less structured ways than many other games allow. They are usually a large area—a city, island, etc.—where the player has lots of activities to choose from, sometimes inclusive of building new level geometry. In single-player games, sandboxes are evident in the *Grand Theft Auto* and *Saints Row* series, where players can choose to follow a story or simply wander. In multiplayer games, sandboxes are present in "battle royale" games such as *PlayerUnknown's Battlegrounds* (*PUBG*) or *Fortnite*, where players compete in large environments that allow building and scavenging. One might imagine that designing sandbox worlds is simple: all you

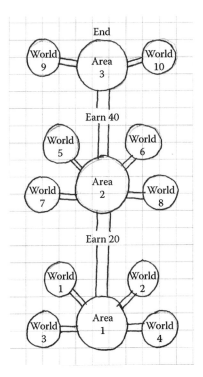

FIGURE 4.35 This diagram shows how hub-based games are typically struc-tured. They represent a ladder of sorts where the overall journey is linear, but the activity of how to overcome each rung is largely determined by the player.

must do is provide the player with a large open set of spaces in which to play and give him or her things to do. However, large spaces carry with them the problems of user orientation and location awareness.

As many real-world spatial designers know, these are problems regu-larly encountered by urban planners. It is perhaps not surprising that many of the most popular sandbox worlds are themselves cities. In this section, we will explore some urban design principles that can be used to build successful sandbox spaces.

Pathfinding with Architectural Weenies

Perhaps one of the most important elements of sandbox spaces comes from creative pioneer Walt Disney. While shooting live action films with dogs, his studio would often need them to run across the set. To accomplish this, they would use sausages, which Disney called weenies, to entice the animals to run in the direction they wanted. Disney described tall build-ings in his parks as having a similar effect for patrons by assisting with directional orientation. Jesse Schell, author of *The Art of Game Design: A Book of Lenses* and one of the designers on *Pirates of the Caribbean: Battle for Buccaneer Gold*, used the term *architectural weenie* to describe landmarks used to attract players to goal points in games.[20]

Architectural weenies are an integral part of sandbox spaces. They allow these worlds to retain their openness but still direct players toward places that designers want them to go. Many designers, such as Scott Rogers, cite Disneyland as inspiration for much of their level design knowledge. In the design of Disneyland, attractions such as Sleeping Beauty Castle or Splash Mountain not only direct visitors to themselves, but allow them to understand where they are by acting like guideposts. In *Grand Theft Auto IV*'s[21] take on Liberty City, landmarks like the Statue of Happiness and Rotterdam Tower serve similar functions: directing players to themselves but also acting as guideposts while players wander the landscape. In Schell's examples, the term *architectural* is used to describe how level designers create not only designed building spaces, but also designed natural spaces. *Battle for Buccaneer Gold* uses volcanoes, burning towns, and other attention-getting sights as weenies, not just buildings. Schell's designation of these objects also shows how architectural weenies can take many forms beyond tall buildings.

One game that cleverly uses architectural weenies is *Half-Life 2: Episode 2*. In one scene, players must use a radio to alert allies of an impending alien attack. The narrative sequence of this scene requires players to enter a building to determine that the radio both exists and cannot power up. Then, players must explore a nearby building to find the power source for the complex and switch it on (Figure 4.36). To keep the open feel of the landscape while directing player action, the developers textured the radio building with bright red and yellow hues and textured the larger tower building in drab browns. Despite its smaller size, this turned the radio building into an architectural weenie by making it stand out more against the natural greens, blues, and browns of the wooded landscape.[22]

Some games use weenies either as, or in concert with, high points so players can see large areas of the world from them. In the *Far Cry* series and in *The Legend of Zelda: Breath of the Wild*, tall towers draw players toward them and allow players to look for their next objective once climbed. In the case of *Breath of the Wild*, unvisited temples have a bright orange glow clearly visible from these towers against the greens and blues of the landscape. *No Man's Sky*, a game with an entire universe to explore, is perhaps one of the most unique uses of high-up architectural weenies.

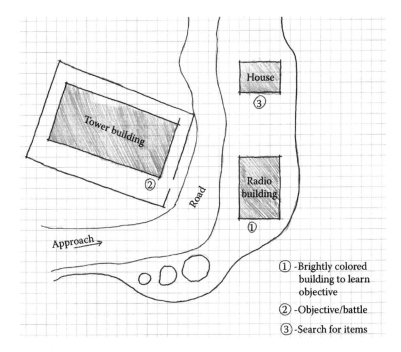

FIGURE 4.36 A plan of the radio tower complex in *Half-Life 2: Episode 2*. While smaller, the radio building is textured with brighter colors that contrast with the greens and blues of the landscape. This directs player attention to it first, rather than the dark browns of the radio tower building itself.

The game's environments are all generated by a computer, but the planet-building algorithm appears to include tall monoliths made of valuable resources located on hilltops. These are handy for several reasons: they provide needed materials for the player to build with but also let players see for miles around. That weenies might be included in an algorithm for procedural world generation is a testament to how versatile and important they are in open-world level design.

Clearly, architectural weenies can take a multitude of forms. They can also serve a variety of tasks, including directing player action and helping players better navigate gamespaces. In the next section, we will explore how this concept and others can further help players navigate sandbox worlds.

Organizing the Sandbox: Kevin Lynch's Image of the City

As stated previously, finding one's way in a large open space can be daunting. For this reason, urban planners have developed a number of organizational principles for how to structure urban spaces. In his influential book *The Image of the City*,[23] urban planner Kevin Lynch reports the results of a five-year study of how people form mental maps of cities. From this study, Lynch advocates aiding visitors by organizing cities with these elements: landmarks, paths, nodes, districts, and boundaries. Organizing cities in this way creates what he calls *legibility* for observers of a city,[24] which is what we should strive to achieve in our own sandbox gamespaces. This section will look at each of these elements to understand how they may be applied to video game sandbox spaces.

Landmarks

Landmarks are recognizable elements that can be guideposts to people in an urban space.[25] This definition should sound very similar to the concept of architectural weenies, as they are the same thing. As we discussed in the previous section, landmarks not only call attention to themselves, but also allow players to orient themselves by observing their relationship to the landmark in space. As many games do not utilize just urban-themed sandbox worlds—with popular choices including fantasy, post-apocalyptic, or historic landscapes—these landmarks can be natural objects or human-made elements that contrast with the rest of the landscape.

Half-Life 2 utilizes landmarks in an interesting way different from how they are typically used in sandbox games. While not a sandbox game itself, *Half-Life 2* strives to create the feeling of a large, seamless world by dividing levels with minimal fanfare: no menus, cutscenes, or other conspicuous scene transitions. The game establishes early on that a distant tower, the Citadel, is the home base of the game's villains, and that the player's final goal is to eventually reach and destroy it (Figure 4.37). This tower is visible from most levels in the game, and players can track their progress by observing how close they are to the structure.

The Citadel shows how versatile landmarks are. They can direct player action, allow them to orient themselves in a large sandbox space, or track their progress by measuring their proximity to them.

Paths

We have already discussed circulation spaces, channels for travel that connect significant gamespaces. Lynch discusses these types of spaces in his book as *paths*.[26] Paths in urban design include roads, sidewalks, and other thoroughfares that allow people to travel through the city.

FIGURE 4.37   The Citadel in *Half-Life 2* is a useful landmark for players to understand not only where they are in the game's large world, but also how far they have progressed in the game itself. The game establishes early on that its climax will take place there.

In terms of molecule design, these paths are the lines that connect significant gamespaces. They can have their own challenges, but are often intimately scaled spaces without significant aesthetic features. Their purpose is to usher players through to the next point of important gameplay. In our previous example of Liberty City, paths are the same types of spaces—streets, sidewalks, etc.—as those suggested by Lynch.

On the other hand, games like *The Elder Scrolls V: Skyrim* do not represent their sandboxes as large urban spaces, but as open landscapes. As such, many of the paths between towns, dungeons, and forts are much less direct and are, in fact, open fields. This allows players to enact their own Steiner points by taking direct routes between landmarks. While these paths might not be explicitly designed as such, they are recognizable. However, they run the risk of getting the player lost in their vast openness. To mitigate this, designers use subtle geographic features such as dirt paths, signposts, or rivers to evoke more direct pathways represented in urban plans.

For designers working in engines such as those described in Chapter 3, keeping these guidelines in mind when working with tools such as in-engine terrain editors is important for creating worlds that are not just aesthetically attractive, but also usable.

Nodes

In many urban spaces, the intersections of pathways offer a variety of opportunities for engaging users. Not only can they be their own guide points for navigation (such as when you direct someone to a business by telling them what corner it is on), but they can also be places for people to gather or interact (Figure 4.38). Lynch calls these intersections *nodes* and highlights how they can be important focal points for large networks of paths.[26]

Nodes can be locations for landmarks to reside, channeling different paths onto one end goal. They can also, as Lynch points out, be strategic *decision points*[27] at which observers can decide what path to take next. In many open-world games such as *Skyrim*, such decision nodes are everywhere, forcing players to prioritize how they wish to spend their time: do you want to go find things to do in a town or explore dungeons?

These decisions become even more interesting when they take on moral or narrative purposes. For example, Rockstar Vancouver's high school-themed sandbox game *Bully*[28] allows players to explore the fictional town and private school campus, taking on missions for various cliques in the school. The reputation the player has with each clique—bullies, jocks, nerds, greasers, and preppies—forms the game's morality system. If the player does something to impress the nerds, he or she may lose the favor of the jocks, etc. Spatially, the game offers many nodes at which the player can not only interact with NPCs, but also choose clique-friendly locations such as the gym, library, or auto shop (Figure 4.39).

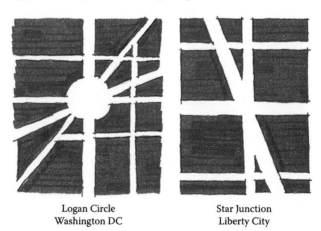

Logan Circle
Washington DC

Star Junction
Liberty City

FIGURE 4.38 Nodes at the intersections of paths offer opportunities for players to make strategic choices of where to go next in a game world and interact with NPCs or other players that may be gathered there.

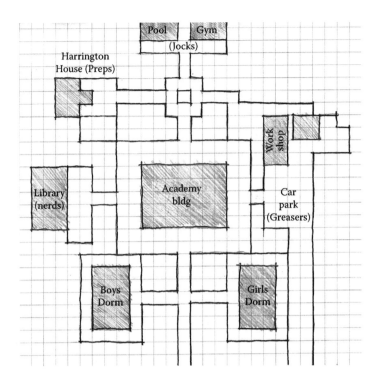

FIGURE 4.39 The grounds immediately outside the Bullworth Academy school building in the game *Bully* are a node that offers access to a number of landmarks important to the game's various cliques. The academy building itself is a landmark that also serves as an architectural weenie, allowing players to orient themselves by their spatial relationship to it.

Edges

Edges, according to Lynch, are boundaries not formed by paths. They are linear elements that mark a transition from one continuous area or condition to the next. Edges can be walls, rows of buildings, changes in vegetation, or other markers that show that an area has changed in character or genius loci.[26] In sandbox games, areas of varying genius loci allow players to feel that the world has variety in the way that games with distinct level theme types—ice, fire, forest, etc.—do (Figure 4.40).

In 1949, mythologist Joseph Campbell described the hero's journey monomyth in his book *The Hero with a Thousand Faces*.[29] As summarized by Campbell, the hero's journey plays out in this manner:

> A hero ventures forth from the world of common day into a region
> of supernatural wonder: fabulous forces are there encountered

and a decisive victory is won: the hero comes back from this mysterious adventure with the power to bestow boons on his fellow man.[30]

In *Origins of Architectural Pleasure*, architect Grant Hildebrand considers a spatial version of the monomyth focused on the journey's *materiality*. Materiality is the understanding of the textural and visual qualities of a surface. As applied to the hero's journey, Hildebrand notes that as the hero ventures from his world, the materiality of his surroundings change from that of comfort, to epic wilderness, and often to a dark, corrupted state when encountering the final enemy.[31] One sees this pattern play out in numerous works of literature, film, and games: from *Beowulf*[32] to *The Legend of Zelda*.

From a production standpoint, edges can mark a change in *art style*. The type of architectural or vegetation models you use can shift, signifying the change to a new area. Likewise, transitions between textures on surfaces can generate player-perceived edges. These transitions can be quick or gradual. A quick transition may mark a defined border, and can often be accompanied by architectural details such as walls or gates, as landscape rarely transitions suddenly. These are especially useful if the area you are entering is the site of an event—a battle, fire, alien

FIGURE 4.40   Different types of edges in sandbox worlds.

encounter, etc.—or if you are transitioning to the realm of a specific group. Gradual transitions, on the other hand, may help build anticipation for reaching a new zone. Burned trees, arrows, and other objects sticking out of the scenery, etc., can give the impression that you are about to enter a dangerous area, creating a tension when approaching it. They can also indicate that you are reaching a natural border between environment types—plains to forest, desert to canyon, etc.

Districts

The last of Lynch's elements is the *district*, which he describes as sections of a city where the observer enters "inside of" and which have some identifying character.[26] In the previous section, we discussed how changes in art style, environment art elements, and texture can indicate changes in environments within a sandbox world. Once past these edges, players find themselves within districts (Figure 4.41).

Beyond changes in style, districts in games differentiate themselves from one another with changes in gameplay: types of NPCs, enemies, events, or mini-games. Districts can be containers for distinct narrative events or gameplay challenges. In the example of Disneyland, the park is divided into distinct districts: Tomorrowland, Fantasyland, Frontierland, and others that have their own distinct character and set of themed attractions. Likewise, *Grand Theft Auto IV*'s Liberty City has several distinct districts of its own: the Algonquin district features skyscrapers and nightclubs, while Broker is a relatively poor district where the player first interacts with several of the city's criminals.

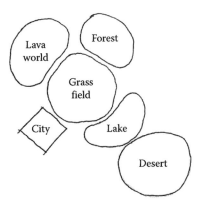

FIGURE 4.41 A theoretical game map showing districts.

If sandbox worlds do not have distinct districts, or if districts do not have their own unique gameplay elements, sandbox worlds can feel empty. In the unfortunate case of Santa Destroy from the game *No More Heroes*,[33] the city has many landmarks but few distinct areas of town. Instead, the entire city is a South Los Angeles-styled environment with a few disparate shops and locations to explore and take on missions. The game's action stages, on the other hand, occur in more distinct linear environments separated from this sandbox world. As reviewer Mark Bozon pointed out, "If the game was based only on the open world style, it would have been a pretty sizable disappointment."[34] If the unique character of the game's action levels were carried over to the sandbox world, the city might have not only been more fun to explore, but also more believable as an urban space.

Clearly, a successful sandbox world is based on how well a player can "read" and understand it. In many games, as in real-world architecture, lines of sight and understanding the point of view of players are of the utmost importance. What, however, is the designer to do with the spatial lessons we have discussed—largely based on real-world first-person points of view—if a game is in the third person, or even in two dimensions? In the next section, we will discuss how a player's point of view impacts gamespace.

WORKING WITH CAMERA VIEWS

Since the release of the German driving game *Nurburgring 1*[35] in 1975 and its American counterpart *Night Driver*[36] in 1976, first-person games have been a part of the gaming landscape. However, it was not until the early 1990s and the release of id Software's *Wolfenstein 3D*[37] that first-person games grew to the dominance they hold today. Indeed, many first-person games prior to *Wolfenstein* had abstract vector graphics or had to show static images rather than displaying a real-time textured 3D environment. Meanwhile, other games utilized 2D viewpoints from the side of the player character, known as *side scrolling* (Figure 4.42), or from above the player character, known as *top down* (Figure 4.43), to show the action of a game. There were even axonometric (popularly called *isometric*) games such as *Zaxxon*[38] and *Q*Bert*[39] (Figure 4.44).

In many modern game engines, point of view is dependent on where the designer places the *camera*, an object from which the player views gameplay. In a first-person game, the camera is located on a player object and given scripts that allow the player to look around freely. In a 2D game,

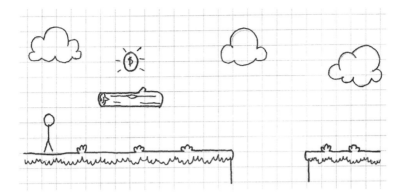

FIGURE 4.42 A 2D side-scrolling game. The view could be said to be a section of the gamespace.

the camera looks from either the top or side and often has options for perspective turned off, giving the camera an *orthographic* view. Axonometric and isometric views often feature cameras that look down on the player from up high. In this section, we will discuss how camera placement offers different limitations and opportunities for how gamespace is viewed.

3D Views

As most modern games are 3D, and since architecture is most often experienced by visitors in a three-dimensional fashion, we will discuss 3D views in games first. The two most popular viewpoints for 3D games are from the first-person view and the *third-person view,* where the camera

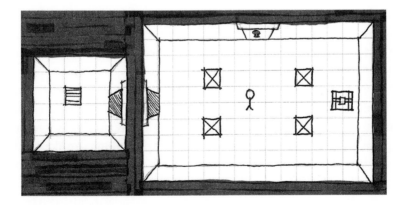

FIGURE 4.43 A 2D top-down game. The view could be said to be a plan of the gamespace.

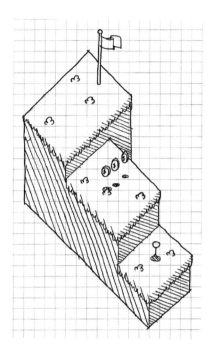

FIGURE 4.44   A 2D axonometric game.

is located outside of the player character's body. While the difference between these two viewpoints is often minimal, there are gameplay situations better suited to one or the other, which we will explore here.

First Person

First-person games are those where the camera is located in the "head" of the player character mesh (if the game uses a defined mesh for the player character at all) and action is viewed from the character's eye level. This is the most natural game view, as it is the view from which we view our own world (Figure 4.45).

It is in first-person games where level designers have full use of many of the architectural concepts discussed in this book. It is also where designers must use the most architectural tricks to capture players' attention, as the player has control over where the camera is looking, unlike in other game types. In *Half-Life 2* and games that have since taken cues from its use of non-passive story scenes, designers have to find ways to keep players near narrative events when NPCs act out a scene. Indeed, during narrative events and gameplay, designers must create lines of sight to direct player attention to details or direct their movement. The exterior contours of a

FIGURE 4.45 Cameras in first-person games are located at the eye level of a player character and allow for maximum use of sight lines.

gamespace are not visible from this point of view, so spatial size types, architectural weenies, and other design arrangements must be used to usher players through the gamespace.

From a gameplay perspective, first-person games can be very immersive, allowing the player to better take on the role of the game's protagonist. There are things that can also be limiting in first-person views, such as platform jumping and melee fighting mechanics that often benefit from a wider perspective.

Third Person

Third-person games are those in which the viewport camera is placed somewhere outside of the player character's body. Even among third-person games, there are many different varieties of view types. The first is *rotating camera*, which has the camera move around the player either in or out of his or her control. The second is *behind*, where the camera stays at a fixed point behind the player, typically by making the camera a *child object* of the player object. The third is *over-the-shoulder*, a semi-hybrid of first and third person where the camera is close behind the player character and allows the player to move the camera to look where the character is looking (Figure 4.46).

Third-person games offer many of the same spatial opportunities as first-person games, most notably the ability to create full 3D environments where lines of sight and other visual tricks can be used to direct player attention. They also offer opportunities to play with a camera's sense of perspective: by changing viewing angle options that many game engine third-person cameras have, designers can get trippy Tim Burton-esque angles and perspectives[40] (Figure 4.47). Third-person cameras are

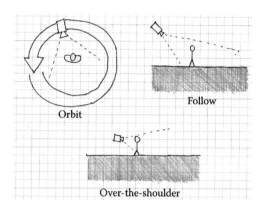

FIGURE 4.46 Three common types of third-person perspective in games.

also used in *fixed-perspective* games such as *Resident Evil*[41] or *Killer 7*[42] to create cinematic camera angles: shots from below, in front, close up, or others. These can greatly increase the dramatic effect of certain scenes, though often come at the cost of ease of control of the player character.

Third-person games offer additional opportunities for 3D game types that first-person games often struggle with. The most notable is platform jumping, since the player can see where the player character's feet will land. Designers often add a shadow underneath the player character to further help players find their way, such as in *3D platformers*. This is even

FIGURE 4.47 In this screenshot from the short game *The Nightmare Over Innsmouth*, prepared for a presentation at the Game Developers Conference (GDC) in China, I modified the camera lens angle to get a warped perspective effect.

more helpful in games with more acrobatic platforming, such as *The Prince of Persia: Sands of Time*,[43] where players can take time to line their character up with poles, swings, ledges, and other obstacles that the Prince can climb on. This game also features brawler-style melee combat where players must move in and out of groups of enemies, something that would be difficult to do in first person.

Third-person games suffer in the area that first-person games excel in: aiming. Camera AI is also notoriously difficult to code well, so cameras that "want to kill players" are a common problem in third-person games. Over-the-shoulder third person mitigates this to a point, though some line-of-sight spatial relationships are better understood in first person.

2D Views

Before good-looking 3D was technologically possible, 2D games dominated the industry. Visually, a textured surface in 2D was more believable than the vector-generated surfaces of many early 3D games. In terms of mechanics, many of the things one can do in a 3D game can be done in a 2D game: platform jumping, shooting, exploration, and others. Since the heyday of 2D was when gaming devices were not powerful enough to create realistic graphics, 3D games were long considered to have a presentational advantage over 2D games. Now, as 2D games are being revisited on modern gaming technology, they are home to presentational styles that mimic handmade arts such as painting, sculpting, crafts, and even knitting.

Games viewed at a 2D perspective have an interesting ability that most 3D games do not: showing the player things that are beyond the eyesight of the player character. In the *Metroid* series, it is common for players to see an upgrade hidden in several feet of rock waiting to be claimed, though the player character would logically have no idea it is there. This technique is very similar to the one employed by director Alfred Hitchcock to create *suspense* in his films.

A favorite example of Hitchcock's was to propose a scene where two people were sitting at a table, but the camera pans down to show that a bomb is underneath. That the diners do not know of the impending doom instills the scene with suspense for the audience that does get to see the bomb.[44] The game *Metroid Fusion*[45] utilizes this when an evil clone of heroine Samus Aran, the SA-X, walks through a hallway that is below the player. While Samus herself would possibly be able to hear the footsteps of the clone, the player gets a suspenseful view of how narrowly he or she is escaping death (Figure 4.48). Sadly, this technique

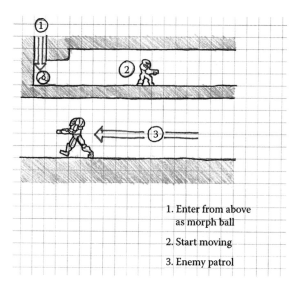

1. Enter from above
   as morph ball
2. Start moving
3. Enemy patrol

FIGURE 4.48   The *Metroid* series uses 2D perspectives to show players the location of hidden items and passages. Likewise, *Metroid Fusion* uses this perspective to create Hitchcock-esque scenes of suspense.

is underused in 2D games, though there are other view-specific techniques that apply to the two most popular types of 2D views: side scrolling and top down.

Side-Scrolling Space

Side-scrolling gamespaces are ones viewed from the side of the player character as though looking at a building section. Side scrollers can be some of the most spatially limiting level types, as there is not much one can design in the way of pathfinding. One's location in a side-scrolling level can also be difficult to track, especially in large open-world 2D games, typically termed Metroidvania for their use in the *Metroid* and *Castlevania* series.

The simplicity of side scrollers makes them effective at teaching their own mechanics: they put everything the player needs to know in a screenshot's distance from his or her avatar. Side-scrolling games often deal with action best understood from a "to the side" point of view, such as jumping, climbing, flying, and shooting. As such, it is important that when designing side-scrolling levels, there are very few "leaps of faith" that the player must take. Even large pitfall obstacles must show you their other end in one screenshot's width from the side where the player is standing (Figure 4.49). It is important for side scrollers to practice their own type

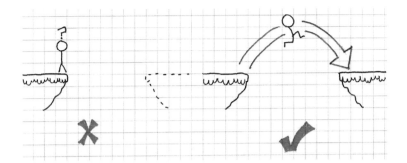

FIGURE 4.49   In 2D side-scrollers, designers should avoid adding "leaps of faith" to their games and always allow players to see the other side of obstacles from within one screen's width.

of *visual level metrics*. Beyond simply making obstacles easily understandable, enemies and enemy projectiles should always leave enough time from when they enter the screen to when they reach the player such that the player has a chance to see and avoid them (Figure 4.50).

Unfortunately, side scrollers render many of the pathfinding and orientation methods we have discussed thus far useless. There are some, however, that experiment with not only height and width, but also depth by putting 2D level environments in layers that can be moved through forward and backward. Games such as *Shantae: Risky's Revenge*[46] utilize this to give in-game villages a more realistic feel. Mazes in this game are more complex, as the player must not only move through left/right (x) and up/down (y) axes, but also forward/backward (z) (Figure 4.51).

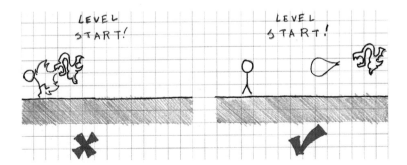

FIGURE 4.50   Enemies and their projectiles in 2D side-scrollers should leave enough time from when they enter the screen to when they reach the player so that the player has a chance to avoid them.

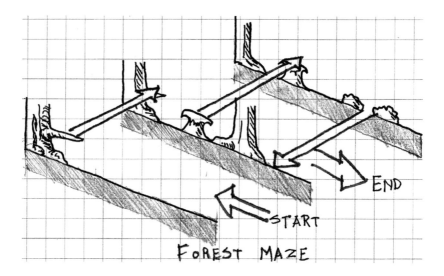

FIGURE 4.51   Many environments in *Shantae: Risky's Revenge* allow the player to move forward and backward through layers of 2D side-scrolling environments. These add another level of depth to in-game mazes and dungeons not common in many side-scrolling games.

Top-Down Space

Top-down gamespaces are ones where gameplay is viewed from above the player character as though looking at a building plan. Indeed, many early games resembled maps and building plans. On one hand, top-down games offer little in terms of creating sight lines and other things that are common in 3D games. However, they excel at creating opportunities for orientation, as many gamespaces can be understood in plan. These spaces can be understood as following the cardinal directions of north, south, east, and west, so devices like landmarks allow players to find their way through large gamespaces (e.g., "I am north of Hyrule Castle").

Like side scrollers, top-down games share the potential for Hitchcock-style suspense due to their ability to show players things that the player character cannot necessarily see (Figure 4.52). Also like side scrollers, enemies should leave enough time between appearing on-screen and when they hit the player such that the player has a chance to move.

Top-down games often feature mechanics that are best enacted in an expansive world, such as exploring or interacting with NPCs, though there are certainly exceptions. Top-down games, like side scrollers, are also well suited to mechanics that involve lining the player character up with a target such as shooting, sword fighting, or even rudimentary jumping. On

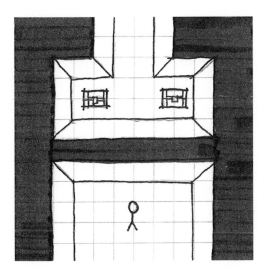

FIGURE 4.52 Like side-scrolling games, top-down games can show players things that the player character cannot necessarily see.

the other hand, top-down games tend to be less reliant on reaction-based action than side scrollers, so more environmental information can be held off-screen (Figure 4.53). In fact, withholding the entirety of a landscape or architectural feature in a top-down gamespace may actually invite players to explore further.

With some creativity in how level geometry and backgrounds are drawn, top-down 2D games can even include the rewarding vistas that 3D games specialize in. *Parallax scrolling* is a technique where layers of sprites on-screen move at different speeds when the screen scrolls. It is used in 2D games to make elements on-screen appear as though they exist in a 3D space, especially in side-scrolling platformers. In top-down games, parallax scrolling gives the impression that backgrounds are far below the actual gameplay space. An early example of this includes the Mountain of Ordeals in *Final Fantasy IV*, where forests below scroll independently of the geometry around the player. Despite the primitive graphic style of that game, featuring particularly blocky levels, the effect communicates the idea of a tall mountain well. A similar effect was achieved early in the 2016 indie game *Hyper Light Drifter*, where players could see a dead giant slumped over a distant mountain peak while standing on a cliff. As players move from area to area, they eventually reach the dead giant, showing how top-down spaces can create 3D-like views and be effective storytelling tools.

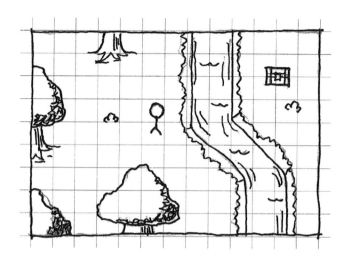

FIGURE 4.53   Since many top-down games involve exploring expansive worlds, information can be withheld off-screen from players. Giving players incomplete information, such as showing part of a landmass or river in one screenshot, invites players to explore further.

Now that we have explored the opportunities present in both 3D and 2D game views, we will look at those present in a type of gamespace that straddles the line between the two.

Axonometric/Isometric Views

In the early 1980s, developers utilized a new game view type—the axonometric game—to create the impression of 3D space while utilizing art that was still actually 2D. Following early axonometric games like *Zaxxon* and *Q*Bert*, this view continued to be popular in games from *Knight Lore*[47] to *Starcraft*.[48] In games, this point of view is often referred to as *isometric*, as that is the type of axonometric projection used to create the game art.

In classic axonometric games, the game is typically viewed without perspectival distortion; that is, the objects on-screen are not on sight lines that meet at a vanishing point. While purely axonometric images can create a dramatic 3D effect, they also come at the cost of depth perception for the player. Axonometric drawings are notorious for the creation of optical illusions such as that shown in Figure 4.54. When constructing axonometric gamespaces, it is important to show the *vertical relationships* between surfaces very clearly so players are not confused by an object's position in space. Likewise, it is important to *occlude*, or disable the rendering of,

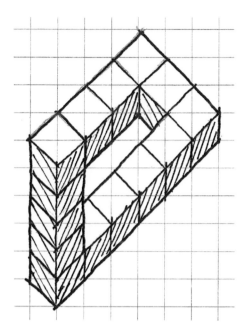

FIGURE 4.54 Axonometric drawings can easily disorient the player if not drawn properly. When making these kinds of gamespaces, make sure you find ways to show vertical spatial relationships.

foreground objects in these spaces so players do not lose their character when they move behind structures.

Isometric as a term has also been adopted by modern 3D game developers to describe a camera that is positioned at an angle above the player character looking down, with perspective options enabled on the camera object itself. This type of perspective is actually described as *three-point perspective*, as edges meet not only at horizontal vanishing points common to two-point perspective, but also at a vertical vanishing point below the level. Unlike actual isometric or axonometric views, changes in height are easily perceived thanks to the perspective option of the camera. This type of view, in both classic and 3D versions, allows for both a detailed 3D environment and for the designer to show the player things that the player character cannot see.

Axonometric views can make it difficult for players to orient themselves in space. Unlike top-down 2D views, the player cannot benefit from the use of cardinal directions. And since the camera is facing downward, they also cannot make use of sight lines, so as much information should be on-screen as possible, unless the world is an expansive one similar to those found in top-down 2D games. However, isometric games allow designers to make dramatic use of spatial size types, as players can easily see how their character relates to the environment around them. Still possible is creating a sense of claustrophobia with narrow spaces or a sense of agoraphobia with prospect spaces. In fact, these spaces' three-point perspective allow for the use of rhythmically arranged vertical elements to create a sense of *epic hugeness* in prospect spaces—creating a sense of *vertigo* as the player looks from the camera down at his or her character (Figure 4.55).

Now that we have discussed camera views and how they correlate with player perceptions of space in games, we will explore one last basic spatial concept. This concept will help us take an element unique to games and utilize it to toy with how a player perceives the nature of space around him or her in games.

ENEMIES AS ALTERNATIVE ARCHITECTURE

In *Chambers for a Memory Palace*, Lyndon and Moore describe the concept of *allies*: statues, short columns, and other architectural elements that are of similar scale to an occupant.[49] Beyond iconographic significance, they point out that allies in a piece of architecture can make spaces more inviting. In games, non-player characters fulfill many of these functions

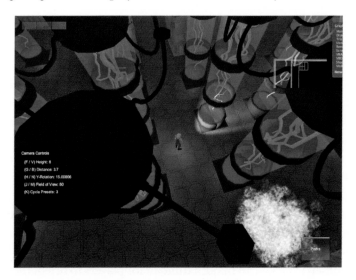

FIGURE 4.55 In this screenshot, regularly spaced biotanks are used in this lab environment to create a sense of vertigo from the camera down to the player character. This emphasizes the verticality of the gamespace, even though the player is viewing the game from a third-person perspective.

and often have their own gameplay reason for being in a space, sending the player on quests, guarding doorways, etc. NPCs that instigate quests often prohibit players from moving through a space until specific tasks are accomplished. As such, NPCs can help designers drive player interaction with the game world.

One key difference between gamespaces and real architecture is that enemies, not just allies, can also inhabit gamespaces. Enemies offer level designers a unique type of architectural ally in their antagonistic relationship with the player. Where friendly NPCs may simply block a space until the player helps them, enemies block spaces by threatening to damage the player. As the player cannot directly pass through enemies without risking damage, game enemies can be seen as *alternative architecture*. In the train station environment at the beginning of *Half-Life 2*, alien soldiers are used as alternative architecture. While many games use locked or non-interactive doors to show a player they cannot enter a room, *Half-Life 2* places sentries throughout a train station. If the player tries to pass, he or she is shoved back. Further attempts by the unarmed player are met with the aliens brandishing their weapons, an effective deterrent. Using interactive enemies rather than plain locked doors does several important things for the game: it builds *Half-Life 2*'s dystopian narrative without exposition, it directs player movement through the station, and it creates the feeling that this station is populated, just as Lyndon and Moore argue is the role of architectural allies.

Using enemies as architectural elements of a level can be a powerful tool for level designers when paired with narrow space as well. In the original *Resident Evil*, for example, zombies fill the narrow hallways of the Spencer Mansion. As they approach players, they block off progress through hallways while shrinking the space the player can safely occupy. Players in this situation must decide whether to risk running past the zombie or shoot it.

As the *Resident Evil* zombies demonstrate, even enemies with simple AI can be powerful spatial tools. In his essay "The Rules of Horror: Procedural Adaptation in *Clock Tower*, *Resident Evil*, and *Dead Rising*," Matthew Weise describes a concept he calls the *shrinking fortress* in zombie films.[50] In shrinking fortress scenarios, such as the one in *Night of the Living Dead*,[51] the protagonists are surrounded by a large group of enemies, which continually advance on them and capture once-safe territory. In *Night of the Living Dead*, for example, survivors fight to protect themselves within a farmhouse. Eventually, the first floor of the house is overrun, and the heroes must retreat into the basement. This scenario can play out in games through story events that cut off previously accessible areas.

An even more powerful application of the shrinking fortress can occur in real time. Strong or difficult-to-kill enemies may be used to *herd* the player where the designer would like him or her to go (Figure 4.56). For this tactic to work, the enemies should be in overwhelming numbers, have powerful attacks, or be difficult to kill. A scenario like this often requires the level space itself to be large, though swarms of enemies will create the feeling of narrow space. Applications like these demonstrate the power that level designers have to use enemies, NPCs, and other game elements not traditionally viewed as architecture for architectural purposes.

SUMMARY

In this chapter, we have explored some basic spatial types that we can use to form our game worlds. From micro-scaled articulations of additive and subtractive space to world structures such as sandboxes, hubs, and classic gamespaces, we now have a set of spatial configurations to create using the game engine tools discussed in Chapter 3. We also know how to cater gamespace to the kinds of gameplay experiences we wish them to house through spatial size types. To pace these elements out or study how they interact with one another, we can utilize molecule and proximity diagrams. We can also organize large worlds of gameplay through urban

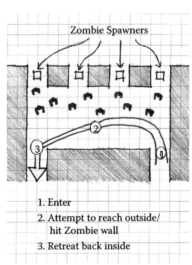

FIGURE 4.56 Enemies may be used to herd players where designers want them to go. For this to work, a large number of difficult-to-kill enemies should be used.

design principles. On the player end, we can cater player experiences of our gamespaces to the point of view they will have through in-game cameras. Lastly, we can use not only friendly NPCs, but also enemies to populate our game worlds, enhance the spatial types we have discussed, and direct player action.

In Chapter 5, we will discuss more directly how to create game levels that teach the mechanics of a game to players and reinforce these mechanics through the entirety of a game.

EXERCISES

1. **Drawing exercise**: Draw a figure–ground image of a level in a video game or a level that you are making. Try to capture how the solid positive masses in a space define their own negative spaces.

2. **Digital exercise**: Graybox an arrival. Use spatial size contrasts or other elements (light, shadow, etc.) so that players know they have arrived in a distinct space.

3. **Writing prompt**: Find a game or level that follows a labyrinth structure, one that is like a maze, and one that is like a rhizome. Describe each and how their worlds and levels are constructed to fit these types.

4. **Digital exercise**: Graybox a narrow space, intimate space, and prospect space for a game you are creating. Describe what type of activity might occur in those spaces.

5. **Drawing exercise**: Draw molecule diagrams for levels that fit these themes: "battle for the high point," "central hub," "one way," "leading with hints."

6. **Digital exercise**: Create a graybox level from a molecule diagram (such as one you drew in the last exercise).

7. **Drawing exercise**: Play a game with a sandbox-style environment. Create a diagram map of the environment showing these elements: Landmarks, Nodes, Edges, Paths, Districts.

ENDNOTES

1. Watanave, Hidenori. Archidemo: The Museum of the Globe. Archidemo. http://archidemo.blogspot.com/2008/07/museum-of-globe.html (accessed February 20, 2013).

2. Watanave, Hidenori. *Archidemo: Oscar Niemeyer in Second Life*. Archidemo. http://archidemo.blogspot.com/p/oscar-niemeyer-in-second-life.html (accessed February 20, 2013).

3. *Second Life*. Linden Research (developer and publisher), June 23, 2003. Online virtual world.

4. Frederick, Matthew. *101 Things I Learned in Architecture School*. Cambridge, MA: MIT Press, 2007, p. 3.

5. Frederick, Matthew. *101 Things I Learned in Architecture School*. Cambridge, MA: MIT Press, 2007, p. 6.

6. Frederick, Matthew. *101 Things I Learned in Architecture School*. Cambridge, MA: MIT Press, 2007, p. 4.

7. Hildebrand, Grant. *Origins of Architectural Pleasure*. Berkeley, CA: University of California Press, 1999, p. 95.

8. Lyndon, Donlyn, and Charles Willard Moore. *Chambers for a Memory Palace*. Cambridge, MA: MIT Press, 1994, p. 212.

9. Borries, Friedrich von, Steffen P. Walz, and Matthias Böttger. *Space Time Play Computer Games, Architecture and Urbanism: The Next Level*. Basel: Birkhauser, 2007.

10. Salen, Katie, and Eric Zimmerman. *Rules of Play: Game Design Fundamentals*. Cambridge, MA: MIT Press, 2003, p. 97.

11. *Slender: The Eight Pages*. Parsec Productions (developer and publisher), June 26, 2012. PC game.

12. Deleuze, Gilles, and Félix Guattari. *A Thousand Plateaus: Capitalism and Schizophrenia*. Minneapolis, MN: University of Minnesota Press, 1987.

13. Koh, Chuen-Ferng. Chapter 1: Internet-Rhyzome. *Internet: Toward a Holistic Ontology*. http://wwwmcc.murdoch.edu.au/ReadingRoom/VID/jfk/thesis/ch1.htm (accessed February 26, 2013).

14. *ActiveWorlds*. ActiveWorlds (developer and publisher), 1997. Online virtual world.

15. Jakobsson, Mikael. Activity Flow Architecture: Environment Design in ActiveWorlds and EverQuest. In Borries, Friedrich von, Steffen P. Walz, and Matthias Böttger. *Space Time Play Computer Games, Architecture and Urbanism: The Next Level*. Basel: Birkhauser, 2007, pp. 164–167.

16. Totten, Christopher W. Designing Better Levels Through Human Survival Instincts. Gamasutra—The Art & Business of Making Games. http://www.gamasutra.com/view/feature/6411/designing_better_levels_through_.php?print=1 (accessed February 27, 2013).

17. *Batman: Arkham Asylum* Video—Silent Knight Challenge Mode Extended Cut | GameTrailers. GameTrailers. http://www.gametrailers.com/videos/dfhan4/batman--arkham-asylum-silent-knight-challenge-mode-extended-cut (accessed February 27, 2013).

18. Hildebrand, Grant. *Origins of Architectural Pleasure*. Berkeley, CA: University of California Press, 1999, p. 22.

19. McMillan, Luke, and Nassib Azar. Gamasutra—Features—The Metrics of Space: Molecule Design. Gamasutra. http://www.gamasutra.com/view/-feature/184783/the_metrics_of_space_molecule_.php (accessed February 27, 2013).

20. Salen, Katie, and Eric Zimmerman. *Rules of Play: Game Design Fundamentals.* Cambridge, MA: MIT Press, 2003, p. 353.
21. *Grand Theft Auto IV.* Rockstar North (developer), Rockstar Games (publisher), 2008. Xbox 360 game.
22. *Half-Life 2: Episode 2.* Valve Corporation (developer and publisher), 2007. PC game. Developer commentary.
23. Lynch, Kevin. *The Image of the City.* Cambridge, MA: MIT Press, 1960.
24. Lynch, Kevin. *The Image of the City.* Cambridge, MA: MIT Press, 1960, p. 2.
25. Lynch, Kevin. *The Image of the City.* Cambridge, MA: MIT Press, 1960, p. 48.
26. Lynch, Kevin. *The Image of the City.* Cambridge, MA: MIT Press, 1960, p. 47.
27. Lynch, Kevin. *The Image of the City.* Cambridge, MA: MIT Press, 1960, p. 72.
28. *Bully.* Rockstar Vancouver (developer), Rockstar Games (publisher), 2006. Playstation 2 game.
29. Campbell, Joseph. *The Hero with a Thousand Faces.* 2nd ed. Princeton, NJ: Princeton University Press, 1968.
30. Campbell, Joseph. *The Hero with a Thousand Faces.* 2nd ed. Princeton, NJ: Princeton University Press, 1968, p. 23.
31. Hildebrand, Grant. *Origins of Architectural Pleasure.* Berkeley, CA: University of California Press, 1999.
32. Heaney, Seamus. *Beowulf: A New Verse Translation.* New York, NY: Farrar, Straus, and Giroux, 2000.
33. *No More Heroes.* Grasshopper Manufacture (developer), Ubisoft (publisher), 2008. Nintendo Wii game.
34. Bozon, Mark. No More Heroes Review—IGN. Video Games, Wikis, Cheats, Walkthroughs, Reviews, News & Videos—IGN. http://www.ign.com/articles/2008/01/22/no-more-heroes-review (accessed March 6, 2013).
35. *Nurburgring 1.* Reiner Foerst GmbH (developer and publisher), 1975. Arcade game.
36. *Night Driver.* Atari (developer and publisher), 1976. Arcade game.
37. *Wolfenstein 3D.* id Software (developer), Apogee Software (publisher), 1992. PC game.
38. *Zaxxon.* Sega (developer and publisher), 1982. Arcade game.
39. *Q*Bert.* Gottlieb (developer and publisher), 1982. Arcade game.
40. *The Nightmare Over Innsmouth.* Chris Totten (developer), 2011. Unreleased PC game.
41. *Resident Evil.* Capcom (developer and publisher), 1996. Sony Playstation game.
42. *Killer 7.* Grasshopper Manufacture (developer), Capcom (publisher), 2005. Nintendo Gamecube game.
43. *The Prince of Persia: Sands of Time.* Ubisoft Montreal (developer), Ubisoft (publisher), 2003. Nintendo Gamecube game.
44. Alfred Hitchcock on Mastering Cinematic Tension. YouTube. http://www.youtube.com/watch?v=DPFsuc_M_3E (accessed March 7, 2013).

45. *Metroid Fusion*. Nintendo R&D1 (developer), Nintendo (publisher), 2002. Game Boy Advance game.

46. *Shantae: Risky's Revenge*. Tim and Chris Stamper (developers), Ultimate Play The Game (publisher), 1984. Sinclair ZX Spectrum game.

47. *Knight Lore*. Way Forward Technologies (developer and publisher), 2010. Nintendo DSiWare game.

48. *Starcraft*. Blizzard Entertainment (developer and publisher), 1998. PC game.

49. Lyndon, Donlyn, and Charles Willard Moore. *Chambers for a Memory Palace*. Cambridge, MA: MIT Press, 1994, p. 164.

50. Weise, Matthew. The Rules of Horror: Procedural Adaptation in *Clock Tower, Resident Evil*, and *Dead Rising*. In Perron, Bernard. *Horror Video Games: Essays on the Fusion of Fear and Play*. Jefferson, NC: McFarland & Co., 2009, pp. 238–266.

51. *Night of the Living Dead*. Film. Directed by George A. Romero. Pittsburgh, PA: The Walter Reade Organization, 1968.

52. Michael, Evans. An Illustrated Fragment of Peraldus's Summa of Vice: Harleian MS 3244. *Journal of the Warburg and Courtauld Institutes* 45 (1982): 14–68. http://www.jstor.org/stable/750966 (accessed February 26, 2013).

INDUSTRY PERSPECTIVES: ALT CTRL LEVEL DESIGN

Jerry Belich

Experimental Game and Experience Designer

INTRODUCTION

Writing about level design, architecture, or space is difficult for me because of the nature of how my game designs usually manifest; which is, I suspect, why Chris challenged me to explore this topic. I create what are most often referred to as alternative controller (alt ctrl), experimental, immersive, or just hardware games. These are games that still harness computing power but with experiences that manifest at least one foot in physical space, necessitating more of an outside-in approach to their spatial design as the actual human players are my "avatars." To give you a better idea of what alt ctrl games are, take a look at the series of three images in Figure 1. The first shows an interactive game called *Please Stand By* made to emulate a 1950s television set. You play by turning the knobs, adjusting the antennas (or rabbit ears as they were colloquially known) and even striking the side of the

FIGURE 1   An alt ctrl game made to emulate a television.

TV! It is a great illusion, but you can see in the second image the relatively simple combination of wiring that provides input from the controls, and a Mac Mini running the software seen booting in image three.

I suspect that most other game designers approach the problem of level design from the inside-out, the inside being a digital space that, as the mathematical confines are expanded, provides more room for exploration by the equally digital avatars inhabiting the space. Expansion is virtually limitless and yet it never touches our physical world space; it stays contained, discrete, firmly set in the "other world" context. Because of my use of immersive technology (a combination of materials, electronics, and software as shown above) to create games and experiences, instead of terms like level design I generally opt for play space design as an analog; fitting, considering the often analog nature of my work. I occasionally drop in other flavor words like "interactive" or "immersive" depending on context and needed clarity.

In fact, let's clarify something before we go on: although much of my work falls into the "game" category, some may only have game-like elements, be interactive like a toy, or merely reactive. I'll use the umbrella term "experience" for my designs and "audience" or "player" for the consumers of an experience. Everything I talk about applies across my work, game or not.

For the sake of time and space, I'm going to focus on two specific topics as I describe how I approached a number of my experiences: boundaries and experience bleed.

BOUNDARIES

I look at boundaries as a bi-directional challenge. I need to determine the boundaries of my design in the play space and also be aware of the boundaries the real world places on my design (I'm careful not to label these "limitations"). Where should the experience start and end? What constraints do the boundaries of reality provide me? As you hopefully have learned already, constraints are a friend in finding your design path, circuitous as it may sometimes be. Digital games have no set boundaries within virtual space, but a hard boundary when it comes to our physical reality. For instance, if you wanted to limit the perception of the player in your digital play space, you would have to design and implement a fog-of-war or view distance feature, where I might be able to simply block your view. A related example…

THE BOUNDARIES OF CYLINDRUS

Imagine a computer screen wrapped around a cylinder where the edges meet to create a continuous display; a video cylinder if you will. Now toss on a simple multi-player arcade game such as Atari's *Combat* (tanks), and place your players around the cylinder, each holding a wireless joystick. That is *Cylindrus* (Figure 2). The boundaries of the digital play space are the cylinder itself and the boundaries of the play space are a concentric circle around the game where the players observe and physically move (or more commonly dart). The affordance of a three-dimensional object in real space is that you can't see all sides of it at once, limiting perception and in this case generating per player fog-of-war on a single display! The arcade style play is familiar to most people, requiring little consideration to experience bleed, which we'll talk about next.

EXPERIENCE BLEED

Those in print media know that bleed is about accommodating something that is inexact in order to get the desired result. To print perfectly edge-to-edge, you print beyond the edges and trim down as needed. When designing an experience, even purely digital, it is important to realize that it doesn't have a hard cutoff, and certainly not where you would expect.

FIGURE 2   *Cylindrus* with two wireless controllers.

The two primary factors in experience bleed are your audience and their context when your experience is introduced or removed. The former, your audience, is out of your control once they become a part of the scenario (your control involves whether or not they ever encounter your experience). The latter, your audience's context, is where you have the most potential for leverage. The moment they decide to play your game their current context will begin to bleed into the one you designed for them, and your designed context will bleed into theirs after their experience ends. Designing in physical space further enhances this effect. By taking this into account you can better control how your experience is affected and even deliberately extend it deeper into your audience's life in a very meaningful way. You can better control the cutoff. Another project example!

THE EXPERIENCE BLEED IN *A.F.T.E.R.G.L.O.W.*

A.F.T.E.R.G.L.O.W. is a physical–electronic game built within a 1970s briefcase. It is modeled with a Soviet-era aesthetic and reuses interface materials, such as the rotary from an old telephone, to enhance the feeling that it is an artifact of a time where spies and espionage were a fact of life (Figure 3). The game itself provides an ultra-minimal display as a ring of LEDs mimicking the layout of the rotary, only viewable through a scope that extends from the open briefcase (an extreme use of boundaries in this case). Closed, it looks identical to any old briefcase, but once open, it immediately feels dangerous, certainly something you wouldn't want to be caught at an airport with!

The experience bleed in *A.F.T.E.R.G.L.O.W.* is extremely deliberate, attempting to create a hard break from reality when beginning play but structured off-boarding when play is finished. This occurs in two ways: first, a thermal printer (keeping with the retro aesthetic) creates an artifact of your play by printing your score and initials (input through the rotary), providing players something shareable and to remind them of the experience. This leads players to the second intervention as the printout further reveals that there is a high score Twitter account that is updated if you are in the top ten. Suddenly the player has standing in a wider community that has also played the game, perhaps inspiring competition and further play.

UTOPIA **ESCAPE ROOM**

Escape rooms (or any live-action game spaces) are an extreme example of what we've already outlined. They encompass more than the volume of an object like a briefcase, but an entire environment like a room, often multiple rooms. I designed and installed a room in Minneapolis, MN (along with my brilliant design partner David Pisa) called *Utopia*, a technology-heavy experience that runs autonomously throughout the hour of play, with a

FIGURE 3   *A.F.T.E.R.G.L.O.W.* briefcase.

heavy dystopian theme. Though I could write a book on that design alone, let's consider how it applies in our case.

Generally, the boundaries of escape rooms are tightly defined by the architecture of the space: the walls, doors, ceiling, and floor. Initially the boundaries in *Utopia* (Figure 4) are stark and uniform, but through play the boundaries begin to give way and the audience gets pulled deeper into the mystery and immersed in the heavy theme of revealing: the chaos behind order, the grime behind what seems clean, and the malevolence behind what seems benign. The boundaries communicate where play can take place and provide opportunity for discovery.

The boundaries which separate reality from the play space are where we can observe the effects of experience bleed and how important it is to compensate or manipulate it to improve the overall experience. What is unique to escape rooms and live-action games spaces is that this is affected by time. An audience will be bringing their current context forward with them. Their worries, stresses, plans for later, how they might handle an upcoming social situation, the tacos they just ate, everything! A common problem I've experienced and witnessed in other escape room audience

FIGURE 4   First view of the *Utopia* escape room upon entering.

members is a loss of play time when first entering the room and beginning the game. I estimate up to a five-minute loss of functional play time, over 8% of the playtime in a sixty-minute game! When cutting prints you start with the definition of the space, then you ensure the bleed goes beyond that definition so the cut doesn't remove important content. Here our definition is sixty minutes of time, so we want the cut to include the entire period, not fifty-five minutes and some waste.

So what do you do about it? Don't stop at the easy boundaries. The game may only begin once inside that room, but the experience can start when the audience enters the building, or even sooner. By applying various amounts of theming leading up to a core experience, you can pull more and more focus from the audience to what they are about to be doing rather than what they have been doing. For an escape room, perhaps the lobby can tie into the theme of the game, or the game master can perform rather than simply read a short blurb describing the scenario. Reminder emails or phone calls can also tie into the narrative while still providing useful information. By the time the audience begins, they should already be focused and ready to live completely within the world you created.

CHOOSATRON

This final example is a bit different from the rest. The *Choosatron* is an interactive fiction thermal printer (Figure 5). Imagine a classic choose-your-own-adventure book that simply prints out the next bit of story when you

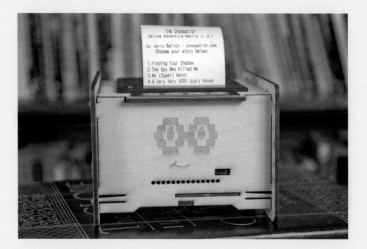

FIGURE 5   The *Choosatron* with the story menu freshly printed.

make a choice, so you end up with a long strip of paper representing your particular path through the variable adventure. While the others focus on building particular narratives and have clear connections (or boundaries) with the surrounding space, *Choosatron* is more of a platform because it can hold many different kinds of stories. As the designer, I can't know what story someone might play when considering how it exists within a play space.

This is important because the driving force of the design became about removing the boundaries between the experience and the physical space the *Choosatron* inhabits, primarily accomplished by removing any evidence of a digital interface or output, like a screen. Physical buttons and paper are how you interact, make decisions, and play. Usually reading is a solitary activity and reading over someone's shoulder a cultural taboo. Even if you were playing a narrative game on your phone, can you imagine how invasive it would feel to realize someone was peeking in to see what happened next?

The paper, especially the act of it printing, is inviting. When standing nearby or in line to play, the noise of the paper and rustle of paper invite onlookers and the device itself sheds the cultural contract for privacy that a mobile device typically promises. All of this provides a positive experience bleed where players feel willing to engage with each other's experiences, providing opinions or warnings about choices only meant for one. This also fuels the strongest part of the bleed, the artifact that players take with them. After a story ends, they tear off and keep the paper, often excited to compare experiences with others or simply share them with friends later on.

The experience lingers and provides an anchorpoint for a memory they can continue to enjoy.

Although my games may be more deeply grounded in the physical world, I hope this helps to show how experience is never confined, even in your all-digital game world. I challenge you to think about the boundaries that you design within, create yourself, or attempt to break and to consider the experience bleed from before your audience enters your world to well after they leave it.

CHAPTER 5

Communicating through Environment Art

To bring his organizing powers into fullest play, the painter must haul his perceptions out of their limbo and annex them to his plan.

—LEO STEINBERG[1]

As systems of communication, game levels utilize sensory information to connect with players. As games are now, this occurs primarily through visual and auditory means and through limited applications of touch.[2] In this chapter, we focus on the visual power of gamespaces, how it can be used to teach, and how it can control a player's understanding of a game.

As we discussed earlier, one of the most important goals of game levels is the *adjustment of behavior* in game players. In earlier chapters, we discussed how modular game assets save time. In this chapter, we will look at how environment art helps designers inform players about the cause-and-effect procedures within a game.

As the above quote from art critic Leo Steinberg points out, visual components of a work must be carefully planned and laid out, rather than haphazardly placed, to be effective communication tools. In this chapter, you will learn about different teaching methods present in modern games. You will also learn how to utilize art assets in such a way that the player associates them with meaningful information, and how they can be organized to teach players through direct or indirect methods. Lastly, we will explore how to use visual information to turn game levels into spaces of information that create feelings of certainty and uncertainty in players.

What you will learn in this chapter:

Teaching theories for game levels

Symbols and visual design in games

Architectural forms and types

Controlling information in memory palaces

TEACHING THEORIES FOR GAME LEVELS

In order to understand the spatial tools we will use to adjust player behavior, we must first understand the theories supporting these methodologies. As we have seen and will continue to see throughout the book, learning from other fields is an important part of the ongoing development of game design. This section will not cover how to construct a tutorial level (that will come later), but it will describe some psychological concepts that inform how visual communication occurs in games. Throughout this chapter, we will reinforce three models of teaching commonly considered by game designers—B.F. Skinner's *operant conditioning* model, the *Montessori method*, and *constructivism*—as the framework of our visual communication methodology.

Behavior Theory and Operant Conditioning

Behavior theory, also referred to as *behaviorism*, is the study of observable behaviors in organisms. John B. Watson established behaviorism as a school of thought in psychology with his 1913 article "Psychology as the Behaviorist Views It."[3] Ivan Pavlov and his famous studies into *classical conditioning*—wherein he would ring a bell before feeding his dogs, thereby causing them to salivate every time he rang a bell—were major influences for behaviorists.[4]

A major evolution of behaviorism came in 1937 when psychologist B.F. Skinner coined the term *operant conditioning*. Skinner rejected Watson and Pavlov's earlier emphasis on reflexive or involuntary actions and "attributed a more active role to the learning subject."[5] Operant conditioning involves changing voluntary actions of subjects via *positive and negative reinforcements*, as well as *punishments*.

In Skinner's experiments with his *operant conditioning chamber* (widely known as the *Skinner box*) he had rats pull a lever in response to a specific stimulus, typically an auditory or visual signal (Figure 5.1). In the version of the experiment for studying positive reinforcement, when the rat pulled the lever in response to the signal, it would receive a food pellet as a *reward*. However, pulling the lever at the wrong time would elicit a punishment, often in the form of an electric shock to the rat's feet. The box could also study negative reinforcement, which teaches the subject to perform actions to remove unfavorable conditions. In the Skinner box experiment, a lever could be used to stop negative stimuli such as mild electric shocks or loud noises, thus strengthening the behavior of pulling the lever in the rats.[6]

Skinner also wrote considerably for the field of education. The current system of grading students—rewarding success with good marks and punishing failure with poor ones—is often seen as an extension of his philosophies. Skinner himself argued for a methodology that avoided emphasis on lectures or tutorials, but rather on breaking large tasks into a series of smaller ones. As each task is performed, correct actions are reinforced so the student learns the proper way of performing his or her tasks.[7] This methodology is also commonly applied to games that seek to do away with extensive explanatory tutorials. When teaching mechanics in the first few levels of a game, such as is done in *Super Meat Boy*, gameplay mechanics are broken into individual tasks that are reinforced and repeated. As we saw in Chapter 2, *Super Meat Boy*[8] focuses its first few short levels on individual mechanics—jumping, running, wall-jumping, introducing obstacles, etc.—that eventually create an extensive knowledge of Meat Boy's capabilities as a playable character.

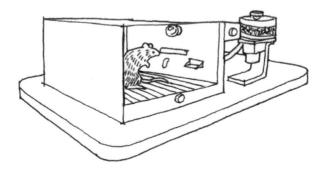

FIGURE 5.1   A typical operant conditioning chamber, or Skinner box. The box is outfitted with devices for several types of experiments, including lights and loudspeakers to be used as stimuli, a food dispenser, a lever, and an electric grid to deliver shocks through the floor.

Skinner-esque reinforcement and teaching models are commonplace in many game levels and puzzles. In many games, solving puzzles or defeating enemies are met with in-game rewards such as resources or new items. Designers often structure game scenes in such a way that players must remove negative conditions—poison gas, constantly spawning enemies, or enemy occupation—to make the territory safe for passage or to continue the narrative (Figure 5.2).

The Skinner box model can be used to describe the repetition of one singular action over and over again. As such, it has been used as a derogatory term for games in the mobile free-to-play market that require players to wait extended periods of time to do simple actions, as in *The Simpsons: Tapped Out* or *Tiny Tower*. For our purposes, we will look at operant conditioning as part of a larger palette of communication devices for educating players on how or when to utilize game mechanics.

Montessori Method

The world didn't want him to fail here. It was pushing him, but gently.

—*THOMAS WAS ALONE*, MIKE BITHELL[9]

Game design is a second-order design problem,[10] meaning that designers are communicating with players indirectly through their games. In this way, we can view our game levels as *prepared environments* of interactive

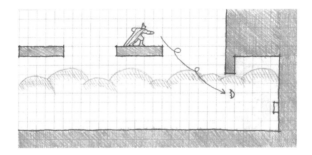

FIGURE 5.2 An early area in *Batman: Arkham Asylum* demonstrates how a negative reinforcement puzzle can transform a space. When the player initially enters a room in the Asylum's Intensive Treatment facility, it is filled with poison gas, requiring Batman to leap on catwalks to progress. When the gas is removed, the room becomes open for regular circulation travel. If viewed in terms of territories, players encounter this area as one that has been corrupted by an enemy and must reclaim it. As one of the first areas to use batarangs for solving puzzles, it is also an important gameplay tutorial.

objects for players to utilize. This is an important distinction for understanding our next educational model for level design: the Montessori Method.

The Montessori Method was developed by Italian physician and educator Maria Montessori beginning in 1897. It emphasizes the senses as a medium for absorbing information that is then interpreted by the intellect into solutions to practical problems. Current Montessori standards enforced by the American Montessori Society (AMS) and Association Montessori International (AMI) highlight the classroom as a free learning environment prepared by a teacher, with multiage learning groups, choices of activities, and uninterrupted work and interaction time.[11,12] Montessori education was accompanied by a set of *Montessori sensorial materials* that included blocks, cylinders, and other objects that would teach students how to utilize their senses to organize or arrange the objects (Figure 5.3). Similar objects, the Froebel gifts, were used in Friedrich Froebel's original *Kindergarten* in Bad Blankenburg, Thuringia, Germany. Frank Lloyd Wright famously received a set in his youth, citing the gifts as a major influence on his own architectural education.[13]

In his book *Persuasive Games*, Ian Bogost suggests the Montessori Method as an alternative view of how games teach players the traditional

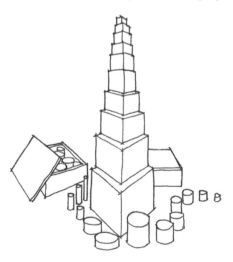

FIGURE 5.3 Two of the Montessori sensorial material sets: the pink tower and the colored cylinders. These objects can be interacted with as the child likes, allowing many types of matching, stacking, and arranging activities. Each object's visual characteristics are meant to reinforce correct arrangements of the objects, such as big to small, tall to short, etc.

behaviorism-centered rhetoric.[14] Montessori views of games, he argues, support the development of player skill and problem solving over the course of an entire game. In a game's early puzzles, players learn the extent of their avatar's movement capabilities before these capabilities are tested in later, more complex, puzzles. Bogost uses *Ninja Gaiden* for the Nintendo Entertainment System (NES) as an example of this:[15] early levels teach players to wall-jump in safe environments where they can try again if they fail before having them use the wall-jump skill over pits or in complex patterns. Designers understanding this method of player-learning can focus early levels on teaching players how to deal with obstacles individually, and then mix and match them later to create more complex puzzles (Figure 5.4). This is especially useful if designers have created a set of modular gameplay assets that they can simply mix and match within their game engine environments.

This outlook on teaching in games differs from the operant conditioning model in that it does not directly address reinforcements or

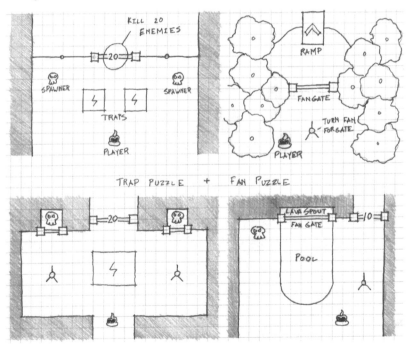

FIGURE 5.4 In *SWARM!*, the designers first introduced two basic puzzles in isolation—one where killing enemies opens gates and another where spinning a fan opens a gate—and then combined them into different orientations that players would have to figure out.

punishments as outcomes to solving in-game situations. The skill gates discussed in Chapter 2, where players cannot progress until they learn the ability that lets them overcome a particular obstacle, are examples of this kind of teaching. Skill gates are *self-reinforcing*, as players are simply stuck if, for example, they do not learn that jumping is a way to pass over a block that is in their way.

Constructivism

The last teaching method we will look at is *constructivism*. Constructivist models have origins in the work of theorists such as Montessori and others who advocate for sensory and activity-based learning methods. Other early influencers of constructivism, such as David Kolb, also advocate for reinforced feedback on the outcome of exercises.[16] Constructivist learning models can be found in modern adult education classes and design or art schools. They are also popular in project and presentation-based coursework such as that in architecture schools. In many studio classes, students are guided through a design problem by teachers who oversee but do not directly intervene in a student's design actions. This combination of freedom and feedback make constructivist methods a better individual descriptor of how players learn in games than either operant conditioning or the Montessori Method alone.

Kolb, along with Ronald Fry, outlined the following methodology for experiential learning: *concrete experience, observation and reflection, forming abstract concepts,* and *testing in new situations*[17] (Figure 5.5). When taken as a methodology for understanding a player's interactions with a game, this can translate to *attempting to overcome an obstacle, observation and reflection of play outcome, forming strategies,* and *testing new strategies*. As pointed out by psychologist Pamela Brown Rutledge[18] and game designer Jane McGonigal,[19] games reinforce a cyclical model of problem-solving through *self-efficacy*, an individual's belief in his or her ability to act and achieve positive results, and by encouraging risk through minimized setbacks.

Constructivist teaching in level design combines Montessori and operant conditioning learning in interactive systems of problem solving. As a designer, you create interactive environments and challenges for players to experiment with. Players, with the system you construct, then have the freedom to solve the problems you set up for them or even experiment with ways to "game the system" with shortcuts, Steiner points, or cheats. As they solve puzzles and problems, you set up places for the players to feel

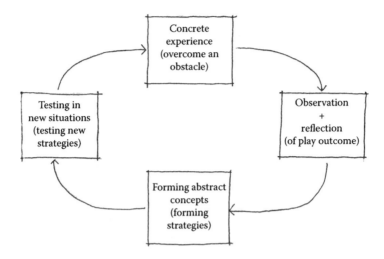

FIGURE 5.5   Kolb and Fry's model of learning follows an iterative spiral through their four elements. When applied to play, it closely mirrors a scientific method-style of interacting with a game.

rewarded for their actions, reinforcing mechanics as they play through a game. Rewarding player action is important, as properly constructed challenges often require several playthroughs before they are overcome. Punishments such as dying or losing progress are also important for the constructivist model, but rather than a severe punishment or setback, players should be only set back to a point where they can comfortably retry a challenge.

Combat games such as those in the *Halo* series[20] excel at constructing iterative challenges when asking players to storm an enemy stronghold. Set placements of enemies allow players to form strategies of how to engage overwhelming forces over several playthroughs. The game also features a generous checkpoint system that stores the game state at locations where a player can easily try a single challenge again rather than restarting a level completely. Additionally, recognizing enemies or their weapons allows players to form strategies based on knowledge from previous encounters.

As evidenced by *Halo* and similar games, modular methods of level construction allow you to use prefabricated assets to create additional challenges. Recognizing assets allows players to interpret new challenges because they recognize game objects from previous encounters. Generous checkpoint systems or distributions of checkpoint objects (however your team implements this functionality) are important for allowing a constructivist gameplay style (Figure 5.6). Checkpoints should generally be placed before significant challenges. In our previously discussed methodology of the *Nintendo Power* method, this would involve placing a checkpoint immediately before your "callout points" on a level map.

In practice, these three styles of learning are often used together to teach players how to utilize a game. Operant conditioning is used to reinforce gameplay mechanics through applications of rewards and other positive game outcomes for success and through punishments for failures. The Montessori Method gives us a framework for understanding how to structure a series of puzzles or challenges over the course of a game so that players can deduce solutions by recognizing elements of previous challenges, even if they are used in new ways. Finally, constructivist methods show us how we can structure challenges, feedback, and punishments in such a way that players are motivated to iterate their play to overcome or master gameplay challenges.

In the next section, we address the modular gameplay or environment art assets mentioned here, and we describe how level designers can use them as vital elements of a level's visual rhetoric.

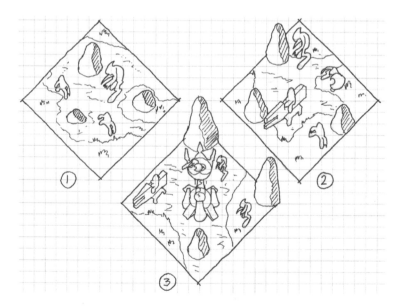

FIGURE 5.6 This diagram illustrates several different enemy strongholds created with a modular set of assets. Recognizable assets allow players to use Montessori-style understanding of the level to form strategies. The checkpoints at the beginning of each challenge help create an iterative problem-solving play style.

SYMBOLS AND VISUAL DESIGN IN GAMES

In the previous section, we delved into teaching methods for game levels—behaviorism, the Montessori Method, and constructivism—with which we create dialogs with players and teach them how to play our games. The common thread between these is that of the modular, reusable asset. In behaviorism, rewards and punishments are used to reinforce positive and negative associations for different types of sensory information. Montessori learning and development over the course of a game hinges upon the player recognizing elements of previous activities, and finally, constructivism speaks to the concept of game levels as spatial puzzles that players must solve through trial-and-error learning of what each level element means.

For reasons even beyond the ways they are constructed in development, games are well suited to these kinds of teaching. The key to teaching through visual communication in games is level geometry and environment art: the 3D models, textures, pixel sprites, and other assets that are used to create believable environments in games. In this section, we will explore functions for environment art that go beyond "cool objects that populate levels" understandings and delve into how environment art helps designers teach gameplay.

Between 1928 and 1929, artist Rene Magritte created the painting *The Treachery of Images*[21] (Figure 5.7), which depicts a smoking pipe and a caption underneath, *Ceci n'est pas une pipe* (this is not a pipe). Magritte, juxtaposing the image and caption, was making the self-referential statement that artists and designers do not create things, but instead create pictorial *representations* of things. The pipe is actually oil paint applied to a canvas in such a way that it forms the image of a pipe, not a pipe from which one can actually smoke tobacco.

FIGURE 5.7 A sketch of The Treachery of Images by Rene Magritte.

Artist Genee Cosden, in a submission to popular t-shirt printing site Threadless,[22] juxtaposed the same caption with a green pipe and Piranha Plant from the game *Super Mario Bros.* (Figure 5.8).[23] This version of the painting, whether intentional or not, applies Magritte's argument to objects in video games: they are not actual objects but are visual representations of objects. Paired with scripted behaviors, these in-game objects take on some of the behaviors of their real-world counterparts: swords and gun objects send damage to "enemy" character-objects, 3D models of first aid kits carry with them behaviors that increase a number related to player health, and so on. The pairing of visual art and procedural behaviors in game objects allows players to build strong associations between game objects and gameplay mechanics. These objects therefore become *symbols* of the gameplay mechanics they represent.

Implementing Symbols in Games

Symbols are a powerful tool in games, both as a construction method and in utilizing the teaching methods discussed earlier in this chapter. The prefabricated assets discussed in our previous examples of *Halo* and similar games are these very same types of symbols. For example, when *Halo* players see a Grunt, the most basic enemy in the game, they know what kinds of tactics Grunts employ and how to defeat them. When designers put such enemies in a game, they typically have a few variations of the prefabricated enemy object that they litter around a level, meaning that not only will their behavior be consistent, but also the player will eventually build a literacy of their habits as defined by their scripted behaviors.

Leci n'est pas une pipe.

FIGURE 5.8   A sketch recreation of Genee Cosden's This Is Not a Pipe t-shirt design.

The same is true of level objects and architecture. As we have seen in our brief explorations of Unity and other engines, an efficient way to construct levels is to reuse prefabricated assets. Once these are created, the designer can use and reuse them throughout his or her games. The player will also recognize the objects and associate them with a specific gameplay mechanic. In *Halo*, players attacking the enemy forts may see a purple platform floating in the air. This object, used throughout the game, typically features an enemy sniper. After one or two experiences seeing this object, they will see it as a symbolic indicator that they will be battling a sniper.

For environment art-intensive games, it is important to establish what portion of the scenery is a gameplay symbol and what is simply environment art. For example, *L.A. Noire*[24] features an extensive environment that simulates the city of Los Angeles in 1947. However, only certain buildings are important to gameplay, and not all can be interacted with. The designers distinguish interactive buildings from non-interactive buildings by coloring the knobs, handles, or other entry hardware of the interactive buildings a gold color.

The difference between *L.A. Noire*'s interactive doors and non-interactive doors goes far beyond the color of their doorknobs. As game objects in an engine, the interactive doors would most likely be 3D models with some sort of script attached that dictate how they respond to player interactivity—either working with collision–interaction scripts attached to the player or entirely driven by the door's own artificial intelligence. Alternatively, the non-interactive doors are just that: 3D models of doors or simply part of a larger 3D model of a building. These objects are just environment art, their interactivity consisting of only their ability to block players from passing through them.

In summary, it is important to follow two rules when building environmental symbols in games:

1. Each symbol must have a unique appearance, even from similar environment art objects.

2. Each symbol must be repeated so the player learns what it means through repetition.

Following these two rules will allow you to use prefabricated game objects as elements of your game's *visual language*. As the player is exposed to your language, he or she will gain literacy of it, knowing how to read it as he or she plays.

Teaching with Symbols in Games

Architect Adolf Loos, in a 1910 lecture, famously argued, "Ornament is a crime."[25] The rationale for this, argued in rebuttal to the ornate art nouveau movement, was a belief that ornament could limit an object's stylistic longevity, and that the use of ornament was therefore unethical. This mindset helped solidify the visual style of architectural Modernism, which often featured clean, plain surfaces and straight lines.

Many of Loos's arguments were focused around ornament as frivolous aesthetic detail. However, as we showed earlier, our own use of environmental objects in games can go beyond mere ornamentation and become symbols: visual objects that carry representative associations with ideas or gameplay mechanics. Games teach through several methods, often in tandem with one another at one time. The repeatability of prefabricated game objects used as gameplay symbols allows these objects to become enforcers of the previously studied teaching methods: operant conditioning, the Montessori Method, and constructivism.

Introducing Symbols

As we saw in discussions of both *Super Mario Bros.* and *Super Meat Boy*, these games introduce symbols in the form of actual game objects or level geometry arrangements by allowing players to interact with them through their avatar's abilities (Figure 5.9). In the example of *Super Meat Boy*, players learn in level 1–2 that vertical walls are interactive and may be gripped by Meat Boy. This is repeated as part of several other puzzles and rewarded by the players reaching Bandage Girl at the

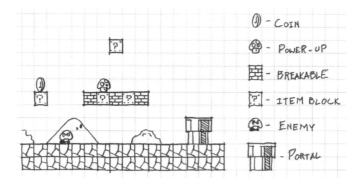

FIGURE 5.9 This famous first area of *Super Mario Bros.* level 1–1 introduces a plethora of visual symbols that will be important repeated gameplay elements during the rest of the game's thirty-two levels.

end of each level. Likewise, players of *Super Mario Bros.* will learn to jump at blocks from underneath after being rewarded with coins and power-ups. As players progress through the game, they will see these symbols again and know what they do because of these first few conditioned encounters.

In *SWARM!* we had the challenge of introducing an unconventional core mechanic to players: luring enemies into traps instead of fighting them directly. This mechanic was further used to unlock doors that would open when all enemies in an area were defeated. To teach the relationship between the player, enemies, and environmental puzzles, we first introduced the enemies far from any traps to communicate that the player could not directly defeat them with the default character. Later, enemy spawn points were set up in an area surrounded by traps, so players could watch the enemies hit the traps and explode. Finally, the player was put in a situation where he or she could lead the enemies into the traps, which would open a door (Figure 5.10). The three pieces of this last puzzle—trap, enemies, and door—were all located within one screenshot's view of each other so players could easily see their relationship. In further iterations of this puzzle, the designers could place the elements further apart to create new challenges, having already made the basic puzzle format clear. Once again, we see the usefulness of Anna Anthropy's "scene" concept, a single screen's worth of space, this time as a tool for teaching gameplay.[26]

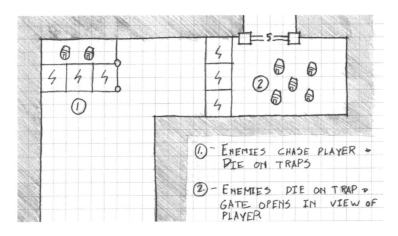

FIGURE 5.10 A level diagram showing the steps taken by the creators of *SWARM!* for introducing the game's enemies and the unusual way the player must defeat them.

Symbols as Guides

As we have seen, symbols are important tools not only for introducing mechanics early, but also for conveying the message of what actions to take throughout entire games. Portal[27] makes excellent use of environmental symbols to indicate gameplay mechanics. On the one hand, there are caution signs at the beginning of the game's test chamber puzzles that describe what hazards are inside. As players visit new rooms, see the symbols, then play the rooms themselves, they learn which symbols correspond to specific mechanics. Another layer of symbol occurs within the level geometry itself, where specific layouts of wall panels and masses are arranged according to the metrics of specific actions. As such, a player who enters a room and sees signs that indicate inertia-based puzzles, and then encounters the deep pit, wide canyon, and tilted wall panels consistent with the game's inertia puzzles will know what actions to take (Figure 5.11).

Portal demonstrates how these early encounters with symbols help designers implement Montessori and constructivist-style models in game levels. As the game is highly modular, elements are used and reused throughout the experience, but shuffled in new and interesting ways. Even the game's textures, which each have their own material properties related to how they

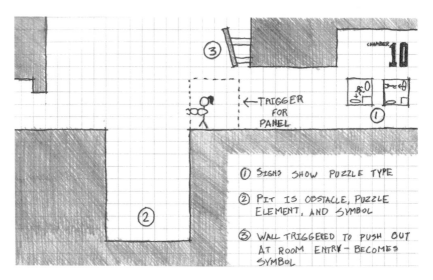

FIGURE 5.11 *Portal* uses detailed signage and consistent level geometry types to indicate what tactics a player must use in puzzles. After establishing these relationships through gameplay and rewards in early encounters, players can recognize and implement these tactics later on.

interact with portals, are symbolic: a white finish indicates that the surface will accept a portal, and a black shiny finish indicates that the player cannot place portals there. In this way, each room develops a rich dialog with players as they experiment and iterate new ways of solving each puzzle through geometry, texture, and symbol. Utilized in this way, newly encountered level environments act like new parts of a conversation for a player to engage in. As players learn what each symbol means, they will train themselves to search for them as indicators of what to do next in your game levels.

I used a similar tactic in my game *Lissitzky's Revenge* with the colors and *patterns* that I used on objects. The game has an art style based on the abstract Bolshevik propaganda poster *Beat the Whites with the Red Wedge* (1920) by the Russian artist El Lissitzky (Figure 5.12). Keeping in line with this poster and others by Lissitzky, the game's graphics are entirely geometric shapes. Playing the game lets players move and change how the shapes are arranged, so any screenshot becomes a unique piece of graphic design. To make the game actually playable though, I kept myself to a strict visual system so that the shapes would still be communicative, even though they were abstract. Red, for example, is always the color of objects "friendly" to the player. Not only does this keep the game in line with the poster—the Red Wedge in the poster is symbolic of the Bolsheviks—but it gives a clear indicator of which pieces in each scene are friendly. Examples of these friendly shapes include the red and burgundy squares from the game's third world, which were taken from Lissitzky's book *About Two Squares* (1922) (Figure 5.13). This level also includes dotted patterns that have multiple functions: early levels introduce them as a way to protect the player character but the squares explode when they hit them. Creating a

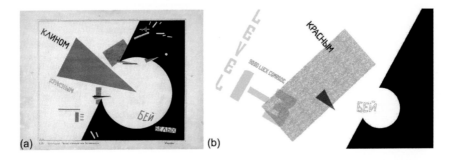

FIGURE 5.12   El Lissitzky's 1920 poster, Beat the Whites with the Red Wedge

(image source: Wikimedia Commons, image in the public domain) next to a screenshot from Lissitzky's Revenge.

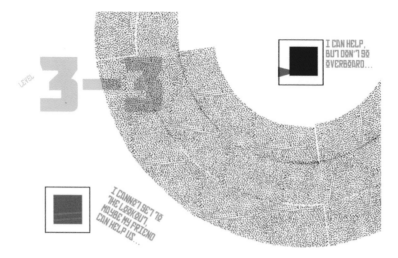

FIGURE 5.13 A screenshot of *Lissitzky's Revenge* showing the player's avatar, the Red Wedge, interacting with friendly squares. Different shades of red were used to make unique "characters" while communicating that these shapes were friendly to the player.

visual language and giving textures and patterns consistent meanings is another way of *juicing* mechanics. This time, new nuances to the meaning of a texture or pattern are revealed over the course of several levels (Figure 5.14). Forms, textures, and patterns are a subtle but equally effective way to include symbols in your levels that evolve as you add new elements to your gameplay.

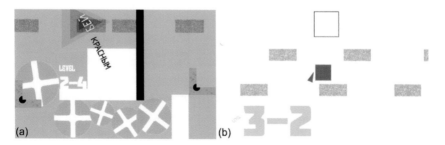

FIGURE 5.14 Two different levels from *Lissitzky's Revenge* featuring the dotted patterned shapes. In one level, they are shields for the player to hide in from enemy shots (the words "beat" and "red" in Cyrillic letters) but in another, important puzzle pieces will explode if they hit them. This gives the visual symbol multiple meanings and multiple gameplay uses. Levels can be constructed that play on this duality. The image on the right is one that recreates the action of the game *Frogger* while players carry a puzzle piece to its resting place.

Designing and Placing Symbols for Effective Communication

As we have seen, establishing which objects are and are not symbols, as well as what each symbol stands for, is important for visually communicating with players. We have also seen that symbols must stand out from other pieces of environment art, such as *L.A. Noire*'s gold doorknobs or *Portal*'s white wall finishes. Good principles of visual communication are vital not only for the aesthetic quality of each symbol, but also to make them stand out from other, non-symbolic pieces of environment art.

Visual communication can aid level design in other ways. The most important is guiding players through environments. As we saw with our studies of Kevin Lynch's urban design principles in Chapter 4, landmarks and other noticeable geometries can help players orient themselves in large environments. However, other subtler principles implemented in a game's environment art can help players find their way through more intimate spaces.

Basic Color Theory

In many games, *color* is a vital tool for communicating with the player. There are two reasons for this: the ways in which colors relate to one another, and the emotional or metaphorical associations colors carry. *Color theory* is a body of knowledge associated with understanding different ways that colors blend with one another. In color theory, there are several *color models* for understanding color.

The first and most commonly used in digital art is the *hue, saturation, and brightness* (HSB) model.[28] This describes colors by their *hue*, the name of a color that most people think of as a color itself; their *saturation*, the purity of a color; and the *brightness*, how much black or white there is in a color. HSB is the model associated with programs like Photoshop or GIMP, as they are the elements of a color that these programs allow users to manipulate.

Other color models include the *additive* color model, which is based on how light behaves, and the *subtractive* model, which is used in painting and printing. Additive color is based on *primary colors* of red, blue, and green. If one looks at a color monitor or television up close, he or she can see that each pixel is comprised of a red, blue, and green element. Adding these primary colors to one another forms different colors, which eventually create white when all three primary additive colors are combined (Figure 5.15). Due to the way this model works, digital art programs have a color mode called *RGB* for creating graphics to be displayed on a screen (like many images and textures used for video games).

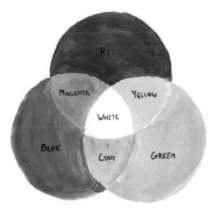

FIGURE 5.15 In the additive color model, the primary colors of light—red, green, and blue—are combined to form new colors, and eventually white light when all three are combined.

The subtractive model is based on two different sets of primary colors: red, yellow, and blue (RYB), or cyan, magenta, and yellow (CMY). When either of these combinations of colors are combined, they form black. CMY is commonly used for three-color printing and graphics. However, it is RYB that gives us the commonly understood *color wheel* (Figure 5.16) of the three primary colors and their *secondary* and *tertiary colors*, which forms our basis of how we use colors in relation to one another.

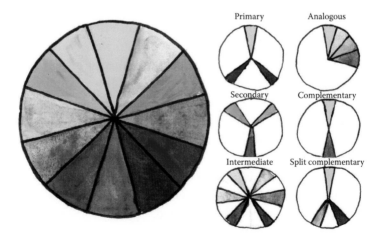

FIGURE 5.16 The color wheel. Groups of three colors next to one another are known as analogous colors, while colors on opposite sides of the wheel are complementary. Using complementing colors in visual design helps contrasting elements stand out.

The color wheel is an important tool for level designers. Groupings of three adjacent colors on the wheel are said to be *analogous* colors, which can help create a harmonious atmosphere based on a particular mood. For example, using blue, blue–purple, and purple together can create a somber or cold feeling in a level. Using *complementary* colors—colors opposite one another on the color wheel—can create a powerful effect, which we will discuss in the next section, on contrast.

It is also important to understand metaphorical associations that particular colors have gained in different cultures. For example, the color combination of blues and purples has been said to create a cold feeling. Likewise, a combination of red, red–orange, and orange creates a warm or hot feeling. Besides temperature, colors can stand for emotions—in Western culture, red is seen as analogous with passion or love, blue with sadness or tranquility, yellow with happiness, etc. These associations carry over to games: one typically sees red or green health items, due to these colors' associations with blood, medicine, or growth. Blue is the color of magic or mana in many games, having a mystical association. Green is also used in many contexts of alien creatures or monsters thanks to associations with nuclear materials or swamps. Level designers would be wise to pay attention to these and other color associations when planning their game environments.

On the flip side to all of this: level designers should also be sensitive to how diverse groups perceive color. Colors may mean different things for different cultures: a famous example is that western brides wear a white gown to their weddings while in India that color is worn to funerals. Being sensitive to cultural differences increases the resonance of your game with people beyond your immediate culture. Accessibility is another thing to keep in mind: designers should make sure that color indicators in their games are perceptible by colorblind players. Options for these audiences include creating accessible color palettes or including different display modes for the various types of colorblindness in your options menu. It is outside the scope of this book to give a complete breakdown of how to design color palettes for diverse players, but it is a good idea for helping players of different groups feel represented.

Contrast

An element of using not only color, but also shape, object size, and other visual elements of game worlds, is *contrast*. Contrast is the juxtaposition of objects such that one is meant to be directly opposite another in some quality such as size, color, shape, or style. When a designer uses contrast, it is typically to call attention to the unusual element. Common contrasts include using a bright object among darker ones, coloring an object a complementary color to the predominant color of a scene, or putting a tall object among a collection of short ones.

An excellent example of using complementary colors to contrast environmental elements is in *Bioshock Infinite*.[29] The chapel where player character Booker DeWitt enters the floating city of Columbia is predominantly blue and dimly lit. Each room has multiple passages into other rooms, but ones on the main path that will lead players out of the chapel contain bright elements such as a worshipper in white robes (to contrast the lighting condition) or bright yellow–orange lighting (to contrast the predominant color of the environment). The other passages, which often contain collectable resources, are analogous colors to the blues of the scene: purples and blue–purples.

Contrast is an important factor in leading players through a game environment. We have already discussed the radio tower area in *Half-Life 2: Episode 2*, where environment art is used to lead players between different buildings to broadcast a message to their allies. We saw that bright, warm-colored textures used for important locations in this puzzle contrasted the cool blues and greens of the background as well as the dark browns and blacks of unimportant buildings. Contrast is important for creating landmarks not only in open worlds, but also within smaller areas: hallways, courtyards, and rooms.

Framing

Another element of visual design of great use to level designers is the concept of *framing*. Framing describes the use of foreground elements to surround the view of something important in an environment as though it were in a frame (Figure 5.17). Framing is a technique useful for enhancing the approach to important game environments: as the player moves through a gamespace, framed openings or expansions of space can enhance or foreshadow the player's arrival at a point.

This simple but crucial aspect of visual composition is an effective tool for turning environmental transitions into guideposts. Combined with environmental techniques such as color theory and contrast, pathways and arrivals in games can be easy to navigate and dramatic.

Bioshock Infinite's introductory gamespaces provide a powerful example of framing. Important architectural areas along the player's intended

FIGURE 5.17 Vertical elements such as trees, columns, or doorframes are effective at helping designers frame scenes, adding to the drama of environmental transitions and approaches.

path are framed with brightly lit embellishments: embedded columns and sculptural ornaments. These pieces of environmental artwork also feature engraved sayings by famous in-game figures—building the characterization of the game's alternative America through embedded environmental narrative.

Rule of Thirds

The last visual design concept we will highlight here is the *rule of thirds*. The rule of thirds dictates that a designer should divide an image into thirds both vertically and horizontally (creating nine total divisions), and then place elements of the composition along the lines (Figure 5.18). This produces more visually interesting compositions than if the designer had simply centered the subjects.

This concept is based on the idea that a visual composition should allow viewers' eyes to travel around the image rather than stay in one place. Subjects placed at the dividing lines in a rule-of-thirds image will keep the viewer's eyes moving around the image rather than staying at the center. Moving objects off center can help designers change the balance of an image or imply movement.

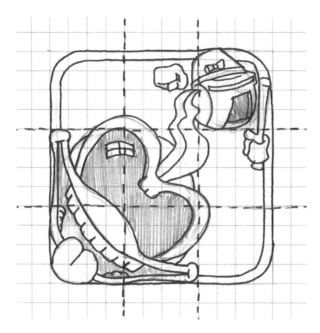

FIGURE 5.18 This diagram shows how an image is composed with the rule of thirds.

In game levels, subtle shifts of level objects to the side of a view can create more visually interesting lines of sight. In Thatgamecompany's *Journey*,[30] the player character tends to occupy the first third of the screen. In the first level, the player character is placed to the left of centrally placed landmarks. Elements placed to the sides of the centrally located markers, such as those found in the game's first screen, for example, direct the player's gaze toward important elements (Figure 5.19). Other markers require players to move slightly right or left, creating a more interesting path than if the player simply had to move straight. At the end of each of these shifts in path are also game objects that become symbols of specific mechanics, so the *visual rhetoric* of the scene is incredibly rich from both the visual composition and symbol-making standpoints.

Symbols are indeed an important element of teaching in levels with visual communication. Through the teaching methods we have explored, designers can introduce and reinforce the meaning of symbols or familiar level geometries. Effective uses of color, contrast, and composition allow symbolic geometries to stand out from other parts of a gamespace. In the next section, we will learn how preformed symbolic associations with architectural forms may also be used to communicate with players in large game worlds.

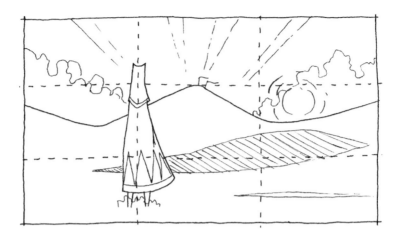

FIGURE 5.19 This sketch of the first level of *Journey* shows how visual elements are placed in thirds on-screen, including the player character itself. The off-centered elements direct the player gaze to the landmark in the center of the view.

ARCHITECTURAL FORMS AND TYPES

We have just discussed how game objects and level geometry are used as symbols: visually representing gameplay mechanics. When teaching a player how to play your game with environments, these associations must be built through a combination of training methods such as those previously discussed. However, there are also symbolic associations that we can take from everyday architecture to guide players in games: architectural *types*.

Architectural types describe a building's use through its *form* (Figure 5.20). In many cultures, buildings of the same use are built with similar forms. Over time, the form becomes associated with the building use, and a type is established. For example, a square building with a pitched roof is often understood as a house in Western cultures. Likewise, *torii*, Japanese gates, would conjure strong associations with temples to a Japanese person. Like symbols, formal building types carry strong associations of ideas beyond the architecture itself.

In games, building types can serve a similar purpose to their real-world counterparts. Games in the *Dragon Quest*[31] series (known as *Dragon Warrior* in the United States until 2005) utilize building types to help players find their way around in-game towns. Like symbols, these types are associated with gameplay through training and demonstration. For example, players of *Dragon Quest* games who need to resurrect fallen party

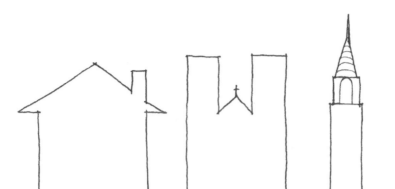

FIGURE 5.20 These shapes represent different building types in Western culture. Based on societal associations of building use with building form, types allow observers to understand their environment.

members or remove curses must find a church—the gameplay functions of which are removing status effects and saving the game. As a formal type, churches can be recognized by the religious symbols incorporated into their architectures—stars, crosses, and others—similar to how symbols are displayed on real churches and temples (Figure 5.21). These types often borrow heavily from the forms of real-world architectural types

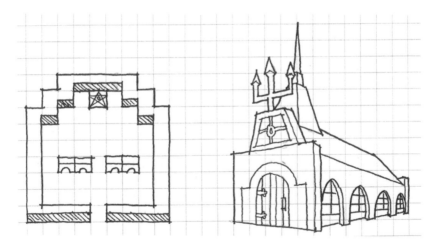

FIGURE 5.21 Sketches of churches from early and newer *Dragon Quest* games. In early entries in the series where building exteriors were not shown, churches were indicated through religious symbols and the shapes of their plans. In later entries the designers made the exteriors of the buildings resemble real-world Western churches.

to communicate their purpose. Churches in *Dragon Quest*, for example, incorporate formal elements such as a narthex or apse in their plans (especially in earlier games where the exteriors of buildings were not shown) or aesthetic elements like stained glass or religious symbols.

Even more overt are the types used in the *Pokémon*[32] series. Like many roleplaying games (RPGs), in *Pokémon* each town contains several building types consistent with different gameplay functions. This includes a Pokémon Center for healing and communicating with other players, a Poké Mart for buying items, and often a Pokémon Gym containing one of the game's bosses. As in *Dragon Quest*, these buildings are recognizable by their outward appearances consistent with their architectural type. Unlike *Dragon Quest* games, however, building types in *Pokémon* games utilize the same sprite or 3D model for each iteration of the type. In this way, building types in *Pokémon* games demonstrate building types as modular assets: the buildings communicate through their building type and are reusable from town to town. Even more graphically sophisticated games like *The Elder Scrolls V: Skyrim*[33] utilize consistent assets when communicating building type: smithies have anvils and stoves, merchants can be found in booths or behind counters, and horses can be bought at barn-like stables. While *Skyrim*'s wealth of detail allows many buildings to be unique, consistent elements like those mentioned above still allow these buildings to communicate their function to players.

The concept of gamespaces as systems of language and communication is an important one for level design. In the next section, we explore an architectural philosophy that applies the methods described in this chapter to control how players absorb and utilize information.

CONTROLLING INFORMATION IN MEMORY PALACES

As we have seen, gamespaces can contain a great deal of information that is not only stored, but also communicated to players in both overt and subtle ways. Game spaces can be considered *memory palaces*. Memory palaces were a pneumonic device employed by Cicero, the Roman orator, philosopher, and statesman, for remembering the content of his speeches.[34] Also called the *method of loci*, this technique has users constructing a palace or other architectural space in their minds. Each room has its own architectural style and stands in for a piece of information. While speaking, the orator imagine themselves moving from room to room—from talking point to talking point.

Chapter 4 mentioned the customization features of games like *Second Life*, which allowed users to create digital museums or sculptures for presenting information to other players. *Minecraft* and *Little Big Planet* users often erect elaborate structures as monuments to their favorite media franchises,[35] explorations of theoretical systems,[36] or even as working computers.[37] These types of structures are pervasive in digital games as functional systems of communication: displaying the ideas of designers for others to see.

It is through these kinds of knowledge-embedding in game levels that we can utilize gamespaces as instruments with which to create emotional experiences for players. In their book *Chambers for a Memory Palace*,[38] Donlyn Lyndon and Charles W. Moore describe how pieces of architecture can become memory palaces through the use of memorable communicative moments. In many ways, these pieces of architecture can help level designers manipulate the type and amount of information that they transmit to players: plot elements, enemy and obstacle locations, puzzle components, etc. In *Rules of Play: Game Design Fundamentals*,[39] Katie Salen and Eric Zimmerman describe three levels of information contained within games: *certainty*, *uncertainty*, and *risk*, based on the work of mathematician Richard Epstein. Through different methods for the creation of emotional experiences in game levels, designers can carefully pace how players experience these levels of information in games. Before we explore the emotional experiences possible through using architectural experience concepts, we must understand these levels of information.

Certainty

The first level of information described by Epstein, and by extension, Salen and Zimmerman, is certainty. A certain game is one in which the outcome is known. Salen and Zimmerman point out that in terms of measuring game outcomes, a game with a certain outcome is hardly a game at all. It is indeed far less exciting to watch a practiced player defeat a novice in a multiplayer video game or to see a sports team get completely shut out by its more skilled opponents.

On a more micro-level in a game, creating certainty within levels through consistent level elements can be a powerful tool for enticing players to explore or continue playing. Much of this chapter has been devoted to understanding symbol-making and the use of modular assets in communicating gameplay elements through visual systems. As players learn how to recognize symbols in games, they will also learn to recognize the conditions under which those symbols reveal themselves. In games such as *Super Metroid*,[40] for example, rooms for recharging weapons are typically placed near rooms containing boss enemies. Also, a reward of some kind (typically in the form of a new weapon or ability) is placed after the boss room. This *pattern* is established early in the game and continued throughout.

Horror games such as *Dead Space*[41] establish patterns with their save rooms. While the overall tone of the game is one of dread and horror at the possibility of enemies jumping out at any time, the game's save rooms are established as safe zones early on in the game. This is done without exposition or other narrative devices, but simply through the player's experience of encountering a number of save rooms that do not contain enemies. Examples such as this and those found in *Super Metroid* communicate the game's pacing to the player. Patterns of certainty help players know when to unwind or prepare for big action. They also feed players' excitement for the game as they play or as they shut the current play session down; knowing that something exciting is coming up soon will make players continue their current session or motivate them to come back to the game after shutting it down. Certainty also gives designers the opportunity to make big dramatic reveals: imagine a threat so powerful that it could destroy one of your save rooms or otherwise safe level zones. That would be terrifying!

Uncertainty

While certainty describes conditions where game outcomes are completely known, uncertainty describes a condition where the player has no concept of what to expect from a game. According to Salen and Zimmerman, this occurs in scenarios such as when someone is playing a game with a person he or she has never met before, like two strangers sitting down at a chess table in a park.[39]

There are different ways to view uncertainty in level design. On one hand, a level space of pure uncertainty can be frustrating to players who may be killed by an obstacle they did not know was there. Level designers should attempt to minimize situations where the player must go blindly into danger. If the point of a game is to bring players back for more, then uncertainty in level design can seem unfair.

Uncertainty in level design is a symptom of poor design or environmental art direction. If players find themselves at a T-junction within a level where they cannot surmise the best direction to go in next, they will feel that their choice may be arbitrary or that they may be forced to backtrack so they may see what lies in the direction they did not choose. The reason for such confusing game areas is typically bland and repetitive environment art, or the overuse of meaningless spatial configurations (as opposed to the purposeful use of special rooms for saving, healing, and other repeatable symbolic forms). Conversely, a junction that communicates what each branch holds, even subtly, allows the player to make informed decisions on where to go in a level. Returning to our theoretical T-junction, if the player finds his or her faction's logo spray-painted on the left passage while the right passage contains stacks of crates suitable for taking cover or signs of a previous struggle, this creates a much more communicative space. Based on the recurrence of these symbols in previous levels, the player may be able to infer that the left passage contains resources that will prepare him or her for a battle in the right passage (Figure 5.22).

Uncertainty, however, has its uses. In many games with experimental mechanics or that want to subvert gameplay standards, uncertainty can be a powerful tool for establishing trust between player and designer. Games such as Jonathan Blow's *Braid*[42] or Terry Cavanagh's *Don't Look*

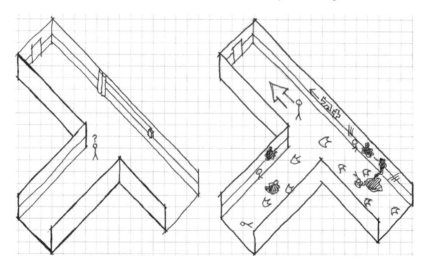

FIGURE 5.22 These two sketches of a T-junction in a first-person shooter level show how proper inclusion of varied environment art can reduce arbitrary uncertainty in a gamespace. The first example offers little to the player in the way of communicating which direction he or she should go. To understand what happens down each hall, the player would have to backtrack. In the second example, the environment gives the player the cognitive tools to make an informed decision on which path to take.

Back[43] feature gameplay moments where players must jump off a large cliff toward a bottom they cannot see. *Braid* utilizes a mechanic where the player can rewind time, so each jump off of the cliff is an opportunity to learn where obstacles are for when the player tries again. This allows the cliff scene of the game to be an iterative experience of trial and error until the player finally reaches the bottom.

Don't Look Back is a modernization of the myth of Morpheus and Eurydice where the player must jump off a cliff to enter the Underworld. At the point of the game where the cliff is encountered, players can only move horizontally and jump. The few previous screens of the game at that point are also very sparsely populated with objects, so the player knows there is nothing for him or her to go back and find. With these factors in mind, the player comes to the realization that his or her only option is to jump off the cliff. As such, he or she is choosing to trust that the designer has not placed an instant death object below him or her. Moments like this, where the player must blindly trust the designer, can provide interesting moments of emotional gameplay.

Risk

The examples of *Braid* and *Don't Look Back* show that even in player–designer trust-building uses of uncertainty, there are opportunities to get as much information on the uncertainty as possible. According to Salen and Zimmerman, uncertainty where the player knows the nature of the uncertainty is actually risk.[39] Risk is a modified version of uncertainty where the player has incomplete information on what lies beyond the point of uncertainty or can make inferences on what to do next based on outside information. Risk is potentially the most powerful of the three levels of information within games, as it is what makes games feel exciting. Risk allows players to feel that their decisions may allow them to come to some successful outcome. If they do not, the attempt gives them enough information to risk another try: fitting the constructivist model outlined earlier in the chapter.

In game levels, the play between risk and rewarding players, often discussed in the design of games as *risk–reward*, is of utmost importance in creating interesting emotional experiences. Risk is created by playing communicative symbols (certainty) against new and ambiguous challenges (uncertainty), such as moving through the previously discussed first-person shooter hallway or a dark cave.

Putting It All Together in a Memory palace

We have seen how each level of information works, but how do visual symbols, teaching, and information types come together in an actual gamespace? Again, this chapter is not going to dive into how to design tutorials (that comes later), but we can for now analyze how a designer might combine these things into a communication system.

The Hyrule of *The Legend of Zelda: Breath of the Wild* is a vast, expansive world with lots of embedded information. It is also a world constructed of very concise and readable communication systems. The beginning of the game is a plateau that the player character, Link, cannot leave without falling to his death. To escape, he must overcome a series of challenges and earn a hang glider to reach the fields below. Players start the game with Link inside a tomb within which he has been asleep for a century. He is guided through a few actions by a mysterious voice but can otherwise wander around the tomb freely and collect items inside. There are no enemies in this space, so the player can begin identifying objects and their functions: treasure chests contain upgrades, glowing pedestals open locked doors, short walls can be scaled, etc. Escaping the tomb leads players to a cliff from which Link sees a sweeping vista as the game's camera orbits around him. While this impressive artwork is a reward, it contains several important pieces of information in the form of architectural landmarks that will later be goals: a volcano with lava spewing smoke and lava, a castle, and jagged cliffs. In review: by opening chests, this behavior is reinforced as the player is rewarded with gear. By solving a simple skill gate puzzle (unlocking a door), the player then gets a visual reward in the form of a dramatic reveal—another reinforcement.

When the player regains control of Link, he or she comes across several resources on the ground, a rudimentary weapon and some health items, and is prompted to pick them up. Based on their previous interactions with gear in the tomb, they can infer that they can interact with these new items in the same way. Now the player knows the basics of item-gathering and what benefits can be gleaned from stocking up. As the player explores, they encounters more new game objects: enemies who attack but yield rewards when defeated (new weapons and food), trees to climb, and eventually, temples.

While this sounds similar to many other open-world games, *Breath of the Wild* stands out in how often core symbols are repeated. The game features a few distinct towns, but the most common settlements are horse stables that are copy-and-pasted versions of one another. Rather than the strikingly different dungeons of previous *Zelda* games, every temple looks the same. Far from laziness on the part of developers, it instead makes what could be an unwieldly open world manageable. Players can find their next goals by recognizing architectural types. There are so many of these types in a single screen's view of the Hyrule landscape that players find themselves always moving to their next goal. This makes unique areas: landmarks, towns, or level-sized creatures, even more enticing to players.

Compared to other open-world games, *Breath of the Wild* features a relatively small number of enemy types. Again, this serves the readability of the gamespace and the player's condition in it. Small groups of enemies are easily beaten even by an ill-equipped player, making it certain that players can get gear from these groups. Later, players encounter larger groups that either require strong equipment or skill at sneaking to beat, but which are guarding large treasures. Uncertainty and risk come in to play here. Players understand that storming enemy camps is a high-risk/high-reward scenario but identifying the number of advantageous objects (red exploding barrels) vs. disadvantageous objects (strong silver-colored enemies) helps them assess that risk. Players who are overly rash in combat can use their mental understanding of the world's symbols to hide or heal up before moving on.

Breath of the Wild's take on Hyrule is, in terms of square footage, quite a bit bigger than a single palace, but the way it introduces then functions on identifiable information makes it a strong memory space. Smaller examples might include a space like Dracula's Castle in *Castlevania: Symphony of the Night*, which is a literal palace with differently styled rooms. Players wandering these spaces can orient themselves by the character of the environment. They can also identify how to proceed next to see if the next architectural form in their way can be overcome by their current set of powers. On an even smaller scale, the Distillery District in *Dishonored* has a visual language that changes several times during the game. In different visits, hazards are added and deactivated and the player's powers expand. Over time, strategies for navigating the District's balconies and alleyways change as the language changes. The player has to modify their memory palace.

Constructing level geometry that players can identify as useful will be of primary importance in the next chapter. There, we will push onward to see how level design becomes not only communicative, but also emotionally resonant.

SUMMARY

This chapter has provided a useful bridge between the construction of gamespaces with reusable assets and the emotions of players. Designers can teach players about their games through different psychological methodologies. They can reward players for utilizing level elements in the proper way. They can allow players to explore levels through interaction and reuse their encounters in earlier levels to inform their later successes. They can also guide players to mastery of their games by allowing them to learn from previous mistakes.

We have also seen that reusable art assets and architectural types can be used to communicate with players. These symbolic assets create dialogs between the design of a level and the player's interactions with it. Visual communication principles such as color theory, contrast, and others help make this process simpler, by allowing symbolic assets and geometries to stand out from other information. Finally, we have seen how these symbols come to embody gameplay through the controlling of information, turning our levels into emotionally evocative memory palaces. As we move forward, scenarios like these will shape how we discuss players' experiences within gamespaces throughout the rest of the book.

EXERCISES

1. **Writing prompt**: Name a game where you encountered behavioral teaching systems and how it used those systems. Do the same for Montessori and constructivist systems. What kinds of things are these systems used to teach in these games?

2. **Drawing exercise**: Play a game and sketch the symbolic assets you see in the game. Make notes of what each symbolic asset represents (game mechanic, indicator, etc.)

3. **Digital exercise**: Create a symbolic asset for use in your levels.

4. **Drawing exercise**: Diagram a level from a game you have played according to its color and lighting scheme. Make note or add a graphic indicator to show any times that color is used to communicate a pathway, provide hints to the player, or create a mood in the space.

5. **Digital exercise**: Create a graybox for an approach (or use one from another chapter). Integrate framing into the approach space in some

way (framing the transition from the approach to the arrival, using multiple frames along the approach, etc.)

6. **Drawing exercise**: Play a game with a large open-world environment. How does the environment integrate architectural types as symbols so the player understands how to use the space (e.g., forts filled with enemies, buildings for healing, shopping plazas, etc.) Sketch examples of architectural or graphic elements that define those types.

7. **Digital exercises**: Graybox a space that builds risk. Use symbolic assets to give hints of what may or may not be in the space, but do not overtly reveal anything to the player so his or her curiosity is piqued.

ENDNOTES

1. Steinberg, Leo. The Eye Is Part of the Mind. In *Reflections on Art: A Source Book of Writings by Artists, Critics, and Philosophers*, ed. Susanne Katherina Knauth Langer. Baltimore, MD: Johns Hopkins Press, 1959–1958.
2. Rumble features of many game controllers, introduced with the Nintendo 64 Rumble Pack in 1997, provide touch-based feedback during game events such as collisions or climactic events. They also have potential to allow players to navigate space by feeling around and finding where level geometry is with rumble feedback. Mobile devices allow players to interact directly with their hands, but require them to see or hear what is happening on the screen in order to understand what it is they are "touching."
3. Watson, John B. Psychology as the Behaviorist Views It. *Psychological Review* 20 (1913): 158–177. http://psychclassics.yorku.ca/Watson/views.htm (accessed April 6, 2013).
4. Pavlov, Ivan P. Classics in the History of Psychology. http://psychclassics.yorku.ca/Pavlov/ (accessed April 6, 2013).
5. Salen, Katie, and Eric Zimmerman. *Rules of Play: Game Design Fundamentals*. Cambridge, MA: MIT Press, 2003, p. 345.
6. What Is Negative Reinforcement? Maricopa Center for Learning and Instruction. http://www.mcli.dist.maricopa.edu/proj/nru/nr.html (accessed April 6, 2013).
7. Skinner, B.F. *The Technology of Teaching*. New York, NY: Appleton-Century-Crofts, 1968, pp. 93–113.
8. *Super Meat Boy*. Team Meat (developer and publisher), October 20, 2010. Xbox Live arcade game.
9. *Thomas Was Alone*. Mike Bithell (developer and publisher), July 24, 2012. PC game.
10. Salen, Katie, and Eric Zimmerman. *Rules of Play: Game Design Fundamentals*. Cambridge, MA: MIT Press, 2003, p. 168.

11. Introduction to Montessori. American Montessori Society. http://www.amshq.org/Montessori%20Education/Introduction%20to%20Montessori.aspx (accessed April 6, 2013).

12. Montessori in the Home. Association Montessori International USA. http://www.amiusa.org/montessori-in-the-home/ (accessed April 6, 2013).

13. Hersey, George L. *Architecture and Geometry in the Age of the Baroque.* Chicago, IL: University of Chicago Press, 2000.

14. Bogost, Ian. *Persuasive Games: The Expressive Power of Videogames.* Cambridge, MA: MIT Press, 2007, pp. 238–239.

15. *Ninja Gaiden.* Tecmo (developer and publisher), March 1989. NES game.

16. Kolb, David A. *Experiential Learning: Experience as the Source of Learning and Development.* Englewood Cliffs, NJ: Prentice-Hall, 1984.

17. Kolb, David A., and Ronald Fry. Toward an Applied Theory of Experiential Learning. In *Theories of Group Process*, ed. C. Cooper. London: John Wiley, 1975.

18. Rutledge, Pamela Brown. Video Games, Problem-Solving and Self-Efficacy Part 1. *Psychology Today.* http://www.psychologytoday.com/blog/positively-media/201208/video-games-problem-solving-and-self-efficacy-part-1 (accessed April 6, 2013).

19. McGonigal, Jane. Jane McGonigal: Gaming Can Make a Better World. Video on TED.com. TED: Ideas Worth Spreading. http://www.ted.com/talks/jane_mcgonigal_gaming_can_make_a_better_world.html (accessed April 6, 2013).

20. *Halo 4.* 343 Industries (developer), Microsoft Game Studios (publisher), November 8, 2012. Xbox 360 game.

21. Magritte, Rene. *The Treachery of Images.* Oil on canvas, 1928–1929. Los Angeles County Museum of Art, Los Angeles, CA.

22. www.threadless.com.

23. Cosden, Genee. *This Is Not a Pipe.* T-shirt design, 2006. Threadless.com.

24. *L.A. Noire.* Team Bondi (developer), Rockstar Games (publisher), May 17, 2011. Xbox 360 game.

25. Loos, Adolf. *Ornament and Crime: Selected Essays.* Riverside, CA: Ariadne Press, 1998.

26. Totten, Christopher W. *SWARM!*—An Academic Postmortem. Game career guide. http://gamecareerguide.com/features/1181/swarm_an_academic_.php (accessed April 15, 2013).

27. *Portal.* Valve Corporation (developer and publisher), October 9, 2007. PC game.

28. Ahearn, Luke. *3D Game Textures: Create Professional Art Using Photoshop.* 2nd ed. Amsterdam: Focal Press/Elsevier, 2009, pp. 18–28.

29. *Bioshock Infinite.* Irrational Games (developer), 2K Games (publisher), March 26, 2013. Xbox 360 game.

30. *Journey.* Thatgamecompany (developer), Sony Computer Entertainment (publisher), March 13, 2012. Playstation 3 game.

31. *Dragon Quest.* Chunsoft (developer), Enix (publisher), May 27, 1986. Nintendo Entertainment System game.

32. *Pokémon Red and Blue.* Game Freak (developer), Nintendo (publisher), September 30, 1998. Game Boy game.

33. *The Elder Scrolls V: Skyrim.* Bethesda Game Studios (developer), Bethesda Softworks (publisher), November 11, 2011. Xbox 360 game.

34. Lyndon, Donlyn, and Charles Willard Moore. *Chambers for a Memory Palace.* Cambridge, MA: MIT Press, 1994, p. xi.

35. *Minecraft.* Pixel Art Templates. http://www.minecraftpixelarttemplates. com/(accessed May 21, 2013).

36. meunierc2008. Turing Machine in *Little Big Planet*—LittleTuringMachine. YouTube. http://www.youtube.com/watch?v=eUXgfnC9Tao (accessed May 21, 2013).

37. Tutorials/Redstone Computers—*Minecraft* Wiki. *Minecraft* Wiki—The Ultimate Resource for All Things *Minecraft.* http://www.minecraftwiki. net/wiki/Tutorials/Redstone_Computers (accessed May 21, 2013).

38. Lyndon, Donlyn, and Charles Willard Moore. *Chambers for a Memory Palace.* Cambridge, MA: MIT Press, 1994.

39. Salen, Katie, and Eric Zimmerman. *Rules of Play: Game Design Fundamentals.* Cambridge, MA: MIT Press, 2003, p. 175.

40. *Super Metroid.* Nintendo R&D1 (developer), Nintendo (publisher), March 19, 1994. Super Nintendo game.

41. *Dead Space.* Visceral Games (developer), EA (publisher), October 14, 2008. Xbox 360 game.

42. *Braid.* Number None (developer), Microsoft Game Studios (publisher), August 6, 2008. Xbox Live arcade game.

43. *Don't Look Back.* Distractionware (developer), Kongregate (publisher), 2009. Internet Flash game. http://www.distractionware.com/games/flash/ dontlookback/.

INDUSTRY PERSPECTIVES: INTERVIEW: GREG GRIMSBY

I conducted this interview with Greg Grimsby in 2013. Greg is a fourteen-year veteran of the game industry who has worked on titles such as the *Dark Age of Camelot* series and *Ultima Forever*. He was the Art Director on *Warhammer Online: Age of Reckoning (WAR)*, overseeing construction of the game's world. He has a BFA in painting and drawing from James Madison University and is on the faculty at George Mason University, where he teaches many of the 3D art, modeling, and animation courses.

Can you name a game, level, or level designer that has left an impression on you? Why?

Although old school, I was always very impressed by the level design work of *Epic Games* in the *Unreal Tournament* series. Their deathmatch level designs were always executed with such a strong understanding of flow, landmarking, and visual impact. I learned a lot from the level design work in those games since deathmatch level design requires such tight and controlled synergy between layout and looks. The layout makes or breaks the play experience. Sure, players could have fun deathmatching in a big open pit, but that thrill wears off in about thirty seconds. A great deathmatch level provides opportunities for players to master the layout of the level, to work the level to their advantage. A great deathmatch map is like a good story—it has important parts, quiet passages of exposition, and a climax. A deathmatch map has these same elements designed into its structure via its flow and foci. Layer on top of this functionality a great-looking environment with awesome architectural design and weenies and you have the makings of a great level.

Are there any media outside of gaming that you find inspire your work?

I am inspired by old master paintings of all kinds, from portraits to landscapes. Their understanding of color, composition, narrative, symbolism, and lighting show the potential we have to understand why things look good and how to achieve great works of art ourselves.

Describe your level design process—how do you begin? What tools do you use (on or off the computer)?

1. **Gameplay goals**. My level design process begins with building familiarity with the gameplay goals and needs of the level. If a designer does not intimately know the gameplay goals of a level, then the process begins with learning, via design docs or conversations with designers, what the level needs to do from a gameplay functionality point of view. Then we proceed to step 2.

2. **Theme**. I brainstorm ideas for the visual theme or environment of the level. Is the level an adventure in the bowels of hell? Is it a deathmatch in a wrecked space hulk? Is it a paintball battle in a low-gravity house of bounce? I try to think of a visually compelling and kick-ass environment.

3. **Points of interest (POIs)**. Once I know the visual theme and location, I sketch points of interests and brainstorm vignettes of awesomeness that may make their way into the level. I ask myself lots of questions like: where can we tease or foreshadow? What are some potentially cool "money shots"? What makes the player go "this looks frickin' awesome"? I sketch and write down encounters and combat situations that could be cool.

4. **Brainstorm and sketch flow**. Next I nail down the basic flow of the map. Is it linear? Does it loop back on itself? Is it a hub-and-spoke design?

5. **Sketch the map**. In this step, I take all of the hodgepodge ideas and pull them together into a series of maps or concept roughs of the entire map.

6. **Whitebox prototype**. With a map in hand, I then get into the 3D software and make a whitebox prototype. The goal is to get the basic shell in to test stuff. I test the flow, the vistas, the running times, and lines of sight. Are they cool? I consider where more landmarks are needed and other changes for better flow and breadcrumbing. More testing follows and more iterations.

7. **Making it "purdy."** Once the layout has been validated via testing, it's time to make final art.

What is your process for playtesting your levels?

It depends upon what the playtest is trying to discover. If it's a gameplay test, then I get in there and test the level—walk through the space, battle enemies, etc. I evaluate the visual design and critique if the gameplay is being helped or hindered by the layout. I ask what can be moved, added, adjusted, or removed to bolster the gameplay goals. A visual playtest is looking at very different, very "art director-y" things.

Do you find art and atmospheric effects an important tool for communicating with players? Any specific examples?

There are many tools in our visual language to communicate to the player what we want to say. We use these tools, art and effects included, to convey a mood to the player and support the gameplay pillars. Sure, a level can function on some basic level with whiteboxing, and it may even be entertaining depending upon the dependency of the game on visuals, lighting, and effects to set the needed mood. *Dead Space* is not as scary without the lighting and all the atmosphere that the art and effects provide. Beyond communicating a mood, art can help a world feel like it has a history about it and make it feel lived in and believable. Architectural design, runes and signage, costume design, surface treatments, and color usage can communicate to the player who lives in your game world about what that world is like. We used this a great deal in *Warhammer Online* to heavily imprint each zone with a different feel and a strong sense of which unique races lived in each environment.

How do you teach players to utilize your levels (without use of the GUI)?

The best levels have so many affordances that lead the player, such as pathways, weenies, lighting, vistas, etc., that there isn't much to teach. Players know to follow the yellow brick road because we, as humans, understand certain conventions of how we interact with spaces. Rewarding players with cool visuals, encounters, or gameplay loot certainly helps incentivize them to follow your intended path through the level.

How do you entice players to explore game levels (without use of the GUI)?

Weenies work wonders to draw players' attention to a distant location. We can use POIs to lead the player around and utilize as much of our map as we want them to. Oftentimes we don't want players to explore every inch of a level. In the huge zones of *WAR*, a player certainly could go off the roads and wander over the hills and mountains, but there are fewer encounters out there. In essence, their ratio of time spent in game to experience points (XP) earned was very poor if you wandered and explored. Now, if your game is trying to entice players to explore, then you need to make it potentially more worth their time than grinding along your storyline. You can entice them with a random chance to encounter a rare mob or item. So there is basic carrot-dangling you can do to get players to explore. The question is, do you want to? Can you craft the art across your *entire* game world to look equally cool? No. So do you want players seeing your weaker artistic efforts way off in the corners of your map?

> *If a player is lost in one of your levels, how can he or she get back to where he or she is supposed to be (without using the GUI)?*

Players use their recall ring to teleport back. A hub-and-spoke design can certainly help along with visual clues, as can landmark weenies that players can see from a distance.

> *How do you direct the actions of players in your levels? How do you encourage players to play in undirected ways?*

Flow directs the action. How you funnel and channel the player with roads, walls, and passages dictates where they can go and what they do. Players will tend to follow the right-hand wall. Players will gravitate toward open spaces over constricted ones. The layout of the map, how it's connected, and what you can see from each part of the level direct the player without having to communicate any meta-goals to him or her. Visual points of interest and lighting play a great role in focusing the player as well. We are drawn to elements that stand out visually—that feel more important because of their scale, lighting, or content. The level designer needs to maintain a hierarchy of importance in his or her work—subduing parts of the level that are not of primary importance. So there is art and design content of primary importance, secondary importance, etc. A designer will not be able to lead the player to every bit of content directly, and there may be content available for free-range grazing, like trash mobs roaming a dungeon. The very existence of other paths of travel and of content that is not directly tied to your main storyline promotes undirected play, but you must be careful to control your signal-to-noise ratio. That is, all content competes for the players' time and attention—and you want players spending their time on your best stuff.

> *What "laws of level design" have you developed in your own work that any designer should know? What should they avoid?*

1. Spend your art efforts where players will see it the most.
2. Simple layouts should act as a framework for your complex visual designs, but underneath a yummy detailed veneer is an easy-to--understand flow.
3. There should be something visually cool on screen at all times.

4. Understand the anatomy of your environment and build that into your worlds. A ruleset based on real architectural structures or mother nature should show in your work. Forests have trees. Trees die. So forests have dead trees. Grass is sparse under trees where light doesn't reach. This is an example of a ruleset based on the anatomy of real forests. Your levels need to reflect this. If you are making up your own world, then design your own ruleset and stick to it.

5. Get your placeholders in early, and that includes color placeholders. On *WAR* we created simple solid color textures and used cutouts from our concept art to approximate and validate our color palettes very early.

6. Use foreground, middle ground, the horizon, and parallaxing to develop rich vistas.

Of course, there is a ton of other important stuff, but those rules help, especially from the artistic side of things.

As an art director, how do you address the issue of creating artworks for game worlds? Do you think of their functional game use first or their aesthetic elements?

Creating a world of game art means the art team must execute on the vision for everything that goes in it, and that is both an artistic act and a project management task. Even with a perfectly clear idea of how a game will look and what will be in it, all that artwork has to be built, support the gameplay, and meet the technical limitations of the engine. It is almost impossible to divorce the look of the game from what the capabilities of your game are. Similarly, if the art doesn't facilitate great gameplay, what's the point? This relationship requires a great deal of communication to happen between the game development team to ensure all these goals are being met. This communication happens in preproduction when decisions are being made about the vision of the game, and that vision is not just its look, but its feel, its core gameplay, its tone, and its underlying design philosophy and goals. Communication and collaboration continue until the game is done and beyond. That is how you build worlds that work and look great.

Do you see environment art more as a tool for adding aesthetic value or as gameplay indicators?

Coming from the visual side of production, I think artists will tend to always be biased to a visual point of view first. It is their torch to bear—to protect the visual quality of the game and to make sure that only gameplay goals that can be executed with visual quality make it into the product. So environment art in the hands of an artist will always aim to fulfill visual goals first, just as assets in the hands of a game designer will fulfill gameplay needs first and visuals second.

In Warhammer Online, *each quest is given out at camps as part of a story chapter. How are these camps designed to be hubs for multiple tasks within the game?*

Each chapter in *WAR* is centered on a zone of the world. The writers and quest designers build storylines and content to match the look and theme of that area. They accommodate the difficulty level associated with that zone. They continue the plot lines that occur throughout the entire game. The chapter hubs are centered on visual landmarks—towns and warcamps usually. The artists and designers work together to build these chapter hubs, starting with a written document of all the quests that will occur there. The quests required additional, unique art, so the designers were given, in essence, a budget of new NPCs, props, and points of interest that the artists could specify to make for a hub and still finish the game on time. A lot of iterative design and playtesting ensured that each hub flows well and is sized appropriately to match the content there, and that the player is directed to the next hub as the general quest line nears completion in each area. Players are directed to the next hub via quests in most cases.

How does a multiplayer world like that in Warhammer Online *facilitate cooperation between players working together toward common goals? How does it enhance conflict?*

WAR introduced the concept of public quests to massively multiplayer onlines. Public quests are quests that players in an area can automatically join just by being at the questing area. A public quest, for example, may be to battle undead at an ancient ruin, and any characters that enter the ruin join in on the fun. This is one way in which *WAR* promoted cooperation between players—to complete the public quest and get a chance at cool quest loot. Even in locations of the game where public quests have not been designed, there is always the potential for players to form pickup groups with others in the area. There obviously is a huge amount of cooperation and teamwork in a game like *WAR* with its realm vs. realm (RvR) system, as players must work together to battle enemy realms in the RvR scenarios and battlefields.

As someone with a fine arts background, where do you see opportunities to educate game developers with more traditional media forms? How can games and art form dialogs to create new experiences?

There are universal principles of design at work in any creative process, and these principles are strongly emphasized in the fine arts. Artists are taught to evaluate every design decision, to look and see with a discerning eye, to strive for continuity and harmony in the work. Form meets function. They are taught many rules of visual communication, and that is what games are—visual communication. This is why any game designer, whether a coder, content designer, writer, or, of course, game artist, benefits from a background in the fine arts. If everyone on the game team has at least a basic understanding of composition, color, and continuity of design, then we would make better games. Of course I could flip this argument around and say that every artist could use some training in software engineering so they learn the principles of system-oriented design, state machines, and a general awareness of coding practices.

CHAPTER 6

Building Exciting Levels with Dangerous Architecture

This all seemed a little dangerous. The world was not to be trusted. It was unstable, and it seemed to Thomas that it could let him down at any moment.

—*THOMAS WAS ALONE*, MIKE BITHELL[1]

Simultaneous perception of a multiplicity of levels involves struggles and hesitations for the observer, and makes his perception more vivid.

Examples which are both good and bad at the same time will perhaps in one way explain Kahn's enigmatic remark: "architecture must have bad spaces as well as good spaces."

—*COMPLEXITY AND CONTRADICTION IN ARCHITECTURE*, ROBERT VENTURI[2]

A mantra of the past few chapters has been that level design is an art of *contrasts*: that making exciting levels requires moments of silent gameplay, that bright colors should stand out among dark backgrounds, that tall structures should be guideposts, and so on. In *Complexity and*

Contradiction in Architecture, architect Robert Venturi argues for the use of subtle "contradictions" in buildings to give them "richness of meaning rather than clarity of meaning."[3] So far in this book, we have looked at ideas that lead to level design *clarity*: centering levels around a core mechanic, symbolic assets with clear meanings, and others. In this chapter and the next, we will more deeply explore how these elements may be used to make a space rich and exciting through contrasts. For this chapter, we will acknowledge a tool that games have that (most) architecture does not: danger.

Designers of both games and architecture acknowledge humanity's survival instincts as a key to pleasurable design. For architecture, it is adherence to spatial principles that humanity has historically identified as safe that creates the feeling of pleasure.[3] Games, however, utilize the emotional release after overcoming danger as a source of pleasure:[4] defeating a large boss monster, successfully crossing a bottomless pit, or breaking into an enemy fortress. In this chapter, we will discuss how level designers can play with the laws of pleasurable and unpleasant architecture to create exciting gameplay experiences.

What you will learn in this chapter:

Survival instincts and game complexity

Prospect and refuge spatial design

Shade, shadow, and survival

Loving and hating height

SURVIVAL INSTINCTS AND GAME COMPLEXITY

Gamespaces create dramatic tension by addressing both the survival of player avatars and historic notions of safe spaces. To achieve this, we must look at our gamespaces as not only levels meant to maximize mechanics, but also spaces for creating dramatic tension and offering choice. Modernist architects dealt with buildings as places for enacting the actions of living, with Le Corbusier famously arguing that the house was "a machine for living." Architect Robert Venturi argued that the modernists perhaps did this a little too well. In his book, he says that while the modernists succeeded in creating simplified plans, they did so by solving only certain design problems while ignoring others. To Mies van der Rohe's maxim "less is more," Venturi retorted, "Less is a bore."

I bring this up because level design needs complexity and nuance to be interesting. In 2011 I wrote, "If to architects the house was the machine for living, the game level should be the machine for living, dying, and creating tension by exploiting everything in between." Building levels that pull this off involves understanding a bit of spatial psychology and an understanding of how to use contrasts and subtleties in level design.

Let us revisit Blake Rebouche's GDC Level Design Workshop talk on *Horizon: Zero Dawn*. Several spaces from that game evolved from overly simplistic to nuanced when spatial contradictions were added. Rebouche's first version of one space, where the player must get past a patrolling group of enemies, was rejected as a poor design for being just a large open space with some walls for cover. Figure 6.1 reviews our look at this space from earlier in the book. As covered in Chapter 3, part of improving this space was enhancing how players arrived in it. However, Rebouche included other improvements in his final design: changes in elevation, improved vantage points, places to hide, etc. Figure 6.2 once again shows the final space. This example is worth revisiting because it shows how the concepts we have explored up until now are less interesting when used in isolation.

Rebouche's early version is a pure *prospect* in that it is a large open space with a few masses to take cover behind. We have also briefly discussed finding multiple uses for game mechanics, or *juicing* them, as the practice

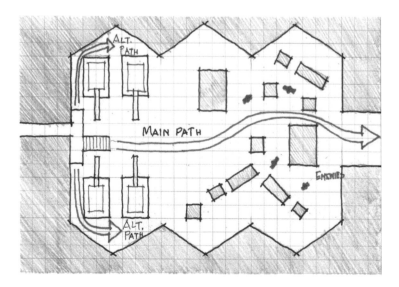

FIGURE 6.1   An early version of a space from *Horizon: Zero Dawn*. This version was cited as too simplistic by the designer's superiors.

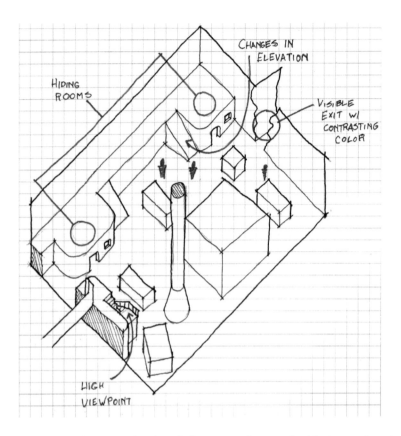

FIGURE 6.2 A diagram of Rebouche's improved space, highlighting elevation changes, hiding places, and other complexities that led to it being a more interesting level.

is known in indie game development circles. Rebouche's final version of the room is more "juiced": the player's ability to sneak is at times strengthened and at other times threatened by the elevation changes and hiding spots in the room. Venturi discusses architectural spaces that are *both-and* and *either-or*, meaning that one space can have multiple functions: structural, spiritual, programmatic, etc.[4] Players of stealth games know this feeling well: with the right strategy, a space can become a weapon against your enemies. One wrong route or error in judgment, though, can turn the same space into a liability.

Contradictions in level design are great ways to make engaging spaces and, in this chapter, we will discuss how a foundational part of gameplay, failure and loss states, can be used to engage players.

Maslow's Hierarchy of Needs

In game design theory, especially sociology-focused academic theory, the metaphor of death as a stand-in for losing games is a popular topic. Losing the game is losing our ability to continue playing. In early arcade games, this idea was translated into game economics: "dying" in the game required a player to insert another coin to keep playing. Even today, when fewer games rely on "lives" as a foundational mechanic, mechanics that halt forward momentum are a big part of games. If we still think of avoiding in-game death as a motivating factor for players, this gives level designers a tool for engaging players: their survival instincts. In his paper "A Theory of Human Motivation," Abraham Maslow proposed a *hierarchy of needs* that describes how humans prioritize their motivations. In this hierarchy, physiological needs such as shelter, food, and sleep rank among the most important, while self-actualization needs such as creativity and problem-solving are among the least important[5] (Figure 6.3). Even now, these hierarchical needs influence our feelings toward much in the world around us. In *Origins of Architectural Pleasure*, architect Grant Hildebrand studies humanity's shelter-based survival instincts and proposes a series of spatial principles for creating pleasurable spaces based on architectures that humanity has historically found safe.

"Bad Spaces": Vulnerability as a Game Mechanic

The game avatar's ability to fail is one way that it becomes relatable for game players. As a resource for continued gameplay, the avatar is valuable and

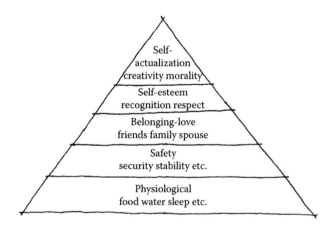

FIGURE 6.3   Maslow's hierarchy of needs.

must be protected. Its vulnerability taps into our own survival instincts and need to protect ourselves from exterior dangers. Architecture and level design differ from one another in the way they handle dangers. According to Hildebrand, architects should strive for pleasurable spaces through the contrast of safe and unsafe architectures that ultimately favor safety. In level design, we can be much more heavy-handed with utilization of dangerous elements, as the risk of failure through loss of life or gameplay chances is ingrained in the experience. This also extends to gaming's use of enemies. Except for Daedalus and the Minotaur, few architects design structures with monsters as part of the design. However, enemies can be an important element of many video game levels and should be carefully planned as part of the experience of gamespaces.

In the last chapter, we saw that levels become *memory palaces* through the relationship between player abilities and level geometry. In a game like *Metal Gear Solid*, the player avatar (in this case, Solid Snake) has abilities that let it directly interact with level geometry, in this case hiding under objects, leaning against walls, and so on. In this way, the design of a space becomes a set of pieces that a player can use in his or her strategy for winning the game. In games like *Dishonored* or *Metroid*, the player avatar's set of moves can be upgraded or expanded, changing how the player uses the environment. This creates several opportunities for complex gameplay. Players must find enhancements that enable them to increase their capabilities and access more of the game world. This structure can be regulated by the design of the game's world and provides opportunities for exploration and achievement-based goals.

Levels that use complex paths that play at survival mechanics make achieving these goals a risky and exciting proposition. Borrowing a phrase from Venturi's quoting of Louis Kahn, "bad spaces" in games are ones we design to put players in specific and exhilarating danger. Creating contrasts of safe and dangerous spaces from scene to scene, or even within a single scene, is one way to create gameplay complexity and "juice" level design. First, we need to understand how a player's vulnerability works in the structure of both an entire game and in micro-scaled game scenes.

Vulnerability as a Game Structure

Games that allow players to minimize their vulnerability over time tap into our own quest for natural growth and enhancement. Adventure games such as *The Legend of Zelda*[6] and *Metroid*[7] and roleplaying games such as *Dragon Quest*[8] base their overall structures on this idea. Players

are confined to a small territory of a large map by either powerful enemies or an environmental obstacle they cannot cross. As players explore
this limited space, they can find enhancements that allow them to move
outside the territory or more easily defeat monsters that previously held
them back. This pattern is repeated throughout a game, with the game
environment continually expanding as the player explores and progresses.
Eventually the player avatar can explore the entire map and easily overcome dangers he or she once found insurmountable. As a game structure,
vulnerability-based design is very environmental in nature and can create
memorable worlds, such as *Zelda*'s Hyrule or *Metroid*'s planet Zebes.

Vulnerability in Individual Game Challenges

While vulnerability-based game structures are not overly complex in pure
spatial terms, they offer a nice feeling of achievement and drama as players
see how far they can push their limits. If we try to think more in terms of
scenes, however, we can put these same experiences into individual high
or low moments of gameplay. As we will see, the implementation of these
systems depends greatly on the survival mechanics in the game itself.

In the article "Seeing Red: The Pitfalls of Regenerating Health," Eric
Schwarz argues that the addition of regenerating health in games, a system
where an avatar's health state increases over time while not being dam-
aged, fundamentally changed how game levels and challenges are structured.[9] This mechanic, he contends, made game challenges more even and
immediate by allowing players to pause, regenerate, then move forward to
the next challenge without having to explore for resources—a mechanic
very conducive to the pacing of online multiplayer games. However, he
also argues that regenerating health diminishes the pleasure of finding
hidden objects through exploration and the drama of surviving challenges
with low health. At the time of his article, Schwarz could only rely on single-player games as examples of the latter style of gameplay. However, the
rejuvenation of resource-based health mechanics in games like *Fortnite*,
that combine a large open world with multiplayer combat, have provided
case studies of levels that plan for both competition and exploration.

Understanding health systems is central to our exploration of survival
in level design and how to deal with avatar survival mechanics in individual encounters. If form indeed follows core mechanics, we must understand how drama is created in individual scenes through a game's system
of survival mechanics and structure our level's design around maximizing these mechanics. Games where avatars internalize many resource

functions through regeneration, such as those in the *Halo* series,[10] structure high and low moments much more straightforwardly: battles occur
in large areas where players defend themselves by finding cover or stealing
enemy tools (Figure 6.4).

In games where players must manage exterior survival resources, spaces
where players encounter enemies can be experienced differently based on
the combination of spatial design and player condition. This is due to these
games' ability to have varied *game states*, which in design terminology
refers to the condition of a game's players at any one time. Games in which
game states change over small periods of time, such as games where players must manage survival-related resources, can provide opportunities for
dramatic emotional experiences and risk–reward scenarios through their
level design.

For example, a narrow maze where hidden enemies stalk the player can
create vastly different experiences depending on what state the player avatar is in when they enter (Figure 6.5). For players who are low on health,
such a scenario is intensely stressful, as the player is at his or her most
vulnerable and is entering a space in which he or she has a disadvantage.
For players with high health, this kind of space can still represent a significant risk: will they be able to maintain their healthy state through the
dangerous territory? The maze also presents opportunities for risk–reward

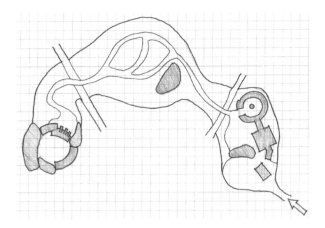

FIGURE 6.4   In games where resource management is dealt with through regenerating systems, levels tend to be very linear and focus on ushering players from
one challenge to another. Moments of high gameplay see the most intricate
environments, which must handle the protagonist's issues of sheltering against
enemies and finding new tools, such as enhanced weaponry from enemy drops.

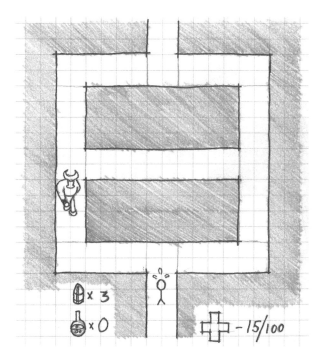

FIGURE 6.5 In games where the game state can change depending on the player's number of resources, level design can be used to create the opportunity for dramatic moments.

gameplay by allowing players to risk extra attack by exploring the entire maze, possibly earning helpful items as a reward. The result of this type of challenge–reward relationship is a level design far less linear than one in a game where resources regenerate (Figure 6.6).

As we have seen, vulnerability, as an element of many games, entices the exploration of gamespaces not just as a game structure, but also as a way to implement risk–reward gameplay. Now that we have explored the foundations of how survival scenarios form emotional experiences in games, we can explore how different formal and atmospheric elements of levels create dramatic gameplay scenarios.

PROSPECT AND REFUGE SPATIAL DESIGN

In Chapter 4, "Basic Gamespaces," we defined three spatial size types: narrow spaces, intimate spaces, and prospect spaces. These size types help designers create emotional experiences by contrasting level form against player metrics in different ways. The results are varying degrees of comfort within gamespaces.

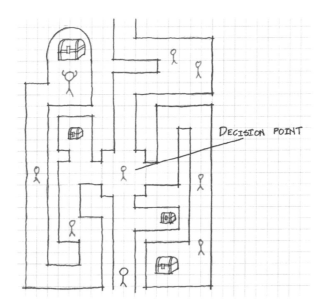

FIGURE 6.6   In games where players must manage their survival resources, level design can take on a much less linear form if the designer creates opportunities for players to risk losing health so they may explore for powerful rewards.

A core element of Hildebrand's survival-based architectural concepts stems from how such spaces are contrasted against one another to create linked sequences of safe and unsafe spaces. He calls these spaces *prospects* and *refuges*.[11] How we contrast them in our levels is one way to create satisfying level complexity.

We have defined prospect spaces as open spaces where one is vulnerable to attack, such as those encountered by early humans who had to explore wide plains to find food and other resources. A refuge, on the other hand, is the contrast to prospect spaces that early humans would return to after their hunt: an intimately sized space that was shielded from view and from which humans could look out onto prospect spaces to evaluate threats (Figure 6.7). The ability to evaluate threats is important when discussing prospect and refuge spaces, as it is this relationship between refuges and prospects that allows us to create gamespaces with this concept.

Creating Paths with Refuges, Prospects, and Secondary Refuges

While one would typically assume that refuges describe permanent living structures, this is not always the case. Borrowing from D.M. Woodcock,[12] Hildebrand divides prospect and refuge further into *primary prospects*,

FIGURE 6.7 Refuge spaces provide protection from external dangers and a place from which to plan how to move forward.

primary refuges, *secondary prospects*, and *secondary refuges*. Primary prospects and refuges are those we are immediately engaged in: the refuge we currently occupy and the prospect we are looking out onto from our refuge. Secondary refuges and prospects are those in the distance—the refuge on the other side of the primary prospect, and the prospect beyond that (Figure 6.8).

FIGURE 6.8 Secondary refuges are protective spaces seen at a distance from refuges and across prospect spaces. Alternations between refuge, prospect, and secondary refuge spaces can create interesting gameplay scenarios.

From a level design standpoint, we are concerned with planning all of these spatial types. However, from a player perspective, we are concerned mainly with the relationships between refuges, prospects, and secondary refuges. These spaces can create exciting gameplay scenarios when used in proper sequence: running from cover point to cover point in a combat game, moving from one hiding spot to another in a stealth game, and many others (Figure 6.9). This type of articulation can be done in spaces of many different sizes too, from a small arena to large landscape. How far a player has to move from refuge to refuge can greatly impact a game's pace.

Prospects and Refuges in Architecture

Prospects and refuges are a mainstay in real-world architecture. In many works, prospect and refuge spaces are used to create a sense of *public–private* contrast: where there are separate spaces for both social and individual activities in a design. When dealing with public–private in the context of prospect–refuge, spaces for private actions are placed in enclosed refuges, while public gathering or circulation spaces are larger prospect spaces. As Hildebrand points out, architectural refuge spaces are often on a different horizontal plane than prospect spaces: higher to provide an advantageous view or lower to provide a cloistered hiding space. He also emphasizes *ceiling height* as essential for differentiating the two: lower ceilings create the feeling of greater protection.[13] So prospect spaces are understood as uncomfortable for humans to linger in, and their uses are typically movement-based, while the uses of refuge spaces in buildings are typically static.

FIGURE 6.9 Refuge–prospect–secondary refuge alternations can create interesting gameplay scenarios.

The IT University of Copenhagen's atrium, designed by Henning Larsen Architects, is one example of how prospect–refuge forms become public–private spaces (Figure 6.10). The atrium is a large public prospect space whose primary function is to allow students to circulate between classrooms. The classrooms, on the other hand, are private enclosed refuge spaces that hang over the atrium and allow occupants to see into the atrium outside.

Issues of prospect and refuge are deeply engrained in the design ideals of two of the most famous modern architects, Le Corbusier and Frank Lloyd Wright. Le Corbusier's architecture has been described as largely prospect dominant.[14] In his book, *Toward an Architecture*[15] (known widely as *Towards a New Architecture*), Le Corbusier outlines his *five points of architecture* (Figure 6.11):

Piloti: thin concrete columns that form the structure of a building, typically arranged in a grid.

Free façade: since the façade is also non-structural, it can be designed freely without the need to have structural elements.

Ribbon windows: long horizontal windows that let in large amounts of light and air.

Open floor plan: unrestrained design of interior rooms since none of the walls are structural.

Roof terrace: a flat roof that can be utilized by occupants.

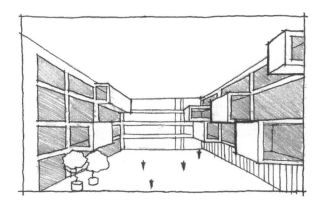

FIGURE 6.10   The IT University of Copenhagen's atrium is a large prospect space through which students can move to the private classrooms, protruding refuge spaces overseeing the atrium.

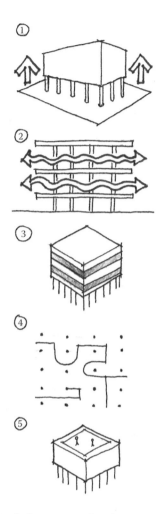

FIGURE 6.11   Le Corbusier's five points of architecture.

Le Corbusier's points emphasize openness and the ability to see from one space to another. This is evident in his most famous work, Villa Savoye—built at Poissy-sur-Seine in 1929—whose wide living spaces are lifted by thin columns and surrounded by wide views of the house's exterior (Figure 6.12). Ramps rise from the ground floor, which houses servants' quarters, to the roof terrace on the third level, with each level having a better view of the wide-open spaces underneath (Figure 6.13). The materiality of the space, lightly colored and unadorned concrete walls, aids in the open feeling of the space by allowing light to reflect throughout.

Frank Lloyd Wright's architecture, on the other hand, is largely refuge-based. His works feature low, broad ceilings, natural materials,

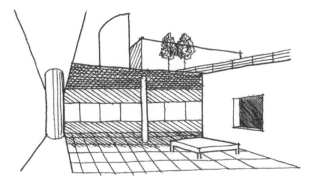

FIGURE 6.12 Sketch of the living space within the second level of Villa Savoye.

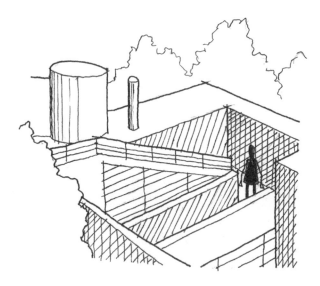

FIGURE 6.13 Sketch of Villa Savoye's ramps as seen from the roof terrace.

and expansive views of the outside consistent with the Prairie School style of architecture. It was a belief of Wright's that the hearth was a central element of the house, and he featured them prominently in the center of many of his most famous works.[16] He utilized depressed sitting areas (Figure 6.14), large exterior overhangs that concealed those within (Figure 6.15), and dictated that perspective drawings of his designs be shown surrounded by trees (Figure 6.16). As Hildebrand suggests, this suggests a tendency toward concealment[17] in many of Wright's works.

FIGURE 6.14   Section of a sitting area typical of Frank Lloyd Wright's building style.

FIGURE 6.15   Reproduction of a section of the Robie House comparing sight lines from outside the house and inside.

Prospects and Refuges in Video Games

An obvious application of prospects and refuges in video games comes from the stealth subgenre in games such as *Metal Gear Solid*.[18] In *Metal Gear Solid*, players progress through the game's levels by finding refuges from which they can discern the placement of enemy guards in prospect territories. Once they have done so, they can move through the prospect spaces to secondary refuges, and so on (Figure 6.17). This shows how prospects and refuges can be used to create discrete paths in games.

When utilizing prospect and refuge gameplay in this way, enemies become important architectural elements and the level itself a spatial puzzle. In *The Nightmare Over Innsmouth*,[19] a companion game I created for my GDC

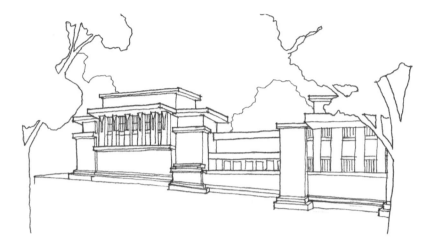

FIGURE 6.16 Exterior sketch of Frank Lloyd Wright's Unity Temple, built in Oak Park, Illinois, between 1905 and 1908. Wright's drawings show the temple nestled among heavy tree cover, though it is actually in a suburban area outside of Chicago.

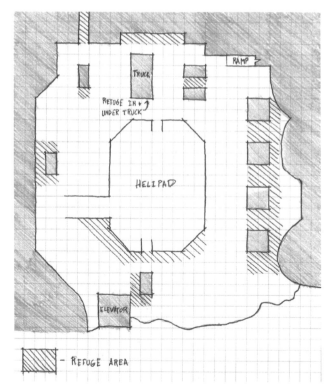

FIGURE 6.17 A plan diagram of a level from *Metal Gear Solid* showing prospect and refuge spaces.

China presentation "Designing Better Levels Through Human Survival Instincts,"[20] enemy behavior design and placement was imperative for turning a courtyard into a prospect–refuge gamespace. In this game, based on the H.P. Lovecraft novella *The Shadow Over Innsmouth*,[21] the player must escape his or her hotel room by crossing rooftop beams, descending into a courtyard, and escaping through an empty house while evil townspeople pursue him or her. The courtyard is designed to utilize prospects and refuges in different ways. Players enter the courtyard from the lower level of a house, whose bottom door is on a lower level than the courtyard itself (Figure 6.18). This refuge creates the sort of arrival that Rebouche created in *Horizon*: a space on a different vertical plane than the area around it from which the player could observe enemies. From here they can look into the courtyard and see the entrance to the safe house, highlighted with orange light to contrast with the blue coloring of the courtyard, as well as the patrol paths of several townspeople. These enemies were scripted to patrol between waypoints, which were placed within the direct path from the courtyard entrance to the safe house (Figure 6.19). Players who did not want to have encounters with the enemies had to use their time in refuges studying enemies' patrol patterns and finding the most advantageous time to move to secondary refuges.

The examples of architectural prospects and refuges in the previous section also allow us to understand more subtle uses of prospects and refuges in video games. Le Corbusier's Villa Savoye shows how wide spaces, views from above, and open planning can create a prospect-oriented space. These types of spaces are common in the multiplayer maps of first-person shooters.[22] With its lightly colored architecture, the Boardwalk

FIGURE 6.18 In *The Nightmare Over Innsmouth*, players can use the depressed entrance to the courtyard as a refuge.

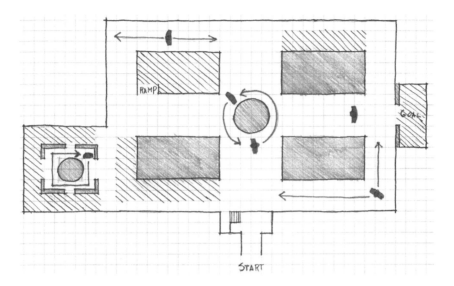

FIGURE 6.19 This plan diagram of the courtyard from *The Nightmare Over Innsmouth* shows enemy paths and refuges.

map of *Halo: Reach*[23] could be taken straight from Le Corbusier's Ville Contemporaine—a "radiant city" with expansive parks, huge causeways, and gleaming towers[24] (Figure 6.20).

Refuges, on the other hand, factor greatly into games where the player must search for hidden passages and secrets, such as *Metroid Prime*.[25] Spaces in this game feature obscure alcoves and cantilevers that hide the game's many hidden items (Figure 6.21). These environments reflect the design values of Frank Lloyd Wright with their often intimate and organic atmosphere.

FIGURE 6.20 Comparison of *Halo: Reach*'s Boardwalk map (right) with Le Corbusier's Ville Contemporaine (left).

FIGURE 6.21   Sketches of environments from the *Metroid Prime* series show how these gamespaces employ Wright-esque details and natural materials to create a secretive, organic look.

Prospects and refuges within level design can be utilized to create vastly different gameplay experiences within one set of gameplay mechanics. Games in the *Mega Man*[26] series, for example, change the experience of their simple core mechanics—run, jump, and shoot—by varying the environmental conditions of battles. For battles with flying enemies, the room may feature several ledges for dodging around Mega Man's freely moving adversaries. Encounters with the Sniper Joe enemy, who hides behind a shield before shooting several bullets in succession, often occur near areas where Mega Man can jump in and out of cover. Boss rooms in these games are often entirely devoid of refuges and are pure prospect spaces, so players can have theatrical showdowns with these unique enemies (Figure 6.22).

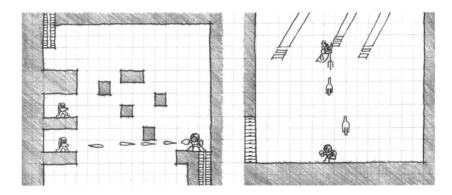

FIGURE 6.22   Despite keeping consistent core mechanics, environments in *Mega Man* games create varied gameplay experiences by changing the prospect–refuge conditions in which players encounter certain enemies.

It is worth noting a unique prospect–refuge experience used in *Half-Life 2*[27] where the prospect space itself is actually dangerous to the player avatar. In a reinvention of the children's game *Hot Lava*, where participants must avoid touching the floor, players must cross a beach under which dangerous alien insects live without touching the sand. They can move across the sand by moving debris with the Gravity Gun weapon to create bridges between rocky cliffs. In this case, the beach is the prospect space and the rocks are the refuges. Unlike the typical employment of prospect and refuge, everything is open. However, using the spatial experience of safe–unsafe contrasts creates a unique and memorable gameplay experience.

Even in a single small gamespace or scene, level designers can create rich spatial experiences by contrasting prospects and refuges. This type of contrast is particularly versatile in creating both linear sequences and multicursal spaces with multiple refuges. In the next section, we will delve even deeper into contrasts by exploring a spatial condition that flips between safe and dangerous: lighting.

SHADE, SHADOW, AND AMBIGUITY

We have just explored prospects and refuges—wide-open bright spaces and comfortably enclosed dark spaces. These spaces can be played against one another to create interesting sequences of gameplay or in the same space to enrich it with complexity. Lacking in complexity is a person's reactions to the space size types that are part of the prospect–refuge relationship. If a space is too big or too small as to be constricting, the player will be uncomfortable. On the other hand, if a space is accommodating to the abilities of a human or game avatar, it is pleasurable.

Our relationships with the *lighting conditions* of these spaces, however, are not so clearly defined. While discussing refuges, Hildebrand suggests that their low lighting conditions offer concealment from exterior dangers located in the brightly lit prospect. However, he later describes other transitions from light to dark as "not so pleasant."[28] He attributes this to the strategic advantage of "seeing without being seen"[28] when one is hiding in the dark. As one moves from dark to light, he or she may instead be the one who is being watched.

Architect Christopher Alexander, on the other hand, advocates for lighting conditions as a device for pulling occupants through space. In *A Pattern Language: Towns, Buildings, Construction*,[29] Alexander describes how light may be used at junctions where the designer would like to lead

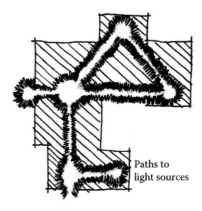

FIGURE 6.23 This sketch, modeled after one drawn by Christopher Alexander, diagrams how light can be used at important junctions along a path.

occupants (Figure 6.23). In discussing complexity, Venturi praises formal and functional *ambiguity*, where one architectural element or space can serve multiple functions under different conditions. In game design, one finds this type of ambiguity in level mechanisms that have multiple uses, especially if those uses contradict one another: dangerous in one version and useful in another. An example might be switches that activate hidden ledges when pressed while deactivating others. In one type of scene, they might help players progress and in another be a hazard if a switch were to deactivate the ledge under it (Figure 6.24). Lighting has a similarly

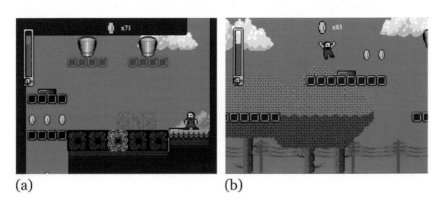

(a)   (b)

FIGURE 6.24 These screenshots from a game I created, *Ice Bucket Challenge*, show how a game object can have ambiguous meanings and functions. In one orientation, the switch helps the player traverse the level by activating helpful ledges and deactivating ones that block the way. In another, the switch is a hazard that deactivates the ledge under the player and plunges him or her into a pit.

ambiguous meaning. In our previous discussions of color and visual communication, lighting was an important element of emphasizing points along a path. Here we explore the contradictory elements of light and dark, and how they create dramatic gameplay experiences.

Shade

The discussions of purely light and dark conditions do not touch upon the many other possibilities available to level designers within their gamespaces. One such possibility is *shade*. Shade is accomplished by allowing diffused lighting into a space through curtains, screens, or stained glass. It was a major feature of Gothic architecture, which strove to create an ethereal experience called *lux nova*, or "new light." This condition was also known as "mystic light" and was used to bring occupants of these churches closer to God. Shade is also a mainstay of the horror genre, with danger obscured by walls of mist.

Whether it is ultimately used to enhance beneficial or dangerous spaces, shade is known to create a sense of *enticement* in humans. As Hildebrand points out, incomplete visual information entices humans to explore and complete their knowledge of what they see.[30] Rhythmic elements such as the columns in the Great Mosque of Cordoba (Figure 6.25) or the pattern of openings and partially revealed galleries in Carlos Scarpa's Castelvecchio

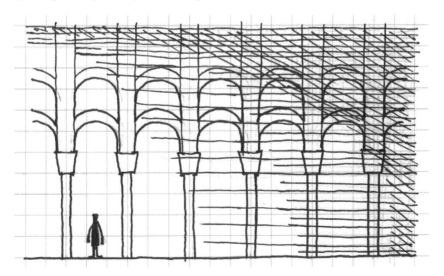

FIGURE 6.25 The shaded conditions inside the Great Mosque of Cordoba (ca. 600 AD) work together with the rhythmic columns to create an enticing space that occupants want to explore.

Museum (Figure 6.26) further entice occupants to move through a space. Combined with shade, the result is a nearly inescapable need to explore.

Shade is an important element of many video games, as its ability to represent both sacred and malevolent spaces allows it to create *atmospheric ambiguity*—a condition where the player is unsure of whether a space is safe or unsafe due to a combination of friendly, unfriendly, and ambiguous spatial indicators. *The Legend of Zelda: Twilight Princess,*[31] for example, utilizes both shade and prospect spaces for the interiors of many dungeons. As players wander through environments, they are left to wonder whether some large spaces are cathedrals that hold an important, sacred item or are the den of an evil monster (Figure 6.27).

The Nightmare Over Innsmouth utilizes shade and colored lighting to create atmospheric ambiguity as players descend into the prospect–refuge courtyard. After navigating a series of rooftop beams, players must enter the window of a house. While the space is safe—actually a moment of low action between a tense balance challenge and an upcoming stealth challenge—the area maintains the level's emotional intensity while giving

FIGURE 6.26 Carlos Scarpa's Castelvecchio Museum in Verona, Italy (1972–1975), features openings between adjacent gallery spaces that entice both through rhythm and the obscuring of what is to the right and left of each portal.

FIGURE 6.27 *Zelda* games often use a combination of shade and prospect spaces to create ambiguous dungeon environments: is the player about to receive an important item or be attacked?

players a break from gameplay intensity. From within the house are the sounds of cultists chanting and an eerie green light—the product of candles encircling a small altar. The visual of the altar (with no actual cultists) and the lighting effect is revealed to players as they descend a tall staircase (Figure 6.28).

Such effects can be created in engines by thoughtfully placing light objects. While one must be mindful of the graphical expense of real-time lighting, dramatic lighting can be accomplished via *light baking* in content creation programs—having the program render a color text for the environment that includes lighting information. Many engines feature *light mapping* capabilities, which produce a texture that contains lighting information, reducing the need for real-time lighting in areas where lighting will not change significantly.

In the mobile game *SWARM!*,[32] the limitations of the target devices only allowed for one directional light: a light object that casts an infinite beam of light in a single direction, much like the sun. Therefore, I had to place each light at the angle that our team wished the light in the scene to come from and tweak the object's settings. As *SWARM!* was built in

FIGURE 6.28 *The Nightmare Over Innsmouth* uses shade to create ambiguous moments of gameplay between points of high action. This allows the game to maintain a tense atmosphere despite a rest from challenges.

Unity, these settings included the ambient lighting color of the level scene, the intensity of the light itself, and its color. With some creative tweaking, many different lighting conditions could be created with only one light (Figure 6.29).

On her blog Love Conquers All Games, game designer Christine Love describes how similar effects were created by the very limited four-shades-of-gray color palettes available on the Nintendo Game Boy and colorized on the Super Game Boy. In her article on colorization on the Super Game Boy, she describes how being able to only use four colors for an entire environment led to more evocative moods in games like *World Heroes 2 Jet*[33] or *King of Fighters'96*[34] when compared to their fully colored arcade counterparts.[35] Though modern 2D color palettes vary, one can see how shade effects can be accomplished by creating scenes with dominant color palettes.

Shadow

While shade is a diffusion of light that presents a mid-ground between light and dark, *shadow* is the condition created when an object obscures the light source and leaves a lack of light. Like shade, shadow has both positive and negative uses. For example, shadows fulfill Hildebrand's

FIGURE 6.29 Screenshots from *SWARM!* demonstrate that different light-ing conditions can be accomplished while still limited to one light per level environment.

aforementioned description of the lighting within refuge spaces. They obscure those within from view and allow them to have a strategic advantage over opponents. This mirrors the friendly associations shadows hold for writers such as Jun'ichiro Tanizaki, who, in his essay *In Praise of Shadows*,[36] reflects on the Japanese's relationship with shadows in their aesthetics, praising their subtlety and contemplative nature against the garish shine and brightness of Western objects.

The developers of the original *Tom Clancy's Splinter Cell*[37] understood this when designing levels for their game, and conceived of the shadows in the game's environments as different spaces than those in the light. For this, they coined the term *shadowspace* to describe the unique areas where the game's protagonist, Sam Fisher, could move around undetected.[38] The Court of the Lions in the Alhambra, located in Granada, Spain, utilizes shadowspace to create the perception of a separate space (Figure 6.30). An arcade surrounds the court and separates the space underneath from the brightly lit courtyard itself. Even though the spaces are fully open to one another, the columns and lighting create the perception of their being separate.

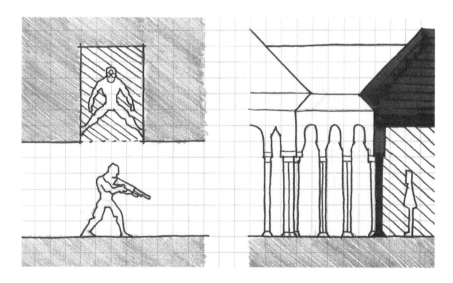

FIGURE 6.30 Shadowspace is when shadows are used to create the perception of separate spaces by changing the lighting conditions within a single space. The term itself was coined by the developers of *Splinter Cell* and can be applied to architectural works such as the Court of the Lions in the Alhambra, Granada, Spain, built between 1362 and 1391 AD.

Shadows can, like physical architectural elements, also create the perception of rhythm. In *The Nightmare Over Innsmouth*, shadows coming from exterior windows of the character's hotel room and laid perpendicular to the player's line of sight are used to establish a rhythm and pull the player further along the main path (Figure 6.31). As pointed out by Valve artist Randy Lundeen, shadows can also be used to create linear elements on surfaces parallel to the player's line of sight that pull the player toward their endpoint.[39] Due to perspective distortion, lines such as those created by the shadows of structural elements will converge on a vanishing point. Used horizontally, this can create a dramatic sign for players to move certain directions in games (Figure 6.32).

Shadows' harmful associations should also be noted. Shadows work against humans when viewed from the light. They create the perception that they are hiding danger, which may very well be true in video games. In games such as *Half-Life 2*, dark alcoves are harbingers of enemy headcrabs, small creatures that leap at the player or turn non-player characters (NPCs) into zombies. This motif is also present in nearly every horror-themed game, where darkness may not only hide enemies, but also affect players in much more powerful ways.

Negative Space

Even when there is no danger within dark corners of caves or gamespaces, the psychological effect of the unknown cannot be ignored. In games, architecture, and media, darkness is just one way that designers build the perception of *negative space*. In art and graphic design, negative space is unused or blank space in a work, the exposure of the background. For our purposes, negative space refers to that which is unknown to the player,

FIGURE 6.31 This rendered plan view of the beginning of *The Nightmare Over Innsmouth* shows how shadows can be baked into an environment to create the perception of rhythmic architectural elements. The layout of this portion of the level also recalls Scarpa's Castelvecchio Museum to create a sense of mystery and excitement in the horror-themed level.

FIGURE 6.32 This perspective sketch shows how shadows can create powerful linear elements that draw a player's eye, and eventually his or her avatar, through a space.

viewer, or occupant. In storytelling this can be the mystery surrounding the motivations of the player. In level design, this can apply to creating anxiety by making players unaware of what surrounds them.

In many ways, negative space is a way to bolster the effectiveness of prospect spaces as it works best when there is a perception of a *beyond* to the gamespace, or that it extends past what the player can see. One such example is the game *Slender: The Eight Pages* by Parsec Productions.[40] In this game, players must search dark woods for eight pages armed with only a flashlight as they are pursued by a malevolent entity known as the Slender Man. The game's very structure is negative space: the environment is a large wooded prospect space shrouded in thick shadows. Slender Man is not a character with a set location or set movement capabilities, but rather is scripted to randomly[41] spawn around the player. This lends an air of mystery to him, as players are unsure of where he will be as they move around. The combination of the heavily shadowed environment and Slender Man's method of movement give Slender Man omnipotence over the gameplay. Even when he is not on screen, the player is aware that he may be anywhere in the environment—a feeling enhanced by the game's sound design. Thus, Slender Man ceases to be simply a humanoid figure, but also is embodied by the shadows.

In addition to its use with shadow, negative space has been used to add a feeling of malevolent unknown to environmental elements, such as bodies of water or architectural spaces. In the film *Jaws*,[42] director Stephen Spielberg withheld a view of the film's monster, a great white shark, for an hour—showing only views from the shark's perspective whenever it was stalking bathers. This decision on Spielberg's part made the shark synonymous with the water itself. Similarly, many science fiction-themed games utilize sound effects to create the impression that the world surrounding the player is bigger than the space directly around the player avatar. *Dead Space*[43] utilizes shadow and sound effects to create the impression that monsters are running through ventilation ducts and other structures within a large space ship. The *Metroid* series utilizes musical themes that are at times more like *soundscapes* rather than actual melodies.

Lighting conditions and negative space are both useful methods of not only putting players in interesting survival scenarios where their enemies are unknown, but also enticing players with withheld information or atmospheric ambiguity.

In the final section of this chapter, we will look at one more dangerous spatial tool that can be contrasted for rich gameplay experiences: height.

LOVING AND HATING HEIGHT

In many of the examples we have seen from popular commercial games, an element consistent in the most interesting levels has been *elevation changes*. Changes in height, whether they be via floating platforms, ramps, stairs, catwalks, or other mechanisms, are a way for level designers to create visually interesting spaces. When we consider dangerous spaces as a way to create spatial drama though, elevation changes gain entirely new and ambiguous meanings. While it is common to have a fear of heights, heights can also give a strategic advantage by allowing occupants of high places to look down on opponents below. In multiplayer games, sniping spots are valuable areas for players to have control of, as they offer a refuge with a wide view of the map. Many strategy games feature mechanics where extra offensive or defensive capabilities are given to units located on higher terrain. In these ways, height is very beneficial indeed.

However, height can also provide an overwhelming sense of danger in gamespaces. While being situated comfortably on a high precipice gives a sense that the high place is a refuge, placing an occupant at a high point with little between him or her and the fall creates a stressful experience (Figure 6.33).

The Nightmare Over Innsmouth explores both elements of height early in the level (Figure 6.34). Near the beginning, the player is forced to cross the structural beams of caved-in rooftops to reach safety. As the beams are the width of the character, crossing them is perilous and requires the player to move slowly. Adding to the perception of height are the caved-in building's windows and the columns holding up the beams that the player is standing on. These vertical elements have the same effect as the shadow lines discussed earlier. Because they appear to converge at a point because of perspective distortion, they create a visual pull toward the bottom of the pit, making the height more intense (Figure 6.35). This is an architectural method modeled after Gothic churches such as the Notre Dame Cathedral in Chartres, France, in which structural columns were not represented as a singular monolithic piece, but as many smaller linear elements. These linear elements would be drawn upward from the floor of the church to the top of the vaulted ceiling to create the experience of peering into

FIGURE 6.33   An occupant's or player's relationship with the edge of a high space determines the experience it creates. When there is an architectural mediation between the occupant and the fall the height is comfortable and advantageous. When there is nothing the height is perilous.

FIGURE 6.34 *The Nightmare Over Innsmouth* demonstrates both uses of height in games: as an advantage and as a danger.

the heavens (Figure 6.36). This method is also used in *Half-Life 2*, which utilizes vertical shadows on the Combine Citadel much in the same way shadows are used inside the structure: to create linear elements that draw the eye toward the shadows' vanishing point. When used vertically, the shadows emphasize the danger of the height.

FIGURE 6.35 In this screenshot, vertical structural elements and windows draw the eye toward the bottom of a pit, making the height feel more intense.

FIGURE 6.36 This sketch of Chartres Cathedral, built between 1194 and 1230, shows how structural elements begin at the floor and are then drawn upward to the top of the church. This draws the eye upward toward the heavens.

The *Innsmouth* level also demonstrates height's beneficial uses. After surviving the walk across the beams, players can look down upon their next major challenge—the prospect–refuge courtyard. This allows players to scout the enemy patterns as though looking at a plan of the level, rather than having to do so from the ground level where the enemies are actually dangerous (Figure 6.37). Like many spatial concepts discussed in this chapter, height can be used by level designers to create interesting experiences for players by utilizing its dualistic nature.

SUMMARY

We have begun our explorations of how to create emotionally evocative gamespaces by investigating spatial orientations related to primal survival

FIGURE 6.37 This screenshot shows how height allows players to look down upon enemies and have a tactical advantage on them. The character in the screenshot can use the time spent on the roof memorizing enemy movement patterns to make the upcoming stealth gameplay easier.

instincts and contrast. While previous sections talked about pure concepts in levels, we are now starting to see how contrasting elements as well as elements with which humans have ambiguous relationships—light, dark, high, low, and so on—can be used for dramatic effect. We also explored the architecture of survival, which provided insights for creating spaces through the use of prospects and refuges.

While many of these architectures correspond with another primal emotion, fear, they can also be used to evoke other emotions by subverting a player's vulnerability to the architectures themselves. This is another aspect of the spatial complexity and ambiguity: taking something that is supposed to be dangerous and subverting it to make it advantageous. Thatgamecompany's *Flower*[44] has players breaking through shadowy environments, bringing light and color to a monochromatic world. *Batman: Arkham Asylum*[45] turns the idea of prospect and refuge on its head by making the game's prospect spaces intimate to Batman's abilities, making him the lurking horror in it. Empowering players in this way can create exhilarating experiences and adds another aspect to our study of contrasts. What do we do when the player successfully navigates or utilizes our contrasted space? We will explore this idea in the next chapter on reward spaces.

EXERCISES

1. **Writing prompt**: Think of a game that uses your player avatar's vulnerability as a way to limit your progress through the game. What kinds of roadblocks did the game put in place to limit your travel? Were some of these roadblocks not doors or walls?

2. **Drawing exercise**: Using a molecule diagram, plot out a level that uses prospect and refuge.

3. **Digital exercise**: Create a graybox of a prospect–refuge level (such as the one you mapped out with the molecule diagram in the last exercise). Take care to use the visual relationships between prospect and refuge spaces into account in your planning.

4. **Digital exercise**: Use the lighting tools of a game engine to add different lighting conditions to a level you are currently working on. Use shade and shadow to build spaces that fit these themes: "pathway," "safety and tension," "curiosity," "wonder."

5. **Writing exercise**: Play a game that utilizes unseen or "negative space" elements to create an emotional experience such as fear. How does the level design of that game emphasize that emotion? How do other elements of the game such as sound effects, physics, or environment art enhance the negative space?

6. **Digital exercise**: Graybox a level that alternates between different experiences of height: safe/advantageous height and unsafe height.

ENDNOTES

1. *Thomas Was Alone*. Mike Bithell (developer and publisher), July 24, 2012. PC game.
2. Venturi, Robert. *Complexity and Contradiction in Architecture*. Second Edition. New York, NY: Museum of Modern Art Department of Publications, 1977.
3. Venturi, Robert. *Complexity and Contradiction in Architecture*. Second Edition. New York, NY: Museum of Modern Art Department of Publications, 1977: p. 16.
4. Venturi, Robert. *Complexity and Contradiction in Architecture*. Second Edition. New York, NY: Museum of Modern Art Department of Publications, 1977: p. 26.
5. Maslow, A.H. A Theory of Human Motivation. *Psychological Review* 50, no. 4 (1943): pp. 370–396.
6. *The Legend of Zelda*. Nintendo (developer and publisher), February 21, 1986. Nintendo Entertainment System game.

7. *Metroid*. Nintendo R&D1 (developer), Nintendo (publisher), August 6, 1986. Nintendo Entertainment System game.
8. *Dragon Quest*. Chunsoft (developer), Enix (publisher), May 27, 1986. Nintendo Entertainment System game.
9. Schwarz, Eric. Gamasutra: Eric Schwarz's Blog—Seeing Red: The Pitfalls of Regenerating Health. Gamasutra—The Art & Business of Making Games. http://gamasutra.com/blogs/EricSchwarz/20120902/176928/Seeing_Red_The_Pitfalls_of_Regenerating_Health.php (accessed May 29, 2013).
10. *Halo: Reach*. Bungie (developer), Microsoft Game Studios (publisher), September 14, 2010. Xbox 360 game.
11. Hildebrand, Grant. *Origins of Architectural Pleasure*. Berkeley, CA: University of California Press, 1999, pp. 24–28.
12. Woodcock, D.M. Functionalist Approach to Environmental Preference. Ph.D. dissertation, University of Michigan, 1982.
13. Hildebrand, Grant. *Origins of Architectural Pleasure*. Berkeley, CA: University of California Press, 1999, p. 32.
14. Hildebrand, Grant. *Origins of Architectural Pleasure*. Berkeley, CA: University of California Press, 1999, p. 39.
15. Le Corbusier. *Towards a New Architecture*. New York, NY: Dover Publications, 1986.
16. Frank Lloyd Wright—The Prairie Style: From Theory to Practice. Frank Lloyd Wright's Westcott House. http://www.westcotthouse.org/prairie_style.html (accessed May 29, 2013).
17. Hildebrand, Grant. *Origins of Architectural Pleasure*. Berkeley, CA: University of California Press, 1999, p. 33.
18. *Metal Gear Solid*. Konami Computer Entertainment Japan (developer), Konami (publisher), September 3, 1998. Sony Playstation game.
19. *The Nightmare Over Innsmouth*. Christopher Totten (developer), 2011. Demonstrative PC game for GDC China presentation.
20. Totten, Christopher. Designing Better Levels Through Human Survival Instincts. Half-day tutorial presentation at the Game Developers Conference, Shanghai, China, November 12–14, 2011.
21. Lovecraft, H.P., and S.T. Joshi, eds. The Shadow Over Innsmouth. In *The Call of Cthulhu and Other Weird Stories*. New York, NY: Penguin Books, 1999, pp. 268–335.
22. It is this author's belief that Le Corbusier would have been an amazing designer of FPS deathmatch maps.
23. *Halo: Reach*. Bungie (developer), Microsoft Game Studios (publisher), September 14, 2010. Xbox game.
24. It should be noted that (as will be discussed in a later chapter) Ville Contemporaine was built to separate the mechanics of one's life—living, working, shopping, etc.—into discrete districts separate from one another, so the comparison to Boardwalk is mainly a stylistic one. The city's own scale was massive, as Le Corbusier designed the city around the use of cars and airplanes, which he loved and figured everyone would have in the future. If Boardwalk were to truly be something out of Ville Contemporaine, players would never even see one another, much less have a deathmatch.

25. *Metroid Prime*. Retro Studios (developer), Nintendo (publisher), November 17, 2002. Nintendo Gamecube game.

26. *Mega Man*. Capcom (developer and publisher), December 17, 1987. Nintendo Entertainment System game.

27. *Half-Life 2*. Valve Corporation (developer and publisher), November 16, 2004. PC game.

28. Hildebrand, Grant. *Origins of Architectural Pleasure*. Berkeley, CA: University of California Press, 1999, p. 54.

29. Alexander, Christopher, Sara Ishikawa, and Murray Silverstein. *A Pattern Language: Towns, Buildings, Construction*. New York, NY: Oxford University Press, 1977, pp. 645–646.

30. Hildebrand, Grant. *Origins of Architectural Pleasure*. Berkeley, CA: University of California Press, 1999, p. 51.

31. *The Legend of Zelda: Twilight Princess*. Nintendo EAD Group No. 3 (developer), Nintendo (publisher), November 19, 2006. Nintendo Wii game.

32. *SWARM!*. e4 Software (developer and publisher), January 2, 2013. Mobile device game.

33. *World Heroes 2 Jet*. ADK (developer and publisher), April 26, 1994. Game Boy game.

34. *King of Fighters '96*. SNK (developer and publisher), July 30, 1996. Game Boy game.

35. Love, Christine. Fuck the Super Game Boy: Fighting Games. Love Conquers All Games. http://loveconquersallgam.es/post/2361219481/fuck-the-super-game-boy-fighting-games (accessed May 31, 2013).

36. Tanizaki, Jun'ichiro. *In Praise of Shadows*. New Haven, CT: Leete's Island Books, 1977.

37. *Tom Clancy's Splinter Cell*. Ubisoft Montreal (developer), Ubisoft (publisher), November 17, 2002. Xbox game.

38. Borries, Friedrich von, Steffen P. Walz, and Matthias Böttger. *Space Time Play Computer Games, Architecture and Urbanism: The Next Level*. Basel: Birkhauser, 2007, pp. 84–85.

39. Lundeen, Randy. Interview by author. Personal. Valve Corporation, Bellvue, WA, October 27, 2008.

40. *Slender: The Eight Pages*. Parsec Productions (developer and publisher), June 26, 2012. PC game.

41. Technically there's no such thing as true randomness with scripting, but this is the best word for it.

42. *Jaws*. DVD. Directed by Steven Spielberg. Universal City, CA: Universal Home Video, 1975.

43. *Dead Space*. Visceral Games (developer), Electronic Arts (publisher), October 14, 2008. Xbox 360 game.

44. *Flower*. Thatgamecompany (developer), Sony Computer Entertainment (publisher), February 12, 2009. Sony Playstation 3 game.

45. *Batman: Arkham Asylum*. Rocksteady Studios (developer), Eidos Interactive (publisher), August 25, 2009. Xbox 360 game.

INDUSTRY PERSPECTIVES: A COMMON LANGUAGE FOR LEVEL DESIGN

Camden Bayer

Level Architect, Arkane Studios

My experience with environment art and level design has been gained by immersion. I'd fire up the editor (or other 3D tool) and make stuff, then my peers or my lead would look at and play what I made, and then I'd iterate based on their feedback. Critiquing each other's work often exposed gaps in our language to describe what the level design was actually doing. We'd talk in circles, trying to describe why something was or was not working. Usually, I didn't know what was right until after a variety of people had a chance to play my work.

It was like we drove with our eyes on the rearview mirror, while wishing there was a way to look forward.

What was needed was a "critical language" for level design. An example learning loop from before we had one comes from eight years ago:

"Why is everyone standing THERE?" I thought to myself. I was sitting on the floor in our Usability Research Lab, quietly watching eight people play one of my levels. I was the environment artist for the "infestation mode" of *Red Faction: Armageddon*, a four-player wave-based co-op mode (basically, "horde mode" with jumping aliens, defense points, and destructible buildings).

Over and over, I watched in horror as the players chose tactics that I knew to be suicidal in that level. All the players bunched up in the central kill-zone while waves of aliens savaged them from all sides. Players neglected the outer loops where all the refuge spaces and pickups were—this was prime real estate to create crossfire into the kill-zone! It was a complete inversion of how to best play the level.

I had recently seen [YouTuber] Egoraptor's video on visual conveyance in *Mega Man X*, and had observed many effective eye-leading techniques (and visual symbolism) in *Mass Effect 2*. As the environment artist, I took it as my responsibility to make sure that the visuals compelled the players to make choices that worked with the level design. Why on Earth (or… Mars) were the players just standing THERE?

Then it clicked.

The useful part of the level (with the refuges and strongholds) was themed as an abandoned cave town. To help sell the ruined, abandoned look, I had placed heaps of burning debris everywhere. To escalate the creepiness, I had made some destructible cover pieces that were dressed as spacecraft paneling with the aluminum ribs extending past the frame and sharpened into points—a cool and threatening "jawbone" silhouette. To jive with the creepy vibe I had gone with, the lighting artists did awesome flickering backlight on the cover pieces (using the fire on the debris) and, for background contrast, kept the outer loop dark. Meanwhile, the middle kill-zone was lit with bright, friendly neutral overhead lights.

The kill-zone was bright and friendly, while the useful part of the level was a dark, burning hell-scape: FACEPALM.

I took quick notes, slipped out of the Usability Research Lab, and walked rapidly to the Lighting Team's room. I explained the player confusion that I witnessed, suggested a fix, shared what I planned to do, apologized profusely for requesting rework, told them I really dug what they had done with the fire and was sad to see that go, and then hurried to my own workstation.

I promptly deleted much of the fire, added some ceiling light fixtures to the outer loop, and added a ton of blood and gore decals to the kill-zone. In a few days, the lighting artist called me over to show me the fixes on his end. It was exactly what we needed, and follow-up playtests showed improved player choices.

I learned the hard way that beautiful art, improperly focused, could hijack your players' instincts and drive them to suicidal game tactics. Frustrated players will then blame your game for being unfair, and will abandon it for other entertainment. Therefore, the art and the gameplay must work together on a subtle, emotional level. That means that the artists and designers on your team need to be able to talk (for planning and coordination) about the art and the design from an emotion-inducing perspective.

We have tons of information from centuries of art theory terminology that was refined by marketing psychology and film study over the last century, and this is covered at any effective art program. You have to dig a little more to learn about the psychology of level design, and that's where Chris' work comes in.

Have you ever heard an idea so profound that you had to reassess everything you thought you knew before into a new framework of thinking?

Jeff Touchstone, one of my co-workers, introduced me to examples of critical language about level design, including terminology about survival-based design, as part of a workshop on level design. Having a shared language was a pivotal moment in my personal growth as a developer and helped our team advance our craft.

Shortly after the workshop, I noticed all the survival space elements described in our workshop that were designed into my daughter's favorite indoor playgrounds. These playgrounds were dotted with refuge spaces of varying kinds for smaller kids to shelter themselves from faster-moving big kids. Meanwhile, the bigger kids spent more time in the prospect spaces and expanded out to master more advanced (often elevated) areas of the playground, like a progression-based videogame!

As I thought more about these elements found in many game levels, I found myself not just thinking about basic tactical choices in my own levels (like cover, flow, fanning, and funneling), but also about the emotional intent of affordance interplay with refuge, prospect, intimate space (sphere of influence), and narrow space. This shift improved my creative clarity and mental variety when I gathered reference and sketched new spaces. It helped me to understand more how art and design blend together into an experience.

As we integrated this terminology into practice, our shared level design critiques at work also benefited from clearer thinking. "We need to add a refuge space just past this entrance, with some elevation to better frame the prospect space so players can plan their route, and add some leading lines and maybe a color or light element back to the exit in case they get turned around while flanking" is more helpful and creatively engaging than a tired mantra like, "Player keeps getting shot, we need more cover."

It is still vital for us to play each other's work and learn afterwards, but by starting with stronger spaces our critiques are faster and more effective. Also, having resources that we can refer back to that describe theories relevant to our work in the industry is pretty awesome.

CHAPTER 7

Rewards in Gamespaces

Golf can best be defined as an endless series of tragedies obscured by the occasional miracle.

—UNKNOWN AUTHOR[1]

What if everything that you see, is more than what you see? The person next to you is a warrior and the space that appears empty is a door to another world? What if something appears that shouldn't? You either dismiss it or accept that there is more to the world than you think. Perhaps it is really a doorway, and if you choose to go inside, you'll find many unexpected things.

—SHIGERU MIYAMOTO[2]

The above quotes highlight the cause-and-effect nature of this chapter, which explores rewards in games and spatial orientations that can make them more rewarding. We have previously discussed elements of rewards—how they may be used to teach, and the challenges that often precede them. The last chapter explored concepts of contrast and ambiguity: elements like shadows, height, refuges, and so on give spaces a positive or negative character based on their use. Now we explore another element of contrast in game levels, the pleasurable rewards that break up moments of danger and conflict. Beyond teaching, these rewards help us as level designers pace our gameplay and urge players to further explore our worlds.

This chapter focuses on the experience of the rewards themselves, particularly what makes them satisfying to obtain and how we can make players aware of them in the first place. We look at how rewards contribute to the psychological journeys players take through our games. Next, we explore the types of rewards found in games, and how they facilitate movement through gamespaces. Finally, we explore how rewards become goals that create the structure for entire game worlds.

What you will learn in this chapter:

The purpose of rewards

The types of rewards in gamespaces

Making rewards exciting through denial

Goals and reward schedules

THE PURPOSE OF REWARDS

At first glance, the purpose of rewards in games should be obvious: to give players a payoff for engaging a game, achieving specific goals, or improving their performance. However, in level design, designers can provide players with options of how to proceed through a gamespace, straight through the main action pieces or on longer paths of exploration, by suggesting the presence of rewards. Therefore, we may say that the purposes of rewards in level design are:

Incentivizing in-game behaviors

Enticing exploration

Creating a sense of curiosity

These three goals will form the basis of how we view rewards in this chapter and how we define how rewards are utilized in gamespaces. Before moving forward, we shall further explore these goals.

Incentivizing In-Game Behaviors

Much of how we utilize rewards in game design is derived from the work of Ivan Pavlov, B.F. Skinner, and other behaviorists. Behaviorists are psychologists who concern themselves with observable behaviors in organisms and how to change those behaviors. Classic experiments by behaviorists such as Pavlov and Skinner included using rewards as a way to teach subjects that certain behaviors were desirable.

As with classical behaviorism, rewards are useful in games for incentivizing and reinforcing gameplay mechanics. Incentivizing is a useful method of teaching players how to play a game by rewarding them when they correctly execute gameplay mechanics. Rewards are also useful for attracting players to games and convincing them to spend more time in a game. As argued by Bernard Suits in *The Grasshopper: Games, Life, and Utopia*, games employ *indirect* methods toward accomplishing goals that seem inefficient compared to how one would accomplish the same goal outside of a game. He uses the examples of boxing and golf—if you want to make someone stay down for 10 seconds, you would use a force much greater than punches; if you want to get a ball into a cup, you would not hit it with a stick from hundreds of yards away.[3] However, the boxer who knocks down his opponent wins the fight and moves up in ranking, and a successful golfer can boast about completing a hole under par—the standard number of strokes it takes to complete a given hole. The pleasure of earning in-game rewards for these actions gives a reason to play despite what appear to be real-world inefficiencies.

In a spatial sense, rewards are useful for making a player take risks or leave the game's "main path" in favor of exploration. In Chapter 6, we explored a number of spatial arrangements that humans consider dangerous: areas where people are open to attack, shadowed spaces, and heights. There are also spaces that seem illogical to travel through: if you have ever "taken the scenic route" instead of going straight to your destination, you have experienced this. Just as pleasurable scenery or a memorable landmark entice people to take alternative routes in the real world, extra rewards incentivize extra exploration of a game world.

Enticing Exploration

As resources, rewards have some type of scarcity or use that makes them valuable: enhancements to or refilling of the player's health, new weapons, ammunition, or an important quest item. For the level designer providing players with opportunities for exploration within his or her gamespaces, directly alerting players to the presence of rewards is an effective tool. It is here where the concept of a player's sight lines, which have been very important throughout the book, once again comes into play. Rewards that are put into the player's line of sight (Figure 7.1) but kept out of reach can be powerful motivators to explore the level he or she currently inhabits beyond any obvious routes.

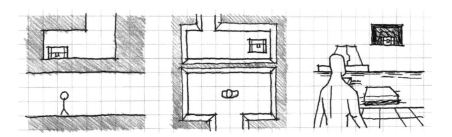

FIGURE 7.1 These sketches demonstrate how rewards can be shown to a player in different camera orientations. By making a reward visible within the player's line of sight, but obscuring the path to that reward, the player is enticed to explore further.

I.M. Pei uses this method in the National Gallery of Art's East Wing in Washington, D.C. Visitors that enter the building's large atrium can see exhibits and other amenities along with pathways to these spaces. In this way, the visitor is motivated to choose a route and find his or her way to one of these enticing experiences. An example that combines both real and game-world instances of this sort of exploration is Niantic's *Pokémon GO!*. In this game, players are shown a map of their real-world location overlaid with images of Pokémon characters. If players reach these characters, they can add them to their collection or even travel with them as partners. In my own *Pokémon GO!* adventures, I would turn the game on during the walking portion of my commute and stop to find new monsters. In more than one case, this led me not only off my direct path, but also to parks, monuments, and public art that I would not have otherwise found.

This reaction is stronger in levels where the designer shows the reward but obscures or merely hints at the path to the reward itself. This can be accomplished by requiring the player to go through other rooms to reach the reward, placing the path behind walls that hint at the path through windows or cracks, etc. This places responsibility for finding the path in the hands of the player, giving him or her a mystery to solve.

Creating a Sense of Curiosity

Curiosity is an important emotion in game development. While the concept of eliciting curiosity is similar to enticement, it is much more abstract. Rather than directly showing a reward to a player, the player gets clues that a reward may be nearby and is thus curious to see if the reward is indeed there. This can be accomplished with the use of modular assets, textures, lighting techniques, or anything that can be prefabricated and reused throughout a game as a symbol.

Once again, I.M. Pei exemplifies this concept with a museum, in this case the Rock and Roll Hall of Fame in Cleveland, Ohio. Unlike the National Gallery's East Wing, exhibits are only partially visible on the Rock Hall's terraced balconies and the circulation spaces are partially obscured. Neon signs and artifacts from more recent artists like Moby, Gwen Stefani, and Weezer draw visitors toward paths that lead to more arcane and historic pieces. This creates the feeling that the museum is a shelf of mysterious objects inviting the visitor to find them. Searching for these spaces moves visitors past attractions they may not have otherwise visited.

As discussed in Chapter 2, "Drawing for Level Designers," a main goal of level design is the augmentation of space with information. Establishing *rewarded patterns* of gamespaces or modular assets is one way to feed information to players as they play (Figure 7.2). As these patterns of rewards are demonstrated, such as the lambda symbol in *Half-Life 2*[4] near friendly bases or weapon caches, players will know to look for further opportunities to be rewarded. In games where players must hunt down metric-expanding rewards to progress, curiosity can be a vital part of the game's core experience for finding both required and extra items. In *Castlevania: Symphony of the Night*, players explore a castle where they are regularly teased with out-of-reach ledges or doorways they cannot open. These are made very visible and apparent to players so when they receive a

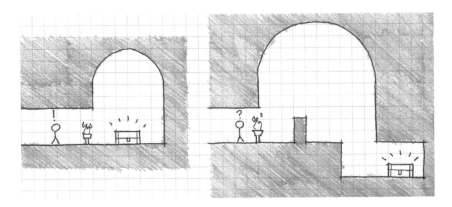

FIGURE 7.2   If players are rewarded for exploring spaces of a type or with certain visual elements, they will learn to recognize that rewards may be nearby if they recognize similar areas later in the game. This will make them curious to explore.

new ability, such as a higher jump or a door-opening spell, they can recall and return to the places those abilities can be used.

The ways in which rewards entice further engagement into a gamespace and reinforce game mechanics depend on the types of rewards utilized. We will explore several types of rewards in games and how they apply to spatial design in games.

THE TYPES OF REWARDS IN GAMESPACES

Now that we understand what rewards are for in game levels, we can discuss the types of game rewards that can be utilized in gamespaces. In *Rules of Play: Game Design Fundamentals*, Katie Salen and Eric Zimmerman describe the following types of rewards:

> Rewards of glory: a sense of achievement gained by overcoming challenges in a game or winning a game. These rewards are not necessarily part of a game's mechanics.[5]
>
> Rewards of sustenance: in-game objects that allow players to maintain their avatar in some way: health, ammo, magic, etc.
>
> Rewards of access: an item or other gained resource that allows players to access a previously inaccessible area, such as a locked door. These are often one-time-use items such as keys. These may also include access to narrative items, such as video logs, or out-of-game information, such as concept art.
>
> Rewards of facility: a new ability for a player that expands his or her moveset in some way. These may or may not also allow access to new areas.[6]

These rewards work within general game design to describe a game's effect on players and how resources can be allocated as a reward for overcoming obstacles. Our goals for rewards in level design describe a lot of these, especially rewards of facility and rewards of sustenance. However, these rewards are largely item-based: resource recharges, keys, power-ups, and the like. While in level design we are concerned with the *placement* of these reward items in space, as discussed in using rewards for enticement, there are also types of level spaces or experiences that can themselves be rewards. This section discusses the types of *reward spaces* and how they correspond to the item and mechanic rewards identified by Salen and Zimmerman. These spaces are:

Reward vaults

Rewarding vistas

Meditative space

Narrative stages

As we will see, these spaces address issues of pacing, sight lines, and scripted events. By exploring what makes these spaces rewarding, we can understand how to create interesting levels with them.

Reward Vaults

The first and most obvious reward space in games is the reward vault. These spaces contain items, information, and other resources that constitute Salen and Zimmerman's gameplay reward types. They can be used for gameplay management opportunities such as save rooms. In terms of form and construction, these spaces frequently distinguish themselves from other level spaces in terms of lighting, music, or spatial character. Like the apse of a church, they are often intimately sized and may feature high ceilings or *vaulting*, the use of arches to create a ceiling or roof, to architecturally celebrate the space (Figure 7.3).

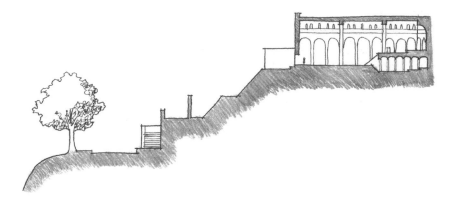

FIGURE 7.3 In many Western Christian churches, the altar is often located at the end of the longitudinal axis of the church and celebrated with a half-domed ceiling structure such as in this sectional sketch of the church of St. Miniato Al Monte in Florence, Italy (built 1062–1090). This is referred to in architectural design as the apse of a church. Visitors reach the church and this important interior space after climbing a series of staircases both outside and inside the building.

A prime example of reward vaults is the item rooms from the *Metroid* series. In the original *Metroid*,[7] these rooms feature a consistent architectural language throughout and have their own music. This uniqueness reinforces the idea that the space is for a function apart from typical gameplay. Also, ceremonial statues with outstretched hands, evoking the architecture of ancient temples, hold reward items. Later games in the series would further embellish these spaces with columns, arches, and other temple forms.

A less obvious example of reward vaults comes in *Bioshock Infinite*,[8] in which the player can find caches of items in storerooms off of the game's main pathways. These vaults require short bouts of exploration and often the use of lock picks to reach. While not celebrated architectural spaces, they still contain rewards of sustenance, such as health, ammo, and salts (the game's mana resource); or rewards of access, such as audio logs.

Rewarding Vistas

An important but often overlooked reward in gamespaces is rewarding vistas, or impressive views of scenery. Like rewards of glory, these do not often offer anything in terms of gameplay resources. However, they are important for pacing purposes, providing a moment of catharsis after areas of high-action gameplay (Figure 7.4).

Rewarding vistas attract players to linger at them by offering interesting or unique game art to look at: wooded valleys, sunsets, the energy cores of alien architecture, cities, or other "eye candy." Coined by designers at Valve, rewarding vistas are used heavily throughout both *Half-Life 2: Episode 1*[9] and *Half-Life 2: Episode 2*.[10] As these are first-person shooter games, the tendency of players is to run through the game to the next gunfight. However, with an interesting visual asset or animation to look at, players will pause for the intended rest. In games conducive to nearly constant action, like first-person shooters, rewarding vistas help create a pleasantly contrasted moment of quiet gameplay without greatly slowing down the game's pace.

Beyond pacing concerns, rewarding vistas can also be utilized to celebrate spatial achievements such as climbing high structures. In *Batman: Arkham Asylum*,[11] players who explore the high structures outside the asylum can view Gotham City in the distance. Likewise, *The Legend of Zelda: A Link to the Past*[12] rewards players for climbing the maze-like caves of Death Mountain by showing forests and clouds beyond the environment of the game itself.

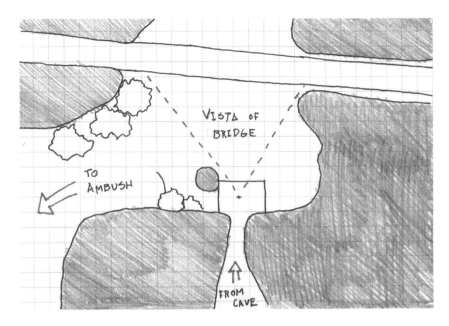

FIGURE 7.4   Rewarding vistas provide a moment of calm after high-paced action gameplay.

Meditative Space

A more extreme version of the rewarding vista is the meditative space. Like rewarding vistas, meditative spaces offer the moments of low-intensity gameplay that are vital for proper game-pacing. Meditative spaces are intimately sized and either provide opportunities for players to enjoy the movement metrics of their avatar or provide an actually meditative atmosphere.

In *The Prince of Persia: The Sands of Time*,[13] water fountains break up the game's intense combat and platforming moments. These spaces offer a relaxing atmosphere with soft lighting and the sound of water as the Prince moves around in the fountain. While also an example of a reward vault, as players can make the Prince drink water to heal himself, these spaces provide a pause in the game's otherwise intense action.

The *Portal*[14] games have players use elevators to travel between puzzle chambers. These spaces offer neither rewarding views nor resources, but break up gameplay so players may mentally recover from the puzzle they just completed and prepare for the puzzle to come.

Narrative Stages

A reward type not addressed by Salen and Zimmerman is the reward of narrative *exposition*, the portion of a story that describes background information to viewers. As an interactive narrative medium, games may utilize storytelling as a reward for completing in-game challenges such as large battles or skill challenges. While the use of narrative gamespaces will be discussed in greater detail in Chapter 9, "Storytelling in Gamespaces," it is important to know that games often utilize narrative as a form of reward.

When designing levels with scripted narrative events, it is important to provide spaces within which these events occur. Like the other rewarding spaces we have explored, these spaces distinguish themselves from others through celebratory architectures such as vaulting, arches, domes, and other structures (Figure 7.5). Games in the *Final Fantasy* series reserve the most

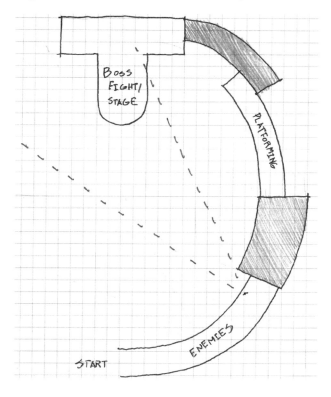

FIGURE 7.5 Narrative reward spaces often have distinguishing architectural characteristics such as domes, towers, or other features. This allows them to both provide an interesting stage at which the often epic narrative events of games may occur and serve as easily identifiable spatial goals.

significant story elements for epic architectural set pieces—the tops of towers, temple interiors, and balconies. In earlier entries, where combat would initiate randomly as players moved through the environment, the spaces approaching narrative stages would also identify themselves through a lack of enemies. Likewise, many of the narrative stages in *Metal Gear Solid*[15] games distinguish themselves with openness—high ceilings and tall monolithic structures for characters to speak from—in a game otherwise focused on alcoves and hiding places. In both examples, the lack of enemies allows players to leave a combat mindset, rest, and prepare to absorb narrative information—even if the narrative scene is followed by a significant battle.

Like rewarding vistas and meditative spaces, narrative stages provide important pacing changes and opportunities for players to rest. These spaces, however, also offer the added reward of allowing players to learn what happens next in a game's story.

These types of reward spaces are not made to stand alone. As examples like the water fountains from *Prince of Persia* show us, reward space types can be mixed together to be both meditative and rewarding, provide both vistas and narrative, or other combinations. Their overall purpose is to give players a sense of achievement and prepare them for upcoming high-intensity gameplay. Reward spaces also interact with spaces that withhold them from players. While we have already explored dangerous spaces, there are other spatial orientations that, when used together with rewards and reward spaces, can entice greater exploration of game levels.

MAKING REWARDS EXCITING THROUGH DENIAL

One aspect of what makes reward spaces rewarding is that they come after other spaces—dangerous spaces or other transitory areas—that make players feel as though they earned the reward. In this way, these spaces enhance the effect of reward spaces through *spatial denial*—the act of withholding rewards from players. While the dangerous spaces that we previously explored provide denial, there are others that, when utilized, hint at rewards while keeping their true nature a secret from players. These denial spaces entice exploration by making players aware of rewards and encouraging curiosity by providing incomplete information. In this section, we will explore several spatial orientations that architects have identified as useful for spatial denial.

Zen Views

As spatial orientations for affecting a user or player's experience within a space, denial is based on controlling a player's line of sight to or awareness of reward spaces. The first comes from an entry in Christopher Alexander's *A Pattern Language*, the *Zen view*, in which Alexander describes its origin:

> A Buddhist monk lived high in the mountains, in a small stone house. Far, far in the distance was the ocean, visible and beautiful from the mountains. But it was not visible from the monk's house itself, nor from the approach road to the house. However, in front of the house there stood a courtyard surrounded by a thick stone wall. As one came to the house, one passed through a gate into this court, and then diagonally across the court to the front door of the house. On the far side of the courtyard there was a slit in the wall, narrow and diagonal, cut through the thickness of the wall. As a person walked across the court, at one spot, where his position lined up with the slit in the wall, for an instant, he could see the ocean. And then he was past it once again and went into the house.[16]

Alexander's tale of the courtyard window describes the Zen view, named for its origin in a Buddhist monk's house, as a deliberate and fleeting experience of a spatial reward experienced when traveling to a destination (in this case, the monk's house, as sketched in Figure 7.6). Alexander contrasts this experience to that of a house where such a view is celebrated with wide picture windows: when the view is constantly exposed and treated as a destination, it eventually loses its power. The monk's small window only allows the view to be experienced for a short while and does not treat it as a destination, allowing the landscape to keep its experiential power.

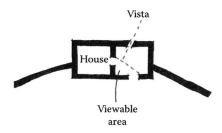

FIGURE 7.6 A sketch of the monk's house as described by Christopher Alexander. The window in the courtyard's stone wall controls occupants' view of the landscape beyond. This denial of a wide view makes the limited experience more rewarding.

In games, Zen views are often the first cognitive interaction that players have with rewards or reward spaces (Figure 7.7). These types of views interact with different reward spaces in different ways. For rewarding vistas and narrative spaces—which, as we have seen, often feature architecture of epic scale—Zen views function much in the same way that they do in Alexander's example: offering a fleeting glimpse of the reward so players will strive to reach it. In the case of reward vaults, the player is often shown a reward—item, treasure chest, etc.—but the path to the reward is somehow obscured, leaving responsibility for reaching the reward in the hands of players.

It should be noted that meditative spaces could be hinted at, but that Zen views are not always sufficient for doing so. These types of spaces work best as surprises or refuges, and are often separated from the rest of a gamespace as part of a narrative device. In *Abzu*, for example, the player occasionally enters a place that is both a significant element of the player's journey, but that also takes place in a dimension separate from the rest of the game world. This makes arrival in that space and in spaces like it in other games surprising and difficult to telegraph. Beyond Zen views, other elements such as music may be used to hint at such spaces. Having music fade in as a player approaches these areas not only entices exploration, but may change the player's interaction pattern: an injured player will dash toward the music for a space that might offer safety and healing. Spatially,

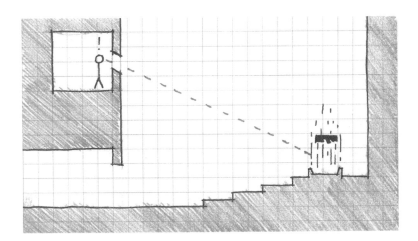

FIGURE 7.7 Zen views in games function in different ways: rewarding vistas and narrative spaces are often hinted at through actual Zen views. While reward vaults can be shown to players, the path to the reward is obscured.

previewing meditative spaces is much subtler, with entryways partially obscured by forking paths. These subtle previews are an important element of one of Frank Lloyd Wright's house designs, which we explore next.

Frank Lloyd Wright's Hanna House

Hanna House, located on the Stanford University campus in California, distinguishes itself from Wright's other designs in several ways, the most important being the architect's first use of a honeycomb grid for the building's plan rather than rectangles (Figure 7.8). While a square or rectangular grid would create 90-degree-angled corners that are difficult to see around for occupants, Wright's design for Hanna House utilizes six-sided shapes with 120-degree corners. The effect allows occupants to partially see around the obtusely angled corners. This provides incomplete information of what lies beyond, requiring visitors to move around the corner to see a complete view of rooms.

The human brain has a remarkable ability to process partial visual information and automatically complete the picture. If part of an image

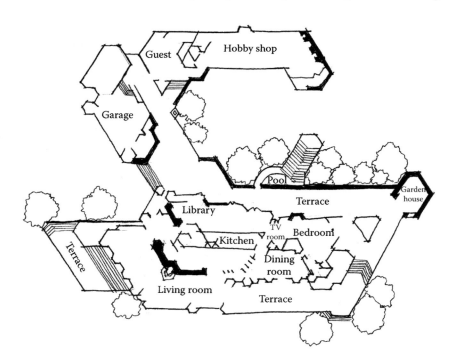

FIGURE 7.8 Plan sketch of Hanna House by Frank Lloyd Wright, built in 1937 in Stanford, California.

that a viewer is familiar with, such as a letter, symbol, or common item in a video game, is obscured, the brain will still be able to understand what the object is. This ability is often used by graphic designers to create optical illusions—such as Rubin's vase, the image that can be interpreted as a vase or two faces looking at one another—or to create incomplete but still readable fonts (Figure 7.9). Hildebrand describes this ability as an important survival tactic: the brain can parse and organize complex or incomplete information into something that can be easily recognized.[17] Hildebrand also highlights this instinct for its ability to incite curiosity: the brain will assume the identity of the incomplete information and seek verification.

Obtuse angles can be utilized in games to partially reveal rewards, enemy encounters, or other important events. They can hint at or warn of things to come or elicit exploration by offering players ambiguous information. This creates a sense of risk: what is around the wide corner may be a reward or may be something dangerous. Passages of this type may obscure meditative reward spaces, keeping them off a level's main path but offering hints at them through partial reveals.

In terms of actual level construction, Hanna House-style passages can be difficult to create. Many engines often work best when utilizing prefabricated square or rectangular objects (in both two and three dimensions). However, creating hexagonal level objects in an external content creation program or through careful design in an engine's internal level editor is possible and has the added benefit of "breaking the grid," obscuring the blocky grids on which the level construction tools of most engines are based (Figure 7.10). The result is an aesthetically pleasing and emotionally evocative gamespace design.

Emotional experiences are core to the design of our next denial space, one that utilizes spatial denial to embody ethereal concepts.

Religious Structures and Eastern Garden Design

Historically, religious spaces or places with spiritual significance have been architecturally separated from their surroundings while

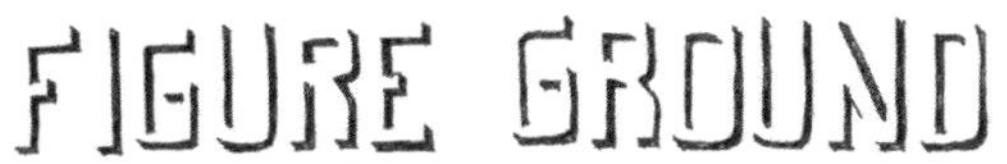

FIGURE GROUND

FIGURE 7.9 Even with incomplete visual information, these letters are still recognizable.

FIGURE 7.10 Honeycomb grids or obtusely angled spaces elicit curiosity by showing players partial information, create a sense of risk, and are useful for "breaking the grid" utilized by many modern game engines.

maintaining connection with them. As seen in Chapter 1, "A Brief History of Architecture and Level Design," early tombs and religious structures in the United Kingdom utilized shafts to allow light into blocked-off inner structures. The biblical Solomon's temple featured a special room for housing the Ark of the Covenant, the Holy of Holies, which could only be entered by the temple's high priest. In Eastern cultures, visitors to temples and houses must often pass through several layers of garden space, each meant to separate visitors from the business of the outside world and spiritually cleanse them before reaching their destination.

The theme of progressing through layers is common in video game dungeon design such as that found in many roleplaying or action games. In *God of War*,[18] player character Kratos must penetrate several layers of a temple to find Pandora's box. Likewise, many games with dungeons utilize the theme of descending—moving downward through floors to the destination of the level. *Quests: Design, Theory, and History in Games and Narratives* author Jeff Howard highlights the theme of descent as one demarcating the progression of players from one goal to another. As players descend through the layers of a dungeon or labyrinth, they are met with both greater challenges and greater rewards. Howard says the layered form of descending spaces allows players to anticipate the rhythm of puzzle and reward challenges.[19]

As the previous examples demonstrate, moving through layers of denial space before reaching a reward can be accomplished horizontally or vertically. As is demonstrated by the example of Eastern garden design, layered denial can be created with several iterations of similar challenges in Montessori-style succession. For example, if a player must pass through three rooms to reach a reward, the first should feature a simple iteration of a challenge to demonstrate how the challenge functions, the second room should be a bit more complex, and the third should be the most difficult (Figure 7.11).

For descent, moving through outer layers, and sequential gardens, these spaces work best when the player is aware that a reward is coming at the end of the sequence, even though the reward is often not shown to players beforehand. In *God of War*, it is well established through storytelling that an important quest item is hidden in the temple. Likewise, dungeons in games like *The Elder Scrolls V: Skyrim*[20] hint at the presence of useful items with environmental cues: tombs and caves are littered with useful items and artifacts that lead to bigger rewards. Such dungeons communicate their own significance through environment art: banners and stone line the walls of tombs instead of blank rock. Such embellishments conjure illustrative associations with hidden items.

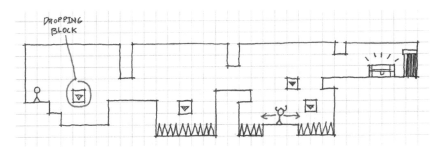

FIGURE 7.11 Layered denial spaces that follow the precedents of religious structures can occur both horizontally and vertically. They can also utilize Montessori-style successions of puzzles and challenges.

While this type of denial space acts more as a level structure, there are also ways to create similar experiences with individual assets.

Layered Walls

As we have seen in the example of Hanna House, interiors are more interesting when occupants are aware of what else is occurring in other spaces. In the case of Hanna House, angles hint at but partially obscure what is around each corner. There are, however, other ways to hint at what is occurring throughout a building. One useful method that both hints at what occurs in other spaces and utilizes the concept of denial through layers is *layered walls*. Rather than creating solid barriers to distinguish one space from another, spaces can be divided with structures that allow the spaces to interact with each other: doorways, windows, trellises, and screens.

In my studio's game *Dead Man's Trail*,[21] in which players must loot towns for supplies, we utilized environment art as denial screens. The game's isometric view allows players to see through fences and behind walls to assess whether a space has enough loot to be worth visiting. While the debris still denies players access to the loot, it also shows what they can find if they explore. Given the game's mechanic of needing to loot towns quickly before a horde reaches the player, enticing exploration in this way makes players weigh the risk of taking extra time to explore against the possibility of finding better supplies.

Layered walls can also deny players access to rewards but may be used to keep players aware of their goals during challenges. *The Legend of Zelda* games apply layered walls in this way regularly. In *Ocarina of Time*,[22] the endpoint of the Gerudo's Fortress level is a maze that players must navigate by utilizing keys gained elsewhere in the dungeon (Figure 7.12). The reward at the end is the Ice Arrow, a powerful magical weapon. Rather than solid stone walls, the designers utilized transparent metal fence textures, so players can see their goal through corridors of the maze. The Temple of Time dungeon of *Twilight Princess* has a room where players must progress by flipping a switch several times to reorient the layered walls in the room between two arrangements. Each wall layer has an opening through which Link may shoot arrows at the switch. While providing a method for the player to progress through the puzzle, the voids in the wall also reveal the player's destination. As the player deals with enemies and collects treasure in the room, the view of the end goal keeps players on task.

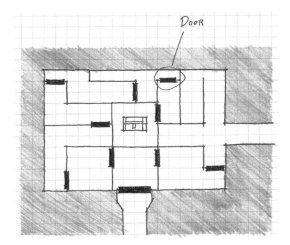

FIGURE 7.12 The Gerudo Fortress environment in *The Legend of Zelda: Ocarina of Time* features a maze of fences so that players can see the goal of the maze, a large treasure chest at the center. This keeps players aware of the goal throughout the dungeon.

The last denial space will also address layered walls that hint at other spaces and combine them with the type of layering found in religious structures.

Oku

In Japanese spatial design, there is a concept known as *oku*. As described by Japanese architect Fumihiko Maki, *oku* is a spatial layout in which the streets, alleyways, and other spaces wind around one another like the layers of an onion. These layers conceal small sitting areas, squares, and gathering spaces that can only be found as someone explores the winding pathways (Figure 7.13). Some of these layers offer opportunities for seeing these spatial rewards through other layers, offering them to explorers who take the time to hunt for them.

In many ways, *oku* is an amalgamation of all of the previously discussed denial spaces: it offers Zen views of other layers of the city through layered walls of urban fabric, features non-90-degree corners that goad explorers, and denies reward spaces with layers of winding passages. *Oku* also shows the power of labyrinths and mazes—the ability not only to be tour puzzles, but also to communicate with players through selective revealing of information. In scenarios where players can view other layers of a maze, there are opportunities for players to gain advantages by observing enemies,

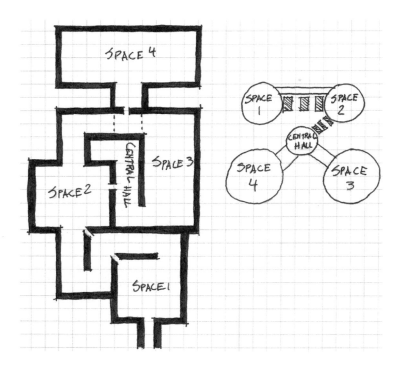

FIGURE 7.13   Spaces laid out according to the principles of *oku* have winding layers of walkways that conceal but hint at places for gathering and rest. *Oku* spaces utilize many different types of denial to create a powerful sense of curiosity.

collecting information on challenges, and finding rewards, among other things.

Oku does not have to exist solely in first- and third-person 3D games. In many ways, the maze from *Pac-Man*[23] follows principles of *oku*. There are winding layers of maze with periodic rewards scattered throughout: power pellets and fruits. Awareness of the reward spaces allowed by the top-down 2D point of view motivates players to rush toward these rewards when necessary to escape enemies or gain points.

Now that we've discussed rewards and the types of spaces that can deny direct access to them, we will explore how we can use rewards on schedules that motivate players to continue moving through games.

GOALS AND REWARD SCHEDULES

As we have seen, rewards and reward spaces of many kinds can be utilized to entice players to continue playing a game. They can be made more exciting to earn through the use of spatial denial that postpones a player's access to the reward. In many ways, the alternation between denial spaces and rewards is core to level design—challenges are designed around player metrics and rewards incentivize playing the challenges.

When designers make players aware of upcoming rewards and motivate the player to reach them—through either showing the reward, describing it through storytelling, or other means—the reward becomes a *goal*. Goals are an essential component of game design. On the one hand, there are often narrative goals that the player achieves through winning a game: saving your beau, bringing peace to the galaxy, creating new planets, etc. Often these goals have little to do with the game's actual mechanics, but help flavor in-game actions in exciting ways. On the other hand, gameplay goals like reaching a high score, finding an item that allows access to new areas, or reaching an important location can be arranged within game levels to create certain experiences. In this section, we will explore different aspects of game goals to discover how they motivate gameplay and keep players engaged for longer.

Long- and Short-Term Goals

Depending on their complexity and length, games typically have more than one goal. For example, the long-term goal of *Super Mario Bros.* is saving Princess Toadstool from Bowser, the evil Koopa King. However, there are thirty-two levels in the original *Super Mario Bros.* If the only mark of success in the game was whether Mario saves the princess, there would be a lot of wasted gameplay and angry players. However, the game has other goals: eliminating enemies, earning power-ups, collecting coins and extra lives, and reaching the end of each individual stage. The game's mechanics are even conducive to players setting their own goals. During the Art of Video Games[24] exhibition at the Smithsonian American Art Museum in Washington, D.C., visitors had a competition to reach level 8–1 in the three minutes of playtime allotted by the exhibit's copy of the game.

Super Mario Bros. and many other games retain player interest because they have *long-term goals*, *short-term goals*, and allow opportunities for *player-defined goals*. These demonstrate how goals are *scalable* throughout a game. Long-term goals are typically important narrative rewards or the ends of quests. These goals provide a distant achievement that players must work for over time. Short-term goals are much more immediate: beat a stage, defeat an enemy, find a health power-up, etc.

Many games that feature *quests*, missions during which players must retrieve an item or complete an action, utilize long strings of long- and short-term goals to move players through the game. In *Ultima IV: Quest of the Avatar*, players must master eight virtues by entering eight temples and exercising the virtues in the game's overworld. There are also quests for artifacts and dungeons to explore. While mastering the virtues and becoming the avatar are long-term goals of the game as a whole, mastering each individual virtue can also be a long-term goal based on where a player is in the game. For example, entering a virtue's shrine requires possessing its rune. When the player is retrieving a rune, that is the immediate short-term goal, while mastering the virtue itself is a longer-term goal that serves the even longer-term goal of mastering the eight virtues.

The Rod of Many Parts

This quest structure—finding or earning a number of items that facilitate the end of a game—is frequently used in games. Examples include *Ultima IV*'s mastering of virtues, *Super Mario Land 2*'s[25] six golden coins for unlocking Mario's castle, and activating elemental lighthouses in *Golden Sun*.[26] Howard compares these types of quests to the Rod of Many Parts, a story structure in which characters must collect seven parts of a magical artifact. Howard cites this structure as a mechanism for marking the progression through game levels and game narratives; the first piece of the rod may be acquired by accident in the game's narrative, but subsequent pieces are the result of the player progressing through further conflicts.[27]

While often used in games, this structure is also useful for establishing a consistent schedule of goals and rewards in game levels. One part of the rod (or one of the crystals, coins, maidens, etc.) is often the goal of one of the game's levels (dungeons, etc.) Each level is divided into a string of smaller challenges: puzzles, enemy encounters, obstacle courses, etc.

Reward Schedules

Doling out goals and rewards in a predictable schedule allows players to *anticipate* upcoming rewards. In many ways, this resembles the classical conditioning practiced by Ivan Pavlov—players will know that after defeating dungeons, for example, they will receive an item. Goal and reward schedules are vital for holding player engagement in games—they keep players aware of when to expect payoffs for their gameplay, and therefore will motivate them to keep playing.

The Rod of Many Parts is far from the only reward schedule used in games. In arcade games, players are rewarded bonuses after each level, and can often rely on special bonus stages to appear incrementally—after two or three regular stages. If a player were to die halfway through the third stage, he or she would be motivated to feed more quarters into the arcade machine to reach the bonus. Similarly, online games like *Fortnite* offer "seasons," where players reap incremental rewards by playing consistently during a period of real-world time. This facilitates a "just one more" scenario in these games, where players keep coming back to build currency and earn desired items.

In terms of level design, reward schedules are important for incentivizing in-game behaviors, enticing exploration, and creating a sense of curiosity through *consistency*. If players know that rewards and items come at a consistent pace, every x number of rooms in a dungeon, for example, they will continue playing to get the next bonus. Players may even be motivated to explore the room in which they expect a reward even if they do not find it immediately accessible.

This extends to symbolic art assets. If it is established that resources can be found by smashing crates or pots, then players will explore a gamespace to find these items. Rewards provide important motivation to explore a gamespace, and consistency in reward schedule helps build expectation of when to expect the next payoff.

SUMMARY

In this chapter, we have explored game rewards as a motivating factor in game levels. We have looked at the effects that game rewards have in game levels, incentivizing in-game behaviors, enticing exploration, and creating a sense of curiosity. We have also explored the types of rewards in both games and gamespaces, including rewarding spatial types that hold items, allowing the player to take a break from quickly paced action, and seeing more of a game's story. We have explored spaces that make rewards more rewarding by denying players immediate access to them, and how these spaces and rewards can be paced to create goal and reward schedules. In their own way, each of the topics we have covered contribute to a player's own narrative of how he or she experiences a game.

Now that we have discussed communication, contrast, danger, and rewards, we will take a step backwards—WAY backwards—and explore the first levels of games. Though these levels seem simple, they present level designers with one of the most difficult jobs of all: teaching players to play the game. It is dangerous to go alone, but we can take the techniques we have learned so far and more that we will see in the next chapter to make excellent tutorial levels.

EXERCISES

1. **Drawing exercise**: Create a molecule diagram for a level that shows a player a reward but denies them access to it initially, forcing them to search.

2. **Digital exercise**: Graybox a level that shows players rewards but denies them access to it unless they search (you may use the molecule diagram from the last exercise).

3. **Game-testing exercise**: Have a player play either a popular commercial game that teases rewards with denial (or one that you have created yourself such as in the graybox level from the last exercise). Observe the player's behavior and try to see how/if his or her path through the level changes upon discovery of the rewards.

4. **Writing prompt**: Find a game that uses at least three of the four types of reward spaces covered in the chapter (Reward Vaults, Rewarding Vistas, Meditative Space, Narrative Stages). How does the game alternate them? How do these different kinds of rewards pull players through the space? How are they spaced out?

5. **Game-testing exercise**: Pick a 3D game or level (or build one) that uses non-orthogonal (non-90-degree) grids in a level and one that uses an orthogonal grid. Have a player play that level and observe how his or her exploration does or does not change based on how views draw him or her to points of interest.

ENDNOTES

1. Furlong, Ron. 50 Greatest Golf Quotes of All Time Bleacher Report. http://bleacherreport.com/articles/540759-50-greatest-golf-quotes-of-all-time/page/30 (accessed June 5, 2013).
2. Sheff, David. *Game Over: Press Start to Continue.* New York, NY: Cyberactive, 1999.
3. Suits, Bernard Herbert. *The Grasshopper: Games, Life, and Utopia.* Toronto: University of Toronto Press, 1978.
4. *Half-Life 2.* Valve Corporation (developer and publisher), November 16, 2004. PC game.
5. Since *Rules of Play*'s publication, many game consoles and online services have begun offering achievement systems that, in a way, quantify these types of rewards.
6. Salen, Katie, and Eric Zimmerman. *Rules of Play: Game Design Fundamentals.* Cambridge, MA: MIT Press, 2003, p. 346.

7. *Metroid.* Nintendo R&D1 (developer), Nintendo (publisher), August 6, 1986. Nintendo Entertainment System game.
8. *Bioshock Infinite.* Irrational Games (developer), 2K Games (publisher), March 26, 2013. Xbox 360 game.
9. *Half-Life 2: Episode 1.* Valve Corporation (developer and publisher), June 1, 2006. PC game.
10. *Half-Life 2: Episode 2.* Valve Corporation (developer and publisher), October 10, 2007. PC game.
11. *Batman: Arkham Asylum.* Rocksteady Studios (developer), Eidos Interactive (publisher), August 25, 2009. Xbox game.
12. *The Legend of Zelda: A Link to the Past.* Nintendo EAD (developer), Nintendo (publisher), November 21, 1991. Super Nintendo game.
13. *The Prince of Persia: Sands of Time.* Ubisoft Montreal (developer), Ubisoft (publisher), 2003. Nintendo GameCube game.
14. *Portal.* Valve Corporation (developer and publisher), 2007. PC game.
15. *Metal Gear Solid.* Konami Computer Entertainment Japan (developer), Konami (publisher), September 3, 1998. Sony Playstation game.
16. Alexander, Christopher, Sara Ishikawa, and Murray Silverstein. *A Pattern Language: Towns, Buildings, Construction.* New York, NY: Oxford University Press, 1977, p. 642.
17. Hildebrand, Grant. *Origins of Architectural Pleasure.* Berkeley, CA: University of California Press, 1999, pp. 92–97.
18. *God of War.* SCE Santa Monica Studios (developer), Sony Computer Entertainment (publisher), March 22, 2005. Playstation 2 game.
19. Howard, Jeff. *Quests: Design, Theory, and History in Games and Narratives.* Wellesley, MA: A.K. Peters, 2008, pp. 50–51.
20. *The Elder Scrolls V: Skyrim.* Bethesda Game Studios (developer), Bethesda Softworks (publisher), November 11, 2011. Xbox 360 game.
21. *Dead Man's Trail.* Pie For Breakfast Games and e4 Software (developers), upcoming. Indie game on Steam.
22. *The Legend of Zelda: Ocarina of Time.* Nintendo EAD (developer), Nintendo (publisher), November 23, 1998. Nintendo 64 game.
23. *Pac-Man.* Namco (developer and publisher), 1981. Arcade game.
24. *The Art of Video Games.* Smithsonian American Art Museum, Washington, DC, March 16–September 30, 2012.
25. *Super Mario Land 2: 6 Golden Coins.* Nintendo R&D1 (developer), Nintendo (publisher), November 2, 1992. Nintendo Game Boy game.
26. *Golden Sun.* Camelot Software Planning (developer), Nintendo (publisher), November 11, 2001. Nintendo Game Boy Advance game.
27. Howard, Jeff. *Quests: Design, Theory, and History in Games and Narratives.* Wellesley, MA: A.K. Peters, 2008, pp. 87–88.

CHAPTER 8

Level 1–1

The Tutorial Level

The definition of a good game is therefore "one that teaches everything it has to offer before the player stops playing."

—RAPH KOSTER[1]

Be proud of your Death Count! The more you die, the more you're learning. Keep going!

—*CELESTE*, LOADING SCREEN GRAPHIC[2]

So far, we have learned about historical game and game-like spaces, how spaces communicate, how contrasts and danger help us make dramatic space, and how spaces reward occupants. Now we go forward to discuss a user's first introduction to a space and how initial encounters with a game introduce players to its mechanics. Here in our eighth chapter, we are discussing first levels.

Wait…what?

While it may seem out of place to discuss the design of first levels so late, there are many reasons to delay both our investigation of these levels and when you design them in your projects. In this chapter, we will discuss the special purpose of first levels and the building blocks that help them reach their goals. Beyond the teaching itself, we will look at how to determine what to teach with your levels and methods that level designers use to introduce game mechanics.

What you will learn in this chapter:

The many functions of first levels

Building blocks for tutorial design

Determining player needs

Playtesting in-game teaching

Tutorial assets and media

Teaching gameplay through advertising methods

THE MANY FUNCTIONS OF FIRST LEVELS

Imagine loading up a digital game, any game, for the first time. Beyond the logos, title screens, and menus, you are probably introduced to the game with a specifically designed introductory level. Likewise, imagine entering a building you have never entered before, especially a public one such as an office, church, or museum. What is the space you enter in either case like? Is it open and welcoming or small and unimportant? Does it entice you with visible passages, hallways, and interactive objects you will find as you explore further or does it list things with text as in a directory or tutorial (Figure 8.1)? Does it let you take your time or does it tell you to get on the elevator already because there is no loitering in the lobby? Does it give you an idea of what is in the building at all?

More than any level in your game, your first level has the most lifting to do. The first level (or section, area, etc. depending on how your gamespaces relate to one another) should excite the player and make him or her want to play more of your game. If your game has a strong narrative, the first part of the game is where the player will be introduced to the world you are building and its characters. Many games use first levels to teach the player how to play the game either with a special tutorial or with spaces that let players discover the game's mechanics. Some games do all of this and provide a *hook*: an epic and seemingly climactic confrontation that shows the player just how cool the game will be if he or she spends time with it.

Architectural Arrivals

A lot of the architectural examples in this book have thus far included *arrivals*, where an occupant reaches a space after occupying one with a different condition. The specific construct where a player or occupant makes

FIGURE 8.1   The interior of the Cleveland Arcade is organized such that a visitor can see the shops and pathways inside once he or she has entered the building. Compare the amount of information you receive in this exploratory experience to an office building with just a text directory and elevators.

such a transition is a *portal*. Architectural historian Philippa Lewis, in *Portals: Gates, Stiles, Windows, Bridges & Other Crossings*, says that a portal can be a "door, window, arch, gateway, or just a gap in a hedge."[3] She elaborates on the symbolic importance of portals by saying that a portal "encapsulates the idea of passing through, to a new opportunity, to making progress or moving forward, to entering fresh new worlds."[3] The goals of good architectural arrivals and the goals of good game introductions are very similar: the most exciting ones are those that invite you to explore the building further. I have mentioned the atria of I.M. Pei's museums, specifically the National Gallery of Art's East Wing and the Rock and Roll Hall of Fame several times already. The place which visitors arrive to when they enter these buildings showcases the exhibits in the museums and the passages that the visitors will use to reach those exhibits. Likewise, Christopher Alexander's pattern of "paths and goals" emphasizes the creation of pathways with multiple areas of interest. Travelers on the path are drawn from one to another, and networks of paths can be created that offer them multiple choices of destinations (Figure 8.2). These examples

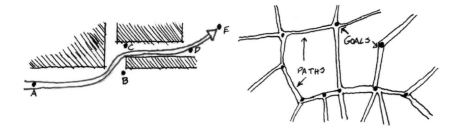

FIGURE 8.2   A recreation of Christopher Alexander's diagram of a network of pathways and goals.

emphasize interactivity and exploration: occupants are shown rather than told the contents of a space and given an idea of how they will reach their destinations.

Interactive Arrivals

One of my favorite first levels of all time is the "Death Star Attack" level from *Star Wars Rogue Squadron II: Rogue Leader*.[4] In terms of the "lifting" that a first level has to do, it performs all of the described functions in an unobtrusive and exciting way. The level opens by recreating the rebel pilots' approach to the Death Star from *Star Wars Episode IV: A New Hope* with in-game graphics. Beyond serving as a technical showcase for the then-recently-released Nintendo Gamecube, this sends a message to the player: in this game you will play your favorite moments from the original *Star Wars* films. The gameplay of the level itself spans several set-pieces, each with its own objective: destroy towers, fight off incoming imperial fighters, and fly down a narrow trench to fire torpedoes into the space station's core.

In reality, these are three scaffolded lessons on operating the game (Figure 8.3). The first section presents the player with minimal resistance but lets him or her practice basic flying and aiming with no time limit. The next section gives the player moving enemies who offer more, but still limited, resistance as players learn to dogfight, again with no time limit. Finally, the player enters the narrow "trench run," which applies what he or she has learned about moving and shooting in an environment that demands more skill. In both the film and game, the rebel pilots communicate via radios in their ships, meaning that story content and tutorial information can be relayed in voiceover that fits the setting. Combining audio and subtle visual or user-interface clues makes this seem even more natural: your character says to his wingmen, "Biggs,

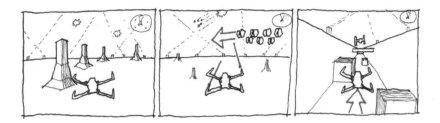

FIGURE 8.3   The three tutorial areas of the "Death Star Attack" level from *Star Wars Rogue Squadron II: Rogue Leader*. The first two scenes offer a wide-open plane on which players can practice flying, shooting, and dogfighting with little resistance. The level ends with a narrow trench of obstacles and enemies that tests these skills. By recreating the final battle from a movie, this tutorial level's slow gameplay feels faster and more satisfying than it would in another setting.

Wedge, follow me" as the interface element that lets you issue commands to your squadron first appears.

Playing the level provides the player with practice in the game's basic functions, but in a backdrop that creates the illusion of tension: turrets unload fire in no particular direction, countless fighters fly and shoot aimlessly, all to John Williams' driving score. Levels after this are quieter and more complex, with a select few—the ones that also recreate scenes from the films—feeling as climactic as this one. Still, such a level says to the player, especially one who enjoys the films, "Welcome to our game; blow up this Death Star! Wasn't that fun? Okay now we're going to take it back a notch but there will be more of this later if you stay with us for a while." At no time does the game stop play or interrupt the player to teach him or her how to play: experienced players can return to it and still have a satisfying experience.

This level is the player's portal to *Rogue Leader*: a space that introduces the ideas that make up the game and telegraph what is to come. Other games follow this trend: each *God of War* game starts with a battle against a large mythological creature or deity, an early area of *Super Mario Odyssey* lets players control a dinosaur, and so on. Not all games include large set-pieces like this, though. Earlier *Mario* series games have levels that introduce the game's mechanics in comfortable ways but create excitement by rewarding high-level play. In *Super Mario World*, the "Dinosaur Island 1" level lets new players become accustomed to Mario's movements with few major challenges. Players more familiar with Mario's abilities will find secrets such as a pipe that launches them like a cannon and a moon that gives three extra lives.

Despite being from different types of games with different mechanics, this small selection of first levels has several things in common: they let players interact with game mechanics in a safe way, they offer the illusion of tension or rewards to make play exciting, they use non-intrusive or optional tutorial content when necessary, and they introduce concepts that will be elaborated on later in the game. Like the architectural examples we briefly covered, they show instead of tell, and let users find information in their own way. Throughout this chapter, we will explore the elements of great first level design, starting with spatial elements that create exciting portals into our games.

BUILDING BLOCKS FOR TUTORIAL DESIGN

While set-pieces involve their own planning and work—especially scripting unique elements like giant monsters, moving vehicles, or moving environmental elements—the main focus of this chapter will be on how first levels teach players to play the game. Sociologist David Sudnow, in his book *Pilgrim in the Microworld*, describes the sensation of learning Atari's *Breakout* and using its controller in this way:

> Within fifteen minutes I'm no longer conscious of the knob's gearing and I'm not jerking around too much. So far so good. Slow down, get rid of the neighbor, get a little rhythm going, and in no time at all you've got a workable eye-hand partnership. The calibrating movement quickly passes beneath awareness, and in the slow phase the game is a breeze...[5]

What this quote demonstrates is how engaging a clean learning environment within a game can be. Never does Sudnow describe a section of Breakout where a window pops up to explain the game to you or a section where control is taken from him. Like many early console games, the cartridge housing Breakout lacked the memory to feature an extensive tutorial and thus designers had to invent ways for their games to support learning. While instructional manuals came with many early games, few players (at least if what my friends told me as a kid are to be believed) bothered to read them. To have games properly explain themselves, they had to be designed to both teach and engage.

For Sudnow and other players, Breakout presented an environment where he could interact with the game and learn its operation quickly. Several paragraphs of Sudnow's book describe his finding the proper hand position with which to hold the Atari "paddle" controller. The memory limitations and simple gameplay of Breakout help make it an easily learned system: players who struggle at first can easily restart with a fresh batch of lives without having to sit through a replay of a tutorial. Similarly, the first screens of *Super Mario Bros.* help players learn the game by presenting most of the game's relevant environmental symbols in one screen's space and forcing players to interact with objects like enemies and the Super Mushroom. This screen is informative for the information it shows the player but engaging because first-time players are delighted when they squish the enemy and grow with the Super Mushroom.

These examples and others in the chapter highlight the type of interesting first levels championed by game designers like Matthew M. White in his book *Learn to Play: Designing Tutorials for Video Games.*[6] It is one thing to describe what is an interesting experience and another to break down why these levels are effective. In this section, we will look at the building blocks of creating interesting and informative first levels by revisiting some of the concepts and teaching methods we explored earlier.

Spatial Building Blocks

Before describing how the content of gamespaces is used to create effective introductory levels, we should explore how these gamespaces are structured. Throughout the book, we have looked at spaces that accomplish a variety of experiential goals from allowing for effective navigation to setting or disrupting moods. In this section, we will concentrate on spaces that introduce or present information in an easily understood way for new visitors or players. While this list is not exhaustive, it revisits some easily employed spatial features that we have discussed before in the context of teaching.

Scenes

First, and perhaps most importantly, we will revisit Anna Anthropy's concept of scenes. Scenes, if you recall, are single screen-sized portions of designed level space that represent what a player is seeing on the screen as he or she plays. By designing in such a way where you are thinking about what is "current" in the minds of players, or the information they have to process in an instant of gameplay, you can divide your level into easily understood chunks.

In *Origins of Architectural Pleasure*, Grant Hildebrand talks about *order* and *complexity* as aesthetic components of space that make a them pleasurable or oppressive.[7] These components aid humans in *categorizing* and *differentiating* the large amounts of visual information[8] that is presented to them in something like a building (or a game). Hildebrand highlights several ways that order and complexity coexist in a piece of architecture and likewise presents ways that buildings are designed so that observers can differentiate their elements. The façade of Louis Kahn's library at the Phillips Exeter Academy has a subtle contrast that makes it both ordered and easy to understand, but complex such that it begs repeated examination. The façade appears to be a simple grid of rectangles, but the top of each window void features a slight curvature such that they are actually arches[9] (Figure 8.4). Hildebrand also argues that repetition or elements that occur in visual rhythm help to make order out of even the most chaotic elements. He uses the example of Laon Cathedral, a French Gothic church built between the twelfth and thirteenth centuries. The towers feature a myriad of architectural ornaments: complex masonry, arches, small columns, and gargoyles. However, each of these elements are of a similar scale and occur in regularly repeating increments, creating a pattern that is easy for casual observers to understand.

In games, categorizing and differentiating visual information is imperative for overcoming challenges and achieving high-level play. These processes are even more important in levels where gameplay information is being presented for the first time, as players should be able to take their time

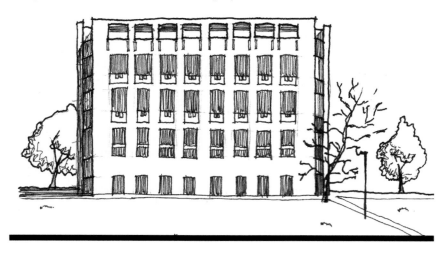

FIGURE 8.4 The façade of Phillips Exeter Academy's Library is simple and repetitive, but Kahn gave the top of each window a barely perceptible curvature that adds a layer of complexity and attracts repeated viewings.

to internalize how to react to symbols. Scene-based design, which forces a designer to put a concise amount of gameplay information in an area of a map, is an important tool for this. Like Hildebrand's recommendations to use contrast, designing in scenes allows you to contrast tutorial-important mechanisms against "normal" geometry in a small space conducive to teaching. Contrast in tutorial scenes also helps these scenes feel exciting: the distant laser barrages of the Death Star Attack level accomplish the same thing that Louis Kahn's slight arches do: they add the perception of visual complexity to a scene that is otherwise pretty simple. Scenes are also great for establishing a rhythm for your tutorial. Rather than trying to put all of the elements you are teaching a player in one scene, you can spread them out over several scenes so the player learns a new thing on each screen. Repeating this "one scene–one mechanic" pattern with several "practice scenes" where players can master newly learned mechanics makes it easy to design whole levels that feel very rich (Figure 8.5).

Designer beware though: while it can be tempting to put everything you've got into a single "uber level," putting too many complex mechanics in a single level makes it overwhelming for new players. Designers should think about the amount and type of gameplay information being presented at one time as they design tutorial levels. That famous first screen of *Super Mario Bros.* is a scene that presents nearly all of the relevant information for the game in one screenspace. Alternatively, modern indie games often break up tutorial information into several scenes or across different levels: new gameplay mechanisms in *Celeste*[9] are introduced in isolation via single-screen scenes and one at a time (Figure 8.6). The number of new objects or mechanisms you introduce in scenes may depend on the complexity of those objects. Scenes in *Super Mario Bros.* can contain more objects because the objects are simple (static bricks, question blocks,

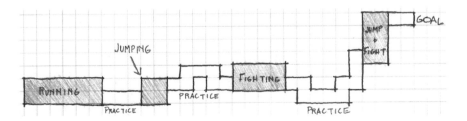

FIGURE 8.5 When you space out scenes where you teach or introduce new mechanics or ways to use mechanics, you may suddenly find yourself with an entire finished level.

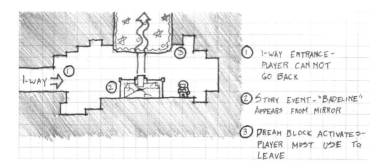

FIGURE 8.6 This diagram from the indie game *Celeste* is typical of how the game introduces new level mechanisms: in a single-screen space and away from other mechanisms.

etc.) when compared to the highly interactive environmental mechanisms found in modern games.

Once again, scenes prove to be an important tool for presenting information to players. In this case, I would consider scene-based design "rule number one" for designing introductory or tutorial levels. They provide a structure that forces designers to put information on the screen in an ordered way, which in turn allows players to categorize gameplay mechanisms for effective use later.

Portals and Thresholds

In Chapter 3's discussion of scenes, we saw that the next stage of scene-based design was controlling how the player is introduced to our scenes. Especially in 3D games, how scenes are first revealed to players means the difference between a readable scene and a confusing one. This means that portals, thresholds, and other arrivals are an integral part of our kit of building blocks for tutorial design.

Earlier, I discussed how the player's arrival into an enemy-filled room in *Horizon: Zero Dawn* was designed to let the player read the space, enemy positions, and so on, before actually entering. In the example, players entered a room and could pause on a small staircase from which they could scan the room and plan their moves. The principle of *readability*, how well the elements of a space can be evaluated by an occupant upon entry, is an important principle here[10] (Figure 8.7). The thresholds I described from *Horizon: Zero Dawn* are mainly strategic: they allow players familiar with the game to plan their next moves. However, the first job of thresholds in tutorial spaces is to teach rather than to provide

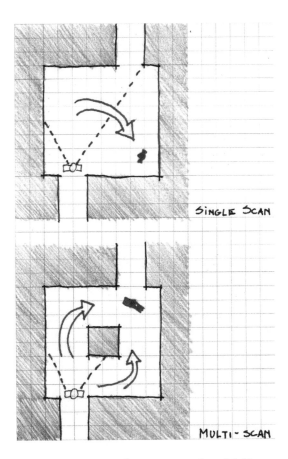

SINGLE SCAN

MULTI- SCAN

FIGURE 8.7   A diagram reviewing the concepts of readability.

opportunities for deep strategy: the players they are serving are the ones unfamiliar with the game.

Early thresholds in the same game perform this job admirably. Very early in the game, the player plays the main character, Aloy, when she is six years old. This sequence allows the developers to show her development as a hunter in a way that does not detract from the game's fiction. During the main game, Aloy is already capable of advanced techniques and acrobatic movements—a tutorial where such a character would learn basic movements like aiming a bow would not make much sense. Through both scenes, tutorial content is provided both as visual pop-ups on the screen, and as lines of audio spoken by characters to one another. Characters like Aloy's mentor, Rost, and Aloy herself speak lines that tell players what they are trying to accomplish, while the on-screen text tells players which button combinations make those actions happen. The tutorial is split into two levels: a cave where players learn to use the game's environmental scanning features and a hunting trip where they learn to fight robotic animals.

In each environment, thresholds serve many important functions for the tutorial (Figure 8.8). In the earlier cave section, thresholds are human-made doors, platforms, and staircases that let the player pause and look around a room before fully entering. While there are no immediate dangers in this area, the scene builds atmospheric ambiguity with its lighting, motivating players to be cautious. Once players find the Focus device (which allows them to scan the environment), thresholds let players look around the environment for scannable objects, which reward the player with story content. The cave also features thresholds that the player cannot pass through, but can see through. These are used to show players their next goal or, in the case of a lock puzzle, to allow them to watch how the door they are trying to open changes while they are doing the puzzle. The later hunting section takes place in an open outdoor area, so thresholds are much less overt than in an interior area like a cave. While this area is open Rost encourages players to follow him, creating a "linear" path. Rost guides the player to bluffs and other high points from which the player can practice hunting skills like aiming a bow and scanning robotic prey. Lastly, the tutorial ends with a tense section where Aloy (and the player) must save a boy from dangerous Watcher robots using the skills she has learned. As the player approaches, he or she gets a short time to observe the location and movements of the Watchers from the bluff before entering the area to save the boy.

FIGURE 8.8 Thresholds in the tutorial levels of *Horizon: Zero Dawn* use thresholds to let players read areas before entering them, find objectives, learn the function of environmental mechanisms, practice new skills safely, and plan strategies.

Thresholds do not need to be literal doors or architectural features. As with level design in general, natural features such as bluffs, cliffs, mountains, caves, trees, and so on are part of your palette. In *Portals: Gates, Stiles, Windows, Bridges, & Other Crossings*, Philippa Lewis lists not only humanmade structures, but also valleys, gorges, canyons, harbors, and other landmass features[11] (Figure 8.9). *The Legend of Zelda: Breath of the Wild* introduces the entire game at the beginning with one such natural threshold. After leaving the cave where the hero, Link, wakes up after one hundred years of sleep, the player is guided to a cliff edge overlooking most of the game world. Landmarks such as Hyrule Castle and Death Mountain, places that will be visited later in the game, are visible. This cliff is a threshold in that it stages a few pieces of information that will be necessary later in the game.

Controlled Approaches

In *101 Things I Learned in Architecture School*, architect Matthew Frederick describes the types of spaces where people move and others where they stay in this way: "We move through negative spaces and dwell in positive spaces" (Figure 8.10).[12] Previously in this section, we saw that scenes where players learn new mechanics should not necessarily come one right after another. Instead, they should be spaced out by scenes where the player is practicing new skills. We also saw a similar concept by Christopher Alexander, where networks of paths and goals are created that draw a user through a space.

FIGURE 8.9 Portals can be manmade or natural features that frame and showcase things that you want players to see in your game.

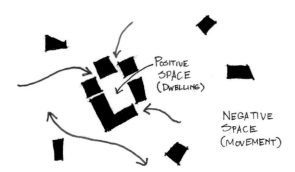

FIGURE 8.10   A recreation of Matthew Frederick's illustration of the concept of positive and negative path and arrival spaces.

These concepts are useful for a variety of level designs, but in tutorial levels, we can think of places or scenes where the player is actively learning new information as our *positive spaces* and paths where players practice their skills as *negative space*. Frederick says of arriving in a space that "our experience of an architectural space is strongly influenced by how we arrive in it."[13] Already, we have seen that the contrast between an approach and an arrival can produce a variety of experiences: arriving in a high-ceilinged space from a smaller space makes the tall space more impressive, dark spaces are scarier if approached from a light space, and so on. The contrast between positive spaces where players are learning and the negative spaces where they are practicing can produce similar effects.

Where do we learn and where do we practice though? In some games, learning occurs in those high-ceilinged, celebrated spaces. Games in *The Legend of Zelda* series make destinations of their tutorial spaces: dojos for learning from old masters, ethereal planes for learning from ghosts of heroes past, and so on. Games in the *God of War* series reverse this dynamic. In *God of War II*,[14] players learn how Kratos moves and interacts with objects along pathways that lead the player to rewarding encounters with a giant enemy: an animated Colossus of Rhodes. Though we could still call the spaces where players learn positive and the places players practice negative, the negative spaces where practice occurs are treated as a reward for the boring tutorial stuff.

Meeting Spaces

One last spatial building block that I will briefly describe is *meeting spaces*. These very literally embody Frederick's idea of positive meeting spaces as he described in his book in how they represent places for people to stop and socialize with others. In the real world, these meeting spaces might be courtyards, town squares, green spaces, meeting rooms, or classrooms.

These types of spaces are important to remember for those rare situations where you have a tutorial that absolutely must stop the player for a demonstration. The meeting before the player takes on the Strider invasion in *Half-life 2: Episode 2*[15] is such a scene. While moving through the friendly White Forest base, the player comes upon a presentation on how to use an important bomb item. Valve playtested this scene multiple times and found that the best way to discourage players from running straight through the room was to model it after a real-world office presentation or class lecture (Figure 8.11). The speaker is in the front of the room next to the exit door and the player enters through the back such that they immediately recognize the social context of the scene. I cite this example because it manages to stop the player when he or she technically has the freedom to leave out the door without hearing the tutorial. The scene avoids taking control away from the player and instead shows how developers can use playtesting and human psychology to encourage players to listen. Having the players attend a meeting with a single speaker also fits

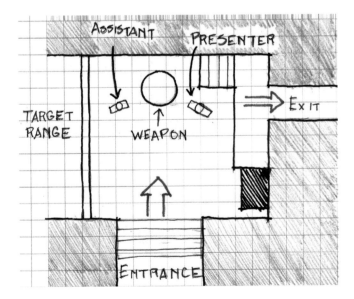

FIGURE 8.11 Valve playtesters found that structuring the space where players learn about the Magnusson Device in *Half-Life 2: Episode 2* as a lecture that the player is arriving late to stops players from running through the scene and missing important information.

in with the game's narrative: the speaker is a scientist that has invented a special bomb for taking down Striders, a large and difficult enemy.

The other time where meeting spaces are useful are in online multiplayer games where players can gather and discuss strategy before leaving for raids or other encounters. In the *Left 4 Dead* series, each campaign has several spaces, often before climactic zombie horde encounters, where players can stop and plan their strategies. These games also begin and end every level with safe houses where zombies cannot enter that serve the same purpose. In massively multiplayer online games, players can meet in spaces that are quite literally the types of positive spaces discussed by Frederick: town squares, taverns, and so on.

Now that we have discussed a few spatial types useful while building tutorial levels, we will revisit previously explored teaching methods in the context of tutorial-building.

Behavioral building blocks

Games that teach and behaviorism have a mixed history. On one hand, using certain behavioral aspects to motivate actions with rewards in free-to-play games and gamified platforms—where game reward systems are applied to real world actions—is seen as shallow game design. On the other, when used in tandem with other teaching models, behavioral game elements are a great tool for motivating player actions. In particular, the understanding of the different types of rewards explored in Chapter 6 can help us define behavioral building blocks that we can use to plan our tutorial levels. In this section, we will discuss how these rewards might be utilized in tutorial scenarios and describe what kinds of assets game developers can use in their levels as rewards.

Rewards in Tutorials

A key component of any system based on behaviorism is the reward. As we have already seen, rewards are a common and, in some cases, powerful part of moving a player through a game. Also as we have seen, the best games use rewards as part of a larger system of visual symbols, non-verbal association-building, and other methods that create a complex system of communication between designer and player.

The earlier examples in this chapter from *Rogue Leader*, *Super Mario Bros.*, *God of War*, and *Horizon: Zero Dawn* each use a variety of different reward types in their introductory levels. A key difference between games that misuse behaviorism (gamification, free-to-play Skinner Boxes) and those that use it well are how reward types are varied in even short bits of gameplay. Keep in mind that I am talking about "reward types" in the sense of those discussed in Chapter 7, i.e., rewards of glory, access, narrative, and so on, rather than different types of guns or hats (which would both be rewards of access).

Let's return to *Rogue Leader*. Since its first level is based on a famous scene from a movie, *Rogue Leader* players are rewarded by watching the scene unfold (reward of narrative and/or access). Likewise, since the scene depicts a climactic battle, feedback for player actions like destroying an enemy tower are very visceral: big noises and explosion effects. These are simple "rewards of glory" that have little bearing on gameplay itself, but are part of our modern study of *game feel* (often also called *game juice*). Game feel is a concept popularly understood as how a game can give meaningful and effective feedback for the player's actions.[16] Particle effects (the systems that exist in game engines to simulate water, fire, explosions, dust, and so forth), screen shake effects, sound effects, and other elements can be used to make a game "feel" satisfying to play. In tutorial levels, these virtual sensations do a lot to attract players to your game and reinforce when the player is playing the game well.

The first three *God of War* games likewise make great use of big, visceral moments to give their introductions weight: giant boss fights, crumbling scenery, and extra powers for the player. As discussed earlier, these happen in-reverse of the positive/negative space concept: the moments where you are fighting a giant monster usually come between moments of learning. These games offer other, subtler, rewards as well. The tutorial levels of the *God of War* games are those where you first encounter resources that the game's enemies drop. These resources sustain the player character, Kratos, and allow him to earn new powers. These "rewards of sustenance" are common throughout many games, but are folded into the tutorial as content that the player will need to know about later.

Super Mario Bros. features only subtle game feel elements (one could argue that the main "game feel" of *Mario* games is not in its feedback, but in the satisfying way Mario is controlled). Despite this, the game offers rewards for the player's experimentation with the game's symbols. If the player stomps on the first enemy, a Goomba, he or she is rewarded with an appealing sound effect, the visual of the flattened Goomba, and one hundred points. Likewise, players that explore the question blocks in the first scene are rewarded with a Super Mushroom that enhances Mario's abilities and awards points. Few modern games tally points, but a game player in the mid-1980s would have been attracted to the prospect of earning a high score, even in a game not necessarily formatted around this mechanism.

Horizon: Zero Dawn's introduction is delivered amidst important narrative moments that set up Aloy's backstory. She and her mentor, Rost, are outsiders that are not allowed to interact with members of a nearby tribe. The tutorial occurs when Aloy is six years old and first emotionally understanding her place as an outcast. This gives the tutorial, set first in a cave full of ancient technology and then in a place where Aloy meets a boy from the tribe, narrative motivation. Rewards in these levels are rewards of narrative that hint at bigger revelations to come. In the cave, players learn to use the game's scanning system to read the environment. As players learn this mechanic, they are rewarded with text logs from the cave's former occupants that hint at large-scale catastrophic events (Figure 8.12). The latter level allows players to observe the tribe's interactions with Aloy: children are told not to play with her, and the boy she saves during a stealth tutorial is scolded for thanking her. Again, these narrative moments come after the player has completed sections of the level that teach game mechanics. While the story content is not as climactic as say, blowing up a Death Star, these levels nevertheless provide interesting narrative threads that are carried into the game's main sections. The way that the tutorial

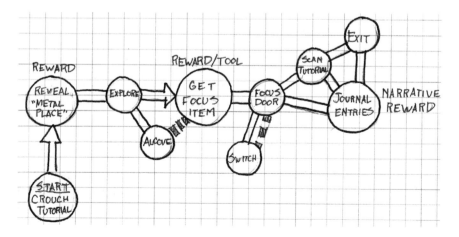

FIGURE 8.12   This molecule diagram of the cave section of *Horizon: Zero Dawn*'s tutorial levels shows the proximity of new learning spaces to places where there are narrative rewards. Molecule diagrams can be a useful tool for mapping out how you will coordinate learning with rewards in your levels.

content is integrated neatly with the narrative rewards of revealing Aloy's motivations makes this section of the game required playing.

As you can see through these case studies, rewards in tutorials go beyond giving the player a simple prize for performing the right action. Remember that there are many types of rewards in games and that these rewards can be mixed and matched to make interesting first level experiences that are worth replaying. Tutorials are a good way to set up the stakes of your game and your character's motivations. Likewise, they are great places to demonstrate what the game has to offer with climactic content that make the player "feel" powerful. Even when you do offer item- or resource-based rewards, you can do so in a way that teaches the player what benefits those resources have to the overall game system.

Access as a First Level Reward

I want to take a moment also to describe game tutorials' use of *rewards of access* in more detail. Salen and Zimmerman describe rewards of access as elements that let players move forward in a limited way, usually a key or another resource that is used once.[17] We can abstract this a bit as a way to discuss *skill gates* as an effective tutorial mechanism. Skill gates are sections of levels that require players to successfully execute an in-game action to progress.[18] Some skill gates feature actual gates that are unlocked via keys and other rewards of access fitting Salen and Zimmerman's definition. You see these occur in levels like *The Legend of Zelda: A Link to the Past's*[19] Hyrule Castle Dungeon, where doors are unlocked as players learn skills like fighting, using switches, and lighting torches.

A more modern use of skill gates still blocks the player until he or she executes an important game mechanic (running, jumping, dashing, etc.) but without literal keys. *Hyper Light Drifter*[20] is a 2016 game that greatly resembles *A Link to the Past* by providing a large explorable world and similar melee combat mechanics. However, many of the skill gates in the game's brief tutorial avoid keys as a blocking mechanism. Instead, the game uses pits that the player must dash over, switches for extending bridges, and boxes in the player's path that he or she must attack to destroy (Figure 8.13). This makes the world feel very organic and open as opposed to built with "video game logic." When the game does use a literal gate to block player progress (as is done when the player encounters the first enemy), the gate falls immediately after without the need to be unlocked via a key.

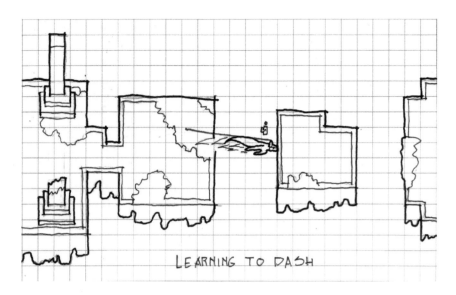

FIGURE 8.13 The tutorial area of *Hyper Light Drifter* blocks player progress to set up skill gates and rewards of access, but avoids doing so by using environmental features instead of lock-and-key mechanisms.

None of this is to say that keys in games are bad design (they are not), but only to point out that the idea of "rewards of access" can be further abstracted beyond literal lock-and-key mechanisms. Games like *Braid* and *Super Meat Boy* use subtle level geometry as skill gates: a short cliff blocks the player's progress until he or she jumps over it (Figure 8.14). While not the most exciting reward, rewards of access—where they player is rewarded by merely being able to progress in the game—are an important tool for designers designing the first levels of a game.

FIGURE 8.14 The first level of *Braid* uses a tutorial graphic integrated into its environment to invite players to jump over a short cliff, making for an unobtrusive learning experience.

In the next section, we will move on from rewards and describe the other side of the action/reward relationship to see how player interactions with tutorial levels are crafted.

Montessori Building Blocks

Rewards on their own, when used well, do a lot for building enjoyable tutorial experiences, but we should also pay attention to how players interact with our tutorial levels. When designing an introductory or tutorial level, it is important to lay out a "lesson plan" for your level (Figure 8.15). It should include things like figuring out what you want to teach players in the level such as mechanics or associations with specific graphics or symbols. When you do this for levels beyond your first level, you should also build on lessons from previous levels. If this sounds like designing the curriculum for a class: it is! For each lesson or level, it is important to not overload players with information, but to ramp up both the difficulty of the game and the amount of information gradually.

In my own teaching experiences, I have found that it is important to list for students at the beginning of lessons the concepts that I will be covering that day. This is not only good for telegraphing information of what

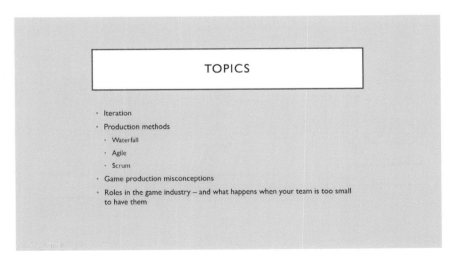

FIGURE 8.15 A screenshot from one of my PowerPoint slide decks for a game production course. At the beginning of each lesson, I lay out a list of topics so students know the boundaries of what we will cover that day. Making a similar list of gameplay mechanics to teach when you start a tutorial level will help you set your goals for your level.

will be discussed, but also for setting limits on content for the lesson. In Chapter 5, we discussed the Montessori-style methods that games use to establish and expand player knowledge of how to play a game. In short: early in a game, players will learn a skill and overcome several challenges using a basic version of that skill (e.g., using a wall jump to reach high platforms). Over time, the player will encounter challenges that either involve a more advanced version of the skill (making several wall jumps in a row to reach higher platforms) or using the skill in tandem with other skills (wall-jumping then shooting an enemy's weak point) (Figure 8.16).

The idea of having a lesson plan for these types of interactions is integral to this chapter and its late placement in this book. Level designers, especially newer ones, are often tempted to include any and every version of a challenge they can in a level. Early in the development of the 2013 mobile game *SWARM!*,[21] I was so excited that we were finished developing individual level mechanisms that I designed a "level 1" that would use these objects to their full extent. What I created was fun, but playtesters had a hard time beating the level: their skills were not developed enough to beat the challenges. Instead of scrapping the level, we moved it to be the third level and designed two levels that prepared players for it. Similarly, in my game *Lissitzky's Revenge*,[22] I based each "world"—or set of levels that share a theme—on an artwork by the Russian Constructivist artist

FIGURE 8.16 The stages of developing a skill may take several levels. In this example, we see a scene from the tutorial level of *Mega Man X* where players first learn about wall-jumping. Later in the game, players encounter other iterations of wall-jumping challenges that advance the skill, leading to a final boss that challenges the skill and blends it with others as a "final exam" for the game. By resisting putting every iteration of wall-jumping in one level, the designers made this one skill relevant to the entire game.

El Lissitzky. Playtests showed that my game had a very strange *difficulty curve*, where World 1 introduced the basic mechanics but World 2, which introduced puzzles where you move colored blocks around, added so much that it spiked the game's difficulty too severely. Likewise, the penultimate World 4 used the basic mechanics again, but with puzzles that developed the basics: it was much easier than earlier levels (Figure 8.17). As a result, I changed the order of the game worlds: what was once World 2 became World 3; World 3 (which featured more advanced block puzzles) became World 4; and what was once World 4 became World 2. This allowed for a more gradual difficulty curve so players were prepared for the later puzzles.

When I play tutorial levels, I pay attention to how focused the level is on a lesson plan and how they limit the players possibilities. One way that these levels work is by using a linear space or enforcing a linear set of actions in a non-spatial way. In *Horizon: Zero Dawn*, the first level in the cave not only denies the player weapons and other tools that would enable the game's combat mechanics, but also follows a strictly linear path. In a game whose main selling point is a large open world, this linearity focuses player actions until they have all of their skills. Likewise, the second level where players learn hunting skills has Rost lead Aloy through the environment. If players veer from the level's path, Aloy is chastised by Rost: even with a more open environment, the designers found a way to enforce a limited possibility space.

Some games also limit the player by making it dangerous to leave a certain part of the game world. *The Legend of Zelda: Breath of the Wild*, which has similar open-world survival mechanics as *Horizon*, has a more open

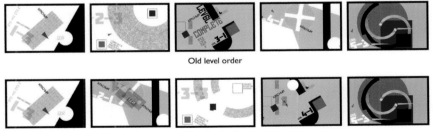

Old level order

New level order

FIGURE 8.17 I put too many new mechanics into the second world of *Lissitzky's Revenge*, creating a very sudden increase in difficulty that I did not intend. Changing the order of levels so that the increase in complexity was more gradual resulted in a better game.

tutorial section that limits the player in other ways. For one, players are limited to a small area of the map because they are on a high plateau with no way to escape: jumping off the sides kills Link. Each shrine in this area enforces a lesson plan built on one of Link's tools and little else. Lastly, at this point in the game, Link does not have as much health or stamina as he will later on. Exploration is limited by his vulnerability to enemies and the environment. The plateau is a tutorial space that gives the illusion of openness, but still finds ways to stick to a limited lesson plan. Once players overcome the challenges on the plateau, they earn the hang glider, which lets Link fly off the plateau without getting hurt.

As new players to *Breath of the Wild* know, the plateau's status as a tutorial space does little to block players from failing: Link dies a lot in the opening parts of that game. That tutorial's openness allows for the possibility of failure, but is still very compelling. Balancing the interactivity of Montessori learning with challenges is important in revisiting our third teaching method, constructivism, in the context of first levels.

Constructivist Building Blocks

When we discussed constructivist learning in Chapter 5, we focused on how games allow players to learn about a game by failing and retrying at challenges. As with behavioral systems (rewarding reactions or objects) and Montessori systems (controlling possibility via linearity or limited character ability), constructivist concepts can easily translate into gameplay systems, especially those regarding failure and reloading a level.

Proximity of Checkpoints

Sometimes failing at something is part of learning. Part of what makes games appealing is that losing at them is a non-permanent condition. Players who fail to complete a game level usually have a means to return and try again. In older games, punishments for losing were severe: often a player would have to restart a game or level from the beginning. In the 1970s and 1980s, this was the norm, but it makes some classic games unplayable for modern audiences. Coupled with the mechanics of *lives*, where players have a limited set of chances to complete a level before having to restart, losing these early games could be a frustrating experience. Now that we are several decades removed from arcade-style mechanics, where games were designed so players would pay for new chances at regular intervals, designers are finding new failure mechanics that encourage players to continue.

For level designers, supporting the player's ability to fail and retry in a quick and satisfying fashion is a matter of level length or checkpoint placement. Indie games have a long history with skill-based games where failure often means falling into an obstacle or otherwise "killing" the player's avatar. *Celeste* is one such game: the player is a woman named Madeline climbing a mountain to confront personal demons and prove that she can finish goals. Failure often means falling into pits, spikes, or being killed by demonic enemies. Each level is quite long, but is also broken into scenes that span no more than a few screens in size, with many being a single screen. Each scene has a *checkpoint*, a place where the player will restart if he or she fails, so when a player fails at one of these areas, he or she can quickly restart and try a new strategy. The game even makes a point to tell players to "take pride in your Death Count" and that it "means that you are learning." The game reloads so quickly that the cycle of dying and retrying becomes zen-like, even giving the player a sense of empathy for Madeline's plight. *Celeste* is the latest in a series of games that patterns its levels as a series of rooms. This is efficient from both a memory standpoint (less to load at one time) but also as a convenient way to space out checkpoints. Other games that do this include *Portal* (each level is an individual "test chamber"), *Super Meat Boy*, and *SUPERHOT* (whose levels are a series of action movie scenario vignettes like "The Deal is Off").[23]

This is not to say that every game that uses constructivist teaching methods in its levels has to be structured on single room scenes. *Owlboy*[24] is a game that features a large and freely explorable world with many difficult stealth challenges, obstacle courses, and battles with enemies to overcome. Levels are designed with frequent checkpoints so that losing at a challenge is not a major setback. The game overall has a light and breezy tone, so getting caught in a difficult section does little to detract from the atmosphere.

This section has discussed elements that help developers teach and reinforce gameplay mechanics in their introductory or tutorial levels. By following specific spatial guidelines or using spatial constructs, levels can be made to show players the information they need to know to play a game in an easily understood way. By reinforcing mechanics via the classical teaching theories we discussed earlier in the book, players can practice and master this knowledge. You may be wondering though, how does a designer even decide which knowledge to teach players? When you make a game, how do you discover what mechanics players need to be taught vs. which ones you can expect them to come to your game with? In the next section, we will look at how designers learn more about their players and their needs.

DETERMINING PLAYER NEEDS

In the last section, we talked about using lesson plans and building blocks to plan and construct good tutorials for players. Knowing what the building blocks for tutorials are and how to use them is important, but how do you determine where to use those techniques? What if you spend lots of time developing a tutorial for a skill that most players will know intuitively? What if that results in your game having a long period of boring gameplay?

This is yet another reason why you may want to design your first levels later in your development cycle: so that you can take the time to learn what players already know and what they need to learn about playing your game. In this section, we will look at some common assumptions about game players that designers make and how they impact gameplay. We also look at some case studies of recent educational games to see how their designers adjusted their content to match the knowledge players had when starting the game. Lastly, we will see how designers use the *playtesting* process, where multiple members of your audience play your game during development, to determine how they structure their introductory levels.

The first step in determining your players' needs comes (or should come) while your game is in the "idea" phase: choosing your target audience. A target audience is the main group of people that you will market your game to. There are plenty of internet and print resources on game design that cover this topic from a marketing standpoint, so we will stick to discussing this from a teaching point of view. In terms of planning your tutorials, the question of *player experience* is the most important: what prior knowledge do players have coming to your game? In marketing terms, this is where a designer decides whether their game should be marketed to "casual" audiences (those that do not play games very often and want simple experiences) or "hardcore" audiences (those that are looking for a more in-depth experience). Though these might be over-simplifications of how actual people play games, the notion that a player might be familiar with certain norms of computer, controller, and game interaction is important as we think of what content to build into a tutorial. Even if you have a good idea of which audience your game is for, however, be prepared to test your game to confirm your assumptions.

For *Dead Man's Trail*, a zombie survival adventure game that friends of mine and I have been developing in our spare time, making the wrong assumptions resulted in some uncomfortable playtests. The game has two modes: "travel mode" where players manage resources on a cross-country trip and "looting mode" a mode where players run into a town and get supplies in isometric 3D. The game also has a robust system of weapons and items to collect, so we focused on a more "hardcore" audience of game players. This shaped several of the assumptions we made when drafting what we told visitors to our convention booths and when making our game's tutorial. We assumed, for example, that most players would use the popular "WASD" control scheme, where the fingers on the left hand stay on the W, A, S, and D keys of a standard English keyboard. This proved only somewhat true: most players did use WASD, but nearly as many tried the arrow keys on the other side of the keyboard as well. We decided it was wise to offer both. More disastrously, we gave only light guidance to players in our shooting mechanics: players click on a zombie with the left mouse button to attack them. One visitor to our booth thought we meant that the character attacked zombies when the left mouse button was clicked anywhere. They repeated several times "I think your game is broken," causing several people in line to walk away. In this case, our assumption that our game would appeal to hardcore audiences, meaning that we could take a light touch with teaching the game's controls, hurt us.

This is not to say that assumptions are always wrong. *Dead Man's Trail* imitates many of the mechanics of *The Oregon Trail*[25] and this makes it an easy game to teach to players familiar with that game. If you are a developer that can determine your own marketing approach, then your choice of whom to market your game to can lead you to productive "givens" about your players. *20XX*[26] is an indie game that models much of its gameplay on classic *Mega Man X* (MMX) games. The game was originally called *Echoes of Eridu* but closer to release, the name was changed to be a reference to the ambiguous year "20XX" that the *MMX* games take place in. This reference attracts players who are fans of the *MMX* games and would need less explanation. Even if your game is not patterned on a retro game or classic franchise, having some knowledge of your core audience gives you an idea of the skills players will likely come to your game with.

What this adds up to is that you can make assumptions as a starting point, but you should view them with a healthy dose of skepticism until they are either confirmed or proven wrong through playtesting. In the next section, we will look at several games for which learning was a major goal and how they approach determining what information to teach players.

PLAYTESTING IN-GAME TEACHING

This section is about educational games, how their designers approach determining player knowledge level, and how they design for players that know very little about the game's subject matter. As you have probably guessed by now, this chapter is not one about making "games for education," which is documented very well elsewhere. However, we can learn a lot about how concepts are taught in games by looking at the design of educational games and how playtesting and game design go hand-in-hand to make them successful. Through three case studies, this section shows how designers of several educational games have used playtesting to evaluate the amount of knowledge that a typical new player had when coming to the game. It also describes how each designer modified their game to account for situations where players had no familiarity with the game's topic. This will give us insight into how to design so your game can accommodate players of any experience level.

A Literature Game for Those Who Have Not Read the Book

The first case study is a non-digital game with a simple card-based story-telling core mechanic. In 2017, a friend of mine in my board game-playing group sent a challenge: design a game and bring it to our next play session. I had just read *Don Quixote* by Miguel de Cervantes and wanted to make a game about it. *Don Quixote* is the story of a man who grows bored of his mundane life and decides to become a knight in an era where knights and chivalry are long forgotten. I thought this would be a great opportunity to do some tabletop game design, so I created *La Mancha*. *La Mancha* is a card game where players tell stories about knights using Chivalry Cards with quotes from medieval books (Figure 8.18). Story prompts would be based on mundane situations and the goal would be to use Chivalry Cards to turn these situations into epic adventures. The first playtest was fun, but confused a lot of players at the table—testers wondered how the mundane prompts blended with the epic quotes. Cervantes' novel is very funny because of how Don Quixote tries to solve ordinary problems in extraordinary ways, but the game was not matching that tone at all. What was wrong and how could I fix it?

While neither digital nor having levels, simple tabletop games are great for observing game design problems without the extra baggage that big

FIGURE 8.18 An image of *La Mancha*, an educational card game based on the novel *Don Quixote*. I had to discover the best way to write card text so players who had not read the novel could enjoy the game. The takeaway lesson is that more explanation is always better.

digital projects bring. In this case, we have an easy-to-understand example of how a designer works around situations where players are missing prerequisite knowledge. In the case of *La Mancha*, many playtesters had not previously read the nearly 1,000-page *Don Quixote* novel. By questioning testers about their understanding of the novel, I would find out later that many assumed that *Don Quixote* was a regular fantasy story rather than a parody. Once I had figured this out, the fix was simple: change the story prompt text to be actual situations from the novel that explained the comedic context. For example, the first version of the card depicting the famous scene where Don Quixote attacks the windmills said "you see windmills" and assumed that players would know to pretend they were monsters. The fixed version not only tells the player that they find the windmills, but that they also imagine that they are giants (Figure 8.19). It then asks the player to tell the table how the battle goes. Once this change was implemented, the game became not only more fun, but also funny. A few testers who had not read the book remarked that they would like to after playing the game

Hark! In the distance, you spy

———

approaching!

THE GLITTERING HELMET

Don Quixote, Vol 1: Chapter XXI

You pass a barber on the road carrying his shaving basin on his head. You instead think that he is a knight with a glittering helmet.

You want the helmet...

FIGURE 8.19 Comparison between a prototype Encounter card from *La Mancha* and the final "Glittering Helmet" Encounter card. Playtesters without the full context of the *Don Quixote* novel did not understand why a knight would imagine mundane things as fantasies, so their ability to tell funny stories in the game was limited. Fixing the cards also gave the game additional value as an educational game.

and had learned a lot about the novel. For this reason, I marketed it as an educational game and entered it into educational game festivals, at which it earned several awards.[27]

Our first takeaway from these educational game case studies is that you may find that you need to explain more about your game than you had originally assumed. Lots of people know about the "tilting at windmills" scene in *Don Quixote*, but fewer people know the novel's premise and how that scene fits into it. I originally thought that explaining or directing players to tell their stories a certain way (e.g., telling the player to imagine the windmills to be giants) would limit the types of stories they could tell. Instead, it informed players without prerequisite knowledge of *Don Quixote* enough so they could have the best time possible during the game. In the last section, we saw that a developer cannot always assume that players will have the knowledge to be able to operate a game. In a digital game, it may be worthwhile to provide detailed instruction on basic operations such as controlling the game and performing basic gameplay actions. As with the examples we have seen throughout the chapter, this does not need to stop the game or take control away from the player; we can provide these things in ways that blend well with our gameplay.

Teaching Molecular Immunology in Only Four Levels

Our second case study is a game from biologist Melanie Stegman, Ph.D., and her studio Molecular Jig Games, called *Immune Defense*.[28] *Immune Defense* is an educational strategy game where players use white blood cells to fight pathogens in realistic simulations of the human body's immune system[29] (Figure 8.20). The game's goals are to create a system that realistically depicts the ways that pathogens are warded off in the body while providing an exciting game experience. Needless to say, the educational subject that *Immune Defense* depicts is a complex one that not many game players are familiar with. However, I have seen the game at several conventions, always with a large crowd of happy kids and parents around it. How does it manage this?

In my own conversations with the developer she says that helping a player learn the game's systems is a process of creating a set of challenges

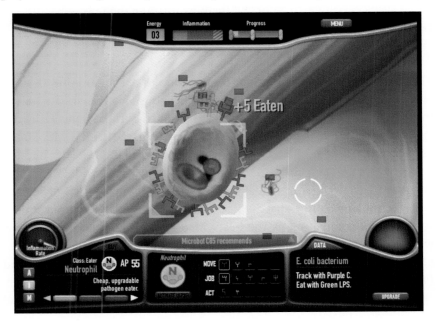

FIGURE 8.20 *Immune Defense* uses carefully planned introductory levels to introduce complex immunology topics one at a time. By the fourth level, players have full control over the process of targeting and attacking pathogens.

that lead them toward mastery. The game's website states that a goal of the game is that the player should always be engaged in exploring the immune system's different functions.[30] As such, the first levels focus on immediate and satisfying scenarios such as having parts of the immune system eat bacteria. The animation of bacteria dissolving in acid is graphic (as much as possible at a microscopic level) and satisfying, giving these scenes good "game feel." Each of the first few levels walk players through a part of the overall process of targeting pathogens and sending cells to destroy them. In the first levels, players enact individual stages of the process of signaling cells to attack certain types of pathogens. In the fourth level, they enact the process in full and from then on are able to freely interact with the game's (and body's) systems to form strategies.

Immune Defense is a digital game with levels, albeit not spatial ones as covered in much of the rest of this book. Regardless, it does show that teaching a few mechanics at a time in levels and training players over several levels are effective tutorial methods. Popular games such as *Super Meat Boy*, *Portal*, and *Celeste* do this as well. While not teaching anything nearly as complex as biology, they allow players to practice the reaction-based skills necessary to complete them by introducing new mechanics in carefully timed increments.

Developing Concepts into Challenges in a Math Game

The last case study is unique among these examples, as the game has an audience with a pre-determined level of expertise. It is also the game with the most typically spatial levels of these studies, letting the designers directly apply level design to teaching. *Function Force* is a game initially developed as part of the 2014 White House Educational Game Jam and later iterated on through a partnership with the Educational Testing Service (ETS). This jam was an event organized by President Barack Obama's Office of Science and Technology Policy that invited game studios to make educational software "as compelling as the best video game."[30] Development teams were given a choice of topic areas to make a game about based on portions of the US Common Core Education Standards. The team that developed *Function Force*: Mike Treanor, Joshua McCoy, Lucien Parsons, and myself, chose the grade 6–8 standards for mathematics focusing on graphing and transforming trigonometric functions.[31] The resulting game was a "shoot-em-up" (popularly called "schmup") style game, a genre that popularly features spaceships that move automatically in obstacle-rich environments and shoot at enemy fighters. Schmups are also heavy in-game feel components like over-the-top special effects (lasers and explosions) so they natively contain behavioral elements friendly to in-game learning. *Function Force* allows players to change the shape and direction of their ship's weapon by changing the values in a mathematical function pictured onscreen or by choosing new functions. By using different types of functions, players could change the shape of their laser to overcome different types of environmental puzzles (Figure 8.21). This turns a complicated mathematical topic into an engaging system that players can interact and practice with until they master it.

Under the guidance of ETS, we continued developing this game with several of our students, Dan Petricca, Kirby Cofino, and Gray Leonard. It now had the goal of assessment (testing whether the user has learned a subject) rather than pure teaching. As such, we could now assume that the player had already had some experience with the graphing functions. Apart from the game's assessment goals, our goal with the design was to see whether level design could be a viable medium for structuring educational content.

Puzzles as Problems, Levels as Lessons

Based on a learning model from ETS and the steps of the Common Core curriculum, we determined that we would structure our levels as lesson plans. Common Core features "subject clusters" that cover a topic (in our

$$y = 1.80\sin(1.24x)$$

FIGURE 8.21 The first prototype of *Function Force* allowed players to change the direction and shape of their weapon to solve puzzles.

case, trigonometric functions) and each concept within that topic is represented by an individual lesson. Working from a micro- to a macro-scale, we thought of puzzle scenes as math problems and levels as lessons that contained several puzzle/problems about the same concept. The game itself then became the equivalent of a subject cluster, or a chapter of a textbook.[32] Again, this reflects the level organization employed by *Immune Defense* and *Celeste*: a series of spaces that teach the steps to master a whole concept individually. In the case of *Immune Defense*, the first four levels teach the steps that a player must take to have a unit attack an enemy (therefore learning how cells attack pathogens). For *Celeste*, this means that early scenes in a level teach the level's concepts so that later scenes in the same level can test the player's mastery.

Four-Step Tutorial Design

Since *Function Force* also had assessment goals, it let us test a concept called *kishotenketsu*, a level design concept for introducing new gameplay mechanics, as an educational tool. Kishotenketsu is based on a storytelling technique in Japanese Manga comics and is used widely in Nintendo's games, notably *Super Mario 3D World* and *Donkey Kong Country: Tropical Freeze*.[33,34] The method has four steps:

1. Introduce a concept in a safe environment that allows practice.

2. Develop the concept by adding or introducing a more complex iteration.

3. Introduce a twist on the concept.

4. Test the player's mastery of the concept.

This method is central to many modern Nintendo platformers[35] (Figure 8.22). In Chapter 3, we discussed how *Donkey Kong Country: Tropical Freeze* introduces new mechanics then develops them into a challenge by scaffolding new concepts on top of familiar ones. Levels in that game separately introduce concepts like water-filled berries that Donkey Kong can throw or burning platforms, then make challenges by mixing them.

Many indie games follow this pattern as well. Beyond the platformers already discussed in this chapter, *Golf Story*[37] uses kishotenketsu to make distinct levels in a sports game. Each golf course that the player can visit has a special mechanic: one is a country club where elderly members

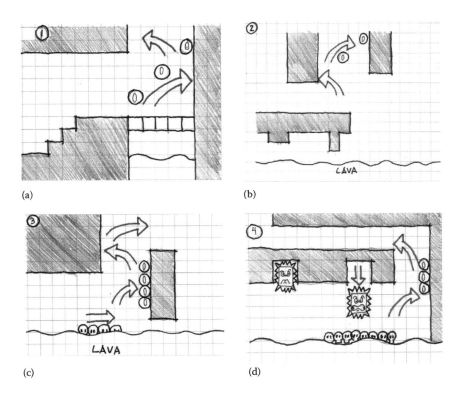

(a)   (b)

(c)   (d)

FIGURE 8.22 Diagrams from a *Super Mario Maker*[36] level made to practice applying kishotenketsu. It is based on the mechanic of wall-jumping, a move where Mario jumps at a wall then quickly executes another jump in the opposite direction. The first screenshot is a skill gate that requires players to wall-jump to proceed, but does not penalize them for failing. The next version is a wall jump over lava: still simple, but now with higher stakes. The third twists the mechanic by requiring the player to string together wall jumps and also introduces floating rafts. The "final exam" requires the player to dodge enemies on a floating raft then make a carefully timed wall jump over lava.

berate you for being too aggressive while another has colored birds take your ball to different types of terrain. When players visit a course, they first find characters that give them small-scale golfing challenges based on the course's conditions. This lets the player learn and practice these new mechanics. These challenges usually escalate in difficulty as the player explores the grounds, so early challenges cover the first two steps of kishotenketsu. Then, a rival golfer challenges the player to a grudge match around the course, typically with a special rule for how to golf during the match: this is the third "with a twist" step. Finally, the player can compete for the course championship as a "final exam" of their mastery of the course's mechanics.

In *Function Force*, kishotenketsu helped us teach gameplay and administer math lessons as game design mastery challenges (Figure 8.23). The first level starts by letting players shoot enemies in a conventional way, letting them get used to the basic mechanics: this is kishotenketsu step 1. Then, the game forces the player to collect an item that changes the slope of their laser: this is step 2. Then, the player must fight enemies with the modified laser, but can collect items to further modify the laser's slope: step 3. Finally, the player reaches a locked door and must shoot a target to open it. To aim at the target, the player must collect enough items to transform the function and give his or her laser the proper slope. This twist takes what was previously a mechanic they could experiment with and makes a more traditional math problem out of it: step 4.

The results from all of these games after testing with audiences was that they teach their topics effectively. While the goal of this chapter and book are not necessarily educational games, the ways that these games present information to players can be adapted to entertainment-focused games. Sometimes players need gameplay information spelled out in more specific terms than you might originally think is appropriate. Likewise, mechanics may be very complicated, so players should be given an appropriate amount of time to master them, be it part of a level or several levels. If you are teaching something very complicated, you can plan your levels as a lesson plan and guide players to mastery in steps. Taking them along steps also helps you turn your tutorials into challenges. Scenes get more and more complex in the Montessori-style until you are giving the player the most advanced and interesting iteration of a mechanic. The thread that ties these all together is playtesting: playing your games with your target audience multiple times is the only way to find out what your players need to know and how to make the best tutorials for them.

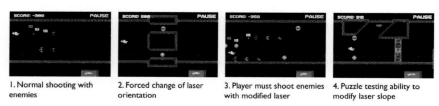

1. Normal shooting with enemies　　2. Forced change of laser orientation　　3. Player must shoot enemies with modified laser　　4. Puzzle testing ability to modify laser slope

FIGURE 8.23　The first level of *Function Force* teaches the gameplay and assesses the player's mastery of linear function transformations using four-step kishoten-ketsu design.

So far, we have focused on the design elements of how tutorials are constructed in games. What about the assets that need to be made to support those tutorials: artwork, audio, interface graphics, and so on? In the next section, we will discuss the types of media you can create to support your tutorial's design.

TUTORIAL ASSETS AND MEDIA

The description of the Death Star Attack level from *Rogue Leader* earlier in this chapter highlighted several elements that make it a great tutorial level, including how it directs the player. Many games stop gameplay to deliver tutorial directions, but Death Star Attack keeps the player in the action of *A New Hope*'s finale. Visually, it gives subtle hints and shows any pop-up graphics in the game's regular interface only when they are needed, keeping them unobtrusive. It also uses audio from the film and that replicates the film's dialogue to give gameplay directions. While it is easy to criticize some games for using text instead of audio, not every game has enough memory for a voice-acted script. Using audio when it is available, however, does deliver a more seamless experience, as in *Rogue Leader*. Game designer and university professor Matthew M. White has studied game tutorials extensively and, in his book *Learn to Play*,[6] describes methods for using media to deliver tutorials that feel like integral parts of a game.

Among his major points, White describes several theories of how information is processed and, if taught effectively, transferred to a learner's long-term memory. He cites the Bruce Mann's Attentional Control Theory of Multimedia Learning, which argues that multimedia creates effective learning by using multiple senses repeatedly[38] (Figure 8.24). Later theories cited in White's book argue that audio and video are better used in tandem rather than alone[39] and that designers should not overwhelm players with too much to learn at once. For the latter argument, we have mainly described this as good design, but White's argument is that we should avoid exceeding the player's *cognitive load*, the effort required to understand something.[40] This reflects what we discussed earlier with Hildebrand's ideas of categorizing and differentiating: humans feel more comfortable when they are not overloaded with information.

I will not discuss all of his points here, but the ones listed above are those which have already been covered in some form in this chapter (particularly in regards to pacing tutorials) or which will be covered here. This section applies some of his methods to level construction, specifically in the use of multimedia assets.

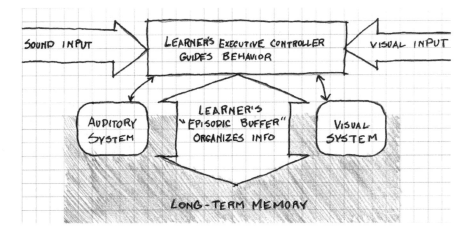

FIGURE 8.24 A diagram of the Attentional Control Theory of Multimedia Learning, adapted from the original by Bruce Mann.

Effective Visual Elements

Early in his book, White condemns games that make exclusive use of interface pop-ups to teach game mechanics. White pejoratively calls these "flash cards,"[41] citing them as trying to describe complex information with an overly simple method. These may sound like the types of methods utilized in effective tutorials described throughout the chapter, but all of the prior examples discussed here have key differences that make them work. For example, some are utilized in tandem with other multimedia assets, notably lines of voice-acted dialog that give the same information. The combination of sounds and visuals delivers the information to our senses in a way that makes the tutorial more effective.

Let us revisit *Horizon: Zero Dawn*. Characters throughout the game's tutorial levels talk in in-universe language about things that the player should do. In the first level, Aloy talks to herself about the next steps she should take, and what she is seeing when the player does things like activate the scanning system. This is coupled not only with the game's graphics but also with flash card graphics that reinforce this information, meaning that it is not the sole delivery system. In the second level, Rost gives Aloy information and commands meant to teach the player and have him or her practice Aloy's moves. Positioning Rost as a mentor adds another element advocated by White: having characters demonstrate things to the player.[42] Rost leads Aloy through the environment and in doing so, shows players many of the actions they should take just ahead. Similarly, allies in *Rogue*

Leader fly toward objectives and attack targets, signaling to players to do the same. Interface pop-ups in this game are kept to a minimum and only appear when contextually necessary.

Not all games have the budget to do these things though: voice acting greatly increases file sizes, actors are expensive, and extra animation can mean months of additional time. In these cases, simple graphics can be presented in interesting ways that help them transcend "flash card" status. I struggled with these factors during the development of my abstract art game *Lissitzky's Revenge*. The goal of each level is to destroy a white circle by charging your avatar, a red wedge, in special safe zones then attacking the circle. Attacking the circle while un-charged moves obstacles aside, but does nothing to the circle itself. These mechanics are based on the game's gameplay inspiration, Atari's *Yar's Revenge*,[43] so I was reluctant to change them because I wanted to maintain that connection. The solution was to do a tutorial, but I could only afford to add simple graphics to the game. Rather than break up the aesthetic with flash cards, I integrated the text into the game's graphic designed environments (Figure 8.25). I also decided that these bits of text should have the "voice" of an unseen totalitarian commander giving orders and feeding the wedge propaganda, adding some story to the game. There is even subversive text challenging this overlord hidden throughout the game, written in the grunge font of some

FIGURE 8.25 The first level of *Lissitzky's Revenge*. The game was made quickly and on a minimal budget, so I could not spend extra on voice-acting for a tutorial. I integrated tutorial text into the game's graphic design, gave it a "voice" so it seemed to be coming from an in-game character, and let gameplay teach the rest.

implied rebels. The rest of the teaching would be done with the teaching theories described earlier in this chapter, delivered through gameplay: successes had big visual effects, the environment had lots of things to experiment with, and levels reloaded quickly if failed. Playtests showed that these were sufficient for teaching the game and players appreciated the added narrative flavor provided by the text's tone.

Popular games like *Portal* and *Dishonored*[44] use environmental text in similar ways. While much of *Portal*'s story is delivered via audio from the murderous computer, GLaDOS, the game's environmental text reveals other characters in the game's lore. While not instructional, the text sets a tone and foreshadows the player's conflict with GLaDOS later in the game. *Dishonored*'s graffiti likewise flavors the game's world and expands on characters, such as the mysterious Outsider, beyond what the player sees in direct cutscenes. This text can be painted into textures or placed as a texture *decal* into environment art. *The Stanley Parable*[45] does this with big yellow text that the player cannot help but see. This text is deceiving: it leads players on a path through the game they are actually meant to deviate from in a parody of how games lead players. That a game was made where the player has to actively resist environmental tutorial text, though, shows how effective it can be.

Audio Elements

Not all developers have the budget to hire actors and schedule studio spaces. If you do have that capability, audio is a great way to deliver story content and reinforce tutorial information. By itself, audio is a great tool for fleshing out your world via radio plays and recordings that require no visuals or animation. This makes it less expensive and time-consuming than other multimedia such as cutscenes or special animations. As already explored, audio and visual information together make for more effective learning in games.

In terms of level design, delivering audio requires careful planning on the part of the designer. Most game engines allow the designer to play audio when a player character enters a *trigger*, an invisible object that players walk through to initiate scripted events. As I stated previously when talking about our game *Dead Man's Trail*, we playtested extensively to determine what players needed to learn in the game. Our eventual tutorial level would be a series of small scenes where players would learn the game's basic mechanics and participate in the beginning of the game's story. Designing in scenes was helpful for maintaining a simple language among developers for where audio prompts would go. The eventual script for these scenes resembled a gameplay description as much as it did a document from which an actor would read lines (Figure 8.26).

The detailed instructions we did eventually write, based on learning what players needed to be taught in playtests, were to be delivered via walky-talky broadcast by an unseen character named Norm. Norm would

---

Dead Man's Trail tutorial outline

Game introduction/looting level

Setting: fortified small town - a "Woodbury"-like town without all the sociopathy

Tiles (areas): Barracks, firing range, outer fence, main-street, escape area

Level/game starts with a character selection window labeled "select your first team member" on a black screen.

After player selects a team member, the party member window disappears and text fades in,

Ashland, VA
15 miles north of the Richmond outbreak zone

Note: Tutorials in this document are written assuming some basic context-sensitive functionality based on the guidelines from *Learn to Play* by Matthew White where tutorial info is delivered in audio with simple visual input and tutorial content is only played if the player needs it (to not condescend to players who already know how to play.) The beginning of the first tutorial line spoken in the looting intro level is:

"Hey it's me again: I found some old operations manuals. Does this make sense to you?"

This text will be referred to with the indicator [Tutorial Start text if needed] on all lines where applicable.

The player's selected party member is standing outside a small barrack building. They are in the barracks area of the level.

First line by Norm, the tutorial narrator, is spoken a second or two after the game begins to tell the player where to go:

"Hey it's me, Norm. You're wanted at the firing range for some practice."

Input needed: WASD movement or point/click movement

FIGURE 8.26 A page from *Dead Man's Trail's* tutorial script. While I do not pretend that the format used here is industry standard, it helped our team rough out the sequence of gameplay steps that needed to occur to trigger each line of dialogue.

be reading "old operations manuals" and would call you to ask what you thought weird instructions like "press the WASD keys to move" meant. In this way, we dictated often-awkward tutorial information in audio, but did so in a way that matched our game's fiction and slightly snarky tone. We scripted certain lines (like the aforementioned one about how to move) to not play if the player uses them before the tutorial plays them: the player does not need to hear tutorials for already mastered. Likewise, other lines play when the player fails to perform an action in a certain amount of time: failing to head to the firing range for the shooting tutorial prompts Norm to ask if your gun skills are getting rusty (Figure 8.27).

Once players have picked up, equipped, and fired the gun at a training dummy, the next section opens and Norm asks if the player would go check the fort's outer wall. The people he sent have not come back yet. The player has mastered the main mechanics of the game's looting mode at this point, so audio is delivered via triggers placed at specific story-important locations that build tension. After players find a wall breach and the team Norm sent out, the game shifts to an escape sequence where players fight a zombie horde (Figure 8.28). Norm directs players toward the exit of the level, but as hurried appeals for them to escape rather than distant orders.

FIGURE 8.27 The shooting range portion of the tutorial level in *Dead Man's Trail* includes a number of audio recordings scripted to occur if players do or do not do certain actions quickly enough. If the player fails to pick up the weapon, equip it, or fire it within a certain amount of time, he or she will be prompted by an unseen character on how to do so. If these actions are done quickly, a gate opens and the player is ushered to move the story forward.

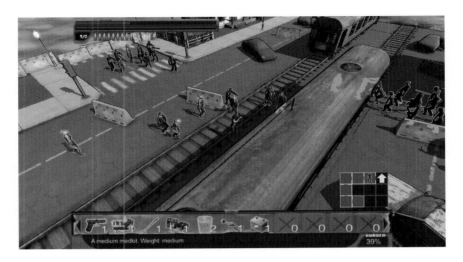

FIGURE 8.28 After a quiet start, the tutorial level of *Dead Man's Trail* eventually delivers a "hook" via a chase sequence with a zombie horde. This is also a chance for skilled players to get extra supplies if they take some risky routes through the level. This rewards experienced players who may be replaying this part of the game.

This teaches players that *Dead Man's Trail* is about running from zombies instead of mowing them down.

Further testing has shown that the tutorial is effective both for teaching the game's mechanics and giving players context for the game's story. While such a level is work-intensive, it is a good case study for the power of well-integrated audio assets in tutorial levels. Rather than a straight recitation, scripting certain lines to play while others stay silent depending on player actions makes the audio feel organic to what the player is doing. This level also integrates other subtle design methods we discussed in this chapter, such as rewarding skilled players by hiding extra rewards (in this case, supplies) and using an early action sequence as a "hook" to build excitement.

Not every developer has access to every type of multimedia useful in tutorials. With some careful planning and knowledge of how to integrate even fragments of a multimedia package effectively, you can maximize their effect. In the last section of this chapter we will look at methods that advertisers use to describe products and elicit responses in customers. These will show us even more ways to integrate visuals, audio, and interactivity into our tutorials while building powerful associations with our game's environmental assets.

TEACHING GAMEPLAY THROUGH ADVERTISING METHODS

In his book *Persuasive Games*, game designer Ian Bogost discusses how methods from the field of advertising can help designers communicate with players through visual and procedural means.[46] Bogost describes three methodologies: *demonstrative advertising*, *illustrative advertising*, and *associative advertising*. These methods are extremely important to level designers, as they describe different methods of how we can communicate information to players. In this section, we will explore what each method of advertising is and how it represents a different style of communication.

Demonstrative Advertising with Scripted Events and Triggers

The first of these methods described by Bogost is demonstrative advertising. Ads that practice demonstrative advertising typically show a product, describe how it is used, and tell how it can help the consumer (Figure 8.29). When advertising video games, for example, this advertising style takes the form of "back-of-the-box" descriptions of a game that describe the number of levels or list a game's features. Products such as cars or tools often use demonstrative advertising to show the utility of the product for the user.

Demonstrations can be a powerful tool for communicating gameplay information to players. We can build associations between gameplay

FIGURE 8.29 A demonstrative advertisement shows a product and introduces its useful or appealing features through copy text.

symbols and gameplay actions through controlled interactions with in-game objects. A demonstration of a certain gameplay element that play-ers can watch but cannot directly interact with can also be an important tool for demonstrating potentially dangerous obstacles or enemy encoun-ters. These demonstrations occur when a player is in view of a danger-ous obstacle, but far enough away that the player cannot interfere with the demonstrative action. For example, the *Half-Life* series typically uses demonstrations to introduce players to the barnacle enemy—a stationary alien character that eats any creature unfortunate to get stuck to its long tongue. Rather than introducing the player to these enemies by letting him or her get caught in the trap, which could be potentially disorienting and create a negative gameplay experience, the designers chose to allow players to watch another creature get caught before they themselves reach the barnacle (Figure 8.30).

In *SWARM!*, the method for destroying enemies—luring them into electrified traps—is introduced by placing the traps between the approach to a room and the enemies' spawn point (Figure 8.31). Building these dem-onstrations in game engines involves careful placement of *scripted game events*, gameplay events that are controlled and activated through a game engine's internal logic-building language. Like many scripted in-game events, demonstrations also require the use of triggers, invisible colli-sion objects that activate scripted events when the player character passes through them. Like other gameplay elements, carefully understanding or defining the metrics of how triggers and scripted events work (adjusting

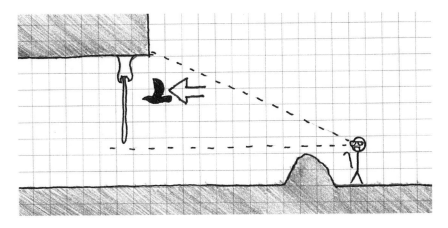

FIGURE 8.30 In-game demonstrative scenarios show players how hazardous gameplay elements work in a safe way so that players can build associations.

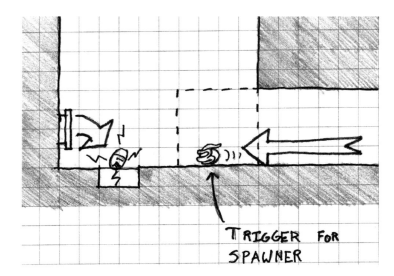

FIGURE 8.31 *SWARM!* introduces the indirect way players must kill enemies by placing traps between the player's entry point to a room and the enemy spawn points. Many demonstrations are based on the timing of scripted events and the placement of event triggers.

the distance of a trigger against the time it takes for the triggered event to occur, adjusting the size of triggers, etc.) is vital for setting up a successful demonstration of gameplay.

While in-game demonstrations involve objects that must be carefully constructed so they create specific gameplay experiences, the other advertising methods are much less concrete in how they engage players.

Illustrative Advertising through Environmental Narrative

Like demonstrative advertising, illustrative advertising shows the product in the ad. However, unlike demonstrative advertising, illustrative advertising omits information on how the product is used or what features could be helpful to consumers, and instead shows the product in an appealing context. This is the "sex sells" method of advertising, where a product is shown being used by someone who then gains favor with those who find him or her attractive. This type of advertising is about promoting a product based on building its image—this car helps you look good at fancy clubs, that cologne will attract beautiful women, our detergent will make your family happy, etc. (Figure 8.32).

Within games, illustrative advertising can be accomplished by building symbols through *environmental narrative detailing*. In *Half-Life 2*,[47] for

FIGURE 8.32 Illustrative advertising shows a product in an appealing context so the viewer builds associations between the product and an image he or she would like to possess.

example, it is established that the lambda symbol (λ) is associated with the heroic resistance movement through environmental and contextual clues—the symbol is used on the player character's armor, in friendly bases, etc. As the player progresses through the game, he or she encounters the symbol many times, typically near caches of helpful items or breaks in long action sequences. Similarly, *Resident Evil 4* utilizes ominously crafted signposts before enemy territories, traps, or encounters. After several iterations of signpost = danger sequences, the player learns that the signs are a warning by the level designers that something dangerous is about to occur. Like *Half-Life 2*'s use of λ, the designers craft a symbol by illustrative means, reinforcing that signposts are followed by danger. Used in conjunction with behavioral and Montessori teaching methods, illustrated symbols become a powerful teaching tool in games.

Associative Advertising as Deconstruction

Associative advertising is the least concrete of the advertising methods discussed by Bogost. Like illustrative advertising, it builds a product's image by associating it with an appealing environment. However, associative advertisements show only the context and leave the product's usage to the viewer's imagination. These kinds of advertisements are popular with car, beer, liquor, and cigarette companies, with their ads often showing implied users enjoying the company of friends, attending stylish parties, or fulfilling male power fantasies (Figure 8.33).

Associative advertising is the product of centuries of development in how advertisements are employed. Many early nineteenth- and twentieth-century ads featured lots of copy describing how a product is used. Over time, advertisers focused on quick, eye-catching image-building ads over descriptive ones—the result of consumers gradually spending less time interacting with each single advertisement.[48] Likewise, associative methods within games are the result of the designer building a system of information over the course of a game. As players are taught how symbols, sounds, or game objects correspond to gameplay through demonstrations, reinforcement, or other methods, they learn the game's visual and auditory language. Players can, through Montessori learning, internalize how a game's symbolic communication system works and interpret even small variations on established patterns if they recognize familiar elements. Associative methods in games allow designers to show a symbol to communicate that the associated gameplay is nearby, even as the designer increasingly adds obstacles between symbol and associated element (Figure 8.34). This can be used, in a way similar to *Half-Life 2* and *Resident Evil 4*, not only to build symbol = gameplay relationships, but also to deconstruct familiar gameplay elements or subvert established patterns.

FIGURE 8.33 Associative advertising works similarly to illustrative advertising, but omits the advertised product entirely in favor of building an image for the product.

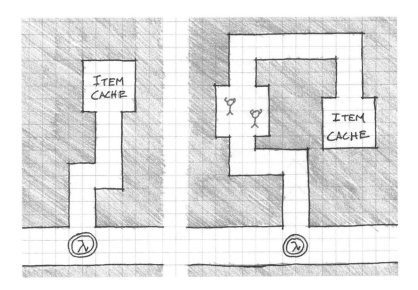

FIGURE 8.34 Building strong associations in games allows designers to increasingly deconstruct the symbol = gameplay relationship. In this example, a symbol that indicates nearby rewards is placed farther and farther from the payoff. Building associations allows for gameplay elements to be mixed and matched with other puzzles or hazards.

Limbo excels at this type of deconstruction by playing its silhouetted art style against a player's relationship with established gameplay conventions. In an early puzzle, players encounter a large press with what appears to be a raised button directly underneath. Gameplay conventions dictate that the raised portion must be the button that operates the press, so the player should avoid it to stay alive. However, when the player moves next to the button so he or she may jump over it, he or she learns that the depressed ground next to the button is actually the mechanism that activates the lethal press (Figure 8.35).

Such subversions could even be utilized in gameplay narratives. Imagine a scenario where in a *Half-Life 2* map, the player encounters what appears to be a friendly base and must choose whether to trust the characters within. However, contextual clues such as missing λ symbols could be used to communicate to observant players that the base is a trap. Such scenarios can provide the player with exciting choices to make if they are accompanied by opportunities to determine whether gameplay scenarios are consistent or inconsistent with the game's system of visual language.

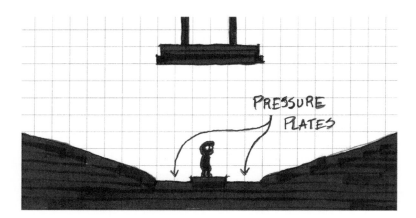

FIGURE 8.35 Associations built in one or more games may be used by game designers to create gameplay scenarios that remix previous puzzles or subvert accepted game conventions. Games such as *Limbo* utilize gameplay tropes to make players reinvent how they are trained to solve certain challenges.

SUMMARY

In this chapter, we went backwards to the beginnings of our games to discover how to teach players to play them. Well-crafted tutorial levels excite, entice, and prepare players to utilize the game's mechanics in a fun and non-intrusive way. Tutorials may seem like black magic, but they do not have to be. By playing lots of them or observing how players interact with them, we can learn the psychology of helping players internalize game skills. By structuring the lessons we teach and the building blocks we use to craft these lessons, we can teach players a variety of mechanics. Visual communication plays a role as well: by using symbolic repeated assets, we can build strong associations that affect player behavior and inform their interactions.

Players who have effectively mastered a game's mechanics can do some really great things, such as telling their own stories using games. In the next chapter, we further explore how gamespaces can be used as facilitators of narrative, both pre-created by designers and created through the player's interaction.

EXERCISES

1. **Game-testing exercise**: Choose a popular commercial game with a tutorial level that does not interrupt the player. Have a player play it and observe his or her behaviors during interactions with the

tutorials and how quickly mastery of the game's mechanics occurs. If he or she does not master the game quickly, ask questions afterward about how and why he or she was getting stuck.

2. **Game-testing exercise**: Choose a popular commercial game with a tutorial level that DOES interrupt the player. Have a player play it and observe his or her behaviors during interactions with the tutorials. Ask, after gameplay is over, how he or she felt about the interruptions.

3. **Drawing exercise**: Design a gameplay mechanism that a player character must react to in a level (like the tilting flowers or rolling spiky fruits in *Donkey Kong Country: Tropical Freeze*). Sketch individual areas of a level for each of these: (1) introducing the mechanism to the player under "safe" conditions; (2) having the player react to the mechanism with his or her character in a little danger; (3) providing a "twist" on the mechanism—presenting it in a new way; (4) "final exam," or having the player react to the twisted mechanism while his or her character is in a lot of danger.

4. **Digital exercise**: Graybox a level that develops a mechanic from a safe tutorial to a "final test" state—at least four or five different scenes. Add checkpoints that are spaced far apart (maybe only one or two in the whole level) and test with a player. See how he or she feels if and when he or she fails challenging puzzles and has to go back. Then add checkpoints at frequent intervals (at the beginning of each challenge scene) and test again. Ask the player how being able to quickly retry challenging areas felt vs. having to navigate back before retrying.

5. **Game-testing exercise**: Have a player that does not play games play a popular commercial game with a tutorial level. What does he or she have a difficult time learning? What assumptions does the game make about the player's background in game-playing? Does the player get stuck on anything that is "normal" in game playing (such as using W, A, S, D to move, etc.)?

6. **Paper prototyping exercise**: Create a paper prototype of a level and design some rules for movement. Write the rules down and have a player read them and try to execute them. What was clear and what did the player get wrong? Try reading the rules to the player and see

if anything changes. How can you change the wording of the rules to be more effective?

7. **Digital exercise**: Graybox a level where the player has to learn two or three mechanics (this can include how to move the player avatar) and create sound and graphics that trigger when the player reaches teaching areas of the level. Test by having only the graphics appear, then test with only the sound playing in these sections. Then try having both appear. Do this with several playtesters and log the results: how often was one of the lone methods (sounds or visuals) better than the other? How often was the combined version (sounds and visuals) best?

8. **Drawing exercise**: Sketch a level or a scene from a game that utilizes each of the advertising methods described in the chapter as a teaching device. Try to diagram them so that you include your thoughts on where event triggers (if the scene has them) might be.

ENDNOTES

1. Koster, Raph. *A Theory of Fun for Game Design*. Sebastopol, CA: O'Reilly Media, 2004.
2. *Celeste*. Matt Thorson (Designer). January 25, 2018. Indie game for Nintendo Switch.
3. Lewis, Philippa. *Portals: Gates, Stiles, Windows, Bridges, & Other Crossings*. New York, NY: Bloomsbury US, 2018, p. 1.
4. *Star Wars Rogue Squadron II: Rogue Leader*. Factor 5 (developer) and Lucasarts (developer and publisher). November 18, 2001. Nintendo Gamecube game.
5. Sudnow, David. *Pilgrim in the Microworld*. New York, NY: Warner Books, 1983, p. 39.
6. White, Matthew M. *Learn To Play: Designing Tutorials for Video Games*. Boca Raton, FL: CRC Press, 2014.
7. Hildebrand, Grant. *Origins of Architectural Pleasure*. Los Angeles, CA: University of California Press, 1999. p. 91.
8. Hildebrand, Grant. *Origins of Architectural Pleasure*. Los Angeles, CA: University of California Press, 1999. p. 92.
9. Hildebrand, Grant. *Origins of Architectural Pleasure*. Los Angeles, CA: University of California Press, 1999. p. 126.
10. Yoder, Andrew. "The Holy Grail of Multiplayer Level Design". Conference presentation. Game Developers Conference 2018, San Francisco, CA.
11. Lewis, Philippa. *Portals: Gates, Stiles, Windows, Bridges, & Other Crossings*. New York, NY: Bloomsbury US, 2018, pp. 4–5.

12. Frederick, Matthew. *101 Things I Learned in Architecture School*. Cambridge, MA: MIT Press, 2007, p. 6.

13. Frederick, Matthew. *101 Things I Learned in Architecture School*. Cambridge, MA: MIT Press, 2007, p. 10.

14. *God of War II*. SCE Santa Monica Studio (developer) and Sony Computer Entertainment (publisher). March 13, 2007. Sony Playstation 2 game.

15. *Half-life 2: Episode 2*. Valve Corporation (developer and publisher). October 10, 2007. PC game.

16. Swink, Steve. *Game Feel: A Game Designer's Guide to Virtual Sensation*. Burlington, MA: Morgan Kaufmann, 2008.

17. Salen, Katie and Eric Zimmerman. *Rules of Play: Game Design Fundamentals*. Cambridge, MA: MIT Press, 2003, p. 346.

18. Kremers, Rudolf. *Level Design: Concept, Theory, and Practice*. Wellesley, MA: A.K. Peters, 2009, p. 33.

19. *The Legend of Zelda: A Link to the Past*. Nintendo EAD (developer) and Nintendo (publisher), November 21, 1991. Super Nintendo game.

20. *Hyper Light Drifter*. Heart Machine (developer), March 31, 2016. Downloadable indie game on Steam.

21. *SWARM!*. E4 Software (developer), January 2013. Indie mobile phone and tablet game.

22. *Lissitzky's Revenge*. Pie for Breakfast Studios (developer), March 2015. Downloadable indie game on GameJolt.

23. *SUPERHOT*. Superhot Team (developer), February 25, 2016. Indie game on Steam.

24. *Owlboy*. D-Pad Studio (developer), November 1, 2016. Indie game on Steam.

25. *The Oregon Trail*. Minnesota Educational Computing Consortium (developer) and The Learning Company (publisher), 1985. Apple II game.

26. *20XX*. Batterystaple Games and Fire Hose Games (developers), August 16, 2017. Indie game on Steam.

27. At the time of this writing, *La Mancha* has earned a bronze medal in the 2018 International Serious Play Educational Game Awards and was an official selection in the 2018 Meaningful Play educational game showcase.

28. *Immune Defense*. Molecular Jig Games (developer), 2015. Downloadable Indie game on GameJolt.

29. Stegman, Melanie. "Immune Defense". MolecularJig.com. http://www.molecularjig.com/

30. DeLoura, Mark. "The White House Education Game Jam". The Obama White House Archive. Created October 4, 2014. https://obamawhitehouse.archives.gov/blog/2014/10/06/white-house-education-game-jam (accessed May 19, 2017).

31. McREL International, 2014. "Common Core Mathematics 6–8". Content Knowledge: A Compendium of Standards and Benchmarks for K-12 Education: Online Edition. Retrieved from: http://www2.mcrel.org/compendium/standardDetails.asp?subjectID=34&standardID=23

32. Treanor, Mike and Christopher W. Totten, Joshua McCoy, and G. Tanner Jackson, 2018. "Merging Education, Assessment, and Entertainment in Math Games: A Case Study of *Function Force*. *International Academic Conference on Meaningful Play*, October 11–13, 2018, East Lansing, Michigan.

33. Nutt, Christian. "The Structure of Fun: Learning from *Super Mario 3D Land's* Director". Gamasutra, April 13, 2012. http://www.gamasutra.com/view/feature/168460/the_structure_of_fun_learning_.php (accessed September 2, 2018).

34. Brown, Mark. "*Super Mario 3D World's* 4 Step Level Design". March 16, 2015. https://www.youtube.com/watch?v=dBmIkEvEBtA (accessed September 2, 2018).

35. Totten, Christopher. "Day 4: Wall Jump Keep". *Adventures in Mario Maker*, September 15, 2015. https://30daysofmariomaker.tumblr.com/post/129145992339/day-4-wall-jump-keep-course-id (accessed September 2, 2018).

36. *Super Mario Maker*. Nintendo EAD (developer) and Nintendo (Publisher), September 10, 2015. Nintendo Wii U game.

37. *Golf Story*. Sidebar Games (developer), September 28, 2017. Nintendo Switch game.

38. White, Matthew M. *Learn to Play: Designing Tutorials for Video Games*. Boca Raton, FL: CRC Press, 2014, pp. 41–42.

39. White, Matthew M. *Learn to Play: Designing Tutorials for Video Games*. Boca Raton, FL: CRC Press, 2014, p. 98.

40. White, Matthew M. *Learn to Play: Designing Tutorials for Video Games*. Boca Raton, FL: CRC Press, 2014, p. 99.

41. White, Matthew M. *Learn to Play: Designing Tutorials for Video Games*. Boca Raton, FL: CRC Press, 2014, p. 27.

42. White, Matthew M. *Learn to Play: Designing Tutorials for Video Games*. Boca Raton, FL: CRC Press, 2014, p. 115.

43. *Yar's Revenge*. Atari (developer and publisher), 1982. Atari 2600 game.

44. *Dishonored*. Arkane Studios (developer) and Bethesda Softworks (publisher), October 9, 2012. Playstation 3 game.

45. *The Stanley Parable*. Galactic Café (developer). October 17, 2013. Downloadable indie game on Steam.

46. Bogost, Ian. *Persuasive Games: The Expressive Power of Videogames*. Cambridge, MA: MIT Press, 2007, pp. 153–162.

47. *Half-Life 2*. Valve Corporation (developer and publisher), November 16, 2004. PC game.

48. McKenna, Stephen. History of Advertising. Class lecture, The Rhetoric of Advertising. Catholic University of America, Washington, DC, January 2009.

INDUSTRY PERSPECTIVES: CASE STUDY: IMMUNE DEFENSE

Melanie Stegman, Ph.D.

PROJECT HISTORY

I am very motivated to teach people molecular cell biology. People should understand the basics of nutrition, clean environment, and vaccination for themselves and for others. People should understand that the current state of medical research is wildly exciting and that we could be discovering so much more with more funding. People should understand how their own fascinating bodies work, before they get depressed for the first time and absolutely before they must make life and death decisions about chemotherapy.

The Federation of American Scientists (FAS), under the leadership of Dr. Henry Kelly, created the third person shooter, *Immune Attack*.[1] Three months before it was released, I happened upon the trailer online. I was a biochemistry post doc at the time, studying how tuberculosis bacteria evade our immune system. I had been looking for a way to teach non-scientists about molecular biology. Biomedical research depends on tax dollars and its effectiveness depends on its adoption. I saw in *Immune Attack* a brilliant method of educating the public on the basics of molecular cell biology. Within two weeks of watching the trailer, I was employed by the FAS and manager of the *Immune Attack* project.

My goal was to evaluate *Immune Attack* as a teaching tool and develop more games based on my research. I was employed with the condition that I would find outside funding within a year to support my work. *Immune Attack* was released Spring of 2008. Howard Young, Ph.D., an accomplished immunologist at the National Cancer Institute reached out wanting to help. Bette Manchester, who started the first one-to-one laptop program in the U.S., called to say she had 40,000 students with laptops and could she please put *Immune Attack* on them. I did a Google search for biology and immunology games and found Leslie Miller, Ph.D. at Rice University, who had created the *MedMyst* series. With these collaborators at my side I wrote and won an R25 research grant from the National Institute of Allergy and Infectious Diseases to evaluate what students learn from playing *Immune Attack* and to use my research to develop the game further.

My three-year controlled quantitative study of learning and confidence gains in 6th–12th grade students who played *Immune Attack* in their classrooms revealed important facts that formed the basis of my research-based design of the game, *Immune Defense*.[2] (1) Students learned molecules' cell biology by playing and they gained confidence in their ability to comprehend molecular cell biology diagrams. (2) Self-reported gamers and non-gamers were equally likely to finish the game, to report that the game was easy to play, to learn molecular biology, and to gain confidence. (3) Students who reported that *Immune Attack* was not "easy to play" still learned significantly more than the control group, however, they did not gain confidence compared to their control classmates. It is important to note that they did not lose confidence, either. (4) The name, function, and real-life identity of cells and proteins in the game were remembered, if using them was required in the game.

My conclusion was that games can teach abstract complex concepts like molecular cell biology, and a game that is "easy to play" can make novices confident in their ability to learn more. My goal was clear: create a casual game, that a wide audience finds easy to play, that gets players using cells and proteins.

LISTENING TO INFLUENCES

My biggest influence is my audience. I am always caught off guard when people ask me "But how do you get kids to play these games?" I honestly have no answer to that question. Kids see the first screen of *Immune Defense* or *Immune Attack* and they play. They laugh, they yell out hints across the room, they complain about the controls and they play. I have asked about 1,000 kids what the most fun part of *Immune Attack* is and the two most common answers are "seeing the inside of the body" and "flying and shooting." OK, some students have refused to play until I tell them the game is actually accurate. My audience wants to see real stuff.

The fantastic thing about *Immune Attack* is that it puts the player inside the body and not in a lab. I was lucky that this fantastic game was my starting point. We scientists do not do lab work because we like flasks. We do lab work because we want answers about what proteins and cells are doing. We can see proteins in our minds and I want to share that ability.

Others have done mind-opening work since I began my journey. Their work points even more clearly to the fact that a successful game will put the player at the heart of the mystery. Soren Johnson's discussion of theme and meaning,[3] Diane Ketelhut's work on *Sheep Trouble*,[4,5] Cornielia Brunner's work on *Ruby Realms*,[6,7] and Jodie Jenkinson's work on video presentations of protein behavior to students.[8] Together these disparate works showed that the mechanic is what players remember and learn from, your students will not shy away from "hard" problems to solve if they are in a well-designed game and that adding more details can improve understanding, especially when those details are key to understanding. These works strengthened my resolve to create a game in which players could manipulate real cells and proteins.

The other one-third of my influences was *Plants vs Zombies*. I love how clever that game makes me feel. Everyone loves that game, certainly, this is the "easy to play, casual game style" that I needed. Then, sitting in the audience at GDC, I hear George Fan talk about how to make an easy to play, widely popular, casual game. Step one: start with easy to interpret actors, like a pea shooter that shoots. I almost cried: proteins all look like blobs, no one can guess their function from their appearance. The rest of Fan's advice is to involve the player in the core mechanic as soon as possible and to introduce the gameplay in small steps that require less than eight words to explain. I tried my best to adhere to this advice. Figure 1 demonstrates how I took this advice to heart. Incidentally, the diagrammatic presentation of proteins I used is exactly how biochemists draw their own models, and often how science is described in articles.

STAGES OF ID GAME DEVELOPMENT, AKA, MELANIE'S GAME DEVELOPMENT EDUCATION

Here are some of the big moments in the development of *Immune Defense*.

1. *Stage one: Listening to our play testers and being willing to change*. In its paper prototype stage, *Immune Defense* was a tower defense game. Players placed cells near a wound and bacteria moved through the wound. Players could place cells in "available spaces" just like any other, sensible, straightforward tower defense style game. In our case, the available spaces were defined by clouds of cytokine molecules, which are the proteins that attract white blood cells to wounds. On paper this meant that available places for placing cells were marked by a bunch of tiny polka dots. However, in our first

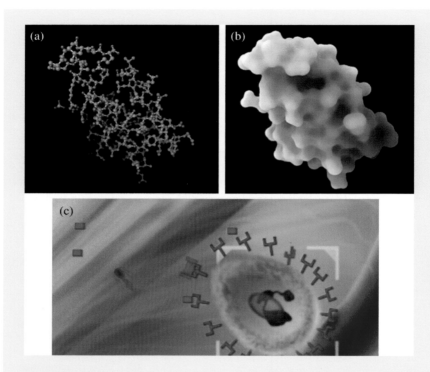

FIGURE 1   (a) The surface diagram of a protein in the game. (b) Another common representation of the same protein. (c) That protein in action in the game: the rectangle is the protein and the receptor that binds it is helpfully drawn as a fork that obviously fits a rectangle.

digital prototype we made the cytokines move around and our play testers were captivated by the moving proteins. They tried to click on then and grab them. Molecules were clearly more fun to play with than cells. We started designing ways to let our players manipulate molecules. We began to treat our cells more like troops in a real-time strategy game: instead of putting the cells down in a known place we now could give them a general direction by giving them some cytokine molecules to follow.

At the end of stage 1: Immune Defense developed into a real-time strategy (RTS) style game. Real-time action made the game more like being in the real body. I also choose the RTS game interface style to promote familiarity, for people who were familiar with RTS games.

2. *To make a popular game, test it where players can freely walk away.* Testing Immune Defense in biology and other kinds of middle school and high school classrooms, we found that our games were very well received. However, when I showed the same version in an expo where

people could come and go freely or at after-school programs where the students could do other things, I learned quickly that players did not pay attention long enough to get engaged. I flailed around a big trying to solve this problem. Many players asked, "What is this?" and "What am I doing?" So my first attempt at a game introduction was to create a tutorial that showed the player the names of the cell, receptors, and proteins. But players clicked through it, said, "Cool," and put the game down.

The answer was to get players to use the objects and to give them very clear feedback about what the objects do. One step was to describe each object in a game-based manner, not a real-life manner. In our user interface we would describe the receptors and the cells as any strategy game does. I originally tried "This is a receptor" and then I wrote "This will let your cell catch the bacteria." This focus on the in-game function let players learn in context of the game and was useful in creating engagement. I learned that when players ask "What is this?" they really mean, "What can I do with this in this game?" All information we show on screen during gameplay is immediately relevant to game plan in that level. After playing a few levels, people start asking, "Is this real?" Then they are ready to read more info in our database, that is accessible when gameplay is paused. Even in our database, most of the words and images are about how to use the object to win. Figure 2 shows the database entry for one of the cells in *Immune Defense*.

Creating extremely easy steps in the beginning that also draw the player into the action was the key to our success. It took me three years to get to where the steps were easy enough. Part of the problem was that biochemistry is very familiar to me, so I always over estimate how easy things are. Part of the problem is that when (many) people hear that the game is a learning game, they walk away without looking at it (yes, not even looking). Another problem is that people get anxious before they even start playing because "It is science and I am supposed to know this already." But honestly, this issue is something every game struggles with: getting the player trained before they decide to quit. A casual game on the app store needs to capture its players in about 30 seconds. A game designed for classrooms has 5–10 minutes during which students will read and try to figure the game out.

3. *Make everything be really obvious and let it be obvious over and over.* The play field has a boundary. All games need one and all games have one. In the beginning levels, the width of the screen was the same as the width of the playable area. This was so the player doesn't need to zoom in or look around: all of the action should happen right in front of the player. The core game loop in *Immune Defense* is the cell tracking, binding, swallowing, and then dissolving of bacteria. But the binding and swallowing sometimes happened off screen. The cell

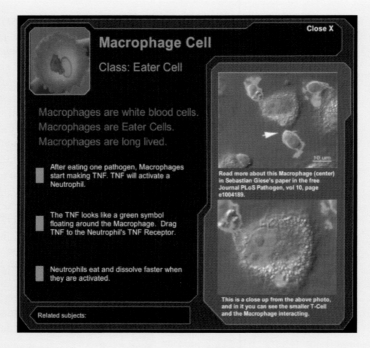

FIGURE 2   The database gives players some hints and also gives them some real-life information.

would track a bacterium to the edge of the screen, and then extend itself to capture the bacterium, but at this point the cell had pushed the bacterium off screen. So the binding and swallowing part of the core game loop was sometimes happening off screen.

It sounds like a no-brainer: just force everything to happen on screen. But (1) it didn't happen all the time and players still had other opportunities to see the binding and phagocytosis; (2) I did not want to use an invisible boundary, because I knew in this game, in which every aspect was 100% foreign, players would not know whether or not WBC had boundaries in real life; and (3) what kind of visible boundary would there be inside the body?

I ended up moving the boundary in closer, making the play field smaller than the screen, so that the bacteria binding and swallowing was always on screen. It really did increase comprehension of what was happening. Then I let the boundary be marked by the ugly same white lines we used for ourselves in the game engine. I designed the white lines to seem like part of the radar system that we had already in the game. It worked because the white lines came and went like the radar grid, it looks really out of place. It looks like an unnatural projection created by our nanobot's computer. I think it works well to make learning to play manageable for our players without misleading them about cells' abilities to locate bacteria.

SCIENCE GAMES

This chapter is just a brief list of moments in the design process where I made big changes. I could list more revelations. But everything I learned led me to realize that *Immune Defense* is a science game. The great joy of being a scientist is asking questions and finding answers. The natural world is unpredictable, the functions the natural world can perform are not cataloged on any website, the methods used to answer our questions about the natural world may need to be invented by you, before you can begin to answer your questions. So, science games will need to have some really unique game mechanics. What guidance can I give to someone trying to create a game mechanic that helps them explain their particular science concepts?

To create a great science game, a designer should let the player be a scientist. A player should be able to Gather data, Make a hypothesis, Experiment, See feedback (GMES). A player in every game is actually conducting experiments constantly: what should I do next? Where should I go? What is the secret in this room? What is interactable? Is it important? Our players are always gathering data and well-designed levels provide them with feedback. A science game differs from a "commercial" game only in that the mechanic is based on the universe we live in. Follow the same steps you do for game design in general: give your players interesting, meaningful problems to solve. And help them find their way by making sure they can always, every moment, guess and get clear feedback. Sometimes the clarity comes from simplifying what is on the screen, sometimes from adding things. Test early and test often with your chosen audience!

ENDNOTES

1. Kelly, H., Howell, K., Glinert, E., Holding, L., Swain, C., Burrowbridge, A., and Roper, M. (2007). How to build serious games. *Commun. ACM, 50*(7), 44–49.
2. Stegman, M. (2014). Immune Attack players perform better on a test of cellular immunology and self confidence than their classmates who play a control video game. *Faraday Discussions, 169*, 403–423.
3. Soren Johnson, Game Design Blog. https://www.designer-notes.com/?p=237.
4. Ketelhut, D.J., Dede, C., Clarke, J., and Nelson, B. (2006). *A multi-user virtual environment for building higher order inquiry skills in science.* Paper presented at the 2006 AERA Annual Meeting, San Francisco, CA, April. Available: http://muve.gse.harvard.edu/rivercityproject/documents/rivercity-sympinq1.pdf [accessed March 2009].

5. Ketelhut, D.J. (2007). The impact of student self-efficacy on scientific inquiry skills: an exploratory investigation in River City, a multi-user virtual environment. *Journal of Science Education and Technology, 16*(1), 99–111.
6. Digital game: *The Ruby Realm*, the adventure game about photosynthesis. https://educators.brainpop.com/lesson-plan/ruby-realm-game.
7. Photosynthesis lesson plan: *The Ruby Realm* game, by BrainPOP Educators, Retrieved August, 2018.
8. Jenkinson, J. and McGill, G. (2012). Visualizing protein interactions and dynamics: evolving a visual language for molecular animation. *CBE life sciences education,* 11(1), 103–110.

CHAPTER 9

Storytelling in Gamespaces

A S WE HAVE SEEN, games are a powerful medium for designers to communicate with audiences through visual communication, feedback, and spatial contrasts. Games are systems that create meaning—through games, designers have the power to shape experience and emotion. Emotions play a vital role in bringing players back to games and making their experience with your games memorable. So far, we have seen that emotions can be evoked through the qualities of space—size, orientation, lighting, and views, among others. In this chapter we will see how to use these methods to tell stories with our gamespaces.

Games are unique from other media in their interactivity, allowing players to have agency over their experience with a story rather than passively absorbing it. In the interest of creating dialogs with our players, level designers can utilize the unique opportunities games present both to convey pre-created stories with their levels and to allow opportunities for players to create their own stories through gameplay.

In this chapter, we explore how game mechanics and art create storytelling opportunities. We also explore the different types of narrative spaces, as well as how modular level assets can be utilized to create environmental narratives or even show narrative progression. With these elements in mind, we reexamine narrative rewards to illustrate how narrative may be used to allow players opportunities for exploration, discovery, and writing their own narratives through gameplay.

What you will learn in this chapter:

Expressive design

Mechanics vs. motif

Narrative spaces

Environment art storytelling

Materiality and the hero's journey

Pacing and narrative rewards

EXPRESSIVE DESIGN

In 1607, Emperor Shah Jahan, then the Mughal Prince Khurrum, was betrothed to Arjumand Banu Begum, a granddaughter of Persian nobles. When they were married five years later, Khurrum gave Begum the title of Mumtaz Mahal, the Jewel of the Palace, declaring her "elect among all women of the time."[1] When Mumtaz died in childbirth in 1631, Jahan was inconsolable. After two years of grieving, he commissioned a tomb be built for her in Agra, Uttar Pradesh, India. To capture the memory of Mumtaz's beauty, architects and artisans from around the Muslim world built the tomb with precise proportions and calligraphic ornamentation of passages from the Qur'an.[2] The surrounding gardens are based on Persian Charbagh (paradise gardens), with abundant trees, flowers, plants and prominent use of water to represent the four rivers of Paradise.[3] The result is the Taj Mahal, one of the most significant and evocative architectural works in human history (Figure 9.1). Through the Taj Mahal's design, the emperor embodied what he believed to be the beauty of Mumtaz, and an expression of his love for her.

In a similar—though much more commonplace—case, design guru Donald Norman, in his book *Emotional Design: Why We Love (or Hate) Everyday Things*, discusses his collection of three unusual teapots, each having a significant narrative or experience.[4] One, designed by French artist Jacques Carelman, has the spout on the same side as the handle and is therefore impossible to use. The next, the Nanna Teapot, designed by architect Michael Graves, has a bulbous design of clear glass that shows the tea as it steeps and a tea ball inside that can be raised or lowered with a crank. The third, the Ronnefeldt "Tilting" Teapot, can be stood on its back for steeping, then propped upright for serving (Figure 9.2). Norman keeps

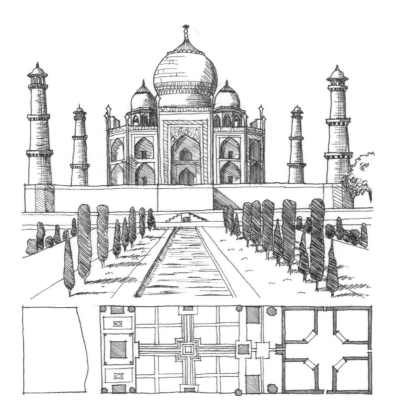

FIGURE 9.1 The Taj Mahal and its surrounding gardens embody a historic love story and the beauty of the woman interred there through ornamentation, proportion, and landscaping.

FIGURE 9.2 An illustration of Donald Norman's teapot collection, as described in the book *Emotional Design*.

the teapots on display because they each evoke different components of product design. However, each also embodies a unique story through the experience of brewing tea: one of snarky impracticality, one offering insight into the transformation of water to tea in an appealing form, and one that describes the readiness of the tea through the practical transformation of the pot itself.

Much like these more classical examples of design—architectural and product design—games have had the power to express narratives, emotions, and ideas. Long before video games gained the expressive power they have today—high-end graphics, media with large storage capacity, sophisticated sound design, and so forth—games, including non-digital ones, embodied a variety of ideas through their mechanics and visual elements. Throughout history, games have been created to simulate important elements of the cultures from which they originated. Chess, for example, was created in India during the Gupta Empire (ca. 320–600 CE) as Chaturanga, which means "four divisions" (of the military).[5] Slave children in the American South played musical, cooperative, and roleplay games (not to be confused with roleplaying games) to cope with their oppressive surroundings.[6] Elizabeth Magie created her *Landlord's Game*, the precursor to *Monopoly*, in 1904 to embody her progressive political beliefs about taxation and wealth.[7]

We have looked at level design in games as a tool for communicating with players. We have also seen game levels as media for teaching or evoking emotional responses such as fear, excitement, or joy. Examples such as the Taj Mahal, Donald Norman's teapots, and historic games, show us that design can embody narrative or cultural ideas as well.

Narrative Design and Worldbuilding

As level designers, we should be concerned with finding the connections between narrative development, the embodiment of cultural ideas, and expressions of usable gamespace. A common expression of these factors is *worldbuilding*, the creation of fictional worlds, geography, and cultures.[8] An important example for game developers comes from the work of J.R.R. Tolkien. Through works such as *The Lord of the Rings*[9] and *The Silmarillion*,[10] Tolkien created Middle Earth: a rich fantasy world beginning with unique languages and then adding political structures and landscapes. As a linguist, Tolkien specialized in ancient English languages, the Germanic languages, and spoke many others.[11] Tolkien acknowledged that languages were central to his works, as Middle Earth was primarily a place for the people who spoke Tolkien's own constructed languages.[12] The cultures he developed influenced his stories and the geography of Middle Earth.

Tolkien's language-centric works show one methodology for world-building, as one might choose to design a world around politics, as a stage for a specific story, or as a home for specific characters. In the case of Middle Earth, the geography is a stage born out of the varied cultures Tolkien created and their relationships with one another. The design of Middle Earth, both visually and culturally, was one element that lent to the success of *The Lord of the Rings* and other works based in that world. Through the detailed descriptions the author provided, readers could envision the world of Middle Earth in their minds and eventually through popular media such as cartoons and film. Tolkien's works, and others like them, would be very influential on narrative-based games, both in setting and in the ability to conjure worlds from designed imaginary elements.

Narrative Worldbuilding in Games

Many modern gamers are familiar with roleplaying games thanks to products like *Dungeons & Dragons*[13] or *Call of Cthulhu*,[14] influenced by the works of Tolkien and horror/sci-fi writer H.P. Lovecraft, respectively. In their most basic form, the physical components of these games include sheets on which players can record their character's abilities, dice, and a guide for the Dungeon Master, the player who runs the game. Gameplay action largely consists of descriptions of events by the Dungeon Master and responses by players, from which epic narratives emerge. Far from the flashy visuals of modern video games, these games have endured for decades and have sold millions of copies. Despite the abstract or text-based nature of these games' presentations, they share the ability to create meaningful narrative worlds through the imaginations and interactions of players. The histories and events of these worlds are often dependent on the actions of players during game sessions.[15]

During the personal computer revolution of the late 1970s and early 1980s, many roleplaying game enthusiasts saw the machines as natural homes for their own designed scenarios: the computer could do the calculations necessary to run the game, allowing players to focus on enjoying the story. Adapting many of their own *Dungeons & Dragons* (*D&D*) scenarios to the computer, designers created early computer roleplaying games such as *Dungeon*[16] and *Akalabeth: World of Doom*,[17] which even featured designer Richard Garriott's own *D&D* character, Lord British. Around the same time, adventure games such as *Zork I*[18] also became popular and featured complex worlds described through text alone (Figure 9.3).

Decades later, independent developers have returned to the text adventure in different ways as a spatial medium. Chris Klimas's popular Twine game engine allows the easy creation of interactive stories through choose-your-own-adventure mechanics and hyperlinks. The structure of developing in Twine allows storytellers to arrange their stories into rooms—a Twine story's flow chart is referred to as a "map"—that can be navigated like an architectural space. While not required, games like *This Book Is a Dungeon*[19] or *The Uncle Who Works for Nintendo*[20] utilize this aspect of Twitch to create mappable spaces—a dungeon and a suburban house respectively. Simogo's mobile game *Device 6*,[21] on the other hand, reimagines the text adventure as an e-book: the player begins by flipping through the story as one would a digital novel. Eventually, as their character, Anna, explores the mysterious castle that she has woken up in, the text takes on the form of a map and changes direction as passages twist and turn. In response, the player must scroll his or her finger in different directions and even rotate the mobile device to navigate the world. Areas where the player must run back and forth between rooms even read the same forwards as backwards. The *Device 6* castle is a memory palace literally made of ideas.

FIGURE 9.3   A portion of the map of *Zork I*. The game used text descriptions and commands based on the player moving in cardinal directions to create a richly detailed world.

While computer roleplaying games (RPGs), adventure games, and text adventures utilize simple displays, they provide engaging narratives that allow player imaginations to fill in any gaps. While this book has been largely about level design based on a game's mechanics, it is important to note that narrative and storytelling are powerful spatial creation engines. When creating game levels that embody both a game's mechanics and story, it is important to find a balance between the gameplay-focused (*ludic*) portions of a game and its narrative elements. In the following sections we explore how this can be accomplished through mechanics, gamespace qualities, and asset placement.

MECHANICS VS. MOTIF

Many game designers begin their work from core mechanics, the basic actions a player takes in a game. In digital games, a lot of games designed this way end up as *action games*, games in which a player performs some action to overcome antagonistic entities or hazards.[22] However, the history of games is full of many examples of design being constructed in the opposite direction, where mechanics are written to support an existing story. A shorthand term I use for mechanic-based design and narrative-based design is *mechanics versus motif.*[23]

Narrative as a Generator of Design

One oft-cited example of beginning game design from a narrative is the creation of the original *Final Fantasy*, the first entry in what is today a lucrative game franchise.[24] Hironobu Sakaguchi created *Final Fantasy* when he was tasked with creating a game to save the nearly bankrupt development studio Square in 1986. Given the freedom to create whatever he wanted, Sakaguchi admitted, "I don't think I have what it takes to make a good action game. I think I'm better at telling a story."[25] From the story, Sakaguchi embedded a ruleset that supported the narrative structure of the game and allowed traditional elements of epic literature such as quests. The character of *Final Fantasy*'s gamespaces, shown through environment art, supports the game's narrative.

In architecture, there is a dissonance between the aesthetics of many buildings and their storytelling abilities. In Chapter 3, "Level Design Workflows," we discussed the *parti*, the formal generator of many building designs. Starting from parti is a product of the Postmodernist focus on form rather than the narrative experience of the building. Meanwhile, our studies of historic buildings up through examples in Modernist architecture show a belief in the power of space to create an expressive experience, such as in the approach to the Acropolis, the simulated heavenly kingdoms of Gothic churches, or the concept of man rising above nature embodied in Le Corbusier's Villa Savoye.

Frank Lloyd Wright's famous Fallingwater parallels *Final Fantasy*'s development by exemplifying design generated through narrative. Fallingwater was built for Edgar Kaufmann, the owner of a chain of department stores near Pittsburgh. Kaufmann's family often vacationed on the land near Bear Run, a stream in Fayette County, Pennsylvania, and hired Wright to build them a new weekend house there. Kaufmann had told Wright about his love of the falls at Bear Run and how he used a boulder at the top of the falls as a favorite sunning spot. Wright decided he would build the house on top of the falls and use the sunning boulder as the base of the house's hearth. The Kaufmanns' desire to entertain large groups at the house required lots of floor space, so Wright designed Fallingwater with generous cantilevers. Wright began his design as an expression of Kaufmann's vacation stories and allowed the form of the building to rise, quite literally, from the narrative.

In truth, designs beginning from either mechanics or narrative in games, and designs from form or expression in architecture, are all equally valid. However, both become more powerful when supporting one another, such as Sakaguchi designing game mechanics to support *Final Fantasy*'s story, and Wright designing a summer house around his client's vacation stories. In this way, designers should strive to find a balance between the game's mechanics and their *motif*—visual themes or narrative patterns. To do this, like Wright, level designers can use their designs to embody both existing narratives and the functional narrative of how a space is used.

Mechanics vs. Story Narrative

The first type of gameplay narrative that designers must balance is *embedded narrative*, the predetermined story that plays out in a game.[26] This kind of narrative can be used as a design generator for games. As we have seen, designs are often generated from embedded narratives: the experience of losing someone you love, a favorite vacation spot, or the story of four warriors trying to save the world.

Narrative takes many forms in games. Some games convey narrative through cutscenes or text that is separate from gameplay. Some convey narrative through the art in the game itself or on the packaging. Salen and Zimmerman describe these methods as *narrative descriptors*, elements that give meaning to game mechanics by placing them contextually in a story.[27] Many games separate their mechanics and narratives in such a way that they can exist without one another: the story is ultimately a backdrop for game mechanics. An exercise I have used when teaching game design in schools is to have students reverse the narrative elements of games. By transforming gritty action games into fairy tales or twisting kid-friendly games into M-rated horror nightmares, new designers see how story and gameplay are kept at arm's length from one another in even the best-made games.

More powerful are the games whose mechanics are an essential part of their narrative experience. The indie game *Thomas Was Alone*,[28] for example, was created to emphasize the concept of friendship. Mike Bithell, the game's creator, utilized level design and characters with different movement capabilities to enforce this theme, requiring players to utilize each character's abilities in tandem to finish levels (Figure 9.4). The concept for *Assassin's Creed*,[29] created by director Patrice Desilets, was based on the life of eleventh-century missionary and assassin Hassan-i-Sabbah.[30] From this narrative concept, the game was eventually given mechanics and level design that embodied elements of an assassin's work: moving stealthily through crowds, scouting locations, and fleeing acrobatically.

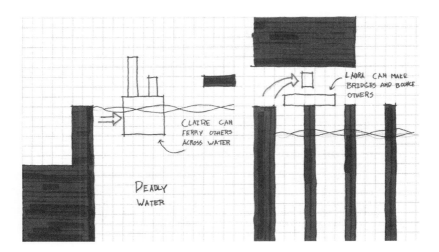

FIGURE 9.4 *Thomas Was Alone* features incredibly simplistic artwork, but the narrative of friendship is enforced primarily in the game's mechanics with additional characterization through voiceovers.

When working from either mechanics or motif as the foundation of your game and level designs, it is important to create a dialog between the two. For those designers who have the time and resources for such development, it is worth asking what the important narrative elements of your game are, what actions will support the narrative, and whether those actions can be translated into gameplay mechanics. For example, if one were to write the character of a hacker in a Japanese-style roleplaying game (JRPG), one would want to understand what types of actions a hacker would take, rather than making the hacker actually play like a JRPG stock character, such as a mage, warrior, or thief. Assuming that the hacker's specialty is opening computerized doors and making robot enemies turn on one another, the designer must design levels around this ability: can the hacker move with stealth through the level, having robots fight for him or her? Can the hacker open passages for rewards that other player characters cannot? And, if this game takes place in the future rather than the medieval fantasy worlds of many RPGs, how does that affect the world and how players interact with it? If the overworld is outer space, can traditional random monster-versus-character battles work, or should designers invent an alternative? This balancing of mechanics and narrative elements is vital to making these elements work harmoniously.

Mechanics vs. Gameplay Narrative

The element of interactivity lends itself to another type of narrative in games: *emergent narrative*.[26] As players engage the rules of a game system, they create their own series of events that drives the game action forward. The set of actions taken by one player is usually different from the actions of his or her friends or other players around the world. Throughout this book, we have discussed games as second-order design problems—products where the direct behaviors of users are out of the control of, though guided by, the work of the designer. While this presents a difficulty for designers intending to create specific experiences in their gamespaces, it is not impossible. Designers may guide players toward intended emotional responses, even if the exact experience of these responses is different for every player. A helpful method for laying the foundations of an intended user experience is to establish a *gameplay narrative* for your levels.

Gameplay narratives address the emergent aspects of game narratives by envisioning the experience of a player interacting with a game level. The embedded narrative of a level from the futuristic space JRPG imagined in the previous section would look like this:

This level is set on the planet of Majon, which features an enemy military base and surrounding slum towns. The level progresses from a town square where the characters' ship lands, then to the planet's complicated waterworks system. The player characters sneak through this into the base's main tower. Eventually players reach a large lab halfway up the tower where one of the experiments crashes out of its containment unit, initiating a mini-boss fight. A cutscene after this fight reveals that the game's main villain is in the base, and the player must fight to the top of the tower. Players fight the main villain at the end of the level with little success, and the level's story ends when the main characters narrowly escape death in their ship and pass out.

This type of level summary gives several important pieces of information: general information on the setting and locations, an idea of pacing through the progression of verbs (from *sneak* to *fight* describing movement through the level), and plot components of the level itself. A gameplay narrative, however, would allude to these narrative elements but also include information on the theoretical experience of a player interacting with the game:

The level opens with a text display that says "Planet Majon." Players choose two party members to travel with for the level. Play begins in the marketplace of a dilapidated and seedy slum town, where players can move north toward their goal on the map, west and east to explorable areas of the marketplace featuring item shops, and south to return to their ship. Moving north takes players near large lakes of water with pipes emerging upward and terminating into the side of a large tower with severe vertical lines. Entering the water and the pipes takes players through a dimly lit maze where they must open and shut valves to reach the inside of the tower. Inside, they can stealthily kill guards until they reach a lab where a mini-boss fight occurs. After this, enemy encounters increase in frequency and are impossible to sneak past, forcing direct combat. Reaching the top of the tower, players find a large windowed room with rewarding vistas where they will see the narrative end of the level.

This summary, rather than focusing entirely on narrative events, addresses some of what the player does from a gameplay perspective.

It also lays out the mechanics of each part of this theoretical level and opportunities for exploration and secrets. Phrases like "dilapidated and seedy slum town" and "dimly lit maze" give hints to the spatial qualities of these areas, describing how a level designer might utilize lighting, textures, soundscapes, or other environmental assets. Such a narrative can even be expanded upon to include information about emotions players should feel as they play certain parts of the level, or experiences they have outside of mechanics ("the player should feel dread as he or she moves through the dark and narrow hallway," "jumping from the cliff to the brightly colored platforms below should be a joyful experience," etc.)

These two types of narratives create distinct, but equally useful, planning tools for level designers. Stories can provide opportunities to flesh out ideas described in the game's plot. They can also help designers put themselves into the mind of potential players by describing the choices different types of players might make. In the next section, we further address spatial types useful for delivering these types of narratives in gamespaces.

NARRATIVE SPACES

Thus far, we have dealt with gamespace as an instrument for supporting game narratives or as the result of the game narrative as a design generator. However, level designs may be used to tell game narratives themselves. In Chapter 7, "Rewards in Gamespaces," we discussed narrative stages, reward spaces where important narrative events play out. These are only one type of narrative space utilized in games. Designers should be familiar with the following four types of narrative space and how they embody and support different types of game narratives:

Evocative spaces

Staging spaces

Embedded spaces

Resource-providing spaces

Through these types of spaces, level designers can create exceptionally expressive game worlds.

Evocative Spaces

The first type of narrative space was defined by American media scholar Henry Jenkins in his essay "Game Design as Narrative Architecture."[26] Jenkins describes amusement park attractions that use familiar shows, films, or genre traditions as their topic, such as Disney's *Haunted Mansion, Back to the Future,*[31] and others as evoking audience memories of familiar media. He also describes *American McGee's Alice*[32] as evoking familiar imagery from Lewis Carroll's Wonderland stories while providing its own nightmarish take on them. Evocative spaces utilize familiar elements to set a mood, establish the fiction of a game story, or communicate positive or negative events. In the case of Wonderland—a normally cheerful, albeit absurd, place—*Alice*'s version utilizes twisted recreations of familiar locales, establishing the narrative of a Wonderland ruled by the Queen of Hearts. Similarly, concepts discussed earlier in the book—symbolic assets, intimate spaces, etc.—can be used to describe a game's narrative state through evocative means. In *Bioshock Infinite,*[33] the character Elizabeth can create alternative versions of the world the game takes place in. In one scene, players jump from the main game world, where the xenophobic government is in control, to an alternative one where rebels have taken control of the city. To establish this switch while allowing gameplay to continue, propaganda posters switch from government-focused to rebel-focused, while the city architecture remains the same (Figure 9.5). The effect is one of quick transition from a hopeless gunfight to a *Les*

FIGURE 9.5 *Bioshock Infinite* shows sudden switches in action through texture swaps in familiar locales.

Misérables-esque revolution—the meaning and tone of the environment changes from negative to positive with the swapping of a few textures.

Evocative spaces work because of our understanding of the *vernacular*, the architectural language of certain locales, established through symbol-building. The U.S. Holocaust Memorial Museum in Washington, D.C. uses the vernacular of European train stations and ghettos to evoke the stories of Holocaust victims (Figure 9.6). Postmodernists such as Michael Graves and Robert Venturi are known for making architectural references to previous works and media in their own work. Michael Graves's Michael D. Eisner Building at the Walt Disney Studios in Burbank, California, for example, evokes both the history of the company and classical architecture through ornamentation. On the façade, Graves used *atlas* or *telamon* figures, male counterparts to *caryatids*—structural columns in the shape of women—of the seven dwarves supporting a large pediment (Figure 9.7).

Vernacular is useful for contrasting evocative art assets with one another in a scene, showing decay, corruption, or the passage of time. *The Last of Us*[34] utilizes the vernacular of urban environments and overgrown forests against one another to create a world twenty years into a zombie apocalypse. Safe zones are mainly urban with militaristic outposts littered throughout, while areas outside the safe zones contrast urban architecture with overgrowth to give a long-abandoned feel.

FIGURE 9.6   The U.S. Holocaust Memorial Museum in Washington, D.C., built in 1995 and designed by James Ingo Freed. The architecture was designed to mimic post-WWII German architecture.

FIGURE 9.7 The Michael D. Eisner Building (formerly the Team Disney Building) at Walt Disney Studios in Burbank, California, completed in 1990.

Evocative vernacular is vital for establishing story, tone, and giving the player some idea of what has happened in a place. A small town with tanks and cars littered through the streets in a zombie game may show that there was at one point a chaotic clash. Vines growing on ruins show that a structure has been long abandoned. When a story becomes more specific, however, subtle environmental storytelling may not be enough. This is why we use the next type of narrative space, staging spaces.

Staging Spaces

In Chapter 7, we described narrative stages as both enticing and rewarding spaces where a player feels that important game events will happen. Staging spaces are often unique and of large scale. They are easy to see as a player approaches them and often call attention to themselves through monumental architecture or unique features. They may house either gameplay events such as climactic battles or narrative events such as cutscenes, or scripted events where characters move around the player as he or she plays. There may also be staged background events, such as in the intro to *The Last of Us*, where players run through a linear city streetscape while scripted zombie apocalypse events happen around them.

In many ways, staging spaces that are important to actual gameplay can be atmospherically ambiguous. They may be where a player gains an important item, such as the pedestal of the Master Sword in *Zelda*[35] games. They may also be staging spaces for large battles. *Metal Gear Solid 3: Snake Eater*[36] has a unique staging area for two potentially different battle events in the game. In the Sokrovenno region, players either engage in a sniper's duel with The End, a boss character, or are ambushed by the Ocelot Unit, an elite military group. For these two distinct battle styles, the level needed to have both large-scale outlook points from which players and The End could use sniper rifles and smaller hiding spaces for taking cover during the more active Ocelot Unit fight (Figure 9.8).

Staging spaces do not have to encompass in-game action, but can be exactly what their name implies: stages. In this way, staging spaces can be set up like the set of a film or play, to support the action that characters are taking within a game. *Half-Life 2*[37] utilizes staging space to tell stories and break up intense action throughout the game. Dr. Kleiner's laboratory near the beginning of the game is a staging space where non-player characters roam and interact with the player and one another, giving expositionary dialog. The scene is set accordingly to evoke a sense of busyness through scattered objects and machine parts. It has places for the events of its specific scene to occur. Such staging spaces are often goals for the player to reach, and can therefore be used as rewards or as a way to control game-pacing. In the case of Kleiner's lab, the player is then directed to escape the city and reach another staging space, Black Mesa East.

While Kleiner's lab has elements of a staging space, there are also game objects that allude to experiments prior to the player reaching it or even to the original *Half-Life*. These types of environmental references bring us to the next type of narrative space.

Embedded Spaces

While there are embedded narratives in games—pre-scripted stories and scenes that form a game's primary narrative arc—there can also be *embedded narrative spaces*, spaces that contain narrative information in the architecture itself. Embedding narrative in architecture is

FIGURE 9.8   This section of the Sokrovenno region in *Metal Gear Solid 3: Snake Eater* shows how the space is designed to stage battles of two different scales: a widely scaled sniper duel and a tightly scaled "run and gun" action.

an old tradition. Before the invention of the printing press in the 1450s by Johannes Gutenberg, books were expensive and typically owned by nobles. As a result, much of the population of Western countries was illiterate. Religious officials needed to find a way to expose commoners as well as nobility to the stories in the Bible, so they stipulated that churches be built with biblical stories embedded in the architecture through sculpture, mosaics, and stained glass windows. Similarly, classical Greek temples often contained relief sculpture in the tympanum of their façades (Figure 9.9). Islamic architecture utilizes calligraphy in many important structures, such as the Taj Mahal and the Dome of the Rock in Jerusalem. The Dome of the Rock is an embedded narrative space, as it surrounds Mount Moriah, where Abraham is believed to have offered his son Isaac as a sacrifice, where the temple of Solomon is believed to have been built, and where Muhammad is believed to have taken his night journey to heaven.[2]

Embedded narrative spaces can be created with environment art by leaving evidence of use by characters or events that previously transpired in the space. *Portal*[38] and *Left 4 Dead*[39] use embedded narratives in their side chambers and safe houses, respectively. In *Portal*, a character known as the Rat Man hides outside of the testing chambers and leaves used food containers and erratic graffiti for the player to find. These subtle narrative hints develop an entirely unseen character, and foreshadow many of the events in the main narrative. *Left 4 Dead* players can see the writings of previous survivors who passed through safe houses, leaving information about the zombie plague, establishing the scope of the outbreak, and developing other unseen characters.

The game designers determine these types of narrative spaces and what information they contain. However, we have already established that there is not only embedded narrative, but also emergent narratives. The next

FIGURE 9.9 Embedding narrative within religious structures has been an architectural tradition for millennia. In many cases, this was a response to the illiteracy of the general populace who worshipped in these buildings—allowing religious narratives to be understood by as many people as possible.

type of narrative space will help players take advantage of the potential to make their own stories in games.

Resource-Providing Spaces

Previous examples of narrative space have shown how spaces are created to embody narrative context through environment art, spatial quality, or as capsules for character dialog. These examples can, however, be passive if not used in the context of interactive narrative. As discussed throughout this book, both architecture and gamespace have the advantage of inter-activity—user interaction gives them meaning. Long after the original creators are gone, buildings may often be repurposed for new uses. For example, Hagia Sophia, a Byzantine church in Istanbul built between 532 and 537 CE and regarded as one of the most beautiful structures in the world, has been adapted for many uses over the centuries (Figure 9.10). Hagia Sophia was originally constructed as a Byzantine Christian church

FIGURE 9.10 An interior perspective of Hagia Sophia (built 532–537), designed by Anthemius of Tralles and Isidorus of Miletus. The building's impressive architecture and important cultural status has led it to be a prized possession for conquering forces in Istanbul.

but was converted to a mosque when the Ottoman Turks conquered Constantinople in 1453 CE, changing the iconography inside to fit Islamic traditions. Since 1935, it has been a museum displaying artifacts and art from the building's history. This building, as an important cultural and historic landmark, has been adapted over time to fit the purposes of whoever resided in the city and has even been featured in films such as the James Bond movie *From Russia with Love*. Other adaptive reuses of buildings can be seen in urban redevelopment projects and gentrification efforts, taking something originally for one purpose and using it for another.

The key element of these examples in providing resources for emergent narrative is that they have some identifiable quality and that they have inherently interactive features. Hagia Sophia is a status symbol. Buildings that are renovated for new uses usually have some marketable quality, such as being on a waterfront or near amenities. In games, landmarks and interactive elements give users incentives to utilize level spaces for more than just travel. In many RPGs and massively multiplayer online RPGs (MMORPGs), towns are important spaces for structured user interaction. Towns such as Goldshire in *World of Warcraft*[40] become hubs for player activity (some positive and some negative) through a central location and having many opportunities for quests and interactions. Games like *Ultima Online* foster player activity by setting up a morality system through which entry to certain towns is forbidden if one acts hostilely to other players. This creates a sense that the game has territories that are unsafe for travel.

Emergent narrative space is not unique to MMORPGs or other games where large groups of players can interact with one another. Environments that provide many opportunities for interactivity, such as physics objects or other interactive environment pieces, can create some very influential emergent narratives. In the playtesting process for *Half-Life 2*, testers discovered that it was possible to kill barnacle enemies by allowing them to pick up exploding barrels with their tongues and shoot them upon reaching the creatures' mouths. Valve designers were so delighted by this discovery that they added it to several levels, providing the player with exploding barrels, a downward ramp, and a group of barnacles at the bottom, and called it barnacle bowling.[41] Multiplayer party fighting games such as *Towerfall*[42] include many interactive objects in tightly confined arenas (Figure 9.11). The use of these objects gives players various ways of dispatching one another beyond core mechanics, allowing for rich

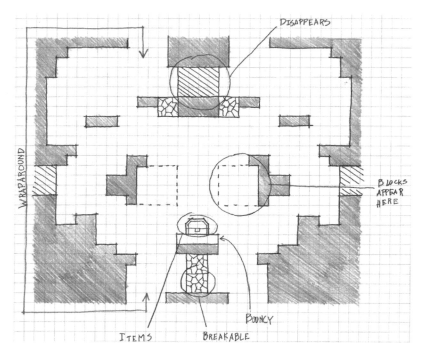

FIGURE 9.11 The arenas in party-fighting games such as *Towerfall* include many interactive objects within a confined space that provide rich opportunities for emergent narratives.

meta-game narratives that are fondly remembered long after players have put the game away ("Dude, remember that time I was about to shoot you but you dropped a crystal ball on my head?") Some live on for years, such as Lord British's accidental assassination during the beta-testing of *Ultima Online*[43] or the ill-advised charge of Leeroy Jenkins, a player who famously stormed individually into a boss room designed to be raided by teams in the MMO *World of Warcraft*.[44]

So far we have mainly focused on the theory and planning stages of spatial narratives, with a few mentions of practical construction elements such as modular assets and spatial quality. In the next section, we discuss practical methods for creating narrative space with modular assets.

ENVIRONMENT ART STORYTELLING

Imagine playing a game where you are walking slowly down a dark hallway, debris crunching under your character's feet. You walk into what appears to have once been a small lounge. On a table, there is an abandoned gun and a half-filled clip; bullets are scattered around and some have dropped onto the floor. Next to the gun is a tipped-over bottle of whiskey. Under an overturned chair next to the table is a smeared path of blood that leads into another doorway lit up by a spotlight (Figure 9.12). As a player, what do you think happened there? What do you want to do next? How does this scene make you feel?

Storytelling with Modular Assets

This scene may or may not have anything to do with the main plot of the game. Players who open the doorway the blood leads to may or may not find anything inside. What this scene does, however, is create a mini-narrative with environment art. It's not difficult to imagine that the player may be able to collect the gun and ammunition on the table to bolster his or her own reserves or that these assets are the same ammo assets used throughout the game. However, the placing and arrangement of such assets tell a story: some person was hastily loading a clip when he or she was attacked and dragged off violently. The whiskey bottle provides slight character development and calls into question the skill of the person: was he or she dragged off due to being drunk, or was the thing so terrifying

FIGURE 9.12 This type of scene is incredibly evocative from a narrative standpoint, and can be constructed by arranging prefabricated environment art assets in specific ways. Even if the player has seen similar assets elsewhere in the game, the arrangement is what makes the scene evocative.

that the person turned to the bottle to calm down? The story told by these objects contains no words, but helps establish tone, create tension, and provide foreshadowing of things that the player may encounter later in the game.

As this demonstrates, modular art can be an effective tool for telling environmental narratives as well as communicating between designer and player. As we have seen with our explorations of narrative space, assets embedded in a gamespace can develop unseen characters or provide narrative clues to game action. In games, art assets have the power to be evocative. In my studio's game *Dead Man's Trail*,[45] for example, we have mixed and matched the placement of environmental assets, pickup items, and zombie spawners to create mini-narratives within levels. As players loot for supplies, they come across areas designed to look like unlucky characters had passed through them. One such example is in a level with hiking trails: designers scattered hunting rifle ammo around a tent and an abandoned vehicle. Zombie spawners were placed such that zombies would appear to come out of the woods—hinting at the fate of the group whose tent the player was looting (Figure 9.13).

FIGURE 9.13 These screenshots from *Dead Man's Trail* show how environment art can be used to hint at what has happened in a scene: vehicles and barriers are arranged to look like a terrified bus driver has tried to run through a blockade. Tents, hunting rifles, and zombie spawners are juxtaposed to hint at the story of an unlucky group.

Environment Art and Cinematography

The juxtaposition of contrasting elements—guns and shelters, vehicles and barriers, etc.—has a great impact on the type of scene you are creating. The way in which the player views these objects is of utmost importance. Camera is an important consideration for storytelling in games, as level designers can utilize a game's *cinematography* to highlight spatial narrative. Cinematography is the study of film techniques, though it is often used to discuss the composition of scenes on film. For game designers, the relationship between camera and object position can be a powerful tool.

When discussing camera usage in games, we discovered that an important element was drawing a player's attention to environmental elements the designer wished him or her to see. In first-person games, this often includes drawing the player's view to objects with visual components such as lines, contrasting colors, or lighting. In 2D or top-down games, cinematography can be used to show something to the player that the player's character may not be aware of—oncoming monsters or objects important to a level's plot.

An innovator in modern cinematographic storytelling techniques was Orson Welles in his 1941 classic film *Citizen Kane*.[46] Welles used a technique in *Citizen Kane* known as *deep focus*, where objects in both the foreground and background are in focus as the result of layering pieces of film on top of each other.[47] Two important scenes in *Citizen Kane* use deep focus or deep focus-like effects to convey narrative that would otherwise be told simply with dialog. The first is a scene where Kane's mother and father are arguing over whether to put Kane in the care of a wealthy banker or let him grow up in an impoverished Colorado town. As the adults—the father, who does not want to lose Kane, on one side of the room and the mother with the banker on the other—discuss the fate of the boy, he can be seen playing in the snow out of a window positioned between the adults (Figure 9.14). A later scene, composed by shooting a scene twice with the same piece of film to capture both foreground and background in focus, has Kane and an associate finding Kane's wife passed out from what they discuss as illness, but a medicine bottle and spoon in the foreground reveal to be a suicide attempt (Figure 9.15). Scenarios like this show how assets may be positioned in such a way that they tell an environmental narrative outside of the immediate action of a scene.

While not all games utilize environmental storytelling at the level of subtlety of *Citizen Kane*, some utilize foreground, background, or even in-game action elements to alert the players to various narrative

FIGURE 9.14 An early scene in *Citizen Kane* positions two arguing factions on either side of a shot, while the object of the argument, a young Charles Foster Kane, is seen through a window in between the two.

FIGURE 9.15 This later scene of the film has the characters finding Kane's wife unconscious, while the scenery informs the audience that she had attempted suicide by careful placement of a medicine bottle.

elements. In *Another World*,[48] the game's side-scrolling gameplay view is treated as one camera angle of several in a cinematic experience. Early in the game, a large monster can be seen stalking the player through the background of several screens. The "to the side" camera is used to show the player's alien ally (nicknamed Buddy) evading captors in other corridors while the two characters are separated later in the game (Figure 9.16). The second act of *Sonic the Hedgehog 3 & Knuckles's*[49] Launch Base Zone depicts the launch of Dr. Robotnik's super weapon, the Death Egg, by including the weapon in the level's background and having it launch at the level's end. In a way, the game also offers this launch as a rewarding vista for the players making it through the level and allows them to watch the climactic launch during a moment of gameplay downtime before a boss fight. Even for games without fixed cameras, such as first- or third-person 3D games, the player's arrival at an embedded environmental object narrative and how it is highlighted through other environmental elements—shadows, lighting, environmental contrast—is vital.

In this section, we have looked at how individual pieces of environment art may be arranged to create environmental narrative. We also looked at the influence of camera position in telling such stories: carefully placing objects in or out of frame so they give players narrative information in addition to the gameplay action on a screen. Next, we use a story structure common in games to describe an approach to using environment art for storytelling.

MATERIALITY AND THE HERO'S JOURNEY

In his book *The Hero with a Thousand Faces*,[50] Joseph Campbell describes the idea of the monomyth, a basic pattern that many heroic narratives throughout the world follow. Campbell summarizes the fundamental

FIGURE 9.16 *Another World* uses the side-scrolling camera angle as a way to convey what is happening to a friendly character that the player is separated from.

elements of heroic narratives from different cultures in this way: "A hero ventures forth from the world of common day into a region of supernatural wonder: fabulous forces are there encountered and a decisive victory is won: the hero comes back from this mysterious adventure with the power to bestow boons on his fellow man."[51]

This structure has the hero follow some variation of a *call to adventure* (which is often initially *refused*), followed by a *road of trials* and enemies to overcome. The hero then meets with a *supernatural benevolent force* (often referred to as the goddess), either realizing that it is a protection he or she has always had or finding it to be a new protection and being blessed by it. The hero must face a *powerful malevolent force*, overcoming both its power and the hero's own demons. The hero must finally *gain and escape with a boon* of some sort (important quest item) and return to his or her normal world, *where his or her newfound power enables a life of peace* (Figure 9.17).

The hero's journey is nothing new in literature or game design—in many ways it is almost a cliché. For our purposes, we can still get some use out of it as a metaphor for using environment art assets to support our games' narratives. In *Origins of Architectural Pleasure*, Grant Hildebrand argues that

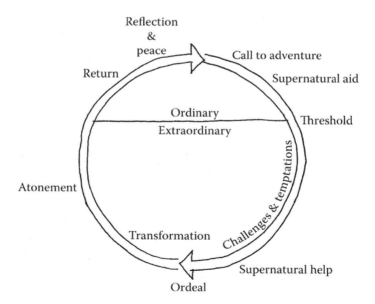

FIGURE 9.17 The hero's journey is a pattern common to narratives of many cultures throughout human history. It is a popular narrative structure for modern video games.

architecture can embody the stages of the hero's journey with both spatial quality and materiality.[52] Hildebrand suggests that in many heroic narratives, landscape makes its challenge to the hero visibly noticeable by being "deficient, one way or another, in support or reassurance."[53] As evidence, he suggests the ruins of Mycenaean forts or the American West as examples of such landscapes, and posits that their visual characteristics help create the heroic narrative itself. Hildebrand argues that buildings such as the Phillips Exeter Library and Salk Institute, both designed by Louis Kahn, embody the hero's journey through a contrast between intimately scaled "safe" study spaces and "dangerous" public transitory spaces. The study spaces in each building are finished in comfortable wood, carpet, and brick finishes, while the public spaces are finished in cold concrete[54] (Figure 9.18). Studies of heroic fiction reveal Hildebrand's assertions to be valid: Odysseus's travels take him from the safety of his home in the green lands of Ithaca to war in Troy, around the Aegean, Mediterranean, and Ionian Seas—deserts of water instead of sand—and finally back home.[55] Similarly, Frodo Baggins must travel from the comfortable farmland of the Shire and through the increasingly bleak lands of Middle Earth to the volcanic Mount Doom, where he can destroy the evil Sauron's One Ring in *The Lord of the Rings*. Materiality can even be an indicator that story expectations are about to be subverted: the final battle in *Star Wars: The Last Jedi*[56] is set up to reflect the snowy Battle of Hoth from *The Empire Strikes Back*,[57] but a minor character mentions that the planet is covered with white salt, not snow. Despite appearing similar to the scene from *Empire* where the heroes lose in a conventional battle, a series of inventive fake-outs allow the heroes of *Last Jedi* to emerge victorious.

Games often utilize materiality, specifically in the tile art or texturing of a game's level surfaces, as an indicator of a place's character and place along a hero's journey. The original *Super Mario Bros.* utilizes a micro-hero's journey in each world of the game: Mario begins each world in a comparatively friendly level with cheerful music, trees, bushes, clouds, and few gaps. He then often (not always) descends into an underground world of some sort filled with new dangers: narrower spaces, aggressive enemies, and shadowy coloration. Upon leaving this, he is in a stage that is above ground but has more perils: wider gaps, moving ledges, or narrow bridges that test his skills gained in the previous two levels. Finally, he must go to Bowser's castle where he encounters cold stone, boiling lava, and a climactic battle with Bowser himself. Upon reaching the captive at the end of the world, he is informed, "The Princess is in another castle,"

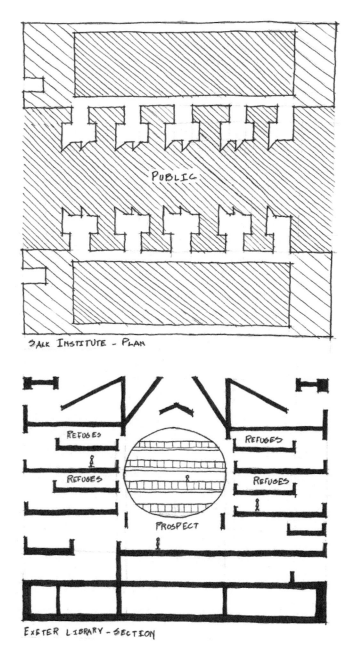

SALK INSTITUTE - PLAN

EXETER LIBRARY - SECTION

FIGURE 9.18 Louis Kahn's Phillips Exeter Library and Salk Institute both use natural materials such as wood and stone in intimately scaled refuge spaces and harsher materials such as concrete in public spaces.

and begins anew (Figure 9.19). Environments in the original *The Legend of Zelda*[58] follow a similar pattern: players begin in a forested area of Hyrule with abundant shops, wander through bleak and dangerous wilderness, and then descend into dimly lit dungeons.

When following a similar pattern in your own games, you can utilize different tile sets and color (diffuse or albedo, depending on the engine you use) maps to create the desired environmental effect. Safe or homely places should feature natural or rich materials: grass, wood, brick, stone, and other Wrightian materials. As the hero moves forward in his or her quest, use increasingly harsh or battle-damaged materials: bigger or more roughly hewn stones, machines, alien technologies, iron, lava, acid, etc. (Figure 9.20). It is also fashionable to use "grunge" textures in modern games—textures that show wear, tear, or damage through dirtiness. Grunge is useful for showing corroded or corrupted areas that were once safe, in contrast to safe areas being clean, tidy, and inviting.

In many ways, movement through a game's narrative is its own reward. While a great story does not make a bad game good, it can make playing

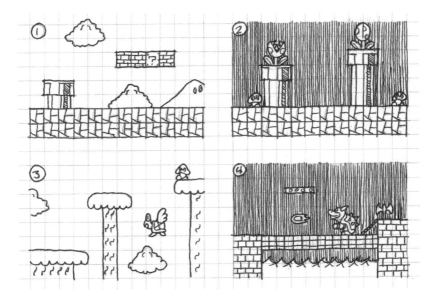

FIGURE 9.19   Each world of the original *Super Mario Bros.* embodies a miniature hero's journey: (1) Mario begins in a relatively friendly landscape, (2) descends into a darker vault separated from previous comforts, (3) returns to the surface to be tested by the environment, and (4) has a climactic battle where he rescues a captive.

FIGURE 9.20 Tile sets and textures can do a lot to convey a sense of place in game environments. As players move through a hero's journey, their environment should go from friendly and inviting to harsh or corrupted.

a bad game tolerable. In the final section of this chapter, we look at how expanded narrative can be used for in-game rewards and how narrative rewards can help us pace our game levels.

PACING AND NARRATIVE REWARDS

While we have discussed narrative spaces throughout this chapter and earlier in the book, there has been only brief mention of narrative as a reward. We have discussed narrative stages as rewards in games: places where story events happen and the player can see from a distance. While we have explored the experience of such narrative spaces in terms of exploration, we have not yet viewed them from the standpoint of game-pacing.

The Dramatic Arc as a Pacing Tool

In 1863, German novelist and playwright Gustav Freytag wrote *Die Technik des Dramas*, which studied dramatic stories in five acts: *exposition, rising action, climax, falling action,* and *dénouement*.[59] This structure formed what is known today as the *dramatic arc*, often visualized as a graphic called Freytag's pyramid (Figure 9.21).

The dramatic arc is a useful tool for tracking throughout fiction. Stories can contain one dramatic arc over the course of the entire narrative, or several. In the example of *The Lord of the Rings*, which was split into three smaller books, *The Fellowship of the Ring*, *The Two Towers*, and *The Return of the King*, each book has its own dramatic arc. Similarly, each chapter of each book often has a situation that follows its own arc. When Frodo and his party are attacked by Ringwraiths at Weathertop, for example, exposition sets up why the characters are there, the action rises as the Ringwraiths approach, the stabbing of Frodo is the climax, and Aragorn's driving off of the wraiths and the aftermath of the event are the falling action and dénouement.

Games also use the dramatic arc to tell stories. *Donkey Kong*[60] uses the dramatic arc across its four story levels thus: exposition is the opening scene where Pauline is shown being kidnapped by Donkey Kong. The rising action is where Mario (then known as Jumpman) pursues Donkey Kong up increasingly complex levels of the skyscraper. The climax comes in the fourth level, where Mario must remove rivets holding Donkey Kong's platform up, and the falling action and dénouement occur as Donkey Kong himself falls and Mario is reunited with Pauline.[61]

In many gamespaces, action is organized into geographic designations: worlds, territories, etc., that have a common thematic factor. *Super Mario Bros.* games often have eight worlds with a series of sub-levels in each and a castle level at the end. *Batman: Arkham City*,[62] which has a large open world, has territories belonging to members of Batman's "rogues gallery," and thus makes each territory represent that character's gimmick:

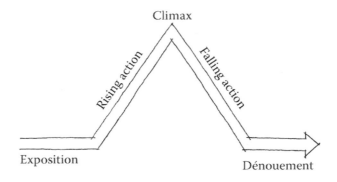

FIGURE 9.21 Freytag's pyramid shows the stages of the dramatic arc.

ice, plants, circuses, etc. In both cases, each territory follows a dramatic arc: Mario must travel through increasingly difficult levels to destroy the Koopa stronghold in each world, and Batman often has a mission to accomplish in each villain's hideout, which includes twisted puzzles and ends in a climactic confrontation.

Rewarding Exploration with Embedded Narrative

The level-by-level dramatic arcs in these games allow players to move easily through the games. As discussed in Chapter 3, it is important to keep a contrast of high and low action to properly pace a game. By structuring game levels with dramatic arcs—arrive in the level, overcome obstacles and challenges, overcome a large challenge or enemy, reach the goal of the level, emerge victorious—players feel as though they have accomplished something.

Falling action and dénouement are both important elements of this structure for game designers, as they are opportunities for players to slow down and breathe. They are also where we can position rewards for players: a dramatic escape, an item that replenishes lost resources, or a sought-after artifact. Embedded narrative delivered at the end of dramatic arcs helps the player feel as though he or she is making progress through a game, whether this narrative is delivered environmentally, through scripted in-game events, or through cutscenes.

This type of pacing also connects narrative structure to long- and short-term goals in games, offering the quest for a short-term goal as a satisfying dramatic arc of its own before pausing and moving on to the next in a larger long-term arc structure.

Rewarding Exploration with Optional Narrative and Easter Eggs

While the dramatic arc structure can give us a feeling for how to structure game levels and reward players by progressing them through a story, there are also opportunities to reward players with optional narrative for exploring gamespace on their own. Optional narratives can be important for games, as they give players additional incentives to test the limits of the gamespace and make players feel as though they are privy to privileged information. These types of narratives can be rewards of glory in game levels, the discovery of which can enhance a player's interaction with a gamespace.

The implementation of these types of narratives often depends on the development resources of studios or how a project is managed. For example, *The Legend of Zelda: Majora's Mask*[63] features a standard *Zelda* narrative structure: overcome a number of dungeons to gain passage to the final enemy's stronghold for a climactic showdown. However, the game also allows players the optional quest of collecting masks, which often involves helping non-player characters (NPCs). Many of these side quests have their own embedded narratives, such as one where the player must reunite two estranged lovers. Each mask quest features special characters, text, assets, and animations, making them more robust than the side quests in other games.

While the example from *Majora's Mask* is possible with a larger development studio, smaller studios may not have the resources for additional content on that level in a 3D game. However, optional narrative rewards can even be created with simplistic storytelling methods. The Rat Man's hideouts in *Portal* are technically optional: they are not required for passage through the main game, and a player's understanding of the story does not suffer if he or she does not find them. However, Valve placed these stories closely enough to the main gamespace that players could find them easily. These assets are much more simplistic: special textures applied to game geometry. For many games, big or small, such assets could be created quickly by an artist, and then added in out-of-the-way places by a level designer. Alternatively, the indie masterpiece *Undertale*[64] features multiple endings, character-based side quests, and mini-games. Its visual style is simple, clean, and mimics the look of 8-bit games, allowing the developer to emphasize a rich story experience.

Half-Life 2 features an optional character that is a little more difficult to find, the All-Knowing Vortigaunt. By entering a tunnel full of radioactive waste in an early level, players can find this character, who speaks cryptically about in-game events and roasts a headcrab over a fire. Creating such a character is as simple as creating textural optional narratives. The designers used common assets—a vortigaunt alien, a headcrab, and a fire particle effect—and recorded some new lines for the alien to speak.

This is an example of an "Easter egg," hidden jokes, messages, or other rewards for looking closely at a work. Easter eggs have been used in many media, such as art, film, or software, often with the author hiding himself or herself somewhere in the work. The term *Easter egg* was coined for this type of hidden object by Atari staff after game programmer Warren Robinett included a hidden room in the 1979 game *Adventure*. This room contained the message "Created by Warren Robinett," an act of defiance against bosses who would not let Atari game designers put their names on their work.[43]

Finding such a reward in a game level, often at great risk, as with the All-Knowing Vortigaunt, or through a complex puzzle, as with the Warren Robinett message, can become an emergent narrative all its own—something for players to brag about to friends. Hiding these types of narrative components in levels can make your own gamespaces fun to interact with both in and out of the game.

SUMMARY

In this chapter we have considered level design from another perspective, that of meaning and narrative. We have seen that design is not the product of mechanical prompts alone, but also of stories. We have also seen how spaces, both digital and architectural, tell stories through architectural vernacular, set construction, and art assets, and we have seen how designed space can transform over time as different users interact with it, changing its use or interacting with it in surprising ways.

In terms of constructing levels, we have seen how environment art and prefabricated gameplay assets may be arranged to build narrative and how the positioning of a game's camera provides opportunity for delivering this narrative. We have also seen how environment art can indicate the progression of players through game narratives, such as those following Joseph Campbell's hero's journey. And finally, we have explored how story structures such as the dramatic arc can be used as pacing mechanisms, and how narrative can be used as goals and rewards within this pacing, for both required game actions and testing the boundaries of game worlds.

In Chapter 10, we continue our exploration of how players test the limits of game worlds and how communicating them to players helps build realms of possibility.

EXERCISES

1. **Writing exercise**: Write a gameplay narrative for a level that you are designing or one you play in a popular commercial game (written as though you were going to design it). Describe the things that the player will see on the screen and the choices he or she need to make. Describe how a theoretical player might react to these prompts. How should players feel in different parts of your level?

2. **Writing exercise**: Play a game that utilizes at least three of the four types of narrative spaces described by Henry Jenkins. Describe how

the game utilizes the narrative space types and what that tells you about the game's story or world.

3. **Digital exercise**: Create a scene built around a bookshelf, table, or other piece of furniture with objects on it. Use modular environment art assets to express these narrative themes: "left in a hurry," "lived in," "not what it seems," "years of knowledge."

4. **Digital exercise**: Develop a "material storyboard" for a level or game (either one you are working on or a popular commercial one). Plot out the story progression via the types of textures used in each part of the game.

5. **Writing exercise**: Play a game enough that you experience a few quests or levels. Describe the narrative arc of each. How do they express (or not express) the type of story structure described by Freytag's pyramid?

ENDNOTES

1. Koch, Ebba, and Richard André Barraud. *The Complete Taj Mahal: And the Riverfront Gardens of Agra*. London: Thames & Hudson, 2006.
2. Fazio, Michael W., Marian Moffett, and Lawrence Wodehouse. *A World History of Architecture*. 2nd ed. Boston, MA: McGraw-Hill, 2008.
3. In most Charbagh, the tomb is at the crossing of the canals, since the rivers of Paradise are said to start at a central mountain. Koch suggests that the Yamuna River, which is next to the tomb, and the gardens across from the tomb are integral parts of the Charbagh plan in addition to the garden's canals.
4. Norman, Donald A. *Emotional Design: Why We Love (or Hate) Everyday Things*. New York, NY: Basic Books, 2004, pp. 3–6.
5. Murray, H.J.R. *A History of Chess*. Oxford: Clarendon Press, 1962.
6. Wiggins, David K. The Play of Slave Children in the Plantation Communities of the Old South, 1820–1860. *Journal of Sport History* 7, no. 2 (1980): 21–39. http://library.la84.org/SportsLibrary/JSH/JSH1980/JSH0702/jsh0702c.pdf (accessed July 1, 2013).
7. Pilon, Mary. "The secret history of Monopoly: the capitalist board game's leftwing origins". *The Guardian*. April 11, 2015. https://www.theguardian.com/lifeandstyle/2015/apr/11/secret-history-monopoly-capitalist-game-leftwing-origins. Accessed June 25, 2018.
8. Wolf, Mark J.P. 2014. *Building Imaginary Worlds: The Theory and History of Subcreation*. Abingdon, United Kingdom: Routledge.
9. Tolkien, J.R.R. *The Lord of the Rings*. 2nd ed. Boston, MA: Houghton Mifflin, 1967.
10. Tolkien, J.R.R. *The Silmarillion*. Boston, MA: Houghton Mifflin, 1977.

11. Jeffrey, Henning. On Tolkien: Growing Up with Language. *Model Languages* 1, no. 8 (1996). http://www.langmaker.com/ml0108.htm.
12. Tolkien, J.R.R., Humphrey Carpenter, and Christopher Tolkien. *The Letters of J.R.R. Tolkien.* Boston, MA: Houghton Mifflin, 1981.
13. *Dungeons & Dragons.* Gary Gygax and Dave Arneson (original designers), 1974. Role-playing game.
14. *Call of Cthulhu.* Sandy Peterson (original designer), 1981. Role-playing game.
15. Kushner, David. *Masters of Doom: How Two Guys Created an Empire and Transformed Pop Culture.* New York, NY: Random House, 2003.
16. *Dungeon.* Don Daglow (designer), ca. 1975. Computer role-playing game on a PDP-10 computer.
17. *Akalabeth: World of Doom.* Richard Garriott (developer), California Pacific Computer Co. (publisher), ca. 1979. Computer role-playing game on Apple II.
18. *Zork I.* Infocom (developer and publisher), 1980. Computer text adventure.
19. *This Book Is a Dungeon.* Nathan Meunier (author), 2015. Twine game.
20. *The Uncle Who Works for Nintendo.* Ztul (author), 2014. Twine game. Accessed at ztul.itch.io/the-uncle-who-works-for-nintendo
21. *Device 6.* Simogo (developer and publisher), 2013. Mobile text adventure game.
22. The term *action game* is also often understood as a game with guns or other trappings of action movies, such as explosions, intense combat, etc. Action games, as a broad genre, is separated into the sub-genres of shooters, platformers, and many others.
23. I wanted to note that I'm specifically not using the terms "narratology" and "ludology" here, lest any reader think that I'm not aware of them. First, I wanted to avoid them since they usually refer to how games are understood and analyzed by game studies academics instead of designed by game industry developers. Secondly, at the time of this writing (2018), the debate between those schools of thought has largely been resolved and is years behind us so it doesn't warrant additional commentary here.
24. *Final Fantasy.* Square (developer and publisher), December 17, 1987. Nintendo Entertainment System game.
25. *Final Fantasy.* Retrospective: Part I. GameTrailers. http://www.gametrailers.com/full-episodes/bx14k1/gt-retrospectives-final-fantasy-retrospective--part-i (accessed July 1, 2013).
26. Jenkins, Henry. Game Design as Narrative Architecture. MIT—Massachusetts Institute of Technology. http://web.mit.edu/cms/People/henry3/games&narrative.html (accessed July 2, 2013).
27. Salen, Katie, and Eric Zimmerman. *Rules of Play: Game Design Fundamentals.* Cambridge, MA: MIT Press, 2003, pp. 399–401.
28. *Thomas Was Alone.* Mike Bithell (developer and publisher), July 24, 2012. PC game.
29. *Assassin's Creed.* Ubisoft Montreal (developer), Ubisoft (publisher), November 13, 2007. Xbox 360 game.

30. The Making Of: Assassin's Creed. *Edge Magazine*. http://www.edge-online. com/features/the-making-of-assassins-creed/ (accessed July 2, 2013).
31. *Back to the Future*. DVD. Directed by Robert Zemeckis. Universal City, CA: Universal Studios Home Entertainment, 1985.
32. *American McGee's Alice*. Rogue Entertainment (developer), Electronic Arts (publisher), October 6, 2000. PC game.
33. *Bioshock Infinite*. Irrational Games (developer), 2K Games (publisher), March 26, 2013. Xbox 360 game.
34. *The Last of Us*. Naughty Dog (developer), Sony Computer Entertainment (publisher), June 14, 2013. Playstation 3 game.
35. *The Legend of Zelda*. Nintendo EAD (developer), Nintendo (publisher), February 21, 1986. Nintendo Entertainment System game.
36. *Metal Gear Solid 3: Snake Eater*. Konami Computer Entertainment Japan (developer), Konami (publisher), November 17, 2004. Playstation 2 game.
37. *Half-Life 2*. Valve Corporation (developer and publisher), November 16, 2004. PC game.
38. *Portal*. Valve Corporation (developer and publisher), October 9, 2007. PC game.
39. *Left 4 Dead*. Turtle Rock Studios/Valve South (developer), Valve Corporation (publisher), October 2008. PC game.
40. *World of Warcraft*. Blizzard Entertainment (developer and publisher), November 23, 2004. PC game.
41. Jacobson, Brian, and David Speyrer. Valve's Design Process for Creating *Half-Life 2*. Speech, Game Developers Conference from UBM, San Jose, CA, March 2006.
42. *Towerfall*. Matt Thorson (developer and publisher), June 25, 2013. Ouya game.
43. Donovan, Tristan. *Replay: The History of Video Games*. East Sussex, England: Yellow Ant, 2010.
44. Leeroy Jenkins—YouTube. YouTube. http://www.youtube.com/ watch?v=LkCNJRfSZBU (accessed July 4, 2013).
45. *Dead Man's Trail*. Pie For Breakfast Studios and e4 Software (developers), upcoming. Indie game on Steam.
46. *Citizen Kane*. DVD. Directed by Orson Welles. Burbank, CA: Warner Home Video, 1941.
47. Ogle, Patrick L., and Bill Nichols. Technological and Aesthetic Influences upon the Development of Deep Focus Cinematography in the United States. In *Movies and Methods*. Berkeley, CA: University of California Press, 1985, p. 73.
48. *Another World*. Delphine Software (developer and publisher), 1991. Amiga game.
49. *Sonic the Hedgehog 3 and Knuckles*. Sonic Team (developer), Sega (publisher), October 18, 1994. Sega Genesis game.
50. Campbell, Joseph. *The Hero with a Thousand Faces*. Princeton, NJ: Princeton University Press, 1949.

51. Campbell, Joseph. *The Hero with a Thousand Faces.* Princeton, NJ: Princeton University Press, 1949, p. 23.
52. Hildebrand, Grant. *Origins of Architectural Pleasure.* Berkeley, CA: University of California Press, 1999, pp. 84–88.
53. Hildebrand, Grant. *Origins of Architectural Pleasure.* Berkeley, CA: University of California Press, 1999, p. 84.
54. Hildebrand, Grant. *Origins of Architectural Pleasure.* Berkeley, CA: University of California Press, 1999, p. 87.
55. Fagles, Robert. *The Odyssey.* New York, NY: Viking, 1996.
56. *Star Wars: The Last Jedi.* Blu-ray. Directed by Rian Johnson. Los Angeles, CA: Walt Disney Home Video, 2017.
57. *Star Wars: The Empire Strikes Back.* Blu-ray. Directed by Irvin Kershner. 20th Century Fox Home Video, 1980.
58. *The Legend of Zelda.* Nintendo (developer and publisher), February 21, 1986. Nintendo Entertainment System game.
59. Freytag, Gustav, and Elias J. MacEwan. Freytag's Technique of the Drama: An Exposition of Dramatic Composition and Art. Internet Archive: Digital Library of Free Books, Movies, Music and Wayback Machine. http://archive. org/details/freytagstechniqu00freyuoft (accessed July 6, 2013).
60. *Donkey Kong.* Nintendo (developer and publisher), July 9, 1981. Arcade game.
61. Fullerton, Tracy, Christopher Swain, and Steven Hoffman. *Game Design Workshop: A Playcentric Approach to Creating Innovative Games.* 2nd ed. Amsterdam: Elsevier Morgan Kaufman, 2008.
62. *Batman: Arkham City.* Rocksteady Studios (developer), Warner Bros. Interactive (publisher), October 18, 2011. Xbox 360 game.
63. *The Legend of Zelda: Majora's Mask.* Nintendo EAD (developer), Nintendo (publisher), October 26, 2000. Nintendo 64 game.
64. *Undertale.* Toby Fox (developer), September 15, 2015. Steam PC game.

INDUSTRY PERSPECTIVES: PSYCHOLOGICAL CHARACTER DEVELOPMENT IN HALO LEVELS

Kelli Dunlap, PsyD

game designer and psychologist

When you design a game world, you project your values, perspectives, and who you are as a person into the design; a veritable Rorschach test of code and art rather than ink. As such, games are cultural artifacts which reflect internalized norms of the community in which they're made. When designing your worlds, it's critical to consider what your design is saying and what aspects of society you are promoting, ignoring, or challenging. This channeling of internalized social values is especially prevalent when it comes to creating narratives and environments that address mental health. As a society,* we hold certain beliefs and stereotypes about persons who have a mental illness and these schemas are often used as emotional and thematic shortcuts in games. For example, horror games frequently use insane asylums or psychiatric settings to prime players to be afraid. Although a designer's probably not intentionally designing to perpetuate harmful stereotypes around mental illness, it is not an accident that games like *Outlast, The Evil Within, Sanitarium Massacre, Injustice: Gods Among Us, Asylum, Shutter Island, Dementium II, Hitman: Codename 47, American McGee's Alice*—just to name a few—all draw on this imagery.

But more interesting and pervasive than the exaggerated portrayals of insane asylums, straightjackets, and homicidal villains who are psychopathic or otherwise insane are the portrayals of mental illness that so directly align with social norms that they are nearly invisible to both designer and player.

HALO: A CASE STUDY

In *Halo: Combat Evolved*, the player–character and protagonist Master Chief is an artificially enhanced super soldier saving the universe from a collection of alien zealots known as the Covenant and intergalactic space zombies called The Flood. While exploring the level 343 Guilty Spark, Master Chief discovers a non-player character (NPC) named AWOL Marine. The NPC is huddled on the floor and begins to yell and shoot at Chief as soon as the player steps into view. The NPC's dialogue contains statements such as, "I'll blow your brains out! Get away from me!" and "Play dead! That's what I did… played dead. They took the live ones… Oh, God, I can still hear them!" As long as the player is within sight, AWOL Marine will continue to shoot at the player and is capable of killing Master Chief. The player has two options: ignore the marine and continue on or shoot the marine. Furthermore, should the player choose to shoot the marine, it only takes one shot to kill him.

These attributes differentiate AWOL Marine from all other marine NPCs. Marines in *Halo* are always presented as helpful, as teammates, as people in need of assistance but still capable and worthy of respect. The player always has the option to act aggressively against the NPC marines, but it comes with a price. If a player harms an NPC marine, the other Marines turn on and eventually kill the player. There are also NPCs whose deaths are major events in the game. For example, "Truth and Reconciliation," the third level of *Halo*, requires the player to protect Captain Keys, an NPC, from the villainous Covenant. If Keys dies during this time, the player has to restart from the last checkpoint. In fact, at no point in *Halo: Combat Evolved* or any of the *Halo* series campaigns is the player required or encouraged to kill a human being. This is not true of AWOL Marine. Because he shoots at Chief, AWOL Marine encourages the player to shoot back. Also of interest is that AWOL Marine does not register on the player's radar. The radar is a small circle instrument overlay on the bottom right of the screen which displays enemies as red dots and friendlies as yellow dots.

This interaction between player and AWOL Marine takes less than a few seconds but coveys several different cultural beliefs and values. Something terrible has happened to this character and he is obviously in distress. He is instantly violent toward the player who has been conditioned to shoot anything that shoots at Chief. This perpetuates the fear and stigma of persons with a mental illness as being inherently dangerous and violent. Furthermore, the player has no option to help the marine despite being allowed to interact positively with other marines (i.e. swapping weapons, trading spaces with marines in the Warthog, being able to call marines to join Chief in the Warthog). AWOL Marine can be killed with a single shot anywhere, even to a non-vital location like the foot, whereas killing the other NPC Marines require at least two shots, even to the head. In this way, AWOL Marine is literally depicted as being weaker than other marines, and unlike aggression toward the other NPC marines, there are no consequences or penalties for killing him.

Another way of evaluating player interaction with AWOL Marine is that killing him costs almost nothing. It takes a single bullet to kill him, so the player is wasting very little in terms of resources and is not required to think twice about the decision to kill AWOL Marine. If it took ten bullets to kill him, for example, players would have the opportunity to reconsider their decision and would likely decide against killing AWOL Marine if for no other reason than the resources required to do so. Furthermore, the scene is deployed in such a way that killing the marine feels almost like a mercy, which is unsettlingly reflective of the historical treatment of the mentally ill. Finally, AWOL Marine not appearing on the player's radar is oddly symbolic in that mental health issues frequently do not appear on society's radar. By not appearing on radar, AWOL Marine is neither friend nor enemy; he is nothing.

At some point in time during the development of *Halo: Combat Evolved*, the decision was made to create AWOL Marine, have him exhibit psychological distress, act aggressively, and be isolated both physically, mentally, and behaviorally from all other Marines. This demarcation of healthy versus sick, strong versus weak is common in human psychology. Being able to identify and label some people as "us" and place "us" at a higher level than "others" may reinforce a sense of self-identity and self-worth. While some game design decisions are conscious applications of cultural values, AWOL Marine exemplifies that some applied ideologies lurk beyond conscious awareness.

In *Halo 3*'s Floodgate level, there is a soldier called the Suicidal Marine. Like his *Halo: Combat Evolved* predecessor, Suicidal Marine is huddled in a corner talking to himself and does not appear on the player's radar. Although he does not shoot at Chief, he does sometimes hold a pistol to his own head while saying things like, "Oh, God! Their voices! Oh, God! No, make them stop! I did them a favor... y-yeah that's it; I helped them! Maybe... maybe I need to do myself... a fav..." Around him are the bodies of several other marines without any sign of infection by the Flood suggesting Suicidal Marine killed his team and is now contemplating killing himself. Physically he is shaking and alternates between putting the gun at his temple and lowering it. Also like the AWOL Marine, there is no option to help Suicidal Marine and he is easier to kill than other Marines. Suicidal Marine does not ever actually shoot himself and eventually will stand in a combat-ready stance on his own. However, he will not trade weapons with the Chief like all the other Marines do.

Suicide is not a psychological diagnosis, but suicidal ideation is a symptom of several severe mental disorders. Suicidal Marine's statement of "Maybe I need to do myself a favor" is indicative of self-harm considering the "favor" he did for his teammates was to kill them. Once again, the game design prohibits the player from interacting in any meaningful way with an obviously distressed individual. The action of not allowing the marine to trade weapons with the Chief could symbolize him being shut off from the rest of the world, unresponsive, or perhaps that individuals experiencing trauma or crisis simply cannot be engaged. Like AWOL Marine he does not show on the player's radar, in effect rendering him invisible, but the weapon reticule does go green when placed on him indicating he is a friendly rather than an enemy or unidentified. Rather than being completely isolated in terms of affiliation, Suicidal Marine at least is identified as a teammate. Although he is not actively violent, the proof of his actions is evident, as is the homicidal maniac trope.

By examining the *Halo* series in depth, several representations of mental illness have been identified. Several characters in the series demonstrate mild to severe psychopathological symptoms and exhibit varying degrees of mental distress. The narrative around these characters (i.e. Cortana's rampancy, the Marine's exposure to the Flood) also tells a story of how mental illness may manifest and influence the thoughts and behaviors of those coping with a mental illness as well as the thoughts and behaviors of others. Game mechanics including who can be shot, how difficult it is to shoot someone, and who appears on radar is another reflection of what kind of people are of value. The strong and healthy are worth protecting, the vulnerable or ill are to be shot, ignored, or sometimes rescued.

CHAPTER 10

Possibility Spaces and Worldbuilding

You should design each part of the garden tastefully, recalling your memories of how nature presented itself for each feature... Think over the famous pieces of scenic beauty throughout the land, and... design your garden with the mood of harmony, modeling after the general air of such places.

—FROM SAKUTEIKI, AUTHORSHIP ATTRIBUTED
TO TACHIBANA TOSHITSUNA[1]

The enjoyment of scenery employs the mind without fatigue and yet exercises it; tranquilizes it and yet enlivens it; and thus, through the influence of the mind over the body, gives the effect of refreshing rest and reinvigoration to the whole system.

—LANDSCAPE ARCHITECT FREDERICK LAW OLMSTEAD[2]

Emergent narrative is a powerful tool to help game players create their own stories. Levels with rich systems of interactive mechanics, objects, and spaces for different play styles are what offer players the chance to make these stories. In addition to previously discussed embedded narrative elements, designers develop game worlds by crafting the rules of how they work and communicating these rules to players through gameplay.

Spatial designers—architects, landscape architects, and garden designers—have their own methods for developing worlds through the orientations of features and materials. In this chapter, we explore how to synthesize the methods of these more classical design fields in the worlds of digital games. We explore how players understand the possibilities present in interactive spaces and how designers inform players about the scope of these spaces. Also, we revisit elements of communication, decision-making, and choice to learn how designers make explorable worlds. Lastly, we see how the designers of these worlds break their own rules to create engaging surprises for players to discover.

What you will learn in this chapter:

Understanding immersion and player individuality

Architectural phenomenology and play

Emergent spaces

Miniature garden aesthetic

Japanese garden design and worldbuilding

Offering experiential choice

Degenerative design

UNDERSTANDING IMMERSION AND PLAYER INDIVIDUALITY

I have spoken several times about level design as a second-order design problem. Designers cannot directly control the behavior of a product's users but can control the rules of a system that users interact with. The late film critic Roger Ebert famously cited this as a reason that he believed that games were not art. Ebert felt that the player's ability to control his or her experience of games diminished the designer's authorship.[3] However, game designers utilize this as a way to build replayability into their products—the ability for players to have varied experiences with a game on repeated interactions. Some designers think replayability and the potential for users to craft their own experiences creates *immersion*, a complete acceptance of virtual game worlds as reality. Others, however, believe that the notion of total immersion defeats the promise of games as media that can be experienced by many different individuals. As we will see, this debate and a similar one within the field of architecture can give us insight into how different players use space. As designers, our goal should be to facilitate a dialog between users and a space's unique qualities.

Immersion is a popular game industry buzzword for a game's ability to engage players. It is often cited as a goal of designers crafting a game, or as a positive quality. However, as is common with buzzwords, its true meaning is lost in its overuse. Katie Salen and Eric Zimmerman turn to the essay "Immersion" by François Dominic Laramee to readdress immersion's true meaning: "a state in which the player's mind forgets that it is being subjected to entertainment and instead accepts what it perceives as reality."[4]

The Immersive Fallacy

Salen and Zimmerman respond to Laramee's definition of immersion with the *immersive fallacy,* a statement of rejection against true immersion that argues that games instead deal in *metacommunication*—expressions that take into account their own state of unreality. They use anthropologist Gregory Bateson's example of a dog biting another dog in play: the bite signifies a real bite, but is at the same time not a real bite; it is a simulated play of biting. Salen and Zimmerman respond with examples from the games *Spin the Bottle* and *Quake.* Players of *Spin the Bottle* kiss but are not expressing love, just as *Quake* deathmatch players are shooting one another but do not hate each other.[5] While players may be engaged in these games and their dramatic elements, they are aware of the game within the context of the game's placement in the real world and within the scope of their own life experiences.

As we have seen in our explorations of how players learn within gamespaces, the content of the space is highly important to showing players how the game functions. Experienced players bring prior experience of the game they are playing or similar games they have previously played. These players assume upon loading a new first-person game that they will have the same controls as many they have previously experienced: the W, A, S, and D keys control player movement, while the mouse is moved to look around and aim. Many players of old Nintendo Entertainment System games were scandalized when they rented a game that used the B button for jump instead of the traditional A button. New players may need guidance based on the complexity of controls, but likely bring some other competencies that will help them see the experience in unique ways. Either way, the people playing your game will bring some amount of prior external knowledge to your game, which contradicts pure immersion.

Player Personalities

Moving even further away from total immersion in a game, *player personalities* are often considered when crafting game experiences. Games such as *Dragon Quest III*[6] or *Ultima IV: Quest of the Avatar*[7] ask players a series of questions at the beginning of the game to determine the stats of player characters. Numerous studies and published works have referenced player types in games. Richard Bartle famously defined the types *achievers, explorers, socializers,* and *killers* to describe the players in *multiuser dungeons* (MUDs), a type of interactive space he helped create with Roy Trubshaw in 1978.[8] Newer editions of the *Dungeon Master's Guide* for *Dungeons & Dragons* describe common "player motivations" and how players functioning as "Dungeon Master," the player who designs gameplay scenarios and acts as the voice of the game itself, can engage each of these player types.[9]

In his Game Developers Conference (GDC) 2013 talk, "Applying the 5 Domains of Play,"[10] Ubisoft creative director Jason VandenBerghe expanded the Bartle types to take into account five elements of personality: *openness to experience, conscientiousness, extraversion, agreeableness,* and *neuroticism.* These were compared to the titular five domains of play— *novelty, challenge, stimulation, harmony,* and *threat*—to determine where players fit on a chart of the first four domains (threat is left out and applied to its own set of criteria), each divided into four quadrants (Figure 10.1). As players answer where they fit on each quadrant of the chart, they can visualize their player personality on a 4×4 grid diagram. VandenBerghe proposes that the test be used as a method for applying "accurate empathy" to a designer's gameplay, allowing him or her to think like different kinds of players as he or she designs. He visualizes this by likening different styles to well-known fictional characters playing well-known games and says, "Play these games like these people."

The suggestion that player personalities factor greatly into the type of character one might build in a game, or that the types of games people play are dependent on their personalities, weighs heavily against the idea of total immersion in games. While the ideas of Bateson, Bartle, and VandenBerghe factor greatly into the subject matter of games themselves, they say little of how users engage gamespace. Architects have been struggling with notions of total spatial immersion versus metacommunication. It is this struggle that will help us explore how the spirit of individual gamespaces can be used in concert with player individuality.

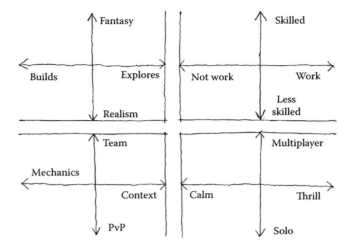

FIGURE 10.1 Jason VandenBerghe's chart for player personality types tracks how players' personalities react to different domains of play: novelty, challenge, harmony, and stimulation. A player's answers to what he or she likes in each quadrant result in a simple player personality diagram.

ARCHITECTURAL PHENOMENOLOGY AND PLAY

In Chapter 4, "Basic Gamespaces," we discussed the concept of *genius loci*, or "spirit of place." This element of architectural design challenges designers to give places their own individual character or transmit meaning through unique spatial experiences. While originally referring to a town's guardian spirit in Roman culture, the term gained its current usage by those applying the philosophy of *phenomenology* to architecture.

Architectural phenomenology was greatly inspired by the works of German philosopher Martin Heidegger, whose application of phenomenology argued against understanding the world in scientific or objective abstracts, but rather in empirical terms based on one's sensory information at any given moment.[11] Architect Christian Norberg-Schultz applied Heidegger's thinking to architectural space, arguing that spaces should be understood for their own elements rather than through the lens of previous experience.[12] As such, practitioners of architectural phenomenology are often concerned with creating spaces with a strong experiential element or that maximize some element of the building's site while shutting out exterior influences or symbols. Architect Peter Zumthor, a noted phenomenologist, stated that he begins projects by thinking which emotions or experiences he wishes to convey, while staying true to elements of site and material.[13] For one piece, the St. Benedict's Chapel in Sumvitg, Graubunden, Switzerland (Figure 10.2), he emphasized the wood used to create the building by purposely adding a creaking floorboard. Zumthor described this addition as one that would "exist just below your level of consciousness."[14]

Phenomenology's supporters argue that works such as those by Zumthor are to be enjoyed for their own sake, without influence from *a priori* knowledge (knowledge known inherently without sensory input). Immersion seems to be the phenomenology of play: enjoying a game without input from the outside world. Some people take the concept of roleplay to heart when playing, enacting what they would not in real-life situations, such as being an evil warlord, fighting powerful foes, or playing a member of the opposite sex. On the other hand, Salen and Zimmerman's immersive fallacy points to even this kind of play as engaging the meta-elements of games.

The phenomenology of gamespace is a mix of self-contained elements that also engage in meta-dialogs with players and culture. On the one hand, we have thus far explored how games utilize symbolic assets to modify player behavior or communicate with players and other cultural elements

FIGURE 10.2 Peter Zumthor's St. Benedict's Chapel, built in Sumvitg, Graubunden, Switzerland, in 1989, clings to its mountainside site while contrasting the forms of surrounding vernacular architecture. An intentionally warped floorboard inside emphasizes the materiality of the building.

outside the game itself. On the other hand, level design seeks to emphasize the unique mechanics of games, as phenomenologist architects seek to emphasize a building's unique materials and experience. Therefore, the same elements that work to emphasize the unique parts of the game they are in—modular assets used for behavior modification, asset arrangements for communication, etc.—can also engage meta-elements of games. Game world architecture can help facilitate player interaction, but it can create surprising game events by providing resources for different types of players.

In this sense, gamespace rejects architectural phenomenology. Gamespaces can be encountered by many different people in many different ways. The way that two players interact with a level, even if they share player personalities, will be completely different unless the developer forces players to play in a specific way. While such games better address concerns over authorship of gameplay experiences in games by taking *choice* away from players, they often are not remembered very fondly or do not have gameplay longevity—*replay value*. When players play a game, they wish to become attached to it: games that fail to "grab" players tend to go unplayed and become part of a game player's "backlog of shame"—unfinished games. Heidegger refers to a similar attachment to spaces, citing the concept of *dwelling* in a space as finding an "existential foothold" in it.[15] A player's ability to dwell, find a foothold to attach to, in a gamespace is important for making a level memorable and feel like a real *place* for them. This attachment brings players back.

Even games that are ultimately linear, such as those in the *Final Fantasy*[16] series, offer players some choices: character customization, job selection, side quests, etc. When these choices are stripped away, leaving less choice in gameplay, the response is not as warm—players are less attached. This was the case with *Final Fantasy XIII*.[17] In terms of level and world design, the game was much more linear than some considered acceptable, described by some reviewers as a "long hallway."[18] Modern first-person shooter level design has likewise been criticized for being a string of cutscenes and high-action encounters linked by hallways (Figure 10.3). While these spaces may succeed at maximizing a game's mechanics, they leave little ability for players to create their own experience of the game to compare with others' experiences. In this way, we must seek to have a simultaneously phenomenological and metacommunicative approach to level design to help players form attachments with your game spaces.

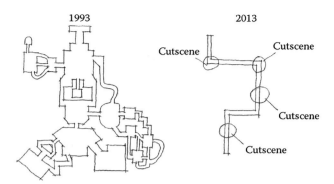

FIGURE 10.3   A recreation of a popular Internet image that describes the seemingly complex nature of older first-person shooter maps compared with the linear nature of modern ones.

In the next section we further explore the elements of gamespace that allow players of different types to have their own experiences with gamespace and how gamespaces use their phenomenological elements to create emergent experiences.

EMERGENT SPACES

Throughout the book, we have looked at complexity as a byproduct of contrasting features played off of one another as described by Robert Venturi. So far, we have used this to describe how contrasts add drama to space. However, we can extend this to mechanisms and spaces that support play styles: worlds that reward different types of players are richer and lead to more attachment. Venturi describes how if systems are placed adjacent to or superimposed over one another, it creates increasingly satisfying complexities.[19] We have also discussed games as *systems*. In *Rules of Play*, Salen and Zimmerman address the *complexity* of systems through the lens of Jeremy Campbell, author of *Grammatical Man*.[20] Campbell describes complexity in systems as "enabling them to do things and be things we might not have expected."[21] Part of what makes games unique is that human players and their wildly divergent personalities act as part of the interactive systems of games and space. Putting players among a variety of spaces that reward different behaviors is therefore a great way to create complexity. This complexity leads to an element of systems that Salen and Zimmerman describe as "crucial" for understanding how they become meaningful for players:[22] *emergence*.

Emergence

In the previous chapter, we discussed how users interacting with games create *emergent narratives*, stories created by how one plays a game. As a concept, emergence refers to unexpected outcomes of systems in which unique components interact with one another. One of the most famous examples of emergence in the field of computer science is *The Game of Life*, a cellular automation created by John Conway in 1970. As the simulation runs, geometric patterns emerge due to the rules of the simulation that could not be predicted by reading the rules alone. Some are temporary, while others actually create new cellular bodies (Figure 10.4).[23]

Rules and interaction are what make emergent outcomes *possible* within systems such as architecture and games. In Chapter 9's example of the Hagia Sophia in Istanbul, Turkey, cultural and geographic factors led to the church being an important status symbol for conquering armies in the area. Such factors exist outside the structural systems of the building itself (which in the case of Hagia Sophia has created an emergent narrative of its own: the central dome has collapsed twice), but are no less part of its history.

Systems like games and architecture are subject to what tabletop game designer Jason Morningstar has called the *fruitful void*, the intersection of a game's rules and the players' personalities.[24] In a larger sense, the fruitful void applies when a work of art or design is subject to reimaginings by human culture over time. In the case of architecture, cultural factors affect the fate of a building and give it new meanings, perhaps even leading to personal attachment. Games with rich potential for emergence function the same way as players make them their own through play. Two players'

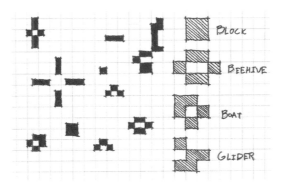

FIGURE 10.4 A sketch of Conway's *Game of Life* showing different patterns that are emergent results of the automation's rules.

stories of how they heroically vanquished the same monster are often very different. Through their rules and design, gamespaces offer players *possibilities* in how they can play.

Possibility Spaces

We have explored the idea of gamespace as emergent worlds from a theoretical perspective, through player personalities, phenomenology, and emergence itself. The question is how to create worlds appropriate for emergent behavior through the largely phenomenological mindset we have used thus far throughout the book: emphasizing a game's rules and expressive elements through modular symbolic assets. Warren Spector, a designer whose credits include *Deus Ex*, *System Shock*, and *Wing Commander*, has said that games create *possibility spaces*. Possibility spaces "provide compelling problems within an overarching narrative, afford creative opportunities for dealing with these problems, and then respond to player choices with meaningful consequences."[25]

The idea that games are spaces where players can address problems through creative solutions is useful for defining how we must think of game worlds as emergent spaces. As illustrated by Conway's *Game of Life*, predefined rules or pieces with programmed behaviors can have unpredictable results. However, that illustration and those like it demonstrate emergence through barely interactive computer simulations. Possibility spaces still address this emergent element of predefined elements of games, but do so in such a way that brings the player into the fold. My own game, *La Mancha*[26]—a card game based on Miguel de Cervantes' 1605 novel *Don Quixote*—uses possibility space as a way to reinterpret classic literature. Players draw cards from a "journey" deck, which contains story prompts based on the novel: people, places, and things that Don Quixote and Sancho Panza see on their quests. Players respond with stories they create by stringing together phrases on the chivalry cards, cards with phrases from books of chivalry, in their hand. The game is light on game mechanics but creates a rich possibility space by prompting the players to roleplay as quixotic characters. In the case of *La Mancha*, this has even resulted in players retelling parts of Cervantes' novel in new ways: having unrelated characters fall in love, finding new outcomes to famous scenes, and so on. In Chapter 9, "Storytelling in Gamespace," we discussed gamespaces that provide resources for emergent narrative and the example of the *Half-Life 2*[27] playtesters killing barnacles by rolling exploding barrels at them. This action could take place because developers created procedures that allowed these things to happen, placed them in an environment that invited exploration, and allowed players to play. Both examples show how games that provide even a few deeply interactive elements can create a rich possibility space (even the one around a table).

Setting the rules for worlds then allowing players to explore their possibilities is a powerful tool for in-game worldbuilding. Worldbuilding through possibility space encourages the creation of interactive elements that can be given narrative context with art, writing, and other expressive methods. This creates a world that is not only narratively expressive in the way Tolkien's Middle Earth is, but also interactively expressive in ways that only interactive designed spaces can be. In the next section, we discuss the actual construction of such worlds and how one designer introduces players to them.

MINIATURE GARDEN AESTHETIC

In *Spore Creature Creator* designer Chaim Gingold's thesis, "Miniature Gardens and Magic Crayons: Games, Spaces, and Worlds,"[28] he writes about the spatial aesthetics of the legendary Shigeru Miyamoto. In particular, he interprets an often mentioned but never explained aspect of his worlds, where large natural landscapes are created in easily explored gamespaces, as *miniature gardens*. According to Gingold, miniature gardens reflect the design principles of Japanese gardens: miniaturized worlds in which occupants can explore a "multiplicity of landscapes"[29] within a short period of time. Examples include the land of Hyrule in the *Zelda* series (Figure 10.5), the various environments in *Super Mario* games, and the explorable alien planets in *Pikmin*.[30] He describes these worlds as complete and self-contained, citing three elements that make them both manageable and believable for players:

Clear boundaries

Overviews

Consistent abstraction[31]

The construction of Miyamoto's worlds, and how they are introduced to players, factors heavily into their success. As possibility spaces, they have a limited and clear set of rules and objects that the player can interact with

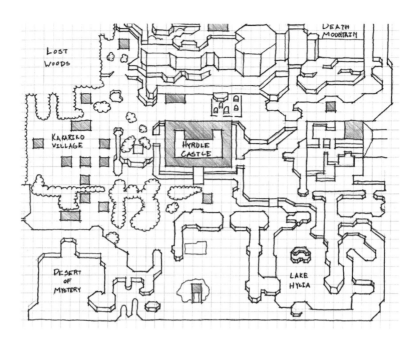

FIGURE 10.5   The map of Hyrule from *The Legend of Zelda: A Link to the Past* has within it a variety of environments for players to explore that are quickly accessible, have clear limits, and are abstracted by their construction with symbolic game assets.

in the world. For ease of both a designer's construction and the players' ability to understand them (not to mention memory limitations of games), these gamespaces are constructed with richly interactive modular assets rather than custom-built. This makes the world and its possibilities easy for players to understand: assets and their variations create a rich system of communication that players come to know as representational of gameplay mechanics. Likewise, keeping this world contained to clear boundaries and a limited set of assets also allows players to learn and interact with the symbolic system more effectively (Figure 10.6). It is the player's freedom to interact with these assets, however, that produces the possibility of gameplay emergence.

While Miyamoto's miniature gardens provide opportunities for player emergence, Gingold also points out that these spaces have methods for introducing these opportunities to players through linear means. It is this mix of linear and emergent that can show us how to craft the gameplay of our own game worlds.

FIGURE 10.6   Some symbolic assets from *A Link to the Past*. These objects have a clear meaning and are therefore repeated across the game to allow communication of gameplay possibilities to players.

Overviews

The first method of introducing possibility space in miniature gardens is through overviews. As stated by Gingold, "Miniature Gardens are scale models of bigger phenomena. Fish tanks and gardens are scale representations of systems bigger than people."[32] The miniature nature of game worlds has not gone unnoticed by writers throughout the history of the medium. In 1983, David Sudnow published *Pilgrim in the Microworld*, a "stream of conciousness"[33] retelling of his experiences with the Atari 2600 game *Breakout*.[34] Sudnow, over the course of several months, feverishly practiced the game until achieving mastery of it. Throughout the book are increasingly complex diagrams of the gameplay mechanics, especially the physics of how the ball and paddle interact with one another.[35] The title is a reference to the miniature nature of the game's reality—a single-screen world that lives in a pocket-sized cartridge—and conveys Sudnow's efforts to master its rich but constrained possibility space.

Breakout and many games of the 1970s and early 1980s single-screen era are great at showing how even a single screen, or scene, can provide a rich overview. The first screen from *Super Mario Bros.* holds another such overview that instead teaches players about the large world beyond that first scene.[36] The player can see a variety of important symbols from the game, as well as an enemy and a power-up item. This provides an introduction to many of the rules of *Super Mario Bros.*'s possibility space that are repeated through subsequent screens and levels.

Overviews in Historic Games

Both *Breakout* and *Super Mario Bros.* are viewed from angles that render game action from outside the game world. In the case of these and other games from the 1970s and 1980s, the metaphor of a fish tank is an apt one: players interact with the game world from a perspective of omnipotence—they can see more than what the game character could conceivably see. This point of view works well in point-and-click adventures such as *The Secret of Monkey Island*,[37] where players must find objects on detailed story screens—any given puzzle can typically be solved with what is visible (Figure 10.7).

Top-down games such as *The Legend of Zelda* and *Dragon Quest* share this same ability to great effect: designers are not limited to the character's point of view when showing or hinting at secrets beyond their current geographic location. From a miniature garden perspective, this also affords the ability to give players an overview of game possibilities. In many ways, we can attract players with new possibilities in the same way we do with rewards: by showing something previously unseen in a place that the player must explore to find.

Overviews in 3D

Three-dimensional games such as first- and third-person games in which the player is viewing the game from very close to or from the avatar present

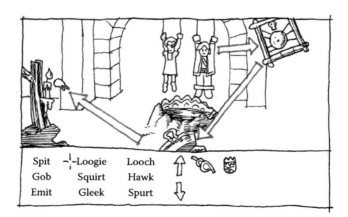

FIGURE 10.7   In adventure games like *The Secret of Monkey Island*, each scene or location conveys its own possibility space. Puzzles are typically solvable with the items visible on the screen during the puzzle itself and with inventory items earned prior to the puzzle.

their own challenges for integrating overviews. Some games provide a cutscene that flies over the level prior to the beginning of gameplay. In some cases this can be convenient, showing players what they will encounter or showing mission-important locations in a game world that allows lots of otherwise free exploration. These can also feel artificial and break the sense that the player is in a space where he or she can be surprised or make discoveries.

The work of Chinese architect I.M. Pei provides insight into how three-dimensional space can have the overviews common in older video games. In buildings such as the Rock and Roll Hall of Fame in Cleveland, Ohio, Pei uses a glass wall as the façade to show viewers outside what is contained within. Upon entering the building, the museum exhibits are revealed on a series of stacked floors arranged like a collector's shelves (Figure 10.8). The building provides a summary of its contents with this reveal, but rewards those who explore further with more information.

Pei's design for the East Wing of the National Gallery of Art in Washington, D.C., alerts visitors to their options for exploration when they walk into the large atrium (Figure 10.9). Angular balconies and walkways protrude into the space from floors above, offering glimpses of the

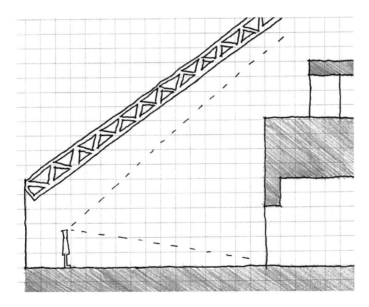

FIGURE 10.8 The arrangement of floors in the Rock and Roll Hall of Fame in Cleveland, Ohio—designed by I.M. Pei and opened in 1995—gives visitors an overview of the exhibits contained within when they enter the lobby.

FIGURE 10.9   A sketch of the atrium of the National Gallery of Art's East Wing in Washington, D.C.—designed by I.M. Pei and built in 1978. This space offers overviews of the spaces contained in the rest of the museum, but denies full access to them unless the visitor explores further.

exhibits contained within, but requiring visitors to explore to receive the full experience. Like the Rock and Roll Hall of Fame, the overview gives a summary of what each section of the building contains but denies full knowledge unless the visitor penetrates further into the space. Both buildings use their entrances, where a visitor *arrives* in the space, carefully as a scene. The visitor's path is controlled such that they must get a framed overview before proceeding further.

As Pei's architecture shows us, overviews can be accomplished with first- or third-person views through the creation of vistas. These vistas allow players in games to see out over the game world and discover the limits of its possibility space. This is another scenario in which height in level design can be beneficial, allowing players to get an overview of 3D game worlds. In games such as *Dragon Quest VIII: Journey of the Cursed King*,[38] players can often gaze out from the top of cliffs to the world below, seeing distant landmarks. Many worlds in *Super Mario 64*[39] also feature a high point from which players may look out onto the environment, seeing red coins, item boxes, enemies, obstacles, and other gameplay elements. Such vistas go beyond rewards, tactics, or scenery, and can give players an impression of the possibility spaces of 3D worlds. Combined with Lynch-esque elements such as landmarks, boundaries, and recognizable districts, players can make informed decisions about the path they will take through a space, just as a visitor to the Rock and Roll Hall of Fame can plan which exhibits he or she would like to see first.

While view-based overviews are great ways to convey the possibility spaces of games, they can also be a passive experience. When used too often, they can make the pacing of games feel stagnant. However, Gingold also highlights another form of overview that better utilizes games' interactivity.

Tours

Another method for introducing possibility spaces to players in miniature gardens is the *tour*. A tour is an initial introduction to gamespaces and their mechanics through a linear level experience. These tours often also show players game mechanics or elements that they may revisit at another time, teasing gameplay to come.[40] In the example of the Rock and Roll Hall of Fame, the architecture of the space requires visitors to enter a lin-ear exhibit on the history of rock music after seeing the lobby overview but before actually getting the opportunity to explore the previewed exhibits. Such a tour gives the teased exhibits a sense of historical context and offers the ability to explore them freely as a *reward of facility*, a reward that offers new abilities.

Game designer Doug Church describes similar experiences in the levels of *Super Mario 64*. He describes how the first power star, an object in the game whose retrieval is the goal of most levels, requires that players travel a path that encompasses the entire environment (Figure 10.10). These challenges show previews of other challenges that the player will encoun-ter later, much like the overviews from high places do. Church argues that in subsequent visits to the world, players will know where to find other stars or challenges, as they have already seen much of what the world has to offer.[41]

Like Pei's linear history exhibit in the Rock and Roll Hall of Fame, tours can also give players an introduction to many of a game's mechanics without resorting to a ham-handed tutorial where the game talks at the player. In *The Legend of Zelda: A Link to the Past*,[42] the introduction to the game, where Link must follow his uncle into the dungeons of Hyrule Castle, introduces many of the game's mechanics: combat, unlocking doors, avoiding pitfalls, pushing and lifting objects, and puzzle-solving.

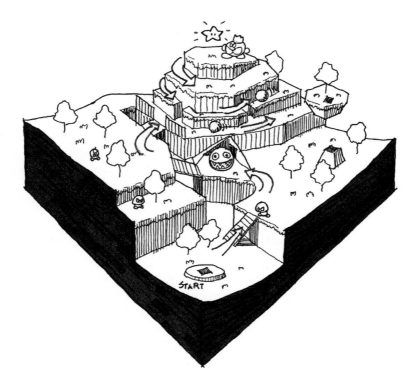

FIGURE 10.10 The first star of many worlds in *Super Mario 64* often requires players to visit most of the gamespace and teases challenges to come. Some, such as Bob-Omb Battlefield, feature a tour-like exploration of the level that ends with an overview from a high place.

Likewise, *The Last of Us* guides players through a series of challenges that teach the game's many mechanics—solving environmental puzzles, combat, stealth, and dealing with different zombie types—during the game's first chapter. Both examples package their tutorials within narrative scenarios rather than training sequences where players are told the mechanics by another character. This allows players to engage the game's action right away while being acquainted with the game's system of mechanics and symbols.

Possibility Space and Procedural Literacy

By now, it should be clear that a primary concern of miniature gardens is allowing players to maximize their possibilities by giving them a thorough understanding of what can be done in the space. In this chapter, we have thus far explored how space can be constructed to introduce what is possible within gamespaces. The introduction of game mechanics in possibility spaces aids the development of what designer Ian Bogost calls *procedural literacy*.[43] Procedural literacy is a familiarity with the rules of a game and how they function within an established possibility space. Consistent, communicative assets are an element of this: players learn that certain textured surfaces are solid while others may cause damage, slipping, and so on. They may learn the identity of items, gates, puzzle elements, objects that can weigh others down, etc. In terms of pure mechanics, this can also translate into an understanding of metrics, character abilities, or when players may encounter obstacles in games. These assets are the building blocks of levels, but are also the procedural language of gamespaces.

Bogost highlights the communicative power of such cause-and-effect procedures, arguing that developing procedural literacy in players can allow them not only to be better players of a certain game, but also help in the creation of *procedural rhetoric*—using game rules as a system of communication. Game rules and the construction of gamespaces as a system of communication between the designer and player are a central theme of this book: designers must create a dialog with their players to make the best play experience possible.

Developing both procedural literacy and rhetoric helps players understand gamespaces and their possibilities better. In the previous examples of *Super Mario 64* and *A Link to the Past*, players are guided through the mechanics that they will use throughout the entire game during tour levels. They are also given overviews that allow them to see other gamespaces where these mechanics will be useful.

Building procedural literacy and then exhausting player possibilities can create powerful game experiences. A previous example utilized Terry Cavanaugh's *Don't Look Back*[44] to discuss uncertainty—the feeling of having no information of how to address game scenarios—and how it may help subvert game design standards. The example of a cliff that the player must jump off of blindly also helps demonstrate how designers can use exhausted game possibilities to guide players through the next steps of a game. Players who reach this cliff know that they have completed everything there is to do in each previous screen, and so know that their only option is to leap off the cliff (Figure 10.11). Galactic Café's *The Stanley Parable*[45] plays with this procedural literacy to create a biting satire of games and game design. It presents players with a disconnect between the choices you have (such as having two doors to go through) and the suggestions the game gives you on where to go ("through the left door"). In

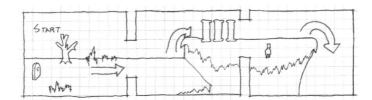

FIGURE 10.11   The cliff screen in *Don't Look Back* comes after a series of simple platforming screens in which the player easily accomplishes everything there is to do in them. As such, the player knows that there are no more gameplay possibilities left to explore when he or she reaches the cliff except to leap from it.

doing so, the player can think about the nature of choice, symbolism, and freedom in games. In one of my favorite examples, the player finds a single button "art game" that the narrator describes through a longwinded diatribe of its meaning. The contrast between the rhetoric (a dump truck of symbolism) and the procedure (pushing a single button) show how overloaded with rhetoric some mechanics can get.

Designers must be careful that well developed procedural literacy does not break the experience of their game. If players can recognize the systemic elements of a game too well, they may dismiss otherwise effective atmosphere-building areas of your levels. In *Dead Space*,[46] for example, players must often traverse narrow ventilation shafts where they cannot attack. Observant players will notice that while they cannot attack, and are otherwise very open to attack, they also never encounter enemies in the vents beyond a few non-confrontational jump scares. As with the art game example from *The Stanley Parable*, players will be quick to point out when this disconnect breaks them out of the game experience. In *The Stanley Parable*, this is played for laughs, but in *Dead Space*, it breaks the game's tension and actually makes the player feel safe.

Envisioning levels as possibility spaces is a very effective way to communicate your game's mechanics to players. Effective possibility spaces introduce a game's mechanics and system of symbolic assets to players in such a way where they understand symbols when they are repeated. They also give players opportunities for creating their own emergent narratives by becoming procedurally literate about a game and testing the limits of what they can do in your gamespaces. In the next section, we will discuss the aesthetic elements of miniature gardens in games and how they can be used to build exciting game worlds.

JAPANESE GARDEN DESIGN AND WORLDBUILDING

According to Gingold's interpretation, Miyamoto's miniature garden aesthetic borrows heavily from the design traditions of Japanese gardens. This is especially true when observing Japanese garden design's use of boundaries and abstraction. In *Secret Teachings in the Art of Japanese Gardens*,[47] David Slawson explores the purpose of these gardens in the larger framework of Japanese culture. In the West, he observes, many Japanese gardens utilize vernacular Japanese architecture: pagodas, *torii* gates, lanterns, etc., to give the garden "a Disneyland quality."[48] However, the true purpose of such gardens is to give the impression of natural landscapes in a small, explorable area. Depending on the scale one wishes to convey, these landscapes are created through the use of various landscaping features meant to represent natural formations: rocks may be placed as mountains, cliffs, or land forms; raked gravel may be used to represent bodies of water, as may small ponds (Figure 10.12). Vegetation also varies based on the scale of the garden; moss may be used as trees if the garden shows something very far away, or as grass if the garden represents something closer. Small pines are also used to create forest-like areas. Such gardens transport viewers to landscapes outside of their immediate surroundings within quick overviews and tours.

FIGURE 10.12   A turtle rock, formed from a rock with moss in the middle of a small pond, represents an island in the middle of a vast ocean. Such formations demonstrate how landscaping creates simulated landscapes within Japanese gardens.

In video games, Miyamoto's Mushroom World and Hyrule are primary examples of this. In early *Legend of Zelda* games, players move through Hyrule in a largely non-linear fashion and may visit a variety of different landscape types: deserts, lakes, forests, mountains, and others within the boundaries of the game world. *Super Mario Bros.* games feature tours of differing landscapes as each in-game world utilizes a different theme: grass, desert, tropics, ice, etc. *New Super Mario Bros. U*[49] for the Wii U even utilizes the likeness of traditional Chinese scholars' stones—naturally formed stones with asymmetrical forms and perforations (Figure 10.13) that are popular features in Chinese gardens—as a backdrop for its mountain-themed world. Some of these worlds are largely interactive, such as Hyrule, and others are simply overviews of interactive spaces, such as those in *Super Mario Bros.* games. This allows us to explore how Japanese gardens treat points of view and what they can tell us about game worlds.

FIGURE 10.13 A scholar's stone. They are traditional features of Chinese gardens and are formed naturally by water and weather conditions in coastal regions. *New Super Mario Bros. U* utilizes stones like these as a backdrop for the mountain world portion of its world map, lending to its miniature garden quality.

Points of View in Japanese Gardens

In his book, Slawson addresses two types of Japanese gardens—those viewed from fixed vantage points in a building or structure and those that the user can interact with (Figure 10.14). As with camera angles in games, each type offers its own advantages and disadvantages when discussing how one sees the miniature world of the garden. The vantage point gardens allow viewers to see exotic landscapes from outside, giving an overview of everything within. Like 2D top-down or side-scrolling games, they express their worlds through controlled points of view from which the user can take in points of interest. The overworlds of *Super Mario* games are like these overview gardens, giving an overview of landscapes and describing to the user the types of adventures that may be contained within. In *Super Mario Bros. 3*,[50] each world has its own map that uses symbolic assets to convey to players the contents of each level: numbered blocks denote normal obstacle courses, forts are mini-fortresses full of skeletons and ghosts, mushroom houses yield power-ups, and castles feature boss battles with Bowser's children. In *Super Mario World*,[51] the maps of each world are linked into one continuous whole, offering players an overview of different landscapes at once (Figure 10.15).

The interactive tea or stroll gardens, on the other hand, allow users to explore their simulated environments. This allows designers to guide users through gardens with communicative views. Hyrule in early *Zelda* games was a mix of vantage point and stroll garden types. These early

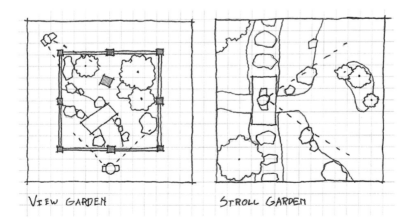

VIEW GARDEN   STROLL GARDEN

FIGURE 10.14 Two types of Japanese gardens: ones viewed from outside and ones that are interactive.

FIGURE 10.15   The map of *Super Mario World* is structured similarly to a vantage point Japanese garden and shows the fictional islands of Dinosaur Land. One might imagine it as a series of rocks with moss and small pines surrounded by raked gravel (as sketched here).

games offered overviews based on their point of view that had the *Citizen Kane* effect of allowing players to see things that their avatar could not. As these games evolved to 3D, they became more purely exploratory spaces, able to take advantage of more traditional viewpoint-based enticement strategies in their designs. The Hyrule of *The Legend of Zelda: Ocarina of Time*,[52] for example, utilizes landmarks in a Kevin Lynch-esque fashion to entice players toward narrative-important quests. *Breath of the Wild* uses landmarks in a similar fashion and has puzzles where the player must visit places where a photo has been taken from. Landmarks visible in these photos are vital for solving these puzzles, which unlock the game's full backstory.

Most importantly, the work of Slawson and his predecessors of over a thousand years gives insight into how game designers may use artificial landscapes and controlled user interaction to create possibility spaces that feel like expansive game worlds. Slawson specifically utilizes two schemas that are of great importance to level designers, *scenic effects* and *sensory effects*, which we will briefly explore to understand how Japanese gardens can help us build emergent game worlds.

Scenic Effects

Slawson's first schema of Japanese garden design is scenic effects: the ability to create visual representations of memorable landscapes. Historically, Slawson writes, such an element of garden design was important to Japanese aristocrats who traveled to China and Korea during the T'ang Dynasty,[53] as it allowed them to re-create sights they had seen in their travels. This, he claims, leads to a *feature-oriented* design aesthetic, where certain features are recreated to evoke feelings that one has when viewing them in nature.[54]

Designers therefore often seek to develop scenic effects in such a way that reflects how something would happen in nature. Slawson uses the example of a gnarled tree:

> A gnarled pine from the mountains (or a similar one from the nursery) serves in the garden not merely as a weathered tree but also, by virtue of the way it is planted in a composition of rocks, as a powerful agent for evoking the atmosphere of craggy mountains far from civilization.[55]

Creating landscapes in accordance with how they occur in nature helps give landscapes their individual character, or *yo*. The rocks, plants, water, and earth elements used by designers become a symbolic language through which the Japanese garden designer speaks to viewers about what type of landscape he or she is creating.

Such ideas are important in creating the feeling of possibility space worlds as representations of a landscape and for giving them their own genius loci. When creating game worlds as illustrative landscapes, designers can arrange art assets in a way that reflects environmental storytelling methods. These establish the narrative reality of the game world. A world with a properly defined sense of place is a world that players can learn to use, form attachments to, and think of as well remembered places they have "visited." As we have seen, consistent symbolic assets help create a rich system of communication between designer and player. Putting boundaries on this system in a miniature garden helps define the possibilities of a gamespace.

Gingold argues that clear boundaries help miniature gardens be "intelligible and plastic,"[56] or understandable and moldable. A game with a clearly defined set of possibilities is easy for someone to pick up and play. *Minecraft*[57] is an excellent example of such a world: clearly defined block objects form the world's geometry and have clearly defined relationships with one another. From these relationships, many potential combinations of materials are possible. Online players have created everything from giant 8-bit sprites to recreations of famous real-world and game architecture.

While such elements create visually appealing landscapes in gardens and possibility spaces, they can also be used for creating interesting spatial experiences. Slawson covers this in his next schema.

Sensory Effects

Slawson's description of sensory effects in Japanese gardens reflects the ideas that drive much of this book. He discusses the use of scenic elements as a medium for directing the experience of viewers. He also suggests directing visitors through gardens with hearing-based stimuli, like the sound of running water, or with the kinesthetic sensations of touch and movement through spaces. It is in his discussions of garden formations, however, that the lines between Japanese gardens and Gingold's miniature garden possibility spaces begin to blur.

As we have seen, carefully defining the boundaries of possibility space helps us teach players how to engage our games. Slawson uses the term *scroll* garden to describe what he and we have been discussing as vantage point gardens, likening the experience of early Japanese gardens to unrolling a scroll and viewing it from above. Such gardens, he states, must fit within a single frame, and he likens them to composing shots on film.[58] In the possibility spaces of games, both 2D and 3D, the way in which a designer frames a view can have great impact on how a player understands what he or she is supposed to do.

This emphasis on scene composition addresses a problem that many new designers have when designing miniature garden spaces, exterior environments, and large game worlds: perceived randomness. In nature, trees, rocks, cliffs, and other natural features place themselves over time in unplanned ways. New designers often haphazardly place trees, rocks, and even buildings randomly on their maps, unaware of the importance of their positioning. Directing players toward carefully placed scenic assets, however, is how we help them understand our worlds.

As we saw in our earlier explorations of overviews and tours, many 3D miniature gardens direct the gaze of their players with carefully chosen high points or arrivals from which the world can be viewed. When composing such views, it is important to understand how to direct the player's eye throughout your scene. Slawson describes the use of the two *visual planes*, horizontal and vertical, for this purpose, and recommends engaging both (Figure 10.16). He describes vertical, horizontal, and *diagonal* forces of objects in a garden, which dictate the direction in which a feature's energy flows and therefore its ability to point views in a certain direction. In terms of these planes, we have already seen how textural elements on the ground of a game world can direct the player's eye, such as with stripes of shadows leading into doorways in *Half-Life 2*. Diagonal forces, representing the visual forces of humankind in Japanese gardens, can direct views both upward and forward from a player's point of view. Diagonal elements like landscaping features or fallen debris can both frame and be visual launch pads to important landmarks. These landmarks are typically vertical elements such as tall buildings, mountains, and others, useful for directing user attention[59] (Figure 10.17).

It is the relationship between landmarks and the less obvious elements of a view that can truly cement our ability to direct players through game worlds. The orientations of the most noticeable elements and the less noticeable elements are of equal importance to these designers. For example, gardens often feature rocks laid out in *horizontal triad* (Figure 10.18) and *Buddhist triad* (Figure 10.19) formations. Horizontal triad rocks are laid in such a way that each formation points to one another, while the formations themselves imply stability through triangular form. These formations emphasize horizontal motion. Buddhist triad rocks show how short complementary rocks emphasize a central landmark rock, highlighting its vertical motion. Supporting this idea, Slawson describes a garden he once watched Professor Kinsaku Nakane build. Professor Nakane first placed a rock of middle height to establish a base height for the composition, and then placed the tallest rock to the right of it.[60] An excerpt from

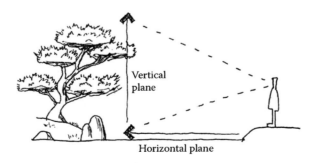

FIGURE 10.16 Scenery in miniature garden worlds directs player views across horizontal and vertical planes.

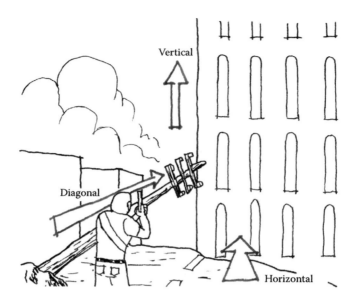

FIGURE 10.17 Scenery elements can be said to have forces in Japanese garden design based on how their shape directs the user's gaze. In games, horizontal forces lead across the horizontal plane of an environment. Vertical forces lead upward and are often used as landmarks, and diagonal forces emanate from the player avatar upward and outward.

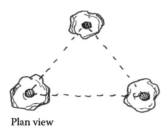

FIGURE 10.18 Horizontal triad formation rocks. These rocks mainly address the horizontal plane and imply movement along it.

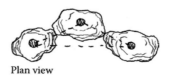

FIGURE 10.19 Buddhist triad formation rocks. These rocks have a minor triangulation along the horizontal plane but stretch vertically, resembling Buddhist deities as depicted in traditional statues: two lesser deities flank a major one.

the fifteenth-century text *Senzui Narabi ni Yagyo no Zu* (*Illustrations for Designing Mountain, Water, Field, and Hillside Landscapes*) illustrates an additional example of such a formation that it calls the *master* and *attendant* rocks. The master rock in a formation is the central and tallest figure, while the attendant rocks flank the master rock and are lowered "resembling persons with their heads lowered respectfully saying something to the Master rock."[61] Establishing the size of a middle object to create the normal scale of a scene, and then developing more hierarchically important objects, is a good methodology for environment artists. In any game project, it is important to set up the metrics of your space before creating moments of high gameplay. Without establishing the norm, gameplay or visual elements may be mismatched or unplayable.

Through these explorations of vertical and horizontal forces as well as the relationships between landmark assets and the environment around them, we can understand how designers can direct players through large game worlds. Composing views—overview, tour, or simply a normal game view—in such a way that emphasizes choices for player action highlights the actions available within a game's possibility space (Figure 10.20). When combined with environments that teach players their limits for in-game

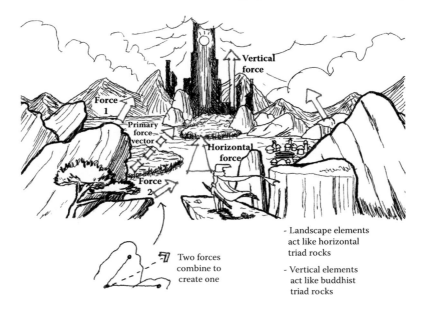

FIGURE 10.20   In this theoretical game view, landscaping elements and their directional forces are used to emphasize landmarks on the vertical plane. When forces are combined, they create what Slawson calls a primary force vector.

actions, these create a powerful spatial dynamic between player abilities, environmental choices, and game goals. The levels in *Journey*[62] produce such an effect. Players may run, jump, and glide in the game, and their goal for each area is to reach a gateway to the next area, often situated in a vertically emphasized mountainside or gateway. Understanding the limits of their avatar and their goal, players may then roam around the largely open level space, directed by environmental cues—architectural elements, cliffs, rocks, and others—that allow views of one another.

Player choice is another ingredient to in-game worldbuilding: offering choices or the perception of choices allows us to make impactful game worlds. The next section will further explore how to emphasize player choice and discuss spaces that emphasize simultaneously limited but undirected exploration.

OFFERING EXPERIENTIAL CHOICE

Gameplay emergence can be a product of both phenomenological elements, such as symbolic assets that are unique to certain games, and the uniqueness that each player brings to all games. We have learned how miniature gardens, spaces that introduce players to their gameplay possibilities and offer the ability to explore multiple landscapes while directing player attention to important features, enable such emergence. Now we will look at spatial orientations that help us develop an awareness of player choice and discuss gamespace types that offer directed choice to players within explorable worlds.

Introducing Choice

When starting a single-player game of *Minecraft*, players awaken on an island with no resources and must find shelter before night falls and enemies appear. At this early stage, players may only move, jump, and punch, but may punch anything they wish. Upon punching blocks in the environment, they learn that the blocks break apart, can be collected, and can subsequently be placed elsewhere in the world. Given the short time limit the player has to gather resources on this first day, successful players will seek easy-to-gather resources and make their shelter from them, often a simple hut or hole. However, the next days will see players expanding their resource pool and crafting tools. These tools allow the gathering of more powerful resources and eventually, the crafting of better tools. In time, the game opens up and the goal is less one of surviving nightly raids and becomes user defined: users can create what they want in *Minecraft*'s sandbox world.

In many ways, the single-player experience of Mojang's *Minecraft* has much in common with I.M. Pei's architecture. Like the Rock and Roll Hall of Fame, the experience of *Minecraft* begins as one of linear discovery and becomes one of freedom within a defined world. Both works show how one introduces the element of choice in many games by initially guiding players through the rules in a directed or limited manner and then allowing players to explore on their own. In *Minecraft*, this process introduces players to the game's symbolic system of blocks. Each has uses and may be combined with other objects and is described by consistent artwork. However, this process also involves the player's *a priori* knowledge: gathering wood has certain connotations in human society, as does crafting a sword or pickaxe. The owner of a new pickaxe is likely to seek rock to use it on. This play between linearity and freedom, as well as unique and prior knowledge, helps direct players through the game. In this way, introductions into the symbols that enable player choice both are phenomenological and involve metacommunication. Players are introduced to unique symbols that they can interact with but that invite association with familiar objects.

Beyond the visual symbols themselves, that they were introduced in a limited fashion has much to tell us about the boundaries of miniature garden worlds such as *Minecraft* and how we introduce large systems of choice to players.

Intelligible Choice

To acclimatize players to its large system of possibilities, *Minecraft* models choice by giving limited options to players in the beginning, but slowly expanding it as players learn new things. At the beginning of the game, players are limited by what resources they can quickly gather, and thus the areas they have access to are limited. As they create new tools and learn more about the world, players gain access to more parts of their island and more resources, and get the impression that their own possibility space is expanding.

Minecraft and other sandbox games, such as *Grand Theft Auto IV*,[63] carefully limit player choice at first and slowly reveal new possibilities as players master each part of the game. These miniature garden spaces take Gingold's idea of establishing clear boundaries and use it as a teaching method: imposing limited boundaries at the beginning and expanding them as players learn the game. If these games gave players access to their entire possibility spaces at the beginning, it would be too big, too unintelligible. Framing portions of the world and possibility space into districts helps players master a few commands, and then move on to new ones when they are ready for boundaries to be pushed aside.

Lyndon and Moore discuss architectural boundaries and breaking them in *Chambers for a Memory Palace*.[64] Humans place boundaries to organize space and mark territory. As Lynch points out, many of these territories have their own individual character that sets them apart from others. Lyndon and Moore go on to explore Japanese design elements such as *shoji*, rice paper screens that slide to reveal the outdoors, and the lack of interior furniture on *tatami* mat floors, which suggests continuous interior space. The edges of individual mats work much in the same way that horizontal shadows do, drawing the user's eye across the horizontal plane of the floor and into the outdoors, which are revealed by an open *shoji* (Figure 10.21). In game design terms, a player of a game is like the person inside the *tatami* matted room: he or she must perform the actions one would inside, and can then have the *shoji* pulled aside to reveal the next part of the environment. The relationship between districts should be established, as the *tatami*'s horizontal lines draw the eye to the outside, both to transition to the next district and as an act of denial when the player has not yet earned entry to the new district. This gives players a tantalizing goal to look forward to as they explore.

Shaping Choice, Risk, and Reward

The border between these distinct districts—outdoors and indoors—gives occupants a choice of whether to remain indoors and view from within,

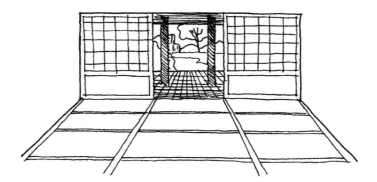

FIGURE 10.21 Japanese houses mark the transition from interior to exterior with a thin membrane of *shoji* screens. A relationship between these two districts is created by architectural details that draw the eye from one district to another.

or to explore the newly revealed environment. Outdoors may offer more possibilities for movement than the previous confines of the indoor space. Such is true of sandbox environments: players in *Grand Theft Auto IV* initially take on missions within a limited area of Liberty City, but are introduced to new districts as the game progresses. As they master the choices available to them in one district, new districts and new choices open up (Figure 10.22).

When developing such environments, designers can treat the borders between districts as skill gates that remain closed until the player has learned all there is to learn in the first district. The mastery of the last skill of a district acts as a trigger to open the path to the next one. *Earthbound*[65] for the Super Nintendo addresses this dynamic in an amusingly self-aware way, having police characters barricade the paths from town to town, claiming that it is their "claim to fame." These barricades are not removed until the player completes the main quests in each town or powers himself or herself up to appropriate levels to survive the next area of the game. Once each barricade is overcome, the world becomes openly explorable. In

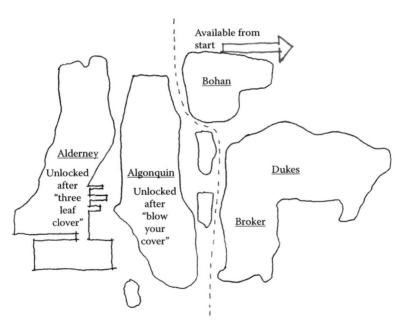

FIGURE 10.22 *Grand Theft Auto IV*'s districts each contain a set number of tasks to perform before a new one is opened up. This forces players to master the possibilities of one space before moving on to the next one that offers additional choices.

sandbox worlds, this often means that the player has agency to test all of the world's limits: *Grand Theft Auto* players can spend hours piloting boats and helicopters, *Minecraft* players can build their own structures, etc.

Behavioral biologist Karen Pryor calls this process of slowly introducing new information on a set of actions *shaping*. Shaping, she argues, takes the components of a complex action and breaks them into steps that can be individually mastered and built on. Her process of shaping behaviors focuses on increasing the criteria for positive feedback as new actions are learned: a reward is given first for something simple and then for increasingly complex steps. She argues for each action to be taught one at a time in isolation. She likens this method to learning a golf swing: players first learn how to grip the club, and then learn successive parts of the action. Rewards are given at first for mastering the grip, then for having a proper grip and backswing, then for properly moving from grip and backswing through to proper weight-shifting, and so on. Lessons are kept interesting by keeping tasks "ahead of the subject"—always teaching the next action as each is learned rather than resting on already mastered ones.[66]

Shaping choice in the way that miniature garden games do allows players to understand the certain, uncertain, and risky elements of worlds. By understanding the choices available to them, players are able to interpret the best path to take when given a choice—elements they are familiar with lead them on paths where they can take educated risks or engage in actions they are certain they can perform. However, such gamespaces can subvert these choices by offering little indication of what is down multiple pathways. In the case of *Earthbound*, caves and dungeons often show multiple passageways on one screen (Figure 10.23) without indicators as to what the correct passage is to reach the end. In these cases where the game has shaped players' understanding of its possibility space, players are actually motivated to explore all of these passages in case one could contain extra treasures, despite the possibility that they could be attacked.

Beyond their use in roleplaying and sandbox worlds, shaping, choices, and risks are also the basis of game worlds that offer both linear progression and opportunities for player exploration. These worlds deserve their own investigation as they create very dynamic spaces driven by rewards and expanding possibility.

"Metroidvania": Worlds of Rewards and Possibility

Throughout the book, we have discussed games in the *Metroid* and *Castlevania* series and their unique style of gamespace popularly dubbed

FIGURE 10.23 This sketch of the Giant Step level of *Earthbound* shows how players are offered multiple passageways through a level with no indication of which one to take. Rather than making players uncomfortable with how to move on, such choices motivate players to try all of them if the designer has properly introduced his or her game's possibility space—risking spending extra time and resources in the dungeon to reap potential rewards.

"Metroidvania"—so named for their dominant applications in those two franchises. The popular definition of Metroidvania is an action game where players move around a continuous and persistent gamespace via platform-jumping. Progressing in these games requires players to collect items and expand their avatar's moveset to reach the end of the game.[67] Classification of which games are and are not Metroidvanias depends on whom you ask. Some feel that Metroidvania games *must* include the level-based character progression found in many roleplaying games. Others feel that Metroidvanias *must* be two-dimensional and reject classifying games that feature persistent exploration in world maps, isometric spaces, and 3D worlds in the genre. Taken as a classification of level style rather than game style, though, Metroidvania is a useful term for describing a particular type of movement and exploration (RPG elements or not).

Many of these spaces are mazes, as discussed in Chapter 4, tour puzzles with multiple branching pathways and dead ends. They are also miniature garden-like in that they have distinct districts and boundaries that offer players the opportunity to explore multiple environment types. Finally, they employ the shaping and expanding possibility spaces of sandbox worlds: players begin in confined areas with a limited number of abilities and gain access to new areas as they learn new moves (Figure 10.24).

Movement through Metroidvania worlds is facilitated through exploration and rewards. Levels in these games greatly employ denial methods to goad players into exploration. Players who explore such mazes are rewarded with power-ups, such as expanded jumping capabilities, better armor, or new weapons that allow access to new areas.

The reliance on rewards for advancement makes finding them critical to moving through the game. As such, these games often employ

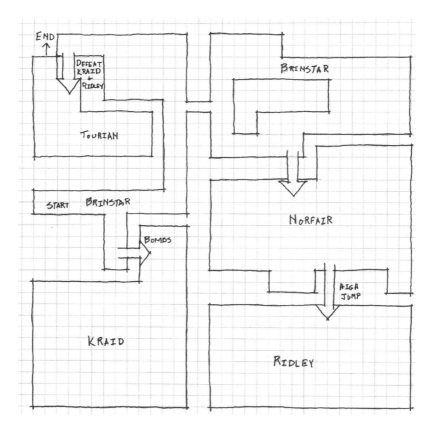

FIGURE 10.24 This sketch of the map from *Metroid* shows how areas are divided into distinct districts and also inaccessible without specific abilities. These worlds are both miniature gardens and shaping spaces that expand as players gain new powers.

the risk–reward uncertainty described in the previous section's *Earthbound* example: showing multiple passages without specifying which one is correct. We may call these *uncertainty nodes*. Lyndon and Moore describe such a node in Eliel Saarinen's Cranbrook Academy of Art. At the end of an important axis on the grounds, Saarinen placed a portico that opens to a pond on the north side, the Cranbrook Art Museum to the east, and the Cranbrook Academy of Art Library to the west (Figure 10.25). This portico, as the climax of the axis, offers a choice of spaces rather than one distinct one. Each path likewise offers its own rich opportunities for exploration rather than a singular space.[68]

Metroidvania worlds rely on uncertainty nodes to encourage back-tracking. If a player chooses a particular path and discovers a new power along the way, he or she is often encouraged to return to explore previously visited spaces with his or her newfound powers. Many of these

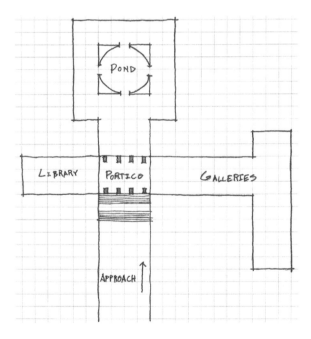

FIGURE 10.25 Eliel Saarinen's Cranbrook Academy of Art, built in Bloomfield Hills, Michigan, in the 1940s. These sketches show how the portico at the end of an important axis on the grounds offers a choice between multiple spatial experiences. Each choice is hierarchically equal to one another, and therefore leaves the choice completely to the occupant.

FIGURE 10.26 *Super Metroid* uses symbolic assets to show players what tool to use to destroy barriers long before they have the proper tool. When players finally gain the tool and understand what wall types to use it on, they can backtrack to open new areas.

spaces have a particular spatial orientation or visual symbol associated with them. In *Super Metroid*,[69] for example, players may from the beginning of the game uncover hidden blocks with weapon symbols drawn onto them (Figure 10.26). These assets consistently appear throughout the game and show players which tool they will eventually find that will allow them to break through. Once the required ability is found, the game shows the player that his or her new power destroys blocks of a certain type, encouraging players to backtrack and enter previously inaccessible areas. The blocks for the Speed Booster are an example of these kinds of symbols. *Batman: Arkham Asylum*[70] utilizes actual level geometry as symbols for using specific tools. Batman's Line Launcher, for example, allows him to cross long horizontal pits over which he cannot gain enough verticality to cross with his default glide. These are introduced soon before Batman gains the launcher. When it is finally received, players know that the mysteriously uncrossable gaps are now within Batman's range of metric possibilities.

Much of how players understand Metroidvania worlds and miniature gardens depends on how designers inform them about the rules of these worlds. However, there are instances where breaking one's own rules can be advantageous. In the last section of this chapter, we discuss the benefits of defining rules and then breaking them.

DEGENERATIVE DESIGN

We have described how designers can build possibility spaces by clearly defining and communicating the rules of game worlds to players, and then letting them have rein to explore them. Such spaces may offer plenty of opportunity for players to stay occupied with possibility space worlds. However, as we saw in the previous chapter, hidden surprises beyond the boundaries of established gamespaces can offer an incredible sense of discovery for players that would otherwise be testing the limits of your game worlds without reward.

Throughout this and other chapters, we have discussed ways to encourage players to explore our games: enticing with denial, rewards, uncertainty nodes, etc. Shigeru Miyamoto's quote from *Game Over: Press Start to Continue* that prefaced Chapter 7 applies here: "What if something appears that should not, according to our game rules, exist?"[71] Such is the purpose of *degenerative design*, design that breaks the established rules of a game and gamespace.

Salen and Zimmerman use the term *degenerate strategies* to describe what is commonly known as *cheating*: utilizing hacks and loopholes in game rules to gain an advantage. In some ways, these can break the reality of the game world, allowing players to move outside its boundaries or uncover the world's artificiality. These may also gain these players an unfair advantage over players who are playing by the rules, which can ruin the experience of playing games.[72] Degenerate strategies, however, also allow opportunities for creative strategies within the rules of a game—barnacle bowling in *Half-Life 2*, bomb jumping in *Metroid*, and so on—that become beloved parts of the games.

Gingold references degenerative design when he discusses the concept of *hide-and-reveal*, the revelation of new spaces when players test the boundaries of miniature gardens. He uses the work of Miyamoto as an example, emphasizing his ability to "tease, goad, and lure" players into finding unforeseen areas in his worlds.[73]

Super Mario Bros. is a notable example of hide and reveal, as its place in the history of games and the comparison of its spaces and those of its contemporaries reveal the power of its own degenerative design. *Super Mario Bros.* was one of the first games to feature horizontally scrolling levels that were unique to one another: many players had not seen such gamespaces before. In this way, the ability to scroll left to right already broke many previous gameplay boundaries. However, players who ducked on pipes could find underground passages. Players who jumped in certain spots or at certain blocks that appeared to be plain brick were likewise rewarded with secret treasures or beanstalks into secret cloud worlds. In *Super Mario Bros.*, Miyamoto established that the screen scrolled left to right, that question blocks held items and that brick blocks did not, and then completely threw these rules out the window to surprise and delight players. Once these were a part of the understood logic of *Mario* games, new logic was offered in subsequent titles, such as the white blocks players could duck behind and shortcuts under quicksand found in *Super Mario Bros. 3*. When designers establish rules, they should also be open to the idea of breaking them in ways that do not break the logic of the game, but instead provide exciting discoveries for players.

SUMMARY

In this chapter we have discussed the assumptions of game players, writers, and spatial designers regarding how designed spaces respond to the world around them. We have learned how the design elements described in other chapters support the idea of games as self-contained immersive systems, but how their reliance on players make them systems for meta-communication. We have studied how these competing relationships offer the opportunity for distinct play styles and unique occurrences that result from the rules of games, known as emergence. Emergent elements of games highlight how games are not simply containers for linear stories, but also spaces that offer interactive possibilities to players.

These spaces of possibility are enhanced by visualizing the space as miniature garden worlds that contain myriad environments for players to explore. Visualizing these spaces as miniature gardens in the Japanese tradition gives us guidelines on how to introduce possibility to players: overviews, tours, and defined but ever-expanding boundaries. Japanese garden design also informs the way we direct players through these spaces: through the careful design and placement of landscape features and level geometry that highlights and emphasizes places of interest.

Such miniature garden worlds and possibility spaces benefit from the designer limiting players' interaction until they are ready to learn more about the world's possibilities. We explored this idea as shaping, teaching by slowly introducing the elements of possibility within a space. Worlds that teach through direction but also entice exploration through uncertainty are the calling card of the popular Metroidvania level style. These worlds reinforce exploration through rewards and shaping through denied access to new areas until rewards are earned. These spaces also encourage risk-taking, as they present players with multiple, equally enticing paths.

Finally, we learned how despite the discussion of setting up, teaching, and creating possibility through rules, designers should embrace opportunities to also break their own rules. These expand the possibility spaces of games in ways often delightful to players, and reward those who test the limits of game worlds.

Through this chapter and the ones preceding it, we have seen a variety of spatial types, orientations, methods, and tricks for assembling game worlds. In Chapter 11, we will describe how such built spaces become *patterns* and explore how patterns might be applied in computer-generated game worlds.

EXERCISES

1. **Drawing exercise**: Using Jason VandenBerghe's player personality method, map out your own player personality type.

2. **Writing prompt**: Map out three theoretical player personalities. Describe a game that you would design for each, describing its mechanics, its theme, its depth, etc.

3. **Drawing exercise**: Play a game that could be described as having a "miniature garden" space. Draw a diagram of its world, showing the different regions and how they reflect different landscape types.

4. **Digital exercise**: Graybox a level that gives you a tour or overview. What does the overview show players and how does this prepare the player for interacting with the level?

5. **Drawing exercise**: Find a vista in a game world where you can see a significant portion of the world (common in open-world games or roleplaying games). Diagram the way that elements in a given view create visual "forces" that draw the player's eye. Look for any environmental art assets arranged in triads.

6. **Game-testing exercise**: Create a graybox level meant to direct players to a specific point (or use one that you created in previous exercises from this chapter). Does your use of environment art, overviews, tours, and visual "forces" effectively direct them to the intended goal?

7. **Writing prompt**: Play a Metroidvania-style game. How does the game limit or direct your exploration? How does the game use symbolic assets to build associations that help you figure out your next steps? How does the game employ choices to encourage exploration?

8. **Game-testing exercise**: Have a player play a Metroidvania game he or she has never played before. Does the game effectively communicate potential pathways for the player or does he or she get stuck often? If the latter, what could the game do to better communicate potential pathways for the player?

ENDNOTES

1. Tanaka, Tan. Early Japanese Horticultural Treatises and Pure Land Buddhist Style: Sakuteki and Its Background in Ancient Japan and China. In *Garden History: Issues, Approaches, Methods*, ed. John Dixon Hunt. Washington, DC: Dumbarton Oaks Research Library and Collection, 1992, p. 79.
2. Slawson, David A. *Secret Teachings in the Art of Japanese Gardens: Design Principles, Aesthetic Values*. Tokyo: Kodansha International, 1987, p. 125.
3. Ebert, Roger. Games vs. Art: Ebert vs. Barker | Roger Ebert's Journal | Roger Ebert. Movie Reviews and Ratings by Film Critic Roger Ebert | Roger Ebert. http://www.rogerebert.com/rogers-journal/games-vs-art-ebert-vs-barker (accessed July 14, 2013).
4. Salen, Katie, and Eric Zimmerman. *Rules of Play: Game Design Fundamentals*. Cambridge, MA: MIT Press, 2003, p. 450.
5. Salen, Katie, and Eric Zimmerman. *Rules of Play: Game Design Fundamentals*. Cambridge, MA: MIT Press, 2003, p. 449.
6. *Dragon Quest III*. Chunsoft (developer), Enix (publisher), June 12, 1991. Nintendo Entertainment System game.
7. *Ultima IV: Quest of the Avatar*. Origin Systems (developer and publisher), September 16, 1985. PC game.
8. Bartle, Richard. Hearts, Clubs, Diamonds, Spades: Players Who Suit MUDs. MUSE: Multi-Users Entertainment Limited. www.mud.co.uk/richard/hcds.htm (accessed July 14, 2013).
9. Wyatt, James. *Dungeon Master's Guide*. Renton, WA: Wizards of the Coast, 2008, pp. 8–10.
10. VandenBerghe, Jason. Applying the 5 Domains of Play. Speech given at Game Developers Conference from UBM, San Francisco, CA, March 27, 2013.
11. Heidegger, Martin. *Being and Time*. New York, NY: Harper, 1962.
12. Norberg-Schulz, Christian. *Genius Loci: Toward a Phenomenology of Architecture*. New York, NY: Rizzoli, 1980.

13. Buchanan, Peter. The Big Rethink: Lessons from Peter Zumthor and Other Living Masters | Campaign | Architectural Review. *The Architectural Review.* http://www.architectural-review.com/the-big-rethink-lessons-from-peter-zumthor-and-other-living-masters/8634689.article (accessed July 14, 2013).
14. Kimmelman, Michael. The Ascension of Peter Zumthor. *The New York Times.* http://www.nytimes.com/2011/03/13/magazine/mag-13zumthor-t.html?pagewanted=all&_r=0 (accessed July 15, 2013).
15. Norberg-Schulz, Christian. *Genius Loci: Towards a Phenomenology of Architecture.* New York, NY: Rizzoli. 1979. Print. p. 5.
16. *Final Fantasy.* Square (developer and publisher), December 17, 1987. Nintendo Entertainment System game.
17. *Final Fantasy XIII.* Square Enix (developer and publisher), March 9, 2010. Playstation 3 game.
18. Glasser, A.J. Final Fantasy XIII Review. Game Pro. http://www.gamepro.com (accessed July 18, 2013).
19. Venturi, Robert. *Complexity and Contradiction in Architecture.* Second Edition. New York, NY: Museum of Modern Art Department of Publications, 1977, pp. 56–68.
20. Campbell, Jeremy. *Grammatical Man: Information, Language, and Life.* New York, NY: Simon and Schuster, 1982.
21. Campbell, Jeremy. *Grammatical Man: Information, Language, and Life.* New York, NY: Simon and Schuster, 1982, p. 102.
22. Salen, Katie, and Eric Zimmerman. *Rules of Play: Game Design Fundamentals.* Cambridge, MA: MIT Press, 2003, p. 158.
23. Salen, Katie, and Eric Zimmerman. *Rules of Play: Game Design Fundamentals.* Cambridge, MA: MIT Press, 2003, p. 162.
24. Morningstar, Jason. Tabletop Design Principles. Speech at East Coast Game Conference from IGDA, Raleigh, NC, April 24, 2013.
25. Squire, Kurt, and Henry Jenkins. Henry Jenkins. MIT—Massachusetts Institute of Technology. http://web.mit.edu/cms/People/henry3/contested-spaces.html (accessed July 18, 2013).
26. *La Mancha.* Pie for Breakfast Studios (developer and publisher), 2018. Tabletop literature card game.
27. *Half-Life 2.* Valve Corporation (developer and publisher), November 16, 2004. PC game.
28. Gingold, Chaim. Miniature Gardens and Magic Crayons: Games, Spaces, and Worlds. Master's thesis, Georgia Institute of Technology, 2003.
29. Gingold, Chaim. Miniature Gardens and Magic Crayons: Games, Spaces, and Worlds. Master's thesis, Georgia Institute of Technology, 2003, p. 7.
30. *Pikmin.* Nintendo EAD (developer), Nintendo (publisher), December 2, 2001. Nintendo GameCube game. It is worth noting that this game was inspired by Miyamoto's own gardening hobby. In many ways, the comparison to a miniature garden is very literal here, as the environments in *Pikmin* are conceived as gardens where the miniaturized player and Pikmin can explore.

31. Gingold, Chaim. Miniature Gardens and Magic Crayons: Games, Spaces, and Worlds. Master's thesis, Georgia Institute of Technology, 2003, pp. 7–8.

32. Gingold, Chaim. Miniature Gardens and Magic Crayons: Games, Spaces, and Worlds. Master's thesis, Georgia Institute of Technology, 2003, p. 9.

33. Anthropy, Anna. Pilgrim in the Microworld. Auntie pixelante. http://www.auntiepixelante.com/?p=1244 (accessed July 19, 2013).

34. *Breakout.* Atari (developer and publisher), 1978. Atari 2600 game.

35. Sudnow, David. *Pilgrim in the Microworld.* New York, NY: Warner Books, 1983.

36. *Super Mario Bros.* Nintendo (developer and publisher), September 13, 1985. Nintendo Entertainment System game.

37. *The Secret of Monkey Island.* Lucasfilm Games (developer), Lucasarts (publisher), October 1990. PC game.

38. *Dragon Quest VIII: Journey of the Cursed King.* Level-5 (developer), Square Enix (publisher), November 15, 2005. Playstation 2 game.

39. *Super Mario 64.* Nintendo EAD (developer), Nintendo (publisher), September 26, 1996. Nintendo 64 game.

40. Gingold, Chaim. Miniature Gardens and Magic Crayons: Games, Spaces, and Worlds. Master's thesis, Georgia Institute of Technology, 2003, p. 12.

41. Church, Doug. Formal Abstract Design Tools. Gamasutra. http://www.gamasutra.com/view/feature/131764/formal_abstract_design_tools.php?print=1 (accessed July 20, 2013).

42. *The Legend of Zelda: A Link to the Past.* Nintendo EAD (developer), Nintendo (publisher), November 21, 1991. Super Nintendo game.

43. Bogost, Ian. *Persuasive Games: The Expressive Power of Videogames.* Cambridge, MA: MIT Press, 2007, p. 64.

44. *Don't Look Back.* Distractionware (developer), Kongregate (publisher), 2009. Internet Flash game. http://www.distractionware.com/games/flash/dontlookback/

45. *The Stanley Parable.* Galactic Cafe (developer and publisher), October 17, 2013. PC Steam game.

46. *Dead Space.* Visceral Games (developer), Electronic Arts (publisher), October 14, 2008. Xbox 360 game.

47. Slawson, David A. *Secret Teachings in the Art of Japanese Gardens: Design Principles, Aesthetic Values.* Tokyo: Kodansha International, 1987.

48. Slawson, David A. *Secret Teachings in the Art of Japanese Gardens: Design Principles, Aesthetic Values.* Tokyo: Kodansha International, 1987, p. 15.

49. *New Super Mario Bros. U.* Nintendo EAD Group No. 4 (developer), Nintendo (publisher), November 18, 2012. Nintendo Wii U game.

50. *Super Mario Bros. 3.* Nintendo EAD (developer), Nintendo (publisher), October 23, 1988. Nintendo Entertainment System game.

51. *Super Mario World.* Nintendo EAD (developer), Nintendo (publisher), November 21, 1990. Super Nintendo game.

52. *The Legend of Zelda: Ocarina of Time.* Nintendo EAD (developer), Nintendo (publisher), November 21, 1998. Nintendo 64 game.

53. Slawson, David A. *Secret Teachings in the Art of Japanese Gardens: Design Principles, Aesthetic Values.* Tokyo: Kodansha International, 1987, pp. 56–57. This is around the same time that the board game Go, originally known in China as Weiqi, is said to have appeared in Japan.

54. Slawson, David A. *Secret Teachings in the Art of Japanese Gardens: Design Principles, Aesthetic Values.* Tokyo: Kodansha International, 1987, p. 58.

55. Slawson, David A. *Secret Teachings in the Art of Japanese Gardens: Design Principles, Aesthetic Values.* Tokyo: Kodansha International, 1987, p. 60.

56. Gingold, Chaim. Miniature Gardens and Magic Crayons: Games, Spaces, and Worlds. Master's thesis, Georgia Institute of Technology, 2003, p. 23.

57. *Minecraft.* Mojang (developer and publisher), November 18, 2011. PC game.

58. Slawson, David A. *Secret Teachings in the Art of Japanese Gardens: Design Principles, Aesthetic Values.* Tokyo: Kodansha International, 1987, p. 82.

59. Slawson, David A. *Secret Teachings in the Art of Japanese Gardens: Design Principles, Aesthetic Values.* Tokyo: Kodansha International, 1987, p. 102.

60. Slawson, David A. *Secret Teachings in the Art of Japanese Gardens: Design Principles, Aesthetic Values.* Tokyo: Kodansha International, 1987, p. 92.

61. Slawson, David A. *Secret Teachings in the Art of Japanese Gardens: Design Principles, Aesthetic Values.* Tokyo: Kodansha International, 1987, pp. 92–93.

62. *Journey.* Thatgamecompany (developer), Sony Computer Entertainment (publisher), March 13, 2012. Playstation 3 game.

63. *Grand Theft Auto IV.* Rockstar North (developer), Rockstar Games (publisher), 2008. Xbox 360 game.

64. Lyndon, Donlyn, and Charles Willard Moore. *Chambers for a Memory Palace.* Cambridge, MA: MIT Press, 1994, pp. 83–86.

65. *Earthbound.* Ape and Hal Laboratory (developers), Nintendo (publisher), June 5, 1995. Super Nintendo game.

66. Pryor, Karen. *Don't Shoot the Dog! The New Art of Teaching and Training.* Rev. ed. New York, NY: Bantam Books, 1999, pp. 35–67.

67. Parish, Jeremy, Benj Edwards, and Chris Sims. "Metroidvania Origins: Vol. 1" *Retronauts.* Podcast Audio. June 19, 2017. https://retronauts.com/article/405/retronauts-episode-104-chronicling-metroidvania

68. Lyndon, Donlyn, and Charles Willard Moore. *Chambers for a Memory Palace.* Cambridge, MA: MIT Press, 1994, pp. 7–10.

69. *Super Metroid.* Nintendo R&D1 (developer), Nintendo (publisher), March 19, 1994. Super Nintendo game.

70. *Batman: Arkham Asylum.* Rocksteady Studios (developer), Eidos Interactive (publisher), August 25, 2009. Xbox 360 game.

71. Sheff, David. *Game Over: Press Start to Continue.* New York, NY: Cyberactive, 1999.

72. Salen, Katie, and Eric Zimmerman. *Rules of Play: Game Design Fundamentals.* Cambridge, MA: MIT Press, 2003, pp. 271–274.

73. Gingold, Chaim. Miniature Gardens and Magic Crayons: Games, Spaces, and Worlds. Master's thesis, Georgia Institute of Technology, 2003, p. 18.

CHAPTER 11

Working with Procedurally Generated Levels

Each pattern describes a problem which occurs over and over again in our environment, and then describes the core of the solution to that problem, in such a way that you can use this solution a million times over, without ever doing it the same way twice.

—CHRISTOPHER ALEXANDER, *A PATTERN LANGUAGE*[1]

We don't want another cheap fantasy universe, we want a cheap fantasy universe generator.

—TARN ADAMS, CREATOR OF *DWARF FORTRESS*[2]

This book is heavily focused on handmade level design, and why not? As we have seen, the design of games and their levels is a highly human-centric discipline: designers create experiences that affect players and give them agency over expressive micro-worlds. Handmade levels can be effective pieces of art and architecture, but sometimes making levels by hand is inefficient: they take too much development time or a dedicated level designer is too expensive. In these cases, there is computer-generated, or *procedural*, level design. While sometimes seen as being at odds with crafted level experiences, procedurally made levels provide lots of content quickly and can even make your game infinitely replayable—a new set of levels every session!

In this chapter, we will discuss approaches to pattern-based and procedurally generated levels that fit into human-centric architectural approaches to level design. We will look at examples of pattern-centric design in architecture that give us an idea of how to implement procedural systems that respond to human needs. We will then use these precedents to understand how level designers might implement systems that mix and match handmade level scenes in procedural ways. Lastly, we will return to our concept of modular assets to show how designers should organize assets for use in procedural systems.

What you will learn in this chapter:

How I learned to stop worrying and love PCG

Pattern languages

Blending handmade design with procedural generation

HOW I LEARNED TO STOP WORRYING AND LOVE PCG

I have to admit, I am a relative newcomer to the world of procedural content generation (PCG), where an artificial intelligence (AI) computer program constructs parts of a game, including environments.[3] Beyond a few adventures in the procedurally generated dungeons of *Diablo* or attempts to learn *Dwarf Fortress*, a fantasy world simulation game with computer-generated histories, PCG was foreign to me. As someone who works with authored environments, I viewed PCG with skepticism: why would anyone want to put artists and level designers out of a job?

This is a completely wrongheaded approach to PCG: the goal is not to eliminate the human portion of visual art and environment design, but to extend a human's ability to create digital worlds. PCG gives games great replayablity without the need for a human to manually create thousands of levels. What turned me around was collaborating on several projects with Mike Treanor and Josh McCoy, who in 2012 worked on *Prom Week*.[4] In *Prom Week*, players shape the interactions between high school students during the week leading up to the prom. These interactions are chosen by the player, but also run by a social simulation program that helps create different stories every time the player plays the game. Working with Treanor and McCoy taught me a lot about the intersections between human-authored content and AI. Likewise, through them I collaborated with Anne Sullivan and Gillian Smith, two PCG researchers whose research focuses on the intersections between AI, electronics, and hand-crafted art (Figure 11.1).

The point of all this is to illustrate how PCG designers are applying their work to areas of human authorship for the purpose of extending or enhancing hand-crafted content. In her essay, "Procedural Content Generation: An Overview," Smith describes several different approaches to PCG, among them *simulation-based, constructionist, constraint-driven,* and *optimization* approaches. Simulation-based approaches construct worlds by starting with a base environment and running a simulation that affects its layout and geometry (Figure 11.2). Smith uses the example of a landmass upon which simulations for erosion and climate would be run.

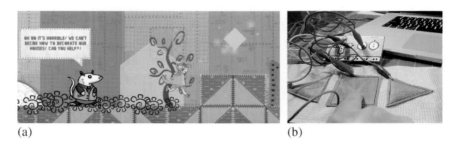

(a)   (b)

FIGURE 11.1   Addie's Patchwork Playground is a game prototype that I created with Anne Sullivan. A player controls an on-screen character (Addie) with a controller made of a quilt with conductive fabric. The game lets players control the environment by collecting and placing quilt patches.

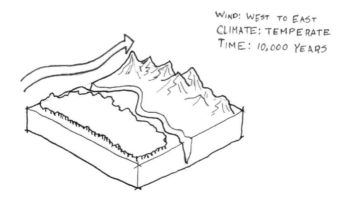

FIGURE 11.2   A sketch showing the basic concept of a simulation-based PCG system.

The amount of in-simulation time that the simulation runs (hundreds or thousands of digital years), determines the state of the world when the player is ready to enter it. Constructionist systems take handcrafted environmental chunks and arrange them randomly to create different types of levels (Figure 11.3). This type of system was used in *Canabalt*[5] and *Spelunky*,[6] where environments are randomly generated constructs built from hand-crafted platforms and rooms. Constraint-driven systems are those where environments are generated by arranging assets whose relationships to other assets are defined by the designer (Figure 11.4). Smith uses the example of an environmental generation AI knowing that table objects should be surrounded by chair objects to describe this system. Lastly, the optimization approach involves humans at an end-user level: educating the game on what to do next either through their play or through a rating system (Figure 11.5).

While not an exhaustive list, these approaches describe ways to blend handmade and procedural level design. Artists and level designers can create level pieces while PCG designers create the rules by which those pieces are assembled. Smith describes several levels of assets used in PCG level design systems, ranging from large *experiential chunks* of levels (big areas of level geometry), down to *subcomponents* (individual

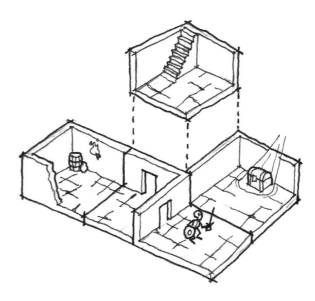

FIGURE 11.3 A sketch showing the basic concept of a constructionist PCG system.

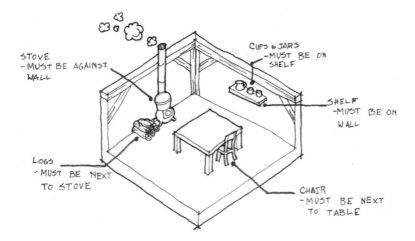

FIGURE 11.4   A sketch showing the basic concept of a constraint-driven PCG system.

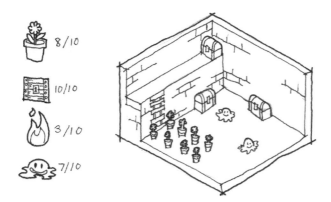

FIGURE 11.5   A sketch showing the basic concept of an optimization PCG system.

art assets). The granularity of the system determines what level of content the level designer should create. For less granular systems a designer might create whole sections of levels, while in more granular systems designers would create assets with constraints defined by a script (Figure 11.6).

Again, this is not an exhaustive explanation of PCG level design systems—many talented people have already published works describing them in more detail. This should at least prepare you, though, for how this chapter will explore the topic. This chapter will mainly focus on

CHUNK

COMPONENT

TEMPLATE

SUB-COMPONENT

FIGURE 11.6 Varying levels of granularity in PCG level systems require different types of assets and different preparation from level designers.

constructionist approaches to PCG. These systems in particular align with architectural pattern languages. With these tools, the level design side of the level designer/PCG designer can take an architectural approach to working with PCG level construction models.

PATTERN LANGUAGES

In 1977, the seminal book *A Pattern Language: Towns, Buildings, Construction*[1] was released. In the front bookflap, author Christopher Alexander writes that a goal of the book is to provide spatial elements and explanations of them so readers could design their own houses.[7] This is accomplished by describing *patterns*—or spatial and material configurations—that create specific life experiences for the occupant. One such pattern, for example, describes how a designer should strive to make living spaces no more than four stories high, since research shows that anxiety increases for occupants at higher levels. Patterns such as *Zen views* or creating paths of well-lit areas, described elsewhere in the book, are other examples of Alexander's patterns.

Alexander's patterns have found their way into building codes and even into the campus plan of the University of Oregon as described in a follow-up to *A Pattern Language* called *The Oregon Experiment*.[8] These patterns have affected industries outside of architecture and urban planning as well such as web development and computer science.

Patterns in Game Design

As a field that is greatly influenced by the history of design, game development has used Alexander's patterns as well. Taking this book out of the picture, influential game developers such as Katie Salen, Eric Zimmerman,[9] and Jesse Schell[10] have all looked to Alexander's patterns as influences on their own game design analysis. Two dissertations, one by Kenneth M. Hullett and another by Denise Bacher, even look at the "patterns" of level design. Hullett's dissertation, "The Science of Level Design: Design Patterns and Analysis of Player Behavior in First-Person Shooter Levels,"[11] presents a kit of parts for first person arenas and how they respond to the needs of player types. Bacher's thesis, "Design Patterns in Level Design: Common Practices in Simulated Environment Construction,"[12] describes patterns found in several game genres including action, strategy, role-playing, adventure, and sport games, describing common elements that they share. These explorations are useful as "designer's notebook"[13] documents—works chronicling common design elements that others may implement in their own work.

In his GDC 2018 talk, "The Nature of Order in Game Narrative," Schell selects fifteen of Alexander's patterns that he believes characterize basic elements of life and compares them to common game narratives. Starting with Alexander's previous book, *A Timeless Way of Building*, Schell describes qualities that create good space, such as completeness, comfort, exactness, egoless-ness, and others. These spaces are pleasing to occupants and exist for their own sake, without calling too much attention to themselves in the way a landmark or other expressive space might. In terms of our previous examples from the work of Hildebrand on architectural pleasure, these qualities have a lot in common with *refuges*, where humans feel safe and comfortable. From this he highlights Alexander's design method, which is patterned on techniques that game designers would later describe as playtesting and iteration. Schell's description of Alexander's patterns focused on those for determining the best design for those who would use a space and finding a spatial language that would meet their needs.

Game designer and educator Chris Barney modeled his Spring 2018 course "Spatial and Temporal Design" at Northwestern University after Alexander's work. The course project was to build a pattern language for level design so students could learn to recognize patterns in game worlds and implement them themselves. On his Medium.com blog, *Perspectives in Game Design*,[14] Barney analyzes the concept of pattern language beyond the patterns and into Alexander's reasons for the patterns as Schell had done. One of his goals was to understand how the *grammar* of using patterns creates a design language that allows for variations in how the patterns are implemented. Core to his explorations are the Alexander quote that begins this chapter, describing the patterns as *solutions to problems* rather than nice spaces. Barney immediately separates himself from previous efforts with this outlook. Rather than finding *tropes*, he searches for the negative player experience that level design patterns are created to fix. In defining patterns then, students had to present a problem, the pattern itself, and examples of the pattern. One student's pattern from Barney's article, "The Pattern of Temporally Available Space," seeks to fix the problem that "architecturally static levels can become predictable and lose player interest." The pattern itself is that spaces are available at only certain times to players, thus creating more interesting navigation puzzles than static space. Examples would include moving platforms or areas that a guard has looked away from in a stealth game.[15]

Working with Patterns in Level Design

All of this is well and good, but how do these patterns become tools for procedurally generated levels? On their surface, patterns understood as repeatable spatial models make great assets for procedural design systems. Returning to Smith's overview of PCG systems, a pattern like a Zen view could be a 3D model you make as an *experiential chunk* that a level design system could call up. However, the *problem-solving* and *linguistic* elements would not be addressed by this. Depending on your and your PCG designers' skills, you can solve this issue in different ways: from simple constructionist systems made of pattern pieces to systems where the pattern language is the grammar.

On the designer end of the spectrum, it is important to know the type and amount of content a modeler or traditional level designer should create for a pattern language-based system. It is well beyond the scope of this book to describe all of the patterns in Alexander's or others' work. However, it is important for level designers who explore patterns in level design to understand how to interpret these patterns for use in their games. Some patterns are very specific spatial constructs that allow only narrow interpretations while others are vague concepts that can be interpreted many ways.

We will use the patterns of *Zen view* and *Temporally Available Space* as examples. In the case of the former, there are very few ways to imagine such a construct (except maybe whether the hole is on a floor, wall, or ceiling). However, the same experience could be created several different ways: windows, holes in a surface, gaps in foliage, and so on. In this way, you create variations that can appear several times while still feeling fresh (Figure 11.7). A pattern like this has very *static interpretations* in that it allows for few variations: it needs a small hole in a surface that gives you a hint of what lies beyond. You can add interest by creating different versions made with different assets or different theming. Something like Temporally Available Space, on the other hand, has very *fluid interpretations*. In one variation it could be a platform that moves back and forth over a pit, in another it could be the area out of a searchlight's view— there are many possibilities (Figure 11.8). From breaking down patterns in this way, we start to see where some of them become larger chunks (the wall for a Zen view and the approach to it) and some are constructed of smaller components and sub-components (a searchlight, a guard, a moving platform, etc.) By understanding how these pieces work, systems of many types can be created: simpler constructionist ones to more complicated grammar-based ones. Likewise, you can see how granular you can get with your assets: some like Zen view can be made from large level

FIGURE 11.7 Sometimes patterns in a pattern language are very specific and allow for fewer spatial variations. Creating them out of different types or differently themed pieces adds variation that keeps them fresh if the player encounters the pattern multiple times.

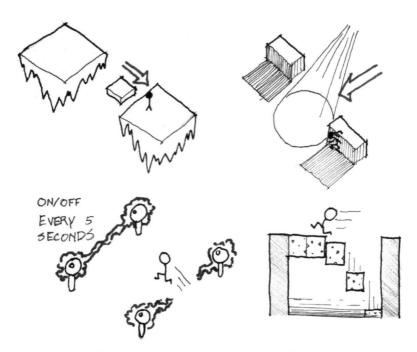

ON/OFF
EVERY 5
SECONDS

TEMPORALLY AVAILABLE SPACE

FIGURE 11.8 Other patterns in a pattern language describe general concepts that can be interpreted in many ways.

pieces. Others like *lights on two sides of a room* can be constructed with individual assets (a model of a lamp) programmed with embedded rules (place across from another light) for the PCG system.

Patterns provide interesting ways to conceive of PCG systems. In my own experience, I have seen lots of PCG level design systems concentrated on the act of constructing a level, but which has no thought given to trying to make the level interesting for players. On the other hand, the best PCG system designers I know have a genuine interest in moving beyond mere creation to generate exciting levels. In the next section, we will look at how these designers are blending handmade level design-thinking with procedural systems to create interesting works.

BLENDING HANDMADE DESIGN WITH PROCEDURAL GENERATION

So far, we have seen what PCG level design systems do, their types, and elements that they use to construct levels. Likewise, we have looked at architectural theories that support this type of design and address a key problem: how do you create a computer algorithm that addresses human spatial experience?

Patterns are a great idea, but ideas are not worth much unless we can use them in a practical way. This section will try to address this by finding ways to tie architectural design theory to PCG system implementation. Earlier in the chapter, I said that a major focus would be constructionist systems because that is where much of my own experience with these systems lies. However, designers of more complex systems should find concepts here that help them extend these ideas into their own work.

Scenes as Patterns

Let us start by bridging a gap between the concepts in this chapter and the methods used in the rest of the book: designing parts of levels that address human experience through patterns is the same as the scene-based design we have focused on so far. Many patterns in Alexander's work share the components of a good scene: an easily understood space that feels complete and self-contained. Thinking of patterns as scenes is important for keeping the problem-solving and language components of pattern language design intact. Connecting patterns to scenes also helps us think of the patterns in a very practical way: as single-screen or room-sized chunks of gameplay.

Smith mentioned the games *Canabalt* and *Spelunky* in her description of constructionist PCG systems, where the generator takes premade level pieces and arranges them. Most of the chunks in these two games are also scenes: they occupy about a screen's worth of space. They are also well designed in how they facilitate player use of their respective games' core mechanics. Players may see scenes multiple times in such a system, but by creating them in such a way that they address player experience, the levels will at least feel interesting. Scene-based design is about creating an experience for the player that addresses the core mechanics and intended experience of the game, so thinking of patterns as scenes bridges the gap between the coldness of computer algorithms and the sensitivity of human design.

As we have seen, thinking of patterns as scenes allows variations on the pattern, allowing even similar scenes to feel different. In *No Man's Sky*,[16] for example, the game regularly uses the pattern of a landmark on a high hill: often a mineral-rich rock (Figure 11.9). Though the pattern is recognizable in multiple environments, it is no less welcome since it usually provides valuable resources and a vantage point.

FIGURE 11.9   In No Man's Sky, patterns emerge in the game's procedurally generated universe, such as landmarks on high hills. This both provides players with valuable resources and gives them a place to look over a planet's landscape. In this way, the pattern supports the core gameplay of exploration.

Throughout the book, we have discussed the benefits of repeating level architecture, from communicative modular assets to repeated challenges that invite mastery. In the case of scenes, patterns, and PCG level design systems, repetition can be a weakness if level chunks are designed without thought, but a strength if they address player needs. Returning to the example of *Canabalt* and *Spelunky*, these games generate levels in large chunks (Figure 11.10). *Spelunky* is a 2D indie game where the players is an explorer diving into procedurally generated caves, fighting monsters, and searching for treasure. It uses a constructionist system where level chunks are pre-designed and arranged by an algorithm. Despite the inherent weaknesses of constructionist systems, many elements can change how one chunk of level is experienced: the placement of enemies (enemies are considered a "component" in PCG systems), the level geometry that is around the chunk, and the theme of the level. *Spelunky* is a game whose level geometry sometimes repeats, but which also has enough "X-factor" elements, such as enemies, that change the experience. According to programmer Darius Kazemi, the game generates levels based on a system that produces a "solution path" to the end of the level and a series of dead end rooms. After this generation, the game does another pass to add enemies and hazards.[17]

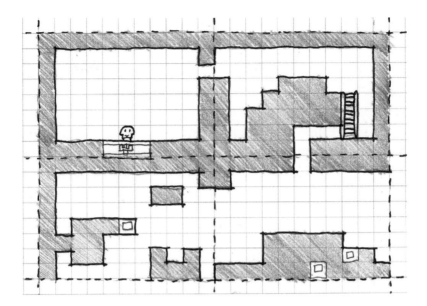

FIGURE 11.10 *Spelunky* creates levels with large level chunks (this diagram just shows what some of these might look like), but the experience of these chunks changes based on the level's theme and the enemies on the screen.

When a game like *Canabalt*, an "endless runner" game where a man in a suit runs across crumbling rooftops, repeats, it is actually a welcome part of the experience. With its arcade-style gameplay, *Canabalt* invites players to dive into its systems and practice toward mastery. Learning how to react to specific scenes is part of this experience, so seeing a specific building that you have already mastered provides a positive rush for players learning the game.

Combining Handmade Design and PCG

One designer specifically researching the intersections between hand-made design and PCG systems is Mark R. Johnson. In his book chapter, "Integrating Procedural and Handmade Level Design,"[18] he describes several games that integrate handmade level content in a PCG system, among them *FTL*,[19] *Spelunky*, and several of his own games. According to Johnson, there are many ways to combine handmade content with PCG systems beyond simply level art assets. In *FTL*, for example, a procedur-ally generated space adventure where players command a starship, the game's map and order of gameplay events is determined by the computer. Players must react to these random events to progress, but at intermittent points there are premade story sections that move the game's plot forward.

We have already described *Spelunky*, but Johnson also highlights how the game includes special quest items in its environments, the order of which was determined by the game's designer Derek Yu. This adds a storytelling component to these games that would not otherwise exist in a purely PCG level design system. In Johnson's own game *Ultima Ratio Regum*, he generates levels based on a system of tagged level elements. He uses the example of an altar, a common element of many levels that is based on both the need for an altar in an area of a level and the theme of a level. Instead of simply implementing an altar in the way a pure PCG system would, the game is concerned with being architecturally consistent, so elements of theming and consistent design are written into the system as well.

Night of the Living Handmade/PCG Case Studies

Johnson shows us that it is important to remember that levels are not just geometry when you are designing your PCG level design systems. Two case studies, both coincidentally featuring zombies, showcase this in different ways: Valve's *Left 4 Dead*[20] series and my own *Dead Man's Trail*.

PCG Alternative Architecture in Left 4 Dead

Left 4 Dead is an online shooter where players team up in groups of four to pass through zombie-infested territories (some modes allow an additional four players to be the zombies). Like many Valve games, the levels are strongly handmade with lots of visual indicators to aid player navigation. The game's PCG component comes in the form of The Director, an AI that evaluates the players' performance and places zombies and resources accordingly. Though the levels never change, the way players experience them from one playthrough to another can be vastly different. In Smith's breakdown of PCG systems, she lists enemies as *components*, which are non-spatial elements that can add variety to PCG environments.

In *Left 4 Dead*, a zombie horde might be a rare sight in games where the players are struggling and might be frequent when players have mastered the game. Likewise, the game features special zombies with their own distinct powers that add challenge to each level. The Tank, for example, is a large and brutishly strong zombie that normally appears in climactic points near the end of campaigns as a boss monster. However, the Tank can appear among regular hordes and in narrower areas. This greatly changes the nature of the matchup between players and this enemy: normally the Tank appears in a prospect-scaled space that allows players to move far away while in narrow spaces it is harder to avoid (Figure 11.11).

FIGURE 11.11   PCG does not only consist of how level geometry is arranged but also how dynamic components, such as enemies, are placed. *Left 4 Dead* uses its special zombies as building blocks for new ways to see familiar handmade levels. The space in which a player encounters an enemy can drastically change his or her experience of fighting it.

The Witch—another powerful zombie that can instantly kill players if she is startled by loud movement—likewise changes the way players use levels, as they must move slowly to avoid being attacked. Remember that enemies are an important part of level design and can become *alternative architecture*, player-sized elements that impact the route players take through a level. Enemies define space as well as level geometry: players change their behaviors to overcome or avoid confrontation with powerful enemies. In PCG systems focused on enemies, this can greatly impact the experience of a level's design.

Mixing Methodologies in Dead Man's Trail

Dead Man's Trail, a zombie survival adventure game that friends of mine and I have been developing in our spare time, utilizes PCG systems in several parts of the game to add replayability. In the game's travel mode, players guide a truck full of survivors across the United States, maintaining their health, supplies, and vehicle integrity. Travel mode incorporates random events, often including moral dilemmas, that can shake up the experience (Figure 11.12). These events are handmade with branching outcomes, dialog boxes, and hand-drawn artwork. In the Unity engine, which we are using to develop the game, the events are represented by GameObjects that contain the scripts and art assets for each event (Figure 11.13). The script that drives the travel mode shuffles these GameObjects like a deck of cards and spawns them at developer-defined intervals.

FIGURE 11.12 A travel event in *Dead Man's Trail*.

FIGURE 11.13 The GameObject that holds the script and assets for the same travel event. The events are listed in the Hierarchy list on the left of the screen and their attributes are listed on the Inspector window on the right. These GameObjects can be shuffled like playing cards so that each journey is unique.

Among these events are also looting events that take players into the second major mode of the game: looting mode. In this mode, players explore 3D isometric cities for supplies and must leave before a zombie horde arrives. Looting mode uses a simple constructionist system to assemble levels. Each level is broken into tiles that are loaded by the game when looting mode starts. Each tile is a scene (in the Unity sense: a file that contains a section of gameplay) with about a city block's worth of gamespace (Figure 11.14). When players reach the exit of a tile, a new file is loaded and gameplay continues. Each tile is a large experiential chunk of level space designed to make players take risks for valuable items. The core mechanics of looting mode are having players "get in and get out" for items while avoiding a zombie horde, so the levels are designed to make players waste time: most item-spawners are located in narrow areas.

Through playtesting, we were able to define a number of patterns that support gameplay and overcome problems that would unfairly get testers killed. One such pattern is *narrow spaces with two exits*, where there is always a way to escape from difficult situations in case zombies clog an area (Figure 11.15). Another is *"rooms" with loops* that allow players to put a piece of level geometry between them and the zombies to find another exit. Sometimes these two patterns were made by the same piece of level geometry. These patterns drove our design for the handmade portions of the levels: each tile could be broken into nine scenes (in the level design theory sense) that represented interesting patterns. In most tiles, four of these scenes were purely for traveling to other areas (empty pathways), but five (the four corners and one in the center) are well suited for gameplay patterns (Figure 11.16).

As I said at the beginning of the chapter, my own personal history with PCG level design is limited and I am still learning the best ways to design for these systems. While repetition can be limited in *Dead Man's Trail* by creating lots of these tiles in several different level themes (small town,

FIGURE 11.14   A level tile from *Dead Man's Trail*, the basic building block of its constructionist-style level building system.

FIGURE 11.15   Defining patterns helped us limit gameplay problems and make more user-responsive level chunks. This one represents narrow spaces with two exits and "rooms" with loops.

farm, forest, mountain, and so on), it still exists if the player sees a theme many times. A way to improve this system in future games might be to avoid using whole tiles as level building blocks and instead use our nine-scene design method. The system could assemble nine smaller chunks into a level tile, increasing variation. As with *Left 4 Dead* though, the

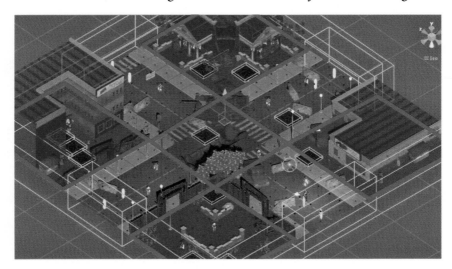

FIGURE 11.16   A tile from *Dead Man's Trail* broken into nine parts. Those shaded in red were designed as gameplay scenes.

FIGURE 11.17 Zombies in *Dead Man's Trail* add an additional layer of randomness to the experience. Even repeated tiles can feel different depending on how zombies have blocked off passage through areas.

procedural way that zombies are added to maps adds an additional layer of randomness to the gameplay, especially since our zombies are supposed to be avoided (Figure 11.17). Testers have noticed repeating tiles, but still experience them differently based on how many zombies are in an area. An easily reached exit might be unavailable if the horde has arrived.

Both games show a variety of ways that handmade content can be arranged in PCG systems. While handmade level chunks can be repetitive, they can be arranged procedurally for more variation. Likewise, enemies, resources, and other gameplay components can be added to change the meaning of repeated spaces: how does a narrow corridor change when you spawn a huge monster or lots of little ones in it?

SUMMARY

This chapter addressed an important force in level design: procedural content generation. PCG systems add replayability to your games and lower the workload on level design teams. While traditionally seen as being at odds, PCG systems and handmade level design can coexist nicely with the implementation of architectural pattern theory. Patterns are interchangeable spatial ideas meant to solve problems of human experience in space, so they make great fits for designing content for PCG construction. The types of assets that can be arranged procedurally can also vary: some games create whole universes procedurally while some arrange enemies and items differently to shake up familiar territories. For the handmade level designer, learning about PCG and how to design for it is an adventure worth taking as it can result in some really cool things.

If you think that PCG systems are random, then the next chapter will explore an even less predictable element of game worlds: the players that use them and their social interactions. In that chapter, you will learn how use urban design principles to plan for social interactions in large worlds that support multiple players.

EXERCISES

1. **Writing prompt**: Based on a game you are working on or a commercial game you have played, define five level design patterns that you see or that could solve problems in the game's design. Can these patterns be interpreted in many ways or in only a few ways?

2. **Digital exercise**: Create a series of hand-designed scenes that could be assembled via a constructionist PCG system.

3. **Drawing exercise**: Play a game that features a PCG system for level design. Sketch different scenes or environmental chunks that you see repeating. Make notes of what is different in those scenes (enemy placement, theming, etc.)

ENDNOTES

1. Alexander, Christopher, Sara Ishikawa, Murray Silverstein, Max Jacobson, Ingrid Fiksdahl-King, and Shlomo Angel. *A Pattern Language: Towns, Buildings, Construction*. New York, NY: Oxford University Press, 1975.
2. Adams, Tarn. Re: Adventure Mode Gripes [Online forum comment], August 12, 2006. Message posted to http://www.bay12forums.com/smf/index.php?topic=948.msg12375#msg12375.
3. Smith, Gillian. "Procedural Content Generation: An Overview". In *Game AI Pro 2*, ed. Steve Rabin. Boca Raton, FL: CRC Press, 2015.
4. *Prom Week*. Josh McCoy, Mike Treanor, Ben Samuel and Aaron A. Reed, 2012. Social simulation game.
5. *Canabalt*. Adam Saltsman, 2009. Browser game on Kongregate.
6. *Spelunky*. Derek Yu, 2008. Indie game on Steam.
7. Alexander, Christopher, Sara Ishikawa, Murray Silverstein, Max Jacobson, Ingrid Fiksdahl-King, and Shlomo Angel. *A Pattern Language: Towns, Buildings, Construction*. New York, NY: Oxford University Press, 1975. Front book flap.

8. Alexander, Christopher, Sara Ishikawa, Murray Silverstein, Shlomo Angel and Denny Abrams. *The Oregon Experiment*. New York, NY: Oxford University Press, 1975.

9. Salen, Katie and Eric Zimmerman. *Rules of Play: Game Design Fundamentals*. Cambridge, MA: MIT Press, 2004. pp. 4–5.

10. Schell, Jesse. "The Nature of Order in Game Narrative". Conference talk, San Francisco, March 20, 2018. Game Developers Conference.

11. Hullett, Kenneth M. "The Science of Level Design: Design Patterns and Analysis of Player Behavior in First-Person Shooter Levels". PhD diss., University of California Santa Cruz, 2012.

12. Bacher, Denise. "Design Patterns in Level Design: Common Practices in Simulated Environment Construction". Master's thesis, Iowa State University, 2008.

13. Rogers, Scott. *Level Up! The Guide to Great Video Game Design*, 2nd edition. San Francisco, CA: Wiley, 2014.

14. Barney, Chris. "A Pattern Language for Games". *Perspectives in Game Design* (blog) Medium.com, May 21, 2018. https://perspectivesingamedesign.com/a-pattern-language-for-games-3d1c6849a3cd

15. Chang, Zhihui. "Design pattern for Temporally Available Space". From Barney, Chris. "A Pattern Language for Games". *Perspectives in Game Design* (blog) Medium.com, May 21, 2018. https://perspectivesingamedesign.com/a-pattern-language-for-games-3d1c6849a3cd

16. *No Man's Sky*. Hello Games (developer), August 9, 2016. Playstation 4 game.

17. Kazemi, Darius. "*Spelunky* Generator Lessons". *Tiny Subdiversions* (blog). http://tinysubversions.com/spelunkyGen/

18. Johnson, Mark R. "Integrating Procedural and Handmade Level Design". In *Level Design: Processes and Experiences*, ed. Christopher W. Totten. Boca Raton, FL: CRC Press, 2016, pp. 218–242.

19. *FTL*. Subset Games (Developer), 2012. Indie game on Steam.

20. *Left 4 Dead*. Valve South (developer) and Valve Corporation (publisher), 2008. PC game on Steam.

INDUSTRY PERSPECTIVES: INTERVIEW: CHRIS PRUETT

I conducted this interview with Chris Pruett in 2013. Chris is the head of 3rd Party Publishing at Oculus VR and is the founder and CEO of Robot Invader. This interview was conducted right after his company released the Android game *Wind-Up Knight*. He was previously Senior Developer Advocate at Google, responsible for bringing games to Android, and a senior programmer at Activision/Vicarious Visions. He is the author of Chris's Survival Horror Quest, an online blog in which he analyzes both famous and obscure horror games.

Can you name a game, level, or level designer that has left an impression on you? Why?

I am continually impressed with the design of the mansion in the original *Resident Evil*. Though the moment-to-moment gameplay involves shooting zombies, finding keys, and solving puzzles, the meta-game is about tracing routes through the maze-like mansion, finding shortcuts, and growing the size of the traversable space. Your job in the early *Resident Evil* games is to recursively unlock areas of the mansion until it becomes a complex, interconnected space, which you must then traverse as efficiently as possible to avoid excessive zombie encounters. In the end, it's the traversal of the (initially simple, eventually complex) map that requires the most brainpower; the zombies and puzzles are simply activities to complete on the way. This sort of design isn't unique to *Resident Evil*, but I think there are few games that do it better. It's very difficult to design this kind of space, but the *Resident Evil* games make it look easy.

Are there any media outside of gaming that you find inspire your work?

I am a big fan of Haruki Murakami's novels, particularly *The Wind-Up Bird Chronicle*. I love the way the events in his writing take place deep below the surface of the narrative.

I really enjoy film as well, though I watch a lot less than I used to. Occasionally I will discover a comic book that sends me reeling for a while. Most recently that award goes to two Japanese books, *Nijigahara Holograph* and *Sayuri*.

Describe your level design process—how do you begin? What tools do you use (on or off the computer)?

The process varies dramatically with the format of the game. For a platformer like *Wind-Up Knight*, the level design cannot be started until the core mechanics are set in stone. So we do a lot of test levels with just boxes hanging in the air until we're able to lock down some of the core move set. From there we block out all of the levels using boxes and (often placeholder) enemies. Only when all of the levels are close to finished do we sit down and sort them into categories (generally by theme and difficulty), and only after that do we start to apply real art. Throughout this process we are constantly throwing things away and reworking ideas. *Wind-Up Knight* went through several months of iteration before we started generating levels that actually appeared in the final game.

For our new, as-yet-unannounced project, the process is extremely different. This game is something a little more akin to the *Resident Evil* example I gave above: it's a space that is slowly opened over time for the player to explore. In this case, I started with a reasonable map layout (architectural plans for a house) and began by mapping the traversal of the player through it over the course of the game. From there I have applied a method called a puzzle dependency diagram which allows me to document the flow of puzzles through the space (puzzle C can't be completed before puzzles A and B are finished, etc.) So the design of the map and the contents of the rooms have been defined since very early in the project, and now our main job is to ensure that the pacing of progression matches the experience we intend to provide to the player.

What is your process for playtesting your levels?

We try to have as many people who are not on our team test as possible. It's useful to watch playtesters, but we also use automated analytics recording to identify issues. On *Replica Island*, I recorded the spots at which players died on a server, and then used that data to generate heat maps over the level geometry, which told me very quickly where the frustration points were.

Do you find art and atmospheric effects an important tool for communicating with players? Any specific examples?

This is also highly dependent on game style, but generally speaking, every tool at your disposal must be used to communicate with players. It's much harder than you might initially assume to send a player a message. Even giant flashing text on the screen will be missed (or ignored, or misunderstood) by some of your audience. So yes, we use art, sound, vibration, animation, user interface—everything we can to get messages through the glass.

More specifically, Thomas Grip, the brains behind *Amnesia: The Dark Descent*, has a very useful idea about sense of presence. This is specifically applicable to atmospheric games. The idea is to remove all elements that might damage the feeling that the player is there in the world. This often causes heads-up display elements to be entirely removed, but it doesn't stop there. Grip talks about removing unbelievable or out-of-place game elements whenever possible to maintain the sense of presence at all costs. For example, some developers like to leave jokes in the background art of their games (e.g., a movie poster named after the developer), but the sense of presence doctrine requires such elements to be removed.

How do you teach players to utilize your levels (without use of the GUI)?

There's nothing wrong with graphical user interface, or more generally, non-worldly elements to ensure communication with the player. For example, *Metal Gear Solid* would be unplayable if it lacked the 2D question mark icons that appear above alerted enemies' heads. Better to ensure that the message is understood than to maintain some concept of realism.

That said, a really good level designer guides the players through a space without them realizing that they are being guided. *Halo 1* does this very well, especially in outdoor environments. Subtle hills and efficient-looking valleys are used to guide the player exactly along the route that the designers want him or her to go without obvious breadcrumb items or GUI.

For our current secret project, we attempt to force the player down a specific path by giving him or her things to do along that path. For example, if players finds themselves with a key in their inventory and one locked door, it is likely that they try the door before exploring other areas. If there is something interesting beyond the door, we expect them to pass through the doorway and explore it. In this way we try to lead players through the game without explicitly forcing them down a fixed path. We also allow for certain areas to be visited in any order before a choke point is reached (which is what the puzzle dependency diagram I mentioned above describes). *Gone Home* is a recent example of a game that does this very well.

How do you entice players to explore game levels (without use of the GUI)?

In a game like *Wind-Up Knight*, which is highly linear and does not require exploration to progress, we do it by dangling hard-to-reach items and secret passages in front of players without telling them exactly where they are. For example, players might see an alternative path, perhaps a subway below their feet, with items to collect. In order to find the entrance to that area, they'll have to go back and look for it, though players who are only interested in progression can skip it and move on.

In our new project, exploration is the core element of the game, so we hope that players approach the experience with a willingness to explore already in their minds. That said, we use narrative (dropping clues for the player to think about while solving other problems), key items (via the recursive unlocking scheme I mentioned above), and puzzles (which often require searching an area to complete) to promote and reward exploration.

If a player is lost in one of your levels, how can he or she get back to where he or she is supposed to be (without using the GUI)?

In *Wind-Up Knight*, this basically isn't possible. It's a platformer, it only moves in two dimensions, and the player's options are to progress or die.

In our new game, we generally prevent players from getting lost by constraining the size of the explorable space. Eventually they will unlock a larger space, but it's a collection of spaces they have explored before, with a few new spaces hanging off the edges. Though the space enlarges, players are already familiar with most of it. We try to ensure that there are only one or two new places to go at any time, so if a player is lost, he or she can simply find an area he or she is unfamiliar with and explore that. That direction is always a forward path.

How do you direct the actions of players in your levels? How do you encourage players to play in undirected ways?

In our new game, we are using a technique common to many adventure games, which is to provide bits and pieces of problems and allow the player to resolve them out of order. For example, at any given time the player should have at most three outstanding problems to solve (where problems are things like a locked door, a combination lock, or the location of an item). These problems can be solved in any order, and once they are solved a new set of problems will be presented. More generally, each problem itself is solved by completing a series of steps, and if the player gets stuck on one step, he or she can go work on a different step for a different problem. The goal is to ensure that we almost never reach a point at which there is only one correct thing to do to progress. When those choke points do arrive, we try to make the next step as obvious as possible.

This way players solve problems at their own pace, in the order that they prefer, but stay within the progression structure that we've defined for them.

What laws of level design have you developed in your own work that any designer should know? What should they avoid?

For platformers: define metrics and use them. All of your jumps should be the same size, or from a small set of predefined sizes. The height of your platforms, the distance from a warning to an enemy, the minimum space between challenges: all of this should be rigorously defined and consistent from level to level. The player is trying to find patterns in your design, and it's your job to provide them.

For adventure-style games: give the player no more than three problems to solve at any given time. Make areas that need to be investigated stand out from the background; the challenge should be to figure out what to do when you get there, not finding the exact pixel to click on. Be very wary of mixing "what do I do next?" challenges with "doing the next thing is mechanically hard" challenges. Give players extra information if they try to investigate something more thoroughly. Close off paths that are no longer relevant to the game.

For all games: checkpoints and save reloads must start players facing the direction that they were facing when the game saved. Make the difference between traversable and non-traversable areas exceedingly obvious.

You've done a considerable amount of game analysis for your blog, Chris's Survival Horror Quest. What spatial elements or types (room sizes, room types, architectural elements, etc.) have you seen throughout multiple games?

One common spatial theme in horror games is descent. Horror games almost always involve delving deeper and deeper underground. The general theme here is areas for which there is no clear escape route. This is often paired with one-way transitions (e.g., jumping into a hole). The message to the player is simple: you can't escape. You must press forward. It is a very oppressive message.

How do you utilize your study of other games to influence your own designs?

For some types of games, such as my current project, horror games provide a direct influence. I'm not making a horror game at the moment, but perhaps a close cousin to the genre, and things like the recursive unlocking setup are extremely valuable. But more generally, I think that thinking about games, and specifically why the designers made the decisions that they did, helps me think much more critically about my own games. Interestingly, I learn a lot more from the games that fail than from the games that succeed.

What place can environment art play in lending to an environ-
ment's mood? How can environment art allow designers to com-
municate with players?

I think this is a big piece of Grip's sense of presence theory. If the art
distracts from the world, it will damage the sense of presence and hurt the
overall effectiveness of the game. If it pulls the player in, the opposite effect
is achieved. *Silent Hill*, with its hellish Otherworld version of the regular
level geometry, is king of this.

Once you've established how player characters move and react
to player input, how do you best design game environments to
address these capabilities?

Player input and mechanics come first. Once those are defined, we
define the basic level metrics (pit sizes, platform heights, etc.) Once we
have those things we can start to combine elements to make for complex
strings of input. It's hard but very fun!

In Wind-Up Knight, *the player has a considerable number of moves*
he or she could utilize—jumping, fighting, shield use, and rolling.
How did you teach players to utilize these actions appropriately in
levels, and how did you reinforce them throughout the game?

We start the player off with just one action—jump—and then slowly
add new moves over time. By level 9 they have the four basic inputs
defined, but it's not until much later, sometime around level 16 or 17, that
they actually have access to all of the Knight's moves. This is tricky—we
want to ease the player into the game, but we also want to get to the complex move sets as quickly as possible, as that's where the really fun level
designs come into play.

CHAPTER 12

Influencing Social Interaction with Level Design

A good city street neighborhood achieves a marvel of balance between its people's determination to have essential privacy and their simultaneous wishes for differing degrees of contact, enjoyment or help from the people around.

—JANE JACOBS, FROM *THE DEATH AND LIFE OF GREAT AMERICAN CITIES*[1]

You have to design and program differently. Combat action in an MMO is so different to combat in a first-person shooter.

—JOHN ROMERO[2]

Thus far, we have explored level design from a generalist point of view, not focusing on any specific genre or play style. Rather, we have looked at how games may use architectural design principles and engage players cognitively through spatial means. While not a specific genre, multiplayer environments—environments in which more than one player is active at one time—deserve their own investigation.

Like the levels of all games, multiplayer gamespaces exist to embody a game's mechanics. Whether the game is a first-person shooter game or a massively multiplayer online roleplaying game (MMORPG), it must embody the actions players take in it: shooting, running, exploring, dungeon-crawling, etc. However, games must do so in a way that supports multiple players, either simultaneously or in turns, competitively, cooperatively, or merely coexisting, all in the same space. Beyond having the players in the space, designers of multiplayer levels must also address how to have players within these spaces interact with one another meaningfully.

Urban design professionals have been tackling many of the same challenges for decades. In this chapter we explore several urban design ideas and precedents, and learn how the structures of multiplayer game worlds can help facilitate player interaction.

What you will learn in this chapter:

Emergence and social interaction

Learning from urban emergence

The importance of spawn points and quest hubs

Houses, homes, and hometowns in games

EMERGENCE AND SOCIAL INTERACTION

There is nothing more emergent than the interaction between people. If emergent systems such as Conway's *Game of Life* are the result of exact and perfectly performed rules on a computer, they are much less dramatic than the interactions between human beings. Humans have moods, ups and downs, varying states of health, aches, pains, and varied personal histories that all influence how successful they are at interacting or playing with others.

Let us once again consider Ubisoft creative director Jason VandenBerghe's player type model from "Applying the 5 Domains of Play."[3] VandenBerghe's player personality elements were *openness to experience, conscientiousness, extraversion, agreeableness,* and *neuroticism.* The five domains of play were *novelty, challenge, stimulation, harmony,* and *threat.* The player elements respectively correspond with:

How players feel about entering into a game experience

How they address tasks in the game

Whether they play best alone or with others

Whether they care about a larger narrative

Personal sensitivity to in-game events

Similarly, the domains of play correspond with factors of how game worlds are constructed:

How many interesting things are there to see?

Are challenges immediate and fast, or do they require practice?

When obstacles are met, what amount of action do they call for and with how many people?

Do we cooperate with others, or are they the obstacle?

Do our actions in the game have agency to affect some larger narrative of the game world, or is the current session self-contained?

What are the rules for discouraging bad behavior?

Based on these factors alone, we can already see how design concepts for multiplayer worlds are generated. By entering design with a purpose, we can begin to build our worlds around how we want players within to interact with one another.

In previous chapters, we also described Jason Morningstar's concept of the "fruitful void,"[4] the interactions that occur between the explicit rules of the game and the personalities of individual players. Morningstar argues that rules in a game are just a small piece of the overall social system of multiplayer tabletop games. They "inspire as much as they constrain" players, merely facilitating and focusing interactions that players may have had anyway based on their personalities.

Morningstar's approach is much like the "experience is key" approach that we have been taking with level design. Apart from a core mechanic, there is also a *core shared experience* driving the design of multiplayer gamespaces. If one takes the core mechanics or genre of his or her multiplayer game—a shooter, MMORPG, persistent virtual world, etc.—and asks the questions above of it, he or she can find a set of guidelines for designing his or her world. VandenBerghe's player personality elements allow us to put ourselves in the shoes of different types of players. For example, we might be tasked with creating a first-person shooter deathmatch level for multiple players. What sort of player would that cater to? On the VandenBerghe chart, let us say that the player prefers realism/exploration in the novelty quadrant, not work/skilled[5] in the challenge quadrant, mechanics/player vs. player

(PvP) for the harmony quadrant, and thrill/multiplayer in the stimulation quadrant (Figure 12.1). Now that we have a theoretical player or player type, we should create a map that can best support this type of gameplay. Let us ask ourselves the domains of play-based questions from above to envision our multiplayer first-person shooter (FPS) deathmatch map:

> *How many interesting things are there to see?* There can be interesting things, but players often will not look at them for very long.

> *Are challenges immediate and fast, or do they require practice?* Challenges are immediate, as players will be quickly shooting at one another. Practice occurs over many matches.

> *When obstacles are met, what amount of action do they call for and with how many people?* Assuming even skill levels, the player with the better firing position or better gun will win.

> *Do we cooperate with others, or are they the obstacle?* In deathmatch every other player is an enemy.

> *Do our actions in the game have agency to affect some larger narrative of the game world, or is the current session self-contained?* Sessions are self-contained.

> *What are the rules for discouraging bad behavior?* Players can be banned from games.

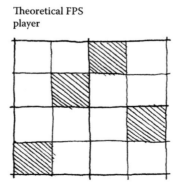

Theoretical FPS
player

FIGURE 12.1 The VandenBerghe chart mapping for a theoretical FPS deathmatch player. Designing a map for such a player can give us insight into what kind of experience we can create with our levels.

Though not a very technical process, we already have insight into what kind of map to create. The map does not need to have a lot of interesting scenery or embedded narrative, but it should be navigable. Spaces should flow easily, feature few dead ends, and lots of loops. Players should not take very long to get to one another, and there should be nodes that channel player activity and allow for large battles. Perhaps some sort of interesting scenery or brighter lighting can be employed in the node areas. The level should have multiple floors so players can gain a prospect–refuge advantage over one another. Lastly, there should be few other obstacles in the level, as the game should focus player attention on one another[6] (Figure 12.2).

From our initial ideas, we can go through the steps outlined in Chapter 3, "Level Design Workflows," including grayboxing and playtesting with the target audience. The hope is that by designing for the right kind of experience and player, the level will be a success by meeting its design goals.

As this example has shown, player personalities and gameplay goals can show us a lot about what kind of map to create. If we keep our eyes on creating a quality experience, our level designs can bring players to

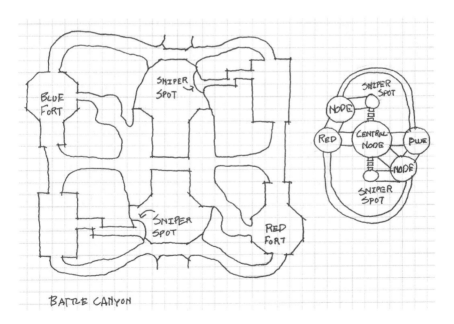

FIGURE 12.2 Sketches of a theoretical level based on the criteria derived from comparing our genre/mechanics (FPS deathmatch) to our player type from FIGURE 12.1, and finally our questions based on the five domains of play.

the fruitful void of memorable gameplay moments. This technique can be applied to many different types of gameplay and many different types of players as well, giving us a strong starting point for many multiplayer levels. In the next section, we explore precedents for facilitating social interactions in urban design and learn what a hotly contested debate over how cities are arranged can teach us about constructing game levels.

LEARNING FROM URBAN EMERGENCE

Cities are always the physical manifestation of the big forces at play: economic forces, social forces, environmental forces.

> The thing that attracts us to the city is the chance encounter, it's the knowledge that you'll be able to start "here" and end up "there" and go "back there," but that something unexpected will happen along the way.

> —QUOTES FROM THE DOCUMENTARY FILM
> *URBANIZED*, DIRECTED BY GARY HUSTWIT[7]

In many ways, cities are the ultimate emergent system: a collection of thousands, if not millions, of people brought together in a space. As the 2011 documentary film *Urbanized* highlights, cities are created and changed by, for, and sometimes even in spite of the wishes of inhabitants. Indeed, the destinies of cities are shaped by citizens, special interest groups, government officials, regulations, and economic and social forces. Due to these factors, studying cities, their design, and the history of urbanism can be helpful for game designers in understanding how space facilitates social interaction and gives players agency over the conditions of multiplayer gamespaces.

As we saw in our explorations of Kevin Lynch's urban design principles, cities utilize discreet elements—landmarks, paths, nodes, edges, and districts—to facilitate movement within. When considering the people part of this environment, Lynch's spatial rules also seem to aid human interaction: people gather around landmarks or run into one another on the paths between them, districts support different types of activity, etc. Perhaps more importantly, neighborhoods bring a sense of home and belonging. They also produce interpersonal relationships that make people feel safe from some of the negative emergent effects of cities: crime, vandalism, and violence. Allowing for the organic mixing of human activities allows such neighborhoods opportunities for interaction to occur. The history of urban design has even shown us examples of what happens when cities are not planned for facilitating positive interactions of residents.

Modernism and Non-Emergent Cities

In the late nineteenth and early twentieth centuries, the city was in a state of flux. Industrialization had packed people into cities looking for work, and cities had therefore become overcrowded. Rich landowners reacted to this demand for housing near industrial sites by packing as many people as possible into tenements for high rents. The result was urban slums like those lamented in the work of Charles Dickens and other nineteenth-century writers.

It was in 1898 that urbanist Ebenezer Howard proposed the *garden city* plan in his book *Garden Cities of To-Morrow*.[8] Howard's plan divided the city into concentric circle districts, which separated the functions of cities, living, working, gathering, moving, etc., from one another (Figure 12.3). The vision of this city was that work could be carried out in manufacturing districts, while housing could be placed among wide country green

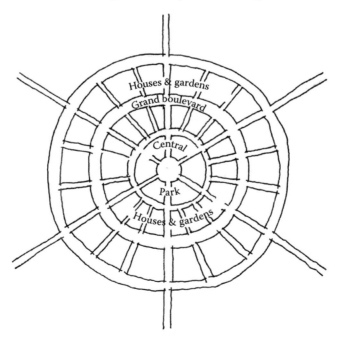

FIGURE 12.3   A sketch reproduction of Ebenezer Howard's garden city plan diagrams from 1898. Each ring of the city houses a separate functional district.

spaces where rent could be kept low. Travel between districts and between interlinked garden cities would occur on large boulevards moving out from the center of the rings.

The garden city movement had a great impact on modern architecture. In particular, Franco–Swiss architect Le Corbusier evangelized the idea of cities where the functions of living were separated. In 1922 he conceived Ville Contemporaine (Figure 12.4), a city plan where inhabitants would live and work within skyscrapers located in the center of the city. Surrounding the skyscrapers were parks and large motorways, which were themselves surrounded by administrative buildings and universities.[9] With Ville Contemporaine, Le Corbusier sought to create the city as a large garden and usher in an age focused on the car and airplane as common transportation types. He saw architecture and urban design as tools for social change and, along with Gerrit Rietveld, Karl Moser, and a number of other famous architects, founded the Congres International d'Architecture Moderne (CIAM) in 1928.[10] This group was responsible not only for formalizing the rules of what is considered to be the modern style of architecture, but also for promoting architecture as a tool for social and political change. Like Le Corbusier, they advocated for urban design to separate

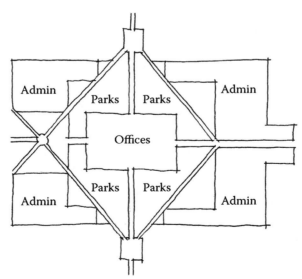

FIGURE 12.4 A plan sketch of Ville Contemporaine, a theoretical city designed by Le Corbusier in 1922. The functions of the city are separated from one another, and transit is done by car and airplane.

the functions of a city into discrete districts; architect Ellen Dunham Jones has described this as being "like modern graphic design" in the tendency to neatly arrange things.[7]

CIAM disbanded in 1959, but its influence on modern architecture is widely felt. While mainly theoretical, several cities were designed by either CIAM architects or architects influenced by their ideas. Le Corbusier himself designed the plan for Chandigarh, India, as the first planned city after India's independence in 1947.[11] Like many of Le Corbusier's theoretical plans, Chandigarh separated different functions into their own districts, with blocks for parkland, industrial areas, and government facilities. Initially, the city was largely empty, though today that has mostly turned around. Even recently, however, visitors have commented that the city is sparsely populated with pedestrians.[12] Attractions such as Le Corbusier's Open Hand statue have had difficulty attracting visitors, but this is felt to be mainly due to government restrictions on visiting these sites.[13]

Another separated-use city, Brasilia, Brazil, makes a somewhat more damning case against Modernist urban planning principles. The city has been described as "beautiful from an airplane, but a complete disaster on foot."[7] Designed by Lucio Costa, the city separates living, working, and administrative facilities among large super-blocks connected with highways. Between are vast green spaces designed to automotive scale. As a result, there are few opportunities for interaction between residents.[14]

Perhaps the most often cited case against Modernist-inspired urban design is the Pruitt–Igoe housing project in St. Louis, Missouri. Completed in 1954 and designed by Minoru Yamasaki, the complex consisted of thirty-three apartment buildings separated by streets and large green lawns. Pruitt–Igoe was originally planned as a publicly owned housing complex in which maintenance money would be generated from rent revenue from the low- and lower-middle-class residents. When new suburban communities enticed middle- and lower-middle-class citizens to leave the city, Pruitt–Igoe was left with only the poorest tenants, and therefore with little opportunity for maintenance income.[15] The decay of the buildings was soon met with decreases in resident population and increases in crime rate. In 1972, demolition on the largely abandoned complex began, which was completed in 1976.[16] Detractors of Modernist planning cited Pruitt–Igoe's design philosophy—isolating the function of living from the rest of the city in favor of having large lawn spaces—as being a major factor in its downfall. Novelist Tom Wolfe commented:

> On each floor there were covered walkways, in keeping with Corbu's idea of "streets in the air." Since there was no other place in the project in which to *sin* in public, whatever might ordinarily have taken place in bars, brothels, social clubs… now took place in the streets in the air.[17]

These examples highlight what happens when interactive elements of space are separated from one another or have large areas of empty space between them. In cities, this can lead to isolation of residents and/or crime. In gamespaces, this has the potential to similarly isolate players from one another or make transitioning between two areas designed for different gameplay styles. While some isolation of the gameplay mechanics in an FPS map is helpful, could you imagine a map where areas for spawning or receiving ammunition are far enough away to make gameplay a chore? Could you imagine an online world where you go to one town to buy armor, another to buy potions, and yet another to receive quests?

A lack of tightly defined mechanics for interaction can lead to anti-social behavior. In the early days of the *Ultima* series, Richard Garriott struggled with how to give players roleplaying freedom while encouraging them to behave in socially positive ways within his worlds. For the single-player experience of *Ultima IV*,[18] this led to the game's theme of becoming a virtuous avatar. An encounter with a player in the wilderness who was enacting the role of a thief a bit too well inspired Garriott to create the reputation system for *Ultima Online*, which kept violent players out of cities and allowed players to police themselves.[19,20]

While these problems with separated interaction and the behavior of players in online worlds seem bleak, Garriott's solutions for mitigating his game's issues through player enforcement resemble urban design principles advocated by a prominent American writer, mother, and advocate for neighborhood preservation.

Jane Jacobs and Mixed-Use Emergent Neighborhoods

In New York City after the Great Depression, a powerful influence on rebuilding the city's broken infrastructure was Robert Moses, an urban planner often called the master builder of New York. Moses was responsible for commissioning many large highways and bridge projects that ran through the city. These structures were responsible for breaking up several neighborhoods and leaving residents isolated from one another. He was also an opponent of public transit and tunnel projects, often opting for bridges and parkways even when other options were less disruptive to the surrounding areas of the city.

One of Moses' strongest opponents was Jane Jacobs, a writer who had lived in Greenwich Village since 1935. In the 1950s, Jacobs began writing for the magazine *Architectural Forum*, focusing on urban development stories. Following a trip to Philadelphia to cover developer Edmund Bacon and his urban design initiatives, Jacobs began to question contemporary urban design practices. She noted that Bacon's plans focused more on high-rise development on sites than the people's ability to use them, which contradicted her own urbanistic ideas: focusing on intimate neighborhoods and interactions between residents. In a lecture she would later give at Harvard University, she said, "The least we can do is to respect—in the deepest sense—strips of chaos that have a weird wisdom of their own not yet encompassed in our concept of urban order."[21]

Jacobs had become a major advocate for neighborhoods once her comments were published in *Architectural Forum*. In the late 1950s she successfully fought against Robert Moses' plans to create an expressway through Greenwich Village. Her struggles with Moses continued over the course of the next decade whenever his plans resurfaced. Jacobs' most influential work in the field of urban design is the book *The Death and Life of Great American Cities*,[22] which outlines Jacobs' own disgust with contemporary urban design principles focused on separated uses and large-scale development. The book instead advocates for preservation of intimate neighborhoods and social spaces.

Key to Jacobs' arguments are her *four generators of diversity* in cities:

1. Multiuse districts that encourage constant use by people

2. Short blocks to allow easy access to amenities and exploration

3. Buildings of varying age so as to vary economic factors

4. Density of population[23]

Jacobs' four generators can greatly influence how we design multiplayer gamespaces to best emphasize the emergence created by the interaction of multiple users. Jacobs uses the term *social capital*, arguing that the socialization that occurs between individuals in a space can yield both social and economic benefits.[24] She cites how a density of people in public places reinforces its safety and develops relationships between users, if only in passing. Eventually, Jacobs' arguments and those of other user-focused urbanists such as Kevin Lynch would become vital to the New Urbanism movement, which emphasized walkable neighborhoods and multiuse districts.

Using our level design vernacular developed throughout this book, it is possible to say that Jacobs' views are well aligned with game designers' seeking of emergent gameplay in multiplayer gamespaces. With a strong focus on planning for the sake of human users, Jacobs' outlook on design can be of great influence for designers of multiplayer spaces.

Integrating Urban Design into Multiplayer Gamespace

Level designers can take both the failures of Modernist urban design and the influences of new Modernism into account when addressing how players may use multiplayer gamespaces. Modeling multiplayer space design principles on Jacobs' own diversity generators and avoiding the pitfalls of Modernist use separations, it is possible to create *four generators of emergence* in multiplayer gamespaces:

1. Multiuse gamespaces that give players access to a variety of mechanics (shopping, talking, fighting, recharging, etc.)

2. Close proximity of functional spaces to one another

3. Spaces for players of different styles, types, or factions

4. Accommodation of player density

To use multiplayer FPS games as an example once again, we may look at how one would model a capture-the-flag level under these principles. Capture-the-flag games divide players into two different teams who compete to capture enemy flags and bring them back to their own base. Maps for this style of game are often symmetrical, with each team having a similar base on a far end of the map on either side of a wide prospect-scaled battle space. The Valhalla map from *Halo 3*[25] is an excellent example of this style, with two bases on either end of a large gulch, featuring intermittent rocks and cliffs for both cover and sniping (Figure 12.5).

Capture-the-flag maps are good examples of how to integrate our four generators into multiplayer worlds. Their rules necessitate certain gameplay styles: defensive shooting by players guarding their team's flag, offensive raiding for those attempting to capture the enemy flag, and runs from

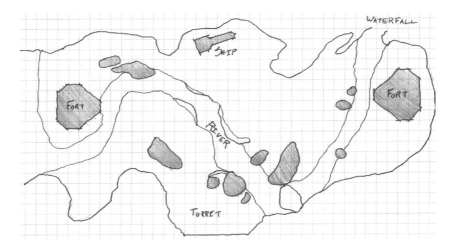

FIGURE 12.5   A plan view of the Valhalla map from *Halo 3*. This map demonstrates the typical structure of a capture-the-flag map: two symmetrically laid out team bases on either side of a large prospect-scaled battle space.

one base to another when the flag has been captured. These requirements also create opportunities for unique gameplay—some players will prefer to hide and snipe into the space between the two bases, and others will take direct paths, fighting opponents head on. Diagrams of the Valhalla map, as shown in Figure 12.6, demonstrate our principles in this fashion. Both bases offer multileveled walkways rather than a direct path to the flag. Flags are cloistered on the bottom level of each base, allowing defensive players the choice to take refuge inside or snipe from upper levels that look out into the gulch. These bases also offer a variety of weapons for players to use: rifles, explosives, etc.

The gulch between the two bases is also multiuse: players can use the tops of cliffs as sniping positions, or sneak between bases or into cover in the river at the bottom. A turret midway through the map offers players the option of gaining a strategic advantage over the other team, and becomes an important landmark for either attacking or defending forces when flags are being transported between bases. While the map as a whole is large, it does not take much time to traverse, so raids can be quick and battle is nearly constant. This largeness offers additional opportunities for the vehicle-based play that is part of the *Halo* franchise, and accommodates the many players that may be in one match. All of this combines to create exceptionally emergent styles of play.

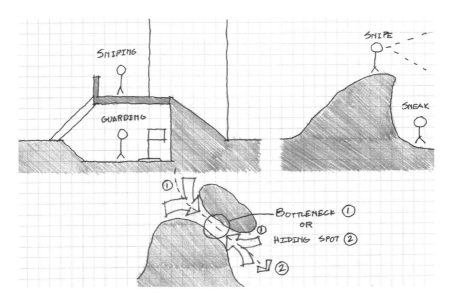

FIGURE 12.6   Diagrams of the Valhalla map show how the design of individual components supports emergent gameplay: bases offer different types of weapons and encourage different defensive styles. Terrain changes in the prospect battlefield allow sniping, vehicle, stealthy, turret, or direct styles of combat.

Towns and cities in massively multiplayer online games such as *World of Warcraft* (*WoW*)[26] also promote emergent social gameplay. In *WoW*, towns contain several gameplay-related amenities such as vendors, places to purchase items, and trainers, non-player characters that help players learn new skills. These may be located on the way to larger settlements or to raiding locations—zones where players and their teams fight game-controlled environmental hazards and foes. Likewise, cities contain many of the amenities of towns, but offer even more gameplay-related functions to further encourage social interaction: inns for rest, taverns for socializing, auction houses for exchanging goods with other players, and banks for storing items. Cities may also feature gathering spaces for specific guilds, organized groups of player characters.

These gamespaces are very much organized under New Urbanist principles and therefore fit into our own gameplay-centered generators for emergence. They feature a mixture of use types that are important for a user's gameplay in *WoW*: training, shopping, socializing, and facilitating quests. The proximity of spaces to one another encourages a constant presence of players traveling between landmarks, and the diversity of vendors or trainers in any given town encourages the mingling of players of different classes and professions (Figure 12.7). In terms of construction, the shops of vendors or trainers within in-game urban spaces utilize consistent symbolic assets: building types and signage. In this way, players of each class can form a language in which symbols are important to them, and seek out these symbols. When buildings of different types intermingle, emergent socialization is not far away.

The islands of battle royale games such as the one found in *Fortnite* mix a large gamespace like an MMORPG world with competitive gameplay. The *Fortnite* island contains urban elements of landmarks, districts, nodes, and so on that facilitate social play, but also types of architecture supporting different competitive styles (Figure 12.8). Players can find high sniping spots, refuge-rich spaces for guerilla tactics, or even isolated spaces for players who prefer to focus on the survival/building mechanics of the game. Since each match takes place on the same island, players also gain familiarity with the space as one would a familiar neighborhood. Combined with the way players enter the environment—jumping from the flying "battle bus" and getting a sky-level overview of the island—players have lots of opportunities to find familiar spaces that fit their play style.

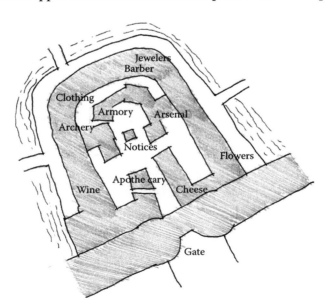

FIGURE 12.7 Urban areas in MMOs such as the Stormwind City's Trade District in *World of Warcraft* offer a multitude of gameplay activities for different types of players within a small proximity, allowing for social interaction to occur.

FIGURE 12.8 The *Fortnite* island follows new urban principles to create a space like an MMO world, but for competitive survival multiplayer. In this way, it balances both social interaction but also the type of small-scale formal elements that encourage different style of competitive play. Players visit this island and get a sky-level overview in each match, so they gain an attachment to the space in a unique way.

The design and the types of functions contained within a multiplayer gamespace help encourage the mingling of different types of players when they follow New Urbanist ideas of multiuse development. While separating uses to focus on singular mechanics may create interesting single-player experiences, multiplayer maps are made more meaningful when they accommodate different types of players. In many ways, the spaces from which players first encounter a gamespace have a lot to do with how they prepare themselves for multiplayer emergence. In the next section, we explore these gamespaces—spawn points and quest hubs—more thoroughly to see how they send players off on the path toward emergent experiences.

THE IMPORTANCE OF SPAWN POINTS AND QUEST HUBS

Throughout the book, we have discussed the importance of pacing in games, alternating high and low action to create manageable gameplay and highlight exciting moments. While many multiplayer games avoid the quiet moments common in single-player experiences, the opportunity to refresh oneself is still a vital part of the experience. In this way, the places in which players appear on multiplayer maps, known as *spawn points*, and the places from which players embark on missions, which we will call *quest hubs*, are of great importance.

Shaping with Spawn Points

In previous explorations of emergent gameplay and possibility spaces, we discussed how games such as *Minecraft*[27] introduce players to the possible mechanics of the game through controlled experiences at the game's opening. As in single-player games, where first levels establish the rules of a world and introduce them to players, the places where players first encounter multiplayer spaces have a great impact on that player's possible strategies. The possibilities present in spawn points and hubs have a great impact on how players may approach their time in a multiplayer game. What weapons are near them as they spawn? What shops can they access? What are the opportunities for leveling up or improving their skills?

Fortnite features a unique take on spawning: players skydive from a flying "battle bus" and get to parachute to a point of their choosing on the game's island environment (within range of the bus's path). This adds an element of risk/reward to spawning—players can choose isolated areas from which they can gear up gradually or urban areas with lots of big upgrades, but likely lots of other players. The overview provided by skydiving lets them assess the risk and shape their initial arrival in the gamespace.

The size of these spaces can greatly affect pacing. In action-oriented multiplayer games such as deathmatch shooter games, spawn points are small and offer a few nearby weapons to get a player moving along—there is no time to linger, only to jump into the game's action. For players appearing on a map, spawn points are often in defensible places isolated from main action nodes but close enough to them so the spawning player can rejoin the fight quickly, as shown in Figure 12.2 and other similar diagrams throughout the book.

In the cooperative multiplayer shooter game *Left 4 Dead*,[28] players begin each level in safe houses—sheltered areas with extra ammunition and health packs. These spaces are in many ways similar to spawn points in other shooter games, as they allow players to quickly recharge and go if they choose. However, they are largely inaccessible to the computer-controlled zombies in the game, and therefore allow players the opportunity to stay and plan their next moves. In this way, these spaces encourage socialization by letting players plan strategies for moving forward through *Left 4 Dead*'s gamespace. The game also features weapon and health caches throughout levels, especially before important large-scale battles. These not only control pacing for the game, but also let players decide how they will approach upcoming challenges based on their individual strengths and play styles.

In open-world or MMO games, players have similar opportunities—refreshing or outfitting themselves, socializing, planning, etc.—but within much larger spaces. These spaces, which we are calling quest hubs, have a great influence on how players explore and learn about multiplayer game worlds.

Shaping Player Interaction with Quest Hubs

In many MMOs and online worlds, players often enter the gamespace in a centralized town or designated beginner's area. In *ActiveWorlds*,[29] a persistent online world, players begin near coordinates 0, 0 on the world map and may move outward from there. Due to the large numbers of players moving through this area, it has become an important in-game commerce hub. *WoW* players begin in a starting settlement or town dependent on their chosen race. These towns have access to trainers for every class, as well as introductory quests specific to the player's chosen race. These activities give players a sampling of available character types they may choose and teach them how to play the game. They also facilitate the establishing of unique play styles by giving access to the game's available classes.

The starting areas in games like *WoW* work in much slower and more deliberate ways than spawn points in multiplayer action games do. These spaces are larger and meant to be carefully explored. They encourage interaction between players, as they are often laid out with a multitude of things to do and quests to undertake. The multiuser dungeon (MUD) *Federation II* (*Fed II*)[30] utilizes carefully planned initial encounters with the game world to teach players how the game works and shape their interaction and gameplay. New *Fed* players are limited to exploring their starting planet until they can purchase a spaceship, which requires gaining a permit and bank loan by utilizing communication commands. This introduces players to some of the basic mechanics of the game and then allows them to venture further once they have mastered these mechanics. Because many of the economic systems that players must contend with to advance are player-controlled, the social hierarchy of the world facilitates interaction with other players.

In *Quests: Design, Theory, and History in Games and Narratives*,[31] Jeff Howard discusses quest hubs like those in MMOs or MUDs, along with similar spaces in single-player games. These hubs, he says, facilitate outward movement of players into the larger world map through the use of quests or missions given by NPCs. Many of these missions require players to travel to other towns, which are themselves quest hubs. As such, these games use quests as a method by which to create tours of the game's possibility space. As players gain more power, movement between hubs and quest selection become easier, giving players more choice over their gameplay experience. Players may also unlock new mechanics as they complete quests.

Federation II's ranking system is based on this experience of travel, learning, and unlocking new abilities. Each new rank in the game opens opportunities to explore new territories and new game mechanics. For example, after the previously mentioned opening quest to get a spaceship, players must pay off that ship by performing cargo-hauling jobs for the Armstrong Cuthbert Company. These hauling missions act as a tour of the game's early planets, and also as opportunities for players to visit social hotspots such as bars. Once players have completed the early hauling missions, they may venture further into space, encountering other players. Eventually, as they move up in rank, they unlock access to the game's other mechanics—stock trading, managing companies, and eventually administrating governments. At this point, players have become the influential characters that newer players will seek out for help.

Enticing Exploration with Side Quests

While emergence is certainly possible if players each have a list of primary quests to take on, more meaningful emergence can only come if players are allowed to customize their travels. For this reason, designers should offer players choices of tasks that are easily findable from their main paths. In many open-world games, the paths between main quests offer opportunities for side quests, tasks or missions that reward players for extra exploration. This type of structure is common in Bethesda Softworks games such as *Elder Scrolls V: Skyrim,* where the game world entices players with views of caves, tombs, towers, and other side quest locations while they travel between major quest hubs (Figure 12.9).

Quest structures in multiplayer RPGs are different than single-player ones, as multiplayer games do not often have a central plot that is advanced by game quests. Some quests or player-defined tasks in multiplayer games may involve more time, players, traveling, and benefit than others. Bigger quests may therefore seem hierarchically more important. Some quests, such as reputation quests in *WoW,* are smaller repeatable tasks that contribute to a larger-scale goal. Traveling to a bar and buying a round of drinks in *Federation II* is not a specific quest item, but it may reap social rewards and can therefore be considered a player-defined side quest. Multiplayer gamespaces should offer both large-scale main goals and opportunities for smaller player-defined goals. These give players opportunities to define how they spend their time in these worlds.

Quest hubs form important nuclei to large game worlds. Players move outward from hubs and into quests and then return to hubs to refresh supplies, gain new weapons, or get new quests. In games that offer guilds, they

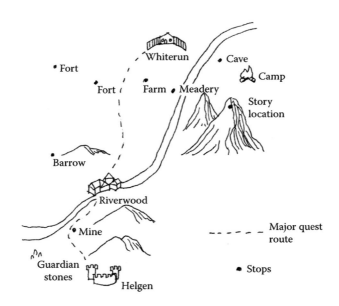

FIGURE 12.9 This diagram of *Skyrim* shows how players are sent from one town to another. Side quests are easily found along the paths between main quest hubs. As such, main quests encourage travel to different parts of the world, within which players may freely access side quest content.

may also be home bases for players to inhabit with social groups. We next explore the concept of a hometown in a game, and discover the benefit that players receive from having personalized territories.

HOUSES, HOMES, AND HOMETOWNS IN GAMES

While quests hubs act as facilitators of travel throughout games, many players may find themselves favoring specific territories based on their level, their progress through a game's story, or the social player groups that frequent these locations. Some games take this idea a bit further and allow players to have customizable places that become their own. The previous example of *ActiveWorlds* allows players to set up their own houses and shops, which helped create the commerce hub surrounding the world's entry point (Figure 12.10). *Second Life*[32] allows players to craft their own houses and shops and even to sell objects in the game.

The ability of players to customize elements of games gives them additional feelings of agency over the gameplay experience. Customization has been an

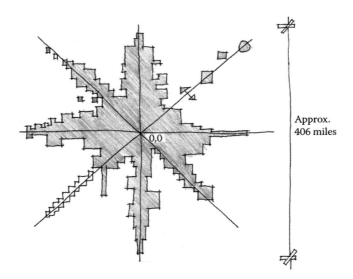

FIGURE 12.10 A map diagram of *ActiveWorlds* when it was known as *Alpha World* showing the world's urban sprawl mass as it emanated from the coordinates 0, 0. The area surrounding coordinates 0, 0 became an important commerce hub, as many players passed through there. The ease of remembering coordinates along the game's x axis (such as coordinates 3, 0), y axis (0, 3), or diagonals (3, 3) allowed these stretches to become similarly valuable as the world sprawled outward.

element of gaming at least as far back as the advent of modern commercial wargaming, which is often attributed to the game *Little Wars* created by H.G. Wells in 1913.[33] These games, such as those in the popular *Warhammer*[34] series, allow players to customize their own figurines with paint and other modifications, even as their stats are determined by common rules. In free-to-play mobile and online games, customization has proven a powerful moneymaking opportunity. In 2011, it was revealed that the economy for hats in the game *Team Fortress 2*,[35] for example, totaled over $50 million.[36]

Beyond the financial benefit to publishers of in-game customization, the ability for players to customize a part of multiplayer gamespaces also has social benefits. Jane Jacobs cites the importance of having a consistent feeling of familiarity with the people in one's neighborhood. Jacobs argues that the consistent presence of "public characters" such as shopkeepers and other residents helps them protect each other or facilitates introductions between residents who are known to have common interests.[37] Having consistent social groups of players is helpful for creating common emergent histories of gameplay events. Clans and guilds can be given the opportunity to meet in in-game social spaces such as towns or taverns. Supplementary spaces ancillary to games, such as chatrooms or forums, likewise allow for the organization of competitions, clans, and rivalries that give multiplayer games meaning.

As mentioned, some game worlds allow players to design and build within them, creating their own home that others may visit. This is useful in games where the primary mechanic is socialization between players, such as *Second Life*. *Second Life* allows players to shape the game world themselves. This allows user-created content to be attractions or allows for socialization through visiting one another's space. This freedom has allowed multiple subcultures to evolve, such as those who use the customizable world for historic reenactments, cultural events, artistic exhibitions, or playing sports.

Animal Crossing: New Leaf[38] utilizes the idea of in-game homes to facilitate interaction between players. Players are the mayor of their own town, and may customize it, their player avatar, and their own house as they wish. Social features of the Nintendo 3DS, such as wireless Internet access and StreetPass—a function that allows passing 3DS devices to communicate and exchange data—allow players to visit each other's towns, exchange items, and give each other gifts. These features allow players to share their in-game achievements and help one another progress through the game by sharing resources.

SUMMARY

In this chapter, we have explored how understanding player personalities can inform decisions we make when creating gamespaces for multiplayer games. Focusing on the development of player interactions rather than simply the execution of gameplay mechanics allows for gameplay to enter the fruitful void where interesting and memorable gameplay events occur.

We also explored historic urban design examples to see how the interaction between large groups of people has been managed. We compared Modernist design principles that separated functions and New Urbanist principles that advocate for mixed-use user-focused urban spaces. We saw how the mistakes of the Modernists should not be repeated in our own multiuser game worlds, and how mixed-use gamespaces can facilitate the interaction between players of different skills, styles, and types.

We saw how the structure of the spaces through which players enter multiplayer worlds, spawn points and quest hubs, affects player interaction with the world. Spawn points provide players with a quick opportunity to refresh resources before entering energetic multiplayer battles. Quest hubs encourage exploration and socialization, and introduce gameplay mechanics through carefully crafted introductory quests. These hubs also encourage the exploration of the larger game world, with quests often sending players to other hubs—cities, towns, planets, etc.—thereby giving them tours of the world. These travels also provide players with the opportunity for self-guided interactions and goals.

Lastly, we discussed how the player's ability to customize his or her own place in these worlds, whether by establishing relationships with specific players or customizing his or her own surroundings, encourages a sense of belonging. These custom in-game "homes" also provide an incentive for socializing in games through visits or gift-giving, allowing players to help one another progress in the game.

In the final chapter, we explore how sound design affects our perceptions of gamespace. Included are explorations of architectural rhythm, ambient sound, and spaces with little or no sound at all.

EXERCISES

1. **Writing exercise**: Map out three theoretical player types according to Jason VandenBerghe's system. Answer the domains of play-based questions from the beginning of the chapter to define an outline for a level you would create for those player types.

2. **Drawing exercise**: Play any online multiplayer game. Sketch diagrams of at least three different spaces that encourage a unique strategy or facilitate a specific style of gameplay.

3. **Drawing exercise**: Using proximity diagrams, plan a map that blends spaces that cater to different styles of players. Do so for these different types of games: a multiplayer first-person-shooter, an MMORPG with multiple character classes (mage, barbarian, thief, cleric, etc.), a battle royale game where players can choose to be aggressive or defensive.

4. **Drawing exercise**: Play an MMO or an open-world game. Travel the primary path between two main story events and document your path with a map. Mark any potential side-quests or other points of interest you find along the way. Notice how they are spaced out. How does this entice exploration or extend gameplay?

ENDNOTES

1. Jacobs, Jane. *The Death and Life of Great American Cities*. New York, NY: Random House, 1961, p. 59.
2. Romero, John. John Romero at BrainyQuote. Famous Quotes at BrainyQuote. http://www.brainyquote.com/quotes/quotes/j/johnromero483970.html (accessed July 30, 2013).
3. VandenBerghe, Jason. Applying the 5 Domains of Play. Speech at Game Developers Conference from UBM, San Francisco, March 27, 2013.
4. Morningstar, Jason. Tabletop Design Principles. Speech at East Coast Game Conference from IGDA, Raleigh, NC, April 24, 2013.
5. I say "not work" for brevity and because these games provide lots of instant gratification. However, many FPS players work very hard to become more skilled at their games, so in reality FPS deathmatches actually fall somewhere in the middle of not work and work.
6. Technically the final question regards banning for bad behavior, but that is more of an administrative question than a level design one.
7. *Urbanized*. DVD. Directed by Gary Hustwit. S.l.: Swiss Dots, 2011.
8. Jacobs, Jane. *The Death and Life of Great American Cities*. New York, NY: Random House, 1961, p. 17.
9. Jacobs, Jane. *The Death and Life of Great American Cities*. New York, NY: Random House, 1961, pp. 21–22.
10. Fazio, Michael W., Marian Moffett, and Lawrence Wodehouse. *A World History of Architecture*, 2nd ed. Boston, MA: McGraw-Hill, 2008, p. 507.
11. Business Portal of India: Investment Opportunities and Incentives: State Level Investment: Chandigarh. Business Portal of India: Government of India, Indian Economy, Investment, Incentives, Trade, Infrastructure,

Legal Aspects. http://business.gov.in/investment_incentives/chandigarh. php (accessed August 1, 2013).

12. Morshed, Adnan. Chandigarh. *Class lecture, Advanced Architectural Theory.* Washington, DC: Catholic University of America, February 7, 2008.

13. Nangia, Ashish. The Town That Corbusier Built. Change Observer: Design Observer. http://changeobserver.designobserver.com/feature/the-town-that-corbusier-built/15028/ (accessed August 1, 2013).

14. Morshed, Adnan. Brasilia. *Class lecture, Advanced Architectural Theory.* Washington, DC: Catholic University of America, February 14, 2008.

15. Husock, Howard. The Myths of the Pruitt-Igoe Myth. *City Journal.* http://www.city-journal.org/2012/bc0217hh.html (accessed August 1, 2013).

16. *The Pruitt-Igoe Myth: An Urban History.* DVD. Directed by Chad Freidrichs. New York, NY: First Run Features, 2011.

17. Wolfe, Tom. *From Bauhaus to Our House.* New York, NY: Farrar, Straus, & Giroux, 1981, pp. 63–64.

18. *Ultima IV: Quest of the Avatar.* Origin Systems (developer), Electronic Arts (publisher), September 16, 1985. PC game.

19. *Ultima Online.* Origin Systems (developer), Electronic Arts (publisher), September 24, 1997. PC game.

20. Donovan, Tristan. *Replay: The History of Video Games.* East Sussex, England: Yellow Ant, 2010.

21. Alexiou, Alice Sparberg. *Jane Jacobs: Urban Visionary.* New Brunswick, NJ: Rutgers University Press, 2006.

22. Jacobs, Jane. *The Death and Life of Great American Cities.* New York, NY: Random House, 1961.

23. Jacobs, Jane. *The Death and Life of Great American Cities.* New York, NY: Random House, 1961, p. 151.

24. Jacobs, Jane. *The Death and Life of Great American Cities.* New York, NY: Random House, 1961, p. 138.

25. *Halo 3.* Bungie (developer), Microsoft Game Studios (publisher), September 25, 2007. Xbox 360 game.

26. *World of Warcraft.* Blizzard Entertainment (developer and publisher), November 23, 2004. PC game.

27. *Minecraft.* Mojang (developer and publisher), November 18, 2011. PC game.

28. *Left 4 Dead.* Turtlerock Studios/Valve South (developer), Valve Corporation (publisher), October 2008. PC game.

29. *ActiveWorlds.* ActiveWorlds (developer and publisher), 1997. Online virtual world.

30. *Federation II.* IBGames (developer and publisher), 2003. Multi-User Dungeon.

31. Howard, Jeff. *Quests: Design, Theory, and History in Games and Narratives.* Wellesley, MA: A.K. Peters, 2008, pp. 47–49.

32. *Second Life.* Linden Research (developer and publisher), June 23, 2003. Online virtual world.

33. History of Wargaming. HMGS. http://www.hmgs.org/history.htm (accessed August 4, 2013). Military strategy games, in reality, date as far

back as Wei-qi (known commonly as Go) in 2000 BC, and others. Miniature wargames were also utilized throughout the nineteenth century by armies to practice battle strategies. However, Wells is one of the first to offer the games commercially.

34. *Warhammer Fantasy Battle.* Games Workshop (developer and publisher), 1983. Tabletop wargame.
35. *Team Fortress 2.* Valve Corporation (developer and publisher), October 9, 2007. PC game.
36. Good, Owen. Analyst Pegs Team Fortress 2 Hat Economy at $50 Million. Kotaku. kotaku.com/5869042/analyst-pegs-team-fortress-2-hat-economy-at-50-million (accessed August 4, 2013).
37. Jacobs, Jane. *The Death and Life of Great American Cities.* New York, NY: Random House, 1961, p. 68.
38. *Animal Crossing: New Leaf.* Nintendo EAD Group No. 2 and Monolith Soft (developer), Nintendo (publisher). June 9, 2013. Nintendo 3DS game.

CHAPTER 13

Sound, Music, and Rhythm in Level Design

I have found, among my papers, a leaf, in which I call architecture frozen music. There is something in the remark; the influence that flows upon us from architecture is like that from music.

—JOHANN WOLFGANG VON GOETHE,
FROM *CONVERSATIONS WITH GOETHE
IN THE LAST YEARS OF HIS LIFE*[1]

When I create soundtracks for games, I don't approach it as myself creating music for the game. I'm just a part of the development team. So, to bring out the game's features, what sound or background music is able to bring out the atmosphere of the game?

I wanted people to feel the music and the atmosphere to be dark and gloomy, to give you a sense of feeling afraid and unsure about things. You're not confident. And then after you clear the game, you feel rewarded and happy that you cleared the game.

—HIROKAZU "HIP" TANAKA, ON HIS CREATIVE
PROCESS AND COMPOSING MUSIC FOR *METROID*[2]

When people think about level design, many think of visual information, interactive game mechanics, or cognitive problem-solving. We have explored level design in this manner: emphasizing visual symbols, spatial communication, and kinesthetic interaction. While often overlooked, audio also plays a major part in our understanding of gamespace.

Game audio is another way in which level designers can augment their gamespaces with information. Audio can entice player movement, help set an atmosphere for gameplay, or reward players for their achievements. Sound design in games can help set the pacing of action, influencing the actions of players interacting with games. In this chapter, we explore sound design in game levels and discover how sound is the final ingredient for engaging players in our constructed game worlds.

What you will learn in this chapter:

The role of rhythm in games and buildings

Complementing level design with ambient sound

Enhancing gameplay experiences with sound design

THE ROLE OF RHYTHM IN GAMES AND BUILDINGS

An essential part of our discussions about game-pacing and architecture has been *rhythm*, the timed repetition of elements or movements. In gameplay, this has meant a steady alternation of high and low moments of gameplay, of dangerous and safe spaces, or of challenges and rewards (Figure 13.1). These changes and contrasts in rhythm add complexity to our games and game worlds. Each of these elements puts players on a schedule, which is internalized, providing powerful enticement through gamespace. In architecture, rhythmic use of visual elements—structure, shadows, etc.—provides a visual draw through space. Rhythmic elements also imply spatial separation, turning a single space into several (Figure 13.2).

Rhythm is also an essential element of music and sound design. In Western musical notation, rhythm is a function of the number and type of notes found in a bar of music. Musical *meter*, often describing the number of patterns and their timing in a piece of music, is another vital element, as it involves the study of specific repeated elements. Justin London, a musical scholar, has said that meter, understood as rhythmic elements repeated over the course of a piece, initially introduces itself to listeners and then forms a schedule on which it is expected.[3]

In these ways, the rhythmic elements of games, architecture, and music are not at all unlike. Rhythm not only provides the structure (pacing of games, spacing of columns, repetition of beats) that holds these media

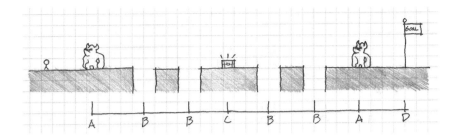

FIGURE 13.1   Examples of rhythmic pacing in gamespaces.

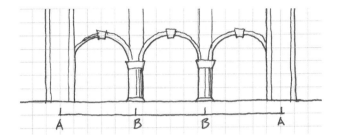

FIGURE 13.2   Examples of rhythmic elements in architecture.

together, but also cognitive responses in consumers. In this section we explore several ways in which rhythmic elements can affect our understanding of gamespaces.

Mood and Music

When discussing sound in games and how it affects player mood and action, the first portion of a game's *soundscape*—the sounds in a game that form a sonic environment—that most people would think about is the game's music. Indeed, music in games is one of the most often noted and remembered elements of the experience. Jack Wall, composer for *Mass Effect* and co-founder of Video Games Live, a traveling video game music concert, said, "Music is the unseen character. It's the emotion behind the actions of a player. It's gently there to show the game designer's intentions. It's totally collaborative with the developer."[4] As the Hip Tanaka quote above describes, game music contributes greatly to worldbuilding in video games. While players are interacting with mechanics, narrative, and other elements of the game world, they are not in the space themselves. Music offers emotional cues to players, and good composition can steer player emotions as deftly as gamespace construction can.

In a 1998 study, researchers at the Institute of HeartMath and the U.S. Naval Postgraduate School tested the ability of certain types of music to affect the mood of listeners.[5] They chose four types of music: classical, new age, grunge rock, and the then-recently created genre of designer music— music designed to affect listeners in specific ways. The designer music is specifically of interest, as it most closely resembles contemporary video game music, with quick beats and atmospheric instrumentation. Using a forty-five-item questionnaire, the researchers tested how the four genres affected these elements of mood: caring, mental clarity, relaxation, vigor, hostility, fatigue, sadness, and tension.[6]

The results supported the hypothesis that all four types of music would affect listeners' emotional states. Classical music was noted to have no significant emotional effects other than lowering tension. New age music yielded increases in relaxation and decreases in hostility and tension, but also lowered mental clarity and vigor. Grunge rock produced increases in hostility, fatigue, sadness, and tension, while decreasing caring, relaxation, mental clarity, and vigor. Finally, the designer music increased caring, relaxation, mental clarity, and vigor while decreasing hostility, fatigue, sadness, and tension.[7]

Studies like this underscore music's ability to reach out to listeners and pull them into the emotion of a piece of gameplay. As we have seen, games are allowed to take us to places typically avoided by other media—fear, tension, aggression, and others—for the sake of creating an imaginary interactive experience. Game developers will often use sophisticated lighting or art to create this tension, as we see in many survival horror games. However, music can be the factor that truly cements the atmosphere hinted at by visual assets. Music may also be the factor that creates an atmosphere in scenarios where sophisticated visuals are not an option.

Metroid II: The Return of Samus[8] for the original black-and-white[9] Game Boy is a great example of how music can be used as a tool to build a tense atmosphere even in the absence of sophisticated graphics. In this game, players must explore the catacombs of a distant planet to hunt Metroids, the titular parasitic aliens featured in the series. Lacking color or high-resolution graphics, the developers still strove to encapsulate the isolated mood of the original through other means. Visually, designers changed the silhouette of Samus as she gained abilities rather than her color, as had been done in the first game. Samus's sprite was also enlarged to show more detail. This had the side effect of turning much of the game levels into narrow spaces (Figure 13.3).

FIGURE 13.3 *Metroid II* utilizes both visual assets and a creative soundscape to recreate the isolated feeling of the original *Metroid* on the NES. Samus's sprite is bigger, causing many of the levels to become narrow spaces. The musical composition enhances the cramped feeling of the game levels by evoking the feeling of being in a nest.

In many ways, the musical composition for the game enhances the feeling of narrow space in *Metroid II*. Of his score for the original *Metroid*, Tanaka said that he wanted to create music that blurred the lines between the game's music and the sound effects of the game's world.[10] Ryoji Yoshitomi's score for *Metroid II* takes this idea further by having extremely minimalistic music throughout the game. The music is often more like rhythmic ambient sound, with electronic cave sounds and the noises of creatures as the instruments. The music switches to a driving riff when players encounter Metroids. This adds to the tension of fighting a large, powerful enemy in a narrow space. Adding to the actual music is a Metroid's screech whenever players shoot it with a missile. This is especially notable, as the distance of the Metroid from Samus facilitates how fast the rhythm of screeches occurs. When there is a short lull in the player's firing, the Metroid can inch closer, and the rhythm of screeches increases—further heightening the scene's tension and the player's awareness of the game action.

Musical composition does not need to be a separate field from sound design. In my studio's PC survival game *Dead Man's Trail*,[11] I had the privilege of working with some great composers: Chris Kukla and early in the project, Akash Thakkar. Akash created musical tracks based on his own *Foley* work, the recording of everyday ambient sounds. For one track, he created sound effects of slamming doors, shooting the last shell in a shotgun, and dragging a cello bow over various household objects.[12] These sounds reflect popular tropes of zombie apocalypse stories: distant battles with hordes, losing the last bit of one's ammunition, the sounds of movement inside buildings. All these things add to the tension of each level and make players aware of the actions they must take to survive. Likewise, Chris's Southern Rock-style soundtrack for scenes where players manage a truck driving across the country contrasted the tradition of American road trips with a feeling of dread.

The musical compositions of *Flower*,[13] on the other hand, are simple guitar and piano arrangements designed to elicit feelings of relaxation and happiness. The player sound effect of the game—a constantly blowing breeze—adds an element of nature to the music. Gameplay sounds are musical—as players hit flowers to open them, piano and violin notes play, adding to the simple background music. As players gain power and speed, so do the notes being played.

As the Institute of HeartMath and the U.S. Naval Postgraduate School's study of mood and music above shows, designed music like that found in games can have a promotional benefit on the listener's positive emotions. Fast-paced songs increase mental clarity, while smoother ones aid in relaxation or concentration. Music with oppressive riffs and a slow tempo, like much of the grunge music used in the study, has negative effects on the emotional state of listeners.

Composer Chanel Summers defines the way that music is used to direct emotions in games and media works as *empathetic* and *anempathetic*.[14] Empathetic music is music that provides the expected feeling for the visuals on a screen: a climactic theme for large battles, quiet music for contemplative scenes, and so on. Anempathetic music expresses an emotion different than, at times completely contrary to, the action on the screen. An example might be the fight against Jenova-LIFE in *Final Fantasy VII*. Instead of high-tempo battle music, the game plays the somber "Aerith's Theme" to punctuate party member Aerith's death in the game's plot and the cruelty of the boss's attack. Every Frame a Painting's mini-documentary, *The Marvel Symphonic Universe*,[15] makes an argument for the impact of unexpected or anempathetic music. The music from the Marvel Cinematic Universe franchise is not as memorable as music from other film franchises, the video argues, because it matches its scenes *too well*.

Musical motifs that appear where not expected, such as when a character's theme plays before they arrive to save the day, stand out. However, music that too closely matches its context and the sound effects of the scene fades into audio obscurity. This is not to say that empathetic music is bad, but it should be used to complete the building of an emotion rather than just supporting what is already there.

The discussion of music and mood in games brings up another potential avenue for music in game levels: becoming interactive. Understanding the concept of interactive game rhythm will have great impact on how we understand the player's relationship with the rhythms of gamespace.

Rhythm and Interactive Sound

Game music often blurs the lines between sound effects and music. Some games, such as *Metroid II* and *Dead Man's Trail*, utilize sound effects in their music to create a hybrid soundscape–song. Others, like *Flower*, utilize musical sound effects so that players feel as though they are contributing to both the game's outcome and music by interacting with the game. Describing this phenomenon of interactive music, interactive audio researcher Karen Collins has called game music *multimodal*—involving more than one sense. Collins argues that games engage three sensory modalities at once: audio, visual, and haptic (interactivity/action-oriented).[16]

Following the mechanics of "call-and-response" toys such as Simon,[17] where players attempted to repeat a pattern of electronic lights and tones by pressing buttons, a new type of game was popularized in the mid-1990s that had players responding to button prompts so a track of music would play—the rhythm game. *PaRappa the Rapper* for the Sony Playstation was one of the first games in this style, requiring players to press a specific sequence of buttons in time with a musical track. If players failed to press the proper buttons, the track would play incorrectly. In this way, the player had agency on how the background music of the game played.

Rez,[18] by United Game Artists, took a different approach. Rather than having players respond to musical prompts to maintain proper sound, *Rez* is a third-person rail shooter where game sound is musical. As players shoot enemies in levels, the music flourishes and different colors permeate the gamespace, building it from a blank grid to an array of complex architectural forms (Figure 13.4). The simultaneity of player action and the development of both game sound and visuals has been described as *synesthesia*, where a person experiences multiple sensory experiences from one

FIGURE 13.4   *Rez* players interact with both the game's sound and level design by moving and shooting enemies. The increasing complexity of sound and space is feedback for the player's actions within the game.

sensory input.[19] A *synesthete*, a person who experiences synesthesia, might perceive letters or numbers as inherently colored.

This type of gameplay, where user input and action affect game assets, produces a unique experience for players. Games in the *Bit.Trip* series, such as *Bit.Trip Beat*[20] and *Bit.Trip Runner*,[21] have an effect similar to that of *Rez*. Players move forward consistently through levels and must respond to musical input in different ways depending on the mechanics of the game. *Beat* involves moving a paddle to hit dots à la *Pong* (Figure 13.5), and *Runner* is a "constant runner"-style game where players must make their character jump and duck to avoid obstacles. The timing of levels, kept consistent since the game automatically propels players forward, corresponds to the timing of a musical track (Figure 13.6). Likewise, interaction with specific bullet types (in the case of *Beat*) or mechanics (in the

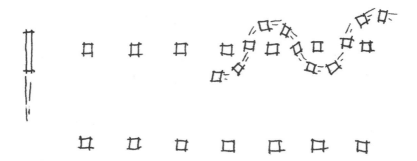

FIGURE 13.5   Bullets fired at players in *Bit.Trip Beat* come in waves synced to musical cues. Players become trained to expect certain rhythmic elements in the music and so begin moving their paddle in time with it.

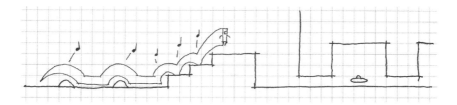

FIGURE 13.6 This diagram of a level in *Bit.Trip Runner* shows how specific obstacles are arranged rhythmically and in repeated movement patterns. Items allow for optional notes in the music.

case of *Runner*) occurs when the player is supposed to hear those sounds. As the player plays, he or she comes to expect these sounds in each track and will move to make them happen. Over time, the player wonders if he or she is playing the game or if the game is playing him or her.

In terms of design, these gamespaces use level geometry as a medium for activating specific musical sounds: *Rez* and *Bit.Trip* players are both adding to and responding to the music of gamespaces by playing the game, yet at times players may feel that since they are anticipating specific rhythms, they know what move to make next in the game.

Rhythmic Entrainment in Games and Spaces

As we have discussed here and in other chapters, patterns and repeated instances of game sounds, objects, or gameplay experiences can train players to expect events to occur or understand what strategies to take. In this way, we can say that entire games or game worlds can have rhythms, much as game music can. Our exploration of rhythmic synesthesia games like *Rez* and *Bit.Trip* shows us that players interacting with rhythms will learn to anticipate when specific movements will occur. This rhythmic synchronization can also occur on a larger scale with game rhythms and with elements of gamespace.

In biomusicology, there is a concept known as *entrainment*, where an organism syncs itself to an external rhythm or to other organisms.[22] A form of entrainment was used to facilitate the enticement practiced by early arcade games: if players are aware that bonuses occur every two levels, they will pay extra money to continue after dying. Entrainment patterns are very common in reward and short- and long-term goal-centric games like the *Zelda* series. Players know that after a short number of tasks in the overworld of many games, they will enter a dungeon, which will often contain a new weapon and an important quest item. The rhythm of *Zelda* gameplay drives players onward and is often enhanced by other elements that highlight this rhythm. For example, the embedded narrative events surrounding each dungeon often follow a dramatic arc. Players learn why they should go into a specific dungeon; they enter, there is a climactic battle, and finally falling action as players reap their rewards and order is restored. The games' status screens often reveal how many quest-important items there are to collect, and therefore how many dungeons. Such games give an overview of their rhythmic system and train players how to recognize it.

In purely spatial terms, buildings and game levels can also utilize rhythm. An example of this is the Great Mosque of Cordoba. On the one hand, it utilizes the shaded lighting condition that was established as having great ability to entice users through space due to its creation of atmospheric ambiguity. On the other hand, its rhythmic arcades and double arches with alternating red and white voussoirs also entice through their physical form by reaching in all directions through the hall. Architecturally, rhythmic components like the columns in the Great Mosque, staircases, shadows, doorways, terraces, or others create a sense of motion and continuity. These draw users through a space in the same way that linear elements, like those seen in Gothic churches or in *Half-Life 2*,[23] do.

The spacing of rhythmic elements in architecture can affect how users move through a space. In department store and mall design, for example, floor tiles are commonly smaller near expensive items. This makes shoppers slow down as their carts begin clicking on tiles faster, creating the feeling that they are moving too fast.[24] Floor tiles between stores in shopping malls are often very large, so users will entrain their steps with the wider pattern. When shoppers reach the front of a store, the tiles at the entrance become smaller, slowing the pace of the walker as he or she entrains to the new shorter pattern (Figure 13.7). The same can be done in gamespace: wider rhythmic architectural elements in prospect spaces, such as buildings in urban driving games or shooters, pull users through large circulation paths, and when players encounter areas where they are immersed in a rhythm of smaller or more intimate elements, they tend to stop and explore the space before moving on.

Varying Structural Rhythms

While gameplay occurs rhythmically and can entrain players to its rhythms to drive them forward, another element of keeping player engagement with rhythmic game structure is to layer rhythms on top of

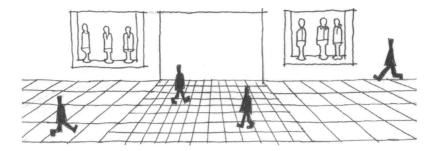

FIGURE 13.7 Even small architectural details like the spacing of floor tiles in a shopping mall can factor greatly into user entrainment. People will widen their pace and move faster over wide floor tiles, and slow down as they shorten their pace for smaller tiles.

one another. This type of layering is evident when designers give players a series of long- and short-term goals in a game. Long-term goals form their own rhythm of "big" events—boss battles, cutscenes, story events, etc. These form the foundational structure of the game, as in, "this game has eight levels," or "this game's story has four chapters." Within these larger structures lie individual stages (worlds 1–1, 1–2, and 1–3), tasks, puzzles, or enemy encounters that create shorter and shorter-term goals.

When diagrammed, these goals begin to form rhythmic patterns. Major game rhythms may be marked with hierarchically more important lines, while other goals are given thinner and thinner lines according to their importance (Figure 13.8). In architectural façade design, such patterns of layered structural elements have been referred to as *tartans*, after the fabric pattern common in Scottish clothing.[25] Architectural tartan patterns are constructed of alternating structural or façade elements of different hierarchical importance: from actual columns to window frames (Figure 13.9). In terms of gamespace rhythms, there can be *entrainment tartans* based on large prospect-space rhythmic elements and more intimate elements. *Bioshock Infinite*[26] utilizes these types of tartans well in the combat-ready streets of Columbia: buildings and islands form large-scale rhythms that draw players from one climactic battle to another. However, players who explore individual structures will find richly developed reward spaces and embedded narrative spaces (Figure 13.10). The development of tartan-like rhythms in gamespace can have great effect on both the large-scale structure of a game and individual level spaces. Layering patterns of gameplay in this way with both large-scale events and individual challenges ensures that gameplay is richer than if only planned from without.

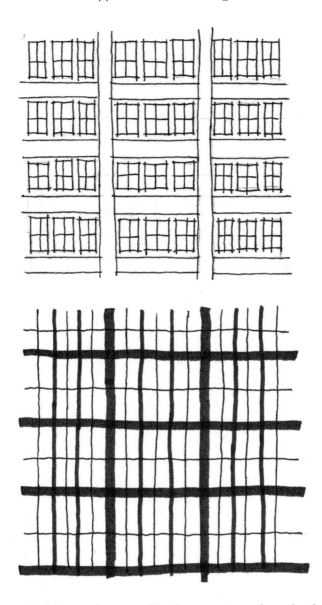

FIGURE 13.8 Architectural tartans like the one pictured can be diagrammed to show the layering of hierarchically different structural elements. Awareness of such layered façade features allows designers to create more visually complex building exteriors.

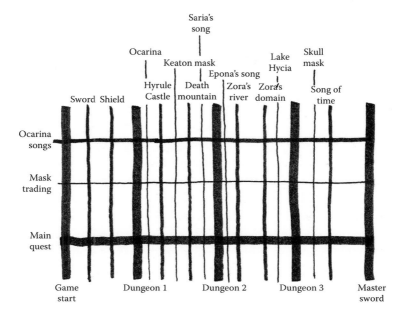

FIGURE 13.9 This diagram shows the layering of rhythms that occurs in *The Legend of Zelda: Ocarina of Time*. Major game events and goals have thicker lines, while other goals are marked with progressively thinner lines based on their scaling.

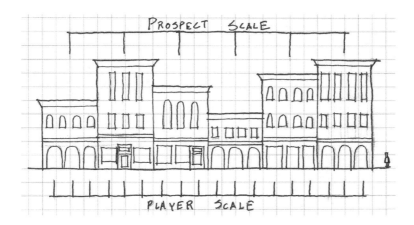

FIGURE 13.10 *Bioshock Infinite* famously features varying layers of gameplay structural experience. The exterior spaces of Columbia work in large-scale patterns of islands and buildings that facilitate quick movement from battle to battle. Players interested in exploration will find more intimately scaled explorable areas and tasks, giving the game a tartan-like structure of gameplay experiences.

While rhythm is the major component in how music contributes to our understanding of architecture and gamespace, there are other opportunities that sound design in games offers for enhancing game levels. In the next section, we look at distinctions between two ways sound is implemented in game engines and how this can be used to draw players through levels.

COMPLEMENTING LEVEL DESIGN WITH AMBIENT SOUND

We have just discussed a major portion of a game's soundscape: music. However, there are other factors that contribute greatly to building a game's audio modality. One of these is *ambient sound*, sound effects that build environmental context. Here we look at two methods for employing ambient sounds and how they enhance our understanding of gamespace. The terminology we use is borrowed from the Unity engine and how it models how sounds work in space: *2D sound* and *3D sound*.

2D Sound

The first and simpler of the two sound models we will explore is 2D sound. Music and contextual environmental sound effects such as wind, rustling trees, or distant urban sounds can be considered 2D sound. These sounds are played over a scene without regard for the distance of the source from the game's viewpoint. For example, a game in which the player character or non-player characters talk will often utilize 2D sound so the dialog can be heard. Game music is typically played over a scene, rather than from a specific source. While these sounds lack actual spatial implementation, they have other uses in building environmental context or atmosphere.

This type of environmental development is exemplified in *Slender: The Eight Pages* by Parsec Productions.[27] The game's developer, Mark Hadley, is a sound designer, and utilizes changes in ambient noise to describe the state of gameplay as players progress. At the beginning of the game, players can hear typical nighttime forest sounds: chirping crickets, wind rustling through trees, etc. As players collect pages, however, the ambient noise becomes increasingly ominous, starting with a steady drumbeat and eventually including different unsettling tones. *Slender* is notable for its use of negative space, building the feeling of being vulnerable within a large prospect space through a thick shroud of darkness. The 2D soundscape of this game aids this notion. The drumming can be described as the footsteps of Slender Man as he stalks players, and sometimes seen as simply scary sound effects. Either way, these sounds, which signal that players have the attention of the titular malevolent entity, give the impression of both distance and closeness. This aids the negative space and the antagonist's random spawning mechanics by making Slender Man's location relative to the player seem ambiguous. The lack of fading in and out for this soundscape likewise gives Slender Man an air of omnipotence in the gamespace, creating a tense atmosphere.

Dead Man's Trail utilizes sound to establish game state and hint at the world beyond the gamespace. Ambient noises of nature are used in many of the game's looting levels to establish setting. However, this quickly fades and becomes a dirge of zombie voices as the horde moves closer. Sound in this game has three purposes: to establish setting, to place the level in a much bigger world, and to inform players of how much time is left to loot. Each looting level allows players only a limited time before a large zombie horde arrives. Instead of a timer, ambient sound forces players to listen for the proximity of the horde and plan their looting accordingly.

Two-dimensional space is useful for scenarios in which the vastness of level space must be established, or for important sounds that must be heard by the player. There are also sounds whose ability to wax and wane with player proximity further enhance gamespace.

3D Sound

Beyond the singular volume of 2D sound is 3D sound, sound that becomes louder as players near its source. Where 2D sound excels at establishing the atmosphere of a gamespace, 3D sound calls attention to specific areas of a level. This can be useful for enhancing the size of a gamespace, guiding players through space, or as audio clues to secret passages.

Of sound effects in landscaping, David Slawson says that "auditory effects, such as the muffled and therefore 'distant' sound of a waterfall, also may be employed to heighten the sense of near and far."[28] These types of sounds can guide players by establishing a sense of proximity to specific objects or areas. In *The Legend of Zelda: Twilight Princess*,[29] this effect is used early in the game to guide players through the Ordon Woods area. Players must listen for the singing of an important character to reach a narrative-important area and learn how to ride Link's horse. In *The Legend of Zelda: Ocarina of Time*,[30] music is used in the Lost Woods area to guide players through a difficult maze. The maze is divided into rooms with four exits, and players must pause near each exit to test whether the music gets louder or softer (Figure 13.11). *Portal*[31] uses a similar tactic to alert players to secrets: radios playing an instrumental version of Jonathan Coulton's

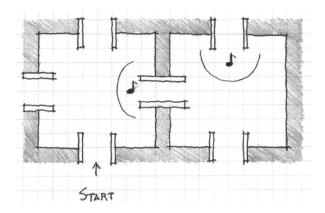

FIGURE 13.11   In *Ocarina of Time*, music is used to guide players through the Lost Woods area of the game. The correct exits to rooms in the maze allow players to hear music more loudly than other exits.

Still Alive are strewn throughout levels. By offering in-game achievements to players for finding them, the developers turn listening for a specific song or sound into an exploration game of its own.

Sounds can create interesting opportunities to alert players to danger or disrupt their play. When creating especially powerful enemies or placing them in levels, you can give them unique sounds to add further tension to encounters with them. In *Half-Life 2*, the poison headcrab enemies, whose attacks leave players greatly weakened, have a distinct rattling sound. Valve employees have noted that during playtesting, testers would drop whatever they were otherwise doing in the game to concentrate on destroying poison headcrabs if they heard the rattling.[32] Likewise, clickers in *The Last of Us*[33] have their own distinctive noise (for which they are named) that alerts players when they are nearby. These enemies cannot see players but have an increased sense of hearing. Thus players may not move too fast around them. As they can instant-kill players, they are powerful blockages to player progress through the game, and their patrol locations often greatly affect the paths players take through levels. Their clicking sounds allow players to detect when these creatures are nearby and adjust their tactics accordingly (Figure 13.12).

Together, 2D and 3D sound can have a great effect on how players experience gamespace. Designers can use 2D sounds to establish the atmosphere of a game or depict a force that envelopes the entire gamespace, and 3D sound can be used as a guide for players or as an alert mechanism.

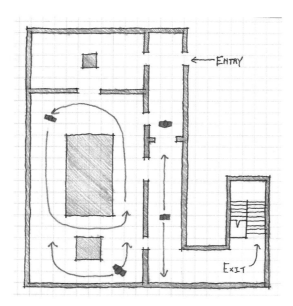

FIGURE 13.12   Clickers in *The Last of Us* alert players to their proximity with distinct clicking sound effects. This allows players to adjust their gameplay strategies to deal with them. Because of their instant-kill abilities, they are also a powerful example of enemies as alternative architecture, as their movements greatly influence how a player must travel through a space.

In the next section, we discuss game sounds that react to player action more strongly, and we see how these types of sounds can enhance the gamespace principles explored in previous chapters.

ENHANCING GAMEPLAY EXPERIENCES WITH SOUND DESIGN

The use of sounds as indicators of approaching enemies or to mark pathways shows us that like art assets, sound assets can be symbolic. As players play *Half-Life 2*, they are trained to understand how a rattling sound indicates the presence of poison headcrabs. Like many *Half-Life* series enemy introductions, the first encounter occurs in an isolated fashion, in a room where they are one of the only enemies, so players can see what effect their attacks have and learn about the sounds they make (Figure 13.13). In *The Last of Us*, players are taught about clickers through a cutscene that clearly shows how they are visually distinguishable from other enemies, and through an easily overcome encounter where players can hear the sounds they make (Figure 13.14).

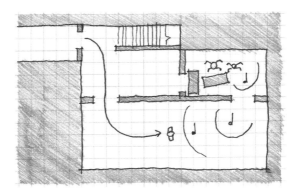

FIGURE 13.13 Poison headcrabs are encountered in an isolated fashion that allows players to see the effect of their attacks without dying and hear their warning sounds.

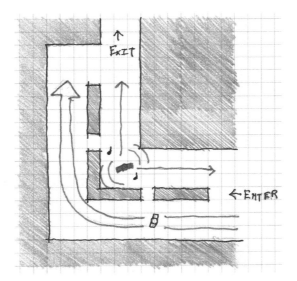

FIGURE 13.14 Clickers in *The Last of Us* are first encountered in an area where they can be observed but easily avoided, and their distinct sound can be heard.

Karen Collins addresses this element of game sound, stating, "The concept of interactive sound as being event-driven suggests that events are repeatable—that if we repeat the action, we will receive the same reaction."[34] She states that this repeatability is important for giving players feedback for their actions in games. Indeed, our idea of sounds as symbolic assets in games is what allows us to use them as another tool for training players, rewarding them, or giving them other feedback for their actions.

Even in situations where the quality of sound design rests on random-ized variations of sounds (such as gunshots or footsteps of characters), she argues, audio feedback gives the impression that the players' actions have agency in the game world.[35] To this end, designers can use symbolic audio assets in several ways to enhance their game's world.

Sound as Gameplay Feedback

We discussed earlier how interaction with elements in gamespace often elicits sound effects or musical tones. In *Flower*, we saw how interacting with closed flowers created notes that were added to the game's music (Figure 13.15). Weapons in many games often play satisfying effects when used: loud bangs for guns, explosions for rocket launchers, and clangs for swords.

If we are to consider sound effects in games as symbolic assets, we have to understand how they produce feelings of agency for player activity. In terms of characters, a pleasant "bwooop" when a character jumps and a jagged "err err err" buzzer when characters are hit become positive rein-forcements and punishments, respectively, in response to player actions. Jumping in games is often a positive action, while being hit by enemy fire is a negative one. In *Bit.Trip* games, successful navigation of the game's envi-ronment plays a pleasant electronic note, while missing these opportuni-ties plays an awkward click or thud sound. This use of sound complements

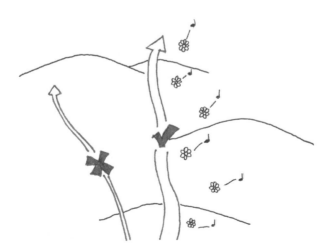

FIGURE 13.15 Moving through the world in *Flower* produces musical tones, which reinforce player interaction.

the training methods discussed that utilize symbolic assets and rewards. As players learn what types of sounds are created by what types of actions, they learn how to properly play the game.

Audio feedback is also useful for directing players within gamespaces. Triggers in certain areas can be scripted to play pleasant melodies when players perform actions there. In *Year Walk*,[36] players must at one point navigate a cave by selecting from an array of identical pathways. By listening for specific notes at each path, players can discern which way to go. The notes that lead players in the proper direction are pleasant and in major keys, while the notes that return players to the beginning of the cave are in harsh minor keys.

In *Slender*, players hear jarring bursts of static whenever Slender Man comes into view. This is an important trigger for players, as a primary mechanic of the game is to avoid seeing the character, which results in the player dying and the game ending. Especially during the early portions of the game, it is possible for Slender Man to be directly in front of players, but far enough away that trees or darkness obscure him. Audio is important here, as it gives players an indication that the antagonist is nearby and they must not continue in his direction. Sound helps dictate the player's interaction with Slender Man, and it also gives players warnings that steer them away from unfair deaths.

Symbolic game objects can have their own symbolic audio assets. Levers can make a satisfying click when pulled, doors can open with a heavy grinding sound, etc. When played in response to player actions in a level, they give the impression that the player has somehow greatly affected the gamespace. When the object that players are interacting with is directly on screen, hearing the sounds an object makes has a similar purpose to the sound effects that characters make: providing satisfying feedback. However, these sounds can also indicate that something has happened elsewhere in the level, as is often the case in dungeon-crawling games (Figure 13.16).

Sound as Reward

Sometimes the audio feedback from important events or difficult puzzles triggers the playing of more triumphant audio assets. Audio feedback is being used here as a reward for in-game actions. In *Zelda* games, jingles play whenever players solve a puzzle in a room or gain a new item. The same is true for most action–adventure games—a unique chime or tune plays in response to player victory. Rewards can be some of the most

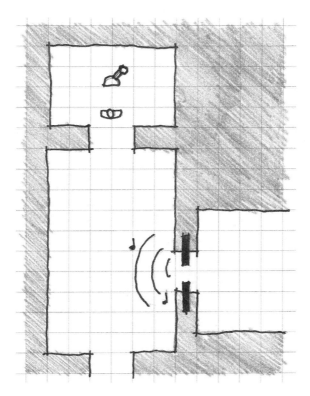

FIGURE 13.16 Environmental sound effects can give feedback for direct inter-activity or alert players that they are affecting something elsewhere in the level.

multimodal experiences in games. In terms of interactivity, they come after players have overcome challenges or performed an important in-game action. Rewards often have a visual component—the sprite or 3D model of the reward object, or some visually rewarding space. Audio also ties the experience together with upbeat celebratory fanfare. Like the link between interactive and visual modalities, the combination of a sound effect with a specific and repeatable game event closely links the sound and game event together. This is an important aspect of enhancing the player's understanding of their agency in a game and the overall game feel.

Audio rewards in games are not necessarily rewards in and of them-selves. They are, however, useful for enhancing other types of rewards or guiding the emotions of players in rewarding scenes. When gaining access to a new weapon or ability, which in Salen and Zimmerman's terms would be a reward of facility,[37] players may hear a heroic tune. The sound played in a reward vault, rewarding vista, or meditative space may have a relaxing melody when compared with the intense rhythms that possibly accompanied any preceding challenges. In these ways, sound in games can move us through the dramatic arcs of individual gameplay challenges.

Sound as Narrative Indicators

Sound can clue players in to the narrative state of a game. As we have seen, sound in games is largely *incidental*, designed for accompaniment of performed events. However, sounds can also give insight into elements of gamespace that are themselves narrative indicators.

In Chapter 9, "Storytelling in Gamespaces," we discussed how textures indicate the narrative state of games with regard to the hero's journey. As a game moves forward, the state or type of materiality indicated through art assets typically deteriorates: green fields give way to the wet stones of dungeons, lava of volcanoes, or ominous metals of alien cities. Sound can fill in gaps of our understanding of gamespace materiality left by our inability to touch gamespace. It can enhance prospects with echoes, make grass in fields seem plush with sumptuous rustling, or enhance the eeriness of swamps with thick sloshing that makes the player's skin crawl when he or she thinks of what his or her avatar is walking in.

Even the music of a gamespace can be a material indicator. In *Sword & Sworcery EP*[38], Jim Guthrie's music not only guides gameplay mood, but also enhances the material awareness of players in specific scenes. The Dream World has slow, melodic music that echoes faintly, making the entire space seem ethereal. Battles with the game's main antagonist, the Gogolithic Mass, feature heavy but sharp percussions that recall the sound of crunching armor and bone. The careful use of these types of evocative music and sound assets greatly enhance the material reality of gamespaces and the experience of interacting with them.

SUMMARY

While level designers and architects mainly consider the visual and interactive elements of space, video games also allow the use of audio enhancements to our designs. In this chapter, we have explored how music and sound affect player moods and can be used to enhance emotional responses to gamespace. We have also seen how sounds in games create rhythms that, if utilized in certain ways, can cause players to expect them. These expected rhythms in musical composition, game structuring, and game level construction can affect the speed of how players interact with games, or offer layered game experiences through differently scaled challenges.

We also explored how game sound exists in video games: through both overlaid 2D sound and location-specific 3D sound. These sounds offer opportunities for describing the nature of gameplay elements and gamespaces in different ways: do certain elements overwhelm a gamespace, as in many horror games where monster effects fill a level, or are they guideposts that lead players to destinations? These types of sounds may also be used to create a sense of great distance through muffled location-specific sound effects or faint 2D soundscapes.

Lastly, we looked at how specific sound effects can enhance gamespace experiences discussed earlier in the book. Sounds can give feedback for specific mechanics or be rewards for important gameplay tasks. These enhance the ways that gamespaces train players and the experience of earning rewards. Sound effects can give narrative context to gamespaces by describing their materiality. Partnered with visual representations of materials, players get a sense of how it feels to be in a gamespace despite not physically inhabiting it.

EXERCISES

1. **Drawing exercise**: Draw a *Nintendo Power*-style map of a game level (either one from a commercial game or one you are making) and highlight significant gameplay areas. How far apart are they spaced? Assign letters to different types of elements or challenges (items, enemies, obstacles, etc.) and see how those are spaced out.

2. **Writing prompt**: Listen to three pieces of game music. Describe what types of emotions they evoke. Watch gameplay of the levels they are from: does the emotional context of the music match the action of the game or does it create a contrast? Do you find areas of contrast memorable?

3. **Digital exercise**: Graybox a level with rhythmic elements (made with architectural elements, shadows, textures, etc.) Have someone playtest this level and see how the rhythmic elements affect his or her play: do they change the player's pace? Is the plyer enticed to follow the elements?

4. **Drawing exercise**: Draw a tartan diagram of a game's goal structure. What do you notice about how short- and long-term goals are spaced out?

5. **Digital exercise**: Graybox an environment that uses different rhythms at different scales such as having tightly packed columns at the player's level and large buildings at a more top-down level. What effect does this have on player exploration? Playtest under different conditions and see under what conditions players will follow the large rhythms and when they will follow the smaller rhythms.

6. **Digital exercise**: Implement 2D and 3D sounds in a level you are designing. In the case of the 3D sound, how do players react to the sound? Does it affect their path through the level? Does the 2D sound affect the player's perception of the level (music providing emotional context, etc.)?

ENDNOTES

1. Goethe, Johann Wolfgang von, and Johann Peter Eckermann. *Conversations with Goethe in the Last Years of His Life*. Boston, MA: Hilliard, Gray, and Co., 1839. http://books.google.com.br/books?id=pN1M2653ViAC&pg=PA 282#v=onepage&q&f=false
2. Parish, Jeremy. A Conversation with Hip Tanaka from 1UP.com. 1UP.com. http://www.1up.com/features/conversation-hip-tanaka (accessed August 5, 2013).
3. London, Justin. *Hearing in Time: Psychological Aspects of Musical Meter*. Oxford: Oxford University Press, 2004, p. 4.
4. Lane, Rick. Different Keys: How Music Works in Games. IGN. http://www.ign.com/articles/2012/07/30/different-keys-how-sound-works-in-games (accessed August 5, 2013).
5. McCraty, Rollin, Bob Barrios-Choplin, Mike Atkinson, and Dana Tomasino. The Effects of Music on Mood, Tension, and Mental Clarity. *Alternative Therapies* 4, no. 1 (1998): 75–84. http://www.musicontap.co.uk/downloads/Music_Mood_Effects.pdf (accessed August 5, 2013).
6. McCraty, Rollin, Bob Barrios-Choplin, Mike Atkinson, and Dana Tomasino. The Effects of Music on Mood, Tension, and Mental Clarity. *Alternative Therapies* 4, no. 1 (1998): 75–84. http://www.musicontap.co.uk/downloads/Music_Mood_Effects.pdf (accessed August 5, 2013), pp. 75–77.
7. McCraty, Rollin, Bob Barrios-Choplin, Mike Atkinson, and Dana Tomasino. The Effects of Music on Mood, Tension, and Mental Clarity. *Alternative Therapies* 4, no. 1 (1998): 75–84. http://www.musicontap.co.uk/downloads/Music_Mood_Effects.pdf (accessed August 5, 2013), p. 79.
8. *Metroid II: The Return of Samus*. Nintendo R&D1 (developer), Nintendo (publisher), November 1991. Nintendo Game Boy game.
9. Some would argue black and green.
10. Brandon, Alexander. Gamasutra—Features—Shooting from the Hip: An Interview with Hip Tanaka. Gamasutra. http://www.gamasutra.com/view/feature/2947/shooting_from_the_hip_an_.php (accessed August 6, 2013).

11. *Dead Man's Trail*. Pie For Breakfast Studios (developer), upcoming. Indie game on Steam.
12. Thakkar, Akash. Akash Thakkar: PAX East 2013 Game Audio panel. SoundCloud. https://soundcloud.com/athakkar/pax-east-2013-game-audio-panel (accessed August 5, 2013).
13. *Flower*. Thatgamecompany (developer), Sony Computer Entertainment (publisher), February 12, 2009. Sony Playstation 3 game.
14. Summers, Chanel. "Making the Most of Audio". In *Level Design: Processes and Experiences*, ed. Christopher W. Totten. Boca Raton, FL: CRC Press, 2016, p. 152.
15. Every Frame a Painting. "The Marvel Symphonic Universe". YouTube video, 13:34. Posted Sept. 12, 2016. https://www.youtube.com/watch?v=7vfqkvwW2fs
16. Collins, Karen. *Playing with Sound: A Theory of Interacting with Sound and Music in Video Games*. Cambridge, MA: MIT Press, 2013, p. 22.
17. Graft, Kris. Before There Was Guitar Hero… — Page 6 of 6 | Features | Edge Online. *Edge Magazine*. http://www.edge-online.com/features/there-was-guitar-hero/6/(accessed August 6, 2013).
18. Rez. United Game Artists (developer), Sony Computer Entertainment (publisher), January 7, 2002. Sony Playstation 2 game.
19. Borries, Friedrich von, Steffen P. Walz, and Matthias Böttger. *Space Time Play Computer Games, Architecture and Urbanism: The Next Level*. Basel: Birkhauser, 2007, p. 115.
20. *Bit.Trip Beat*. Gaijin Games (developer), Aksys Games (publisher), March 16, 2009. Nintendo WiiWare game.
21. *Bit.Trip Runner*. Gaijin Games (developer), Aksys Games (publisher), May 17, 2010. Nintendo WiiWare game.
22. Clayton, Martin, Rebecca Sager, and Udo Will. In Time with the Music: The Concept of Entrainment and Its Significance for Ethnomusicology. *ESEM CounterPoint* 1 (2004): 1–45.
23. *Half-Life 2*. Valve Corporation (developer and publisher), November 16, 2004. PC game.
24. Dan, Lockton. Controlling Shoppers. Architectures | Dan Lockton | Design & human behaviour. http://architectures.danlockton.co.uk/2006/05/12/-controlling-shoppers/ (accessed August 7, 2013).
25. Jenkins, Eric. Diagramming Architectural Tartans. *Class lecture, Design Thinking*. Washington, DC: Catholic University of America, 2004.
26. *Bioshock Infinite*. Irrational Games (developer), 2K Games (publisher), March 26, 2013. Xbox 360 game.
27. *Slender: The Eight Pages*. Parsec Productions (developer and publisher), June 26, 2012. PC game.
28. Slawson, David A. *Secret Teachings in the Art of Japanese Gardens: Design Principles, Aesthetic Values*. Tokyo: Kodansha International, 1987, p. 106.
29. *The Legend of Zelda: Twilight Princess*. Nintendo EAD Group No. 3 (-developer), Nintendo (publisher), November 19, 2006. Nintendo Wii game.

30. *The Legend of Zelda: Ocarina of Time*. Nintendo EAD (developer), Nintendo (publisher), November 23, 1998. Nintendo 64 game.
31. *Portal*. Valve Corporation (developer and publisher), October 9, 2007. PC game.
32. *Half-Life 2: Raising the Bar*. Roseville, CA: Prima Games, 2004.
33. *The Last of Us*. Naughty Dog (developer), Sony Computer Entertainment (publisher), June 14, 2013. Playstation 3 game.
34. Collins, Karen. *Playing with Sound: A Theory of Interacting with Sound and Music in Video Games*. Cambridge, MA: MIT Press, 2013, p. 33.
35. Collins, Karen. *Playing with Sound: A Theory of Interacting with Sound and Music in Video Games*. Cambridge, MA: MIT Press, 2013, p. 34.
36. *Year Walk*. Simogo (developer and publisher), February 21, 2013. iPad game.
37. Salen, Katie, and Eric Zimmerman. *Rules of Play: Game Design Fundamentals*. Cambridge, MA: MIT Press, 2003, p. 346.
38. *Superbrothers: Sword & Sworcery EP*. Capybara games (developer and publisher), March 24, 2011. Apple iPad game.

Conclusion

A s OUR INDUSTRY MOVES forward in developing a critical framework from which to understand game design, we must not leave other vital elements of game development, such as level design, behind. We must learn to balance game design's own *firmitas*, *utilitias*, and *venustas*—functional requirements, usability, and delight—rather than ignore one to focus on another.

We have explored many facets of both architecture and games here. We began with a historical foundation of both arts and discovered ways in which each dealt with technical and societal factors to create meaningful experiences. This led us to explore methods for analyzing spatial design and documenting this analysis through plan, section, elevation, and other representational methods. We explored tools and techniques for designing game levels based on traditional game design methods, as well as some that merge architectural foci on modularity and measurements.

These tools in hand, we studied traditional spatial types in games and how they might be organized like traditional architectural forms. We discovered how the size of spaces and the ways in which they are arranged can influence our experience of them. From some of these practical concerns, we explored spatial design to see how it can fit our goals of level design: the adjustment of behavior, transmission of meaning, and augmentation of space. For this we discovered that gamespaces can utilize art assets to which we can assign game behaviors or associations, making them symbolic art assets. With these we can teach players how to play our games. We also saw how simple manipulations of the way spaces are arranged and presented can create emotional experiences such as suspense, fear, denial, and reward. And, we saw how we may establish rhythms of goals in our level spaces that entice players through our games and how to use those goals and rewards to help teach players how to use our games. We also discussed how many of our art assets can help mark the player's place in a story. This is especially true of textures and materials in environment art, which can be powerful descriptors for working with traditional narrative structures such as the hero's journey.

After illustrating some of these experiential orientations of space, we explored ways in which we may tell stories or provide players with the resources to make their own. As many games create possibility spaces through a set of rules embodied in an environment, we discovered how games build worlds through rules. We also learned how to use systems that build levels for us in such a way that we can still use all of our human-centric design methods. We returned to our spatial learning methods to discover how these possibility spaces slowly shape user behavior through controlled exposure to a game's mechanics that later allow players to freely explore. Such explorations of mechanics formed our discussions of multiplayer gamespaces, and how theories of urbanism demonstrate how we might create exciting multiuser worlds through mixed-use spatial layouts rather than by separating gameplay functions. To complement these discussions of how gameplay is controlled, we further explored rhythms in games—both in architectural spaces and in sound assets. Through this, we discovered how sound and rhythm might be of use for establishing the mood of our game, as well as for directing the pacing of gameplay.

Level design is a rapidly changing sector of the game industry and as more designers write and share their processes, it is important to understand the role of design-thinking in game worlds. These ideas are beyond technology. While they influence how we build levels when we sit down at our 2D art or 3D content creation programs, middleware game engines, or proprietary software, they have a larger meaning. We see games displayed as singular art objects in museums and cultural institutions, but let us not forget that games are made by artists from multiple disciplines bringing together generations of artistic knowledge. By seeing level design as a distinct art, we can make worlds as timeless as the most meaningful pieces of architecture. Many of the most influential works cited in this text are at least fifty years old. Many are hundreds or even thousands of years old, yet the experiences they create through their spatial arrangements have withstood both time and the emergent narratives brought on by intense human interaction. Through these timeless spatial design principles, we hope to build timeless gameplay.

Index

Taylor & Francis Group
an **informa** business

Taylor & Francis eBooks

www.taylorfrancis.com

A single destination for eBooks from Taylor & Francis
with increased functionality and an improved user
experience to meet the needs of our customers.

90,000+ eBooks of award-winning academic content in
Humanities, Social Science, Science, Technology, Engineering,
and Medical written by a global network of editors and authors.

TAYLOR & FRANCIS EBOOKS OFFERS:

A streamlined
experience for
our library
customers

A single point
of discovery
for all of our
eBook content

Improved
search and
discovery of
content at both
book and
chapter level

REQUEST A FREE TRIAL
support@taylorfrancis.com